How CHINA Is Ruled

How CHINA Is Ruled

Alan P. L. Liu

University of California, Santa Barbara

Prentice-Hall, Inc., Englewood Cliffs, New Jersey 07632

Library of Congress Cataloging in Publication Data

Liu, Alan P. L. (date)
    How China is ruled.

    Includes bibliographies and index.
    1. China—Politics and government—
1949-   . I. Title.
DS777.75.L57 1986   951.05   84-26643
ISBN   0-13-396664-X

Printed in the United States of America

10 9 8 7 6 5 4 3 2 1

*Editorial/production supervision and
    interior design: Joan L. Stone*
Cover design: Lundgren Studio
Cover illustration: Karen Goldsmith
Manufacturing buyer: Barbara Kittle

ISBN 0-13-396664-X   01

Prentice-Hall International (UK) Limited, *London*
Prentice-Hall of Australia Pty. Limited, *Sydney*
Editora Prentice-Hall do Brasil, Ltda., *Rio de Janeiro*
Prentice-Hall Canada Inc., *Toronto*
Prentice-Hall Hispanoamericana, S.A., *Mexico*
Prentice-Hall of India Private Limited, *New Delhi*
Prentice-Hall of Japan, Inc., *Tokyo*
Prentice-Hall of Southeast Asia Pte. Ltd., *Singapore*
Whitehall Books Limited, *Wellington, New Zealand*

To Alice, Amy, and Andy—
my three most enduring supporters

Contents

Preface   xiii

PART ONE

The Historical Context

CHAPTER 1

Chinese Ecology and Political Tradition   1

ECOLOGY 2   *POLITICAL TRADITION* 7   *NOTES* 13

CHAPTER 2

The Rise of Communism in China   15

THE DESTRUCTION OF THE QING DYNASTY, 1850-1912 16
CIVIL WARS AMONG WARLORDS, 1913-28 19
THE RISE OF THE COMMUNIST PARTY, 1921-49 20
REVOLUTIONARY LEGACY 34   *NOTES* 36

CHAPTER 3

The People's Republic, 1949-81   38

REVOLUTIONARY DESTRUCTION, 1949-52 40
SOCIALIST CONSTRUCTION, 1953-57 41

*THE GREAT LEAP FORWARD AND THE PEOPLE'S COMMUNE
MOVEMENT, 1958-60* 44
REHABILITATION AND NORMALCY, 1962-65 45
THE GREAT PROLETARIAN CULTURAL REVOLUTION, 1966-69 47
THE STRUGGLE FOR SUCCESSION, 1970-76 50
THE STRUGGLE FOR POWER AFTER THE DEATH OF MAO, 1976-81 53
NOTES 55

PART TWO

Civil Administration

CHAPTER 4

The Communist Party of China 57

THE HIGH COMMAND: NATIONAL ORGANIZATION OF THE CPC 61
THE MIDDLE COMMAND: PROVINCIAL PARTY ORGANIZATIONS 69
THE LOWER COMMAND OF THE CPC 72
THE CPC RANK AND FILE: PRIMARY ORGANIZATIONS 74
THE COMMUNIST PARTY UNDER STRESS 76   *NOTES* 85

CHAPTER 5

Chinese Communist National Government: Structure and Process 88

THE CONSTITUTION OF THE PRC 88
THE NATIONAL PEOPLE'S CONGRESS 91
PRESIDENCY OF THE PRC 94   *STATE COUNCIL* 95
ROLE OF THE STATE IN POLICY MAKING 97   *NOTES* 98

CHAPTER 6

Subnational Government and Politics 100

LOCAL POLITICS 103   *MINORITY NATIONALITIES* 108   *NOTES* 113

CHAPTER 7

Rural Administration and Development 116

LAND REFORM, 1949-52 117   *COLLECTIVIZATION, 1951-80* 118
DECOLLECTIVIZATION, 1977 TO THE PRESENT 129   *NOTES* 132

CHAPTER 8

Parapolitical Organizations   135

UNITED FRONT 135   TRANSMISSION BELT 142   NOTES 156

CHAPTER 9

The Communist Cadre System   159

COMPOSITION OF CADRES 160   CADRE RECRUITMENT 162
TRAINING OF CADRES 165   DANGFEN—CADRES' STYLE OF WORK 170
CONCLUSION 178   NOTES 179

PART THREE

Coercive Organizations

CHAPTER 10

The Judiciary and the Public Security System   181

THE JUDICIARY BEFORE 1977 182   THE JUDICIARY FROM 1977 185
THE PUBLIC SECURITY ESTABLISHMENT 187   NOTES 193

CHAPTER 11

The Role of the Military in Chinese Politics   195

FORMAL POLITICAL STATUS OF THE MILITARY 196
CIVIL—MILITARY RELATIONS, 1949-79 198
CIVIL—MILITARY RELATIONS IN THE 1980s 205
THE PLA AND CHINESE ECONOMIC DEVELOPMENT 210   NOTES 211

CHAPTER 12

The People's Militia   213

1950-57 213   1958-69 214   1970-72 218   1973-76 219   1977-83 220
CONCLUSION 220   NOTES 220

PART FOUR

The Political Process

CHAPTER 13

Ideology and Ideological Style   222

THE FORMAL IDEOLOGY OF THE CPC   224
POST–MAO IDEOLOGICAL TRENDS   226   NOTES   230

CHAPTER 14

Factions, Cliques, and Clientelism   232

STRUCTURAL CONDUCIVENESS   234   PRECIPITANTS   235
TYPES OF FACTIONS   236
CLIENTELISM IN COMMUNIST BUREAUCRACY   241
COPING WITH FACTIONALISM   244   NOTES   245

CHAPTER 15

The Policy-Making Process   247

IDEOLOGY: SUM AND PARTS OF POLICY   247
THE ELITE: POLICY MAKING   249
POLICY MAKING AFTER MAO   254
MASS CAMPAIGNS   256   NOTES   258

CHAPTER 16

Public Opinion
and Political Communication   261

THE OVERALL POLITICAL SYSTEM   261
THE POLITICAL-COMMUNICATION SYSTEM   262
NONINSTITUTIONALIZED COMMUNICATION   271   LEADERSHIP   281
THE POST–MAO APPROACH TO PUBLIC OPINION   283   NOTES   284

PART FIVE

Economic and Social Transformation

CHAPTER 17

The Chinese Political Economy   287

THE STRATEGY OF ECONOMIC DEVELOPMENT 288
THE PERFORMANCE OF THE ECONOMY 290   *STRUCTURAL STRAINS* 295
REFORM 297   *NOTES* 301

CHAPTER 18

Social Change and Modernization   303

POPULATION AND OCCUPATION 303   *THE CHINESE FAMILY* 307
EDUCATION 310   *SOCIAL STRATIFICATION AND MOBILITY* 314
STATUS OF WOMEN 321   *PUBLIC HEALTH* 323
SOCIAL CONSENSUS AND INTEGRATION 326   *NOTES* 333

PART SIX

Conclusion   338

NOTES 343

APPENDIX

Hu Yaobang's Speech   345

HISTORICAL REVIEW 346   *A DECISIVE TURNING POINT* 350
PARTY BUILDING 351   *UNITE AND LOOK FORWARD* 357

Index   359

Preface

I have written this book to satisfy my long-standing desire to understand the totality of the Chinese Communist political system. What precipitated my decision to realize my desire now was the outpouring of new information from China on almost every aspect of Chinese Communist society, politics, and economy after the death of Mao, especially in 1979-80. These candid revelations have given us a much more accurate and insightful view of the Chinese Communist political system and process than we were able to obtain in the past.

As my aim is to provide the reader (both general and specialist) with an up-to-date, accurate, and meaningful interpretation of Chinese Communist politics, I have relied primarily on original sources. I have depended on two qualifications to make what I regard as good use of various reports culled from the Chinese media: an awareness of the broad context (e.g., history of the Communist rule of mainland China and familiarity with the policies and programs of the Communist party since its inception) and case studies of aspects of the Chinese Communist political system, some of which have already been published in scholarly journals. This book enables me to integrate the broad context and case studies with the latest information from China.

In any scholarly study an author may treat a specific topic as the exemplification of a theory that he or she is interested in disseminating. Or the writer may use theories or concepts to shed light on the subject matter under study. In the latter case an eclectic approach is often adopted. I have chosen the second approach since my interest is in Chinese politics, not any grandiose social science theory. Moreover, I have taken the stand that a scholar's first and foremost tasks are analysis and critique. So the reader will find that this book calls a spade a spade, not any other name. The other stand that I have taken is that a book on Chinese politics must approximate the actual experience of Chinese citizens living in the People's Republic of China. This is yet another reason for my reliance on original Chinese sources, especially information released during periods of "liberalization," e.g., the Hundred Flowers Blooming in 1957, the rebellion in the Cultural Revolution of 1967-68, and the self-criticism period of 1979-80. Sometimes one finds studies on Chinese politics in the United States that do not touch on the empirical experience of the great majority of Chinese, dwelling instead on the formal ideology of Chinese Communism and idealistic image of China on the part of the author. My stress, however, is on the empirical experience, not ideological abstraction.

This book would not have been written without the continuous support of my research by the Academic Senate of the University of California at Santa Barbara campus. I am eternally grateful to the faculty and staff of the university. I appreciate greatly the understanding and support that I have received from Stan Wakefield, editor of political science books at Prentice-Hall. Stan's moral support was crucial to my completion of this book. Thanks also to Mrs. Margaret Y. Nee, whose generous contribution to the study of Chinese modernization at the University of California at Santa Barbara provided the funds for typing and reproducing this manuscript. My students Yuan-lin Chao and Pao-chu Wang assisted in producing the graphics for this book, and I am grateful to them.

Alan P. L. Liu

How CHINA Is Ruled

PART ONE

The Historical Context

CHAPTER 1

Chinese Ecology and Political Tradition

The fundamental tasks of politics, in China or elsewhere, are conceptualization and organization for joint action. An essential component of political conceptualization is memory, from which a blueprint for the future springs. Memory is in turn composed of historical experience.

We thus start our analysis of the Chinese Communist political system with three chapters on Chinese historical experience, each constituting a layer of memory in the minds of Chinese leaders and people. There is first the deepest layer of memory—the distant past that began some three thousand years ago. Next is the middle layer, memory of modern China from midnineteenth to midtwentieth century, marked by national disintegration, foreign aggression, civil wars, and Communist revolution. Finally there is the most fresh memory of the first twenty-seven years of the People's Republic, or the era of Mao Zedong (1949-76) which most of the contemporary generation of Chinese personally experienced. Our historical analyses will bear out the fact that the three layers of historical memories tend to reinforce each other and produce some invariable elements in Chinese politics, such as transfer of power through violence, bureaucratic centralism, and personal rulership. Moreover, certain parts of historical memory tend to have more influence on the present than other parts, the most influential being the experience of the Chinese Communists of their own revolutionary way to power. Finally, our historical analyses show that the memory component clashes with the contemporary and cosmopolitan part of Chinese Communist political conceptualization. The latter refers to the incorporation of Western ideas and values, i.e., Marxism-Leninism and industrial development. The interaction of these disparate elements in the Chinese conceptualization accounts for the dynamics of contemporary Chinese politics.

The late Chinese Communist leader Mao Zedong (Mao Tse-tung) once said that the Chinese people, apart from their other characteristics, "have two remarkable peculiarities; they are, first of all, poor and, secondly, blank."[1] Underlying these two peculiarities of China is mutual aggravation of natural and human conditions. Chinese politics, past and present, is but one contributing factor to this dynamic. Hence, to understand Chinese politics one must begin with the ecology of China.

ECOLOGY

In contrast to the Confucian norm of harmony between men and nature, in practice the relationship between Chinese society and its natural environment has been one of, to use Mao's words again, "antagonistic contradiction." A few figures on China bear this out. The total area of Chinese territory, 9.6 million square kilometers (similar to 9.3 million square kilometers of the United States; see map 1-1), seems to be immense. Much of it is uncultivable, however, and hence useless to most Chinese, who are predominantly farmers. According to noted geographer George Cressey, Chinese territory is about evenly divided between mountains and hills, 51 percent, and plains, basins, and plateaus. "Less than 15 percent of all China has suitable land forms, climate, and soil for any agricultural use. Great areas have been so seriously eroded that they are now unproductive for agriculture and have become virtually man-made deserts."[2] Thus historically, China has always had to bear a heavy pressure of population over land. Today the Chinese population (1.008 billion as of July 1982) amounts

MAP 1-1   China and the United States. Adapted from George B. Cressey, *Land of the 500 Million: A Geography of China* (New York: McGraw-Hill Book Company, 1955). Reproduced by permission.

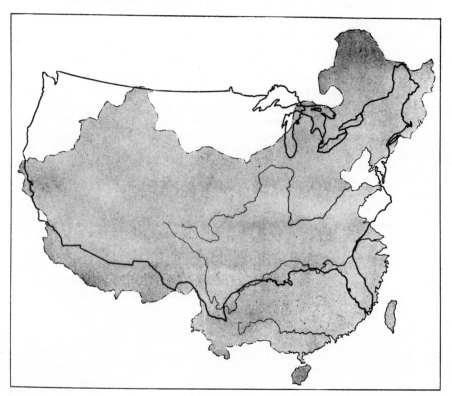

to 22.7 percent of the world population though Chinese territory is but 7 percent of world land area.[3] Owing to the Chinese topography and the fact that the people are predominantly farmers, the population is concentrated in the few plains along the eastern coast and along the fertile river valleys, especially that of the Yangtze (Chang-jiang) (see map 1-2). The result is extreme unevenness in the regional distribution of population. Over 90 percent of the Chinese reside in the eastern and southern coastal areas, which are but 40 percent of the Chinese territory. The vast Northwest, which amounts to 60 percent of the land, has only 10 percent of the Chinese population. According to the census of July 1982, the population density of the eleven coastal provinces is 828 per square mile (the national average density of the United States being 62 per square mile) whereas it is 30.5 in the northwestern provinces such as Tibet, Qinghai, Xinjiang, Gansu, Ningxia, and Inner Mongolia. In Shanghai, an eastern city, the population density reaches 4952 per square mile.[4]

Aside from the unevenness in population distribution, the Chinese terrain causes difficulty in communication and transportation. To begin with, the three major rivers of China, the Yellow River in the North, the Yangtze River in the Central-South and the Xi River (Xijiang or Sikiang) in the South, all flow eastward across the country. There has been no natural waterway to link the North and the South. Though the Chinese emperor of the Sui dynasty (581–618 A.D.) constructed the Grand Canal to link up the Yellow and Yangtze River valleys, communication between these two regions of China has been historically precarious. Because of the segregation between

MAP 1-2   Population density in China

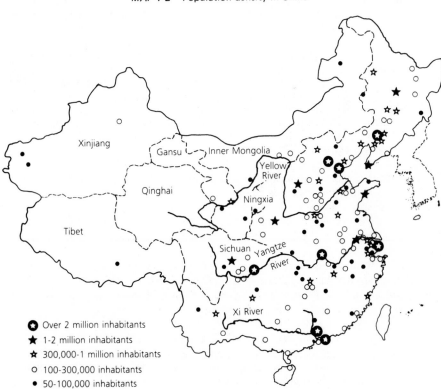

the regions popular stereotypes of northerners and southerners have developed. For example, the people from the North are supposed to be conservative and reliable. The southerners are held to be flexible, active, and radical.[5] In modern times revolutionary leaders and generals are mostly southerners, whereas foot soldiers are men from the North. Elsewhere in China the mountainous nature of the land has made construction of modern roads and railroads very difficult, if not impossible. The building of the Chengdu-Baoji (Chengtu-Paoki) line to link up Sichuan (Szechwan) Province's rich economy with the rest of China (see map 1-2), for example, requires forty-one tunnels in one stretch of twenty-six miles.[6] It is no wonder then that "economic regionalism has always characterized China."[7]

Regionalism, however, is not limited to the economy of China. At the popular level China is also characterized by cultural regionalism in the form of diverse dialects spoken by the people (see map 1-3). According to Cressey:

> China has a uniform written language, but the spoken tongue varies considerably. Across north China people speak an essentially uniform Mandarin, of which Pekinese is the elite version. . . . [However] along the coast, from Shanghai to Canton [Guangzhou today], there is a diversity of dialects, many so different as to be unrecognizable as Chinese. People from adjoining cities have difficulty in understanding one another. The province of Fukien [Fujian today], with more than one hundred dialects, is one of the worst in this respect.[8]

The diversity in language has posed a major problem for the Chinese Communist government to carry out its ambitious program of indoctrinating every Chinese in the ideology of socialism. According to Paul Serruys, at a national conference on language reform, it was reported:

> At the end of 1955 there were fifteen broadcasting stations out of 55 which had programs in local dialects; all together, there were 18 different dialects spoken on the Chinese radio network. In Wenchou [Wenzhou], only 5 percent of the people understand Pekinese. The older workers and women in the factories of Wusih [Wuxi] and even in Shanghai cannot understand Pekinese and want to listen to the dialect programs. In Kuangsi [Guangxi], radio broadcasts are made in Pekinese but are followed by translations in dialects, or the Mandarin variety of Liuchou [Liuzhou].[9]

That language diversity remains a serious problem today may be seen in a reader's letter to the authoritative *People's Daily (Renmin Ribao)* in September 1980 requesting that thereafter movies made in the South be equipped with captions as the people in the North could not understand the "common speech" (revised or popularized Pekinese promoted by the government as the national language) spoken by southern actors and actresses.[10]

So far we have discussed the macro manifestations of Chinese ecology. At micro level the impact of Chinese natural environment has also contributed to China's being "poor and blank." As even to this day 80 percent of Chinese are peasants, we shall discuss the condition in the countryside mainly.

MAP 1-3   Major language groups in China. Adapted from "New Atlas of China," *Sun Pao*, 1948, Institute of History and Language, Academia Sinica, as reprinted in George B. Cressey, *Land of the 500 Million: A Geography of China*, 1955.

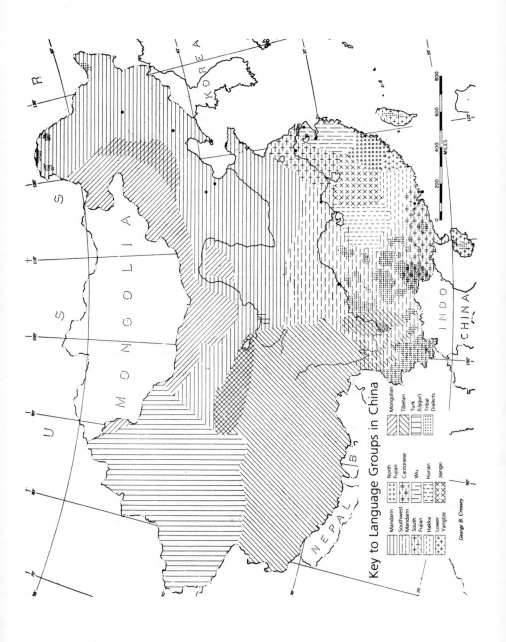

Key to Language Groups in China

Mandarin
Southwest Mandarin
South Fujian
Hakka
Lower Yangtze
North Fujian
Cantonese
Wu
Hunan
Jiangxi
Mongolian
Tibetan
Turk (Uygur)
Tribal
Dialects

George B. Cressey

5

Traditionally Chinese peasants live in compact village communities. Each community centers its economic and social activity in a marketing town where peasants sell whatever they cannot (or will not) consume themselves and buy whatever they cannot produce themselves. The marketing towns are where much of the social interaction of peasants outside of their family circles takes place. Anthropologist William Skinner found that a typical marketing community in premodern China consisted of eighteen satellite villages. Skinner estimated that in 1948 the average size of a marketing area was 25 square miles (64.4 square kilometers) and the average population was a little over seven thousand.[11] Skinner found that the boundaries of the marketing areas do not overlap; thus each area is, by and large, discrete, i.e., a self-contained community. Chinese sociologist Martin Yang has this to say about the autonomy of a rural marketing community: "On the whole, although there is no clear-cut line of demarcation, each market town has a definite and recognizable area, and looks upon the people of certain villages as its primary customers; in turn, it is regarded by the villagers as their own."[12] In general, in traveling from one such community to the other, one finds differences in dialect, units of weights and measures, and religious worship. To this day much of rural China preserves this marketing community structure.

Living in isolation and engaging day in and day out in backbreaking labor, Chinese peasants (or for that matter, all traditional peasants) cannot but develop a very constricted mentality. C. K. Yang describes it well:

> The peasant's personal life was dictated by the schedule of farm chores, many of which, like planting and harvesting, could not be delayed too many days without causing economic loss. . . . he did not have any protracted period of complete leisure which he could devote to the development of other social, economic, or cultural interests.
>
> His mental outlook was conditioned by the simple organic cycle of his crops. His economic ties with the urban centers and his occasional visits there did not change the basic conditioning factors relentlessly exerted upon him by the simple, cyclical, demanding, and poorly remunerated farm schedule. The rich and complex urban culture standing at close proximity to him failed to inculcate in him an urban way of life. . .[13]

The constricted mentality of Chinese peasants, however, does not prevent them from becoming highly skilled producers, skilled albeit in prescientific farming. This qualification is of crucial importance. Almost every Western observer of Chinese farming has been impressed by the efficiency of Chinese peasants, efficiency in a traditional context. R. H. Tawney, who visited China in the late 1920s, for example, writes that a typical Chinese farmer "has acquired an ingenuity which has rarely been surpassed in wringing from the land at his disposal, not, indeed, the most that it could yield—for the output could be increased by the use of modern methods—but the *utmost possible* with the resources that he has hitherto commanded" (emphasis added).[14] The high efficiency of Chinese peasants in prescientific farming, however, has historically played a cruel joke on their lives. For a certain period, Chinese farmers were able to produce enough to sustain a growing population while a brilliant elite culture flourished in the cities. But their efficiency invariably had definite limits. Sooner or later population rise always caught up with the stationary supply of land and resources. Rural indebtedness and destitution gradually increased. As peasants became impoverished, some could no longer make a living in their self-contained community, and more and more of them became beggars or bandits outside their community. Then at a time of crisis, such as a severe drought or disastrous flood, the peasant bandits who had been cast off from their communities were joined by more of their kind. The stage was set for a massive peasant rebellion, which traditionally toppled a dynasty and brought forth a new dynasty whereupon the same cycle of peace-prosperity-population rise-poverty-rebellion began all over again. "Famine is the economic, civil war the political, expression of the pressure of population on the means of subsistence," wrote Tawney.[15] As we shall discuss later, the founding of the People's Republic of China in 1949 by the Communist party of China (hereafter the CPC) did not deviate from this traditional pattern in which politicians rode to power on the crest of peasant discontent.

POLITICAL TRADITION

The social stresses as a result of a combination of natural and human factors described so far cannot but impinge directly and forcefully on Chinese political development. The overall rural framework of Chinese society and the social and economic stresses stemming from these are dynamical factors that channel Chinese political actions and traditions. In this section we shall discuss the four major Chinese political traditions: revolution, regionalism, bureaucratic centralism, and alien rule.

The Revolutionary Tradition

For good or bad, transfer of political power from one group to the other through violence has run through Chinese history like a red thread. The renowned twentieth-century Chinese writer Liang Ch'i-ch'ao (Liang Qichao) compiled a list of *major* revolutions in Chinese history and counted the duration of each revolution (see table 1-1).

Not included in the table is the Qing (Manchu dynasty, 1644-1911). From the first massive peasant rebellion of the Taiping in 1850 to the founding of the Republic of China in 1912, the revolution lasted for sixty-two years. Then it took another thirty-seven years of civil war to transit from the Republic of China in 1912 to the People's Republic of China in 1949. Today the civil war between the Communists and the Nationalists continues, albeit in a prolonged dormant phase.

Compared with the revolutions in the West, Liang observed, the Chinese revolutions have seven unique characteristics. First, Chinese revolutions in history are "private" in contrast with the "public" revolutions in the West. That is, Chinese revolutions are led by individual leaders, who regard the revolution as a personal

TABLE 1-1 Revolutions in Chinese history

DYNASTY TOPPLED	DURATION OF REVOLUTION OR CIVIL WAR
Qin (221–206 B.C.)	16 years
Western Han (206 B.C.–8 A.D.)	26 years
Eastern Han (25–219 A.D.)	97 years
Sui (589–617 A.D.)	20 years
Tang (618–907 A.D.)	104 years
Yuan (1280–1367 A.D.)	23 years
Ming (1368–1643 A.D.)	57 years

Ch'i-ch'ao Liang, *Ying-ping-shih-Wen-chi,* vol. 1 (Taipei: Hsinhsin Shu-chu, 1955), sec. 1: 193–94.

undertaking. In contrast, Western revolutions are staged in the name of an organized group such as the Parliament in the English civil war of 1642–46, the Estates General in the French revolution and the thirteen colonies in the American War of Independence. Second, Chinese revolutions are motivated by active pursuit of personal ambition rather than in defense of group interest, as in Western revolutions. The latter is for defense of middle-class interests, whereas the former is for personal aggrandizement. Third, China has revolution by the upper or the lower class but never by the middle class. In Western revolutions it is the middle class that often takes the lead. Fourth, in terms of the number of participants, Chinese revolutions typically consisted of numerous independent rebel bands, whereas in the West revolutionaries are organized around a single group. Fifth, as table 1-1 illustrates, Chinese revolutions have been extremely protracted and have caused untold millions of casualties. In the West revolutions end quickly, as soon as the ancient regime is toppled. Sixth, with the single exception of the French Revolution, the object of Western revolutions has been the ancient monarch and no others. In China revolutionaries have directed their violence not only against the old dynasty but also against each other. Seventh and finally, Chinese revolutions throughout history more often than not have facilitated the conquest of China by alien races. Sometimes alien tribes capitalized on China's civil war to invade the country. Sometimes revolutionary groups in China induced alien tribes to help fight other Chinese rebel groups. In contrast, Western revolutionaries are always able to rally all the forces to defeat foreign invaders.

It was during the anarchic days of the warlords after the overthrow of the Qing dynasty in 1912 that Liang wrote about these contrasts between revolutions in China and the West. His purpose was to awaken knowledgeable Chinese to the futile and even fraudulent nature of the revolutions in China. But what interests us is the social and economic dynamics underlying the peculiarities of the revolutionary tradition of China. Perhaps the most important cause of the various characteristics of Chinese revolutions is the overwhelming rural framework of Chinese society, which prevented the development of a substantial middle class and a national consciousness. In Europe (more notably in the western than the eastern part of it), the city and its middle class had always played an important role in society, in the economy, and in politics, even in medieval times. Another possible reason for the peculiarities of Chinese revolutions is the predominantly exploitative relationship between the imperial court and the Chinese rural population. Examples of this may be gleaned from Chinese classics. Mencius said to a feudal king some two thousand years ago: "While there is [sic] the finest meats in your own kitchen and sleek horses in your stable, your subjects have a starved look and in your countryside people are dying of hunger."[16] All these factors combined, i.e., the rural, nonpolitical frame of mind of the majority of Chinese people in traditional times, the exploitative relationship between the imperial court and the populace, and the sharp contrast between the high living of the court and the subsistence living of most Chinese, make traditional (and contemporary) Chinese politics the arena for no-holds-barred struggles. The stakes are extraordinarily high for those participating in the political struggle. As an old Chinese saying goes, "The victor is the king whereas the vanquished is a bandit." There is little or no restraint to political struggle, neither national identity nor class interest, least of all, public opinion.

Regionalism

The ecological and social dynamics that have conditioned the revolutionary tradition of Chinese politics have also contributed to political and economic regionalism in China. Chinese since ancient times have accepted disunity and regionalism as facts of life. The popular Chinese novel *The Romance of Three Kingdoms,* written some five hundred years ago, begins with the observation that a period of unity is always followed by a period of disunity, after which a period of unity will return once more.

Though Chinese political theory and most Chinese political leaders almost invariably advocate centralized and unified rule, in practice through most of China's more than two thousand years of history there have been long periods of disunity when China was split up into several independent regional states. For example, in the 2,133 years between the first dynasty of the Qin in 221 B.C. and the end of the Qing (Manchu) dynasty of 1912, for almost half the time (some 963 years) China was split up into regional states. The point is that the centrifugal forces in Chinese society and politics are at least as strong as the centripetal ones. China undoubtedly had some strong and unified dynasties in the past, notably the Han (206 B.C.–222 A.D.) and the Tang (618-907 A.D.). During the latter Chinese political strength reached its zenith. It is said that during the Tang dynasty in the seventh and eighth centuries, China may have been the greatest country in the world in area, population, government, and culture. But we must not lose sight of the equally important tradition of regionalism in Chinese history. As Tawney wrote in the 1920s, "The thought of China, one and indivisible, is no doubt a power; but it is primarily the reflection of a great cultural tradition. As a political force, expressed in the working routine of habits and institutions, it still has to be created."[17] The same can be said of China in the 1980s.

Bureaucratic Centralism

Whether China is unified in a single dynasty or split into several regional states, the form of Chinese political organization has always been the "proprietary state," i.e., the state was a family affair—the reigning family—and the offices of the state were the personal property of the emperor. Power won by force of arms and after a long fight is not likely to be shared by the victor with the rest of the community.

According to scholar Kung-chuan Hsiao, from the first unified dynasty of Qin in 221 B.C. to the last dynasty of Qing (1644-1912), the basic principles of imperial control underwent little modification. Successive Chinese emperors and ministers improved and refined Chinese administration "generally in favor of increased centralization, more minute regulations, stricter surveillance, and tighter control."[18] Yet at the same time this bureaucratic and centralized system was, until the midnineteenth century, hopelessly confused with the domestic service of the imperial court. The officials were the servants of the emperor, who appointed, promoted, dismissed, or punished them as he wished. The standard six ministries of traditional Chinese national government dealt almost exclusively with the maintenance of the bureaucracy itself, not with the welfare of the population. These ministries were in charge of appointment and dismissal of officials (*libu*), military conscription (*pinbu* and *hubu*), construction of palaces (*gongbu*), ceremony (*libu*), and punishment of criminals (*xingbu*).[19] The first Chinese ministry that was separated from the domestic service of the court—the Tsungli Yamen, or ministry of external affairs—was established in 1860 as a result of the imperialist attacks on China from the West. In England the process of divorcing national government from the domestic service of the court began as early as the twelfth century, and the first office to break free was the financial administration.[20] The contrast between China and England both in the time of the separation between the administrative system and the domestic service of the court and in the first type of administration to be independent is of crucial importance in understanding Chinese bureaucratic tradition. Moreover, the implications are of contemporary significance, given (1) the charge of present Chinese Communist leaders that Mao Zedong imposed on the Communist party a "patriarchal system" and (2) the prevalence of corruption in the present Chinese Communist administrative system.[21]

When analyzing the traditional Chinese bureaucratic system, one must not just look at its formal appearance and structure but must also pay close attention to the informal process within Chinese bureaucracy. The formal appearance of the traditional Chinese bureaucracy impresses one with its rationality and efficiency. The bureaucracy exhibits all the necessary qualities of Max Weber's "ideal" bureaucratic organization, namely: (1) organization of official functions bound by rules; (2) officials having a specified sphere of competence; (3) hierarchical organization of offices; (4) official conduct regulated by explicit rules; (5) strict separation between offices and the personal property of officials; and (6) administrative acts, decisions, and rules formulated and recorded in writing.[22] At the national level traditional Chinese bureaucracy typically was composed of a prime minister (zaixiang) who was directly responsible to the emperor and a central government consisting of six ministries or boards. The prime minister was often assisted by coordinating councils of senior officials, such as the Grand Secretariat and the Grand Council during the last Qing dynasty. These officials advised the emperor on major policies and were responsible for day-to-day administration of the empire. While senior officials, especially the prime minister and members of the coordinating councils, were formerly fellow revolutionaries during the emperor's struggle for power, others were recruited after the founding of a new dynasty through the civil service examination, a procedure that is regarded as unique in traditional political systems for its universalistic standard and open accessibility.

Through a system of local governments the power of the Chinese national government was extended to every part of the empire. The Chinese territory was divided into provinces, prefectures, and counties. The emperor personally appointed governors or governor-generals to rule the provinces and magistrates to rule the prefectures and counties. To keep the far-flung local government under the control of the imperial court, the number of local officials was purposely kept small. During the last dynasty of the Qing, there was on the average one magistrate for 100,000 inhabitants in 1749 and 250,000 in 1819. Altogether there were 1,500 magistrates.[23] The conduct and responsibilities of local officials were comprehensively specified by rules handed down from the central government in Peking. "Discretionary power was very sparingly given to officials, even those with great responsibilities. Every administrative decision and action had to be reported to Peking, including matters that were merely routine," Kung-chuan Hsiao wrote about Chinese bureaucracy under the last Qing dynasty.[24] The local government had no revenue of its own. "Officials of the local government . . . acted only as agents of the central government in collecting and delivering taxes in accordance with the quotas set by the central government."[25] Even the operating budget of a local government was determined by the central government.

This highly centralized and formalized administrative system was, of course, designed to enable the emperor to control the officials. But the control measures impeded the actual operation of traditional Chinese bureaucracy for two reasons. First, the number of officials was too small to rule an empire as large as China. Second, regional differences were too great to permit uniform and rigid rules and regulations as specified by the national government. As happens in every overregulated and rigid organization, an informal system developed in traditional Chinese bureaucracy in order for the officials to function. This informal system consisted mainly of the personal retinues of officials. Known as *muliao* (staff or secretary) at upper levels and *shuli* (clerks) at lower levels, these nonofficial officials were employed in great numbers and they made the bureaucracy run.[26] This was especially true in local government, since a single magistrate was responsible for too large a territory and population, and his responsibilities were too numerous. Moreover, owing to another control measure of Chinese emperors, no magistrate was allowed to serve in his home province. So a Chinese magistrate had to employ, on his own, a large number of local people to help him carry out the official duties. Scholar T'ung-tsu Ch'u has done an exhaustive study of this sytem at the local level during the last Qing dynasty. A magistrate, for example, employed four groups of personal retinues: clerks, "government runners" (messengers, guards, and policemen), personal servants, and private secretaries. While exceptions could be found, most of these nonofficial officials were of lower-class or even outcast origin, and their only motive to join the administration was material gain. (The personal servants and private secretaries, however, often came from higher classes, and some did have a sense of "professional calling.") They were chiefly responsible for the image and reality of traditional Chinese bureaucracy as rife with corruption and graft.[27]

As the formal bureaucracy in traditional China was actually run by so many personal retinues of officials, it was pervaded by cliques and personal intrigues. Chang Tsun-ming, a noted Chinese political scientist, attributes to these personal employees of officials in traditional Chinese bureaucracy the four major manifestations of Chinese political culture: emphasis on ideology, cliquishness, formalism, and corruption.[28] Since senior officials were mostly recruited from the civil service examination, which tested almost exclusively a person's mastery of Confucian classics, Chinese officials tended to occupy themselves with moralizing and doctrinal polemics rather than social and economic matters. The use of personal retinues and their dependence on the bureaucracy for their livelihood naturally inclined them to form cliques, engage in graft, and avoid initiative. Historically almost every attempt at reform by conscientious officials—for example, Wang An-shih in the Sung dynasty (907-1127)—went down in defeat at the hands of rival and conservative cliques.[29] The centralized bureaucracy, being placid, could neither stem the tide of social stresses nor resist alien conquerors. As we shall discuss later, there are numerous parallels between the traditional and the contemporary Chinese bureaucracies in mainland China.

So far our discussion of traditional Chinese bureaucracy has been confined to what sociologists call the manifest functions (intended purpose or activity) of an institution. But every institution is likely to have latent functions (unintended purpose or activity). In traditional times the Chinese civil service examination and the bureaucracy were intended to recruit loyal servants for the emperor. Through this system of examination, however, a strategic middle group, variously referred to in Western literature as Chinese Mandarins, scholar-officials, literati, or gentry, was created.[30] Their number was of course small but these Mandarins played a crucial role in Chinese politics and society. Not every one of the Mandarins was employed by the government. Sometimes scholar-officials out of office organized an informal "opinion group" in the capital. Chinese emperors naturally kept a close watch over these unemployed Mandarins, and from time to time in Chinese history the emperor launched persecution campaigns to prevent them from challenging the authority of the court.[31]

Members of the Mandarin class who lived in their own communities rather than in the capital—the gentry—were the crucial link between the thousands of rural communities and the bureaucracy.[32] The formal administration of traditional China was not extended to the lowest level of the empire—the marketing areas, which we mentioned earlier, where the majority of Chinese people lived. The lowest officials were the magistrates, whose offices were located in large towns at some distance from where most Chinese people lived. Consequently, Chinese magistrates cultivated personal relationships with the gentry in rural communities in order to collect taxes and conscript labor. As with any intermediary group, the function of Chinese gentry was complex and ambivalent. T'ung-tsu Ch'u points out, for example: "While the gentry could represent their own interests to the local government, there was no agent to represent other groups in the community. At most, the gentry were likely to be concerned with the welfare of the people only in the interest of general stability in the community."[33] But the important latent function of the gentry is that they were the only *nationalized* group in the particularistic rural communities of old days. To the extent that traditional China was unified, much of the unification whether in the cultural or political sense of the word was forged by the gentry, or the Mandarins, in Chinese society. It is interesting to mention here that according to some American scholars the maintenance of American democracy depends heavily on the strategic middle group—"the influentials, the opinion-leaders, the political activists in the order."[34]

Alien Rule

The traditions of revolution, regionalism, and the peculiar character of Chinese bureaucracy that we have discussed so far all contributed to another major Chinese political tradition: long periods of alien rule. As Liang Ch'i-ch'ao pointed out, revolutions or civil wars in China often induced alien tribes from North China to invade and conquer parts or all of China. Until the coming of Western imperialists in the mid-nineteenth century, the foreign threat to China was always the nomadic tribes in the North, against whom the Great Wall was constructed. Chinese armies of peasant conscripts were no match for mounted archers from either the Mongolian or Turkish tribes in North or Northwest China. The result was that "during the last seven centuries China had been ruled more than half the time by non-Chinese emperors—the Yuan dynasty of the Mongols (1279-1368) and the Ch'ing (Qing) dynasty of the Manchus (1644-1912)."[35]

What is noteworthy is that these alien dynasties did not transform China's sociocultural entity. On the contrary, alien rule further solidified Chinese traditions of regionalism and bureaucratic centralism. As John Fairbank points out, soon after their conquest of China these alien rulers had no alternative but to adopt Chinese bureaucratic rule. "Indeed, since a million or so alien invaders were out-numbered a hundred or more to one by the Chinese populace, they could rule only with Chinese help."[36] But though the Mongols and the Manchus had to use Chinese to administer the empire, they did not have to (but they did) adopt the Chinese way of rule. In the nineteenth century in India the British colonial force was outnumbered by Indians, but the British rulers did not adopt Indian ways. The Mongols and the Manchus, however, were not culturally equipped to rule a densely populated agrarian empire. In terms of modern political science, the alien tribes that conquered China in traditional times had developed in their own lands a primitive political system in which the functions of government were not separated from other functions in society owing to their small numbers and the tribal basis of their communities.[37] China's government, however, had long since evolved into a centralized bureaucratic system capable of administering an extended empire. In the end, the Mongols proved to be incompetent rulers and were overthrown, and the Manchus were absorbed into the Chinese framework. Thus, paradoxically the long years of alien rule in China served to further consolidate Chinese political traditions rather than to transform them. In other words, Chinese cultural complacency, which was very early expressed by Mencius—"I have heard of making Chinese out of barbarians, but I have never heard of making barbarians out of Chinese"—was actually reinforced by alien rule. This cultural complacency on the part of Chinese elites would have serious implications for China's coping with Western imperialism in the nineteenth century, as we shall discuss later. In the meantime, the long alien rule is a further reminder to us of the lack of a politically organized society (in modern context) in China and the peculiarities of Chinese bureaucracy.

With the single exception of alien rule, all the things that we have discussed so far remain dynamical forces in contemporary Chinese politics. Later chapters will show that modern China witnessed extended civil strife with peasant rebellions, numerous other rebel groups, and alien invaders. The victory of the Communist party of China in the struggle for power closely followed the traditional pattern. The way of rule by the Communists replicates and further refines traditional Chinese bureaucratic centralism. In the meantime, the dispersed rural communities remain the primary form of the rural settlement in China, ultimately defeating Mao Zedong's scheme to collectivize Chinese farming into huge people's communes.

NOTES

1. Stuart R. Schram, *The Political Thought of Mao Tse-tung* (New York: Praeger Publishers, 1970), p. 352.

2. George B. Cressey, *Land of the 500 Million: A Geography of China* (New York: McGraw-Hill Book Company, 1955), p. 47.

3. Xueyuan Tian and Yuguang Zhen, "The Population Factor in Economic Adjustment," *Renmin Ribao* (hereafter *RMRB*), May 11, 1981, p. 2.

4. *RMRB*, November 16, 1982, p. 5.

5. Cressey, *Land of the 500 Million*, p. 13.

6. Theodore Shabad, *China's Changing Map: National and Regional Development, 1949–71* (New York: Frederick A. Praeger, 1972), p. 94.

7. Cressey, *Land of the 500 Million*, p. 149.

8. Ibid., p. 13.

9. Paul L. M. Surruys, *Survey of the Chinese Language Reform and the Anti-illiteracy Movement in Communist China* (Berkeley: Center for Chinese Studies, University of California, 1962), pp. 142–43.

10. *RMRB*, September 6, 1980, p. 8.

11. G. William Skinner, "Marketing and Social Structure in Rural China," part I, *Journal of Asian Studies* XXIV, no. 1 (November 1964), 3–43.

12. Martin Yang, *A Chinese Village: Taitou, Shantung Province* (New York: Columbia University Press, 1945), p. 190.

13. C. K. Yang, "A Chinese Village in Early Communist Transition," in *Chinese Communist Society: The Family and the Village* (Cambridge, Mass.: MIT Press, 1972), p. 35.

14. R. H. Tawney, *Land and Labor in China* (Boston: Beacon Press, 1966), p. 45.

15. Ibid., p. 104.

16. James R. Ware, trans., *The Sayings of Mencius* (New York: New American Library, 1960), p. 46.

17. Tawney, *Land and Labor*, p. 163.

18. Kung-chuan Hsiao, *Rural China: Imperial Control in the Nineteenth Century* (Seattle: University of Washington Press, 1960), p. 3.

19. The best book summing up China's political tradition is, alas, in Chinese—*Chungkuo Chengchi Liang-ch'ien-nien (Two Thousand Years of Chinese Politics)* by Chang Tsun-min (Reprinted in Hong Kong: Chung-wen Shu-tien, 1971). Students interested in English sources of traditional Chinese bureaucracy should consult the essays in David S. Nivison and Arthur F. Wright, eds., *Confucianism in Action* (Stanford, Calif.: Stanford University Press, 1959).

20. T. F. Tout, "The Emergence of a Bureaucracy," in Robert K. Merton, Ailsa P. Gray, Barbara Hockey, and Hanan C. Selvin, eds., *Reader in Bureaucracy* (New York: Free Press, 1952), pp. 68–79.

21. For a comprehensive critique and assessment by the Chinese Communists themselves

on Mao and the party see "On Question of Party History," *Beijing Review*, no. 17 (1981), pp. 10–39. For the corruption in Chinese Communist bureaucracy, see Alan P. L. Liu, "The Politics of Corruption in the People's Republic of China," *American Political Science Review* 77, no. 3 (September 1983), 602–63.

22. Max Weber, "The Essentials of Bureaucratic Organization: An Ideal-Type Construction," in Merton et al., *Reader in Bureaucracy*, pp. 19–20.

23. Kung-chuan Hsiao, *Rural China*, p. 5.

24. Ibid.

25. T'ung-tsu Ch'u, *Local Government in China under the Ch'ing* (Stanford, Calif.: Stanford University Press, 1962), p. 194.

26. Ibid. Also, Kenneth E. Folsom, *Friends, Guests, and Colleagues: The Mu-fu System in the Late Ch'ing Period* (Berkeley: University of California Press, 1968).

27. T'ung-tsu Ch'u, *Local Government*.

28. Chang Tsun-min, *Chinese Politics.*

29. John Meskill, *Wang An-shih: Practical Reformer?* (Boston: D. C. Heath and Company, 1963).

30. Ping-ti Ho, *The Ladder of Success in Imperial China* (New York: John Wiley & Sons, 1964).

31. Charles O. Hucker, "The Tung-Lin Movement of the Late Ming Period," in John K. Fairbank, ed., *Chinese Thought and Institutions* (Chicago: University of Chicago Press, 1957).

32. Chung-li Chang, *The Chinese Gentry: Studies on Their Role in Nineteenth-Century Chinese Society* (Seattle: University of Washington Press, 1955).

33. T'ung-tsu Ch'u, *Local Government*, p. 198.

34. V. O. Key, Jr., *Public Opinion and American Democracy* (New York: Alfred A. Knopf, 1963), p. 558.

35. John K. Fairbank, "Synarchy under the Treaties," in Fairbank, *Chinese Thought*, p. 204.

36. Ibid.

37. See the classification of political systems in Gabriel A. Almond and G. Bingham Powell, Jr., *Comparative Politics: A Developmental Approach* (Boston: Little, Brown and Company, 1966), pp. 213–54.

CHAPTER 2

The Rise of Communism in China

From the midnineteenth to the midtwentieth century, China was again plunged into the pattern of severe social stresses, peasant rebellions, foreign invasion, and regionalization of the Chinese state. The Communist party of China grew out of this historical background.[1]

The violence and disorder in modern China was caused not only by the decay of the old dynasty of Qing (Manchu dynasty) but also by an invasion of China, both physically and culturally, by European imperialism. Consequently, the concerns of the Chinese were no longer just who would win in the struggle for power but also what the new order should be like, now that Western imperialism had made it clear that China would not be able to survive as a sovereign nation if she chose to return to the old dynastic rule. Furthermore, the participants in the political change in modern China were also different from traditional ones. Whereas in the past after a dynasty fell, the major actors contesting for power were either members of the old ruling class, peasant rebels, or alien conquerors, in modern times a new group joined in the process. That was the new middle class of China, i.e., young men and women from an upper-class background who had received a modern (Europeanized) education. They were the so-called alienated intellectuals, alienated from the old Chinese culture (as they perceived it) and radical in their desire to build a new China modeled after Western nation-states. In other words, the revolutions in modern China would *no longer conform entirely* to the old peculiarities described by Liang Ch'i-ch'ao. A new middle class had emerged in China and would take the lead in modern Chinese revolutions.

The chaos in modern China resulted from the joining forces of modern and traditional factors. At a phenomenal level political crises unfolded in (1) destruction of the Qing dynasty, 1850-1912, (2) civil war among the warlords, 1913-28, and (3) the rise of the Communist party of China, 1921-49, during which the Japanese invasion of China also took place.

THE DESTRUCTION OF THE QING DYNASTY,
1850–1912

By the midnineteenth century, the Qing dynasty that had ruled China as Manchurian conquerors since 1644 was already in a state of decline. In 1839–42, the Manchu lost to Great Britain in the Opium War and capitulated in the Treaty of Nanking to the British demands for Hong Kong, for the opening of coastal cities of China to trade with the outside, and for diplomatic representation in China. From then on Chinese society was open directly to Western influence, for soon after the British a horde of Western European powers and tsarist Russia followed the example of the Treaty of Nanking, obtaining numerous concessions from the Manchu government.

In the meantime, in the countryside the old social and economic crisis of peasant destitution was developing on its own. In the 1740s the Chinese population was roughly 143 million. By 1851 the Chinese population was estimated to be around 432 million.[2] Natural disasters of various types (drought, flood, hurricane) struck Chinese provinces from 1846 to 1850. In 1849 the province of Guangxi was hit by a widespread famine. In the next year, a massive peasant revolt, known as the Taiping Rebellion, broke out there. The revolt lasted for a decade, ravaged half of China, and caused some 20 million deaths. It provoked other rebellions by peasants and ethnic groups in China down to 1900. Though none of the peasant rebel groups succeeded in toppling the Qing dynasty, each group nevertheless weakened the dynasty and prepared the way for modern middle-class revolution.

Typical of many ancient regimes on the eve of revolution, the Manchu dynasty at first was confronted with internal opposition, i.e., members of the old ruling class who advocated urgent reform in order to save the regime. These moderates almost always were defeated at the hands of the conservatives. The political stage was then cleared for radicals bent on a violent destruction of the old regime. So it was with the Manchu. In 1898 a group of reformers were able to win the confidence of the young Manchu emperor, Guangxu, and designed a comprehensive reform of Chinese government and the educational system. But their scheme was short-lived, for the real power inside the Manchu court was in the hands of Empress Dowager Ci Xi (Tsu-hsi), who staged a palace coup, putting the young emperor under house arrest and executing most reformers. Since reform was not possible, revolution was the only way out.

The revolutionary movement against the Manchu dynasty was led by Dr. Sun Yat-sen, whose background and education symbolized the rising new middle class of China. Dr. Sun came from a wealthy rural family in the province of Guangdong, which was the first Chinese province to have commercial contact with the West, mainly Great Britain. Part of Dr. Sun's family had emigrated to Hawaii, and Dr. Sun received his middle-school education in an English missionary school in Honolulu. Subsequently, Dr. Sun acquired a medical education in Hong Kong. Dismayed and disgusted by the incompetence of the Manchu and influenced by his Western education, Dr. Sun rallied a group of like-minded young Chinese to plot a violent overthrow of the Manchu dynasty. Their movement was precipitated by China's humiliating defeat at the hands of the Japanese in 1894. The year after that Dr. Sun and his followers launched their first urban uprising against the Manchu rulers.

In the meantime, the moribund nature of the Manchu was brought forcefully to the Chinese by their handling of the Boxer Rebellion of 1900. The Boxers were a band of peasant rebels in the province of Shandong (Shangtung) whose avowed goal was to kill Westerners who trampled Chinese land and violated Chinese customs. The cause of the Boxer Rebellion was the same social stress that had motivated the Taiping Rebellion of 1850. Chinese historian Shi-heng Li recounted the woes that befell on Chinese peasants since the midnineteenth century:

> During the period of the Taiping rebellion more than 30,000,000 persons were slain. From 1894 to 1895 in the Mohammedan Rebellion in Kansu [Gansu] 250,000 persons were killed. In the years of 1810, 1811, 1846, and 1849 several famines occurred in wide areas of North China. About 45,000,000 persons starved. During 1877, famine covered three entire provinces of North China, and approximately 9,500,000 persons died from food shortage. In 1888 as a result of the break of the Yellow River dikes approximately 2,000,000 persons were drowned. From 1892 to 1894 there was a big drought in the provinces of Shansi [Shanxi], Shensi [Shaanxi], and Hopei [Hebei], and in Mongolia, and the deaths of the people were enormous in number.[3]

The Boxers came from the regions of North China devastated by drought and famine. Claiming to have acquired immunity from Western bullets, they attracted the attention of the Manchu viceroy of Shandong who then brought the cause of the Boxers to the ignorant Manchu court in Peking. In May 1900 Empress Dowager Ci Xi blessed the Boxers and ordered the Manchu army to admit the Boxers to Peking in order to exterminate Westerners in the city. Thereupon eight Western nations including the United States and Japan formed an allied expeditionary force and invaded Peking, forcing the empress and her court to flee the city. The British, Japanese, and German troops burned, raped, and looted in the capital and executed captured members of the Boxers. The Manchu court capitulated and signed a treaty with the allies, which required China to destroy the coastal defense in the North so that Western and Japanese troops could march into Peking as they wished, to permit the stationing of Western and Japanese troops in Peking and elsewhere in China on a permanent basis, and above all, to pay a huge indemnity fund to all the invasion forces.

Now even the Empress Dowager felt the pressure from Chinese society for urgent reform. Starting in December 1900, the empress went through a series of motions to "reform" the Manchu system. The first measure was to reform the civil service examination so that a new type of officials who were educated in modern schools could be recruited. In 1905 the civil service examination was abolished altogether, thus severing the only tie that hitherto had bound the imperial court to Chinese society. The death of the empress dowager in 1908 and the installation of a minor on the Manchu throne further precipitated more demands from Chinese upper classes in the provinces for rapid change toward a "constitutional monarchy." In 1909 preparliamentary societies in the provinces were organized, and these became the centers for mobilization against the Manchu court. The next year the Manchu court was embroiled in a serious conflict with several provincial Chinese authorities over the right of the court to build railways that would extend the power of the court effectively to the provinces. Local militia controlled by Chinese officials were in open clashes with the Manchu army. As with other moribund ancient regimes, the reforms of the Manchu court merely hastened its own downfall.

It was against this background that the middle-class revolution *nominally* led by Dr. Sun Yat-sen was finally able to overthrow the Manchu dynasty. On October 10, 1911, while Dr. Sun was away in America, a group of dissident army officers in the central Chinese city of Wuchang (now Wuhan) staged a successful insurrection against the Manchu viceroy in town, declaring their independence of the Manchu and allegiance to Dr. Sun's movement. Then, one by one, in the cities and provinces south of the Yangtze River, revolutionaries drove off Manchu officials and declared independence. Dr. Sun returned to China to assume the provisional presidency of the Republic of China. In February 1912, the Manchu government formally abdicated in favor of the Republic.

The Qing dynasty fell primarily for two reasons. First, even with all the encroachments on Chinese soil by Western powers, the Manchu rulers and their Chinese supporters were not entirely convinced of the need for fundamental reforms of Chinese society, economy, and politics. They believed to the very last in the "superiority of Chinese civilization." Hence, even though the Manchu after 1860 did establish some modern institutions such as arsenals, modern army, navy, iron works, and ship-building companies, these were isolated and alien organizations within the overwhelming rural framework of China.[4] There was no will from the Manchu rulers to plan systematically for modernization. The high officials of the Qing dynasty thought that a limited number of technical institutions were enough to resist Western invasion without having to change basic Chinese institutions and values. Second, had the Qing authorities had the will and knowledge to change China fundamentally in the direction of industrialization, it is doubtful that the imperial bureaucracy would be willing, let alone able, to carry out the task. Liang Ch'i-ch'ao described the attitudes of the Qing officials at the time of the abortive reform of 1898:

> The first group of officials does not know the existence of five continents of the world. They, if told of the names of foreign nations, would disbelieve it. When one mentions to them the danger of foreign aggression, these officials would accuse the informer of making traitor's talk. The second group is aware of the danger of foreign aggression. But they reckon that since they are already aged, all they hope for is peace in their last years. . . . The third group is of the view that even if the empire falls, their personal wealth will not be affected so long as the court is allowed to survive (by Westerners). But if the present reformers had their way, then the basis of self-enrichment of these officials would be lost. Moreover, these officials know that being old and useless they would be rejected by the new administration. So they fought desperately to hold on to their present positions.[5]

From the Taiping Rebellion to the Republican Revolution of 1912, sixty-two years had passed. The slow death of the Manchu had deepened the social and economic crises of China. By 1912 Chinese society was torn to fragments. On China's coast were Westernized cities known as treaty ports, many of which, like Shanghai, were actually administered by Western powers. They were, in fact, Western colonies with modern commercial and industrial institutions run by Westerners but worked by Chinese laborers. A small Chinese proletariat grew in the cities. But more important than the proletariat were the students and army officers, who became part of the new middle class of China. Western missionaries had opened schools and universities. Chinese educators established their own modern schools and private military academies. From the new middle class sprang modern Chinese nationalism. As in most developing nations, among the new middle class of China intellectuals and army officers predominated. Intellectual radicalism, combined with the coercive power of army officers, plunged modern China into cycles of civil war and anarchy. In the meantime, the countryside remained as it had been when the Taiping Rebellion began. The dying Manchu dynasty, of course, could not and did not take measures to ameliorate the plight of Chinese peasants. The revolutionaries under Dr. Sun were more politically than socially conscious of China's crisis. Though in the main, Chinese peasants by 1900 had spent their rebellious impulses, peasant unrest continued in isolated places.

CIVIL WARS AMONG WARLORDS, 1913-28

The overthrow of the Manchu dynasty did not bring peace and order to China. Instead China degenerated into anarchy in which private armies led by native leaders known as warlords controlled the provinces, warring with each other continuously from 1913 to 1928.

Dr. Sun had inspired the October 1911 revolution but did not have a civil-military organization to take control of China. Consequently, he yielded his presidency of the Republic to an old Chinese general who had served the Manchu until the latter's abdication. General Yuan Sikai (Yuan Shih-kai) succeeded Dr. Sun as president in April 1912. From then until his death in 1916, General Yuan imposed on China an ineffective and pointless military dictatorship. Political power was decentralized in the hands of Yuan's regional lieutenants. After Yuan's death, no semblance of central authority existed in China, and the regional lieutenants came into their own. Chinese provinces were divided among these lieutenants, known as warlords, who fought one another for control of Peking and of the central government.

Amidst the anarchy of warlords, social fragmentation, and intellectual radicalism, two political parties were formed. The first one, the older of the two, the Nationalist party, was composed of remnants of Dr. Sun's followers. The Kuomintang had wished to organize a parliamentary form of government under Yuan but was outlawed by the latter in 1913. As it was constituted then, the Kuomintang was not a united and disciplined party, lacking a forceful leader and comprehensive social and economic programs. Among the members of the Kuomintang were admirers (like Dr. Sun) of Western democracy, reform-minded traditionalists who still wished to "retain Chinese essence," and those impressed by Japan's militaristic development. The prestige of the Kuomintang was damaged by internal dissension and its inability to resist General Yuan's dictatorship.

In 1921 the younger of the two parties, the Communist party of China, was formed under Soviet sponsorship. The background to the birth of the Communist party of China was both domestic and international. Domestically, educated Chinese, especially college students and professors, were disgusted and shamed by the failure of the Republic to rid China of the warlords and the imperialists, the most aggressive now being Japan. The nationalistically minded Chinese were at first hopeful of the good will and assistance of the United States in restraining Japan's ambition in China. But President Woodrow Wilson's compromise with Japan's design on China at the Versailles Peace Conference in 1919 greatly angered and disillusioned Chinese patriots. Chinese students, intellectuals, and army officers, however, were impressed by the success of the Bolsheviks, who had toppled the tsarist regime in Russia, defeated their domestic opponents, and forced Western troops to withdraw from Russia. In Marxist ideology radical Chinese students and intellectuals also found an emotionally satisfying answer to China's problems and hope for the future. At the same time, in 1920-21, the Soviets were also looking east to China for an ally to prevent another "capitalist encirclement" of Russia. The Soviet government declared their good will to Chinese revolutionaries by offering to relinquish the colonial privileges that old Russia had exacted from Manchu China and to help China unify and develop. Moreover, the Soviets had already established an organization known as the Comintern (Communist

International) to carry out assistance to Chinese or other Asian revolutionaries. So in July 1921 the Communist party of China was formed under the fosterage of the Comintern. The party had then only thirteen members and was headed by Chen Duxiu, a professor of philosophy at Peking University.

In their social background the elites of the Nationalists and the Communists are much alike.[6] The leaders of both parties came from the families of landlords, businessmen, scholars, or officials of the old society. They hailed from the southern and coastal parts of China, where Western influence was the most advanced. The overwhelming majority of the leaders of the Nationalist and the Communist parties had acquired higher education, a rare privilege in China then, and some had even been educated in Western countries or Japan. When the two parties were first formed, most of the leaders were students-turned-organizers. They were alienated intellectuals, caught between tradition and modernity. Few if any of them had acquired modern professional skills, which would have enabled them to earn a living outside of the political arena. Once plunged into the process of power struggle, these alienated young men and a few women soon regarded political agitation and organization as their true and only vocation. Political struggle became intensely personal. As the two parties competed with the warlords and then with each other, they increasingly had to rally professional army officers, who came from a lower-class background. Thus in the ranks of both the Nationalists and the Communists a second elite emerged—men from a plebian background, mostly from hinterland provinces, who rose to leadership position via the barrel of a gun. The radicalness of professional political ideologues was now meshed with the army officers' readiness to use violence. Modern Chinese history was pushed further and further into a self-sustained process of violence.

THE RISE OF THE COMMUNIST PARTY, 1921-49

By the time the Communist party of China was formed in 1921, the Kuomintang had already spent its energy. Dr. Sun was faced with a phantom party. "There were members of the Kuomintang but there was no Kuomintang."[7] Meanwhile, Dr. Sun's tactics to make use of some warlords' forces for his benefit was being turned around by the latter for their benefit. The Chinese Communist party began with youthful vigor and a degree of naiveté. Being mostly young students and intellectuals, the Communists at first worked blindly to implant a Bolshevik-type revolution in China. It was only after a major catastrophe, which almost destroyed the Communist party entirely, that the Communists slowly and painfully discovered their own independent way to political success. We shall discuss the history of the Communist party of China in terms of five periods: (1) urban mass movement, July 1921-April 1927; (2) urban armed uprising, August 1927-October 1930; (3) peasant wars in the countryside, October 1927-October 1934; (4) united front and regional state, October 1935-August 1945; and (5) war of liberation, August 1945-December 1949.

Urban Mass Movement, July 1921-April 1927

Since the Communist party of China (CPC hereafter) was fostered by the Soviets, the latter coached their Chinese disciples in the only type of revolution that they knew—the urban workers' revolution in Russia in 1917. Chinese workers, less than 1 percent of the population in 1921, were concentrated in large, modern cities such as Shanghai, Wuhan, and Canton (Guangzhou), where modern industries, owned largely by Western and Japanese capitalists, were located. Therefore the CPC established its organizations in those cities, with Shanghai as the main base.[8]

From 1922 on, the Communist party organized numerous unions, clubs, and schools for workers in large cities and circulated publications exposing the miserable conditions in which Chinese workers worked and lived. Under the leadership of the CPC, the Chinese workers' movement began to take off. In the meantime, the CPC also initiated agitational and organizational work among students, other youths, women, and to a much lesser extent, peasants. The activities of the CPC gave the modern Chinese revolution a fresh look and a new direction. Hitherto middle-class Chinese revolutionists had focused their movement entirely on political and military issues such as expelling the Manchu, the imperialists, and the warlords. Now the Chinese Communists, under Soviet advisorship, turned Chinese revolutions to social issues.

While the Communists in China were vigorously pushing for mass movement in cities, in 1923 the Comintern directed the CPC to form a united front with the Kuomintang. The reasoning of the Comintern was that China was not yet ready for socialist revolution but that the most crucial task for the moment was a national revolution, i.e., to unify the nation by destroying the warlords, and then, as the Bolsheviks had done in Russia, to force Western imperialists to withdraw from China. Soviet assistance to China was conditioned upon this united front. Reluctantly the Chinese Communists joined hands with Dr. Sun's Kuomintang in 1923 to push for national unification.

From the Soviet Union came civil and military advisers to Dr. Sun. The Kuomintang was reorganized along the line of the Bolshevik party under the guidance of Soviet adviser Michael Borodin. A military academy was established, staffed with Soviet advisers, but the commandant was a young Kuomintang general named Chiang Kai-shek. Chinese Communists were instructed by the Comintern to maintain its own independent organizational entity *within* the Kuomintang and concentrated its work in mass mobilization of workers, students, women, and peasants. Ostensibly this was to revive the Kuomintang, enabling the latter to have a mass base. Secretly the plan of the Comintern was to insure that through the control of the Kuomintang by the CPC from within, the leadership of Chinese revolutionists would be closely allied with the Soviet Union. Ultimately the Comintern hoped to transform the Kuomintang into a Communist party. This is known as the *bloc within* strategy.

Meanwhile the CPC worked effectively in labor movement. As the Communists gained influence among urban Chinese workers, the rank of the CPC grew significantly. In 1925 the CPC organized several large strikes, which provoked brutal repressions by Japanese and British police, the most notorious one being the May 30th massacre in Shanghai in which Japanese and Indian policemen killed some sixty strikers in a series of conflicts with Chinese workers. The membership of the CPC grew precipitously, from 950 in January 1925 to 50,000 in 1926.[9] The Communists were also gaining ground in peasant mobilization. The peasant work section of the Kuomintang was controlled by a member of the CPC named Peng Bai (Peng Pai), who in 1924 had organized a training institute for cadres to work in the countryside. Peng's peasant agitation, however, was confined entirely to Guangdong Province. But it was Peng who founded the peasant movement for the CPC, not Mao Zedong, who learned peasant mobilization from Peng a year or so later. It was clear to everybody then that the CPC, though part of the Kuomintang at that time, was the more dynamic party.

From the very beginning the joining of the CPC with the Kuomintang was opposed by some members of the latter, but the united front was unilaterally decided upon by Dr. Sun, who had lost hope of ever obtaining any aid from the West. With the CPC gaining ever more members after 1923 and all the while maintaining its own "party group" within the Kuomintang, opposition among Kuomintang members to the CPC gained strength. But as long as Dr. Sun was alive, the united front between the left and the right would be maintained. In March 1925 Dr. Sun died of cancer, and the linchpin of the alliance between the Kuomintang and the CPC was removed.

For the moment, the alliance held, though precariously. In 1926 the united front between the Chinese Nationalists and the Communists was supposed to carry out its chief objective, a war against the warlords in the so-called Northern Expedition, the revolutionaries being based in the southern city of Canton, of Guangdong Province. The Communists, however, were the weaker party in the expedition, since the new revolutionary army was commanded by Chiang Kai-shek, whose ideology was closer to that of the reform-minded traditionals than of the radicals inside the Nationalist party. The Northern Expedition started out promisingly, as the revolutionary army, trained and equipped by Russian advisers and politically indoctrinated, was more disciplined and united than the warlord armies. In the meantime, within the Kuomintang sentiment against the Chinese Communists mounted. In April 1927, after occupying the city of Shanghai, General Chiang turned his troops against the Communists in the city in a bloody massacre. Shanghai was then the main operating ground of the Chinese Communists, who had already organized a large contingent of workers' militia armed with weapons that they seized from the defeated warlord army. In fact, it was the Communist workers' militia that had staged a coup against the former warlord commander of the city before the arrival of Chiang's revolutionary army.[10]

The coup by General Chiang against the Communists in Shanghai, however, was not or should not have been a total surprise to the CPC. For, even before the start of the Northern Expedition on March 20, barely fifteen days after the death of Dr. Sun, General Chiang had launched a surprise move in the city of Canton (Guangzhou), arresting a score of CPC members in the revolutionary army and expelling Soviet advisers from the military academy. The Shanghai massacre by Chiang marked his final and decisive break with the Communists. Now the Kuomintang itself was split in two, one faction being still supportive of the alliance with the Communists, and the other faction, the larger one, being behind General Chiang's action. The latter faction called on the whole Nationalist party to "cleanse" the party of Communists. Not long after the Shanghai incident, the proalliance faction (left-wing Kuomintang) within the Nationalist party dissolved. General Chiang and his colleagues pushed for a nationwide purge of the Communists. No exact figure is available as to how many members of the Communist party were executed and how many deserted or defected. On the eve of Chiang's coup in Shanghai, the total membership of the Communist party amounted to 57,962. By the end of 1927, the membership of the Communist party had dwindled to 10,000.[11] Separate bands of Chinese Communists, one led by Mao Zedong, for example, made their way into hinterland provinces to conduct armed resistance against the Nationalist party. Thus the war against the warlords ended only to see the start of civil war between the Kuomintang and the Communists (see figure 2-1).

Urban Armed Uprising, August 1927–October 1930

The Shanghai massacre and subsequent arrest and execution of thousands of CPC members by Kuomintang generals marked the end of the urban mass-movement phase of the CPC. The Chinese Communists, however, had not yet learned, or were

FIGURE 2-1   Evolution of Chinese Nationalist-Communist "United Front," 1923–37

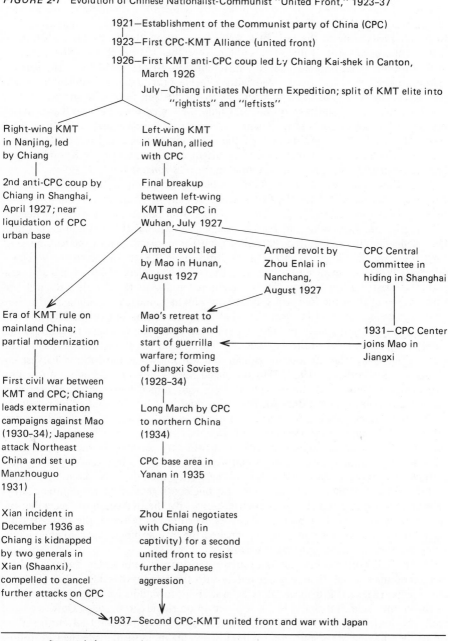

1921—Establishment of the Communist party of China (CPC)

1923—First CPC-KMT Alliance (united front)

1926—First KMT anti-CPC coup led by Chiang Kai-shek in Canton, March 1926

July—Chiang initiates Northern Expedition; split of KMT elite into "rightists" and "leftists"

Right-wing KMT in Nanjing, led by Chiang

Left-wing KMT in Wuhan, allied with CPC

2nd anti-CPC coup by Chiang in Shanghai, April 1927; near liquidation of CPC urban base

Final breakup between left-wing KMT and CPC in Wuhan, July 1927

Armed revolt led by Mao in Hunan, August 1927

Armed revolt by Zhou Enlai in Nanchang, August 1927

CPC Central Committee in hiding in Shanghai

Era of KMT rule on mainland China; partial modernization

Mao's retreat to Jinggangshan and start of guerrilla warfare; forming of Jiangxi Soviets (1928–34)

1931—CPC Center joins Mao in Jiangxi

First civil war between KMT and CPC; Chiang leads extermination campaigns against Mao (1930–34); Japanese attack Northeast China and set up Manzhouguo 1931)

Long March by CPC to northern China (1934)

CPC base area in Yanan in 1935

Xian incident in December 1936 as Chiang is kidnapped by two generals in Xian (Shaanxi), compelled to cancel further attacks on CPC

Zhou Enlai negotiates with Chiang (in captivity) for a second united front to resist further Japanese aggression

1937—Second CPC-KMT united front and war with Japan

⟶ stands for *merge into*

⎯ stands for *develop*

not permitted by the Soviets to learn, the lesson of its debacle. By then, on the Soviet side, Lenin had already died and Stalin controlled the Comintern. Sensing that the disaster of the CPC in China would bring disrepute to the Comintern and to him, Stalin, who was then locked in a succession struggle with Trotsky, ordered the CPC to proceed according to the Bolshevik way of revolution, that is, to stage urban uprisings to take power just as the Soviets did in November 1917 in Russia. Now the situation in China at that time was radically different from Russia in 1917–18. The Russian revolutionaries then had been faced with a feeble provisional government that was surrounded by rebellions from all sides. It was not difficult for the Bolsheviks to stage the November coup and take power. In China the armed power of the Kuomintang, thanks to the Soviets, was at its height subsequent to the Shanghai incident of April 1927. Moreover, the armed strength of the Kuomintang was strongest in cities where the CPC had focused its activity. To stage urban uprisings against the Kuomintang in large cities in 1927 was to hit the Kuomintang at its *strongest* link!

Stalin's order was, however, blindly obeyed, but not by Chen Duxiu, who was later made the scapegoat for the Comintern's mistake in China. In a rump party conference on August 7, 1927, the CPC, on order from Stalin, "elected" a new leader, a young Communist trained in Moscow named Qu Qiubai (Ch'u, Ch'iu-pai). Under Qu's leadership, the CPC staged three abortive urban uprisings against the Kuomintang. First there was the August 1, 1927, armed uprising in the city of Nanchang of Jiangxi (Kiangsi) Province organized by such well-known CPC leaders as Zhou Enlai and General Zhu De (Chu Teh). That date is celebrated today in the People's Republic of China as the birth of the Red Army as General Zhu had induced the municipal garrison troops to defect to the CPC. But the rebel force was driven out of the city and was subsequently exterminated by the Kuomintang Army in Guangdong. Zhou Enlai barely escaped with his life to Hong Kong. The second revolt, more rural than urban, was organized by Mao Zedong in Hunan and was known as the autumn harvest uprising. On September 8, 1927, Mao organized several peasant armies to storm into five towns in Hunan. As the peasant soldiers were armed with spears and were not trained, the fighting lasted only for four days. Mao was briefly arrested by provincial militia but escaped. The most tragic and bloody was the Canton uprising, known as the Canton Commune, of December 11–13, 1927. A group of Chinese Communist military officers rallied some cadets from the military academy in the city, together with workers' militia, and staged a coup on December 11 by attacking the police station, the army arsenals, and public offices. They then declared the establishment of the Canton Commune. The next day a strong contingent of the Kuomintang Army arrived and attacked the city with counter-terror. By the thirteenth of December the rebellion by the CPC had been crushed. As eyewitnesses testified, the three-day uprising of the Communists in Canton drenched the city in blood, most of the victims being members of Communist labor unions.

The survivors of these abortive urban uprisings, including Mao Zedong and his peasant soldiers, made their way separately into the interior, notably Fujian (Fukien) and Jiangxi (Kiangsi) Provinces. The CPC was about to find its own style of revolution in the countryside. But Stalin had not given up on the urban strategy. Qu was ousted from the leadership of the CPC and made to atone for his "blind adventurism" in China by studying Marxism-Leninism in Moscow. Stalin, in turn, made the CPC follow a protégé of his, Li Lisan (Li, Li-san), who assumed the leadership of the CPC in June 1930. Li called on the CPC to achieve victory in a few provinces in order to provoke a nationwide revolt against the Nationalist regime, which was then embroiled in internecine feuds. By then Mao Zedong had already organized a sizeable peasant force in the mountainous regions of Jiangxi. Li ordered Mao and other Communist forces in the countryside to move against the provincial capitals of Hunan and Jiangxi. Mao was notably reluctant to do so. But another Communist force led by General Peng Dehuai (Peng, Teh-huai) briefly occupied the Hunan capital of Changsha. Mao's force attacked but did not succeed in occupying the Jiangxi capital of Nanchang. By the end of October 1930, the urban uprising of Li Lisan was finished. The Chinese Communists would not make another attempt to attack a city until fifteen years later, after the defeat of Japan.

Peasant Wars in the Countryside, October 1927–October 1934

The total failure of the CPC's urban uprisings left the Communists no alternative but to fall back on the score of guerrilla bands in China's hinterland. By the end of 1928, five Communist guerrilla bases had been established in the provinces of Fujian, Jiangxi, Zhejiang (Chekiang), Anhui, Henan, Hunan, Hubei, and Sichuan (see map 2-1). The largest base was controlled by Mao Zedong and General Zhu De in the border regions of Fujian, Jiangxi, and Hunan Provinces, the most famous stronghold being Jingangshan (Chinkangshan). It was then and there that Mao and other Chinese Communists made rendezvous with Chinese revolutionary tradition and thus found their own way to ultimate political victory.

MAP 2-1.   Communist guerrilla base areas and the long march (October 1934–October 1936). Adapted from *The Long March: Eyewitness Accounts* (Peking: Foreign Languages Press, 1963).

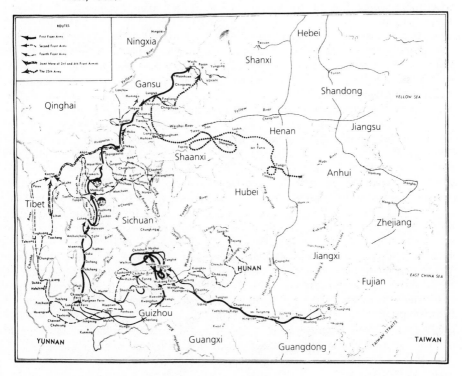

As Mao explained in 1928 in the essay "Why Is It That Red Political Power Can Exist in China?" the rural guerrilla bases were a viable way to wage war against the Kuomintang primarily because of disunity among the forces of the Kuomintang and China's economic regionalism. Both of these traditional factors were strengthened by "the imperialist policy of marking off spheres of influence in order to divide and exploit."[12] Moreover, according to Mao, the Communist base areas were not established at random; they were in regions that had already been politically mobilized during the Northern Expedition of 1926–27. "In many parts of these provinces trade unions and peasant associations were formed on a wide scale, and many economic and political struggles were waged by the working class and the peasantry against the landlord class and the bourgeoisie."[13] Mao, however, did not dwell on another crucial factor in the survival of the guerrilla base areas—they were in the border regions of two or three provinces. That is also a part of Chinese revolutionary legacy. As mentioned previously, in time of social stress destitute Chinese peasants have formed into rebel bands outside their old rural communities, surviving as bandits in "in-between" areas of villages and provinces. It was in these intermediate zones that the power of central and provincial authorities was at its weakest. So the so-called border-region strategy of the CPC after 1928 was borrowed from the tradition of Chinese peasant rebellion.[14]

But those traditional conditions alone could not be depended on for the survival of these Communist guerrilla bases. They merely provided the Communists with a breathing spell. More substantially, the security of the bases hinged on two important tasks: to repulse the relentless attacks by Chiang's forces and to organize the base areas into viable political, economic, and social units. The two tasks were, of course, intimately related. Without political, economic, and social mobilization of the base areas there would not be the wherewithal to resist Chiang's campaigns of "bandit extermination."

To mobilize the rural population in the base areas the CPC under Mao's leadership implemented a land-redistribution policy in which the lands belonging to the landlords were distributed among poor peasants. During the entire period of peasant wars between 1928 and 1934 the land question was a central issue among Communist leaders, who debated endlessly on the optimal combination between the dictates of Marxism and survival.[15] Today Chinese Communists characterize this whole period as "war of land revolution." Accompanying the land policy of the CPC was political and social mobilization of the peasants. In every village Chinese Communists organized "poor peasants' associations" to facilitate land distribution. After that every group of peasants, regardless of age and sex, was organized into some useful auxiliary for the CPC. There were, for example, the Red Defense Army (adult males), Young Pioneers (teenage youth), and Children's Corps. These were assigned tasks, such as sentry duty, scouting, policing, transporting, road repairing, and caring for the wounded. Women were organized to sew uniforms and to perform in song-and-dance troops to entertain soldiers. Schools and literacy classes were set up to teach peasants basic tenets of socialism and, at the minimum, to make them learn the passwords of the Red Army. Young peasant women, as one Communist document records, were extremely enthusiastic about learning to read and write.[16] To feed the thousands of Red Army soldiers and civilian members of the CPC, the Communists organized peasants into cooperatives for production, consumer-goods distribution, credit (money lending), and rice production.[17] These measures granted poor Chinese peasants, both men and women, real participation in community affairs, which hitherto had been monopolized by officials and their personal servants at the expense of peasants. So there was real enthusiasm and excitement among the peasants in Communist base areas even though the burden of peasants was increased under Communist control since the provision of troops and the administration of the CPC must come from the peasants. To give all these demands on the peasants a degree of legitimacy, the CPC proclaimed in November 1931 the establishment of the Chinese Soviet Republic with Mao as its chairman. The capital was the Jiangxi town of Ruijin. A state structure was set up, complete with a constitution and representative assembly. Naturally it was staffed with Communist party members. The Soviet government in Ruijin proclaimed laws on land ownership, labor protection, marriage, and conscription.[18]

With the base areas mobilized, Mao and General Zhu De waited for the inevitable arrival of Nationalist troops. From December 1930 to October 1933 Chiang Kai-shek mounted five "bandit extermination campaigns" against those areas, the main objective being the destruction of Mao's base in Jiangxi-Hunan. Outnumbered and outgunned, Mao and General Zhu relied on their tactical brilliance and the cooperation of the populace to overcome Chiang's attacks. Using "mobile warfare" ("maneuver warfare" in today's concept), Mao and Zhu's guerrilla troops made daring strikes behind enemy lines and launched campaigns of disruption and surprise designed to weaken and collapse the enemy rather than to destroy him physically. In other words, Mao and Zhu constantly created new and dangerous situations with which Chiang's commanders, conditioned by their training in regular conventional warfare, were not prepared to cope. The Red Army thus successfully defeated the first four campaigns of Chiang's forces (December 1930, April 1931, July 1931, and January 1933). In October 1933 Chiang commenced his fifth "bandit extermination campaign." Now both Chiang and the Communists changed their tactics. Chiang was advised by several German generals to surround Communist areas from all sides and build concrete fortresses as the Nationalist troops advanced toward Mao's area. In the meantime, Mao's control over his troops was temporarily taken away and put in the hands of a group of young and inexperienced "returned students" from Moscow. The latter had criticized Mao's guerrilla warfare, which lured the enemy deep into the areas of Communist control. The new leaders of the CPC wished to stabilize the rear by confronting Chiang's forces in positional wars outside of the base areas. In other words, in the fifth campaign the Communists fought a conventional war with Chiang's forces. Under this circumstance the "fortress strategy" of Chiang paid dividends. Chiang's army was able to take one Communist base area after another. Without heavy weapons the Communists were unable to destroy the concrete fortresses. Fortunately for the Communists, Chiang's persistent weakness had been unevenness in the quality of his troops. The western flank of Chiang's troops was negligent in building fortresses and adhering to the overall strategy of attack. So on October 14, 1934, the Communists, with 100,000 soldiers and civilians, abandoned their last base area in Jiangxi and broke through the western flank of Chiang's troops between Jiangxi and Hunan. Thus began the celebrated Long March of the Red Army under the command of Mao and General Zhu De. In the meantime, another Communist guerrilla band also moved west from their base area in the border regions of Anhui, Hubei, and Henan, hoping to join forces with Mao (see map 2-1). The Long March took the Communists through the impoverished southwestern provinces and the dangerous terrain on the eastern edge of Tibet and thence northward toward the province of Shaanxi (Shensi) where a small Communist band had already established a base area. When the Long March ended in October 1935 in the northern region of Shaanxi Province, Mao and his force had marched for some eight thousand miles and lost 80 percent of their men and women. The phase of peasant wars now came to an end for the CPC.

United Front and Regional State, October 1935–August 1945

During the years of Communist guerrilla wars (1930 to 1935), the international situation in China had undergone rapid changes that gratuitously but significantly helped the survival of the CPC. On September 18, 1931, just as Chiang Kia-shek and Mao were locked in their second battle in Jiangxi, Japan attacked and occupied the northeastern provinces of China. The Japanese puppet state of Manzhouguo was subsequently established there. In January 1932 Japan attacked and partially occupied the city of Shanghai. The Chinese Nationalist government under the leadership of Chiang Kai-shek was caught between civil war with the Communists and Japanese conquest of China. The Chinese public, especially college students, was incensed by Chiang's single-minded pursuit of the Communists while he temporized with the Japanese. The CPC quickly capitalized on the Japanese attack to mount a political offense against Chiang's military offense by announcing to the nation the Communists' willingness to cease civil war so as to fight the Japanese. In 1935 while the Communists in China were completing their Long March, the Comintern in Moscow directed the CPC to seek a second unified front with the Kuomintang in order to resist Japan. The Soviet Union was fearful that once Japan conquered all of China, Russia would then be facing a pincer movement from Nazi Germany from the West and Fascist Japan from the East. Thus, in the Kremlin's calculation, China must not be allowed to be overrun by Japan. Following the direction of the Comintern, the CPC announced on August 1, 1935, through its representative in Russia, its willingness to cease armed rebellion and subordinate the party to a "national defense government" to be formed by all parties and patriotic groups in China. Significantly, the CPC did not rule out the participation and even leadership of the Kuomintang in this government.

Chiang Kai-shek, nevertheless, ignored the appeals from the CPC and the mounting student protests that were capitalized by underground CPC agents in cities. In December 1936 Chiang flew to the city of Xian (Sian) of Shaanxi to urge the "Nationalist" troops there to take offensive actions against the Communists, who were reeling from the Long March. But the so-called Nationalist troops in Xian were not really under Chiang's control; these troops were the warlord army of the northeastern provinces that had been occupied in 1936 by Japan. The "Manchurian" soldiers were under the command of the young Marshal Chang Xueliang (Chang, Hsueh-liang), whose late father had been the "Manchurian warlord." Chinese Communists directed their "united front" propaganda to Marshal Chang and his homesick soldiers. Unbeknown to Chiang Kai-shek, secret talks between Marshal Chang and Chinese Communists had already taken place before Chiang's arrival in Xian. Not long after Chiang's arrival, on December 12, 1936 Marshal Chang's troops staged a mutiny and put Chiang Kai-shek under house arrest. This is the famous Xian Incident of December 1936. From the Communist capital of Yanan (Yenan) Zhou Enlai came to join Marshal Chang in persuading Chiang Kai-shek to stop fighting the Communists and form a coalition government to resist Japan's attack. Chiang had no alternative but to agree. Formalistically speaking, the civil war between the Communists and the Nationalists ended for the moment after Chiang's release from captivity on December 25, 1936.

Japanese militarists now decided that they must deliver their final blow before it was too late. So on July 7, 1937, the Japanese army attacked Chinese Nationalist troops on the Marco Polo Bridge outside Peking. Abiding by his agreement with the CPC earlier, Chiang Kai-shek called on the whole nation to unite to fight Japan. On July 15 the CPC announced its second united front with the Kuomintang to resist Japan's aggression. The CPC and its army were formally declared to be part of the national government and of the armed forces under the command of Chiang Kai-shek. Meanwhile the Japanese army quickly occupied one Chinese city after another in eastern and coastal China, thus destroying a decade of Nationalist construction and dislodging the Kuomintang from its urban bases.

Japan's attack and the subsequent united front between the CPC and the Kuomintang gave the former a much needed long breathing spell. Under Mao's concept of guerrilla warfare the CPC had completed its "strategic withdrawal" and would not prepare for "strategic offense" against the Kuomintang. The Yanan period of 1936–45 was the crucial incubation for the CPC's ultimate takeover of national power in China. Hence the tasks of Mao and the CPC in Yanan were much more complex than the ones in the Soviet Republic of Jiangxi. During this period Mao undertook to rebuild the Communist party and the army, expand the areas of Communist control, and organize a national coalition to isolate the Kuomintang.

The relative peace that the CPC enjoyed in Yanan during the war with Japan enabled Mao to transform the Communist party according to his personal wishes. Hitherto Mao's authority over the CPC had been persistently challenged by a group of young Communists, known as the returned students clique, who were trained in Moscow. But they were discredited by the loss of the Jiangxi base. So in a crucial party conference during the Long March in the city of Zunyi (Tsunyi) of Guizhou (Kweichow) Province, Mao reasserted his control of the CPC. In Yanan Mao felt that the most urgent task was to impart a uniform frame of reference among party cadres in order for the CPC to expand its influence in China and still retain its cohesion. Academies of political study, such as the Anti-Japan War College (*Kang Da*), were established in Yanan to indoctrinate party cadres. In 1942 Mao carried out the "party rectification campaign" in which all CPC members were required to listen to speeches by major party leaders, study documents and texts of Marxism-Leninism, engage in self-criticism, and submit to party assignments. At that time the Communist rank and file were of diverse backgrounds. There were poorly educated peasant youths whom the CPC had recruited from the countryside of north China and well-educated Chinese youths from the cities who, as the war went on, fled from Japanese-controlled areas in growing numbers to go to Yanan. To integrate these disparate members of the CPC the rectification campaign subjected them to a heavy dose of Communist indoctrination. The substance of the rectification included basic Communist philosophy, the necessary ethos of being a party member, and a practical guide to political leadership among the rural population.[19] The rectification campaign of 1942 not only gave the members of the CPC a uniform outlook but also enabled Mao to build himself up as the supreme leader of the CPC.

Mao's attention was, of course, not confined to the party. Since its near extermination in 1927, the Communist party, and especially Mao Zedong, had put a premium on the creation of an army of its own. Throughout the war with Japan Mao Zedong carefully nourished the Red Army, sometimes reprimanding Communist generals for unnecessarily engaging the Japanese. The main force of the Red Army would be kept for the final struggle for power with the Nationalists, not to be wasted in war with a

Japanese army that was superior in arms and training. In the meantime, small bands from the army and cadres of the Communist party penetrated behind Japanese lines to set up base areas in various provinces. The work of the Communists was facilitated by Japanese atrocities against Chinese civilians. Also the Communists took care to emphasize only the nationalistic component of their ideology.[20] Gradually the Communist party organized an underground infrastructure in Nationalist- and Japanese-occupied areas. This infrastructure would be activated when the final battle between the Communists and Nationalists took place.

Meanwhile, Japan's war against China not only provided the Chinese Communists with a long breathing spell but also created the most essential condition for any successful revolutionary movement—a coalition of the activists of all classes of society. The second united front with the Nationalists during the war enabled the Chinese Communists to have a liaison office and publish a newspaper in the Nationalist capital, Chongqing (Chungking). While there, the Communist party used the full advantage of an opposition party that had no prospect of assuming formal power. So the Communist party in Chongqing championed every cause of those political groups in opposition to Nationalist one-party rule. Based on this tactic, a unified front was organized by the Communist party with intellectuals, journalists, lawyers, industrialists, and politicians, i.e., the most articulate elements of Chinese society. Even American diplomats and educators were targets of Chinese Communist united front tactics. Thus while the Nationalist party isolated itself during the war, the Chinese Communists expanded their base of support in Chinese society.

Since the breakup of the first united front between the Communists and the Nationalists in 1927, the two parties had developed radically different traditions. The Nationalist party assumed the mantle of the legitimate government of the Republic of China and took up all the tasks of a modern government. The experience of the Nationalists was in administration, planning, economic development, law and order, and diplomacy. The Communist party, on the other hand, had developed a tradition of political and military combat. Members of the Communist party were oriented to the single goal of pursuit of political power. Unlike the Nationalists, who acquired influence and power in a "natural" way because they were the formal authority, the Communists had to accrue power bit by bit in a highly self-conscious and deliberate manner. In political struggle the party that cultivates power consciously is likely to win. Unbeknownst to most Chinese, the fate of postwar China had already been decided during the war with Japan.

By April 1945 when the CPC convened the Seventh Party Congress in Yanan, the Communist party had been transformed. The membership of the CPC had risen from 40,000 in 1937 to 1.2 million in 1945. The armed forces of the CPC now boasted of having 1.2 million regular troops and 2.2 million militia men. The total population under the administration of the CPC in North and Northwest China was said to be 130 million.[21] The Communist party of China was now ready to commence its "strategic offense" against the Nationalist government.

War of Liberation, August 1945–December 1949

Since Japan's attack in 1937, the international situation in China had undergone another drastic change. Both the United States and the Soviet Union became allies of the Nationalist government, while the CPC was left to fend for itself. The United States made continuous efforts to mediate between the Kuomintang and the CPC, hoping to unite the two in order to fight Japan. From Washington came one American official or general after another, including Vice-President Henry Wallace, who visited Chongqing in 1944. In February 1945, despairing of the internal political situation in China, President Roosevelt at the Yalta Conference turned to the Soviet Union for aid to defeat Japan on mainland China. So when Japan finally surrendered on August 10, 1945, the Soviet army had already occupied the northeastern provinces of China. While agreeing to withdraw from Chinese territory, Stalin ordered the Soviet army to remove all valuable industrial equipment from Chinese provinces as "war booty," to hand over surrendered Japanese weapons to Chinese Communist forces, and to prevent Chinese Nationalist forces from taking over the northeastern provinces.[22]

The United States made another attempt to mediate between the Kuomintang and the CPC. American ambassador Patrick Hurley personally escorted Mao Zedong to Chongqing to negotiate peace with Chiang Kai-shek on August 28, 1945. The talk between the two Chinese leaders came to nothing. Meanwhile, throughout China Communist and Nationalist forces clashed, as they raced to take over cities being vacated by surrendering Japanese troops. In northeastern provinces fighting between Chinese Communist forces who had been allowed into the area by the Soviet army and the advancing Nationalist forces was particularly intense. The United States made one last try to mediate by sending General George Marshall to China in 1946. But neither the Chinese Communists nor the Nationalists negotiated with each other in good faith. In 1947 General Marshall abandoned his mission in China. The civil war between the Nationalists and the Communists then became formal. Like the Soviet Comintern, which directed the CPC to transplant the Bolshevik revolution to China in the late 1920s, the Americans sought to make Chinese Nationalists and Communists accept the American political ethos of shared power. The Russians and the Americans, each in their own way, were defeated by Chinese political tradition.

With General Marshall gone, the civil war between the Communists and the Nationalists gathered momentum. In the first half of 1947 the Nationalists were on the offensive and took the Communist capital of Yanan in March. But the Communists were merely marking time and maneuvering their troops to surround Nationalist forces, who were overextended, especially in the northeastern provinces. In May the Communists launched a powerful and well-planned offensive against the Nationalists in the Northeast, where the latter had concentrated the best of the troops, equipped and trained by the United States during the war. In these battles, the Nationalist army was clique ridden, and each unit fought on its own in a fixed position. The Communist army fought as a single unit and took initiative in mobile warfare. By November 1948 the Nationalist troops in the Northeast had been annihilated. For all practical purposes, the Nationalist regime was finished. From then on the Nationalist armed forces no longer had the will to fight. Large-scale defections to the Communist side occurred among Nationalist commanders. In January 1949 the Communist army broke the Nationalist defense in Central China and crossed the Yangtze River. On October 1, 1949, Mao proclaimed the founding of the People's Republic of China in Peking.[23] By the end of the year the Nationalist party, together with remnant armed forces and a valuable corps of civilian administrators and specialists, had retreated to the island of Taiwan.

The defeat of the Nationalist government on mainland China in 1949 has beclouded Western (mostly American) scholarship on the two decades of Nationalist rule, 1928-49. Undoubtedly there were serious shortcomings in the Nationalist rule. In retrospect, however, the Nationalists also accomplished much, although the results were uneven. The Nationalists, after their purge of the Communists in 1927-28, established the first real modern government and administration that the Chinese had ever known. In its first decade the Nationalist government headed by Chiang Kai-shek carried out important reforms in financial and economic organization. The currency system was unified, and a modern paper-money system was adopted. The government established a system of taxation and acquired tariff autonomy. The Nationalists sought technological aid from the League of Nations. Impressive gains were scored in the extension of modern transportation. Industrial development was emphasized by the Nationalists and registered an overall growth in the first decade of Nationalist rule. Arthur N. Young wrote:

> Although the economy as a whole showed little growth in the decade because of the great weight of traditional agriculture, handicrafts, and transport, the aggregate should not obscure the great progress in many fields. Compounded yearly growth rates in 1927 to 1936 were 9.4 percent for electric power, 8.4 to 17.1 percent for modern-type communications with air communications growing spectacularly from nothing, and for a limited but representative group of industries including utilities and mining (in 1931 to 1936) 6.7 percent. For bank deposits the rate was 15.9 percent, with slightly more coverage but with relatively little net price change in the period. These growth rates were accomplished despite worldwide depression, when most economies were deteriorating or only slowly recovering.[24]

Japan's attack in 1937, of course, ended all this hard-won progress.

Nevertheless, the Nationalist rule of mainland China suffered persistently from two weaknesses. The first was limited political unification. Before 1937 the Nationalist government had full financial control in only four provinces: Jiangsu, Zhejiang, Anhui, and Jiangxi. After the Second World War, the enlargement of Communist-controlled areas and the remnant warlord control of some provinces (e.g., Shaanxi and Yunnan) did not enhance the Nationalist government's effective control of the nation. The second major weakness in the Nationalist rule is its inability to incorporate agricultural development into its overall national plan. The Nationalist government had concentrated its reform in the modernized coastal regions without making the vast countryside an integral part of its national development. For fear of alienating the powerful landlord-gentry group, the Nationalists did not dare to tax agriculture or carry out fundamental land reform that would create conditions for self-sustained industrial development. In the meantime, the persistent attempts of the Nationalist government, both in 1927–36 and in the postwar period, to unify China by force of arms resulted in heavy military expenses, which reduced significantly the government's capacity to develop society in an all-round fashion. After the war with Japan ended, the Nationalist government did not carry out sweeping reforms in its finance and economic development. Fighting the Communists became the first and foremost goal of Chiang Kai-shek. The result was financial ruin in the form of runaway inflation. The economy then was segmented. The eastern coastal and urban region to which the government paid most of its attention "became almost self-sufficient, with a basic orientation toward world markets."[25] The government had not taken into account the released purchasing power due to the end of the war and had overestimated the urban areas' ability to absorb the vastly increased governmental outlays for executing the war with the Communists. The resultant inflation in the urban areas in the coastal regions ruined the economy and alienated the population from the Nationalist government. Moreover, the Nationalist government, probably under the influence of the personality of Chiang Kai-shek, was affected by an "administrative mentality." This was aggravated by the one-party rule of the Nationalists. Consequently, the Nationalist government never captured the ideological zeal of the rising young generation and the critical-minded intellectuals of modern China. In an era of war and social unrest such as the Nationalists were faced with before 1949 people, especially the educated ones, long for symbolic appeals. The administrative mentality of the Nationalists proved to be not only inadequate but even anachronistic, in contrast to the Communists' concentration on political symbolism.

One can debate endlessly on the chief cause of the defeat of the Nationalists on the mainland. Some would readily join the Chinese Communists, attributing to the Nationalists all the weaknesses of an "ancient regime," thus putting the Communists in the camp of "the progressives." Others would point to Japan's attack and the Communist rebellion as the major reasons that the Nationalists were distracted from their essentially sound national development strategy, with its emphasis on gradualism, a free-market economy, and international aid and commerce. This second theory is strengthened by the success of the Nationalists on Taiwan. Thirty years after their defeat on the mainland, the Nationalists built Taiwan into one of the most prosperous East Asian nations, with a living standard ten times that of the people on mainland China. Arthur Young, who belongs to the second school of thought on the fate of the Nationalists, wrote: "Had the Nationalists been granted the opportunity, their past record and resourcefulness suggest that they could have found means to promote sustained growth within the framework of a fairly free economic system."[26]

In the final analysis, for a government to weather the kinds of social, economic, and political storms that the Chinese Nationalists faced on the mainland from 1928 to 1949, there are two alternatives. The first alternative is for it to give most people sufficient "payoffs" so that the population has "basic trust" in the government and will give it the needed time to overcome various crises (the American people and government during the time of the Depression being such an example). The other alternative is for the government to be ruthless and effective enough to stamp out all organized opposition so that the people are forced to accept crisis conditions without any recourse to rebellion (the history of the Communist rule on mainland China after 1949 seems to exemplify this). But the Nationalist government before 1949 was not able to achieve either of the two conditions. The government had not given most people a significant payoff to earn their basic trust, and the Nationalists were never able to stamp out organized and armed opposition, Communists or warlords. Former finance minister of the Nationalist government, Chang Kai-ngau put it well: "Into this chaos and political moral vacuum almost any militant group promising a clean sweep could have moved without strong opposition; and the Communists were there to take full advantage of the situation."[27]

Meanwhile, the Chinese Communists, with victory in hand, performed the rite of "summing up experience of history," which is an essential component of Communist ideology. "On the People's Democratic Dictatorship," written by Mao on July 1, 1949, on the twenty-eighth anniversary of the founding of the Communist party, included the following:

> Our twenty-eight years are entirely different [from Sun Yat-sen's forty years of revolutionary work]. We have plenty of invaluable experience. A party with discipline, armed with the theories of Marx, Engels, Lenin, and Stalin, employing the method of self-criticism, and linked up closely with the masses; an army led by such a party; a united front of various revolutionary strata and groups led by

such a party; these three are our main (lessons of) experience. They all mark us off from our predecessors. Relying on these three things, we have won a basic victory. . . . [28]

Party, army, and united front—these constituted the formula of success for the Chinese Communists. This was a completely political formula, designed for the single purpose of capturing political power. Mao Zedong undoubtedly was conscious of the purely political nature of his formula for success. That is why he used the phrase "basic victory." The crucial question now, in October 1949, was whether the Communist formula for success in political struggle would also serve as the formula for the party's ultimate victory—as Mao stated it in "On People's Democratic Dictatorship":

> to enable China to advance steadily, under the leadership of the working class and the Communist party, from an agricultural to an industrial country, and from a New Democratic to a Socialist and Communist society, to eliminate classes and to realize the state of universal fraternity.[29]

REVOLUTIONARY LEGACY

Mao's formula for success deals only with the manifest components of the Communist party's revolutionary tradition. These are presented in ideologically correct and dignified terms. There is also, however, a latent component to the revolution tradition of the Chinese Communist party. That is, the long experience of war and political maneuver has cultivated in the minds of Communist party leaders and the rank and file as well a set of fundamental attitudes that serve as the basic frame of reference for the Communists. Here we shall briefly sum up the latent attitudes of the Chinese Communist leaders and followers that resulted from their experience of revolution.

Accentuation of Ideological Faith

That the Chinese Communist party survived the relentless attacks by the Nationalists in the late 1920s and through the 1930s, suffering from incredible tribulations during the Long March, could be attributed partly to the Nationalist party's brutal treatment of any Communist captured alive and partly to faith in ideology. Hence, after 1949 Mao Zedong would attempt to impart the same degree of ideological commitment to the whole Chinese population with results very different from that of the pre-1949 days.

Personalistic Leadership

Revolutionary movements, especially prolonged ones in the form of guerrilla warfare, always tend to breed a "charismatic" type of leadership. Mao Zedong, Ho Chi Minh, and Fidel Castro are contemporary examples of personalized leadership growing out of armed rebellion. Among the lesser leaders of a revolutionary movement, similar tendencies toward charismatic relationships exist as soldiers and political commissars follow their "old chief." It is only a small step from the charismatic revolutionary tradition to the postrevolution "cult of personality" and factionalism in politics.

Campaign Style of Work

Before 1949 Chinese Communist leaders and followers lived in a state of continuous military campaigns in which a large number of troops and cadres were directed by a high command to storm enemy targets. The Chinese Communists became experts in organizing campaigns of various types, be it "thought rectification" or a rise in grain production in the base areas. The campaign style of work is deeply ingrained among many Chinese Communist leaders and ordinary members. Sociologist C. K. Yang, for example, suggests that Chinese Communists collectivized agriculture in the manner of a military campaign. However, as Yang also points out, the campaign style of work does not take into account the crucial difference in perspective of men in combat from those in time of peace. Soldiers and revolutionaries engaging in deadly political and military struggle temporarily narrow their lives to a single focus, whereas peasants and citizens of China after 1949, living in peace, are subject to the multiple pressures and considerations of a complex social life.[30] In the latter case the campaign style of work has definite limitations in producing the social change desired by the CPC. After the death of Mao and the ascendency of the party pragmatists under Deng Xiaoping, the CPC finally declared that the campaign style of work was unsuitable to the task of building a nation's economy and culture.

Communalization of Life

The Chinese Communist party developed out of a social movement with a comprehensive ideology. It is common in such a movement to demand from its members surrender of individuality to the movement. The practical conditions that the Chinese Communists found themselves in before 1949 also made group living necessary. Hence, a strong preference for a communalized way of living exists among the Chinese Communists. For example, national leaders live in a single residential compound in Peking known as Zhongnanhai, with tall walls separating them from the rest of the city residents. On matters concerning economic and social institutions the Chinese Communists always insisted on the principle of "first, bigness, and second, public ownership" (*yi da er gong*). As a result, the distinction between private and public is blurred in the minds of Communist cadres.

A Political Ethos of "Struggle"

In "On the People's Democratic Dictatorship," Mao spoke of the Communist party as a party "employing the method of self-criticism." That is the ideal, i.e., self-criticism is the way to resolve conflict and correct error. In practice, according to the late Liu Shaoqi (Liu Shao-ch'i) in his famous talk, "On the Intra-Party Struggle," an "unprincipled struggle" took the place of "criticism and self-criticism."[31]

In 1981, five years after the death of Mao Zedong, the leaders of the Chinese Communist party attributed the turmoil of the first three decades of the People's Republic of China partly to its legacy of "struggle." They stated:

> Our party had long existed in circumstances of war and fierce class struggle. It was not fully prepared either ideologically or in terms of scientific study, for the swift advent of the new-born socialist society. . . . we were liable, owing to the historical circumstances in which our party grew, to continue to regard issues unrelated to class struggle as its manifestations when observing and handling new

contradictions and problems. . . . And when confronted with actual class struggle under the new conditions, we habitually fell back on the familiar methods and experiences of the large-scale, turbulent mass struggle of the past, which should no longer have been mechanically followed.[32]

It should be pointed out emphatically here that not every Chinese Communist leader is affected *to the same degree* by the revolutionary legacy of the CPC. The varying impact of the above-mentioned predispositions on Chinese Communist leaders has been one of the most important contributing causes to factionalism among contemporary Chinese leaders. There are those who insist that the Jiangxi or Yanan experience is applicable to post-1949 Chinese society, economy, and culture. There are leaders who regard the pre-1949 style of the CPC as suitable for the situation then but, as a recent CPC resolution points out, not to be "mechanically followed" after the establishment of the People's Republic. To appreciate the serious consequences on contemporary Chinese politics of Chinese Communist leaders' different reception of the revolutionary legacy, we shall review briefly in the next chapter the first thirty years of the Communist rule of mainland China.

NOTES

1. For a short history of modern China with emphasis on revolutions, see Wolfgang Franke, *A Century of Chinese Revolution, 1851-1949* (Columbia: University of South Carolina Press, 1980).

2. Li Sou-k'ung, *Chung-kuo Ching-tai-shih (History of Modern China)* (Taipei: San-min Shuchu, 1964), p. 146.

3. Shi-heng Li, *Hu Kau Tung Hwei* (Shanghai: World Book Company) as quoted in George B. Cressey, *Land of the 500 Million: A Geography of China* (New York: McGraw-Hill Book Company, 1955), p. 11.

4. For an authoritative study of industrialization during the Qing dynasty, see Albert Feuerwerker, *China's Early Industrialization* (New York: Atheneum, 1970).

5. Quoted in Li Sou-k'ung, *Chung-kuo Ching-tai-shih*, p. 545.

6. For a systematic comparison of the social background of Chinese Nationalist and Communist leaders, see Robert C. North with Ithiel de Sola Pool, "Kuomintang and Chinese Communist Elites," in Harold D. Lasswell and Daniel Lerner, *World Revolutionary Elites: Studies in Coercive Ideological Movements* (Cambridge, Mass.: MIT Press, 1966), pp. 319-455.

7. Wang Chien-ming, *Chung-kuo King-chan-tang Shih-kao (History of the Chinese Communist Party)*, vol. I (Taipei: Wang Chien-ming, 1965), p. 126.

8. For a good, brief history of the Communist party of China see Benjamin Schwartz, *Chinese Communism and the Rise of Mao* (Cambridge, Mass.: Harvard University Press, 1958); and Conrad Brandt, *Stalin's Failure in China* (New York: W. W. Norton & Co., 1966). For a longer study of the CPC, see James P. Harrison, *The Long March to Power: A History of the Chinese Communist Party, 1921-1972* (New York: Frederick A. Praeger, 1972).

9. *I-chiu-liu-ch'i Fei-ch'in Nien-pao (1967 Yearbook on Chinese Communism)* (Taipei: Institute for the Study of Chinese Communist Problems, 1967), p. 564.

10. The best account of the conflict in Shanghai is Harold R. Isaacs, *The Tragedy of the Chinese Revolution* (New York: Atheneum, 1966).

11. *I-chiu-liu-ch'i Fei-ch'in Nien-pao*, p. 564.

12. *Selected Works of Mao Tse-tung*, vol. I (Peking: Foreign Languages Press, 1965), p. 65.

13. Ibid.

14. Chang Kuo-t'ao, *Wo-ti-hui-yi (Memoir)*, vol. I (Hong Kong: Ming Pao Monthly, 1971), pp. 6-8.

15. Tso-liang Hsiao, *The Land Revolution in China, 1930-1934: A Study of Documents* (Seattle: University of Washington Press, 1969).

16. Wang Chien-ming, *Chinese Communist Party*, vol. II, p. 304.

17. Tsai Hsiao-chien, *Kiangsi Su Ch'u, Hung-chung Hsi-tswan Hui-yi (My Recollections of the Kiangsi Soviet Area and the Westward Flight of the Chinese Red Army)* (Taipei: Institute for the Study of Chinese Communist Problems, 1970), pp. 119-20.

18. For texts of these documents see Conrad Brandt, Benjamin Schwartz, and John K.

Fairbank, *A Documentary History of Chinese Communism* (New York: Atheneum, 1967), pp. 217-38.

19. Boyd Compton, trans., *Mao's China: Party Reform Documents, 1942-44* (Seattle: University of Washington Press, 1966).

20. Chalmers A. Johnson, *Peasant Nationalism and Communist Power, the Emergence of Revolutionary China, 1937-1945* (Stanford, Calif.: Stanford University Press, 1962).

21. *RMRB*, July 3, 1981, p. 2.

22. Tang Tsou, *America's Failure in China, 1941-50* (Chicago: University of Chicago Press, 1963), pp. 324-40.

23. For study in detail of the military aspect of the war between the CPC and the Kuomintang, see William W. Whitson, *The Chinese High Command: A History of Communist Military Politics, 1927-1971* (New York: Frederick A. Praeger, 1973).

24. Arthur N. Young, *China's Nation-Building Effort, 1927-1937: The Financial and Economic Record* (Stanford, Calif.: Hoover Institution Press, Stanford University, 1971), p. 429.

25. Chang Kia-ngau, "War and Inflation," in Pichon P. Y. Loh, ed., *The Kuomintang Debacle of 1949: Collapse or Conquest?* (Boston: D. C. Heath and Company, 1965), p. 24.

26. Young, *China's Nation-Building Effort*, p. 428.

27. Chang Kai-ngau, "War and Inflation," p. 26. For other references on the defeat of the Nationalists see Albert Feuerwerker, ed., *Modern China* (Englewood Cliffs, N.J.: Prentice-Hall, 1965); Franz Schurmann and Orville Schell, eds., *Republican China: Nationalism, War, and the Rise of Communism, 1911-1949* (New York: Vintage Books, 1967); Suzanne Pepper, *Civil War in China* (Berkeley: University of California Press, 1978).

28. Brandt, Schwartz, and Fairbank, *History of Chinese Communism*, p. 460.

29. Ibid., p. 456.

30. C. K. Yang, "A Chinese Village in Early Communist Transition," in C. K. Yang, *Chinese Communist Society: The Family and the Village* (Cambridge, Mass.: MIT Press, 1965), p. 249.

31. Brandt, Schwartz, and Fairbank, *History of Chinese Communism*, p. 360.

32. "On Questions of Party History," *Beijing Review* 24, no. 17 (July 6, 1981), 10-39.

CHAPTER 3

The People's Republic, 1949-81

Unlike other political contenders in modern China, the Chinese Communists came to power in 1949 with a powerful civil-military machinery. By the end of 1949 the Communist party had four and a half million members and an army of more than two million men. Moreover, there were other favorable conditions to facilitate the Communist party's consolidation of power. For example, the colonial presence on the China coast had been eliminated by the end of the Second World War, thanks to the diplomatic efforts of the Nationalists during the war. Japan's attack and the civil war had also destroyed Chinese warlords for good. Furthermore, public opinion on mainland China in 1949 was receptive to a new order, having been through the runaway inflation and the corrupt administration of the last days of the Nationalist government. Many prominent intellectuals and professionals had stayed behind on the Chinese mainland, willing to cooperate with the Communist authority. Finally, after the battle in Manchuria in 1948, there was only limited destruction of facilities in the major industrial centers in central and south China. Thus the Chinese Communist party was endowed with numerous advantages that neither the warlords nor the Nationalists had ever enjoyed.

However, the first thirty years of the People's Republic have been turbulent. After initial success in establishing a relatively effective administration, starting in the mid-1950s, the Chinese Communist party was entrapped in a series of policy blunders followed by increasingly serious disputes among topmost leaders. In the Great Proletarian Cultural Revolution of 1966–76, the Communist party of China was on the verge of total self-destruction. Meanwhile, as a result of dispute among Communist leaders, policies and programs on agriculture, education, and industry were repeatedly reversed from one period to another. Social problems mounted, especially stagnation in living standard, population explosion, and attendent problems of unemployment and low social mobility. Before we sum up the history of the first three decades of the PRC, we must discuss the causes that have brought about the present crisis.

In retrospect, the defeat of the Kuomintang by the CPC merely changed the nature of, but did not terminate, the power struggle among Chinese political leaders.

Now that the common enemy of the CPC was destroyed on mainland China, differences in political outlook among Chinese Communist leaders hitherto suppressed owing to the threat of the Kuomintang surfaced. For analytical purposes, we shall divide Chinese Communist leaders into two groups, the "radicals" and the "pragmatists." We shall use Bittner's definition of radicalism to interpret the differences between these two groups of Chinese Communist leaders. According to Bittner, radicalism "implies a concentration of the forces of relevance on a particular principle, at the expense of the traditionally sanctioned regard for the complexities of context."[1] That is, radicals tend to align all human activities according to a single principle, which is antithetical to the common-sense notion of pluralistic contexts of everyday life. Rejection of the existing order and projection of a completely new way of life are the two sides of the coin of radicalism. The style of reasoning of radicalism is characterized less by "logically derived conclusions" than by "unity of meaning," i.e., perception of, and attitudes toward, reality being synthesized into an internally coherent outlook. For example, during the last two decades of Mao's rule on mainland China the propaganda media of the CPC exhorted all Chinese to adhere to Mao's dictum: "Class struggle as the key link" in society. Class struggle was, then, the single principle that must be used to align all actions. Soon after Mao's death, Chinese Communist propaganda media began to expose the "pragmatic" line as exemplified in the declaration: "There are laws of revolution and there are laws of production; one must not be substituted for the other."[2] The latter declaration respects pluralism in everyday life. So even though leaders of the CPC all profess to adhere to Marxism, their approach to the translation of ideology into practice is quite different. Hence one of the reasons for the persistent elite conflict in the first three decades of the PRC was the power struggle between the radicals and the pragmatists at the topmost echelon of the CPC.

Another contributing cause to the crisis in the first three decades of the PRC concerned the transition from personalized (or charismatic) leadership to institutionally based authority. As Max Weber pointed out, personalized or charismatic leadership emerges in an extraordinary situation such as revolution or social movement. The personality of a leader and people's belief in the extraordinary ability of the leader in such a time of distress temporarily take the place of law and culture, which bind a people in time of normality. But once the extraordinary character of a period is no longer obtained, personalized or charismatic leadership loses its raison d'être. Weber wrote:

> Charisma is a phenomenon typical of prophetic religious movements or of expansive political movements in their early stages. But as soon as the position of authority is well established, and above all as soon as control over large masses of people exists, it gives way to the forces of everyday routine. . . . As a rule the process of routinization is not free of conflict. In the early stages personal claims on the charisma of the chief are not easily forgotten and the conflict between the charisma of office or of hereditary status with personal charisma is a typical process in many historical situations.[3]

As our subsequent summary of the history of the first thirty years of the PRC will show, Mao Zedong tried to maintain his charismatic domination over the CPC and Chinese society after 1949. Hence Mao repeatedly (perhaps unconsciously) created crisis situations in which his charismatic leadership would be justified. There were Chinese Communist leaders who clearly perceived the need to change the authority pattern of the PRC to a less personal and more impersonal kind. In 1952, for example, a senior Chinese Communist leader named Dong Biwu (Tung Pi-wu) remarked, on the occasion of drafting the first national constitution, that the Chinese Communists had in the past lived by movements, but after the constitution had been adopted they would live by the law.[4] The conflict between Mao's charismatic inclination and other CPC leaders' emphasis on law is joined with the radical and pragmatic division among CPC leaders. The radicals naturally are favorably disposed toward a charismatic leadership, given their rejection of the existing order and their desire for permanent revolution. The pragmatists recognize the diversity of society, which calls for law and institutions to order it.

Closely related to all the foregoing is the difference among Communist leaders with regard to the relevance of pre-1949 experience of the CPC to the national reconstruction after 1949. As mentioned previously, the different approach to the applicability of Chinese Communist revolutionary experience in post-1949 nation building divided Chinese Communist leadership. With their respect for pluralism in everyday life, the party pragmatists were opposed to the "mechanical application" of the CPC's revolutionary legacy to national reconstruction. The radicals, led by Mao Zedong, as expected, wished to transform Chinese society along the revolutionary legacy of the CPC.

The divisions in the outlooks and attitudes among Chinese Communist leaders that we have discussed have greatly contributed to the political turbulence in China from 1949 to 1976 and even today. We shall now sum up the first thirty years of the PRC so as to better understand the contemporary policies and programs of the CPC.

REVOLUTIONARY DESTRUCTION, 1949-52

Mao Zedong had believed that before there is construction, there must first be destruction. Furthermore, a "correct" thought must precede a new institution. Following this logic, the Chinese Communist authorities in 1949 were not in a hurry to establish formal governing institutions. While entrusting the governing of the nation temporarily to military control commissions at various localities, the Communist party organized numerous mass campaigns to destroy old institutions and authorities and, in the process, inculcate a "correct" frame of mind among the populace.

The following is a list of major campaigns carried out in this period:

Campaign	Target of Attack
New Marriage Law, 1950	Traditional family rules
Land Reform, 1950	Landlords and clan authority
Anti-America, Aid-Korea, 1950	Public good will toward America, especially among Chinese intellectuals
Suppression of Counterrevolutionaries, 1950	Urban Chinese suspected of having close ties with the Nationalist party or former American agencies in China
Three-Anti or "Three-Evils" (corruption, waste, and bureaucratism), 1951	Corrupt Communist cadres and urban businessmen

Campaign	Target of Attack
Five-Anti or "Five-Evils" (bribery, tax evasion, theft of state intelligence, cheating on state contracts, and theft of state property), 1951	Urban businessmen
Thought Reform of Intellectuals, 1951	Intellectuals, mostly liberal arts and social science faculty in major universities
Democratic Reform, 1952	Old labor unions

In addition, there were campaigns against the established Christian religion in China. In each of the campaigns, a huge number of Chinese, young and old alike, were organized by the Communist party to engage in such activities as compiling incriminating dossiers on targeted groups, publicly denouncing people singled out for attack, propagandizing policies and programs of the Communist party, and leading public demonstrations and group-study sessions. In campaigns of terror, such as the execution of landlords in the Land Reform campaign and of counterrevolutionaries in the Suppression of Counterrevolutionaries, the masses were made to witness or even take a hand in the terror. The campaigns, wrote Doak Barnett, were "controlled mob actions and disciplined emotional binges on a massive scale."[5]

At the end of each campaign an old institution and the social group connected with it, such as landlords, urban businessmen, liberal intellectuals, labor unions, and the Christian church were either destroyed or totally discredited. On the ruins of the old, the Communist party established a network of new institutions—"mutual-aid teams" in the countryside, state-controlled enterprises in the cities, universities and trade unions modeled after the Russian system, and mass organizations such as the Communist Youth League and women's associations. The mass campaigns also enabled the Communist party to discover "activists" among the masses, and they were used to staff the new institutions. At the same time, through the experience of mass campaigns the public on mainland China was expected to be impressed by the power of the Communist party and henceforth to comply with the command of Communist authorities.

SOCIALIST CONSTRUCTION, 1953-57

Having destroyed the old and "educated" the masses, the Communist party in 1953 commenced the phase of "socialist construction." Politically, construction meant a nationwide "election" for delegates to the National People's Congress, supposedly the highest legislature in the land. The Congress, in turn, enacted a national constitution in 1954. Subnational governments, i.e., in provinces, municipalities, and counties, were also formally established in the form of a people's congress (the legislative branch) and a people's council (the executive branch). In areas where ethnic minorities resided, "autonomous regions" were established.

The installation of new government institutions was accompanied by an overall centralization of control in the hands of the national party authorities. Hitherto the Communist party had delegated power to several regional party bureaus. These bureaus were abolished after 1952 in favor of direct control of the provinces by the national party center in Peking. The concentration of power in Peking provoked the first major political dispute among Communist party leaders in 1953-55. Two powerful regional party leaders, Gao Gang of northeast China and Rao Shushih of East China, differed with Mao and other national leaders over a wide range of issues, political or economic. The dispute ended with Gao's suicide and disappearance of Rao.

Economically the Communist party had decreed in 1953 the "general line of socialist transition" and the beginning of the first five-year plan. The economic life of Chinese people was fundamentally altered. In urban areas private industry of whatever type and commerce were rapidly "socialized," i.e., taken over by the state. By the end of 1956 private enterprise virtually ceased to exist on mainland China. Equally radical changes took place in the countryside. At the start of 1956 only 4 percent of the peasant households on mainland China were members of the "advanced" cooperatives, i.e., Soviet collective farms. By the end of the year, 87.8 percent of peasant households had been transformed into advanced cooperatives, although the original plan had predicted that this change would take ten to fifteen years. The acceleration of rural collectivization began after Mao Zedong, at a conference in July 1955, attacked those who wanted to adhere to the original plan as "tottering along like a woman with bound feet."

Meanwhile, under the first five-year plan, a forced industrialization was carried out under the close supervision of Soviet advisers. Modeled after Soviet industrial planning, the Chinese five-year plan put an overwhelming emphasis on heavy industry at the expense of agriculture and consumer industry. Under the plan 61.8 percent of state investment went to industry and only 6.2 percent to agriculture. Of the investment in industry 88.8 percent was made in heavy industry, leaving only 11.2 percent for light industry.[6]

The gross disparity between industry and agriculture and between heavy and light industry in the very first five-year plan would have severe and long-range social and economic consequences that are still being acutely felt today in mainland China.

Socially, in this period of "socialist transition," a totalitarian order was imposed on the population. People's lives came increasingly under bureaucratic control, with such actions as rationing of necessities, state assignment of jobs, and restriction on residence and movement. In art and literature political regimentation was enhanced. Parallel to the cases of Gao Gang and Rao Shushi, the imposition of literary control provoked a major purge in 1955 against a famed writer named Hu Feng. Hu had remonstrated with Mao against party interference and regimentation of art and literature. Mao responded by denouncing and arresting Hu and his associates. This was followed in 1955-56 with a campaign of repression, the Suppression of Hidden Counterrevolutionaries.

As can be deduced from the foregoing, the radical changes in mainland Chinese society had, by the end of 1956, created numerous contradictions. The situation in the countryside was particularly tense. The exaction from the "advanced cooperatives" and the newly instituted "unified purchase and sale system" had resulted in food shortages and peasant demonstrations.[7] Communist cadres often made peasants work excessively long hours.[8] In August 1956 the Chinese press reported of widespread accidental deaths of rural infants in the countryside due to their mothers' being compelled to work in the field.[9] Elsewhere, the purge of Gao and Ruo and the suppression of dissent within the Communist party over collectivization had a chilling and demoralizing effect. Even Mao complained that after the incident of Gao and Ruo, the atmosphere within the party tended to be stale and disturbingly quiet. The campaign of Suppression of Hidden Counterrevolutionaries in 1955 was widely regarded (as revealed in the speeches during the 1957 "Hundred Flowers Blooming" campaign) as excessively harsh.

The tense situation in mainland China in 1956 was further compounded as word began to spread that the Soviet leader, Khrushchev, had made a secret speech denouncing Stalin as a pathological tyrant at the Twentieth Congress of the Communist party of the Soviet Union in February of that year. This was followed by unrest in Eastern Europe. Communist China could not be immune from these developments. The party pragmatists capitalized on this opportunity of de-Stalinization in Russia by putting forth a program of "less politics but more economics" at the Eighth Congress of the Chinese Communist party in August 1956. The communiqué of the Congress declared that the task of the nation would henceforth be economic development and that class struggle was no longer the principal occupation of the Communist party. The new party constitution then emphasized inner-party democracy and deleted all references to "the thought of Mao Zedong" to prevent "cult of personality." Chinese leader Zhou Enlai announced a new policy toward intellectuals, promising better treatment.

Mao Zedong had sensed quickly that all these developments had put him on the defensive. The reassert his initiative Mao, who had earlier silenced dissenters in and out of the party in order to carry out his radical programs, now decided to outmaneuver other party leaders by being "more liberal than the liberals." Mao's way was to launch the "Hundred Flowers Blooming" campaign in May 1957, in which he called on people outside of the Communist party to voice their views on every aspect of the Communist regime freely without fear of consequence. Mao Zedong apparently sought to realize two aims from this campaign: to separate himself from Stalin and to relieve somewhat the pent-up tension in Chinese society so as to avert a Hungarian-type response. Mao naturally hoped to reap a political windfall out of the campaign of the Hundred Flowers.

Mao's hope, however, vanished soon after when Chinese critics began their barrage of criticism, charges, and denunciations of various aspects of the Communist regime. From mid-May to the first week of June 1957 the attacks continued. The most articulate groups were prominent non-Communist politicians who were supposedly "allies" of the Communist party (democratic personages, as they were called in China), scholars, and college students. The critics focused their attack on the dictatorship of the Communist party, the lack of civil liberties, the privileges and incompetence of party cadres, and the political regimentation of all aspects of life. University students, especially those in Peking who had been the most enthusiastic group in welcoming the victory of the Communist party in 1949, now became the most vehement critics of the party. Moreover, the students backed up their words with actions as student leaders traveled to other campuses and started their own organizations. Meanwhile, peasants took this opportunity of the Communist party's being on the defensive to leave cooperatives in large numbers. Workers capitalized on the events by striking for higher wages and for a genuine labor union. Sensing that the situation was getting out of their hands, the Communist party put a stop to the Hundred Flowers campaign. Mao commenced an Anti-Rightist campaign against the critics. A massive purge of every locality and institution of rightists began in late June 1957 and did not let up until 1959. Many were imprisoned. Even more were dismissed from their jobs and suffered permanent discrimination and ostracism, as did their family members.

Thus the "construction" phase of 1953-57 ended with numerous signs of disquiet in the People's Republic. The pragmatists in the Eighth Congress of 1956 had sought to shift the national task and attention from politics to economics and had planned to make, without fanfare, suitable adjustments to lessen the tension in Chinese society. But Mao had overturned party pragmatists' scheme by launching the Hundred Flowers Blooming campaign, which exacerbated the tension between the party and Chinese society.

THE GREAT LEAP FORWARD
AND THE PEOPLE'S COMMUNE MOVEMENT,
1958-60

Having lost politically in the Hundred Flowers campaign, Mao Zedong sought to regain the image of infallibility of his leadership in economics. The occasion was right for Mao to intervene economically; for the end of the first five-year plan had left Chinese leaders with a major dilemma: lack of significant rise in agricultural productivity threatened to hamper further industrial expansion.

Taking the opportunity of the Anti-Rightist campaign of 1957, which had silenced dissenters within and without the Communist party, Mao Zedong carried out the Great Leap Forward campaign in the summer of 1958 to accelerate agricultural *and* industrial growth in an unprecedented way. Agriculture was to "leap forward," according to Mao's plan, by the establishment of the people's commune, which at its height abolished all forms of private property. The large size and the centralized command structure of the people's commune, in Mao's scheme, laid the necessary ground for mass mobilization of peasant labor for major constructions such as canals, dams, and other irrigation projects. Communes were thought to be able to establish their own "local industry" to make implements for farming. New methods of farming such as deep plowing and close planting were required of peasants in order to increase yield per acre. Since family life was collectivized, women were supposed to be free to work in the field. Thus Mao envisaged a "great leap" in grain production in 1958 and he demanded that industry must accelerate its growth on the basis of the agricultural "leap." In industry, Mao set the strategy of "taking steel as the key link." Steel production was targeted to increase by one fold, from 5.3 to 10.7 million tons in one year. Other industries were to gear up to the growth of iron and steel. Chinese state investments in new heavy-industry projects was doubled from 1957 to 1958. The rate of national saving jumped from 22 percent during the first five-year plan to 34 percent in 1958. To staff the new industrial plants the state induced 20 million laborers to move from the countryside to cities.[10]

The Great Leap Forward was accompanied politically by an intensification of the Anti-Rightist campaign within the Communist party. At the topmost level party pragmatists went into a political eclipse, while Mao cultivated radical clients among provincial party leaders and propagandists so as to spread his Great Leap program all over the nation. Socially, the Great Leap Forward was expressed in a massive campaign of anti-intellectual and populist propaganda. Peasants were told to break free of the "superstition concerning the necessity of scientific and academic learning" for development and to rely on their own native wisdom and activism. Students were told to integrate their book learning with practical work; at every university and college many hours were spent establishing factories or farms. In the meanwhile, "class origin" was strictly enforced in admission to institutes of higher education and a marked rise in political instruction took place in all schools. Moreover, in the countryside, life was being militarized as people's militia were created, enlisting all able-bodied men and women. Mao's vision of turning China into a modern Sparta seemed to be realized in the fall of 1958 when every citizen was supposed to be simultaneously a radical revolutionary, a producer (industrial or agrarian), and a soldier. The radical vision of the Great Leap was completed with a visible "threat of enemy" as the Chinese Communist regime launched an artillery attack on the islands of Quemoy and Matsu off the coast of Fujian, which were held by the Nationalists. The offshore islands crisis, in turn, brought an American warning to the People's Republic of possible military retaliation.

In the end, Mao's hopes for the Great Leap Forward vanished as quickly as his hopes in the Hundred Flowers campaign earlier. The main reason for the failure of the Great Leap, as a recent Chinese press article pointed out, was that it was based on *political* projection and requirement, not on economic assessment.[11] It did not take into consideration resource constraint and human motivation. By July 1959 when the Communist party finally decided to abandon the Great Leap, severe damage was already done to farm production. This situation was further compounded by political and natural crises. The political crisis was Mao's purge of Defense Minister Peng Dehuai and his associates, who had criticized the Great Leap at a top party conference in July 1959. As the party attempted to return the countryside to normalcy, bad weather hampered the effort. The result was famine and starvation, which plagued mainland China from 1959 through the early months of 1962. Twenty years later, in 1981, noted Chinese economist Sung Yefang revealed that in 1959-62, 10 million people died of "unnatural causes" (i.e., starvation).[12]

Like Mao's first major blunder—the Hundred Flowers campaign of 1957—the second one, the Great Leap Forward, eroded the unity of Chinese Communist leadership and tarnished the image and credibility of the Communist party in the eyes of Chinese public.

REHABILITATION AND NORMALCY, 1962-65

The failure of the Great Leap Forward had discredited Mao and his radical associates. Subsequently, in early 1959 Mao resigned his chairmanship of the People's Republic, and Liu Shaoqi took over both the chairmanship of the PRC and the grave task of returning Chinese economy to a healthy footing. Liu made use of the party pragmatists, the major figures being Chen Yun and Deng Xiaoping.

The party pragmatists began their rescue missions in the countryside. Private plots were restored to peasants. Decision on production and disposal of collective income was vested in the smallest unit of the people's commune: a production team, which was composed of an average of twenty peasant families. Free trade among peasants was allowed though to a certain extent confined. Finally, the size of the commune was radically reduced to promote flexible adaptation to local conditions. A "rationalization" was carried out in Chinese industry, including closing down many inefficient plants built during the Great Leap and instituting a system of responsibility and profitability in factories. The state investment in new projects had been reduced from 38.4 billion yuan in 1960 to 5.6 billion yuan in 1962. The rate of national saving or accumulation had been decreased from 39.6 percent in 1960 to 10.4 percent in 1962. The 20 million people who had been recruited from the countryside during the height of the Great Leap Forward were repatriated to rural areas. The party pragmatists, with limited success, sought to have a balanced growth between industry and agriculture and between light and heavy industry. In the meantime, the educational system, which had been disrupted by the emphasis on production during the Great Leap, was restored to normal operation. Intellectuals were paid respect by party pragmatists, who emphasized research and development. By 1965 starvation was a thing of the past, and production had been restored to pre-1958 level. To crown the success of the party moderates, in 1965 China announced the accomplishment of self-sufficiency in petroleum, a milestone in Chinese industrial development.

But the economic success during this period was not given a secure political blessing. From January 11 to February 7, 1962, at the beginning of the reign of the pragmatists, a large party conference was convened, attended by all top party leaders including Mao Zedong, Liu Shaoqi, Zhou Enlai, and Deng Xiaoping as well as seven thousand regional party leaders. In the tradition of the Chinese Communist party, this conference summed up the lessons of the previous decade, especially that of the Great Leap Forward, and announced a new line of development in the light of past mistakes. Mao Zedong felt that as in 1956 he was on the defensive, and he decided to go with the tide by making self-criticism in the conference concerning his responsibility in the disaster of the Great Leap Forward. The party pragmatists apparently regarded this conference of January 1962 as their second chance, after the Eighth Party Congress of 1956, to deradicalize Chinese Communist politics and turn the nation's attention to economic construction. They had designed this conference to be a model of "democratic centralism"; the agenda was set during the conference with all attendants participating in deciding its content. There was relatively free discussion and airing of opinions. For the moment the hope of the public was high that, after the lessons of the Great Leap Forward, an era of economic rationality and political moderation had dawned.

Before the end of 1962, however, the hopes of party pragmatists were once more dashed. In September of that year, during a meeting of the party central committee, Mao Zedong proclaimed that a period of intensified class struggle between the "two roads" of capitalism and socialism lay ahead. Calling on the whole nation to "never forget class struggle," Mao made the Communist party launch a Socialist Education campaign in the countryside to stem what he perceived to be the growth of capitalism: enlarged private plots, free trade, and peasants' leaving farms to take jobs in cities. Next to peasants, Mao's target of socialist education was Chinese youth and students. From 1963 through 1965 a marked rise in political indoctrination in class hatred took place in Chinese schools and the mass media. At the same time Mao openly and repeatedly attacked the entire literary community of China for its lack of enthusiasm for Mao's brand of socialism.

While Mao's general call for "class struggle" continued, from late 1962 on more ominous signs of political storm appeared. It seems that by 1962 Mao had already organized an alliance of civil-military leaders to implement his socialism. On the civilian side Jiang Qing, Mao's wife, became active in the propaganda establishment of the party for the first time since the founding of the People's Republic. Moreover Jiang had recruited two party propagandists from Shanghai, Zhang Chunqiao and Yao Wenyuan, to help her carry out a relentless campaign of vilifying prominent literary figures and promoting a new "proletarian culture." On the military side Defense Military Marshal Lin Biao in 1963 extended his campaign of building Mao's cult of personality, hitherto confined to the armed forces, to the civilian population. At first Marshal Lin's military propagandists called on Chinese youth to emulate a dead soldier named Lei Feng, who was said to have been totally dedicated to the teachings of Mao. Then in 1964 the entire nation was told to "learn from the People's Liberation Army," especially from its devotion to "the thought of Mao Zedong." Beginning with this campaign in 1964, the little red books of "quotations from Chairman Mao" began to circulate in China in massive numbers.

The political pendulum of the People's Republic was swinging to the left once more, and to the extreme left at that.

THE GREAT PROLETARIAN CULTURAL REVOLUTION, 1966-69

Ever since 1926, when Mao Zedong witnessed a spontaneous peasant movement in his home province of Hunan, he had regarded mass movement as the most powerful weapon to win political battles and accomplish great deeds. Mao had also come to see a mass movement as the acid test of a person's revolutionary commitment as he commented on the 1926 peasant movement:

> Every revolutionary party and every revolutionary comrade will be put to the test, to be accepted or rejected as they decide. There are three alternatives. To march at their peasants' head and lead them? To trail behind them, gesticulating and criticizing? Or to stand in their way and oppose them?[13]

As Mao saw it, the mass campaign of socialist education and emulation of model persons in 1963-65 were a test of other party leaders' revolutionary character. In late 1965 Mao apparently had concluded that most party leaders had taken the wrong attitudes toward mass campaigns: trail behind them, or stand in their way. Mao was particularly incensed by members of the Peking party establishment that had been reluctant to follow his lead in attacking prominent literary figures. To Mao Zedong those who had shown reluctance in endorsing the mass campaigns in 1963-65 were no longer revolutionaries but "power holders taking the capitalist road." As Mao told an Albanian military delegation in May 1967:

> During the time of the democratic revolution, these people actively participated in opposing the three big mountains (feudalism, imperialism, bureaucratic capitalism), but once the entire country was liberated, they were not so keen on opposing the bourgeoisie. Though they had actively participated in and endorsed overthrow of local despots and the distribution of land, after the country's liberation when agricultural collectivization was to be implemented, they were not keen on this either. He who would not take the socialist road and is now in power—is it not he who is a power holder taking the road of capitalism![14]

But Mao had suspected a great majority of national, provincial, municipal, and lower party leaders of being "power holders taking the capitalist road." Thus nothing short of a revolution would accomplish Mao's goal of leading China down the path of socialism.

To make revolution, Mao must depart from the norm of the Communist party. As we mentioned earlier, Mao had already organized an ad hoc civil-military group in 1963-65 to carry out his campaigns of proletarian culture, class struggle, and learning the "thought of Mao Zedong." In late 1965, as the first step in launching the Great

Proletarian Cultural Revolution, Mao directed this ad hoc civil-military group to openly attack the Peking Communist party establishment, an unprecedented act, which if undertaken by any other party leader, would certainly be condemned as treason. Mao Zedong described his conspiratorial deed to an Albanian military delegation:

> China's Great Proletarian Cultural Revolution began with Comrade Yao Wenyuan's [Yao Wenyuan] criticism of "Hai Jui Dismissed From Office" in the winter of 1965. At that time, certain departments and certain localities in this country of ours were dominated by revisionism. It was so tight that even water could not seep in and pins could not penetrate. I then suggested to Comrade Chiang Ch'ing [Jiang Qing] that she organize some articles to criticize "Hai Jui Dismissed From Office." But this was impossible to accomplish here in this Red metropolis, and there was no alternative but to go to Shanghai to organize it. Finally the article was written. I read it three times, and considered it basically all right, so I let Comrade Chiang Ch'ing bring it back for publication. I suggested that some of the leading comrades of the Central Committee be allowed to read it, but Comrade Chiang Ch'ing suggested: "The article can be published as it is, and I do not think there is any need to ask Comrade Chou En-lai [Zhou Enlai] and K'ang Sheng [Kang Sheng] to read it." After Yao Wen-yuan's article was published, most of the newspapers in the country published it, but it was not published in Peking and Hunan.[15]

Unbeknownst to most Chinese, the Cultural Revolution, which would eventually result in 20 million deaths and 100 million victims had already begun.[16]

At first the Cultural Revolution directed its terror against literary intellectuals and the propaganda establishment of the CPC. Mao's chief target then was Wu Han, deputy mayor of Peking and famed historian. Wu had published a play entitled "Hai Jui Dismissed From Office," Hai Jui being a Ming dynasty official who had remonstrated with the despotic emperor. Mao suspected Wu of using the play to attack Mao's dismissal of the former defense minister, Marshal Peng Dehuai. Following Wu's downfall (Wu died in prison), a sweeping campaign was unleashed against literary figures in Peking. Mao also purged the presumed patron of these literary figures, the Peking Party Committee (Peng Zhen being its head then). These actions, according to Mao, had prepared the ideological base of the Cultural Revolution.

But no phase of revolution is complete, according to Mao, without a mass movement. So from November 1965 to December 1966 the ideological phase of the Cultural Revolution was accompanied by a student movement. After the dissolution of the Peking Party Committee in May 1966, students at Peking University wrote "big-character posters" accusing chief university administrators of following a "bourgeois line of education." There is no doubt that those students who led the demonstration at Peking University were instigated by the ad hoc group around Mao, which had now been formalized as the Central Cultural Revolution Group, headed by Mao's long-time secretary Chen Boda. Subsequently the Communist party decreed a suspension of all schools so students could participate in "educational revolution." Soon, Red Guards appeared, first in Peking and then in other cities. They were students of the "correct class background" (workers, peasants, martyrs, soldiers and party cadres). The Red Guards attacked violently a selected group of teachers for their "bourgeois" teaching and five categories of "class enemy" (remnants of landlords, rich peasants, counter-revolutionaries, "bad elements" and rightists). To this day there is no public account of the number of deaths in the hands of the Red Guards; it must have been in tens of thousands.[17]

The ideological phase of the Cultural Revolution passed into the "power-seizure phase," beginning in January 1967. At this stage, at the elite level, the focus of attack was on Liu Shaoqi, then vice-chairman of the Communist party and chairman of the People's Republic. Mao had charged that Liu had erred in his handling of the student demonstration at Peking University in June 1966. This was certainly an excuse for Mao's deep resentment over Liu's success in achieving economic recovery after the disaster of the Great Leap Forward. Liu was subjected to public denunciation and dismissed from his formal positions without due process. Later he was ordered out of Peking. Liu died in 1969. At the mass level, the Red Guard organization and action were emulated widely. In Chinese cities workers and employees organized into "rebel associations." All of them were told by the Central Cultural Revolution Group to struggle on behalf of Mao against "power holders taking the capitalist road." But the latter were local party leaders who, driven to desperation, fought back with their own Red Guards and rebel associations. Some of the "power holders" organized peasants from the suburb to storm into cities to fight Red Guards and rebels. Anarchy and violence spread to the entire nation.

The Cultural Revolution rapidly moved to the crisis phase, which began in March 1967. The totalitarian order that the Communist party had established since 1949 broke down as students, workers, and peasants fought one another and, more important, traveled freely to make alliances with other groups in a link-up movement. Control of communication by the party collapsed as students published their own newspapers, journals, and pamphlets, known as Red Guard publications. The crisis was compounded by Mao's ordering the army to intervene on the side of the left. Since it was almost impossible for politically inexperienced army officers to distinguish left from nonleft groups, army intervention added fuel to the fire. In July 1967 a serious clash between the Mao-supported Red Guards and the army command in the city of Wuhan had a sobering effect on Mao, who now feared the army's alienation from his leadership.

In January 1968 Mao attempted to consummate the Cultural Revolution by organizing revolutionary committees, based on a three-way alliance, i.e., an alliance of representatives of soldiers, cadres, and "masses" (Red Guards and workers). The revolutionary committees would be the new institutions of authority in China. The process of reestablishing order was long and intermittent. The Red Guards and the worker-rebels had organized themselves into small cliques and guilds and were fighting and quarreling with one another. But by 1968 Mao Zedong had already expressed his disillusionment with the Red Guards. He stated that the mentality of the Red Guard "is basically bourgeois."[18] Mao, as he had done before, reversed himself; local Party leaders were restored to their former positions. In many instances Red Guard members found themselves to be in a three-way alliance with the same party leaders whom they had violently struggled against a few weeks before. The protests of the Red Guard to Mao were not heeded; for by 1968 Mao feared the Red Guard more than the cadres. Similar to what had happened to the Hundred Flowers campaign of 1957, the movement of the Red Guard threatened to go its own way; some Red Guards demanded genuine elections, and they attacked the party bureaucracy as the "Red capitalist class." Thus with the aid of Marshal Lin's army officers and men, revolutionary committees were forced on the Red Guards and workers throughout the nation in 1968.

Then in April 1969 Mao declared the victory of the Cultural Revolution and convened the Ninth Party Congress. The congress marked the height of Marshal Lin Biao's power. It formalized a new party constitution in which Marshal Lin was named the successor to Mao. Moreover, Lin also succeeded in making Mao accept the composition of the Politburo (Political Bureau of the Central Committee) of which half the members were Lin's military subordinates, including his wife. The power structure that evolved out of the Ninth Party Congress was a complex mishmash. The national core of power was composed of Mao, the Central Cultural Revolution Group, Marshal Lin's military cohort, and the public security (police) leader, Xie Fuzi. The middle and lower-middle layer of the power structure, i.e., those in the provinces, municipalities, and counties, consisted of the old cadres who were initially the target of Red Guard attacks. The "revolutionary masses" (Red Guards and worker rebels) were, at most, admitted selectively at the lowest layer of the power hierarchy, under the thumb of those who had been known at the start of the Cultural Revolution as power holders taking the capitalist road.

THE STRUGGLE FOR SUCCESSION, 1970-76

Mao proclaimed the Ninth Party Congress of 1969 "a congress of unity." Events following the congress soon repudiated that. Since 1949 the source of disunity in the party had always stemmed from its innermost core, i.e., Mao and those around him. In 1970 Chen Boda, who had been Mao's personal secretary for some thirty years and was chief of the Central Cultural Revolution Group, was denounced by Mao and Jiang Qing as a "sham Marxist" and dismissed from his formal positions. Then in September 1971 Marshal Lin Biao, his wife and son (an air force officer), and several members of China's top-rank military leaders were reported to have been killed in a plane crash in the Mongolian People's Republic. Later it was announced that Marshal Lin and company had been involved in an assassination plot against Mao. When the plot was discovered, Lin and his men fled in a hurry in a jet plane, which crashed on its way to the Soviet Union—so the official account by Peking goes.

Two years after Lin's death, in 1973, the Communist party circulated a set of documents purported to be the proof of Lin's assassination plot. These documentary exerpts showed, at best, Lin's disillusionment with Mao and his feelings of extreme insecurity. Other inner-party circulars revealed, however, that Mao had been dissatisfied with Lin as soon as the Ninth Party Congress was over. Basically, both Chen Boda and Lin Biao had tried to fortify their own positions in anticipation of Mao's demise. At that time they would have to face the old party establishment, which was bent on revenge for what Chen and Lin had done in the Cultural Revolution. Accordingly, Chen and Lin had suggested, without prior consultation with Mao, a format for a new national government, including the revival of the chairmanship of the People's Republic, which had been abolished with the dismissal of Liu Shoaqi earlier.[19] In other words, Chen and Lin had shown independence in front of Mao. Moreover, Chen and Lin's attempt to staff the party and state center with their own men disturbed Mao's design to mix the left with the right so as to insure that Mao would not have to deal with a solid wall of bureaucracy that "even water could not seep in[to] and pins could not penetrate." The dilemma of Chen Boda and Lin Biao was that they had thoroughly antagonized the old party establishment by faithfully carrying out Mao's Cultural Revolution without, however, obtaining Mao's complete support to insure their safety after his death. The naming of Lin Biao in the party constitution as successor to Chairman Mao was not enough, since the party or state constitution in the People's Republic is like the traditional "mandate of heaven"—a *post factum* justification of the victor. In the final analysis, the fall of Chen Boda and Marshal Lin Biao points to the overwhelming importance of the patron-client relationship in a totalitarian bureaucracy. The death or uncertain support of a patron spells the doom of his clients.

The incidents involving Chen Boda and Lin Biao signified an intensified and accelerated phase of succession struggle inside the Chinese Communist party. After September 1971 Mao was on the defensive again so the political pendulum in China momentarily swung to the right. Zhou Enlai, who was entrusted by Mao to handle the Lin Biao case, now assumed practical leadership of the party and of the state of China and attempted to restore Chinese economic and cultural life to normality, much as Liu Shaoqi had done after the disaster of the Great Leap. Zhou sought to reverse some of the measures of the Cultural Revolution. In January 1972 Zhou presided over a memorial ceremony for the late foreign minister Chen Yi, who had suffered at the hands of the Red Guard. Mao attended the memorial personally, and the Chinese press showed him bowing before Chen's portrait in a gesture of penitence. From August to October 1972 Zhou launched a press campaign criticizing "ultra-leftism." Discipline of labor and material incentives were emphasized. Professionalism was, at least, not singled out for attack. Excessive administrative interference in agriculture was reduced. But just like Liu Shaoqi's actions in 1960-62, Zhou's measures in 1972 did not have a secure blessing from Mao, who had deliberately fostered a "dialectical" relationship between the left and the right in the party.

The 1973 Tenth Congress of the Communist party of China exemplified Mao's dialectics. In the congress Zhou delivered the political report on the state of the Communist party. But Wang Hongwen, the youngest member of the Gang of Four who rose to national prominence in 1967 after militantly leading a workers' rebel association in Shanghai, made the report on the revision of the party constitution. Wang Hongwen was also "elected" to be a vice-chairman of the party, and all members of the Gang of Four (Jiang Qing, Zhang Chunqiao, Yao Wenyuan, and Wang Hongwen) were made members of the Politburo. On the other hand, Deng Xiaoping, who had been denounced as "China's number two revisionist" during the Cultural Revolution, was formally rehabilitated in the Tenth Party Congress, together with five other old party leaders who had suffered disgrace in the Cultural Revolution.

In the scheme of Mao the Tenth Party Congress of 1973 marked the start of returning China to normalcy but normalcy within the bounds of Mao's socialism. The appointment of leftists to the highest councils of the Communist party was designed by Mao to make sure that the resumption of economic and political life in China would not lead to "creeping revisionism," which in Mao's views had happened in 1960-62 under Liu Shaoqi's leadership. But the four leftists, Jiang Qing, Zhang Chunqiao, Yao Wenyuan and Wang Hongwen, were not content with performing a watchdog function. They feared for their safety like Chen Boda and Lin Biao before them. The rehabilitation of Deng Xiaoping and other veteran party leaders in the Tenth Congress of 1973 meant that the time for the four leftists to build their own power base in the bureaucracy was running out. Jiang Qing and her associates must seize the occasion of the forthcoming Fourth National People's Congress in 1975 to win some major appointments for their own followers.

The four thus set to work in 1974. Their influence was seen in the numerous rebel associations among urban workers and college students. The leftist tactics were to ferment disturbance among these groups, bringing forth a general paralysis in production, and thus discredit and disrupt Zhou's effort to restore production. Consequently, according to the plan of the leftists, Mao would be receptive to selecting state ministers or even the premier from the leftists. Under the instigation of the leftists, a wave of labor unrest swept through China in 1974, especially among railway and steel workers. Many factories and plants stopped functioning, and steel production declined drastically.[20] Mao's response, however, took the leftists by surprise. The labor unrest in the nation had prompted Mao to urge Zhou Enlai to hasten China's return to an orderly life. Mao instructed Zhou Enlai to work toward three basic goals: mass learning of the theory of the dictatorship of the proletariat, national unity and stability, and economic development.

Armed with the instructions from Mao, Zhou Enlai convened the Fourth National People's Congress in January 1975. Capitalizing on Mao's demands for unity, stability, and economic growth, Zhou declared in the People's Congress that agriculture, industry, defense, and science and technology would all be modernized. In the meantime, the leftists sought to embarrass him by organizing one campaign after another with themes such as "Criticize Lin Biao and Confucius!" The idea of these campaigns was "antirestoration," i.e., opposition to Zhou's plan to return China to normalcy. But the leftists went down in defeat as they did not win any major appointment. Zhou Enlai had persuaded Mao to let Deng Xiaoping take charge of China's production and other aspects of national life, for Zhou was then dying of cancer.

In the autumn of 1975 Deng Xiaoping drafted three major guidelines for national development: a general program, a directive on science and technology, and a program for industrial growth. Meanwhile he launched a behind-the-scenes campaign to rally veteran party leaders in support of his programs and to prod them back to work. This then provoked the leftists to react. A select group of college students in Peking were mobilized by the leftists to write polemical articles in the press denouncing Deng's work and to put up wall posters on campus accusing Deng of returning China to the "revisionist path." But as long as Zhou was alive, Deng was safe politically.

Deng's patron, Zhou Enlai, died in January 1976. Zhou's death raised both hope and fear for the leftists—hope that Mao would appoint one of them to succeed Zhou and fear that he would appoint the most logical successor—Deng Xiaoping. The tension and anxiety surrounding the question of Zhou's successor were widespread, from the highest to the lowest point of the Chinese Communist political system. It was clear to everyone that the successor to Zhou would be, in fact, the successor to Mao, who was dying also. Against this background of heightened elite tension and mass anxiety, a riot took place in Peking's Tiananmen Square on April 5, 1976. The night before, groups of people had left wreaths of flowers under the martyrs' memorial in the square, which were intended for the memory of Zhou Enlai. Yao Wenyuan, one of the Gang of Four, interpreted that as an antileft sentiment and ordered the wreaths removed. That, in turn, precipitated a confrontation the next day between visitors to the memorial and the police. The confrontation then led to a spontaneous mass outburst, which at its height involved some 100,000 men and women. The riot was finally put down by the "worker militia" of Peking, which was organized and controlled by the leftists.

Deng Xiaoping was blamed by the leftists for the riot, and since Jiang Qing had direct access to Mao, the latter believed her. Consequently, Deng was dismissed and disgraced for the second time. Deng's latest purge once more shows the importance of patron-client relations in Chinese politics. Without Zhou Enlai as his patron, even so high a leader as Deng could not survive long. The victory of the leftists, however, was a hollow one, for Mao did not appoint any leftist to succeed Zhou. Instead he chose a newcomer to the national politics of China, the former party leader of Hunan (the home province of Mao), Hua Guofeng.

THE STRUGGLE FOR POWER
AFTER THE DEATH OF MAO,
1976-81

Mao Zedong died on September 9, 1976, and the People's Republic of China was, in many ways, like an ancient regime in the throes of a revolution. Politically, Mao left behind a divided national leadership, and factions were entrenched throughout the structure of the Communist party. The political and economic system that Mao had handed down to his successors in September 1976 showed numerous signs of strains and breakdowns; the industrial sector was, on the whole, obsolete, inefficient, and wasteful (exceptions may be made in isolated defense industry). Portents of a violent outburst from society were present: poverty, declining mobility, unemployment, and graft and venality in the bureaucracy. Against this background a serious power struggle took place from October 1976 to January 1979, which ended in the victory of "party pragmatists-turned-reformers." In retrospect, this political turnover, for the time being, saved the Communist regime from a violent overthrow.

The struggle for power after Mao's death involved five discernible power blocs within the Communist party. On the side of the Mao regime were three, by no means consensual, groups with varying degrees of identification with Mao's ideology and program. They were (1) the Gang of Four; (2) the coopted veteran cadres—former provincial leaders or regional army commanders who had been promoted to national leadership by Mao during and after the Cultural Revolution, the most important ones being Hua Guofeng, Wang Dongxin (commander of a special guard division in Peking whose duty is to protect the personal safety of Mao and other high-ranking party leaders), General Chen Xilian (commander of the Peking Military District), and Wu De (mayor of Peking at the time of Mao's death), and (3) the coopted old guards of the party, such as Marshal Ye Jianying and former finance minister Li Xiannian (presently president of the PRC), who had played only ceremonial roles under Mao. Of the three groups naturally the members of the Gang of Four were the closest in identification with Mao's ideology and program and hence most vulnerable to attack by party members who had suffered in the Cultural Revolution. The inner group that was least identified with Mao's regime was the coopted old guards. The challenger to this inner core of Mao's regime consisted of two groups of veteran cadres, one comprising the same party pragmatists (now turned "party reformers") who had been repeatedly suppressed by Mao from 1956 to the end of the Cultural Revolution and the other, the large number of intermediate party leaders who had been known during the Cultural Revolution as "the power holders taking the capitalist road." This last group was the most numerous and carried the most weight in the long run, as the party machinery had always been in their hands. Even Mao had to rehabilitate most of these veteran cadres after 1968. The mentality and interest of these veteran cadres are very straightforward— *status quo ante.* That is, return to the status quo before the Cultural Revolution. To this end removal and punishment of the Gang of Four was the first and foremost goal of the veteran cadres after the death of Mao.

Removing the Gang of Four was also the common goal of the coopted old guards and the coopted veteran cadres, who had belonged to the inner core of Mao's regime. These two groups knew that their own political survival depended on their disassociation from the four radicals. The purge of the Gang of Four was, of course, the goal of the party pragmatists too. So the Gang of Four was dispatched without difficulty. In October 1976 Marshal Ye Jianying, with Hua Guofeng's cooperation, ordered the arrest of the four radicals. So ended the meteoric political career of Jiang Qing and her three associates.

The purge of the Gang of Four, however, won only a temporary reprieve for the coopted old guards and the veteran cadres associated with the old Mao regime. That was due mainly to the numerous social and economic problems in mainland China to which these inner groups had no answer. The political initiative was now in the hands of the party pragmatists, led by Deng Xiaoping. Deng's group enjoyed both prestige and legitimacy. They could always boast of their record of rescuing Chinese economy from the famine days of 1960-62 and of their suffering in the hands of the leftists in the Cultural Revolution. Deng boldly championed the cause of reform. Deng appealed to the intermediate party leaders on the platform of returning China to normalcy and restoration of the authority of old party cadres. He also appealed to the public on the programs of political democratization and economic modernization. Against this background Hua Guofeng, then chairman of the CPC, had no alternative but to restore Deng to his formal positions within the party and the government in July 1977.

Once restored to formal positions, Deng moved with dispatch to return China to normalcy. Deng calmed the most vociferous group, the youth, by quickly reviving national college entrance examinations, which had been suspended for more than ten years under Mao's Cultural Revolution. He then released tens of thousands of intellectuals and former students, condemned earlier as "the rightists," from prison camps. Following these moves, Deng reconvened the united front organization of the Chinese People's Political Consultative Conference, which is composed of prominent non-Communist political and social notables. Other parts of the regular Communist infrastructure were reestablished, such as the trade unions, the youth league, and the women's associations. Moreover, to appease the army, Deng reorganized the militia so as to return the control of the latter to the regular army command. By July 1978 Deng Xiaoping had completed the status quo ante and had thus rallied behind him both the veteran cadres throughout the party and the nonparty influentials in Chinese society.

In December 1978 in the celebrated third plenum of the Eleventh Party Central Committee, Deng unfurled his sweeping program of reform. After having been repeatedly beaten by Mao, the party pragmatists were finally able to lead China in the direction of "less politics, more economics." The third plenum decreed the end of party priority in the class struggle, to be replaced by four modernizations. It announced a new policy in agriculture by allowing peasants to farm on a family basis. Deng's reform called for radical revamping of the Chinese industrial system by importing Western science and technology. The third plenum restored the honor of the party by rehabilitating (in many cases, posthumously) leaders who had been defamed and purged by Mao during the Cultural Revolution.

Naturally Deng's group met strong opposition from the two inner groups associated with Mao, especially the coopted veteran cadres, i.e., Hua Guofeng, Wang Dongxin, Chen Xilian, and Wu De. The latter group accused Deng of "taking down the Red Flag" and countered Deng's reform program with their own line of "following whatever instructions and programs of Chairman Mao." Henceforth Hua's group was referred to in China as the *whatever* group. However, the whatever group could not match Deng in organizational strength, party seniority, or public support. So in February 1979 Wang, Chen, and Wu were forced to resign from their formal positions in the Central Committee. To rid the central party leadership of all the remnants of Mao's associates, Deng's group forced the resignation of Hua from state and party positions in 1980 and 1981. The premiership that Hua formerly held was relinquished to one of Deng's protegés, Zhao Ziyang. The party chairmanship that Hua formerly held was taken over by another of Deng's protegés, Hu Yaobang, in June 1981. At last the struggle for succession was over, and the party pragmatists could now impose their program of reform on the whole Communist party.

Throughout this period of political transition Deng had to face not only internal but also external opposition. His appeal to democracy and attack on the dictatorship of the leftists had encouraged mass protest and demonstration from all walks of life. From November 1978 through April 1979, thousands of petitioners from all corners of China assembled in Peking demanding redress of the wrongs that had been done to them by the party during the Cultural Revolution. Wall posters and underground publications proliferated during this period. Dissident youth groups surfaced, calling for true democracy and respect for human rights. These developments gave outsiders a rare glimpse of an aspect of Chinese Communist society and politics that had been effectively suppressed by the Communist party for a long time. Deng Xiaoping, however, had sufficient command of the party and state machinery to suppress these genuine expressions of public opinion once more. In the meantime, Deng sought to implement reforms in a disciplined manner to solve many fundamental social and economic problems.

In the final analysis, Deng's challenge to the old regime left behind by Mao, though momentarily raising the danger of disintegration, in the long run saved the Communist party and Chinese society from another bloody civil war or revolution. His reform raised the hope of many in China of a liberalized and humanized Communist rule. The Chinese people, after thirty some years of turbulence under Mao's "permanent revolution," longed for peace and normalcy, which is what Deng promised.

If there is any single lesson to learn from the first thirty years of Communist rule of mainland China, it must be the heavy cost of charismatic or personalistic leadership. And this lesson is a general one. As Turner and Killian perceptively put it:

> There is a major tendency in every movement for the leader, by virtue of his elevated position, to be protectively isolated from normal criticism. A man can seldom maintain a balanced perspective regarding himself when his exposure to evaluations by others is highly selective. The public worship and the expressed admiration of those close to him generate in the leader an exaggerated conception of his own capabilities. Such an exaggerated conception leads to arrogance, dependence on his own hunches rather than a careful weighing of viewpoints, and intolerance of all opposition. Thus the personal and impulsive element in decision-making increases, the disproportionate influence of personal favorites becomes greater, and the probability of strategic blunders that will wreck the movement is magnified.[21]

NOTES

1. Egon Bittner, "Radicalism and the Organization of Radical Movements," *American Sociological Review*, no. 28(1963), pp. 928-40. Also, Bittner, "Radicalism," in David Sills, ed., *International Encyclopedia of the Social Sciences*, vol. 3 (New York: Crowell Collier & Macmillian Company, 1968).

2. *RMRB*, September 12, 1977, p. 2.

3. Max Weber, *The Theory of Social and Economic Organization*, trans. A. M. Henderson and Talcott Parsons (New York: Free Press, 1964), p. 370.

4. Chow Ching-wen, *Ten Years of Storm* (New York: Holt, Rinehart & Winston, 1960), pp. 92-93.

5. A. Doak Barnett, *Communist China: The Early Years, 1949-55* (New York: Frederick A. Praeger, 1968), p. 135.

6. Li Choh-ming, *Economic Development of Communist China* (Berkeley: University of California Press, 1959), pp. 9-10.

7. Wang Xuewen, "Critique of Certain Mistaken Views on the System of Compulsory Purchase and Sale," *Xuexi*, no. 7(1956), pp. 25-27.

8. Yang Jiao, "Why We Should Not Neglect Individual and Current Interests of Laborers," *Xuexi*, no. 7(1967), pp. 25-27.

9. "We Should Not Allow Accidental Deaths of Women and Infants to Happen Again in the Countryside," *RMRB*, August 12, 1956, reprinted in *Xinhua Banyuekan*, no. 18(1956), p. 5.

10. "Study of 'On Questions of Party History,'" *RMRB*, July 14, 1981, p. 5.

11. "Answering a Question," *RMRB*, October 18, 1982, p. 1.

12. Sun Yehfang, "Strengthen Statistical Work; Reform System of Statistical Work," *Jingji Guangli*, no. 2(February 1981), as excerpted in *Ming Pao Daily News*, April 26, 1981, p. 1.

13. *Selected Works of Mao Tse-tung*, vol. 1 (Peking: Foreign Languages Press, 1965), p. 24.

14. Mao Tse-tung, "Speech to the Albanian Military Delegation," *Mao Tse-tung Ssu-hsiang Wan-sui* (hereafter *Wan-sui* no. 2) (People's Republic of China, 1969), 677. The translation here is from *Miscellany of Mao Tse-tung Thought (1949-68)*, part II (Arlington, VA.: Joint Publications Research Service, 1974), p. 459.

15. Ibid., pp. 456-57.

16. Fox Butterfield, "Peking Indictment Accuses Radicals of Killing 34,000," *New York Times*, November 17, 1980. Also, Li Huo-cheng, "Chinese Communists Reveal for the First Time the Number of 20 Million Deaths in the Cultural Revolution," *Ming Pao Daily News*, October 26, 1981, p. 3.

17. For more details on the extent of violence in the Cultural Revolution see Ma Sitson, "Cruelty and Insanity Made Me a Fugitive," *Life*, June 2, 1967; and Alan P. L. Liu, *Political Culture and Group Conflict in Communist China* (Santa Barbara, Calif.: Clio Books, 1976).

18. Mao, "Speech to the Albanian Military Delegation," p. 459.

19. "The CCPCC 'Chung-fa (1972) Document #12' plus Supplement: Notes from Chairman Mao's Talks with Leading Comrades on Inspection Trips (mid-August to September 12, 1972)," *Chungkung Yenchiu (Studies on Chinese Communism)* 6, no. 9 (September 10, 1972), 82-97.

20. "A Counterrevolutionary Play of Seizure of Power and Usurpation of the Party," *RMRB*, July 16, 1977, p. 1.

21. Ralph H. Turner and Lewis M. Killian, *Collective Behavior* (Englewood Cliffs, N.J.: Prentice-Hall, 1972), p. 391.

PART TWO

Civil Administration

CHAPTER 4

The Communist Party of China

The formal institutions that the CPC established after 1949 to rule China can be divided into civil and coercive institutions. In part two we shall deal with the civil administration.

The civil administration of the PRC continues and further refines historical Chinese bureaucratic development toward, in Kungchuan Hsiao's words, "increased centralization, more minute regulations, stricter surveillance, and tighter control" (see chapter 1, note 18). The traditional Chinese impulse toward bureaucracy and "statism" was, of course, reinforced and legitimized by three modern conditions: prolonged civil war, the ideology of socialism with its emphasis on central planning and public ownership, and emulation of the Soviet political system.

The structure of formal ruling institutions of the People's Republic of China (PRC) is copied almost entirely from that of the Soviet Union. The core of the ruling institutions is the Communist party, which decides all public policies. The decisions of the party are executed by a civil and a military arm. The civil arm consists of the state or governmental apparatus, formally known in China as People's Government at both national and local level. The military arm is the People's Liberation Army (PLA) that keeps a close surveillance over Chinese society through a system of "military regions" and "military districts," which meshed with the civil administrative divisions of provinces, counties, and townships. The power of these three formal institutions is extended to all the nooks and crannies of Chinese society through what this book will refer to as parapolitical organizations, i.e., organizations that serve as auxiliaries to formal ones. The Communist party has exclusive access to groups with the largest constituents: trade unions, youth leagues, and women's associations. The Chinese People's Government is complemented by the Chinese People's Political Consultative Conference (CPPCC), which is composed of non-Communist notables of Chinese society, e.g., political allies of the CPC before 1949, famed intellectuals, and professionals. The PLA is assisted by the tens of millions of members of the people's militia. The relationship of these organizations is illustrated in figure 4-1. These organizations provide the key to the effective control of China by the Communist party.

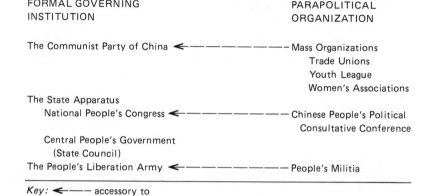

FORMAL GOVERNING INSTITUTION

PARAPOLITICAL ORGANIZATION

The Communist Party of China ◄————————— Mass Organizations
Trade Unions
Youth League
Women's Associations

The State Apparatus
National People's Congress ◄————————— Chinese People's Political
Consultative Conference

Central People's Government
(State Council)

The People's Liberation Army ◄————————— People's Militia

Key: ◄——— accessory to

FIGURE 4-1   Governing institutions of the People's Republic of China

The institutional arrangement of the PRC is justified in the formal political formula, the People's Democratic Dictatorship (PDD), which is used by the CPC to distinguish the Chinese political system from other political forms in the world. According to its original definition in the interim constitution of 1949, the Common Program, "The Chinese people's democratic dictatorship is a political power of the people's democratic united front made of the Chinese working class, peasantry, petty bourbeoisie, national bourgeoisie and other patriotic democratic personages. It is based on the alliance of workers and peasants and is under the leadership of the working class." The People's Democratic Dictatorship thus stipulates that the power relations in the Chinese Communist political system fall into three concentric circles, as shown in figure 4-2.

Institutionally, the three nonproletarian groups in the People's Democratic Dictatorship—the national bourgeoisie, the petty bourgeoisie, and the "patriotic democratic personages"—are organized in the CPPCC. The workers and peasants are represented by the CPC and organizations such as trade unions, militia (mostly peasants), the youth league, and women's associations. In practice, the peasants are uniquely without any formal institutional representation since the peasant associations became defunct as soon as the Land Reform campaign was over.

As a political formula, the People's Democratic Dictatorship is a revision of the Marxist formula, "the dictatorship of the proletariat," which according to Marx should be the political form of a society practicing socialism. The reason for the PDD was that it was invented before 1949 when it was not expedient for the CPC to talk about the dictatorship of the proletariat. Instead, Mao Zedong offered a "joint dictatorship" with the upper classes of China to isolate the Kuomintang politically. The PDD, moreover, satisfied four situational requirements accompanying the victory of the CPC in 1949—all power to the CPC, socialism, nationalism, and democracy. The leadership of the working class in the formal definition of the PDD met the demand of all power to the CPC. The alliance of workers and peasants is the Marxist-Leninist component of the People's Democratic Dictatorship. The democratic united front means rule by the majority, hence the symbol of democracy is upheld. Finally, the People's Democratic Dictatorship satisfies nationalism—the PDD being a "creative" application of Marxism-Leninism to Chinese conditions. In 1956, acknowledging the fact that private means of production in industry and agriculture had been abolished, and hence that the bour-

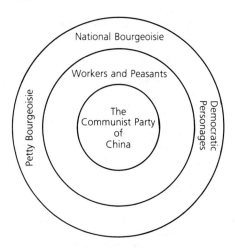

FIGURE 4-2

geoisie no longer had a class base in the PRC, the CPC declared that "the people's democratic dictatorship is in essence the dictatorship of the proletariat." From the Cultural Revolution till the death of Mao, the CPC dropped the PDD altogether so as to emphasize the dictatorship of the proletariat, symbolizing Mao's determination to use dictatorship to transform China into a truly proletarian society. Not surprisingly, the post-Mao leadership of the CPC restored the 1956 formula—"The People's Democratic Dictatorship is in essence the dictatorship of the proletariat." By reviving the PDD, the present leaders of the CPC wish to impress the Chinese public with their intention to practice democracy in contrast to Mao's emphasis on dictatorship.

In practice, the CPC decides when and how much dictatorship or democracy is to be applied to China, who is to be included in "the people" or the "patriotic united front," and when or how fast the nonproletarian groups such as intellectuals, petty bourgeoisie, and national bourgeoisie are to be "transformed" into the working class. After 1950, whenever the top-ranking leaders of CPC felt a degree of defensiveness, such as during the initial period of 1949–52, when the need for legitimacy was paramount, or in 1956–57 (till June) when the CPC had to cope with Khrushchev's de-Stalinization, or in 1961–62, when the PRC suffered severe food shortages, starvation in the countryside, and troop unrest, they would play up the democracy aspect of the People's Democratic Dictatorship in order to achieve national unity. Like most political doctrines, the People's Democratic Dictatorship transforms might to right.

Each of the six chapters that follow deals with a key civil institution in the PRC. We must emphatically point out that these formal institutions are the real substance of Chinese politics—bureaucratic politics. They are the permanent components of the Chinese political process. For the past thirty-four years Chinese Communist policies and programs such as those for agriculture or education have undergone drastic changes and reversals. But the totalitarian-bureuacratic institutions described and analyzed here remain largely intact.

In the institutional framework governing China the first and foremost organization is the Communist party. As the latest party constitution, adopted at the Twelfth National Party Congress on September 2, 1982, states it, the CPC is "the force at the core leading China's cause of socialism."[1] Hu Yaobang, in 1984 the top-ranking leader of the party (formally, general secretary of the Central Committee of CPC), portrays the relationship between the CPC and China as that between a captain and his ship. In Hu's words:

> Whether or not we can steer the ship of the Chinese revolution onward through storm and stress in the new historical period, whether or not we can modernize our agriculture, industry, national defense and science and technology fairly smoothly, avoid suffering such serious setbacks and paying such a huge price as in the past, and achieve results that will satisfy the people and win the praise of posterity, all depends on the efforts of all comrades in the Party in the next decade or two.[2]

Students unfamiliar with the history of the People's Republic of China may not be aware of the implications of CPC's critical role in China that is implicit in Hu's oratory. For, the "serious setbacks" and "a huge price . . . in the past" in Hu's speech are also a result of CPC's captainship of China.

With a current membership of 40 million, one for every 25 citizens of the PRC, the CPC is the largest Communist party in the world. As a political party, the CPC differs from the pragmatic and issue-oriented parties in most Western nations. The CPC shares with (in fact, surpasses) most political parties in the Third World some common characteristics, such as taking on a distinct world view (a comprehensive ideology) and representing a way of life. "Such parties," writes Lucian Pye, "are inclined to feel they have a mission to change all aspects of life within their society, even conceiving of themselves as a prototype of what their society will become in time."[3] The current CPC constitution declares: "The Communist party of China makes the realization of communism its maximum program, to which all its members must devote their entire lives."[4] Hence, though calling itself a party, the CPC does not permit party politics since its self-appointed mission is to abolish all parties and make the state "wither away."

Being an organization dedicated, at least in theory, to bringing about a new society, the CPC, in the language of organizational studies, is a "normative-oriented" institution whose goal is creation of a new culture.[5] This normative goal colors every aspect of CPC operation. For example, like other normative organizations, such as religious institutions, the CPC is supposed to rely primarily on ideological conversion to bind the lower rank to the party. The rank and file of the CPC are expected to identify themselves completely with the party on moral and ideological grounds, not for pecuniary gains or fear of punishment. There should not be any independent sub-groups within the party as there ought to be a close integration in both the higher and the lower ranks and among the ranks, too. A constant stream of ideological communication flows from the top to the bottom layers of the party. Members of the party must live their lives entirely within the norms set by the CPC. Every member of the CPC, in theory, has a charismatic influence on the general public. Deviations from the ideal cause great anxiety on the part of top party leaders and are the basis for organizing regular "rectification campaigns" to bring the members of the CPC closer to the model.

The CPC's relationship with Chinese society is an extension of the "normative ideal" that serves as the *raison d'être* of the party. Hence, in theory, the CPC executes its leadership over China first, by formulating "correct lines, principles and policies," and second, through "the exemplary conduct" of party members.[6] However, the normative ideals of the CPC remain largely just that—ideals—for two reasons. First, the normative ideals represent the perspectives of top party elite. The rank and file of the CPC have very different notions concerning the CPC, most of them highly materialistic and utilitarian. Second, the normative ideals of the CPC collide with the party's worldly aim of monopolizing all power of decision making. Thus in principle the CPC realizes its leadership over society by formulating "correct lines" (i.e., general direction of national development) and by means of persuasion. In reality, the CPC depends on bureaucratic organization to control and mobilize Chinese society.

The CPC developed its bureaucratic organization very much along the lines of the Soviet Communist party. The organizational pattern closely resembles a military hierarchy in which policy directions come from the central command, and the obligation of the subordinate is to carry them out. We shall analyze the CPC in terms of the High Command (national party organization), the Middle Command (provincial and autonomous region party organization), the Lower Command (prefectures, municipality, county and commune party organizations), and the party rank and file (primary organizations).

THE HIGH COMMAND: NATIONAL ORGANIZATION OF THE CPC

In describing and analyzing the various aspects of the CPC, it is useful to divide them into two parts: "dignified" and "efficient." The dignified parts "excite and preserve the reverence of the population" and the efficient part works and rules. In other words, the former gains authority, and the latter uses authority.[7] In the CPC the dignified parts bear the title "Party Congress," which exists primarily to pay deference to the universal demand for democracy. The efficient parts of the CPC come under various titles, usually Party Committee, Standing Committee, or Secretariat. These are the ones who "formulate correct lines, principles and policies."

At the national level, the dignified institution is the National Party Congress which, in the words of the party constitution, is "the highest leading body of the party." The congress, among numerous functions and powers, is "to discuss and decide on major questions concerning the party."[8] Composed of more than a thousand delegates (1,600 in the latest Twelfth Party Congress in September 1982), the National Party Congress meets, in principle, every five years. The delegates to the congress are, in theory, freely elected by the members of the party. In practice, the Congress had met irregularly in the past, since whether or when the Congress is to meet is in the hands of the efficient part of the CPC. For example, eleven years separated the Seventh Party Congress (1945) and the Eighth Party Congress (1956). The Ninth Party Congress was convened thirteen years after the Eighth. Election of delegates is in name only; cooptation is the fact. At each election the rank and file of the party is presented with a slate of candidates by the higher-ups for members to affirm. Technically members of the party *vote* for the delegates to the Party Congress, but they do not *vote freely*.

The power "to discuss and decide on major questions concerning the party," which nominally belongs to the National Party Congress is, in practice, in the hands of the efficient parts of the national CPC machinery. The latter, in ascending order of efficiency, is composed of (1) the Central Committee of the CPC, (2) the Political Bureau (Politburo) of the Central Committee, (3) the Standing Committee of the Politburo, (4) the Secretariat of the Central Committee, and (5) the general secretary of the Central Committee.

The Central Committee

The National Party Congress elects the Central Committee, whose present membership is drastically reduced to 348. That alone shows that the Central Committee, compared with the National Party Congress, is more "efficient." In principle, the Central Committee meets in plenary session at least once a year. But since the convening of the Central Committee is at the convenience of the more efficient Politburo, the former met in irregular intervals as the Party Congress. The functions of the Central Committee are defined constitutionally: "When the National Congress is not in session, the Central Committee carries out its decisions, directs the entire work of the party and represents the Communist party of China in its external relations."[9]

The Central Committee of the CPC, with its large membership and irregular meetings, is still basically a dignified organization, though the values the Central Committee defers to are different from those of the National Party Congress. The composition of Central Committee membership is meant to show support for the current "line" of the elite of the party. For example, the composition of the Eleventh Central Committee of August 1977, the first Central Committee after the death of Mao Zedong, signifies the change in party line. Compared with the membership of the previous Central Committee under Mao's control, the Eleventh Central Committee increased the representation of party *apparatchiki* (colloquial term for officials in the party and government apparatus of Communist systems) from 36 to 50.8 percent. The representation of military men and "revolutionary masses" (model workers, peasants and youth) declined, especially the latter (from 31 to 17 percent).[10] The Eleventh Central Committee shows that Mao's antibureaucratism and "mass line" are things of the past. The authority of veteran party officials at every level of the CPC was restored, whereas the control of the party by the military that began with the Cultural Revolution of 1966–69 had declined, albeit gradually.

The composition of the current Twelfth Central Committee similarly reflects the reformist line of top CPC leaders such as Hu Yaobang, Zhao Ziyang, and Deng Xiaoping. First of all, to signify the present CPC's decision to infuse the party with new and younger blood, 60 percent of the present 348 members (210 voting members, 138 nonvoting members) are first timers. Two-thirds of the new members are below the age of sixty, and the youngest is thirty-eight years old. Second, to give substance to the present CPC leaders' stress on modernization, the number of technical and scientific specialists increased from 9 (2.7 percent) at the Eleventh Central Committee of 1977 to 59 (17 percent) at the Twelfth Central Committee of 1982.[11] The Twelfth Central Committee of 1982 went a step further in consolidating the control of the *apparatchiki* as 69 percent of the full members are either party or state leaders at the national or regional level. The representation of the military, though reduced since 1977, is still substantial, accounting for 24 percent of voting members. The representatives of the revolutionary masses, leftover from the Mao era, were almost totally eliminated from the current Central Committee.[12] For Western students interested in Chinese affairs and the public on mainland China, the Central Committee is both the medium and the message of changing party lines.

We might also use the military metaphor of "strategic reserve" to describe the role of the Central Committee in the power alignment of top CPC leaders. The Central Committee is composed of all major national and subnational leaders, whose cooperation is necessary to execute any party policy and program. The largest contingent in the Central Committee consists of regional party secretaries (provinces and autonomous regions). The next largest group is the state functionaries, especially from industry and finance. Then, as a reflection of CPC's history and the nature of its present power, presence of military officers is always substantial, especially commanders of "great military regions," members of the High Command, and commanders of various services.

The Central Committee is also composed of dignified and efficient parts. The dignified part is the plenary session of the Central Committee. The efficient parts of the Central Committee are its staff departments. The staff departments perform two essential functions for national CPC leadership: managing the growing party apparatus and providing top CPC leadership with information and analysis on the state and society of China. Like the plenary session of the Central Committee, the staff departments underwent changes, qualitative or quantitative, as the orientation of top CPC leaders changed. The post-Mao leaders of the CPC created new staff departments, such as Office for the Research of Party History and Committee for the Collection of the Historical Materials on the Party. The reason for these new staff departments is that during the last decade of Mao's leadership (1966-76), many long-time, senior party leaders, including Hu Yaobang and Deng Xiaoping, were denigrated by Mao and the radicals. To repudiate Mao's distortion of party history and provide ideological sanction to the reformist programs of the present leaders, new staff departments on history and ideology were created in 1980.[13]

Among the various Central Committee staff departments, now numbering thirty, some are more consequential than others. These deal with party and state management. They are permanent and powerful in inner-party decision making. We shall describe briefly each of these departments:

1. The general office of the Central Committee handles internal party communication and, hence, is in a strategic position in case of a power struggle among leaders.

2. The organization department performs what Lenin called "the function to distribute the forces of the party."[14] In other words, the organization department deals with the recruitment, training, and assignment of party cadres (those members of the party who wield authority over others).

3. The propaganda department supervises all forms of ideological communication to party members and the public, encompassing control of mass media, the educational system, and mass organizations.

4. The united front department handles the relationship between the party and major social groups or institutions such as intellectuals, former industrialists and businessmen ("national bourgeoisie"), ethnic minorities, organized religion, and former political parties.

5. The department of investigation is a shadowy institution whose main function seems to be collection of foreign intelligence.

6. The editorial department of *Hongqi* (*Red Flag*) publishes *Hongqi*, which is the most authoritative ideological journal in China, representing the "correct line" of national CPC leadership.

7. The editorial department of *Renmin Ribao* (*People's Daily*) publishes *Renmin Ribao*, which is the most authoritative newspaper in China, setting forth the "correct line" of national party leadership.

8. The central party school gives ideological indoctrination to leading party cadres, e.g., party secretaries who are members of provincial, municipal, and prefectural party committees and those in important positions in national party and state administration. The school is of particular importance in time of leadership turnover when a new party line is to be carried out.

The distribution of these eight most important Central Committee departments makes clear the ideological and bureaucratic substance of the CPC's leadership. Several of the departments are of particular strategic (basic, long-term) importance in time of leadership changeover or power struggle among top leaders. For instance, during the power struggle after the death of Mao, one of the most serious contenders to national power was Wang Dongxin, the former bodyguard of Mao. From 1977 to 1979 Wang held the concurrent positions of the head of the general office, de facto director of the department of propaganda, chief editor of the journal *Hongqi* and of a newly created Committee for the Editing and Publishing of Works of Mao, and deputy principal of the central party school. Thus Wang controlled the communication within the central CPC machinery and the channels that transmit the party line to the party rank and file and the public. To clip the wings of Wang, Deng Xiaoping and his colleagues revived the position of the general secretary of the Central Committee in 1979 the director of which duplicates and thus reduces the "gate-keeping" function of the director of the general office. Hu Yaobang was appointed general secretary, and he assumed also the position of the director of the department of propaganda and deputy principal of the central party school so that the reformist group's line could be put through the party machinery in Peking.[15]

As we mentioned earlier, a vital function of the staff departments of the Central Committee is basic research on major policies and programs of the CPC. So after the consolidation of power of the reformist group in the central CPC machinery in 1980, three new staff departments were established to provide leadership for three major areas of political reform. First, a Committee on Political and Legal Affairs was created to supervise the resurrection and reform of the judiciary in China. Second, a finance and economics group was set up to deal with reform of Chinese finance after 1980, including the installation of a taxation system and provisions for independent accounting of enterprises. Third, in connection with the major reform in the countryside as exemplified in the "production responsibility" system, an Office for the Research of Policy on Agriculture was organized.

The work of the Central Committee staff departments is vital to the leadership of the CPC, but it is also precarious. More often than not major lines and policies of the CPC are ideologically prescribed, such as the decision in 1955 to transform agriculture through collective farms. When a policy such as collectivization encounters difficulty, a relevant staff department of the Central Committee is assigned to investigate and make recommendations to national leaders. Depending on the orientation of top leaders, the proposals from the staff departments may be adopted or rejected. In case of the latter, members of staff departments may be punished for making "ideologically heretical" proposals. For instance, the staff department for agricultural works in 1955 informed Mao of the poor results of collectivation in the countryside, especially lack of peasant incentive to increase production, and hence a widening of the gap of living standards between peasants and workers. The staff department recommended suspension or reduction of collectivization. Mao accused the staff department of advocating "social retrogress" and being guilty of "empiricism." Subsequently Mao ordered an acceleration of collectivization.[16] One deputy director of a Central Committee staff department named Tian Jiayin paid with his life during the terror of the Cultural Revolution because of his suggestion that individualized farming would increase peasants' incentive to produce.[17]

The Politburo, the Standing Committee of Politburo, and the Secretariat

As we stated earlier, the Central Committee, though performing valuable staff functions, is basically a "dignified" organization. The Central Committee is also the crucial transition beyond which party organizations become drastically smaller in membership but higher in "efficiency." There are three such efficient organizations above the Central Committee whose members were all "elected" by the committee. The first one is the Politburo, which at present consists of twenty-eight members. The second is the Standing Committee of the Politburo, which is composed of six members. The third is the Secretariat of the Central Committee, which has eleven members. Topping all three is the general secretary of the Central Committee, the uppermost position of the CPC. Whereas members of the Standing Committee are automatically members of the Politburo, seven of the eleven members of the Secretariat are not members of the Politburo. Hence the effective decision makers of the CPC national organization consists of thirteen people, six from the Standing Committee and seven from the Secretariat.

How these three efficient party organizations distribute their function and power is not exactly clear. The plenary session of the Politburo, judging by the number of its members alone, seems to be less efficient than the Standing Committee or the Secretariat. The Secretariat, being newly revived (it was in existence before 1966), does tend to overshadow the other two. An officially approved article states that "the Secretariat will look after the 'first line,' or day-to-day work, while the Political Bureau and its Standing Committee will man the 'second line.'"[18] The resurrection of the Secretariat is said to enable "members of the Political Bureau and its Standing Committee to concentrate on major international and domestic issues so that they will obtain greater initiative and prescience in their work."[19] Wang Renchong, director of the department of propaganda of the Central Committee and a member of the Secretariat until September 1982, wrote: "Except for some routine and specific tasks which the Secretariat has been entrusted by the Politburo to carry out without prior consultation, anything that touches on major principle or policy must be approved by the Politburo or its Standing Committee."[20]

In its heyday, i.e., before 1958, the Politburo and its Standing Committee were often referred to by Mao as China's "institute for political designing."[21] The Politburo then regularly received reports and briefings from various party and state agencies, out of which broad policies were made. Mao protested in 1958 that some agencies had relegated the Politburo to the role of a stamping machine by submitting completed policy statement.[22] Until the recent resurrection of the Secretariat, the Politburo maintained an "enlarged work conference" in which various party and state leaders at national, regional or lower levels were invited to attend. In these enlarged work conferences, the Politburo would test its "political design" on the participants, especially those representing the provinces and lower organizations whose views on the feasibility of a policy were solicited. The size of these work conferences varied from a few hundred to several thousand. A work conference that is exceptional both in its size (seven thousand participants) and in "inner-party democracy" took place on January 30, 1962, in the midst of China's worst crisis of food shortage and agricultural breakdown since 1949. This conference is regarded as unique because for the first time (and only time so far) the agenda of the conference was decided by all the participants instead of the usual pattern in which it was the Politburo that made up the agenda for partici-pants to accept. As Mao said at the conference: "If we had not used this method [agenda set by participants], but held the conference *in the usual manner,* we would have heard the report first and held a discussion afterwards. Everyone would have ap-proved it with a show of hands" (emphasis added.).[23]

The enlarged work conferences of the Politburo more often than not produced major policy decisions, which would then be dignified in a plenary session of the Cen-tral Committee. For instance, a Politburo work conference was convened in November 1978 in which Deng Xiaoping's major reform programs were decided. Subsequently, the third plenum of the Eleventh Central Committee met in December and announced Deng's comprehensive reform measures, such as the creation of a Central Commission for Discipline Inspection, the end of class struggle, and a shift of the national task to economic development.

Since the restoration of the Secretariat in 1980, however, the role of the Polit-buro and its Standing Committee in inner-party decision making has been much re-duced. The Secretariat has become the executive agency of the Politburo and its Standing Committee. Wang Renchong's statement, mentioned earlier, seems to suggest a limited, housekeeping, function of the Secretariat (see note 20). But that is mislead-ing. We should read Wang's statement to mean that except for decisions of fundamen-tal nature, the Secretariat has been entrusted by the Politburo to decide most policies. The Secretariat is now CPC's "institute for political designing." Chinese press reports nowadays routinely attribute various policy decisions to the Secretariat, be it future development of Peking,[24] new education policy,[25] changeover of the provincial party leadership of Hebei province,[26] punishment of party and state leaders involved in an oil-rig accident in 1980,[27] policy on incentives to peasants,[28] or the use of farmland by rural residents for housing construction.[29]

Inside the Secretariat, the eleven members plus Hu Yaobang divide their labor much like the staff departments of the Central Committee. They are:

1. Hu Yaobang: general secretary, or head of the Secretariat
2. Wan Li: chief assistant to Hu Yaobang, in charge of agricultural work
3. Xi Chongxun: chief assistant to Hu Yaobang, in charge of legal affairs
4. Yu Qiuli: political and party work in the armed forces
5. Yao Yilin: finance and commerce
6. Deng Liqun: propaganda and ideology
7. Chen Peixian: public security and legal affairs
8. Hu Qili: youth and student affairs
9. Gu Mu: economic planning and foreign trade
10. Qiao Shi: relations with socialist nations
11. Hao Jienxiu: trade union and women
12. (A secretarial post for military affairs, vacant since the death of General Yang Yung in 1983)

As another indication of the "efficiency" of the Secretariat in policy making, the Secretariat has its own staff departments. So far we have been able to identify only two such departments, the Office for Research and the Office for Research of Agricultural Policy.[30]

The background of the twelve members of the Secretariat shows the persistent strength of pre-1949 party elite. Table 4-1 gives the year that each of the twelve secretaries joined the CPC. Only one, Hao Jianxiu, joined the party after 1949. The only female in the Secretariat and a model textile worker since 1953, Hao is presently an alternate (nonvoting) member of the Secretariat. The seven senior members of the Secretariat (Xi Chongxun, Yu Qiuli, Yang Yun, Gu Mu, Hu Yaobang, Yao Yilin, and Wan Li) are truly professional revolutionaries as they had joined the CPC in their teens, the exception being Wan Li, who joined at the age of twenty. Before the victory of the CPC in the Chinese civil war, these men worked in various political capacities in the party or army. After 1949 several of them became more or less permanently attached to a special line of work: Wan Li in urban development, Gu Mu in state economic planning, Yu Qiuli in the petroleum industry, and Yao Yilin in state finance. That these politicians-turned-managers or generalists-turned-specialists are in the Secretariat not only reflects the complex bureaucratic management of Chinese economy but also represents the leaders' goal of modernization. But these specialists are always held in check by other secretaries who have persisted in their roles as revolution-generalists; the careers of Hu Yaobang and Xi Chongxun exemplify that. Hu joined the CPC youth corps at the age of fifteen in 1930 and had always worked in youth affairs. Xi also joined the CPC youth corps at the age of thirteen in 1926 and thereafter held a variety of political positions including local party secretary or political commissar in the army before 1949. After the CPC victory, Xi remained in general administrative line of work and was at one time chief secretary to Premier Zhou Enlai. Among the five new members of the Secretariat, i.e., appointed in September 1982, one sees the same situation of revolution-generalists balancing generalists-turned-specialists. Chen Peixian, Deng Liqun, and Hu Qili belong to the generalist category, whereas Qiao Shi developed a second career after 1949 in managing the steel industry. Hao, the model female textile worker, is most likely installed in the Secretariat for "dignified" purposes. Of proletarian origin, she gained prominence in 1953 when a "correct" work ethic (in contrast

TABLE 4-1   Members of the Secretariat

NAME	YEAR OF ADMISSION TO CPC
Xi Chongxun	1928
Yu Qiuli	1929
Yang Yun (deceased in January 1983)	1930
Chen Peixian	1931*
Gu Mu	1931
Hu Yaobang	1933
Yao Yilin	1935
Deng Liqun	1936*
Wan Li	1936
Qiao Shi	1940*
Hu Qili	1948*
Hao Jianxiu (female)	1953*

*Elected to the Secretariat in September 1982.

Source: RMRB, March 2, 1982, p. 2, and September 13, 1982, p. 3.

to the emphasis on revolution and rebellion in the Cultural Revolution) was promoted by the CPC.

Except for Hu Qili and Hao Jianxiu, the rest of the Secretariat was socialized in the era of civil war. Their prolonged experience with wartime mobilization and militarized administration cannot but have left a deep imprint in their minds. Though these senior CPC leaders now espouse reforms, especially turning away from Mao Zedong's bureaucratic and ascetic socialism, they nevertheless share Mao's socialization. This cannot but put a certain limit to their "de-Mao-fication."

The foregoing are the major "dignified" and "efficient" parts of the national organization of the CPC. In addition to these, there are three more national CPC institutions: Central Advisory Commission, Central Military Commission, and Central Commission for Discipline Inspection.

The Central Advisory Commission is totally new, having been established at the Twelfth Party Congress in September 1982. It is a temporary agency to which the CPC retires a number of aged leaders and also a civil way of disposing of politically undesirable leaders. Hence, of the 172 members of the Advisory Commission most are in the age category of seventy to seventy-nine years old. Several members are more than eighty years old. Then there are some who are below the age of seventy; they belong to the "out" group, the former Maoists who had lost in their face-off with the present reformist leadership.

The Central Commission for Discipline Inspection heads the CPC's internal judicial system, which is comparable to the system of ecclesiastical courts. The present commission was established in 1978 and has 132 members. The forerunner of the present commission on discipline was the Central Party Control Commission, which was destroyed during the Cultural Revolution (1966–76) since Mao Zedong wished to establish a new party. The absence of a party judiciary resulted in a problem:

> Many new party members admitted during this period did not understand party rules or regulations. They did not know our Party tradition. Even some party members of long standing, after a decade of unrests, grew weak in their idea of party spirit and disciplines. So bad style of work rose.[31]

One group of commission members consists of senior national party, state, and military leaders. The second group includes leaders representing the provincial and lower party and state and military authorities. The third group is composed of party cadres, who function in "mass organizations" such as trade unions, youth groups, and women's associations. The Central Commission for Discipline Inspection heads a nationwide system of commissions, which runs parallel to the party apparatus at subnational levels.

The last but certainly not the least component of the CPC national organization is the Central Military Commission, whose members *"are decided on* by the Central Committee" (emphasis added).[32] The party charter also stipulates that the chairman of the military commission must be a member of the Standing Committee of the Politburo. At present Deng Xiaoping chairs this military commission, which is the highest decision-making body of the military in China. This commission is almost a permanent fixture at the topmost echelon of the CPC. The history of the CPC or, for that matter, of modern China, bears testimony to the vital role that the military plays in politics. At the same time CPC leaders are painfully aware through personal experience of the disruptive consequence of a military force uncontrolled by a superior and civil authority. The composition of the Central Military Commission as presented in table 4-2

TABLE 4-2   The Central Military Commission of CPC

MEMBER	YEAR OF ADMISSION TO CPC
Deng Xiaoping (chairman)	1924
Marshal Yeh Jianying	1927
Marshal Xu Xianqian	1927
Marshal Nie Rongzheng	1923
Yang Shangkun (vice-chairman)	1926

shows the precaution that civilian leaders have taken to keep the military under the command of the party. We see that both the chairman and vice-chairman are civilian CPC leaders belonging to the founding generation of the CPC. The three aged Marshals are truly old guards who have been with the CPC since the beginning of the party. Unlike the members of the Secretariat, the military commission has no second generation, i.e., leaders who joined the CPC in the 1930s. We shall have more to say on this commission and the military in Chinese Communist politics in a later chapter.

Summing up, the National Party Congress, the Central Committee, the Politburo and Standing Committee, the Secretariat, the Central Advisory Commission, the Central Commission for Discipline Inspection, and the Central Military Commission constitute the national machinery of the CPC or the High Command. They are the nerve center of the Chinese political body. The structure of the present national organization is the work of the Twelfth National Party Congress in September 1982 and is, in theory, a repudiation of the dictatorial leadership by Mao Zedong and a realization of "collective leadership." But the composition of the national leadership is more complex than a simple collective leadership. We see, for example, the continued concentration of power in one leader—Deng Xiaoping. Deng is at this writing (October 1984) a member of the Standing Commission and Chairman of the Central Military Commission. At the same time one does note the active role in policy making on the part of the Secretariat, which seems to be a collegiate body. This then is a "two-line" arrangement. The "old guards" such as Deng Xiaoping and the rest of the Standing Committee of Politburo have opted to stay in the rear, or in the "second line," taking actions only when "major lines or principles" are involved. The Secretariat, with its second generation and some third generation CPC leaders, handles most decision making in party and state affairs. In this way the "old guards" of the CPC hope to accomplish two tasks: a collective leadership and a smooth succession by the second generation of CPC revolutionaries.

THE MIDDLE COMMAND: PROVINCIAL PARTY ORGANIZATIONS

One step below the national leadership of the CPC is the party establishment in the provinces, "autonomous regions" (ethnic minority settlements, e.g., Xinjiang, Nei Monggol, or Inner Mongolia), and municipalities of Peking, Shanghai, and Tianjin. Party leaders at this level are known as party secretaries and constitute the most powerful subnational elite. The top-ranking provincial or "autonomous region" CPC leader, known as first secretary, is always a member of the Central Committee. This CPC middle elite is often present at any enlarged work conference of the Politburo.

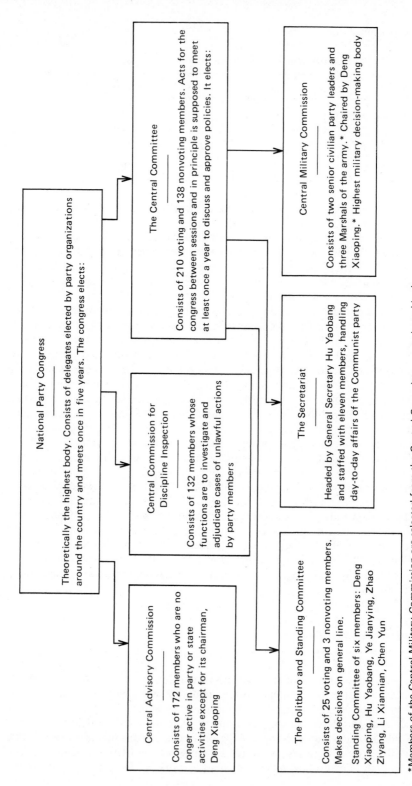

National Party Congress

Theoretically the highest body. Consists of delegates elected by party organizations around the country and meets once in five years. The congress elects:

The Central Committee

Consists of 210 voting and 138 nonvoting members. Acts for the congress between sessions and in principle is supposed to meet at least once a year to discuss and approve policies. It elects:

Central Military Commission

Consists of two senior civilian party leaders and three Marshals of the army.* Chaired by Deng Xiaoping.* Highest military decision-making body

Central Commission for Discipline Inspection

Consists of 132 members whose functions are to investigate and adjudicate cases of unlawful actions by party members

The Secretariat

Headed by General Secretary Hu Yaobang and staffed with eleven members, handling day-to-day affairs of the Communist party

Central Advisory Commission

Consists of 172 members who are no longer active in party or state activities except for its chairman, Deng Xiaoping

The Politburo and Standing Committee

Consists of 25 voting and 3 nonvoting members. Makes decisions on general line.

Standing Committee of six members: Deng Xiaoping, Hu Yaobang, Ye Jianying, Zhao Ziyang, Li Xiannian, Chen Yun

*Members of the Central Military Commission are selected from the Central Committee, not elected by it.

FIGURE 4-3 The national organization of the Communist party of China

When vacancy occurs in the national leadership, it is from the provincial elite that a successor is selected.

The organization of provincial CPC is, in general, a replica of the national party machinery. Constitutionally the highest provincial party institution is the Provincial Party Congress, which "elects" a smaller body of leaders known as the Provincial Party Committee. Parallel to the national organization are a (provincial) Advisory Committee and a (provincial) Committee for Discipline Inspection. But the "efficient" parts of every provincial or autonomous region CPC are the (provincial) Standing Committee and Secretariat. In 1983 as part of the CPC's effort to trim the overblown party bureaucracy, the membership of the Standing Committee of every Provincial Party Committee was reduced to between ten and sixteen people and the Provincial Secretariat has also been reduced to four or five members. Provincial party committees also have their staff departments, such as general office, department of propaganda, and department of organization. Members of the Provincial Party Secretariat divide their functions just as the Secretariat at national level. According to a report by the first secretary of Heilongjiang Province in the Northeast, some ten "leading teams" were formed inside the Party Committee, according to industrial branches. One or two such teams were further supervised by a member of the Standing Committee or the Secretariat.[33]

Though details on the personal background of the provincial elite are not available, the general pattern of their lives is relatively clear. Most of the provincial first secretaries are men in their mid- or late sixties. They had joined the CPC in the 1930s during the early stage of the resistance war against Japan, when they were in their teens. Thereafter they rose from the ranks, and most of them had one time or another served in the guerrilla army in the capacity of political directors (commissars). By the time the CPC won the civil war with the Nationalists in 1949 most of the present provincial elite had already served the party loyally for fifteen to twenty years and had been in the middle level of the growing civil-military apparatus of the CPC. Most important of all, members of this provincial elite had by 1949 already been the protegés of at least one national party leader. Take, for example, the present premier of the PRC, Zhao Ziyang. Until his promotion to the premiership in May 1980, Zhao was the first secretary of Sichuan Province. At the age of thirteen (1932) Zhao was already a member of CPC's youth corps in his native province of Henan, and five years later, at eighteen, Zhao became a formal member of the CPC. During the wars with Japan and later the Nationalists Zhao served under another party leader named Li Xiannian, who is presently one of the six members of the Standing Committee of the Politburo. After 1949 Zhao served in the province of Guandong under another national leader, Marshal Ye Jiangying, presently also a member of the Standing Committee of the Politburo. Zhao, like many other provincial party secretaries, suffered temporary disgrace during the Cultural Revolution and was later rehabilitated. In 1976 Zhao became the first secretary of Sichuan Province, the home of the influential Deng Xiaoping. After the death of Mao, Deng Xiaoping took control of the CPC and entrusted Zhao with the task of making good on Deng's reform programs first in Sichuan Province. Zhao's achievements in Sichuan subsequently earned him the premiership.[34]

Today the provincial CPC elite is plagued by aging and incompetent leaders. As Zhao Ziyang's career makes clear, most provincial first secretaries received only primary or junior high school educations in the early 1930s when they joined the CPC. Their specialty is political agitation and mobilization. After 1949 most of the leaders settled down to bureaucratic careers, being *apparatchiki* for the past thirty years.

Hence in the present restructuring of provincial party committees, specific emphases have been placed on reducing the age of party secretaries and increasing the years of education for future leaders. For example, after streamlining the provincial Party Committee of Sichuan, which has a population of 99 million, the average age of the members of the Standing Committee decreased from 62.6 to 57.1 years, while the percentage of leaders with college educations increased from 17.4 to 43.7. As at the national level, in the provinces those who joined the CPC after 1945 or 1949 are for the first time being coopted, albeit in very small numbers, into top provincial party positions.[35]

THE LOWER COMMAND OF THE CPC

To the national leaders of the CPC the provincial elites are nearby and, on the whole, amenable to central direction. Below them, however, lies a dispersed Lower Command, which consists, in descending order, of party organizations at 208 "prefectures" (*difang*), 230 cities (*shih*), 2,136 counties (xien), and some 55,000 communes (currently being gradually replaced by *xiang* or townships).[36] The secretaries of the party committees at these local administrative divisions are "local emperors" whose local policies (*tu zhengce*) often have greater and more direct impact on the lives of the overwhelming majority of the people than national leaders do.

At the head of the CPC's lower command is the prefectural CPC, which is intermediate between provincial CPCs and municipality and county CPCs. The prefectures are transmission stations designed to enable the higher authorities to control lower units without being saddled with details of governing. Also an intermediate structure such as a prefecture may, in time of need, facilitate flexible adjustment of centrally decided policies to a local situation. Since prefectural CPCs are "dispatched" organizations from provincial CPCs, the former do not have party congresses but are well equipped with staff departments of the usual types: organization, propaganda, industrial and agricultural production, security, and mass organization. The party secretaries of prefectural CPCs are powerful local elites, but they are in the second line in local decision making. In other words, the prefectural party secretaries mainly see to it that major decisions of provincial CPCs are carried out in various localities.

The local elite that has first-line responsibility in China's cities and villages consists of municipal or county party secretaries, especially the latter, as more than 80 percent of Chinese population reside in the countryside. In every county, decision making power is in the hands of members of the county Party Committee and its Standing Committee. Composed, in most cases, of around a dozen men and usually one token woman, the Standing Committee of a county Party Committee is headed by a first party secretary, and the rest of the members are known as party secretaries. Each party secretary is assigned to supervise a special area of work, such as organization, propaganda and education, security, rural work, and industry and trade. The power of the county party secretary is shown dramatically in the question asked by an innocent Hebei farmer in connection with the rights of peasants to retain private plots (private land): "Whose power is greater, county party secretary or the Constitution?"[37] The impact of local policy, set by a county party secretary, on the welfare of rural residents can be seen in the following letter published in the *People's Daily*:

Due to the long standing practice of party cadres being appointed by higher authorities people are accustomed to link the fate of a locality or the life of the people with the personality of a party secretary. The quality of a party secretary is, in turn, entirely in the hands of higher authorities. . . .

In our county since 1969 we have had five county party secretaries and they have done five major deeds. The first party secretary ordered well digging, saying that wells would increase productivity. He required every production team (village) to dig a big well. We spent great manpower and financial resources and were just about to complete our work when a new party secretary was appointed. The second one said that rearing pigs would increase productivity. So every team had to set aside lands to rear pigs and cancel well digging. Then came the third party secretary who ordered ground levelling and achieved some good results. But came the fourth party secretary who launched a "Party Rectification" campaign. After that a fifth party secretary was appointed who ordered us to abandon all previous projects and start a new "farm-land construction" project. Our land was re-divided and broad paths were opened on the field, destroying rice seedlings already planted. Then the secretary designated a part of the land to be used for mechanized farming.

Many local party secretaries have the attitude: the Party and I are one and the same; my will supersedes everything else. Any instruction from the national center must first pass my gate. That which suits me I shall carry out. That which does not suit me I shall resist.[38]

To the national leaders of the CPC the combination of county CPC's power over the population and its great distance from the national center is always a worrisome matter. Chinese leaders, Communist or not, are well aware of the weakness of traditional Chinese administration below county level. To insure effectiveness of central policy at and below county level, Chinese Communist leaders in Peking resort to "divide and rule." That is, in many areas of China, particularly in southern provinces, the most powerful regional positions, such as prefectural, municipal, and county first party secretaries are given to "outsiders." In southern provinces and counties, those who have power are northern cadres. Given the diversity in language and custom in various areas of China, the divide-and-rule policy of the national leaders is bound to provoke conflict between cadres from outside and those recruited from local population. This is particularly true in areas where there were indigenous guerrilla forces before 1949 such as Guangdong and Yunnan. After the establishment of the PRC, the former guerrilla leaders naturally assumed local CPC leadership, but owing to the centralist policy of the national leaders of the CPC, the guerrillas-turned-local-party-leaders were always subordinated to leaders from the North. The degree and extent of conflict between northern cadres and local cadres varied from place to place according to the degree of regional identity. In Guangdong, where there has always been a strong regional identity, conflict between local leaders and northerners persisted throughout the history of PRC. In 1958-59 the national leaders of CPC carried out a campaign of "antiparochialism" to suppress protests by local CPC leaders in Guangdong, Yunnan, Zhejiang, and Shangdong. In each case local CPC leaders resented their northern superiors' carrying out a centrally decided policy without taking into consideration local conditions. Several prominent guerrillas-turned-CPC-leaders in Guangdong, for example, complained that the land reform in their province, carried out under the supervision of northern leaders, was "too violent."[39] Similarly, local leaders in Yunnan criticized their northern superiors for being cruel to peasants who had been forced to work on large-scale water-conservancy projects.[40] Sometimes the conflict between the two groups of lower party leaders took the form of county leaders' confronting provincial party leaders who were predominantly outsiders. When animosity between northern and local cadres was accompanied by geographic separation from mainland China as in Hainan Island, the local cadres of one county staged a "Hungarian incident" in 1957.[41]

Throughout the thirty-year history of the PRC the tension between national leaders of the CPC and local CPC leaders below province level persisted. Mao Zedong had complained bitterly in 1959 that the lower cadres could not be relied upon, as "many of them would pretend to follow but actually deviate from central direction in case they did not like certain decisions; sometimes they disregarded centrally decided policies altogether."[42] It is, of course, easy and expedient for both the national leaders and the general public of China to blame the lower elites for unpopular programs. But objective analysis shows that the conduct of county and commune party secretaries has been conditioned by their past experience of dealing with higher authorities. For example, the immobilism of county and commune CPC leaders in 1978–80 with respect to the present national leaders' policy of individualized farming was clearly a reaction by lower leaders to their experience under Mao when promotion of individualized farming was a serious political crime.[43]

THE CPC RANK AND FILE: PRIMARY ORGANIZATIONS

So far we have discussed the various levels of the CPC's command structure. But the effectiveness of the CPC ultimately depends on the commitment and conduct of its rank and file. To insure the quality and commitment of its members the CPC sets up primary organizations, small groups among party rank and file, so as to involve each member in the affairs of the party on a regular basis. According to the present party constitution: "Primary party organizations are formed in factories, shops, schools, offices, city neighbourhoods, people's communes, cooperatives, farms, townships, towns, companies of the People's Liberation Army and other basic units, where there are three or more full party members."[44] These primary organizations, sometimes referred to as party cells, are like the squads in an army or the Bible classes in religious organizations, all of them being designed to involve members in organizational goals.

The hierarchical principle that governs the higher command structure of the CPC extends also to the primary organization. The latter consists of three echelons: the highest primary organization is the Primary Party Committee; the middle echelon, General Party Branch; and the lowest echelon, Party Branch. Each of these has a "dignified" part, i.e., general membership meeting, and an "efficient" part, i.e., Party Committee. Even as small an element as a Party Committee, a secretary, an organization member, and a propaganda member are to be elected. Each primary organization of the CPC is required to have regular branch committee meetings, general membership meetings, small-section meetings (small sections being components of a party branch) and party study classes. In late 1984, with 40 million members, the CPC has some 2 million primary organizations.[45]

The primary organizations of the CPC, or of any Communist party for that matter, hold a special status in the Communist philosophy of organization. The primary organizations are formally referred to in the party charter as "militant bastions of the party in the basic units of society." In other words, each primary organization of the

CPC *ideally* acts as a combat squad, fighting for socialism amidst a huge population of nonbelievers. Members of a primary organization play the role of exemplary Communist for the rest of society to emulate, leaders in carrying out socialist undertakings and vigilantes against counterrevolutionaries. They are, indeed, fighting missionaries or Communist Jesuits working amidst heathens.

Since 1978 increasing concerns have been voiced by top CPC leaders over the quality of primary organizations. The phenomena of "impurity in membership" and "weakness, feebleness and laxity" are reported to be quite common at the basic levels of the party.[46] The present national leadership blamed part of the weakness at the primary level to the destruction of party discipline in the Cultural Revolution of 1966-76. Of the present membership of the CPC, 40.6 percent were admitted during that time by way of shock tactics (*tuji*).[47] Among these joining the party in 1966-76 were five kinds of people, i.e., rebels, factionalists, rowdies, opponents to the party line of the third plenum of 1978, and grafters. Taking responsibility at primary levels is nowadays avoided by many party members. "In some party branches," it was reported in a newspaper column, "when a new branch secretary is to be elected, everyone declines to assume the position, regarding it as a burden. Some comrades said that a branch secretary has neither financial nor personnel power so it is non-consequential."[48] An investigation of 3,658 party branches in Peking in 1982 found that less than one-third met the standards of "adhering to a correct party line, leaders being united, and fulfilling the functions of being militant bastions." Sixty percent of the branches belonged to the "mediocre" category and "backward" ones were less than 10 percent. The latter branches are characterized by: (1) divided leadership, which is clique ridden and disinterested in assuming responsibility; (2) opposition to the general party line, and passivity in work; (3) corruption and graft; and (4) insubordination toward superiors and dictatorship over subordinates.[49] Whereas in cities the Cultural Revolution is partly responsible for current problems in primary organizations, the serious disarray in rural party primary organizations is caused mainly by the drastic change in production management—decollectivization—brought about by present leaders. The sudden end of collective farming in the Chinese countryside after 1978 has created conditions that are

> sharpening the need for correctly handling the relations among the state, collectivity and individual; [there are] rising instances of gambling and superstitions; increase in civil and criminal lawsuits; rampant spread, in some places, of graft, speculation, smuggling and robbery of state property. . . . All this requires a strong and forceful rural primary organization to overcome it but, instead, some primary organizations of our party display impotence and feebleness. Some have paralyzed completely. Many responsibilities have not been assumed.[50]

Since farming is now through individual contract, party branches are deprived of their past functions of supervising and organizing collective farming. A common saying among rural party leaders is, "The old way no longer works but the new way is incomprehensible."[51] In many rural areas the operation of primary organizations such as regular party branch committees or general membership meetings has been suspended for years. That is why in December 1981 the national department of organization issued a new and comprehensive Working Regulations of Branches in Agricultural Areas (Provisional) to reestablish a system of party primary organizations in the countryside.[52] In 1983, as the people's communes were being formally and gradually separated from the newly revived township (*xiang*) government, demoralization and paralysis of party leaders at primary levels advance simultaneously.[53]

THE COMMUNIST PARTY UNDER STRESS

Our discussion of the structure of the CPC, together with the summing up of the first thirty years of the PRC, has referred to the various stresses and even crises that the CPC has been undergoing. The seriousness of the problems that the CPC is faced with was well stated in 1982 by Song Renqiong, director of the organization department of the Party Central Committee in 1982: "At the start of our state the ratio of party members to the national population was one to one hundred; today the ratio is one to twenty-five, a threefold increase, but why is the effectiveness of our party not as high as at the beginning?"[54] In this section we shall discuss the major inner stresses that the CPC has been subject to since 1949.

Personalization of the CPC

The first and foremost cause of the present malaise that afflicts the CPC was the progressive disintegration of the original core of top leaders. That in turn brought about the present demoralization and degeneration of the rank and file of the Communist party of China. But the root cause was the transformation, after victory, of the party into the personal instrument of its leader, Mao Zedong.

Even before the CPC's victory in the civil war, as we mentioned earlier, the process of shaping the party to suit Mao's conception had already began in the Party Rectification campaign of 1942. By April 1945 when the CPC convened the Seventh Congress, the cult of Mao's personality had been established; ironically the leader mainly responsible for Mao's personality cult then was Liu Shaoqi (Liu Shao-ch'i). During that congress, for the first time, the phrase "the thought of Mao Zedong [Mao Tse-tung then]" was added to the party constitution as a guiding principle of the party, equal to Marxism-Leninism.[55] Liu's report to the Seventh Congress on the revision of the party constitution was profuse with acclamation of Mao:

> Comrade Mao Tse-tung is an outstanding representative of the heroic proletariat of our country and of all that is best in the traditions of our great nation. He is a creative and talented Marxist, combining as he does the universal truth of Marxism—the highest ideology of mankind—with the concrete practice of the Chinese revolution. He has raised the ideology of the Chinese nation to an unprecedented height and shown to the suffering Chinese nation and people the only correct and clear road towards complete liberation—the road of Mao Tse-tung. Following this road, our party and the Chinese people launched the great pre-1927 revolutionary movement, of which Comrade Mao Tse-tung was the organizer. During the Agrarian Revolution, the great Red areas and the Red Army were created with Comrade Mao Tse-tung as their founder and leader. In the War of Resistance to Japanese Aggression, the great liberated areas and the people's armed forces were created—the Eighth Route Army and the New Fourth Army, of which Comrade Mao Tse-tung was again the founder and leader.[56]

The victory of the CPC in 1949 naturally further enhanced the status of Mao, who, like Chinese emperors of traditional time, now would transform the whole nation according to his conception. After 1949 it became clear that the fate and fortune of any CPC leader depended on his support of Mao's policies and programs. The history of the CPC in the past thirty years shows that as Mao's programs failed to accomplish the desired results, his attitude toward other leaders who differed with him became increasingly antagonistic. Thus in 1953 when a party leader named Po I-po did not agree with Mao on rural cooperatives and taxation policy toward urban business, Mao charged Po with having "bourgeois ideas" and ordered Po to conduct self-criticism.[57] In the same year, as noted before, two other leaders (Gao Gang and Rao Shushih) were dismissed from their positions because of their differences with Mao over the implementation of the first five-year plan and other issues. Another inner crisis emerged in 1955 over Mao's acceleration of rural cooperatives. This was the first time that Mao had suspected other CPC leaders of being less than committed socialists.[58] Mao's attitude toward the opposition thereafter became radicalized. When in 1959 several leaders were critical of the Great Leap Forward program, Mao called them "opportunists who had wormed their way into the Party," and accused them of "deliberately attempting to sabotage the dictatorship of the proletariat, divide the party, organize faction, disseminate their views, and dissolve the vanguard of proletariat so to establish their party of opportunism."[59] Subsequently Marshal Peng Dehuai, who was the most prominent critic of the Great Leap Forward, and a group of national and provincial civil and military leaders were purged from their party and state positions. Each of the inner crises so far had resulted in the promotion of leaders who, in Mao's view, would think and act as Mao Zedong did. Marshal Peng's position was taken over by Marshal Lin Biao whose public attitude toward Mao was, as he put it in 1967: "So far as the thought of Mao Zedong is concerned, my stand is that we should carry it out whether we understand it or not."[60]

The transformation of the CPC into a personal instrument of Mao was completed in the Cultural Revolution. In the innermost chamber of party leadership, i.e., the Standing Committee of the Politburo, Mao had coopted those whose social and educational background closely resembled his. After a comprehensive and systematic study of the background of CPC leadership, Robert Scalapino concluded that in the members of the Standing Committee of the Politburo of the Ninth Party Congress (1969) "Mao appeared to have supplemented and recreated himself."[61] Breaking all precedents, the CPC at the Ninth Party Congress wrote into its constitution the name of the late Marshal Lin Biao (Lin Piao) as the successor to Mao. The personalization of the party of 1969 is shown in the words the party constitution employed to justify Lin's position: "Comrade Lin Piao has consistently held high the great red banner of Mao Tse-tung Thought and has most loyally and resolutely carried out and defended comrade Mao Tse-tung's proletarian revolutionary line. Comrade Lin Piao is comrade Mao Tse-tung's close comrade-in-arms and successor."[62] The whole history of the CPC was rewritten subsequently to show that the Communist party of China "has been *nurtured* and built up by . . . Mao" (emphasis added).[63] In the hands of the Maoist party historian, the history of the CPC became a history of "Communists struggling against other Communists,"[64] or, more accurately, "Mao's struggle against other Communists."

Alienation and Dissension in the CPC

The effectiveness of a normative organization such as the CPC hinges on its inner unity, which is in turn based on the identification of all members of the organization with its goals. The unity of top leaders is crucial to the effectiveness of a normative organization since its goals are defined and interpreted by these leaders. Serious and continuous disputes among the leaders at the highest echelon cause disorientation and demoralization of the lower elite and the rank and file. It is not surprising that the personalization of the CPC was accompanied by steady demoralization and disorientation among the lower leaders and ordinary members of the CPC.

Recently published speeches of Mao show that many in the CPC were skeptical of the official accounts of purges of numerous leaders. In a speech to a party gathering in March 1955 Mao declared: "Some comrades say that they have not come across any document [of the] antiparty alliance of Gao and Rao" and he brought up the "doubts expressed by some comrades to the effect that since there was no written agreement, perhaps there wasn't an alliance after all." [65] A significant aspect of this is that doubts and skepticisms about the Gao and Rao case were expressed by members of the Politburo and other party leaders of national and provincial party establishments. For Mao had complained during an enlarged Politburo meeting in April 1956 that because of the Gao and Rao case the atmosphere inside the party (i.e., the Politburo) had become "rigid and stifling" and that there was a tendency "to be extraordinarily cautious and avoid discussing state affairs." [66] The Gao and Rao case revealed that not even members of the Politburo were fully informed of these important personnel matters, and they certainly did not participate in policy debates. Party leaders below the Politburo level were naturally even more cut off from the top elite than were members of the Politburo. Uncertain of what had really happened and unconvinced by the official explanations of these purges, those party members not in the innermost chamber of party leadership chose the natural course of being extraordinarily cautious and withholding their opinion and speech. Thus gaps in inner-party communication caused dissension and alienation on the part of those outside the top elite.

The dismissal of Marshal Peng Dehuai and others in 1959 had similar effects on the corporate body of the CPC. In a party gathering in August 1959 Mao spoke about "many comrades' failure to understand" the cases of Gao, Rao, and now Peng. Many were "surprised." [67] The case of Marshal Peng concerned the destructiveness of the Great Leap Forward program of 1958-59. The severe economic crisis caused by the Great Leap threw into sharp relief the extent of communication gaps and alienation from Mao of many provincial party leaders. Mao's speech to the Central Military Commission on September 11, 1959, testifies to the phenomenon of alienation and communication gaps:

> During the past few weeks at provincial level conferences, quite a few high cadres have been exposed as right-opportunist elements and trouble-makers, whose one fear is that the world should be free of trouble. . . . For example if there is not enough pork, not enough vegetables, not enough soap, not enough women's hair grips, they seize the opportunity to say, "You have done things badly!" *They say it is your affairs and not theirs. When organizations hold meetings and reach decisions they don't utter a murmur.* For instance at the Peitaiho Conference not a murmur, at the Chengchow Conference not a murmur, at the Wuch'ang Conference not a murmur. At the Shanghai Conference they did mumble something but we could not hear. . . . [emphasis added].[68]

Distrust, however, is a mutual process. As the lower elite of the CPC grew distrustful of the high elite, so did the high elite, especially Mao, distrust the lower cadres of the CPC. From 1958 on, one frequently comes across references in inner-party communications to Mao's distrust of cadres. In one intra-party correspondence in early 1959 Mao wrote:

> Please firmly bear in mind that we must not believe too much the statements made by such people as general branch secretaries, secretaries of factories and mines party committees, responsible persons of organizations under the munici-

pal government and secretaries of party groups, and the comrades among bureau and department chiefs at the Central Government level. . . . They feign compliance with, or entirely ignore instructions from higher levels of these instructions that do not suit them.[69]

The irony is that Mao's correspondence was directed at the very persons (secretaries of party committees, party branches, and secretaries of various municipal, provincial, and autonomous-region party committees) that he asked to be distrusted. More instances of this type can be found in Mao's talks. For example, in a conference of provincial party secretaries in February 1959 Mao declared that the confidential journal, *For Internal Reference*, which published reports by the *New China News Agency* on conditions in Chinese society, "should be read, but not too often" since in Mao's views Chinese society was changing so fast in the Great Leap Forward as to make the journal "part of history."[70] In July 1959 Mao spoke about his distrust of an investigation by the Academy of Sciences on peasants' attitudes toward communal mess halls. Mao maintained that the investigation stressed only the negative but not the positive aspects of communal mess halls.[71] In 1964 Mao again expressed his distrust of provincial reports on the critical situation in society (presumably on the severe food shortage and popular demoralization) and his confidence in reports from three army commanders who gave a positive account of society.[72]

Though Mao's personalization of the CPC is one of the fundamental causes of the distrust within the party, another reason for that is the overall manipulative relationship between the top and lower elites of the CPC. This manipulative relationship inside the CPC can be seen in top leaders' handling of internal communication. A crucial source of power inside the CPC is the system of "internal transmission" of decisions made at the highest level. Whether a decision is to be transmitted to certain echelons of the party is obviously controlled by the top leaders. For instance, in April 1956, on the question of Soviet leaders' denunciation of Stalin and disputes within the international Communist movement in connection with de-Stalinization, Mao instructed the Politburo: "On transmission, some matters can be talked about anywhere. Those concerning the misdeeds of Stalin and the Third International should be transmitted to prefectural party committees; it is all right to let county party secretaries know too. But we are not prepared to talk about this in the press or to the masses."[73] In 1957 Mao, in a Central Committee conference, recalled that the decision on the Socialist transition of 1953 was made at a meeting on finance: "At first we did not dare to publicize it to the whole Party but did transmit it to the office of county party committee."[74] In the Cultural Revolution the control of transmission inside the CPC became extreme. Mao told an Albanian military delegation that his first broadside against the Peking CPC establishment was drafted secretly by one of the Gang of Four, Yao Wenyuan. Mao was inclined to show the essay to "some of the leading comrades of the Central Committee" but his wife, Jiang Qing, would not even show it to Zhou Enlai.[75]

This manipulative leadership of topmost CPC leadership could not but alienate the lower elite and rank and file. One might argue that in any corporation as large and bureaucratic as the CPC a degree of manipulation by top leaders exists. This is undoubtedly true. But one must bear in mind that CPC is not just another corporation, though it does share with other corporations some common characteristics. As a prototype of a new community and the sole decision maker in China, the CPC requires a very high degree of consensus within its own rank in order for the party to be effective. Personalization of the party and manipulative leadership sooner or later dissolve inner consensus and unity. The terror in the Cultural Revolution finally brought alienation and dissension within the CPC to the surface. In 1976 a leftist spokesman denounced a prevailing opinion among party members that Mao's so-called struggle between two lines was merely a front for "sectarian struggle for power."[76]

Clique Proliferation

Alienated from Mao and other topmost leaders, cynical about the official ideology, and terrorized by the Cultural Revolution, the rank and file of the CPC formed numerous cliques or factions to protect themselves and to realize their material interests. In 1980 two writers of the CPC declared in the party's chief ideological journal, *Hongqi (Red Flag)*, that if the cliques were allowed to continue, the CPC was in danger of being a "giant with clay feet."[77]

The two major forms of cliques inside the CPC also indicate their causes. The first form is based on formal association. This is reminiscent of the American expression that a city hall is composed of a close-knit group. In China often an entire Party Committee of a province, city, county, or commune forms a clique. These cliques are facilitated by two essential characteristics of the CPC: centralization and concentration of power. Centralization promotes an insular mentality on the part of party members, who are held accountable only to their superiors, not to public opinion or constituents. Concentration of power further accentuates an insular outlook among party leaders. In the structure of the PRC political system one often finds that a provincial first party secretary is concurrently head of the provincial government and political director of the provincial military command. In time of normalcy cliques on the basis of formal association are constrained or permeated by two universalistic forces: members' commitment to the goals of the party and the role of the top leaders as final arbiters in party affairs. But personalization of the CPC, gaps in inner-party communication, manipulative leadership, and insecurity during the Cultural Revolution virtually destroyed whatever restraint on cliques there was. Hence cliques based on formal association came into their own and pervaded the whole CPC after the Cultural Revolution.

The second form of cliques is based on small alliances, or "societies of brotherhood," that were formed among party members during the anarchic days of the Cultural Revolution as either mutual-protection groups or combat groups to seize power from other Party leaders.[78] After the Cultural Revolution these former alliances were transformed into mutual-aid cliques. A top Chinese army general wrote in *Hongqi* that "cliques are invisible until the occasions for consideration of a cadre's promotion, assignment and rank designation."[79]

In terms of organizational effectiveness, cliques have several effects. First, factions or cliques displace the goals of an organization. For example, a *People's Daily* commentator wrote that cliques "take a utilitarian attitude toward party line, principle and policy; [cliques] distort, ignore or attack [party line] from the standpoint of each group's interest."[80] Second, cliques make the establishment of accountability difficult. The work of the Central Commission for Discipline Inspection, for instance, was handicapped by the prevailing network of cliques inside the CPC. Lower branches of the party, more often than not, will not report infractions of their colleagues in the same party committee. The Discipline Inspection Commission has to rely on ordinary cadres' letters to detect even obvious cases of indiscipline or corruption.[81] In almost every case, a cadre under the investigation of the Commission for Discipline Inspection is able to find a patron-protector to intercede for him. As one writer put it, the cliques and personal connection in the party "reduces a big case into a small one and dissolves a small case into dust."[82] Factions and cliques tend to increase intraorganizational conflict and strife. One account described the strife-provocation nature of cliques:

> They [factions] fasten and exaggerate the mistakes and problems of people outside of their clique but ignore or minimize the mistakes of people inside their group. They practice favoritism in matters such as personnel transfer and evaluation and housing allocation. To those who do not belong to their clique, no consideration whatever is shown by them. Because of this, grievances and compliances [within a party unit] rise. The work of four modernizations cannot but be hampered.[83]

Lastly but not leastly, factionalism tends to contribute to "overloading" at the top level of an organization. Because of factional fighting at middle or lower echelons, problems cannot be resolved in time. In the end, the higher-ups must intervene or risk a major incident.[84]

Bureaucratization of the Party

Another major reason for the present malaise of the CPC is bureaucratization. In previous sections we described the hierarchical structure of party committees, which in turn are staffed with party secretaries. The operation of this system follows the dictum: "Party secretaries make decisions; others carry out decisions." This is known in China as "unified leadership of the Party" (*Yiyuanhua lingdao*). Party secretaries became thus preoccupied with day-to-day administration. Li Honglin, a major writer for the reformist group inside the CPC, explained:

> Take, for example, in farming. Not only general planning, but also details such as weeding and fertilizing became the central concern of commune, county and even higher party committees. The day-to-day activity of production teams has been entirely monopolized by party branches. The same is true in other enterprises. Everywhere the party committee (or branch) "leads all." . . . The party sinks into routinism.[85]

The principle of unified party leadership worked hand in glove with the principle of centralization. The combination of the two gave birth to what is known in China as bureaucratism, which was best described by Deng Xiaoping in an enlarged Politburo conference in August 1980:

> Our various leading organs have run many things that they should not have run, did not run well, or could not run them. Many of the things would have been handled well if they were delegated to lower units such as enterprises, professional or social bodies if only we had established rules and adhered to democratic centralism. Once all things were handled by the party and the state at the center then we run into difficulties. No one is so efficacious as to manage well so many complex things. This may be regarded as the root of the peculiar bureaucratism that we have at the present. Another cause of bureaucratism is that our party, state and enterprise, for a long time lacked a set of rules and a system of individual responsibility. There was no stipulation on the scope of one's function or authority. So a majority of our officials could not handle problems inde-

pendently and spent their time in writing reports and passing on documents. With respect to some people whose sectarian spirit is strong, they evade responsibility and struggle for benefit. Furthermore, concerning the cadres, we do not have a system of appointment, promotion, demotion, retirement, dismissal, and circulation. Regardless of a cadre's performance, his job is secure. A logical result of all this is a bloated organization, having numerous layers, a large number of subsidiary and superfluous positions. A bloated organization promotes bureaucratism. This system must be changed in a fundamental way.[86]

In Deng's speech no distinction is made between party or nonparty officials but other information suggests that bureaucratism is especially advanced among party members. This is evidenced in the distribution of party members. Since 1982 Chinese press and journals have frequently expressed a concern over party members' concentration in administrative positions; the closer a position is to the actual production process, the less likelihood there is of the presence of party members.[87] Even in the countryside party members rapidly installed themselves in the administration of county, commune, production brigade, or even the lowest level of production team, detaching themselves from any actual productive tasks. The CPC has, in other words, become a party of true elites, who own and dispose of resources that are generated by others.

Bureaucratization of the party is ideologically inconsistent with the original conception of a Communist party. Following the classical division of function between philosopher and king, the party is to be the philosopher, not the king, whose function is to be assumed by the state apparatus. The party is to set a general line for society to follow, not administering it. In the words of Li Honglin, whose commentaries in Chinese press represent the views of the party reformist group:

> The leadership of the party is political, not administrative. The party leads the masses through its own program, line, principle, and general direction. In other words, the party offers a political program, pointing out clearly the direction, affirming long-range goals and current tasks so that all people will unite marching forward along the line determined by the party. To form people into a revolutionary force, the party must accurately conceptualize and handle class relations. Whom to oppose, whom to rely on, whom to unite with, and whom to neutralize, this is commonly known as the "class line." This is yet another part of political leadership. . . . Every agency, be it military, state, mass, economic, or cultural organization, has its own special task to perform. Uniting all their different tasks on the basis of the party's political program so to mobilize them to focus on the overall objective is another aspect of political leadership.[88]

To sum up Li Honglin's discussion, the "proper" party leadership consists of three things: general line (or program) of development, class line, and setting priority in resource allocation. Bureaucratization of the party displaces the original goals of a Communist party. Instead of conceptualizing the broad direction of national development, nowadays CPC members immerse themselves in bureaucratic busy work. In the words of another party commentator:

> The party is supposed to be the locomotive leading a whole society moving forward. But now it has become a pedestrian carrying a heavy load on its back. In the meantime administrative agencies cannot perform its functions fully, being powerless to make decisions.[89]

No ruling Communist party, however, escapes from bureaucratization. It is easy for national leaders who are not involved in the day-to-day administration of the country to insist on "line" leadership of the party. But for subnational leaders in China the distinction between line leadership and administration is difficult to observe. In the first place, CPC is a highly centralized organization. The substance of line leadership that Li Honglin describes, i.e., general program, class line, and resource allocation, falls into the category of major decisions, which are monopolized by national leaders. There is very little leeway left for subnational leaders to assume line leadership. Politically, it is also risky for subnational leaders to be active in line leadership since the line of national leaders changes rather unpredictably. It is safer for provincial, prefectual, municipal, and county party secretaries to administer a line transmitted from Peking rather than have their own line. But even if there had been sufficient local autonomy in the CPC, the literacy level of most party secretaries would not be adequate for the line leadership that CPC idealists wanted. As discussed earlier, it is only now that advanced education is being stressed in regional party leaderships. Most regional CPC leaders are not prepared to assume either the ideological or the professional type of charismatic leadership, being well versed in neither Marxism-Leninism nor modern social and economic development. Finally, one must also consider Chinese political tradition. One of the most interesting aspects of CPC self-criticism after 1978 is that most party cadres are tainted with feudalism. It had been an established policy of the CPC to recruit lower leaders after 1949 from activists of working class or peasant background. Owing partly to low literacy and partly to the absence of significant social and economic change in the bulk of Chinese countryside before 1980, most lower cadres of CPC are still under the sway of Chinese tradition. The model for local cadres to emulate is traditional Chinese bureaucracy.[90]

The transformation of the CPC into an administrative hierarchy means that the party is losing its identity as a "prototype of a new community." The party is dissolving into the society that the CPC originally intended to change. This situation is known in China as "the party manages everything but not itself" (*dang bu guan dang*). Since the CPC has taken upon itself the sole function of moving society forward and, on that basis, eliminated any other independent institution that might challenge or dilute CPC functions, the loss of "combat capability" of the party means social stagnation and corruption.

Current Party Rectification

To cope with the various problems analyzed above, the national leaders of the CPC have taken numerous measures since 1978.

The first step that the national leaders of the CPC undertook to reestablish the "combat" quality of the party was to involve party members regularly in party activity. This approach is a fundamental method of all normative or ideological organizations, i.e., making their members devote their lives to organizational affairs in order that their commitment to the goals of the organization will be retained and reinforced. The CPC now requires every party member, high or low, to attend regularly two kinds of party activity, one a gathering of a party branch and the other a meeting of party members in their work place. This is known in China as living a double organizational life. In principle, every party member belongs to a party branch, the primary organization of the CPC. A branch is supposed to meet regularly with short intervals in between. In branch meetings members, no matter how different their formal positions, are equal in theory as they associate solely on the basis of party membership. A party secretary and a sanitation worker who happens to belong to the same party branch should, in theory, treat each other as comrades with no status difference. They study policy or ideology together on a regular basis and conduct criticism and self-criticism. The branch gathering is thus designed not only to renew members' belief in Communist ideology and leadership but also to build up comradeship. Numerous Chinese press reports indicated that party branch meetings have atrophied since the destruction of the party in the Cultural Revolution.[91] That was to be expected, given the alienation of lower party echelons from upper echelons, which we analyzed in previous sections. But the paralysis of party branch activity means the hollowing of the CPC.

In addition to the gathering of the party branch, every party member is also an employee whether in party, state, or other organizations. So the second type of organizational life is that of party members' meeting and associating with each other on a regular basis as fellow employees in the same work place. The regular gathering of party members in their work place consists of activities similar to a party branch meeting, i.e., political study, criticism and self-criticism, exchange of views on daily work, and socializing. Through the two types of organizational life the national leaders of CPC hope to make every member deeply committed to the party and serve as a vanguard in society. However, the party spirit is low at present, and many party members do not have the desire to participate in organizational life.[92]

Disappointed by the lack of significant progress in party effectiveness, the national leaders of the CPC declared on the occasion of the Twelfth Party Congress of September 1982 a wholesale Party Rectification campaign in 1983-86. Two important measures of this campaign are a systematic screening of every party member so as to rid the party of undesirable members ("Cultural Revolution 'rebels,' factionalists, rowdies, opponents to reform, and corruptors") and promotion of younger and better-educated members to leading positions, i.e., members of party committees at provincial, municipal, and county level. At the end of this campaign party members would reregister with the CPC to formalize their membership. Apparently the reregistering of party members is the real cutting edge of party rectification. This, then, is the latest inner crisis of the CPC, which is trying to adapt to the new situation of four modernizations.

How shall we evaluate this latest Party Rectification campaign? Is it likely to succeed? The answer to the last question depends on whether the multiple problems that the CPC is faced with are, according to present Communist leaders, due to the Cultural Revolution. That is, the breakdown of the normal operation of the CPC during 1966-76 had enabled many unqualified persons to be admitted into the party. If that is indeed the main reason for the present malaise of the CPC, then as long as the current leaders of the CPC revert to the "normal" operation of the party, the crisis will gradually ease off. But there are facts that refute this explanation, which stresses incidental factors. As early as 1942, during the Party Rectification that went on then, the bureaucratic problems that are being discussed today in Chinese Communist publications had already been pointed out. Those problems included party members' passivity, falsehood, reprisal against people with different opinions, and crude treatment of the population.[93] After victory in civil war, with the CPC the ruling party, these critical manifestations of party members became even more extensive and aggravated than in the past. The disputes among the elite and the Cultural Revolution merely added fuel to the fire; they did not start it. Moreover, when we put the present Chinese Communist reform effort in a contemporary and comparative context, the prospect of the reform effort is not improved either. The bureaucratic inertia and corruption that have plagued the CPC today were the very targets of the late Soviet leader Yuri Andropov's "war on 'shoddy work, inactivity, and irresponsibility.'"[94]

Furthermore, there is an important reason to support our contention that the present party rectification in China will not be a thorough one. Since 1949 the CPC has staged several campaigns of "rectification," such as the Three-Anti (three evils) in 1951, the Antibureaucratism campaign in 1956 (forerunner of the Hundred Flowers Blooming campaign), the Four Cleanups in 1964, and then, of course, the Cultural Revolution. In each case the CPC national leaders called a halt *before* the campaign substantially accomplished its purpose. Even in the Cultural Revolution Mao eventually rehabilitated the overwhelming majority of middle- and lower-echelon cadres, which has been the most important reason for Chinese youth's widespread disillusionment with the CPC. It was not Mao's personality that caused the abortions of the previous campaigns. The fundamental reason for that was the nature of the CPC. In theory, the CPC represents the interest of workers and peasants. In practice, the primary constituents of CPC leaders are the members and cadres of the party. For the latter, top leaders are their protectors or patrons. It is thus implausible that any top Communist leader will carry out a truly thorough party rectification. Mao's Cultural Revolution was the best example of this implausibility. Our hypothesis is corroborated by the CPC leaders' handling of the image of Mao Zedong. In December 1983 on the occasion of the ninetieth anniversary of Mao's birth Chinese Communist leaders staged a return of the cult of Mao's personality. In speeches and essays published on this occasion, the early criticisms of Mao's "mistakes" were absent.[95] As Deng Xiaoping often reminds his fellow Communists, without Mao there would not have been a People's Republic. Similarly, without the 40 million party members who are willing to fight society there would not be a Communist party to take power. One might expect the current party rectification to rid the CPC of the worst abuses or inefficiencies, and that is in the best interest of top leaders. But one should not expect the rectification to produce a rebirth of the CPC.[96]

NOTES

1. "Constitution of the Communist Party of China," *Beijing Review* 25, no. 38 (September 20, 1982), 2.

2. "Hu Yaobang's Speech," *Beijing Review* 24, no. 28 (July 13, 1981), 19.

3. Lucian W. Pye, *Politics, Personality, and Nation Building: Burma's Search for Identity* (New Haven: Yale University Press, 1962), p. 18.

4. "Constitution of the Communist Party," p. 10.

5. Amitai Etzioni, *A Comparative Analysis of Complex Organizations* (New York: Free Press, 1961).

6. Lu Zechao, "The Basic Principle of Building an Advanced Socialist Democracy," *Hongqi*, no. 21 (1982), p. 18.

7. Walter Bagehot, *The English Constitution* (New York: Doubleday & Company), pp. 63–64.

8. "Constitution of the Communist Party," p. 15.

9. Ibid.

10. Feng Chun-kuei, "An Analysis of Members of the 11th Party Congress and Personnel in the Central Leading Organs," *Chung-kung Yen-chiu (Studies on Chinese Communism)* 11, no. 9 (September 15, 1977), 25.

11. *RMRB*, September 12, 1982, p. 2.

12. Kang Feng, "An Analysis of the Members of the 12th Central Leadership," *Chung-kung Yen-chiu (Studies on Chinese Communism)* 16, no. 10 (October 15, 1982), 40.

13. Kang Chiao, "Comments on Party Central Organ Reform," *Chung-kung Yen-chiu (Studies on Chinese Communism)* 16, no. 6 (June 15, 1982), 71.

14. Merle Fainsod, *How Russia Is Ruled* (Cambridge, Mass: Harvard University Press, 1965), p. 179.

15. Fox Butterfield, "Peking Appoints Close Associate of Teng Party Secretary General," *New York Times,* January 5, 1979, p. A7. Also, "Hu Yaobang in Charge of Day-to-Day Work of the Central Committee," *Ming Pao Daily News,* January 8, 1979, p. 3.

16. Mao *Tse-tung Ssu-Hsiang Wan-Sui* (hereon *Wan-Sui*) (People's Republic of China, 1969) no. 2, pp. 16, 21, 23, 28.

17. *Ming Pao Daily News,* April 10, 1980, p. 3.

18. "The Central Committee's Secretariat and Its Work," *Beijing Review* 24, no. 19 (May 11, 1981), 21.

19. Ibid.

20. Wang Renchong, "Unify Thoughts. Rectify Party Style of Work Seriously," *Hongqi,* no. 5 (1982), p. 4.

21. *Wan-Sui,* no. 2, pp. 40 and 148.

22. Ibid.

23. Stuart Schram, ed., *Chairman Mao Talks to the People: Talks and Letters: 1956-1971* (New York: Pantheon, 1974), pp. 158-59. For original text, see *Wan-Sui,* no. 2, pp. 399-422, or *RMRB,* July 1, 1978, pp. 1-4.

24. *RMRB,* May 5, 1980, p. 3.

25. *RMRB,* September 9, 1981, p. 2.

26. *RMRB,* December 11, 1981, p. 3.

27. *RMRB,* August 26, 1980, p. 2.

28. Hu Yaobang, "Talks at the First Plenum of Twelfth Central Committee," *RMRB,* October 22, 1982, p. 1.

29. *RMRB,* November 6, 1982, p. 4.

30. Yang Chia, "The Secretariat Has Established an Office for Research of Agricultural Policy," *Ming Pao Daily News,* May 24, 1982, p. 3. Also Kang Chiao, *Central Organ Reform,* p. 71.

31. *RMRB,* January 28, 1980.

32. "Constitution of the Communist Party," p. 15.

33. Yang Yizheng, "Take the New Path of Joint Industrial and Agricultural Development," *Hongqi,* no. 21 (1982), p. 38.

34. Donald W. Klein and Ann B. Clark, *Biographic Dictionary of Chinese Communism, 1921-1965* (Cambridge, Mass.: Harvard University Press, 1971), pp. 93-194; *RMRB,* March 2, 1980, p. 2; *Ming Pao Daily News,* October 24, 1978, p. 3. *Chung-yan Jih-pao* (overseas edition), September 22, 1980, p. 1.

35. *RMRB,* February 7, 1983, p. 1.

36. "Administrative Divisions of the People's Republic of China," *Beijing Review* 26, no. 1 (January 3, 1983), 25; Christopher S. Wren, "Peking's Farm Policies Beginning to Pay Off," *New York Times,* April 10, 1983, p. 8.

37. *RMRB,* November 30, 1978, p. 1.

38. *RMRB,* November 28, 1978, p. 3.

39. *Survey of Mainland China Press (SCMP),* no. 1899, p. 17.

40. *SCMP,* no. 1856, p. 20.

41. *SCMP,* no. 1899, p. 21.

42. *Wan-Sui,* no. 1, p. 110.

43. I dealt with this in some detail in "Problems in Communications in China's Modernization," *Asian Survey* XXII, no. 5 (May 1982).

44. "Constitution of the Communist Party," p. 17.

45. *RMRB,* June 27, 1982, p. 1.

46. Ibid.

47. *RMRB,* October 29, 1982, p. 1.

48. Special commentator, "To Make the Organizational Life of the Party Healthy," *RMRB,* January 16, 1980, p. 3.

49. Tuan Junyi, "To Rectify Our Party Is a Task of Foremost Importance," *Hongqi,* no. 22 (1982), p. 15.

50. Jing Dong, "Strengthen Party Rural Primary Organizations," *Hongqi,* no. 8 (1982), p. 36.

51. Ibid., p. 37; also *RMRB,* February 19, 1982, p. 1.

52. The full text of this document is in *Chung-kung Yen-chiu* 16, no. 9 (September 15, 1982), 131-50.

53. *RMRB,* March 16, 1983, p. 2.

54. Song Renqiong, "Teach Party Members the New Party Constitution. Be Ideologically Prepared for Party Rectification," *RMRB,* December 18, 1982, p. 4.

55. Conrad Brandt, Benjamin Schwartz, and John K. Fairbank, *A Documentary History of Chinese Communism* (New York: Atheneum, 1967), p. 419.

56. *Collected Works of Liu Shao Ch'i, 1945-1957* (Kowloon, Hong Kong: Union Research Institute, 1969), p. 14.

57. *Selected Works of Mao Tse-tung,* vol. V (Peking: Foreign Languages Press, 1977), pp. 106-7.

58. Ibid., pp. 184–207.

59. *Wan-sui*, no. 1, p. 85.

60. Ibid., p. 674.

61. Robert A. Scalapino, "The Transition in Chinese Party Leadership: A Comparison of the Eighth and Ninth Central Committees," in Robert A. Scalapino, ed., *Elites in the People's Republic of China* (Seattle: University of Washington Press, 1972), p. 91.

62. *The Ninth National Congress of the Communist Party of China* (Documents) (Peking: Foreign Languages Press, 1969), pp. 112–13.

63. Ibid., p. 67.

64. Yang Zhengya, "Correctly Record the History of our Party's Struggles," *RMRB*, November 27, 1979, p. 3.

65. Mao Tse-tung, *Selected Works*, vol. V (Peking: Foreign Languages Press, 1977), pp. 161–62.

66. *Wan-sui*, no. 2, p. 35.

67. Ibid., p. 308.

68. Stuart Schram, ed., *Chairman Mao Talks to the People: Talks and Letters: 1956–1971* (New York: Pantheon, 1974), p. 149. For original text, see *Wan-sui*, no. 2, p. 314.

69. *Miscellany of Mao Tse-tung Thought (1949–1968)*, part I (Arlington, VA.: Joint Publications Research Service, 1974), p. 172.

70. *Wan-sui*, no. 1, p. 272.

71. Ibid., p. 301.

72. Ibid., p. 599.

73. Ibid., p. 40.

74. Ibid., p. 122.

75. *Miscellany of Mao Tse-tung Thought (1949–1968)*, part IV (Arlington, VA.: Joint Publications Research Service, 1974), pp. 456–57.

76. Liang Xiao, "Use Revolutionary Public Opinion to Destroy Counterrevolutionary Public Opinion," *RMRB*, May 5, 1976, p. 1.

77. Yang Fengchum and Zhang Leike, "Resolutely Rectify the Deviation within the Party," *Hongqi* no. 24 (1980), pp. 13–16.

78. *RMRB*, October 22, 1980, p. 3.

79. Zhang Tingfa, "Leading Cadres Must Take the Lead in Being Qualified Party Members," *Hongqi*, no. 13 (1980), p. 5.

80. Commentator, "Resolutely Overcome Factionalism," *RMRB*, August 15, 1979, p. 3.

81. Zhang Zhe, "Thoroughly Implement 'Standard of Inner Party Political Life, Persist on Democratic Centralism,'" *RMRB*, October 4, 1980, p. 3.

82. Zhang Lizhon, "Restrain the Trend of Protecting Deviations," *RMRB*, January 29, 1982, p. 5.

83. Commentator, "Persist on Party Spirit and Rid Factional Spirit," *RMRB*, June 24, 1980, p. 1.

84. *RMRB*, December 17, 1980, p. 3.

85. Li Honglin, "What Kind of Party Leadership Do We Insist Upon?" *RMRB*, October 5, 1979, p. 3.

86. "Teng Hsiao-ping's Speech to the Party Central Political Bureau Enlarged Conference," *Chungkung Yenchiu (Studies on Chinese Communism)* 15, no. 7 (July 15, 1981), 118–19.

87. *RMRB*, April 5, 1982, p. 3.

88. Li Honglin, "What Kind of Party Leadership Do We Insist On?" *RMRB*, October 5, 1980, p. 3.

89. Peng Xianfu and Zheng Zhongping, "On Unified Leadership," *RMRB*, December 12, 1980, p. 5.

90. Xue Muduo, "How to Conduct Struggle With Bureaucratism," *RMRB*, April 28, 1980, p. 5.

91. *RMRB*, January 16, 1980, p. 3.

92. *RMRB*, January 28, 1983, p. 4.

93. *Zhengfeng Wenxian (Documents of Rectification)*, enlarged edition (Hong Kong: New Democracy Publisher, 1949), pp. 299–318. It is too bad that Boyd Compton's *Mao's China, Party Reform Documents, 1942–44* (Seattle: University of Washington Press, 1966) does not incorporate this crucial document by a regional CPC leader named Liu Zejiu.

94. John F. Burns, "Andropov's Tall Order: Rousing the Loafers," *New York Times*, January 4, 1983, p. 1; also, Burns, "Soviet Study Urges Relaxing of Controls to Revive Economy," *New York Times*, August 5, 1983, p. 1.

95. Christopher S. Wren, "China Honors Mao with Selective Fanfare," *New York Times*, December 25, 1983, p. 1.

96. For a thorough analysis of how the Chinese Communist party copes with bureaucracy see Harry Harding, *Organizing China: The Problem of Bureaucracy 1949–1976* (Stanford, Calif.: Stanford University Press, 1981).

Chinese Communist National Government: Structure and Process

Previous discussions on the Chinese Communist party have made the point that the CPC as a normative organization is not supposed to run the day-to-day affairs of the country. The function of administration is assumed by the state or government apparatus of China. Hence parallel to the structure of the CPC is that of the Chinese Communist state, formally called the people's government.

At the head of the people's government of China is the National People's Government in Peking. The structure of the Chinese national government, like that of the CPC, consists of "dignified" and "efficient" parts. The former comprises a national constitution, the National People's Congress, and the president of the PRC. These are, to borrow from Bagehot again, the "comely parts" of Chinese government. The efficient parts of the National People's Government consist of the State Council (*Guo Wu Yuan*), which is equivalent to a cabinet and the various ministries, commissions, and councils under the State Council. In this chapter we shall describe and analyze these national state institutions.

THE CONSTITUTION OF THE PRC

Karl Marx stated in *The Communist Manifesto* that the bourgeoisie in the West had created a world after its own image. Part of this transformation of the whole world after the image of the West is that nowadays almost every nation feels the necessity to have a constitution to obtain (to borrow from Mao Zedong) "world membership," if for no other purpose. However, a constitution, which serves as the fundamental or organic law of Western democracies, undergoes a radical change in its function when it is transplanted to a Third World nation. The constitution of the PRC is no exception.

"The Chinese Constitution," says the observant David Bonavia of *Far Eastern Economic Review*, "is more in the nature of a political manifesto than a basic statement of the rights and duties of citizens. It expresses the ideas of whichever group is in power, and each ruling group has found it both possible and opportune to convene a National People's Congress (NPC) to amend it."[1] Since 1954 the PRC has had four constitutions, the latest one adopted by the NPC in December 1982. Each of the four constitutions represents a major phase of post-1949 political development. A brief comparative analysis of the four constitutions will both illuminate the changing political mood of China from 1954 to 1982 and point out the peculiar function of the constitution in China.

To begin with, we shall follow the thesis of two Chinese scholars that any constitution has two parts, one being programmatic (e.g., a political manifesto) and the other organic, setting forth norms or standards for the structure and function of government, rights and obligations of citizens, and relationships between government and people.[2] As a revolutionary society "settles down," the programmatic parts of a constitution are superseded by organic parts. The first constitution of the PRC, in 1954, is regarded by Chinese leaders today as a good one because it is more organic than programmatic. Consisting of 106 articles, the 1954 constitution represented a relatively consensual leadership of the CPC, hopeful of an orderly process of "transition to socialism." Defining the Chinese state as a "people's democratic state led by the working class," it includes universally "dignified" articles of civil liberties for citizens and provides a government based on elected representatives. The preeminent role of the CPC vis-a-vis the state is mentioned only once in the 1954 constitution. By 1975 when the second constitution was adopted, the political mood in China had changed drastically. The consensual leadership of the CPC had disappeared, and a great purge had just been carried out in the Cultural Revolution. Consequently, the 1975 constitution reflects the uncertainties, antagonism, and anxiety then rife among leaders of the CPC. It characterized China as "a socialist state under proletarian dictatorship" and repeatedly referred to the superior role of the CPC over the Chinese state and society. In the 1975 constitution the Chinese state was deprived of a presidency, and no clear references were made to election of a people's congress. In contrast to 1954, the constitution of 1975 consisted of only thirty articles. In other words, the second constitution is more programmatic than organic. Overall the 1975 constitution symbolized Mao's preoccupation with the absolute power of the CPC, i.e., Mao himself, and his desire for a radical change in Chinese society. So the role of the state was minimized in 1975.[3]

The third constitution was adopted in 1978 and represented another important change in Chinese political development. By then Mao had died and the Gang of Four had been arrested. A degree of "de-radicalization" had already taken place in Chinese politics, economics, and society. But the leadership of the CPC was still in the hands of those who owed their national position to Mao and the Cultural Revolution as exemplified in the career of Hua Guofeng, then chairman of the CPC. Consequently, the 1978 constitution, though it had twice as many articles as the 1975 constitution, was still more programmatic than organic. The 1978 constitution retained the 1975 prescription of the Chinese state—"a socialist state of the dictatorship of the proletariat" —and the superior role of the CPC was stated at the outset. In the 1978 constitution the Chinese state remained without a president. On the other hand, more ground was gained in the organic part of the 1978 constitution by such moves as revival of the judiciary and reaffirmation of the election of People's Congress members by secret ballot.[4] Thus the constitution of 1978 marked another transition in Chinese politics, albeit going from revolution back to normalcy.

The 1982 constitution, the latest, is often compared rather than contrasted with the 1954 constitution. Both marked the end of social unrest and the beginning of a new era of orderly nation building. By 1982 the leftists had been eliminated from the national leadership of the CPC. The reformist group led by Deng Xiaoping and Hu Yaobang had taken over the helm of the party. The 1982 constitution stands for the present emphasis on stability and unity, under which the four modernizations would be carried out. The state of China is once more, in the present constitution, "a socialist state under the people's democratic dictatorship," and the presidency of the PRC is restored. No reference is made to the preeminent role of the CPC though it declares that the state of "people's democratic dictatorship" is "led by the working class." Moreover, article 5 of the present constitution states: "All state organs, the armed forces, *all political parties* and public organizations . . . must abide by the Constitution and the law" (emphasis added).[5] Naturally all the "comely" articles on the civil liberties of Chinese citizens have been restored (with the significant deletion of workers' right to strike). A longer document than the constitution of 1954, with 138 articles, the 1982 one is obviously more organic than programmatic.

The changes in the Chinese constitution provide an example of how a Western institution undergoes a drastic transformation in its function when it is transplanted into another culture. Like the first constitution of Japan, which was presented to Japanese as "a gift of the emperor," so the constitution of the PRC is a gift of the CPC, which may rescind it as the party wishes.

Underlying the fluidity of the Chinese constitution is a basic conflict between the CPC's design to change Chinese society fundamentally and the original function of a constitution, i.e., providing a stable infrastructure for a nation. For example, Mao Zedong in a speech on the first constitution in 1954 stated, on the one hand, that a constitution "is a set of general rules, it is the fundamental law," but on the other hand, he put greater stress on the propaganda effect of a constitution: "In the form of the constitution . . . there will be a clear course before the people of the whole country and they will feel sure they have a clear, definite and correct path to follow—this will heighten their enthusiasm."[6] Also, "We must now unite the people of the whole country and unite all the forces that can and should be united in the struggle to build a great socialist country. *And the constitution has been drawn up specifically for this purpose*" (emphasis added).[7] A more interesting statement on the Chinese constitution was made by Mao in 1958 when he mobilized the whole nation to organize the people's commune:

> Has the people's commune done any damage to the constitution? For example, on the principle of merging government function with the commune, the National People's Congress did not legislate it and it is not mentioned in the constitution. Many articles in the constitution are out of date. But we shall not revise the constitution. After we have overtaken the United States then we shall produce a written constitution. At present we follow the American way, having an unwritten constitution. The constitution of the United States is an unwritten one [*sic*], being patched up piece by piece.[8]

In other words, to Mao the 1954 constitution was an unwritten one, and only after he completed a radical transformation of Chinese society and "overtaken the United States" did he intend to sanction a written constitution.

Undoubtedly, at present the reformist leaders of the CPC are serious about gaining stability and unity by means of the constitution. But the tension between the CPC's impulse to mobilize society as it sees fit and the organic function of a constitution persists. In addition, the Chinese public has learned to treat the constitution as a partisan document. After the adoption of the present constitution in 1982, even among the delegates of the NPC there were doubts about the CPC's seriousness toward it, and some suggested establishing a separate organization to supervise its implementation.[9]

THE NATIONAL PEOPLE'S CONGRESS

Next to the Chinese constitution, the National People's Congress (NPC) is another major "dignified" part of Chinese government apparatus. Like those of the constitution, the functions of the NPC are domestically to "heighten the enthusiasm" of the population and internationally to "gain world membership." Over the decades, however, the original functions of the NPC, similar to those of the constitution, have been superseded by use of the congress for partisan purpose.

According to the latest Chinese constitution, the NPC "is the highest organ of state power," and the NPC and the Standing Committee together "exercise the legislative power of the state."[10] Members of the NPC are not directly elected by voters but are ostensibly "elected" by the delegates of provincial (and autonomous region) people's congresses and delegates of the people's congresses of three "special municipalities," i.e., Shanghai, Peking, and Tianjin. Furthermore, two special groups "elect" their own NPC delegates: the armed forces and ethnic minorities. Based on the latest practice, the delegate-voter ratios are one NPC delegate for every 1,040,000 village residents and one for every 130,000 city residents.[11] The present and Sixth NPC was convened in June 1983 with 2,977 delegates, a reduction of 523 delegates from the previous congress in response to some delegates' request to streamline the NPC to make it more efficient.

In theory, the NPC meets once every year to pass major legislation. In practice, says a long-time student of Chinese Communist affairs, "parliaments in Communist countries are usually summoned to approve the will of a body of rulers well entrenched in power."[12] The lack of representation in the NPC can be shown in numerous ways. First of all, the deputies are actually coopted. That is, in every locality a CPC secretary selects prominent people from every sector of society to be deputies to the NPC—model workers, successful film actors or actresses, athletes, engineers, professors, and meritorious teachers. "Selection of deputies to the people's congress," wrote a reader to the official *People's Daily,* "has become a simple form of political patronage. Gaining some merits in work or fame in society or having made historical contributions are sufficient bases for being elected as people's deputies. Very little consideration is given to whether deputies are capable of speaking on behalf of the people or struggling against phenomena that harm the interest of the people."[13] After being thus "elected," a deputy is, technically speaking, required to conduct "tours of inspection" of his locality to gather information on society. These tours, however, are highly orchestrated affairs. Deputies go in groups like tourists; party or state functionaries receive them in formal briefing sessions. According to a Shanghai deputy, "Since local officials have prepared for these tours, one is not likely to uncover any problem."[14] Thus it is not surprising to hear the account of two deputies from the province of Guizhou on their normal activity: "Except for going to the provincial capital and Peking once each year to attend a congressional session we have nothing else to do."[15] When attending a formal session, the deputies follow the routine of listening to formal reports by top leaders on every aspect of governmental function. After that the deputies go into small-group discussions, organized on the basis of locality. Even in small-group sessions there are seldom really free exchanges or articulation of views because each group is led by a prominent CPC leader. Hence a small-group session becomes another occasion for deputies to pay respect to CPC leadership. During the 1980 session of the NPC the Chinese press unprecedentedly, and obviously for partisan reasons, printed speeches of deputies, who were using this rare opportunity to air their views. A deputy from the special municipality of Tianjin complained about their formalistic role play:

> I do not agree to the way of our congress during the "cultural revolution" in which so many people read from prepared texts. At present, we listen to two or three reports plus group discussion. That completes our work. I do not like this either. Many important problems such as price of commodities and wages are of concern to all of us. The departments in charge of these problems should have discussed it with us so we could report back to the masses.[16]

Whenever an NPC meets, the Chinese press dutifully reports the number of motions made by the deputies, though the motions are never described in any detail, and neither is there any account of the disposal of these motions. For example, the second session of the Fifth NPC in 1980 made 1,890 motions. Among these some were reported to have been immediately adopted, such as suspension of an industrial exhibit on the thirtieth anniversary of the PRC, opening up of the NPC assembly hall to the public for tours, abolishment of bodyguards for ministers, and control of film shows "for internal review."[17] One cannot but note the conformity of these "motions" to the measures of the CPC taken at that time, prior to the NPC session, to control the privileges of high-ranking party cadres.

Structurally, the NPC is not capable of performing its function as the highest legislature of China, with more than two thousand deputies meeting for one week a year. So the NPC delegates its "efficient" functions to the Standing Committee, which at present consists of 155 members. The Standing Committee handles day-to-day affairs of the NPC when the latter is not in session. Since the death of Mao and the beginning of the reform era under Deng Xiaoping, the Standing Committee of the NPC has gained a new lease on life and, at least on paper, has enlarged power in such areas as interpreting the constitution, enacting statutes, examining the budget, annulling rules and regulations of national and local government, and appointing ministers and judicial authorities when the NPC is not in session.[18]

One must put the wide range of the formal functions of the NPC Standing Committee in perspective by pointing out that even if these functions were really performed by the Standing Committee, there still would not be a division of authority between the CPC and the NPC since the control of the NPC Standing Committee is in the hands of CPC leaders. The Standing Committee is composed of a chairman, a number of vice-chairmen, a secretary-general, and ordinary members. As presently constituted, the Standing Committee is headed by Peng Zhen, a member of the CPC Politburo and former mayor of Peking before the Cultural Revolution. Of the twenty vice-chairmen of the Standing Committee, ten are members of the CPC Central Committee, including three generals of the People's Liberation Army. The background of the remaining ten members of the present Standing Committee of the NPC represents the united front strategy of the CPC. Seven of the ten non-CPC vice-chairmen of the Standing Committee are from the "democratic parties" of China (more on these parties in a later chapter). Two vice-chairmen are Tibetan, one being a member of the People's Congress of the Tibetan Autonomous Region and the other a representative of the Tibetans residing in the province of Qinghai and the honorary chairman of the Chinese Buddhists Association. The last non-CPC chairman of the Standing Committee is the executive chairman of the Chinese Academy of Sciences. The composition of the Standing Committee of the NPC thus symbolizes present CPC leaders' strategy of socialist democracy under the leadership of the CPC to accomplish four modernizations.

In addition to the Standing Committee of the NPC, another "efficient" arm of the congress is the special committee. Before 1982 every session of the NPC authorized the organization of a Nationalities Committee, a Budget Committee, and a Motions Examination Committee. Now a new group of special committees has been organized such as Law Committee, Finance and Economic Committee, Education, Science, Culture, and Public Health Committee, Foreign Affairs Committee, and Overseas Chinese Committee. According to the present constitution, "the special committees examine, discuss, and draw up relevant bills and draft resolutions." It is almost a foregone conclusion that the head of each special committee is a top-ranking CPC leader. For example, the Sixth People's Congress of June 1983 "elected" the most important special committee of all: the Central Military Commission, supposedly the highest state organization in military affairs. But the membership of this commission, which is headed by Deng Xiaoping, overlaps completely with that of the CPC Central Military Commission.[19] The other special committees of the NPC are actually supplements to the staff departments of the Central Committee of the CPC.

The NPC as a whole, like the Chinese constitution, has been used by the CPC as another medium of esoteric political communication. Throughout the brief history of the NPC, the ruling factions of the CPC never hesitated to use the NPC for partisan purposes. In the fourth session of the first NPC in July 1957, for example, according to an eye-witness account, deputies' small-group discussions had been turned into "struggle meetings" against rightists, i.e., critics of the CPC during the Hundred Flowers Blooming campaign.[20] In 1961, admidst starvation in the countryside, serious food shortages in the cities, and unrest in the army, the NPC was not convened. When the 1962 session of the NPC met, the sessions were conducted secretly, and texts of addresses were not published. The attendance at the meetings was unusually low.[21] From 1965 to 1974 no NPC was convened since that was during the Cultural Revolution. When the Fifth NPC met in January 1975, no public notice of it was given until after the congress had ended. "Propaganda began after the Congress, not before."[22] Chinese Communists, or for that matter Communists in general, are adept in setting up "front" organizations to realize their goal of turning an existing and non-Communist organization into an auxiliary of the party. For that reason they are careful even with an organization like the NPC, which is entirely orchestrated by the Communist party, so that no individual, let alone group, could turn the tables on the CPC.

Even after the death of Mao and the beginning of Deng's reform administration, partisan use of the NPC continued. The unprecedented practice of publishing verbatim speeches of the deputies of the third session of the Fifth NPC in September 1980 was clearly designed to create the image of Deng's being "for democracy" and thereby isolate the remnants of leftists in the CPC, such as Hua Guofeng. After Hua's resignation, speeches in sessions of the NPC were no longer critical but uniformly supportive of present CPC leadership and its programs. The composition of the Sixth NPC in June 1983 provided a good example of CPC orchestration of the NPC to carry out the current party line of promoting "younger, knowledgeable, and specialist" cadres. First of all, of the 2,977 deputies to the Sixth NPC, 76.5 percent were newly "elected." Second, the social composition of deputies showed an overrepresentation of intellectuals and members of "democratic parties," 23.5 and 18.2 percent respectively. The great majority of Chinese—workers and peasants—account for only 26.6 percent of the total. Third, scientific, technical, and other modern professions constitute 44.5 percent. Also these are mostly in the 30-to-40-year-old group.[23] Whereas in Western democracies parliaments are valued for both their substantive (aggregation of interest) and symbolic (government by the people) role in society, in the PRC, the People's Congress is valued solely for its symbolic function. A Chinese scientist expressed this well when referring to the People's Congress: "Of course, it's a rubber-stamp for the party, but then you don't know what the party is going to do until the Congress has rubber-stamped it."[24] Furthermore, in Western democracies the symbolic role of a parliament is anchored on its substantive function; in the PRC, the symbolic use of the People's Congress by the CPC is not rested on substantive function. Hence the Chinese scientist's statement is not entirely valid since the CPC, especially the Secretariat, legislates for China with or without the NPC rubber-stamp.

PRESIDENCY OF THE PRC

The worldly orientation of present CPC leaders that has produced a new constitution and stressed the formality of the NPC has also caused the resurrection of the presidency of the PRC. For fifteen years (1967-82) the Chinese national government was without a head. Under the 1954 constitution, the head of the government was the chairman of the Republic, a post that Mao Zedong held until 1959. After the debacle of the Great Leap Forward, Liu Shaoqi was chairman. The economic recovery under Liu's administration imparted a degree of charisma and substance to the chairmanship, inspiring Mao's subsequent purge of Liu in the Cultural Revolution and the abolishment of the chairmanship of the PRC. Now, as part of present CPC leaders' stress on normalcy and world membership, the head of state has been reinstated, albeit in the new title of president of the PRC. The Sixth NPC "elected" the seventy-four-year-old Li Xiannian as the current president of the PRC. Li is also a member of the Standing Committee of the CPC Politburo. A former Red Army general, Li had been a finance administrator since 1949.

In discussing the resurrection of the presidency of the Republic, Chinese Communist writers take pain to point out that the position is without substantive power and is almost entirely ritualistic. Thus, it is emphasized, the president does not have any administrative function, except for naming a candidate for the premiership for the NPC to approve (or, to be more exact, to acclaim). The rest of the president's functions are all of "broadcasting" nature: "confers state medals and titles of honor; issues orders of special pardons; proclaims martial law; proclaims a state of war; and issues mobilization orders."[25] The president also performs the routine of receiving foreign representation. Apparently, in their fear of a charismatic and substantive state authority apart from the CPC and their zeal in protecting the "unified leadership" of the CPC, present leaders of the CPC differ from Mao in degrees but not in kind.

STATE COUNCIL

So far, the three major state organizations, i.e., the constitution, People's Congress, and presidency of the PRC, are all dignified rather than efficient. The really efficient part of Chinese Communist national government is the State Council (*Guo Wu Yuan*), which according to the Chinese constitution, "is the executive body of the highest organ of state power; it is the highest organ of state administration." [26] The formal functions of the State Council are vast and among them are the following:

- to exercise unified leadership over the work of local organs of state administration at different levels throughout the country and to lay down the detailed division of functions and powers between the Central Government and the organs of state administration of provinces, autonomous regions, and municipalities directly under the Central Government
- to draw up and implement the plan for national economic and social development and the state budget
- to direct and administer economic work and urban and rural development
- to direct and administer the work concerning education, science, culture, public health, physical culture, and family planning
- to direct and administer the work concerning civil affairs, public security, judicial administration, supervision, and other related matters
- to conduct foreign affairs and conclude treaties and agreements with foreign states
- to direct and administer the building of national defense
- to direct and administer affairs concerning the nationalities and to safeguard the rights of minority nationalities and the right of autonomy of the national autonomous areas
- to protect the legitimate rights and interests of Chinese nationals residing abroad and protect the lawful rights and interests of returned overseas Chinese and of the family members of Chinese nationals residing abroad.[27]

The State Council, in short, is the "motor" of Chinese national development.

As it is presently constituted, the State Council consists of a premier—Zhao Ziyang—and four vice-premiers (all members of the CPC Central Committee), and nine state councilors (all members of the CPC Central Committee). The function of state councilors is to undertake whatever special tasks they are entrusted with by the premier or vice-premiers. The premier, vice-premiers, and state councilors convene "executive meetings" and comprise the highest decision-making body of the State Council.

As the national government of the PRC, the State Council has the usual ministries, commissions, and agencies that one finds in the executive branch of any government. But the "advanced" nature of centralization in the Chinese political system has made the State Council unique in its power over public affairs. Figure 5-1 shows the various ministries and other offices under the State Council. Some agencies, however, are only nominally under the jurisdiction of the State Council, being directly controlled by the CPC Central Committee. These are defense, justice, and public security (police). The State Council is primarily responsible for the economic development of China, especially heavy industry. Mao Zedong, for example, claimed in 1958 that the national leadership of the CPC (i.e., Mao himself), up until then, had monopolized

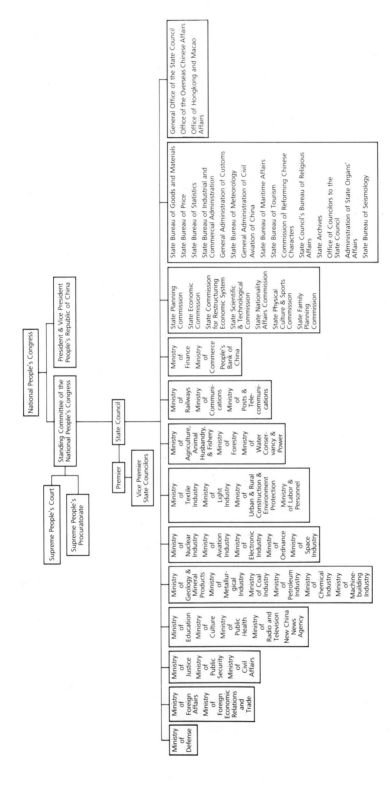

FIGURE 5-1 The national government of the People's Republic of China

decision making on both agricultural policy and "making revolution" (i.e., general political line), "the rest was in the hands of the State Council."[28]

The State Council leads other governmental apparatus in bureaucratism, which is exemplified by a high degree of compartmentalization of jurisdiction, an excess of hierarchical structure, and countless departmental heads and deputy heads. A high-ranking CPC leader disclosed that from 1950 to 1981 the number of ministries and commissions of the State Council grew from 34 to 100. State Council ministries and deputy ministries in 1981 numbered 1,000 and department directors, 5,000. In some agencies the number of deputy directors had grown to 20 or 30. As we discussed in connection with the development of the CPC, the growth in bureaucracy goes hand in hand with reduction of efficiency.[29] Against this background, a major streamlining program was implemented in April 1982 to trim the bureaucracy of the State Council. The result is that the ministries and commissions were cut back, from 52 to 41. The ministries and departmental directors were reduced by 67 and 43 percent respectively.[30] Nevertheless, one must point out that at least twice in the past, in 1958 and 1969, similar streamlining programs were carried out in the State Council. But as long as the basic principle of "major decisions' being monopolized by national leaders" and compartmentalization of jurisdiction remain in effect, bureaucratism is likely to return to the State Council. Almost inevitably, a new coordination agency will have to be created to connect the various ministries. Hence, in February 1983, not long after the reduction of ministries and commissions, the State Council created two more new offices, Commission for Soil Conservation and Leading Group of Science and Technology, whose function is to coordinate the work of ministries and departments performing similar tasks.[31]

In addition to bureaucratism, the State Council also exemplifies the merger of party and state leadership. As mentioned earlier, the premier, vice-premiers, and state councilors are all members of the CPC Central Committee. Among the forty-one ministries and commission directors, twenty-one are members of the CPC Central Committee, and seven are members of the CPC.[32] There is no reason to doubt that of the thirteen unaccounted for ministry and commission directors, CPC membership is not predominant. Despite all the talks on division of functions between the CPC and the state, in practice, party leaders are deeply involved in state administration.

ROLE OF THE STATE IN POLICY MAKING

In formal policy making the national leaders of the CPC always initiate and formulate any major policy. After that, the State Council administers the various programs required by a policy. Members of the NPC may or may not be involved in the formulation of programs, let alone initiate any legislation. The late Mao Zedong, for example, divided policy making into two parts: decisions and rules. Decisions are made in unspecified "meetings" at the highest echelon (most likely Standing Committee) of the CPC. After that, the Politburo makes some revisions of a decision, which is then made public quickly. But rules and regulations, said Mao, "are like secondary constitutions." They must first be put forth by the State Council in draft form and solicit opinions. Then a specific set of rules or regulations would be presented to the National People's Congress for legitimization.[33] In another instance, referring to the program of Forty Articles on Agriculture, Mao reported in 1957 that the forty articles were "from the political design institute of the CPC" (e.g., the Politburo) and had first been tried on an experimental basis for two years. After that, "the CPC will send it to the State Council and the State Council will present it to the National People's Congress."[34] Mao's statements applied, of course, to the "normal" time of the 1950s, before the Cultural Revolution.

Mao's passing has not changed the formal policy-making process of Chinese national politics. A Peking deputy of the National People's Congress reported in 1980: "At present, whatever decision is made by the central leadership of the party is then presented to the National People's Congress for discussion. [The National People's Congress] can hardly assume its role of being the highest organ of state power in this manner."[35] At most, the NPC contributes to policy making in working out specific rules. This is usually done by the special committees of the NPC, for specialists in legal matters are often appointed to these committees. Drafting specific rules of a program will probably be the main function of the NPC under the present CPC leadership. For example, following the CPC's decision in 1982 to transfer the formal administrative function of people's communes to township (*xiang*) government, the Law Committee of the NPC conducted opinion surveys among provincial, county, commune, and production team members. It sponsored symposiums to solicit expert opinions on the separation of function between commune and township government (more on this in a later chapter) and collected necessary source materials for basic research on this major decision, which virtually terminated the people's commune in the Chinese countryside.[36]

In the meantime, because of the overlap of party and state leadership in the State Council the power of the ministries is vast. It was disclosed in the NPC meeting of 1980 that a State Council minister often decides, by himself, on construction projects that cost tens of millions of dollars. "On major construction projects, decisions should not be made by this minister or that vice-premier. If he does not choose to report to the NPC, ignores opinions of others and insists on decisions made by one man or a minority, then what is the need for NPC?"[37]

NOTES

1. "Constitutional Merry-Go-Round," *Far Eastern Economic Review*, March 17, 1978, p. 19.

2. Xu Zhongde and Ho Huahui, "Our Study of Three Chinese Constitutions," *Wuhan Da Xue Xuebao*, no. 6 (1980), pp. 51–55.

3. "The Draft Constitution," *China News Analysis*, no. 823 (December 4, 1970), p. 3; Wang Shao-chi, "An Analysis of the Constitutional Rectification," *Chungkung Yenchiu* 9, no. 2 (February 10, 1975), 10.

4. *The Constitution of the People's Republic of China* (Peking: Foreign Languages Press, 1978).

5. "Constitution of the People's Republic of China," *Beijing Review* 25, no. 52 (December 27, 1982), 10–29.

6. *Selected Works of Mao Tse-Tung*, vol. V (Peking: Foreign Languages Press, 1977), p. 145.

7. Ibid., p. 146.

8. *Wan-sui*, no. 2, p. 257.

9. *RMRB*, December 7, 1982, p. 3.

10. *Constitution of the PRC*, p. 18.

11. Lu Hsiang, "Preliminary Analysis on Fifth Session of the Fifth People's Congress," *Chungkung Yenchiu* 16 (December 15, 1982), 32.

12. "The People's Congress, Part II," *China News Analysis*, no. 990 (February 14, 1975), p. 2.

13. *RMRB*, December 21, 1979, p. 3.

14. *RMRB*, September 9, 1980, p. 2.

15. *RMRB*, September 13, 1980, p. 4.

16. Ibid.

17. *RMRB,* September 5, 1980, p. 4.

18. *Constitution of the PRC,* pp. 20–21.

19. *RMRB,* June 21, 1983, p. 3.

20. Yen I, "I Witnessed That Frightening People's Congress," *Cheng Ming,* no. 36 (October 1980), pp. 34–35.

21. A. M. Halpern, "Between Plenums: A Second Look at the 1962 National People's Congress in China" (Santa Monica, Calif.: RAND Corporation, 1962).

22. "The People's Congress, Part I," *China News Analysis,* no. 989 (February 7, 1975), p. 2.

23. *RMRB,* May 10, 1983, p. 4; June 7, 1983, p. 1; June 16, 1983, p. 1; *Beijing Review* 26, no. 22 (May 30, 1983), 5.

24. *The New York Times,* December 14, 1981, p. 6.

25. Xiao Weiyun, "Reinstatement and Development of the Presidency of Our State," *RMRB,* December 28, 1982, p. 5.

26. *Constitution of the PRC,* p. 23.

27. Ibid.

28. *Wan-sui,* no. 2, p. 153.

29. *RMRB,* December 19, 1981, p. 4.

30. *RMRB,* April 27, 1981, p. 1.

31. *RMRB,* January 28, 1983, p. 1; *Ming Pao Daily News,* February 3, 1983, p. 3.

32. *RMRB,* May 5, 1983, p. 4.

33. *Wan-sui,* no. 2, p. 24.

34. Ibid., p. 141.

35. *RMRB,* September 12, 1980, p. 4.

36. *Nongye Jingji* (September 1982), p. 93.

37. *RMRB,* September 5, 1980, p. 2.

CHAPTER 6

Subnational Government and Politics

The powerful and unitary party-state machinery that we discussed in previous chapters rules over a vast and diverse Chinese landscape. Below the national government, China is divided into three levels of administration: the province, the county, and the township (replacing the commune). These divisions have been the most permanent institutions in Chinese history, surviving numerous domestic political regimes as well as alien conquerors. After the establishment of the PRC, Chinese Communist leaders added a new administrative division, the autonomous region, to govern the 67 million ethnic minorities of China.

Because of the richness and diversity of culture and economy in its various regions, mainland China has the potentiality of developing a vigorous local politics. The late Chairman Mao Zedong, for example, once remarked that China was composed of "twenty-eight nations, some big and some small, such as Tibet and Qinghai, which are sparsely populated."[1] Mao, of course, was referring to the twenty-one provinces, five autonomous regions, and two special municipalities, i.e., Peking and Shanghai. Since then the number of these "nations" within China has been increased to twenty-nine, for the city of Tianjin has become the third special municipality, i.e., under the direct administration of the national government of the PRC. Mao compared these administrative regions of China to nations because of the contrast in their size, population, resources, and economic development (see table 6-1). Take, for example, the contrast in population between Sichuan's 99.7 million and Tibet's 1.8 million. The differences in economic development among the provinces and regions are also dramatic. The official *Beijing (Peking) Review,* for example, speaks about the need for East-West dialogue in China because:

> the eleven coastal provinces, municipalities and autonomous regions, embracing 13 percent of the total national territory, contribute to 56 percent of the nation's total industrial and agricultural output value; the twelve provinces and autonomous regions in central China embrace 32 percent of the national territory and account for 40 percent of the total industrial and agricultural output

TABLE 6-1 Chinese provinces and population

NO.	UNITS AT THE PROVINCIAL LEVEL	CAPITAL	AREA (1,000 sq. km.)	POPULATION	UNITS AT THE PREFECTURAL LEVEL	CITIES	UNITS AT THE COUNTY LEVEL	DISTRICTS UNDER THE CITIES
	Total: 30		9,600	1,031,882,511	208	230	2,136	514
1	Beijing		16.8	9,230,687			9	10
2	Tianjin		11.3	7,764,141			5	13
3	Hebei Prov.	Shijiazhuang	180+	53,005,875	10	10	139	39
4	Shanxi Prov.	Taiyuan	156	25,291,389	7	7	101	15
5	Inner Mongolian Autonomous Region	Hohhot	1,200	19,274,279	9	10	79	13
6	Liaoning Prov.	Shenyang	140+	35,721,693	2	13	45	42
7	Jilin Prov.	Changchun	180+	22,560,053	4	9	37	9
8	Heilongjiang Prov.	Harbin	460+	32,665,546	7	12	66	61
9	Shanghai		6.2	11,859,748			10	12
10	Jiangsu Prov.	Nanjing	100+	60,521,114	7	11	64	33
11	Zhejiang Prov.	Hangzhou	100+	38,884,603	7	9	62	13
12	Anhui Prov.	Hefei	130+	49,665,724	8	12	70	34
13	Fujian Prov.	Fuzhou	120+	25,931,106	7	7	61	10
14	Jiangxi Prov.	Nanchang	160+	33,184,827	6	10	81	16
15	Shandong Prov.	Jinan	150+	74,419,054	9	9	106	21
16	Henan Prov.	Zhengzhou	167	74,422,739	10	17	111	34
17	Hubei Prov.	Wuhan	180+	47,804,150	8	11	73	13
18	Hunan Prov.	Changsha	210	54,008,851	11	14	89	22
19	Guangdong Prov.	Guangzhou	210+	59,299,220	9	14	96	18
20	Guangxi Zhuang Autonomous Region	Nanning	230+	36,420,960	8	7	80	17

TABLE 6-1 (cont.)

NO.	UNITS AT THE PROVINCIAL LEVEL	CAPITAL	AREA (1,000 sq. km.)	POPULATION	UNITS AT THE PREFECTURAL LEVEL	CITIES	UNITS AT THE COUNTY LEVEL	DISTRICTS UNDER THE CITIES
	Total: 30		9,600	1,031,882,511	208	230	2,136	514
21	Sichuan Prov.	Chengdu	560+	99,713,310	14	13	182	22
22	Guizhou Prov.	Guiyang	170+	28,552,997	7	5	79	5
23	Yunnan Prov.	Kunming	390+	32,533,817	15	6	123	4
24	Tibet Autonomous Region	Lhasa	1,200+	1,892,393	5	1	71	1
25	Shaanxi Prov.	Xian	200	28,904,423	7	6	91	11
26	Gansu Prov.	Lanzhou	450	19,569,261	10	5	73	6
27	Qinghai Prov.	Xining	720+	3,895,706	7	2	37	4
28	Ningxia Hui Autonomous Region	Yinchuan	60+	3,895,578	2	2	16	7
29	Xinjiang Uygur Autonomous Region	Urumqi	1,600+	13,081,681	12	8	80	9

Source: Beijing Review 26, no. 1 (January 3, 1983), 25.

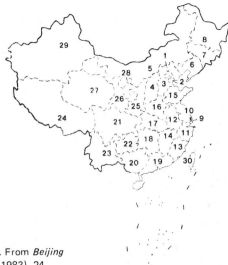

MAP 6-1 Chinese provinces. From *Beijing Review* 26, no. 1 (January 3, 1983), 24.

value. The six provinces and autonomous regions in the northwest make up 6 percent of the total population and 4 percent of the total industrial and agricultural output value.[2]

The diversity of Chinese provinces, however, has not resulted in a distinct local politics. As subsequent discussion will show, the very essence of CPC political culture and strategy is to nationalize local politics. Thus the government and politics in Chinese provinces, municipalities, and counties manifest the same characteristics that one sees in Chinese national politics, that is, the pro forma function of the legislature, CPC monopoly of decision making, and bureaucratism in administration.

In subsequent discussion we shall first describe the government and politics in general in Chinese provinces, municipalities, and counties under the rubric *local politics*. Then we shall deal with the ethnic minorities (the "non-Han" races) in the five autonomous regions.

LOCAL POLITICS

Legislature

The structure of provincial, municipal, and county governments in the PRC is modeled after that of the national government. Hence, at the topmost echelon of a local government is the same two-headed structure: a local people's congress—the legislature—and local people's government—the executive.

Deputies to provincial or special-municipality people's congresses are elected not directly by the people, but by people's congresses at the next lower level (county and city district, respectively). Their tenure is the same five years as that of deputies to the National People's Congress. As at the national level, a provincial, municipal, or county people's congress elects a standing committee to take care of the day-to-day affairs of the congress. The functions of a local people's congress are, first, to ensure the fulfillment of national policy and, second, to implement local policy. The present national constitution states that provincial and other local people's congresses may "adopt and issue resolutions and examine and decide on plans for local economic and cultural development and for the development of public services"[3] within the limits of their authority as prescribed by the constitution.

As presently constituted, local people's congresses cannot fully perform their formal functions. The number of deputies is too large, some provincial people's congresses having more than a thousand deputies.[4] The composition of the standing committee of provincial people's congresses is also characterized by too many members, averaging fifty to sixty, and most of the members are too advanced in age.[5] Moreover, the deputies to local people's congresses are elected in name only; most of them are made deputies to congresses because of their fame or accomplishments—model workers, actors, actresses, athletes, engineers, professors, and teachers. Membership in the standing committee is also used to retire some veteran CPC members. Consequently, whenever a local congressional standing committee convenes, the rate of absenteeism is high.[6] The standing committee is also handicapped by lack of regular funding. Moreover, Chinese press reports reveal utter confusion and an absence of rulings in the national constitution with regard to the division of legislative authority between provincial people's congresses, those below them, and local government, which is also empowered to enact "administrative rules and regulation." Finally, local populace and CPC leaders do not hide their opinion that local people's congresses are superfluous. "The Party Committee has already made decision, why should we go through the formality of people's congress?" is a common complaint against party and state officials.[7]

In spite of the foregoing, two recent developments in local people's congresses must be mentioned. First, the Chinese press suggests that since 1980 some local congressional deputies have taken their duties seriously and achieved positive results. In most cases these deal with local problems that require urgent improvement such as housing shortages, road repair, supply of running water, or inadequacy of public restaurants.[8] The municipal people's congresses at Peking and Shanghai are of special note. Both cities are already industrially advanced, and the population is of high educational standing. Concentrated in these two special municipalities are most of China's highly skilled people. The reformists of the CPC wish to gain credibility for their four modernizations program by first transforming Shanghai and Peking. The people's congresses in those two cities perform the function of mobilizing talents from all walks of life. Thus the activities of the deputies in these two cities have been publicized in the Chinese national press.[9] The standing committee of the people's congress of Shanghai, for example, has organized special subcommittees in charge of law, finance, urban planning, and science and culture.[10]

Local legislation also seems to have made a start. According to an official report, 296 local laws were passed in provinces, municipalities, and autonomous regions from November 1979 to June 1982. Of these, 30.7 percent deal with local law enforcement (e.g., public safety, control of market and price, anticorruption, and speculation), and 26.6 percent concern educational, cultural, and public health matters.[11]

The second noteworthy development on the local scene, which took place in 1980-81, is the direct election by rural residents of deputies to county people's congresses. Before that, only deputies to township (or commune) people's congresses were directly elected by rural residents. Township deputies, in turn, elected deputies to county people's congresses from their own members. In 1980, as a gesture of present CPC leaders' promise of democracy, county people's congresses were open to direct election by county residents. According to the Minister of Civil Affairs, who was in charge of organizing the election, the rate of voter turnout was 96.56 percent. An average of 1,249 voters elected one county deputy. Among the elected deputies, those of CPC members constituted 66.85 percent, but among those deputies elected as leaders of county government, CPC members amounted to 79.87 percent. These percentages, together with proportional representation of workers, peasants, cadres, intellectuals, military personnel, patriotic persons, and overseas Chinese among county deputies, cannot but lead one to suggest that the election was an orchestrated affair.[12] The key to the CPC's control of this election was in the nomination process. Though in theory a county voter could nominate anyone with three or more endorsing voters, the nomination was actually in the hands of the local CPC party committee, which went through three rounds of "discussions and consultations" with voters in each election district to finalize the list of candidates. As another indication of the orchestration of this county election, the Minister of Civil Affairs denounced some "who rejected socialist legalism, democracy under party leadership, disciplined and ordered democracy . . . in order to engage in the so-called campaigning."[13]

So much for the legislative aspect of local politics on mainland China.

The Executive: People's Government

The executive arm of local government in China is known as a people's government. The national constitution states: "Local people's government at different levels are the executive bodies of local organs of state power as well as the local organs of state administration at the corresponding level."[14] In other words, a local people's government in China is formally subordinated to two authorities, one being the national government—the State Council—and the other the local people's congress and its standing committee.[15] In practice, given the centralist strain in the Chinese political system and the pro forma nature of local legislatures, the people's government in a province, municipality, or county is more a subsidiary of national government than the executive arm of a local government.

Local government and politics in the PRC are generally characterized by supremacy of party committees, supremacy of the power of central or national authority, and bureaucracy.

The supremacy of CPC authority in local politics can be readily proved by referring readers to Chinese mass media. One rarely, if ever, reads or hears about the activities of the heads of local government, e.g., governors (*shengzhang*), mayors (*shizhang*), or county heads (*xianzhang*). Local news reports are almost entirely dominated by the party committee (*shenwei, shiwei,* or *xianwei*), especially by the personage of first party secretary (*diyi dangwei shuji*). The supremacy of party authority is formalized in that a first party secretary of any locality almost always occupies either the top position of local government or the second position. In cases where the governship, mayorship, or county leadership is given to a non-CPC member, then the deputy to these offices is certainly a member of the party secretariat of a locality, and no one questions the fact that the deputy is the boss. Recently the national leaders of the CPC launched a campaign to separate party from state functions, and more non-CPC leaders have been made heads or deputy heads of local government. But these non-CPC governmental leaders are powerless figures. A newspaper report illustrates this. The deputy mayor of the metropolitan city of Nanjing is a member of the China Democratic Construction Society, one of the "democratic parties" in the PRC. Once when the deputy mayor made suggestions to the municipal bureau of environmental protection, he was confronted by the bureau chief, who is also the secretary of the CPC branch in the bureau. The latter rejected the deputy mayor's suggestion by saying: "I represent the Communist party; whom does he [the deputy mayor] represent?"[16]

Though in each locality the area's CPC leaders have supremacy in local government and politics, all local authorities, party or state, are subordinated to central party and state authorities. The national government of the PRC has nationalized local politics. Even in time of severe crisis, as during the Cultural Revolution, provincial developments were effects of events at the national center. This has led one veteran China scholar to comment: "Each province has its own history, yet comparing the story of Chekiang [Zhejiang] with that of Kwangtung [Guangdong] . . . one discovers that we are dealing not with local problems but with a huge national issue. China, even in her trials, is one."[17] The Chinese press takes care to maintain a centralist or national perspective in reporting provincial or local developments. One comes frequently across the reference: "Directives from the Center followed by provincial Party Committee's decision."[18]

The national authorities control local government and politics through the centralized structure of the CPC and the centrally planned economy. The state constitution describes the functions of local governments ambiguously:

> Local people's governments at and above the county level, *within the limits of their authority as prescribed by law,* conduct the administrative work concerning the economy, education, science, culture, public health, physical culture, urban and rural development, finance, civil affairs, public security, nationalities affairs, judicial administration, supervision and family planning in their respective administrative areas . . . [emphasis added].[19]

However, the centralized economy of the PRC leaves little opportunity for local governments to develop their culture and economy. Wan Li, former governor of Anhui Province and presently a member of the Central Secretariat of the CPC Central Committee, spoke candidly to a delegation of Japanese journalists in 1979:

> The size of our province is larger than any county of Japan but the power of provincial governor here is less than a county head in Japan. Take, for instance, the resources of this province. We have rich minerals underground and if we exploit it, the economy of this province will expand greatly. Though we have applied for fund from the Center, we do not know when or whether we will obtain it. *We hand over almost our entire income to the state.* The fund that this province can use by itself is very limited. We are now discussing with the Center, trying to gain more power for the province [emphasis added].[20]

The first secretary of the Fujian Provincial Party Committee spoke in a similar vein on the backwardness of the Fujian economy:

> We must firmly take stock of the condition of this province. The average per capita income of Fujian is one-fourth lower than that of the whole nation. But the rate of population growth in Fujian is one-fourth higher than the whole country. With these two contrasts is there any wonder as to the backwardness of Fujian? Because of Fujian's being at the front line [opposing Taiwan], the state did not undertake any major construction in Fujian for the past thirty years. So what weight does Fujian have [in national economy]?[21]

Whereas in the cases of Anhui and Fujian mentioned above the weight of Chinese national government is felt locally in the form of "omission," in other provinces and localities, the power of central government is shown in the form of "commission." The latter refers to those provinces that have been specially favored by national party or state leaders. For example, the three northeastern provinces of Liaoning, Heilongjiang, and Jilin, the northern province of Shanxi, and the central China province of Henan, either because of economic or political reasons or both, had established a special client relationship with Mao long before 1976. Consequently, the party elites of these provinces had substantial resources in their hands for construction. The evidence of that comes from several major cases of graft and corruption in those provinces, which were exposed after the death of Mao. The former mayor of the city of Luda of Liaoning Province, for example, was accused of embezzling public funds to build sixty-four unauthorized buildings, including twenty-eight club houses and a score of office buildings, theatres, and department stores.[22] In Henan Province, present CPC leaders discovered extensive financial irregularity. The entire party committee of a provincial district in Henan was accused of embezzling more than $103 million from a flood-relief fund and engaging in large-scale unauthorized construction projects, including private mansions, club houses, and new office buildings (nicknamed Wall Street).[23] Since 1964 the province of Shanxi had been given substantial state funding because its Dazhai Production Brigade was designated by Mao as a national model. The brigade "received enormous help in the form of material, funds, and manpower from the state and various departments."[24]

The power of central government in the provincial and municipal governments of China also manifests itself structurally. The problem of bureaucratism—e.g., bloated organization, compartmentalization, and multiple layers—which is associated with national government, also plagues local governments. A deputy from Shaanxi Province testified that "seeing that the State Council has 108 offices, the provincial government of Shaanxi also sets up 108 bureaus and offices, an increase by 30 from pre-Cultural Revolution days."[25] A Gansu party official further revealed that emulation of central governmental structure by provincial leaders is for a specific and gainful purpose. As he put it, "Whatever ministry there is in the national government, our province creates a corresponding bureau. The lower governmental structure seeks to parallel the structure of upper government so as to facilitate their acquisition of funds."[26] Municipal governments are no exception to the rule. For example, the city of Xianyang of Shaanxi Province has been reported by the Chinese press as a typical case of municipal bureaucracy. At present, the Xianyang city government has fifty regular offices and fifty-seven "temporary" offices. Fifty-two of the temporary offices duplicate the functions of regular offices. There is a regular Bureau for Agriculture and Forestry, but among the temporary offices there are separate offices each for cotton, pig breeding, domestic animals, and vegetables. In 1965 the total number of the employees of the Xianyang municipal government was 462. By 1979 the number had increased to 1,076.[27]

Hence, the politics of local governments in the PRC is predominantly administrative in essence and bureaucratic in form. The majority of Chinese local elites are preoccupied by bureaucratic busy work, consisting mainly of red tape, endless meetings, and much paperwork. A Chinese writer reported in 1981 that a proposal or application typically went through twelve steps inside a Chinese bureaucracy before a response was given. Two of the twelve steps were the real bottlenecks. The first one was "comments by deputies." A Chinese office head was often assisted by a large number of deputies, from six to double digit. Every decision had to be commented on by these deputies. That was the bottleneck in terms of time. The second hurdle was "consultation with concerned persons." As Chinese bureaucracy is highly compartmentalized, every decision had to be coordinated with numerous other departments, each under a separate chain of command. A proposal or application was, more often than not, stalled at this point and went no further. That was a bottleneck in terms of space. The Chinese bureaucratic pipe was clogged there for months.[28]

In 1983 Chinese national authorities commenced an antibureaucracy campaign aimed at reducing provincial and municipal bureaucracy. As had been done in the State Council, offices of similar functions were merged and unnecessary agencies abolished, thus reducing the number of departments in provincial and municipal governments. The number of deputies was reduced to two or, at most, four.[29] But another measure tends to enlarge the bureaucracy of a selected number of cities. Some highly industrialized municipalities on the coast are now required to administer counties, which used to be subordinate to provincial governments. In this way the leaders of the PRC hope to speed up the process of urbanization in the Chinese countryside.[30]

A recent development in the PRC local governmental structure, as in the legislature, may signal the beginning of a more diversified and vigorous local politics. Reform in the centralized economic system since the death of Mao has allowed provinces to use their resources to develop a more specialized economy. This is especially valuable with regard to eastern and coastal provinces, which are permitted to conduct trade with Western nations. The provinces of Guangdong and Fujian have already constructed a special economic zone to attract foreign or overseas-Chinese investment. In the reorganization of the provincial government of Fujian, for example, economic reform and foreign trade are greatly stressed. Fujian now has its own commission for foreign trade and finance. To cope with the complications brought by private investment from overseas Chinese in Fujian, the provincial government has organized a committee on the reform of the economic system, a center for research on provincial economy, and a center for research on economic law.[31] In the special economic zone of Shenzhen in Guangdong Province, a non-Socialist type of management and production has been installed.[32] If this trend of provincial specialization continues in the future and is extended to all the provinces, it is a potentiality for a more diversified local politics.

MINORITY NATIONALITIES

A unique aspect of Chinese local politics concerns areas where members of non-Chinese or "non-Han" races live. According to the latest census of July 1982, there are fifty such races totaling 67,233,254, which is 6.7 percent of the national population.[33] Chinese leaders often point out that though they are a true minority in China, the non-Han races occupy 50 to 60 percent of Chinese territory. Moreover, the minorities reside in strategically important border areas, such as Inner Mongolia (bordering the Soviet-allied Mongolian People's Republic), Xianjiang (bordering Soviet Kazakh SSR), and Tibet. Nowadays, however, it is no longer meaningful to talk about the non-Han races' occupying 50 to 60 percent of Chinese territory since large-scale colonization of the ethnic minority areas by Chinese has already taken place. In Inner Mongolia, for example, the Chinese are in the majority and in Xinjiang the Chinese population has increased from 25 percent in 1949 to 41 percent today.[34]

Both in population and settlement pattern the minority races of China vary a great deal. Fifteen of the minority races number over a million, according to the

TABLE 6-2   Ethnic minorities in China with populations over one million

RACE	POPULATION (1982)	RESIDENCE (IN PROVINCE)
Zhuang	13,378,162	Guangxi
Hui	7,219,352	Ningxia, Gansu, Yunnan
Uygur	5,957,112	Xingjiang
Yi	5,453,448	Sichuan, Yunnan
Maio	5,030,897	Guizhou, Hunan
Manchu	4,299,159	Northeast China, Inner Mongolia
Tibetan	3,870,068	Tibet, Sichuan, Yunnan, Qinghai
Mongol	3,411,657	Inner Mongolia, Gansu, Northeast China
Tujia	2,832,743	Hunan, Hubei, Sichuan, Guizhou
Buyi	2,120,469	Guizhou
Korean	1,763,870	Jilin
Dong	1,425,100	Guizhou, Hunan, Guangxi
Yao	1,402,676	Guangxi, Hunan, Guangdong, Yunnan
Bai	1,131,124	Yunnan
Hani	1,058,836	Yunnan

Source: *RMRB*, October 29, 1982, p. 4; *China News Analysis* 569 (June 18, 1965).

latest census, and their resident pattern ranges from concentrated to scattered (see table 6-2). According to Ulanhu, the PRC's highest authority on the ethnic-minority question and himself a Mongol: "Historically, the various nationalities of China moved frequently from place to place and inhabited each other's areas. This practice gradually gave rise to a situation in which some nationalities lived in homogeneous communities of various sizes, or settled in isolated areas. But many immigrated to each other's territories and coinhabited one area."[35] The government of the PRC has not yet completed identification of all the minority races. As late as June 1979, the State Council formally acknowledged the existence of one Jinuo race, concentrated in Yunnan Province and numbering ten thousand.[36] The social structure and economic development of the minority races naturally differ drastically from each other and from the Chinese race. According to a Chinese Communist source, in 1949 about 30 million (out of a total 35,320,360) of the minority peoples were more or less at the social and economic level of the Chinese people around them, about one million were still at "slave economy" level, while 700,000 were still "primitive."[37]

To integrate these nationalities into China, the PRC government organized a three-tier system: autonomous regions (*zizhiqu*), autonomous prefectures (*zizhizhou*), and autonomous counties (*zizhixian*). The relationship of this three-tier system to the provinces and other administrative divisions in the rest of China is shown in figure 6-1. There are presently five autonomous regions: Inner Mongolia, Guangxi Zhuang, Tibet, Ningxia Hui, and Xinjiang Uygur. The rest of the nationalities have been grouped into twenty-nine autonomous districts and seventy autonomous counties.[38] However, owing partly to the interpenetration of the races and partly to the CPC's divide-and-rule technique, an autonomous unit does not necessarily include only a single race.

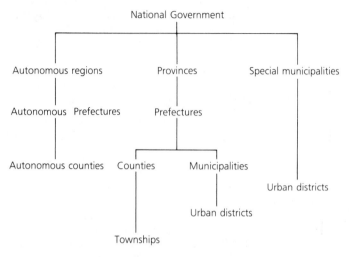

FIGURE 6-1   Levels of local government in the PRC

In some instances one race is scattered in several autonomous districts, and in other cases, several races are grouped in one unit.[39] The internal structure of these autonomous administrative units is no different from that of the provinces, municipalities, and counties in China proper. Each autonomous unit is headed by a people's congress and a people's government. However, the state constitution stipulates that: "The chairmanship and vice-chairmanships of the standing committee of the people's congress of an autonomous region, prefecture, or county shall include a citizen or citizens of the nationality or nationalities exercising regional autonomy in the area concerned."[40] Further, the head of the people's government of an autonomous area must also be "a citizen of the nationality, or of one of the nationalities" in the area.[41]

Now the crucial question is, How autonomous are the autonomous regions, districts, and counties? According to a leading **PRC** official in charge of minority nationalities, *autonomy* refers to (1) government by indigenous leaders, (2) the right to use native language in official business, communication, and teaching, (3) policy in conformity to native conditions, (4) local legislation (it may not contravene the state constitution), (5) financial autonomy greater than corresponding administrative units in China proper, (6) greater control over forests, pastures, and minerals than corresponding administrative units have in China proper, (7) the right to conduct foreign trade on the border, (8) development of indigenous culture, science, and education, and (9) after due notice to the central government, the right to revise or cancel a national program if it does not conform to local needs or conditions.[42] In practice, Chinese policy toward the autonomous areas has differed not only from period to period and in various aspects but also from one race to another.

Generally speaking, before 1957 the CPC followed a "soft" policy toward the ethnic minorities, specifically in terms of coopting the existing native elite into the new autonomous political structure, allowing use of native languages and at the same time open criticism of "great-Han chauvinism" on the part of Chinese cadres. Underneath the soft appeal, however, was a program of "socialist transformation," which the CPC launched in 1952 in ethnic-minority areas, with the single exception of Tibet. In response to this radical change in their way of life, which included such things as land reform and organization of agricultural cooperatives (collectives), the ethnic minorities, elite and commoners alike, expressed strong opposition during the 1957 Hundred Flowers Blooming campaign. To counter this opposition the CPC resorted to a "hard" policy toward minority nationalities. Now instead of denouncing "great-Han chauvinism," Chinese Communist authorities commenced a campaign of "anti-local nationalism." Many native leaders in autonomous regions were denounced and summarily dismissed from formal positions. The CPC authorities followed that with an acceleration of assimilation, mainly by carrying out more socialization programs in minority-nationality areas and forcibly altering the languages of minorities in order to integrate them with the Chinese language. This hard policy continued without letup until 1961, when the entire nation suffered from a severe agricultural crisis, famine, and death due to starvation, the consequence of the Great Leap Forward program of 1958-60. So the CPC switched back to a soft policy in 1962-64. Beginning in 1965, another hard policy, and an extreme one at that, was carried out as part of the Cultural Revolution. Throughout this long period of 1965-76 the left-wing extremists of the CPC headed by Mao advocated the thesis that the nationality problem was, in the last analysis, a class question. According to this "theory," there is no conflict, or even difference, between the Chinese and non-Chinese proletariat, the only difference being between all proletariat and bourgeoisie, irrespective of nationality. Under that interpretation, the leftists of the CPC forbade the use of native language in autonomous areas, virtually eliminated indigenous literature, art, and music, and conducted a class struggle in ethnic areas much as the CPC had in the Chinese population. In the meantime, the minority races, regardless of their social structure or economic condition, were made to adopt people's communes. This hard policy ended with the death of Mao, the arrest of the Gang of Four in 1976, and the rise to power of the reformist faction of the CPC in 1978. The present leaders of the CPC have made a public commitment to abide by a genuine autonomy policy toward the ethnic minorities in China, especially in Tibet, where local nationalism is the strongest.

Concerning each aspect of the autonomy program, it is clear that from the start the CPC had no intention of sharing decision-making power with indigenous leaders of ethnic minorities. Though the Chinese press continuously reports on the "cultivation of minority-nationality cadres," after thirty years, they constitute only 3 to 5 percent of the total number of cadres.[43] The monopoly of decision making in autonomous units by Chinese cadres was one of the things most frequently complained about during the 1957 "free speech" period. From almost every autonomous area came the demand for organizing political parties representing ethnic minorities since the CPC was regarded as "a party for Chinese."[44] There were also demands for a Soviet-type federation in which each nationality would form an independent "union republic."[45]

Though CPC policy toward autonomy in language and culture has fluctuated from period to period, there has been a continuing program to assimilate ethnic minorities. The method the CPC has used is to create written languages for the many races that have only oral traditions and "reform" the languages of other races. In 1965, for example, the CPC forced the Turkic people of Xinjiang to adopt a Chinese-devised Latinized alphabet, replacing the Arabic script of the natives.[46] During the leftist era of 1965-76 suppression of indigenous language and culture in autonomous areas became extreme. "Mongolian cadres did not dare to speak Mongolian; Mongolian teachers did not dare to use Mongolian to teach; and Mongolian actors and actresses did not dare to sing in Mongolian; otherwise they would run the risk of being accused of becoming elements for the separation of nationalities!"[47] Great numbers of minority-nationality books were burned. The library at Northwest Nationality Institute lost 600,000 volumes.[48] Under the great terror of the left, singing folk songs of minority nationalities was a crime punishable by prison sentence.[49] In 1978 delegates to a national conference on the literature of minority nationalities appealed to the government and the public for "urgent rescue" of the literary works of minority nationalities, for as the conference stated it, these works were "on the brink of extermination."[50] That there was destruction of religious institutions and temples in Tibet and elsewhere during the Cultural Revolution is now common knowledge in and out of China.

Given the foregoing, it is not surprising that in social and economic policy there is little autonomy for the minority nationalities in China. Though delayed here and there, the minority races in the PRC went through all the socialization measures that the CPC carried out in China proper. In some areas, such as the agricultural regions of Inner Mongolia, Xinjiang, Gansu, Ningxia, and Guizhou, land reform was carried out in 1952 using the same methods and concepts in ethnic areas as in Chinese areas. The Tibetans living in Sichuan and the smaller ethnic groups in Yunnan underwent similar land reform in 1956. Because of their nomadic nature, the pastoral peoples in Inner Mongolia, Xinjiang, Qinghai, Gansu, and Sichuan were organized into cooperatives in 1956. After its 1959 armed rebellion was suppressed, Tibet underwent "socialization." It was the socialization process that provoked an upsurge of "local nationalism" in 1957, which, said an official report, had "reached a very dangerous point."[51] The sentiments of the minority races were well expressed by the Hui people in Gansu Province: "Cooperativization [sic] . . . undermines our customs and practices [and] destroys our national characteristics."[52]

"The main lesson to be learned," says a long-time scholar on Chinese internal affairs, "is that the territories of the minorities are treated exactly like those inhabited by Chinese only."[53] "Autonomy never meant any kind of administrative independence; it designated only the peculiar population situation of a place."[54]

The following is a comment to balance the discussion so far. Communist leaders in charge of nationality affairs invariably present statistics. From Ulanhu, we learn:

> Since the founding of the People's Republic, socialist construction has made advances in various national autonomous areas. The total output value of industry, agriculture, and animal husbandry in the national autonomous areas in 1979 was 10.26 times that of 1949. Compared with 1952, the enrollment of students of minority nationalities in 1979 was up 13.9-fold in universities, 24.16-fold in middle schools, and 6-fold in primary schools. These achievements would have been unobtainable without the policy of national regional autonomy.[55]

These statistics are not very informative as they do not tell us about the gap between the ethnic minorities and the Chinese, the quality of achievement, or who are the actual beneficiaries of the expansion of industry. What we do know is that the Chinese press still talks about the urgent need to alter "poverty and difficulty" in minority-nationality areas of the PRC.[56] According to another Chinese author, writing in the authoritative *Hongqi (Red Flag),* organ of the CPC Central Committee: "From statistical charts, the number of schools and students [in ethnic minority areas] has gone up. But the rate of securing students in continuing education and that of insuring the qualification of graduates have gone down. So the overall quality of education has declined."[57] With regard to the industrial development in the minority-nationality areas, an article in the *Guangming Ribao,* a paper for a scholarly readership, reported in 1981 that the gross industrial output of Inner Mongolia, Ningxia, Xinjiang, Tibet, Guangxi, Qinghai, Guizhou, Yunnan, and Gansu amounted to 63.3 percent of the industrial output of the city of Shanghai.[58] At the same time, the Chinese press reported extensive ecological destruction of pastoral lands in Inner Mongolia and elsewhere because of industrial development by Chinese officials.[59] A spokesman of the Commission for Nationality Affairs of the State Council admitted in 1980 that in Tibet, Chinese officials in the past neglected the much needed handicraft industry in order to pursue "industry that should not have been built" and planted grain at the expense of animal husbandry in contravention of "natural law and economic law."[60]

In the last analysis, the single most substantial development in the minority-nationality areas of the PRC since 1949 has been heavy penetration of Chinese population, i.e., colonization. For the first time in China's history these border areas have been firmly controlled by the Chinese national government.

Like other aspects of domestic Chinese politics, present CPC policy toward minority nationalities is in transition. Among present CPC leaders are Deng Xiaoping and Yang Jinren (himself a Hui), who have always been noted for advocating a soft approach toward minority nationalities. In a 1967 Red Guard paper these two were denounced for their tolerant view on autonomy of nationalities.[61] Hence, it is not surprising that after the death of Mao and the consolidation of power by Deng, the CPC's policy toward minority nationalities was once more switched to a soft approach. The minority races are now guaranteed full autonomy by the state constitution. The CPC's new policy toward Tibet has been made the cause célèbre. In May 1980 two top CPC leaders, Hu Yaobang and Wan Li, made a highly publicized personal visit to Tibet. There they made known a six-point program for Tibetans. The major measures of this program provide for increasing the number of Tibetan cadres in local government and withdrawing a substantial number of Chinese officials, dissolving collectives, exempting Tibetans from state taxes and requisitions for two years, permitting commerce on borders, and promoting native economy.[62] It was reported recently that since 1980, eleven thousand Chinese officials have been sent from Tibet to east China, and more will soon be repatriated. The percentage of Chinese in the capital city of Lhasa has been reduced from 50 in 1980 to 30 in 1983.[63] However, Tibetan deputies to the National People's Congress of 1982 expressed the fear that the new policy may not be permanent or that it could also be turned into "benign neglect."[64]

In conclusion, the comment on Chinese policy in Tibet by an Asian diplomat based in Peking has wider significance: "In twenty-five years, they have failed to bring the Tibetans into the mainstream of the Chinese nation."[65] If integration of ethnic minorities almost always starts with coercive penetration by the majority race, followed by voluntary identification by the minority with the majority, then the integration of the PRC, after thirty years of hard and soft approaches, is still at the very early stage.

NOTES

1. *Wan-sui*, no. 2, p. 637.
2. "East-West Dialogue in China," *Beijing Review* 25, no. 33 (August 16, 1982), 23–26.
3. *The Constitution of the People's Republic of China* (Peking: Foreign Languages Press, 1978), p. 25.
4. Wu Dauin and Liu Han, "Let Various Local People's Congresses Fully Perform Their Functions," *RMRB*, January 11, 1981, p. 5.

5. Wu Dauin and Liu Han, "Local Legislation Needs to Be Improved Urgently," *RMRB*, November 21, 1980, p. 5.

6. Chen Yunshen, "Strengthen the Organization of Local Congressional Standing Committee," *RMRB*, June 15, 1981, p. 5.

7. Ibid.

8. *RMRB*, August 5, 1981, p. 3.

9. *RMRB*, April 21, 1981, p. 3; April 29, 1981, p. 2; April 30, 1981, p. 3; April 25, 1982, p. 4; May 16, 1982, p. 4; and November 19, 1982, p. 3.

10. *RMRB*, November 19, 1982, p. 3.

11. *Ming Pao Daily News,* October 7, 1982, p. 1.

12. *RMRB*, September 12, 1981, pp. 1 and 4.

13. Ibid.

14. *Constitution of the PRC*, p. 26.

15. Zhang Zhenzhao, "The People's Governments at Various Localities," *RMRB*, January 27, 1983, p. 5.

16. *RMRB*, April 11, 1983, p. 3.

17. *China News Analysis*, no. 731 (November 1, 1968), p. 7.

18. *RMRB*, November 12, 1978, p. 2.

19. *Constitution of the PRC*, p. 26.

20. *Ming Pao Daily News,* July 30, 1979, p. 3.

21. *RMRB*, April 6, 1982, p. 5.

22. *RMRB*, April 6, 1978, p. 1.

23. *RMRB*, September 8, 1978, p. 1.

24. Zhou Jinhua, "Appraising the Dazhai Brigade," *Beijing Review* 24, no. 16 (April 20, 1981), 25.

25. *RMRB*, December 19, 1981, p. 4.

26. Ibid.

27. *RMRB*, January 19, 1979, p. 2.

28. *RMRB*, May 12, 1981, p. 8.

29. *Ming Pao Daily News,* April 3, 1983, p. 1.

30. *RMRB*, January 2, 1983, p. 1.

31. *Ming Pao Daily News,* April 15, 1983, p. 1.

32. *RMRB*, May 6, 1983, p. 5.

33. *RMRB*, October 28, 1982, p. 4.

34. Frank Ching, "Xinjiang Notebook: A Chinese Province Escapes Full Grip of Communist Party," *Wall Street Journal*, June 7, 1982, p. 24.

35. Ulanhu, "National Regional Autonomy," *Beijing Review*, no. 46 (November 16, 1981), p. 15.

36. *RMRB*, June 7, 1979, p. 2.

37. *China News Analysis*, no. 232 (June 13, 1958), p. 1.

38. *RMRB*, September 25, 1979, p. 1.

39. *China News Analysis*, no. 569 (June 18, 1965).

40. *Constitution of the PRC*, p. 27.

41. Ibid.

42. Yang Jinren, "Resolutely Implement Central Directive. Do a Good Job in the Work in Tibet," *Hongqi*, no. 5 (1980), pp. 5-6. For secondary works on Chinese policy toward the minorities see George Moseley, *The Party and the National Question in China* (Cambridge, Mass.: MIT Press, 1966); and June T. Dreyer, *China's Forty Millions* (Cambridge, Mass.: Harvard University Press, 1976).

43. *RMRB*, February 4, 1980, p. 3.

44. *Survey of China Mainland Press (SCMP)*, no. 1672, p. 7.

45. *SCMP*, no. 1698, pp. 1-7.

46. *China News Analysis*, no. 1051 (August 20, 1976).

47. *RMRB*, January 7, 1979, p. 3.

48. *RMRB*, December 9, 1978, p. 2.

49. *RMRB*, October 30, 1979, p. 3.

50. *RMRB*, November 27, 1978, p. 4.

51. *SCMP*, no. 1672, p. 4.

52. *SCMP*, no. 1730, p. 12.

53. *China News Analysis*, no. 831 (February 12, 1971), p. 1.

54. *China News Analysis*, no. 720 (August 9, 1968), p. 2.

55. Ulanhu, ibid., p. 19.

56. *RMRB*, May 3, 1983, p. 5.

57. Zang Boping, "Expanding the Education of Minority Nationalities in a Solid Way," *Hongqi*, no. 12 (1981), p. 36.

58. Yu Ruihou, "Pay Attention to the Research on Theory of Economic Development in Backward Areas," *Guangming Ribao*, January 31, 1981, p. 4.

59. *RMRB,* July 19, 1979, p. 2; December 14, 1980, p. 3; June 12, 1981, p. 1.
60. *Zhonguo Jianshe* 29, no. 10 (1980), 4.
61. *Nongnu Ji,* May 13, 1967, p. 1.
62. *RMRB,* May 31, 1980, p. 1.
63. Christopher S. Wren, "Chinese Trying to Undo Damage in Tibet," *New York Times,* May 3, 1983, p. 5.
64. *RMRB,* December 3, 1983, p. 3.
65. Wren, ibid.

CHAPTER 7

Rural Administration
and Development

In organizing China along the lines of provinces, municipalities, and counties, the CPC could and did follow traditional pattern, albeit reinforced by Soviet totalitarian structure. But the greatest challenge to the CPC's organizational prowess has been the countryside, which had defied the efforts of all past Chinese governments to bring it under effective administration. The functioning of China as a modern industrial nation, however, requires the Chinese government, of whatever ideological persuasion, to administer the countryside effectively, for it is there that the majority of Chinese live. According to the 1982 census, 79.4 percent of the population (1.08 billion) reside in rural areas.[1] As we shall discuss in this chapter, the CPC's administration of the Chinese resembles closely the party's dealings with the minorities.

Any Chinese government that wishes to fundamentally change China's overwhelming rural framework *quickly* finds that its two objectives — political control and economic development — are, *in the short run,* incompatible with each other. The main reason for that is the ecological structure of rural China, which we discussed at the outset, especially the high degree of diversity or particularity in the Chinese countryside. There are not only great differences between one region and another but also significant differences within each region or even within a locality. Traditional Chinese rural settlements and hand farming are closely harmonized with this environment of diversity. Unless the degree of rural diversity is considerably reduced by modern science and technology — which is possible but would take time — rigorous administration of the countryside by the national government (which inevitably stresses uniformity of conduct) will either be resisted strenuously by the rural residents or wreak havoc with rural society and economy. The consequence of the latter would be catastrophic for the nation as a whole, given the subsistence of the Chinese economic base. Traditional Chinese dynasties were aware of the incompatibility between the political and economic objectives and had, for centuries, chosen to favor the economic over the political objectives. That is why in traditional times the formal administration stopped at the country. As we mentioned previously, below the county level the rural communities were largely self-governing, and the connection between these communities and the national government was by personal relations between the county magistrate and the gentry families in the countryside. The Kuomintang government before 1949, preoccupied with fighting the warlords, the Communists, and the Japanese, basically followed the old wisdom (or folly) in the short run. However, the Kuomintang had already made an effort, in areas under its control, to penetrate below the county. A three-tier structure was established by the Nationalists between the county and individual peasant families: district (immediately below county), township (*hsiang* or *xiang*) and village (*ts'un* or *cun*). Within each village the Kuomintang authorities organized among families a system of collective responsibility known as *pao-chia* (*bao jia*) in which ten households formed a *chia* (*jia*), and ten *chia* formed into a *pao* (*bao*) for mutual surveillance against Communist organization in the countryside. These Nationalist measures, however, were more formalistic than substantive.[2] Consequently, the social and economic autarky in the Chinese countryside persisted throughout the Nationalist rule.

The Chinese Communist party, particularly its left wing (as represented by Mao and the Gang of Four), basically does not recognize the division between political and economic objectives. Both its Leninist ideology and its revolutionary legacy predispose the CPC to see the economic as a derivative of the political objective. This is summed up in the Maoist slogan "Grasp Revolution, Promote Production" (*zhua geming, cu shengchan*). There are degrees of adherence to this "politics taking command" view among CPC leaders, dividing them into *radicals* and *pragmatists*. But until the death of Mao in 1976, it was the leftist line that determined the CPC's rural program most of the time. We shall briefly sum up the history of Mao's conquest of the Chinese countryside.

LAND REFORM, 1949-52

Initially, in 1949-50 the CPC, adhering to its emphasis on politics before economics, sought to raise the "revolutionary consciousness" of the peasantry first, before the establishment of any new rural administration. So the CPC maintained the triad of district, township, and village left behind by the Kuomintang. The old *pao-chia* system was abolished quickly since the CPC wanted to organize peasants from the grassroots, and the *pao-chia* was an immediate obstacle. The central CPC measure in this initial period was, of course, the Land Reform, which was designed not to promote production but to instigate a social movement, i.e., class struggle, in the countryside. With Land Reform the CPC wished to create an unshakable bond between the CPC and a group of peasant activists so that the latter would forever be receptive to direction from the CPC. Ideally, from the standpoint of Mao and other CPC leaders, the consciousness of the poor peasants in the Chinese countryside would be so raised in the Land Reform that they would from then on endure hardship and privation in order to accomplish the great design of the CPC or more accurately Mao, to industrialize China just as the poor peasants in Jiangxi and North China did in the thirties and forties to advance the revolution of the CPC. Liu Shaoqi (Liu Shao-ch'i) explains in "On Agrarian Reform Law" in 1950:

> The basic reason for and the aim of agrarian reform are different from the view that agrarian reform is only designed to relieve the poor people . . . . The results of agrarian reform are beneficial to the impoverished laboring peasants, . . . But

the basic aim of agrarian reform is not purely one of relieving the poor peasants. It is designed to set free the rural productive forces from the shackles of the feudal land ownership system of the landlord class in order to develop agricultural production and thus pave the way for New China's industrialization.[3]

Land Reform was carried out in each village, starting formally in June 1950, under the leadership of the Land Reform Work Team, which consisted of urban students and other young intellectuals led by veteran CPC cadres. The work team launched an agitation campaign among poor peasants to instill in their minds class hatred of the landlords. The fruits of this class agitation were the establishment of two new institutions—an association of poor peasants and a peasants' militia. Local members of the association or the militia were then made leaders in the villages, responsive to policies and programs initiated by the CPC. For the moment the CPC retained the old formal position of village head (*cunzhang*), which was now assumed by a member of the peasants' association. In addition, other political organizations were established in villages during and after the land reform, such as the Communist party branch, the women's association, and the youth league. According to C. K. Yang, the Communist party of China cultivated a new group of rural leadership from the Land Reform campaign. The "new men were elevated from the middle and poor peasants, while the old leadership stemmed mainly from the rich peasants and landlords, especially the latter."[4] Consequently, for the first time in the history of China villages were integrated into national political power. The consequence of this loss of rural autonomy is far reaching for all Chinese peasants.

COLLECTIVIZATION, 1951-80

As the Land Reform was clearly a transient program, the CPC moved quickly, almost simultaneously with the Land Reform, to collectivize Chinese agriculture. There was no disagreement among Chinese Communist leaders on the need for collectivization. However, on the speed, extent, and objectives of collectivization, Chinese Communist leaders differed a great deal, setting Mao apart from a considerable number of party pragmatists.

Mao's approach was political. His preference for rapid collectivization and large collectives was based on an early image—an image formed in 1925 and 1930 in his home province of Hunan and the first guerrilla base of Jiangxi—of poor peasants rising in a great tidal wave to destroy the status quo and embrace new forms of social relations and production, i.e., revolution. For that the poor peasants, in Mao's mind, would be willing to endure privation for a long time. The CPC's responsibility—and it called for the art of leadership—according to Mao, was to satisfy this inexhaustible revolutionary desire of the peasants by providing them with concrete programs such as large collectives. The latter would perform two vital functions for Mao's grand design of industrializing China, which had always been Mao's *first and foremost* commitment. Large collectives would, in Mao's thinking, organize production and consumption in the countryside efficiently and economically so as to deliver a large volume of goods to the national government to be used for industry without (and this is important) having to divert precious industrial goods to develop the countryside. The raised consciousness of poor peasants would support such an "industry first" policy of the CPC. Second, according to Mao large collectives would enhance immeasurably the degree of central direction of the countryside. In traditional times central direction had been impossible because of the scattered rural communities. Hence, Mao's scheme hinged on the ideological consciousness of poor peasants, large collectives, and the central direction of the national authority in Peking, i.e., Mao himself. Moreover, it was Mao's deep belief that large-scale collectivization of agriculture and industry, which would eventually culminate in a national "unitary system of the ownership of the means of production by the whole people" represented the "law of social development." Thus Mao spoke about his strategy in 1957 as comprising two rules: Following the "law of social development" and complying with "the will of the proletariat."[5] Mao's approach was vulnerable on one point—the disastrous result of Soviet collectivization under Stalin. Those Communist Chinese leaders who were opposed to Mao's acceleration of the collectivization drive in the countryside in 1953–56 did bring up the Soviet experience in agriculture to caution Mao. However, Mao refuted the dissenters' negative assessment of Soviet collectivization, which he said had enabled the Soviet Union to industrialize. Second, the Soviet Union had not raised the political consciousness of the peasants, but China had (so Mao thought). Mao concluded: "On no account should we allow these comrades to use the Soviet experience as a cover for their idea of moving at a snail's pace."[6]

Opposing Mao was a group of party pragmatists, whose approach to rural development and organization was less politically conceived than Mao. The main figure of the pragmatists was Deng Zihui (Teng Tzu-hui), head of the Rural Work Department of the CPC Central Committee in the early 1950s. Deng Zihui and his fellow pragmatists based their economic approach to collectivization also on their experience before 1949. Deng Zihui was in charge of organizing cooperatives among peasants in Jiangxi in the 1930s, while Mao was then primarily occupied with political and military strategy. Based on his field experience, Deng Zihui advocated small collectives and voluntary participation. Instead of relying, as Mao did, on poor peasants' so-called revolutionary consciousness, the pragmatists would make use of well-to-do middle or rich peasants to make collectives productive. The pragmatists would allow free trade, hiring labor, and the profit motive in the countryside. In other words, the pragmatists in the CPC wished above all to protect and promote peasants' incentives to produce.[7]

But alas for the pragmatists, Mao Zedong since 1950 had regarded agricultural work as his specialty, and he staked his reputation and status as a charismatic leader on the success of his rural collectivization program. As a general rule, when a leader's ego is involved in a program, objective discussion is no longer possible. So the Chinese countryside after 1951 had to withstand Mao's "permanent revolution" in collectivizing production.

Mutual Aid Teams, 1951–53

Even while the Land Reform was not entirely completed, in order to forestall Chinese peasants from developing a strong sense of private ownership of their newly acquired land, the CPC organized in 1951 the most elementary form of collective, known as Mutual Aid Teams. An average of six or seven peasant households formed a team that shared implements, draft animals, and labor. As a form of cooperation among peasant families, the Mutual Aid Teams were not a new thing in the Chinese countryside. Traditionally cooperative arrangements like the Mutual Aid Teams existed in Chinese villages, but they were temporary and seasonal, organized only in busy periods of harvest and planting. When the seasons of heavy work were over, these teams were dissolved. In many Chinese villages in the South, often the families of an entire village were related by clan ties, so cooperation among families was a very natural practice. But the Mutual Aid Teams that the CPC promoted in 1951-53 were permanent, not seasonal, undertakings and had more functions. By 1952, 40 percent of Chinese peasant households were already members of the Mutual Aid Teams.[8]

So far as the reaction of Chinese peasants was concerned, contrary to Mao's expectation that poor peasants would rise in "revolutionary consciousness" following the Land Reform and the formation of the Mutual Aid Teams, Chinese press reports indicated quite a different range of peasant attitudes. Investigatory groups sent by the CPC to the countryside found that poor peasants felt anxious about their newly acquired property and uncertain of the permanency of the arrangement. "They are not clear whether they are free to buy and sell their land. Some have asked that after [land] redistribution, when one member of a family died, whether the government would after a period of time take away his quota of land from the family for redistribution."[9] Others were frightened by the violence inflicted upon landlords and rich peasants during the Land Reform campaign and became afraid of increasing their income. "There is a common tendency of fearing to show any sign of wealth." The peasants were unsure of the meaning of *exploitation*. Instead of having their consciousness raised—Mao's aim—as one report stated it, "The people [were] ideologically confused."[10] The same report commented: "It is only when the peasants realize clearly that land and other properties are completely owned by them and are at their disposal, can they settle down. It is only then that they will be willing to till their land carefully, to apply more fertilizers, to improve the soil, to practice economy and increase production, etc."[11]

Moreover, Chinese peasants felt immediately increased government demand for delivery of produce to the state after the establishment of the Mutual Aid Teams. Another CPC investigating group reported the sentiments of peasants in Fujian Province: "We shall never be able to complete the tasks assigned by superior authorities. As soon as the 'Three Great Tasks' have been completed, here come the 'Six Great Tasks.' Will there ever be an end?"[12] In Guangdong "village cadres became reluctant even to compile records for the agricultural tax and to work out accounts."[13] Further, peasants discovered another means of governmental squeeze. That was the "scissors effect"—the government paid peasants low prices for agricultural goods but sold them industrial goods at a high price. In other words, the fear of the pragmatists of hurting the production incentives of peasants by collectivization had already become real, even in the earliest stage of collectivization.

In the meantime, just as the Mutual Aid Teams had been phased in before the Land Reform was phased out, a new form of collective was phased in before the Mutual Aid Teams were phased out in 1952. That was the lower Agricultural Producers' Cooperatives (APCs).

Agricultural Producers' Cooperatives, 1952-56

The lower APCs pooled all land that was farmed as a collective unit on a permanent basis. Larger than Mutual Aid Teams, the lower APC concentrated decision making in a management committee; hitherto it had been individual peasant families who made decisions on farming, selling, and disposal of income. Each peasant member of the lower APCs in principle retained the ownership of his land and, again in principle, was remunerated partly according to his work in the collectivized land and partly according to his proportionate share of that part of the yield set aside for the recognition of land ownership. The lower APCs thus resembled shareholders' cooperatives in which members possess shares in the capital of the cooperatives in which members themselves work.

The pragmatists in the Rural Work Department of the CPC Central Committee moved gingerly in setting up the lower APCs for fear of hurting production. In 1952 some 3,600 lower APCs were established; the number increased to 14,000 by December 1953. Throughout this first expansion of the lower APCs, the high leaders of the CPS were of divided minds. The cooperatives were apparently meeting resistance from peasants. The directives from the national CPC leaders most likely reflected the division among leaders. Nevertheless, according to Mao, "mass dissolution" of the lower APCs occurred in 1953. In the province of Zhejiang (Chekiang), "Out of 53,000 cooperatives . . . some 15,000 were dissolved at one fell swoop" in 1953.[14] The disbanding of the lower APCs in 1953 greatly angered Mao, who ordered the leaders of the pragmatists to conduct self-criticism (admission of error in party conference). As a result of Mao's insistence on expansion, the number of lower APCs increased from 100,000 in 1954 to 670,000 in the first half of 1955. But that was not enough for Mao, who then decided to take stronger measures to push for further expansion. In July 1955 Mao made the celebrated speech, "On the Question of Agricultural Cooperation," in which he described the cautious action of the pragmatists in establishing the lower APCs as "tottering along like a woman with bound feet." Mao justified his call for expansion of the cooperatives on the ground that an "upsurge in the socialist mass movement is imminent throughout the countryside." In other words, Mao revived his 1925 image of Hunanese peasants rising in a mass movement to overthrow the landlords.[15] Whereas before Mao's speech in July 1955 only 13.6 percent of Chinese peasant households were organized into lower APCs, within a year of Mao's call for an "upsurge," by July 1956, 96 percent of Chinese peasant households were made members of lower APCs. Moreover, while the lower APCs were being widely and hastily organized, even larger collectives were also being formed, known as the higher APCs. Of the 96 percent of peasant households in the cooperatives, by July 1955, 88 (!) percent had already been collectivized into higher APCs.[16] A hypothesis is almost inescapable: Mao Zedong wished to make the cooperatives an accomplished fact before the opposition in society and in the CPC became too strong to cope with.

The higher APC were even larger than the lower APCs, which meant that the decision-making body—known in China as the accounting unit—was further removed from peasant families and concentrated in the "higher APC management committee." The shareholder nature of the lower APCs was eliminated in the higher APCs and Chinese peasants lost their private claim on lands that they had brought into the cooperatives. Chinese peasants became agricultural wage earners in the higher APCs, similar to urban workers. As a concession to the peasants' desire for private land, each peasant family in the higher APCs was allocated a private plot of land, the total size of which was no more that 6 percent of the size of a higher APC, and over which the peasants, *in principle,* had total freedom of use. The higher APCs were, in other words, exact copies of the Soviet collective farms. With the establishment of the higher APCs, a rural bureaucracy based on cooperatives was organized. Decision making was centralized in the higher APC management committee, which was further directed by the county CPC. Below the higher APC management committee there were production teams (former lower APCs) and production groups (former Mutual Aid Teams). So by the end of 1956 Chinese peasants had lost their land and decision-making power entirely to the state, an unprecedented phenomenon in Chinese history.

On the surface, Mao achieved a great victory in changing the institutional structure of rural production. In practice, it was easier to set up the cooperatives than to make them work. The cooperatives, whether in lower or higher form, were beset with administrative and social problems that were never resolved. First of all, in rushing through the cooperatives, Mao alienated the new rural leadership that was created after the Land Reform. The rural cadres were at first bewildered by Mao's declaration that an "upsurge" or "tide" was imminent in the countryside for "socialist" transformation of production. It was reported in the Chinese press then that some rural cadres replied: "Where is the high tide? . . . If the superior authorities say there is a high tide, we count it so."[17] Afterwards rural cadres naively believed the official explanations that the cooperatives had to be formed on a voluntary basis and that the cooperatives were for the improvement of the living standard of the peasants. Following this logic, rural cadres wished to count on the well-to-do peasants (known in China as upper-middle, or rich, peasants) to form and lead the production of the cooperatives. As the cadres maintained: "The rich peasants have three good possessions (good farm implements, good livestock, and good management) and three capacities (capacity for talking, capacity for writing, and capacity for calculation)."[18] But the Maoist line was that poor peasants ought to be relied upon by cadres to initiate and consolidate cooperatives because the poor peasants were "the semi-proletariat in rural areas" and so were enthusiastic about collectivization. Rural cadres' observations on poor peasants differed from Mao's. The cadres maintained that the poor peasants in the Chinese countryside "have no capacity for production, no [labor] power, no grain to meet unified [compulsory state] purchase, no end [to their] demand [for] . . . supply and are weaklings. . . ."[19] Having no alternative but to comply with upper directives, rural cadres then had to face the resistance of well-to-do peasants who did what Russian peasants had done during collectivization: carried out mass slaughter of livestock, felled timber, and refused to work.[20] Under such cross-pressures, rural cadres chose the only way out—refused to continue as cadres or did very little work. The Chinese press in 1955 and 1956 reported that cadres' inactivity and disinterest in serving the CPC was widespread.[21] As a party branch secretary in the province of Qinghai told a reporter in October 1955: "I have been the party branch secretary for a year, my work became difficult *only after* the movement to form cooperatives" (emphasis added).[22]

The difficulty in managing the cooperatives was also caused by the low educational qualification of rural cadres and the complexity (if not the impossibility) of standardizing work and remuneration norms. As we repeatedly mentioned, the diversity in the rural conditions of China has been extensive, and only science and genuine economic development would gradually reduce rural particularity. For example, should one hour of weeding be paid the same as one hour of watering? Multiply this question by a hundred times, and one begins to appreciate the complicated tasks of rural cadres. It is no wonder that the Chinese press reported "improper job recording and income distribution" in the APCs.[23] In a 1957 overall assessment of the APCs the authoritative *People's Daily* (*Renmin Ribao*, formerly *Jen-min Jih-pao*) reported that APC cadres were "spending money carelessly and unnecessarily . . . not taking good care of the communal property . . . much communal property [being] damaged and lost," and a "tendency [to] record work points [in a] disorderly [manner]."[24]

In the meantime, the APCs collectivized not only farming but also trading. Hitherto Chinese peasants had been free to buy and sell their produce. Tawney found that in the Chinese countryside "more than a quarter of the goods consumed by agricultural families are purchased."[25] After the setting up of the APCs, all buying and selling in the countryside were monopolized and centralized in Supply and Marketing Cooperatives. The official explanation to the peasants was that the latter "liberated" the peasants from the past exaction by the middle men in trade. But in practice, Chinese peasants immediately felt shortages in supplies of daily necessities as the cooperatives were subordinated to a national ministry and became more interested in fulfilling their assigned quotas of compulsory purchases from peasants than in supplying villages with goods.[26] Meanwhile the abolishment of free trade in rural areas following the APCs significantly threatened the cash crops that peasants depended on to provide income for day-to-day living expenses. In fact the cash crops were eliminated after the APCs, and the living standard of peasants in the APC suffered greatly, as noted Chinese sociologist Fei Xiaotong (Hsiao-tung Fei) discovered when he investigated in 1957.[27]

Moreover, the APCs aggravated the problems of heavy state exaction on peasants by increasing the quotas on compulsory purchase of grains and exacerbating the scissors effect, both of which the peasants had already complained about during the formation of the Mutual Aid Teams. Peasants had to bear the burden not only of the national agricultural tax and the compulsory grain purchase but also of various deductions for maintaining the APCs. Even before the acceleration of the formation of the APCs in July 1955, the *People's Daily* had already reported that "in some instances, the peasants practically have nothing left after the [expenses] are deducted. Such [expenses] include: shares for the credit cooperatives, shares for the Supply and Marketing Cooperative, repayments of loans, bond subscription and others . . . the peasants do not even have pocket-money left. . . ."[28] Meanwhile, believing that the "superiority" of the APCs would raise production, the national leaders of the CPC increased demand on rural cadres to deliver more grain to the state. Driven to desperation, rural cadres forced peasant women to work in the fields. Death of young children because of the absence of their mothers reached an alarming degree in May 1956, and national authorities finally stepped in to put a halt to the forced labor.[29]

Last but not least, the fundamental question on the optimal size of an APC was never resolved. It was natural for peasants to prefer small cooperatives in which they would be working with relatives rather than strangers so that the problem of equity was minimized. But the preference of Mao and other national leaders was otherwise. As we mentioned before, Mao believed that the "law of social development" was for ever larger cooperatives. Furthermore, larger collectives would reduce the influence of kinships, thus making the collectives receptive to central direction. Large cooperatives, however, inevitably alienated peasants, whose individual interest was always made to yield to the collective interest.

Against this background, in late 1956, there was a wave of withdrawals by peasants from the APCs. This phenomenon was possible, as we explained in chapter 3, because Mao was under the pressure of Soviet leader Khrushchev's denunciation of Stalin. Consequently, political regimentation in China was relaxed, leading to the Hundred Flowers Blooming campaign in May 1957. After the suppression of the Hundred Flowers Blooming campaign, peasants were made to return to the APC once more, and throughout China "a large-scale Socialist Education" campaign was carried out in order to raise the socialist consciousness of peasants.[30]

None of the problems concerning the APCs dissuaded Mao from his scheme of collectivization. As mentioned earlier, Mao had personally taken charge of the agricultural collectivization, believing that he had a superior understanding of the peasants wishes. One of Mao's colleagues, who was also in charge of rural work, recalled in 1983 after the CPC finally abandoned the people's commune altogether:

The earliest mistake made by Comrade Mao was his critique of others' "tottering along like a woman with bound feet." At that time, Comrade Mao Zedong spent a great deal of time and effort to take charge of agricultural collectivization. In July 1955 he published the essay "On the Question of Agricultural Co-opera-tion" and he edited the book *Problems in Agricultural Co-operation* for which he personally wrote the preface and the annotations. . . . By then he had already lost touch with reality and was not willing to listen to different opinions, thus betraying his own principle of seeking truth from facts and following the mass line.[31]

As we said before, the ego-involvement of a leader in any public program spells the death knell of objective assessment of it. The collectivization of Chinese villages into higher APCs, which was originally projected by CPC pragmatists to take at least fifteen years to accomplish was rushed through by Mao in *one year*! The idea of the Great Leap Forward was already stirring in Mao's mind by 1957.

The People's Commune, 1958-80

Mao Zedong's taking charge of agricultural collectivization does not, however, mean that he was committed primarily to developing Chinese agriculture. On the con-trary, Mao's commitment after 1949 had always been first and foremost to industry. His close direction of agricultural collectivization was designed to carry out his scheme of making agriculture pay for China's industrialization *and* for its own survival and growth. We must view the next stage of agricultural collectivization in China—the set-ting up of the people's commune as part of the Great Leap Forward campaign—in this context.

All the measures of agricultural collectivization that we have discussed so far, from the Mutual Aid Teams to the higher APCs, were designed to synchronize with China's first five-year plan of 1953-57. As mentioned in chapter 3, the first five-year plan emphasized overwhelmingly heavy industry at the expense of agriculture and light industry. To heavy industry went all the tangible resources, such as skilled manpower, raw materials, equipment, and all the foreign reserves that China could marshal as well as Soviet aid, which was considerable then. Agricultural growth was, in Mao's scheme, to depend on intangible resources, mainly the "ideological consciousness" of peasants and organizational manipulation by such things as the cooperatives. The projected rise in agricultural production would then fuel China's great push for industry. The year 1957 marked the end of the first five-year plan, and Mao was faced with a dilemma and an embarrassment. The dilemma was that the high rate of industrial growth in the first five-year plan was being threatened in 1957 with agricultural stagnancy. The em-barrassment was that the APCs had not lived up to Mao's expectation of "liberating the productive forces" of Chinese peasants. "Even the official data show [in 1957] that the rise in food crop production per capita was confined to the years before 1955. Production remained more or less stationary between 1955 and 1957."[32] The threat of agricultural stagnancy to further industrial development in 1957 took two forms: "tight urban food supplies on the one hand and agricultural raw materials shortages for industry on the other."[33]

Faced with such a dilemma in 1957, Mao decided to radicalize his original strategy of making agriculture shoulder the twin burdens of supplying industrialization and maintaining itself. The possible option of diverting tangible resources such as skilled manpower and state investment from industry to agriculture was out of the question. Mao lashed out at a Chinese scholar and rural reformer named Liang Shumin (Liang Shu-ming), who had suggested the need to develop the countryside first in 1953: "If your ideas were adopted, wouldn't that spell the destruction of China's industry? Such a diversion of the workers' earnings would mean the ruin of our country and our parties." [34]

So Mao, with his mind squarely fixed on industrial growth at an even higher rate than during the first five-year plan, conceived of a Great Leap Forward in agriculture to support the rise in Chinese industry. Starting in 1958, the industrial development was to be led by steel production, which was projected to increase by 100 percent in one year, from 5 million in 1957 to 10 million tons in 1958. "Steel as the key link" was the slogan of the Great Leap Forward. The investment of the state in new industrial construction was also expected to increase by 100 percent. The rate of saving in national income was to be raised to 33.9 percent (the optimal rate without creating undue hardship on the population was 22 to 25 percent). The number of employees for the planned new industries was expected to increase by 20 million. [35] Agriculture was made to bear the burden of all these increases. To accomplish such a feat Mao called for further collectivization of the higher APCs: the people's communes.

When the people's communes were first introduced to China in August 1958, Chinese villages had already been collectivized into 740,000 higher APCs. The people's communes merged these higher APCs into 24,000 communes. This was accomplished in two months! [36] The old township administration was formally abolished and absorbed by the commune management committee. As communes managed both production and general administration below the county level, Chinese villages resembled company towns or Latin American plantation towns. In terms of size, people's communes leaped over the higher APCs and also the natural exchange and trade community of the old days. Each commune consisted of well over five thousand households. Though initially, national leaders called on the lower cadres to form communes on the basis of "one township–one commune," in practice Mao favored large communes that merged several townships. The most advanced communes were county federated communes, a county being a federation of several large communes. In these "advanced" communes, the accounting unit was the county government that was empowered to use labor, materials, and funds in a unified way for the purpose of constructing large projects (see figure 7-1).

The people's communes collectivized every aspect of peasant life, including family life. All able-bodied males were organized into mobile labor gangs to work on large-scale irrigation projects at the direction of the newly established commune management committee and higher CPC authorities. Adult females were to take over farming work, which had previously been done by males. Children were to be housed in communal nurseries and taken care of by old and retired peasant women. All members of the people's communes were to eat in communal mess halls, so peasants, male and female, could devote a maximum amount of time to labor-intensive construction and farming. According to Mao's scheme, the "liberated" male and female peasants in the people's communes would provide enough labor to create a whole range of local industry to supply the needs of agriculture—back-yard steel furnaces (i.e., the old blacksmith's way of making steel), small-scale fertilizer plants, and small-scale electric power plants. Through all this, no tangible resources were to be diverted from modern industry to the countryside of China. Peasants must find ways and means to do all the above-mentioned things and achieve a phenomenal growth in production to supply industry. The result was well described by Alexander Eckstein:

The technical problems were solved by "letting all teachings contend"—that is, through free debate and practice. Locally manufactured cement and steel were used; and wood, bamboo, tile, and other materials were substituted freely for steel, iron, and cement. There probably were as many "formulas" for concrete as there were construction sites. One such "formula" called for 70 percent powder ground from old brick, 25 percent lime, and 5 percent gypsum; and a *hsien* (county) in Ningsia [Ningxia] was said to be making concrete with clay as the principal component.

The zeal of the cadres and the pressure from above led to a miscalculation of resources in many other ways as well. In the attempt to mobilize fully all the underemployed labor, even labor needed in farm production was caught up in the construction of irrigation canals, dams, and other water conservation projects. As a result, acute labor shortages developed in 1958 and 1959—to the point that in some places fields were overgrown because they were insufficiently weeded or were left uncultivated altogether.[37]

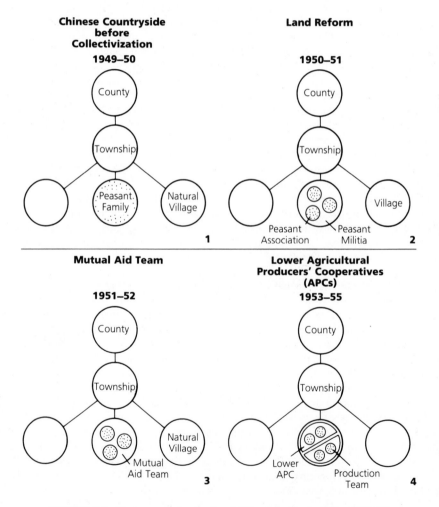

FIGURE 7-1 The process of agricultural collectivization in China 1949-83

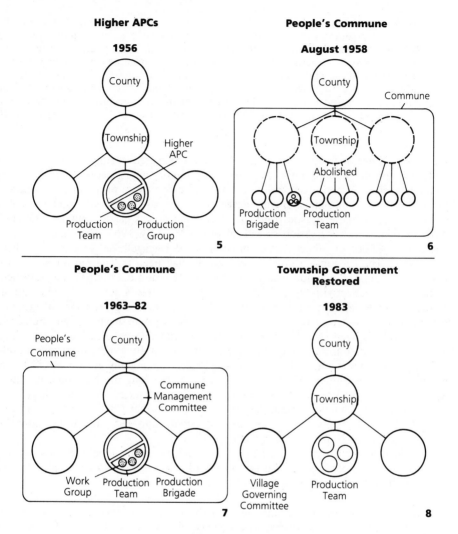

FIGURE 7-1 (con't.)

Socially the people's communes were to approximate genuine communism. So wages were abolished and replaced by "free supply." Peasants were guaranteed six things: food, medical care, education, funerals, movies, and haircuts—all to be supplied by communes free of charge. The daily life of peasants was regimented in military fashion. Initially the organizational designations of communes bore the military titles of regiment, battalion, campany, platoon, and squad. Peasants worked in serried ranks under the command of cadres. After farming was done, able-bodied male and female peasants were organized into the People's Militia, modeled after the communal guards of the Paris Commune of 1871.

The people's commune in its pristine form (as just described), however, lasted only from August to December 1958, before it was ended by widespread peasant resistance. Mao Zedong reported in March, 1959:

After the autumn harvest of 1958, a wave of "inadequate supply" of grain, oil, meat and vegetables took place. This is a concentrated expression of resistance. On the one hand, national, provincial, prefectural, county and commune authorities severely castigated production teams or production groups for their sectarian attitude and their hiding the amount of production and secret distribution of grain among themselves. On the other hand, it is a widespread practice among production teams to hide the amount of production, even to the extent of burying grain deep underground or posting sentries to protect their produce.[38]

Beginning in December 1958, national CPC leaders retreated steadily from their initial model for the people's commune. At first, only minor "adjustments" were made on communes, such as permitting peasants to own some private property (e.g., houses, quilts, furniture, bank deposits) and engage in limited sideline production (vegetables and chickens). A more drastic overhaul of communes was carried out in 1960 and 1961, as famine and starvation spread all over China. By 1963 the number was increased to 74,000. In other words, communes had been reduced to a third of their 1959 size.[39] The accounting units of communes had been transferred downward to production teams, so decision making over production and distribution was returned to the smallest collectivity, a production team being simply a neighborhood group of twenty to thirty families. Each peasant family was allowed a private plot of ground. Remuneration was based on work, the free-supply system having been abolished. Public mess halls were closed. The many commune-run enterprises, which drained and wasted precious resources of the villages, were shut down. By 1963 a press report indicated that communes and brigades were no longer running any enterprises.[40] These measures did save Chinese agricultural economy in the long run but could not stop famine, which according to recent popoulation figures, caused the death of at least 20 to 25 million Chinese.[41] Mao, despite warnings by other CPC leaders, reaped the same results as had Stalin's "war on *kulaks*," which precipitated a disastrous famine in Russia that claimed 10 to 11 million deaths in 1931-33.

William Skinner argues that the commune failed organizationally because of "its grotesquely large mold," which did not align with the natural socioeconomic systems shaped by rural trade. Furthermore, wrote Skinner:

> Intensified by the preoccupation with sheer survival, "local particularism" at first hampered, then frustrated, and finally defeated the efforts of Communist cademen to organize collectivized units at a level above that of basic marketing systems. By the winter of 1960-1961, Communist planners and cademen alike had gained new respect for the enduring significance of natural social systems, and were seeking ways to use traditional solidarities for their own organizational ends.[42]

But *economically*, the people's commune failed because, as pointed out by Eckstein, it "represented a last desperate attempt to bypass the agricultural problem and to avoid facing up to the necessity of channeling modern technical inputs into agriculture."[43]

But Mao, with his ego-involvement in agricultural collectivization, did not give up. Not long after starvation in the countryside and severe food shortage in the cities subsided in 1964, Mao planned for a return of his agricultural policy. In that year he called on the whole nation to emulate the production brigade known as the Tachai brigade (Dazhai brigade today), of Shanxi (Shansi) Province. (A production brigade was the production unit one level lower than the commune management committee; the lowest unit was the production team.) According to the official account, the Tachai brigade had not retreated from the original design of the Great Leap Forward after 1958. "Tachai embarked upon new labor-intensive capital projects, terracing the surrounding mountainsides by hand and carving from them an intricate irrigation system of channels and small reservoirs. From 1960 to 1962, while crop failures and malnutrition plagued most of China, the peasants of Tachai according to official accounts annually sold to the State double their assigned grain quota."[44] In August 1963 Tachai, again according to the official account, suffered a severe natural disaster (flood), but the peasants "armed with Mao Thought, raised up the flattened crops plant by plant, bringing in a good harvest."[45] Though the provincial party authorities of Shanxi accused the party secretary of Tachai, Chen Yonggui, of lying and falsification of records, Mao overruled them and promoted Chen to the vice-premiership of the National People's Government. In 1965 some fifty Tachai-type communes were set up all over China to persuade the rest of the Chinese peasants to return to the original plan of the Great Leap Forward in agriculture.[46] An official report about these models did not hide the fact that these communes had received extra funds and materials from the state.[47] In the 1970s, after the reestablishment of diplomatic relations between the PRC and the United States, many American visitors to the PRC were shown these model communes, and they returned to the United States with glowing accounts of China as a model for the nations in the Third World. After the death of Mao, the Tachai model was declared a fraud.[48]

Though Mao was unsuccessful in convincing the Chinese people of the credibility of the Tachai or Dazhai model, he refused to retreat further on the commune system after 1962. From 1964 on, he launched campaigns such as Socialist Education and Four Cleanups (first, clean up finance, warehouses, accounts and labor points; later, clean up politics, economics, thought, and organizations) to prevent further "corruption" of the commune system. During the ten years of leftism (1966-76) Mao kept up pressure on villages in three ways. First, the size and operation of the private plot of each peasant household were kept fluid. Chinese peasants were threatened from time to time with the loss of their plots, in order to make them work on communal land. Second, there was continuous manipulation by national, county, and commune leaders of the remuneration of peasants. The stress by the CPC was to equalize income among peasants. Third, there was a persistent attempt to transfer the accounting unit upward, from the production team to the brigade or, in some cases, back to commune management. Because of this, the commune still operated various enterprises in 1966-76 that were financed by resources and labor taken from production teams. According to later accounts, pressure on peasants to yield their private plots and return to collectivized life was intensified in 1970 and continued after Mao's death, until 1978.

DECOLLECTIVIZATION, 1977 TO THE PRESENT

The death of Mao Zedong in 1976 marked the beginning of the end of the people's commune in China. After the purge of the Gang of Four and other followers of Mao Zedong in 1977-78, Chinese Communist leaders were able to sum up the CPC's experience in economic development, especially agriculture, in a frank and objective manner. The Chinese economy at the time of Mao's death was "on the verge of total collapse" owing to previous policies of heavy spending on basic construction of capital industry, a squeeze on agriculture, and an unreasonably high rate of saving.[49] The condition of the countryside in mainland China was especially critical. A high-ranking CPC leader wrote in the *People's Daily*:

> Both the number and composition of our population indicate the backwardness of our economy and the low standard of our productive force. That 800 million peasants are preoccupied with raising food shows that the peasants still labor with their hands, productivity being low, and that the broad countryside remains as a semi-self-sufficient economy.[50]

Another Chinese provincial leader likened the people's commune to life in a primitive society. The group work routine in the commune was like "primitive people hunting a deer in a noisy and collective way. . . . If the deer is caught, then everyone is fed; if not, everyone goes hungry."[51]

All the problems associated with the Mutual Aid Teams and the APCs, such as official exactions from the peasants, incompetence and corruption of rural cadres, and lack of incentive to produce, persisted and were aggravated by the people's communes. In some production teams, exactions by commune authorities amounted to 86.97 percent of their total annual cash income.[52] That must be one of the chief reasons for the strange phenomenon in the people's commune: "increase in production but no increase in the income of commune members."

Hence, the first step toward the dismantling of the people's commune in China after 1977 was to restrain the commune bureaucracy's squeeze on production teams. The second step, taken in 1979, was to allow contract farming. That is, individual peasant households or groups of households that were formed voluntarily contracted with production team management for farming a certain amount of land. Various forms of contracting were permitted.[53] In other words, the accounting unit in the countryside was being transferred gradually back to peasant households.

By 1983 the contracting system (also called the production responsibility system) had already been installed in 92 percent of the production teams in the nation. Of these, 78.7 percent were "contracting on the basis of individual households."[54] In short, Chinese villages have gone back to household farming. Accompanying this move has been a reduction of commune bureaucracy. In one commune, for example, the number of cadres in production teams was reduced by 60 percent, as a result of the contracting system.[55] The raison d'être of the people's commune was now entirely undermined. The former company-town status of communes could no longer be maintained. Hence, in 1983 the old township, which had been absorbed by the people's commune in 1958, was resurrected (see figure 7-1).

The present leadership of the CPC gave four reasons for the separation of township government and commune organization: (1) to deprive commune management the power to make exactions on villages (i.e., production teams); (2) to enable peasants to organize new collective economic groups flexibly and voluntarily (e.g., transteam, transcommune, and transregional economic joint enterprises); (3) to achieve greater efficiency and productivity on the part of the township administration and farming through a division of labor between administration and production; and (4) (most interesting) to return politics to where it belongs. On the last point, two Chinese writers stated:

Since 1979, the production responsibility system has been popularized throughout the country. The material interests of individual peasants are now recognized and protected. This mobilizes the peasants' initiative for production. As a result, the tasks of mediating disputes, maintaining public security, tax collection, village construction and providing welfare facilities have become heavier. They require stronger local political organizations.

However, under the present system, when the busy farming seasons come, commune leaders have to devote all their energy to production. Their work as political leaders cannot but be weakened. The separation of the two will lead to the establishment of township governments and villagers' committees that can devote all their time to political power building and administration. This will contribute to peace and stability in the rural areas.[56]

In other words, the dismantling of the people's commune does not mean returning to the old days when the national government left the villages to govern themselves. The new township government is supposed to assume genuine "political functions," i.e., maintaining law and order, collecting taxes, building basic facilities such as roads, dams, and canals, and administering social welfare. A noteworthy omission from the functions of township government is economic planning. The communes suffer a quiet death. According to one report: "The name of the commune may still be used, or the communes may be reorganized into other suitable economic organizations."[57]

At the villages no formal governing structure, at this writing (October 1984), seems to have evolved. The Chinese press reports mention village committees, but no details have been given. As villagers' lives revolve around production of food, the production team remains the most important organization in the national villages. The production team is the main contractor in villages with whom peasant households sign an agreement on farming. The production team is also the lowest taxing and requisition unit accountable to administrative authorities at township and county seats. The production team seems to have assumed the status of the old *pao-chia* system in villages, though the function of the team is more economic than political.

The dissolution of the people's communes and the return of household farming have had a "depoliticalization" effect in villages. Both the youth league and the Communist party branches in the villages suffered serious disintegration with the dismantling of communes. The head of the Communist Youth League spoke of the "loosening and scattering" of league branches in the countryside in 1981. In 1980 the number of villages without a youth league branch increased by 1,685 over the previous year.[58] Other reports revealed similar tendencies toward "paralysis and disintegration" on the part of party branches in villages.[59] In December 1981 the national CPC leadership publicized a program for organizing and revitalizing party branches in villages.[60] The irony is that both documents, the youth league's and the CPC's, are now obsolete as its program of strengthening rural organizations was, in 1981, still premised on the existence of the people's commune.

The dissolution of the people's commune and subsequent political disorganization in villages led to a vigorous revival of traditional practices in the Chinese countryside, especially a return of folk religion, superstition, clan activity, arranged marriages, gambling, and gross discrimination against women. Members of the party in rural areas actively participate in these "feudal" practices.

"Overnight we return to pre-liberation days after thirty years of hard work." That has been the lament of some CPC cadres on the demise of the people's commune.[61] According to some Chinese writers, the reasons for the failure of the people's commune, or of even the advanced APCs earlier, can be summed in three Chinese characters: *quan* (power), *ze* (responsibility), and *li* (payoff). The people's commune took away the peasants' power to make decisions for themselves, depriving them of responsibility for their own livelihood without giving them a real payoff.[62]

From the standpoint of a political historian, the agricultural collectivization program of Mao Zedong and the CPC, from its inception to its demise, is a microcosm of Chinese Communist political culture, the components of which we have mentioned in different contexts previously. There is first the charismatic leadership, as in Mao's ego-involvement in agricultural collectives and the serious consequence of Mao's staking his personal status and prestige in the undertaking. Second, there is the revolutionary legacy of the CPC, especially Mao's image of the "socialist consciousness" of poor peasants, which dated from 1925 and 1930. Third, there is the CPC impulse to centralize or militarize Chinese society, the people's commune being the most telling example. Last but not least, there is the Marxist-Leninist ideology. As Benjamin Schwartz reminds us, even though Chinese Communist leaders such as Mao Zedong, forced by circumstances, had to work with and use peasants before 1949, "we must not overlook the abiding conviction of the Chinese Communists themselves that they are unswerving Marxist-Leninists."[63] Lucien Bianco rounds out the implications for Chinese peasants of Mao's deep commitment to Marxism-Leninism: "From the sarcasm of Marx, Engels, and Trotsky toward 'the class that represents barbarism within civilization' to Stalin's bloody expeditions against the 'blood drinkers' who resisted forced collectivization, Marxism was in theory as in practice the deadly antagonist of the peasantry. Among other things, Marxism may be seen as an ideological expression of the age of urbanization and industrialization."[64]

For students of administration and political development, the dissolution of the people's commune confirms two observations made by some scholars on modernization. First, centralization must be accompanied by growth of knowledge. If not, the probability is high that any error on the part of the central planner will result in what Marion Levy, Jr., called "*stupidity* or *ignorance* death."[65] Second, in a social environment consisting of small-scale, self-sufficient, and mutually independent economies, a decentralized administration is more efficient than centralized ones.[66] In dealing with both minority nationalities and Chinese peasants, the CPC stressed centralization excessively, with detrimental effects to political integration and economic development.

NOTES

1. *RMRB*, November 16, 1982, p. 5.

2. For more on Chinese villages before 1949 see Hsiao-tung Fei, *China's Gentry* (Chicago: University of Chicago Press, 1953); and C. K. Yang, "A Chinese Village in Early Communist Transition," in C. K. Yang, *Chinese Communist Society: The Family and the Village* (Cambridge, Mass.: MIT Press, 1965).

3. *Collected Works of Liu Shao-ch'i, 1945–1957* (Kowloon, Hong Kong: Union Research Institute, 1969), p. 220.

4. C. K. Yang, "A Chinese Village," p. 173.

5. *Wan-sui*, no. 2, p. 132.

6. Mao Tse-tung, *On the Question of Agricultural Co-operation* (Peking: Foreign Languages Press, 1966), p. 21.

7. One can gather these views of the pragmatists from Mao's criticisms of them in *Selected Works of Mao Tse-tung*, vol. V (Peking: Foreign Languages Press, 1977), pp. 211–26.

8. *RMRB*, July 10, 1981, p. 5.

9. *Nan Fang Jih Pao (Southern Daily)*, February 19, 1953, as translated in *SCMP (Survey of China Mainland Press)*, no. 527, p. 21.

10. Ibid.

11. Ibid., p. 22.

12. *Chieh Fang Jih Pao*, November 8, 1951, as translated in *SCMP*, no. 219, p. 19.

13. See note 9. For other reports of peasants' reaction to the Land Reform, see Shang Gedong, "The Division in Small Farm Economy after the Land Reform," *Xuexi* 2, no. 9 (July 16, 1950), 10-11.

14. Mao Tse-tung, *On the Question*, p. 9.

15. For Mao's description of the Hunanese peasant movement in 1925-27, see Mao Tse-tung, "Report on an Investigation of the Peasant Movement in Hunan," in *Selected Works of Mao Tse-tung*, vol. I (Peking: Foreign Languages Press, 1965).

16. The figures on the Mutual Aid Teams and the APCs cited here are all from *RMRB*, July 10, 1981, p. 5.

17. Hsiao Chen-tao, "Empiricism, Doctrinairism and the Rightist Mentality in the Agricultural Cooperative Movement," *Hsin Chien She*, no. 88 (January 1956), as translated in *Extracts from China Mainland Magazines (ECMM* hereafter), no. 39, p. 36.

18. Liu Lan-tao, "Implement Correctly the Party's Rural Class Policy," *Jen-min Jih-pao (RMRB)*, November 20, 1955, as translated in *SCMP*, no. 1181, pp. 20-26.

19. Ibid.

20. Wang Jui-ting, "It Is Wrong to Stress that 'Fluctuation of Peasants' Thought Is Inevitable,'" *Cheng Chih Hsueh Hsi*, no. 5 (1955), as translated in *ECMM*, no. 15, pp. 12-15. Also, "Stop Indiscriminate Slaughter of Draft Cattle," *Chekiang Jih Pao*, February 24, 1957, in *SCMP*, no. 1500, pp. 8-9.

21. *Shansi Jih Pao (Shanxi Ribao)*, May 31, 1955; *Heilunkiang Jih Pao (Heilongjiang Ribao)*, September 12, 1956. These regional papers are available on microfilms made at the Union Research Institute (Kowloon, Hong Kong) and are available at the Center for Chinese Studies, University of California, Berkeley.

22. *Ch'inghai Jih Pao (Qinghai Ribao)*, October 26, 1956.

23. *Chung Kuo Ch'ing Nien Pao*, December 19, 1956, in *SCMP*, no. 1447, pp. 9-12.

24. *Jen-min Jih-pao (RMRB)*, April 21, 1957, in *SCMP*, no. 1521, pp. 9-11.

25. R. H. Tawney, *Land and Labor in China* (Boston: Beacon Press, 1966), pp. 54-55.

26. *Jen-min Jih-pao (RMRB)*, November 12, 1955, in *SCMP*, no. 1178, pp. 11-14.

27. Fei Xiaotong, "Revisit Jiang Village," *Xinguancha (Hsin Kuan Ch'a)*, no. 11 (June 1, 1957) and no. 12 (June 16, 1957).

28. *Jen-min Jih-pao (RMRB)*, March 3, 1955, in *SCMP*, no. 1004, pp. 5-6.

29. *Xinhua Banyuekan (New China Fortnightly)*, no. 18 (1956), p. 67; *Jen-min Jih-pao*, August 12, 1956.

30. *RMRB*, August 7, 1957.

31. Tang Zhenlin, "Inherit and Develop the Thought of Mao Zedong," *RMRB*, December 7, 1983, p. 5.

32. Alexander Eckstein, *Communist China's Economic Growth and Foreign Trade: Implications for U.S. Policy* (New York: McGraw-Hill Book Company, 1966), p. 58.

33. Alexander Eckstein, *China's Economic Revolution* (Cambridge: Cambridge University Press, 1977), p. 54.

34. *Selected Works of Mao Tse-tung*, vol. V (Peking: Foreign Languages Press, 1977), p. 127.

35. *RMRB*, July 14, 1981, p. 5.

36. Ibid.

37. Eckstein, *China's Economic Growth*, p. 72.

38. *Wan-sui*, no. 2, p. 284.

39. G. William Skinner, "Marketing and Social Structure in Rural China," part III, *Journal of Asian Studies* XXIV, no. 3 (May 1965), 394.

40. *RMRB*, January 31, 1963.

41. John S. Aird, "Recent Demographic Data from China: Problems and Prospects," *China under the Four Modernizations*, part 1. Selected papers submitted to the Joint Economic Committee, Congress of the United States, August 13, 1982 (Washington, D.C.: Government Printing Office), p. 182.

42. Skinner, *Marketing and Social Structure*, pp. 395-96.

43. Eckstein, *China's Economic Revolution*, p. 59.

44. Jonathan Unger, "'Learn From Tachai': China's Agricultural Model," *Current Scene: Developments in Mainland China* IX, no. 9 (September 7, 1971), 2.

45. Ibid.

46. *Jen-min Jih-pao (RMRB)*, November 1, 1965, as translated in *SCMP*, no. 3576, pp. 13-16.

47. Chang P'ing-hua, "On Operation of Pilot Scheme," *Jen-min Jih-pao (RMRB)*, March 7, 1966, as in *SCMP*, no. 3661, pp. 9-17.

48. *Beijing Review* 24, no. 16 (1981), 24-28.

49. *RMRB,* April 9, 1981, p. 5.
50. Ibid.
51. Xiang Nan, "On Seeking Truth from Facts," *RMRB,* April 6, 1982, p. 5.
52. *RMRB,* November 30, 1980, p. 3.
53. *Beijing Review* 24, no. 17 (April 27, 1981), 6-8.
54. *RMRB,* February 9, 1983, p. 1.
55. *RMRB,* February 4, 1983, p. 11.
56. Song Dahan and Zhang Chunsheng, "Important Change in the System of People's Communes," *Beijing Review* 25, no. 29 (July 19, 1982), 17.
57. Ibid.
58. *Chung-Kung Yen-chiu* 16, no. 8 (August 15, 1982), 108-9.
59. Jin Tong, "Strengthen Party Basic Organization in Villages," *Hongqi,* no. 8 (1982), pp. 36-43.
60. *Chung-kung Yen-chiu* 16, no. 9 (September 15, 1982), 131-50.
61. *RMRB,* December 22, 1981, p. 2.
62. An Gang, Song Zhen, and Huang Yuechun, "The Prospect for Revitalizing Chinese Agriculture Is Good," *RMRB,* July 9, 1981, p. 2. For excellent accounts by American scholars on rural life in China today see Steven W. Mosher, *Broken Earth: The Rural Chinese* (New York: Free Press, 1983); and Anita Chan, Richard Madsen, and Jonathan Unger, *Chen Village: The Recent History of a Peasant Community in Mao's China* (Berkeley: University of California Press, 1984).
63. Benjamin I. Schwartz, *Chinese Communism and the Rise of Mao* (New York: Harper & Row, 1967), p. 202.
64. Lucien Bianco, *Origins of the Chinese Revolution, 1915-1949,* translated by Muriel Bell (Stanford, Calif.: Stanford University Press, 1971), p. 74.
65. Marion J. Levy, Jr., *Modernization: Latecomers and Survivors* (New York: Basic Books, 1972), p. 72.
66. Robert T. Holt and John E. Turner, *The Political Basis of Economic Development* (Princeton, N.J.: D. Van Nostrand Company, 1966), p. 298.

CHAPTER 8

Parapolitical
Organizations

From our discussion of the way the CPC organized the rural areas of China one can see that the Chinese Communists are adept at creating seemingly populist organizations such as the Peasant Militia and Peasant Association to extend the power of the party. Moreover, as mentioned previously, the formal ideology of the People's Democratic Dictatorship prescribes that the rule of the CPC is to be based on the alliance of workers and peasants and a "united front" with "national bourgeoisie," "petty bourgeoisie," and "democratic personages." Hence, in the formal governing institutions of the PRC there are what we refer to as parapolitical organizations, which ostensibly belong to various groups such as workers, youth, women, the bourgeoisie, and "democratic personages." These organizations are associated with the formal structures of power, i.e., the CPC and the People's Government, in a subsidiary or accessory capacity.

The parapolitical organizations in the PRC can be divided into two major types in terms of the functions that these groups are assigned by the CPC. First, the united front organizations are intended to unite the CPC with the upper classes of Chinese society. The second type of parapolitical organizations enables the CPC to mobilize the working class, the young, and the women; these organizations perform the so-called transmission-belt function, i.e., transmitting the policy and program of the CPC to the working people of China.

UNITED FRONT

The united front strategy of the CPC originated in the late 1930s when the CPC sought to launch a political offensive against the Nationalist party. The tactics of the CPC then were to ally itself with several non-Communist political groups in the name of the anti-Japanese patriotic front. But the goal of the CPC united front changes as the need of the CPC changes. From 1940 until the victory of the CPC in the civil war, the CPC used the united front to isolate the Nationalist regime politically by joining with other anti-Nationalist parties, groups, and individuals in a demand for democracy and coalition government. In late 1948, as the civil war between the Nationalists and Communists turned more and more in the Communists' favor, the CPC united front strategy assumed a new function: to provide the forthcoming Communist regime with a legitimate base. Until then the CPC had dealt with each political party or group individually. Now in August 1948 the CPC decided to unify all the parties and groups allied with the Communist party in an umbrella organization named the Chinese People's Political Consultative Conference (CPPCC). In September 1949, after the CPC took over Peking, the first meeting of the CPPCC was convened. From all over China and especially Hong Kong, where many opponents of the Nationalist party operated then, the CPC invited individuals, groups, and "parties" who were in varying degree opposed to the Nationalists or were prominent nationally to attend the first conference of the CPPCC. Included was a dissident group from the Nationalist party under the name Revolutionary Committee of Chinese Nationalist Party. The emissaries that the CPC sent to invite the non-Communist groups informed the latter that the purpose of the CPPCC was to form a coalition government of all "democratic" parties and individuals and that the head of the new government would be a non-CPC person.[1] The first CPPCC in September 1949 formally performed the function of a temporary parliament. It announced the birth of the People's Republic of China and "elected" Mao Zedong chairman of both the PRC and the CPPCC. The first CPPCC also passed a Common Program to serve as the provisional constitution of China. Aside from being the midwife of the PRC, the first CPPCC performed a very important function: to create a favorable image of the CPC among the upper classes. The daughter of a prominent Shanghai business family recalled the mood in 1949: "We watched to see who went over to the Communist side and what positions they took. If a sufficient number of 'responsible leaders' joined the coalition government being put together by the Communists, my uncle would stay. Otherwise we would leave for Hong Kong."[2]

The temporary parliamentary function of the CPPCC ceased in September 1954 when the formal National People's Congress was convened for the first time and a state constitution was also enacted. Nevertheless the CPPCC continued to operate as the most important organization of the CPC's united front strategy. The CPPCC after 1954 played both "dignified" and "efficient" roles in the Chinese Communist political system. The dignified role of the CPPCC was to assist the CPC in governing China by making suggestions on state policy. Hence the activity of the CPPCC paralleled that of the National People's Congress. Members of the CPPCC, like deputies to the National People's Congress, conducted investigations of society and submitted bills to the government. The national conference of the CPPCC was always convened simultaneously with that of the National People's Congress. Sometimes the standing committees of the CPPCC and the National People's Congress held joint sessions to listen to the reports of government leaders. In 1957 during the brief period of free speech (Hundred Flowers Blooming), one of the vice-chairmen of the CPPCC, Zhang Bochun (Chang Pao-chun), suggested that the CPPCC and the National People's Congress resembled the bicameral legislatures in some socialist and capitalist nations. Zhang fell short of proposing to make the CPPCC the upper house.[3] But in the final analysis, like the National People's Congress, the CPPCC was a rubber-stamp body. During the 1957 Hundred Flowers Blooming campaign, members of the CPPCC spoke out bitterly of their powerlessness and demanded a share of decision-making power. Zhang Bochun proposed that the CPC set up a political design institute (department) in which "the Communist party should fully cooperate with the People's Political Consultative

Conference national committee, the standing committee of the National People's Congress, the democratic parties and groups, and the people's organizations in discussing the important policies and problems of the state."[4] Mao Zedong rejected Zhang's suggestion by saying that what Zhang wanted was a "political design institute for the bourgeoisie" and what the CPC wanted was a "political design institute for the proletariat."[5]

There was never any doubt that Mao Zedong and his colleagues deeply distrusted the most important component of the CPPCC—the democratic parties. In April 1956 in his celebrated speech "On Ten Great Relations," Mao had this to say about the democratic parties:

> Formally speaking there is no opposition party in China; all democratic parties accept the leadership of the Communist party. But in reality some among the democratic parties are the opposition party. On questions such as "carrying the revolution to the end," "lean to one side" in foreign relations, Anti-America and Aid-Korea and Land Reform, they are partly opposed to it and partly in support of it. They have reservations on suppression of counter-revolutionaries. They said that the "Common Program" was very good and were not willing to have a constitution. But once a draft of the constitution was made, they raised both arms in a show of support.[6]

Again in January 1957, even before the launching of the Hundred Flowers Blooming campaign, Mao Zedong in a speech to provincial and municipal party secretaries referred to Chinese landlords, bourgeoisie, and democratic parties as agents of American imperialism engaging in subversive activities in China.[7] Given Mao's distrust of the members of the CPPCC, why then was the CPPCC allowed to exist and even increase its membership? The increase in the membership of the national committee of the CPPCC in Mao's time is presented below:[8]

1949:   180 members
1954:   559 members
1959: 1,041 members
1964: 1,199 members

In addition, the CPPCC had been transformed, after 1954, into an association of Chinese intelligentsia. In 1959 the second national committee of the CPPCC showed an increase in natural scientists (up by 2.6 times since 1949), intellectuals from art and literary circles (their number having been doubled since 1949), educators, and medical workers.[9] There were two possible reasons underlying this increase, both having to do with the CPPCC's "efficient" role as designated by the CPC. First, the CPPCC enabled the CPC to have an easy access to these suspected groups. Through the CPPCC, Communist leaders carried out a "thought remolding" program among members of the democratic parties, intellectuals, and former business people. It was known as self-education and self-remolding.[10] Second, by transforming the CPPCC into an association of modern Chinese intelligentsia whose political reliability was uncertain, the CPC made these suspected groups highly identifiable and thus easily isolated and controlled. During the Hundred Flowers Blooming campaign of 1957, Lo Lungji (Lo Lung-chi), a leader of the most important democratic parties—the Democratic League—alluded to the CPC's tactics: "The Communist Party recruited members from the masses of the workers and the peasants, whereas the democratic parties and groups were not allowed to. The latter might recruit members from among the intellectuals and, what was more, only from among the old style intellectuals who were quite old now."[11] The strategy of the CPC was to keep the working class and peasantry as the exclusive clients of the party so as to maintain the party's distinct identity and basic strength. The suspected bourgeois elements, in the CPC's scheme of things, are "quarantined" in the CPPCC and to be used or dispensed with as the CPC sees fit.

After the death of Mao, against the background of serious political division and mounting social unrest, present CPC leaders declared a new era of united front. The goal of the present united front is to "mobilize all positive factors, unite all those that may be united and transform all passive elements into active elements to carry out the current task [of modernization]."[12] Thus the new line of the united front calls for the broadest possible support for the CPC. Specifically, ten groups are the objects of the united front strategy. They are (1) democratic parties, (2) prominent people without party affiliations, (3) non-CPC intellectual leaders, (4) defectors from the Nationalist regime, (5) former businessmen and industrialists, (6) the upper classes of ethnic minorities, (7) "patriotic" religious leaders, (8) dependents of Nationalist party officials who now reside in Taiwan, (9) Chinese people residing in Taiwan, Hong Kong, and Macao, and (10) overseas Chinese and their dependents in China.[13]

The CPPCC, as the most important agent of the CPC united front strategy, naturally greatly expanded its ranks. In September 1984 it was reported that the CPPCC had a total membership of 281,000 and 2,645 local committees.[14] There has been a great increase in the number of intellectuals in the CPPCC, from 16 percent in 1978 to 40 percent in 1983. These are representatives from art and literary groups and professionals in science and technology, social science, education, journalism, medicine, and sports.[15] At the same time, the percentage of CPC members in the national committee of the CPPCC has been reduced from 60 percent in 1978 to 40 percent in 1983.[16] But the most remarkable development of the CPPCC in 1983 was the prominence given to a score of former Nationalist government leaders and generals, including some who had surrendered to the CPC in 1948–49 and others who had recently returned to the PRC from Taiwan via the United States.[17] Apparently CPC leaders wish to induce a sufficient number of Nationalist party leaders on Taiwan to come to terms with the party through the examples of these former Nationalist officials.

As happened briefly in 1956 and early 1957, the CPPCC at present has been allowed to assume its "dignified" role of an opinion forum. Members of the CPPCC are again conducting "social inspection." But as expected, this is a highly orchestrated affair. A Peking member of the CPPCC revealed at the sixth conference in June 1983 that during her formal inspection of certain department stores, she found that stores were stocked with goods usually in short supply and that the manner of store clerks was civil. She was then accompanied by reporters and photographers. But afterward she made an informal and unannounced visit to the same stores and found the situation very different from her formal visit, including a return of uncivil conduct of store clerks.[18] More substantial than these formalistic social inspections is the CPPCC's acting as an interest group for its real clients—intellectuals, former bourgeoisie, and dependents of overseas Chinese. In 1982, for example, the CPPCC, in response to appeals from the faculty of Hunan University on the mistreatment of professors by party leaders on campus, sent an investigation team to the university. Subsequently the CPPCC submitted a lengthy report to the CPC providing details of party leaders' persecution of professors at Hunan University. The CPPCC report was refuted by the Hunan provincial CPC. But luckily for the CPPCC, the national leaders of the party supported it. As a result, the case of Hunan University was exposed in the national paper *People's Daily*.[19] But this is more an exception than the rule. There were two reasons that the CPPCC investigation of Hunan University received the support of national leaders of the CPC: (1) the overall policy of present CPC leaders to gain the good will of intellectuals, and (2) national CPC leaders' desire to purge the Hunan CPC, which is known to be a stronghold of leftists, Hunan being the home province of Mao and governed for a long time by Hua Guofeng, the heir designated by Mao. Though national leaders of the CPC are genuine in their support of CPPCC activities, regional CPC leaders persist in treating the CPPCC with contempt, as exemplified in the case of Zhoukou city of Henan Province. Responding to the call of national CPC leaders to marshal their knowledge to contribute to China's modernization, the CPPCC at Zhoukou organized forums of specialists in industry, science, and technology and published a journal discussing problems and ways of developing local industry and technology. This angered the municipal CPC at Zhoukou, which suppressed the journal and openly insulted leaders of the CPPCC. Those specialists participating in CPPCC forums were panic stricken, afraid of being made objects of struggle. Subsequently the CPPCC at Zhoukou ceased operation.[20]

The CPPCC, as mentioned earlier, is an umbrella organization. Its constituent members are parties and organized groups. Most important among the member organizations of the CPPCC are the eight democratic parties. They are: (1) the Revolutionary Committee of Guomindang (Kuomintang), i.e., the Chinese Nationalist Party, (2) the Democratic League, (3) the Democratic Construction Society, (4) the Promotion of Democracy Society, (5) the Democratic Party of Workers and Peasants, (6) the Zigong party, (7) the September 3rd Society, and (8) the League for Democratic Self-Government of Taiwan. After 1949 the CPC assigned each of the eight parties a specific function and client group. We shall describe each party briefly.[21]

The Revolutionary Committee of Guomindang (RCG)

Established in Hong Kong in 1948, the RCG combines three dissident groups of the original Chinese Nationalist party. Of all the democratic parties, the RCG has been restricted most in activity; the CPC directed it to recruit and work only among former members of the Nationalist party or "those who have historical ties with the Nationalist party" now residing on mainland China. Before the Cultural Revolution, the total membership of the RCG was 24,000.[22]

Democratic League (DL)

Established in 1941 in the wartime capital, Chongqing (Chungking), the DL was the most prominent third party in China before 1949. Originally the DL was an umbrella organization of six minority parties. Its initial goal was to offer a third choice between the warring Chinese Nationalist party and Chinese Communist party. After Japan's surrender, the DL focused its attack on the one-party rule of the Nationalist party and moved closer to the political line of the CPC as civil war took place. In 1947 the Nationalist government outlawed the DL, which then moved to Hong Kong. After that, the DL openly aligned its policy with that of the CPC, abandoning its original stand of neutrality between the Nationalists and the Communists.[23] In the ranking of political parties in the first CPPCC conference in September 1949, the DL was ranked third, coming after the CPC and the RCG. In 1954 the DL was directed by the CPC to operate among Chinese intellectuals in cultural and educational circles. The newspaper *Guangming Ribao* is the official outlet of the DL, specializing in academic subjects. The members of the DL suffered most in the aftermath of the Hundred Flowers Blooming campaign since many outspoken critics of the CPC were leaders of the DL.

According to the CPC's own admission in 1981, in the Anti-Rightist campaign of 1957-58 "one-third of the Central Committee members of the DL were classified as 'rightists.' . . . [and] a large number of comrades [of the DL] suffered politically and *economically* for some twenty years, and [were] thus unable to use their talent in socialist construction" (emphasis added).[24] The DL had 33,000 members in 1966 before the Cultural Revolution.

Democratic Construction Society (DCS)

The DCS was started during the war with Japan among a group of Chinese businessmen and industrialists, possibly instigated by the CPC. The members of the DCS are the national bourgeoisie in the united front strategy of the CPC. After 1949 the DCS was directed by the CPC to work among "capitalists in industry and commerce and those intellectuals related to industry and commerce." In a 1956 talk with the All-China Federation of Industry and Commerce, Mao Zedong explained that the DCS, being the organization of the national bourgeoisie, concerned itself with "big issues," whereas the federation represented middle and lower bourgeoisie.[25] In 1966 the DCS had 25,000 members.

Promotion of Democracy Society (PDS)

Established in Shanghai in 1945, the PDS was initiated by three prominent and left-leaning Shanghai educators and writers. Its first leader, Ma Sulung, at one time served as education minister in the Chinese Nationalist government. After 1949 the PDS was assigned to work with high school teachers and the publishing business. The membership of the PDS in 1966 was 10,000.

Democratic Party of Workers and Peasants (DPWP)

The oldest of all democratic parties, the DPWP was first established in 1927 by Deng Yanda (Teng Yen-ta), who had at one time served under the Nationalist leader Chiang Kai-shek. At that time Deng called his party Provisional Action Committee of the Kuomintang. He advocated the merger of the Communists and the Nationalists into one party. His movement was regarded as the beginning of the third-party movement in China.[26] After Deng's execution by the Nationalists in 1931, his party was renamed the Liberation Action Committee of the Chinese People and was headed by Zhang Bochun (Chang Pao-chun), who later became a vice-chairman of the CPPCC. But in 1947 Zhang's group changed its name to the present DPWP. In a 1957 talk in Shanghai Mao Zedong said, "The DPWP has neither workers nor peasants. But we shall give it work to do."[27] So the DPWP was assigned by the CPC to work among the professionals in medicine and public health. Before the outbreak of the Cultural Revolution in 1966, the DPWP had about 10,000 members.

China Zigong Party (CZP)

The CZP was at one time a secret society among overseas Chinese in America. In reality the society's purpose was to assist new Chinese immigrants to America. Chinese revolutionaries since Dr. Sun Yat-sen had solicited aid from overseas Chinese communities in the West, the United States in particular. So the CPC promoted the CZP among relatives of overseas Chinese residing in mainland China in order to maintain contact with Chinese overseas. In 1966 the CZP had 3,000 members.

September 3rd Society

Established in the wartime capital, Chongqing, in 1944 by a group of natural scientists and educators, the September 3rd Society was originally named Forum for Democracy and Science. On September 3, 1945, in celebration of China's victory in the Second World War, the forum changed its name to the September 3rd Society. After 1949 the CPC directed the society to work among scientific and technical professions. In 1957 the September 3rd Society claimed to have 6,000 members.

League for Democratic Self-Government of Taiwan (LDST)

Organized in November 1947 in Hong Kong, the LDST was at first composed of a few native Taiwanese activists who had participated in the abortive February 28, 1947, uprising on Taiwan in opposition to Nationalist rule. Its leader then was a woman named Xie Xue-hong (Hsieh Hsueh-hung). In 1948 Xie responded to the CPC's call for convening the CPPCC, and the LDST became a member of the CPPCC. Because of Xie's criticism of the CPC in the 1957 Hundred Flowers Blooming campaign, she was denounced as a rightist, and her membership in the CPC was canceled. Almost the entire leadership of the LDST was purged in the Anti-Rightist campaign. That the LDST has never recovered from the purge in 1957 may be seen from recent CPC action to set up a new organization known as All-China Association of Fellow Countrymen from Taiwan. Before 1966 the LDST had fewer than 1,000 members.

All-China Federation of Industry and Commerce (ACFIC)

Always classed in the same league as the eight democratic parties is the All-China Federation of Industry and Commerce (ACFIC), which was established in 1953. The ACFIC is a CPC-sponsored interest group. Members of the ACFIC were petty bourgeoisie whose means of production were nationalized by the CPC in 1953–56. As mentioned earlier, Mao had distinguished the ACFIC from the DCS. The latter was for the national bourgeoisie with whom, in theory, the CPC discussed "big issues." But the ACFIC, said Mao, should be concerned only with "medium and small issues" such as compensation for property taken over by the state. Mao had pledged in 1956 to assist members of the ACFIC to solve their practical problems.[28]

The predicament of the democratic parties in the PRC was well described by none other than Mao Zedong. In a 1957 talk in Shanghai Mao spoke of a deep moat separating the CPC from the democratic parties. "The democratic parties," said Mao, "have their grievances. They are not allowed to listen, to see, or to know the true intention of the Communist party." Mao then urged local party leaders to have regular talks with the democratic parties "to let them know our true intention." But Mao quickly added that that was "to lure enemy deep into our territory."[29] Lo Lungji of the Democratic League spoke out during the 1957 Hundred Flowers Blooming campaign:

> What embarrassed the democratic parties and groups most was the lack of information required for study of policies. At the standing committee meetings of

the National People's Congress and the People's Political Consultative Conference, the democratic parties and groups could not voice any effective opinion on matters under discussion because they were not informed in advance of the matters to be discussed, and they had no time to study them at the moment of discussion.[30]

As we pointed out earlier, the democratic parties bore the brunt of the Anti-Rightist campaign in 1957–58. After that, the CPC launched the Heart-Surrendering campaign among democratic parties. In one instance in March 1958, "Ten thousand members of democratic parties, deputies of the people, scientists, educators, doctors, engineers, capitalists, writers and artists, and former Kuomintang officers" were at a rally and announced "surrendering" of their hearts to the CPC.[31] The democratic parties ceased all formal functions long before the Cultural Revolution. In October 1979 the *People's Daily* reported that the eight democratic parties and the ACFIC had convened their national conferences "for the first time in twenty years."[32]

In conformity with present CPC leaders' stress on the broadest possible united front, the democratic parties were allowed after 1979 to recruit new members in their designated population group. In 1983 the Chinese press reported that the eight democratic parties had admitted 50,000 new members, with 800 regional offices and 5,000 "basic level branches."[33] In the meantime, Communist leaders have made some gestures to bring the democratic parties into inner-party decision making. For example, one finds the rare move by the CPC in transmitting a secret party document—a speech by Deng Xiaoping on the need for organizational retrenchment—to members of the democratic parties in 1980.[34] More substantial roles are being played by the democratic parties in China's drive for four modernizations. The DL, PDS, and September 3rd Society have been allowed to open private schools that train accountants and teach other useful commercial skills. In 1981 the *People's Daily* published a sample of opinions and suggestions made by the DCS and ACFIC: change the shape of pencils, guarantee of the supply of raw materials for exported goods, establish companies specializing in certain goods, set rational prices for hog bristles, establish opinion and suggestion committees in business enterprises, and manufacture wet paper towels for tourists.[35] Lately the CPC had promoted a new task for the democratic parties—aid frontier regions. Since China's intelligentsia are concentrated in the democratic parties, they are now called upon to go to the aid of Xinjiang, Inner Mongolia, and Tibet for cultural and economic development.[36] The old desire of democratic parties to participate in a political designing institute with the CPC remained unfulfilled even after the death of Mao.

TRANSMISSION BELT

Whereas the united front strategy, according to the CPC, operates in the realm of superstructure, i.e., the functioning of the state, the organizations that are designated to perform the "transmission-belt" function form the infrastructure of the Communist party. The latter organizations enable the CPC to move society and constantly replenish the party membership. The transmission-belt organizations are also known in China as mass or people's organizations, e.g., trade unions, youth leagues, and women's associations. The concept of transmission belt originated in the Soviet Union. As Stalin explained it:

The proletariat has also a number of other organizations without which it cannot wage a successful struggle against capital: trade unions, co-operatives, factory organizations, parliamentary groups, nonparty women's associations, the press, cultural and educational organizations, youth leagues. But how can a single leadership be exercised with such an abundance of organizations? What guarantee is there that this multiplicity of organizations will not lead to divergency in leadership? . . . the party, as the best school for training leaders of the working class, is, by reason of its experience and prestige, the only organization capable of centralizing the leadership of the struggle of the proletariat, thus transforming each and every nonparty organization of the working class into an auxiliary body and transmission belt linking the party with the class.[37]

The ideas of independence or neutrality of these nonparty organizations, Stalin said, were "wholly incompatible" with the Leninist theory of revolution. What is noteworthy is that the emphasis on single leadership was at first made *before* the victory of the Communist party in capturing national power and was justified on the ground of the exigency of combating an "armed counterrevolution." But in both Soviet Russia and the PRC, approach and practice first adopted for the war situation were carried over to the postwar period. In other words, no formal or informal groups in the PRC are allowed to be independent or neutral. These nonparty organizations exist, as Stalin put it, to carry out "the line, the general direction" determined by the Communist party.

Formally, aside from the united front organizations (CPPCC, democratic parties, and ACFIC), there are the mass organizations in the PRC.[38] They are the All-China Federation of Trade Unions (ACFTU), the Communist Youth League (CYL), the All-China Youth Association, the All-China Student Association, the Young Pioneers, the All-China Women's Federation (ACWF), the Chinese Society of Science and Technology, the All-China Art and Literary Association, the All-China Association of Returned Overseas Chinese, and the China Welfare Society. But not all these ten mass organizations are of equal weight in the Chinese political system. We shall describe briefly the three most important mass organizations: ACFTU, CYL, and ACWF.

All-China Federation of Trade Unions (ACFTU)

Though the present ACFTU was established in May 1953, the CPC's organization of labor began in the very first year of the birth of the CPC, 1921. Under the fosterage of the Soviets, the CPC at first regarded the mobilization of urban workers as its primary task. But the CPC lost contact with urban workers after 1927, when the party was forced to flee to the rural areas of China. The CPC was not able to resume its work among urban working classes until 1948. When the ACFTU convened a national conference in 1953, it claimed a 1.02 million membership.[39] By 1983 the membership of the ACFTU had grown to 73 million, testifying to the great industrial expansion since 1949.[40]

According to the wording of the ACFTU charter, trade union membership is extended to "all manual and *non-manual workers* living entirely or mainly on their wages" (emphasis added).[41] Hence, employees in government offices, schools, cultural organizations, and other white-collar occupations may all join Chinese unions. Nevertheless, when the Chinese Communist press speaks of trade union activities, it refers primarily to trade unions in industries. Trade unions in the PRC are organized according to both trade and geographical administrative units. In counties and provinces there is a federation of trade unions, and these are all united in ACFTU. The national leadership of Chinese trade unions is in the Executive Committee of the ACFTU.

According to the formal charter of the ACFTU, the main functions of Chinese trade unions are to promote production and to "insure the fulfillment and overfulfillment of the construction plans of the state." Then, ambiguously, the charter states, *"On the basis of developing production,* the trade unions should *gradually* improve the material and cultural life of the workers" (emphasis added).[42] Not surprisingly, the ACFTU since its formal inception in 1953 has been rife with conflict between the official transmission-belt concept and Chinese workers' interest in using the unions to raise their living standard. The latter attitude, which is taken for granted in Western nations, is referred to derogatively in the Chinese Communist press as manifestations of syndicalism or economism.

Twice before 1958 Chinese Communist leaders dismissed top leaders of the ACFTU for siding with workers on using the unions for the material improvement of workers' lives. The union newspaper, *Daily Worker,* informed the cadres on union work in 1958:

> The good union worker takes his stand on the side of the proletariat; he does not accept the demands of the workers indiscriminately; he explains what is right and criticizes what is wrong; he raises the communist consciousness of the workers, and implements the party policy; he does not consider the improper demands of backward workers as the demand of the whole body of the worker's masses; he does not run here and there asking the party and the government to accept the demands, nor is he opposed to the party's and the government's supremacy over the trade unions, for that would be an extremely grave error. All should know that our party is the party of the working class.[43]

Because of this orthodox line on unions, the ACFTU and its member unions were not able to protect Chinese workers' interest in 1957-58 when the government implemented five new regulations about wages, benefits, and leave for clerks and workers. As one account on these measures described it: "The effect of these was to reduce the pay of the lowest categories of employees, to lengthen the period of apprenticeship during which a mere pittance of a living allowance was paid, to regulate the pensioning of employees and make pensioning off dependent on the needs of the enterprise."[44] Neither had the ACFTU been able to make the management willing to reduce the occupational hazards of workers. In 1955 ACFTU leader Lai Ruoyu protested about sickness and casualties among workers due to exhaustion.[45] By December 1957 while Lai claimed that "the number of injuries to men and equipment had decreased year after year," he nevertheless added: "In a number of industrial units and enterprises, however, many mishaps . . . still occur. Occupational diseases are still *prevalent* in some cases" (emphasis added).[46] Because of Chinese unions' inability to protect the interest of workers, Lai's worst fear was realized: ". . . divorcement from the masses is to the union . . . the greatest of all perils."[47] And Lai warned in 1957 that this divorce of unions from workers would lead to workers' pushing aside unions and organizing their own. Both in the 1957 Hundred Flowers Blooming campaign and the 1966 Cultural Revolution Chinese workers did ignore their formal unions and organized their own guilds.[48]

After the climax of the Cultural Revolution in 1975, the CPC, then dominated by Mao and his left-wing disciples, made an attempt to revive the unions. But only regional unions were reestablished and the national Executive Committee of the ACFTU remained suspended until 1978. No meaningful union work was undertaken from 1973 to 1978 since the leftists were even more orthodox in their view of unions than CPC leaders before 1967. During this leftist interlude unions were hamstrung not only by the usual strictures of economism and syndicalism but also by additional censures against concepts of production union, welfare union, and popular union,[49] for the leftists had wanted to turn urban workers into a tool of the power struggle by organizing urban workers' militia. Consequently, the leftists attacked the unions' emphasis on production, welfare, and popular acceptance.

After the death of Mao and the arrest of the Gang of Four, Chinese union work underwent phases of a short-lived "thaw" in 1978-80 and returned to the orthodox line in 1981. In October 1978, the Ninth National Conference of the ACFTU was convened, the first such conference since 1957. During 1978 Deng Xiaoping mounted a political offensive against the remaining leftists in the top echelon of the CPC. The Chinese public was encouraged by Deng to air their views freely in the name of "emancipation of thinking." Union leaders also took this opportunity to make their views known. We present here a sample of these views expressed in 1978-80 so as to reveal the state of unionism in China.

- The deputy director of Hebei Provincial Federation of Trade Unions:
   At present many "taboos" still exist in the minds of union cadres. If the cadres are told that workers are allowed to supervise leading cadres, they are afraid of being accused of "imposing supremacy over the party." If we suggest protection of the democratic rights of workers, then the cadres fear being charged with "syndicalism."[50]
- *People's Daily* editorial:
   Union leaders must remember that being responsible to the party and to the masses is one and the same. They must overcome the erroneous idea: "fear not offending the masses, fear only offending the party secretary." Union leaders must be daring in leading workers to combat bureaucraticism, subjectivism, violation of law and discipline.[51]
- CPPCC member Zhen Yu:
   In the past we dared not acknowledge the independence of unions and the unique function and rights of unions. For years, unions have had no power. Lin Biao and the "Gang of Four" had brought the unions to a state of paralysis. Before the "Cultural Revolution," as soon as a union mentioned independence, it was immediately labelled "syndicalism." In reality, independence of unions and syndicalism have no common ground. . . . the unions must protect the democratic rights and immediate interests of workers. Otherwise unions would be officially sponsored organizations and are meaningless. Since you do not protect their interests, the masses push you to one side as they rise. . . .[52]

By 1981 Deng's reformist group had already consolidated its control over the national machinery of the CPC. Deng and his colleagues had promulgated a series of reforms that included ridding Chinese industry of inefficient and obsolete plants, and they naturally feared the social consequences. So a degree of return to the orthodox line on unions was reimposed. Once more party leadership and the status of unions as the transmission belt of the CPC were stressed. An editorial of the *Workers' Daily* stated:

> Our unions are the mass organizations of the leading class. This peculiar social and political status [of the unions] distinguishes it not only from the unions before [the Communist party's] acquisition of power but also from the unions in capitalist nations. Our unions are not in an adversary position toward [their] own government and management. On the contrary they are intimate collaborators.[53]

Nevertheless this was not a total reversal to the orthodox line. Present CPC leaders need unions to report to it the reaction of those workers whose plants are to be shut down; otherwise the CPC might have to face a serious demonstration from workers. In the meantime, the CPC is promoting a Congress of Workers and Staff in every factory or enterprise to enable workers to have a say in the management and allocation of resources of their work unit. The Congresses of Workers and Staff, in theory,

> are empowered to examine reports made by the enterprise leadership, as well as to discuss major matters such as production plans, the organization of labor force, the use of enterprise funds and other financial matters. . . . [They] also oversee welfare and labor protection, make criticisms and suggestions regarding all fields of work, and exercise supervision over the work of the leadership.[54]

This "new" measure, at best, represents the wishes of top CPC leaders to satisfy the desire of Chinese workers to have a say in the condition of their work place. At the same time, if the Congresses of Workers and Staff lived up to its purpose, that would confine workers' grievances at the lowest unit and obtain resolution quickly so that a Polish-type workers' movement would not rise in China. But the Congresses of Workers and Staff face numerous difficulties in operation. First, the congresses are to be convened by the party secretary of each enterprise. Since bureaucraticism is prevalent in China, there is very little incentive for party leaders in enterprises to convene the congresses. As one deputy to the National People's Congress of 1980 pointed out, "some enterprise leaders are afraid of difficulty in meeting the demand of workers and staff, so they will not convene the congresses of workers and staff."[55] Second, the Congresses of Workers and Staff also have unrealistic goals. Chinese workers, like workers everywhere, are more interested in the material improvement of their life than in having a role in the administration of enterprise. Moreover, Chinese workers as a whole are culturally and educationally unprepared to assume administrative functions or evaluate them intelligently. A 1979 survey of 20 million workers (out of 94 million in total) found that 80 percent have less than junior middle school education, and of these, 7.8 percent are illiterate or semiliterate.[56] Another authoritative press article reported that the criteria for being an advanced worker in Chinese industry consisted mainly of "putting in more labor, enduring hardship and standing hard work." Absent from the merits of Chinese advanced workers were "experimenting with new products, innovation in production technique and adoption of new and advanced technology, enhancement of efficiency and strengthening of scientific management."[57] Third, the Congresses of Workers and Staff are nothing new to Chinese workers. The congresses were installed together with the establishment of the ACFTU in 1953. In 1962 when the PRC was under the "revisionist" leadership of Liu Shaoqi (Liu Shao-ch'i), the Congresses of Workers and Staff were stressed in the same way as today.[58] In other words, whatever alienation exists between unions and workers also exists between the Congresses of Workers and Staff and the workers of China. Chinese workers have long been accustomed to the situation described succinctly in a common saying: "Party secretary makes decisions; plant manager delivers reports; the masses play the role of fools; and the unions play a bit role."[59]

In the last analysis, be it the ACFTU or the Congresses of Workers and Staff, their function of being the transmission belt of the CPC is severely handicapped today by the mood of Chinese workers. We may gather that by first examining the composition of Chinese workers. According to the authoritative *Hongqi,* a 1981 study found that 60 percent of Chinese workers have joined the rank of the working class since 1966 and are under the age of thirty-five. They amount to 60 million. Moreover, 80 percent of these young workers are from urban working-class families, unlike the workers in the 1950s, who were predominantly fresh from the countryside.[60] In other words, the young workers of China today underwent the profound experience of violence, interruption in schooling, minimal social mobility, and political disillusionment as a result of the Cultural Revolution. These young workers are part of the "youth problem" in the PRC today. The workers share with many Chinese youth and students a general skepticism of the party line that socialism is the most superior social system in the world. A press report on the political outlook of a Peking chemical plant indicated that the most difficult question for party propagandists to explain is "the superiority of socialism," on which more than one hundred questions were asked by workers.[61] Another journal article, apparently based on public opinion polls, estimated that on average, about 20 percent of young workers may be said to be ideologically motivated.[62] Young workers are said to be so influenced by the Cultural Revolution that they are prone to factionalism, materialism, individualism, and violence.[63] As a measure of the attitudes of young workers, codes of conduct for young workers were established in some cities.[64] The overall attitude of Chinese workers may be gleaned from the title of a *Hongqi* article: "Re-imbue the Working Class with Communist Ideas."[65] Against this background, the work of Chinese unions is both difficult and vital. Whether the CPC is able to survive the social consequences of long-accumulated socioeconomic problems and the present reform depends partly on the union's ability to deal with workers' discontent. A *People's Daily* editorial revealed the anxiety of top CPC leaders over the mood of Chinese workers:

> To protect the *fundamental interest of the working class,* union organizations must confront contradictions and manage well their work. They must do their utmost to nip in the bud all factors that cause unrest, solving them at the basic level. Unions must support the legitimate demand and correct views of the masses. Toward illegitimate demand and incorrect views of the masses, unions must patiently educate and persuade so to make sure that contradictions are solved quickly. To those who are determined to ferment unrest, unions must expose them so to isolate them completely [emphasis added].[66]

The crucial question is whether, in addition to the psychological strictures in the minds of union staffs, Chinese unions have the organizational strength to accomplish what CPC national leaders wish.

The Communist Youth League (CYL)

The second most consequential mass organization in the PRC is the Communist Youth League (CYL), whose members are youths in the age group of fourteen to twenty-eight. Like union work, Chinese Communist mobilization of youth started from the very beginning of the formation of the Communist party in 1921. Today the CYL claims to have 48 million members, which is 19 percent of Chinese youth of the CYL age group.[67]

As pointed out by several writers, modern radical totalitarian regimes, be they of right or left ideology, pay special attention to the mobilization of youth. Friedrich and Brzezinski, for example, wrote:

> The totalitarian dictatorship, because of its sense of mission, is vitally concerned with the transmission of its power and ideological program to the younger generation. Indeed, it is upon the young that the hopes of the dictatorship are focused, and the totalitarian regime never tires of asserting that the future belongs to the youth.[68]

Transmission of power, however, is only one reason for the Communist party's great emphasis on youth work. Another reason for the Communists' concern over youth mobilization is their personal experience. Communist leaders such as Mao Zedong, Lenin, and Stalin began their careers as professional revolutionaries at relatively young ages, and they undoubtedly took cognizance of this fact. Scholars interested in the psychological basis of political activity, such as Harold Lasswell and Erik Erikson, have noted the ideological inclination of adolescence.[69] Before the coming of modern totalitarian regimes, organized religions had already set an example of tapping the ideological fervor of youth (i.e., the Jesuits and the Christian missionaries in the Afro-Asian world). After a totalitarian regime establishes itself, there is yet another reason for its emphasis on youth work: the youth must be kept away from the influence of rival ideologies. Youths may be useful because of their idealism, but that same idealistic inclination also makes them radical critics of any status quo.

As a mass organization, the CYL has a special status with regard to both the Communist party and other youth organizations in China. First of all, the CYL is constitutionally subordinated to the CPC. Article 49 of the present charter of the CPC states:

> The Communist Youth League of China is a mass organization of advanced young people under the leadership of the Communist party of China; it is a school where large numbers of young people will learn about communism through practice; it is the party's assistant and reserve force. The Central Committee of the Communist Youth League functions under the leadership of the Central Committee of the party. The local organizations of the Communist Youth League are under the leadership of the party committees at the corresponding levels of the higher organizations of the League itself.[70]

The key phrase in article 49 is that the CYL is the "reserve force" of the CPC. In other words, the CYL is the "prep" of the Communist party. No other mass organization in the PRC has that unique function. Quite a number of present top-ranking CPC leaders, including Hu Yaobang, were once officials of the CYL. Hu Yaobang led the youth league from 1950 until his recent appointment to national CPC leadership. Of the eleven members of the Central Secretariat of the CPC, six were once officials of the CYL.[71] That membership in the CYL is a stepping-stone to the CPC is taken for granted among the rank and file of the CYL. A former student and CYL member recalled his school days in China: "We League members were the most active students who played a leading role in all activities. . . . We had hopes of entering the Party as soon as possible and knew that this would depend upon the record we made while in the Young Communist League." [72]

Just as the Communist party has the Youth League as its "prep," the Youth League has its own "prep"—the Young Pioneers (*Shaoxiandui*). The age group for the

Young Pioneers is nine to fourteen. It was reported in 1982 that more than 70 percent of Chinese children in the age group of the Young Pioneers have joined it. The formal charter of the Youth League has a provision for the Young Pioneers, the wording of which is identical to the CPC provision for the CYL: "The Young Pioneers of China is a mass organization of young Chinese; it is a school for learning communism; it is the reserve force for the construction of socialism and communism. The Communist Youth League of China is entrusted by the Communist party of China to lead the work of the Young Pioneers." [73] Furthermore, like the relationship between the CPC—the "vanguard of the working class"—and the trade unions—the "working class"—CYL is the vanguard for two other youth organizations—the All-China Student Association (*Xuelien*) and the All-China Youth Association (*Qinglien*). In practice, these two youth organizations are perfunctory, designed mainly for activity in Communist-controlled international youth forums. Organization and control of Chinese students and young workers are entirely in the hands of the CYL.

The most "efficient" component of the CYL is its primary organizations, the smallest of which is a league branch with three to fifty members. The primary organizations of the CYL, like those of the Communist party, are established in factories, shops, schools, offices, city neighborhoods, people's communes, cooperatives, farms, townships, towns, companies of the People's Liberation Army, and other basic units. In December 1982 the CYL claimed to have more than 2 million primary organizations. [74] The official functions of league primary organizations are mainly what is known as political socialization. So the primary organizations of the CYL are supposed to organize its members to study Communist ideology and current party line and programs, propagandize party policy among the masses, and inform the CPC of the sentiment of Chinese youth in general.

The actual operation and development of the CYL over the past three decades parallel those of the trade unions. League leaders who showed any tendency toward independence were quickly removed by the Communist party. In 1952, for example, the first secretary of the Standing Committee of the CYL, Feng Wenbin, was removed from his position because of his emphasis on the youth league's special characteristics, i.e., special interest and character of the young. [75] Furthermore, as the CYL is a reserve force of the Communist party, the latter took precautionary measures to insure the "class purity" of the league. Three "class-cleansing" campaigns were carried out in the league from 1953 to 1957, ridding the league of "alien classes," i.e., children of landlords, rich peasants, and other "undesirable" families, and in 1957 rightists were removed from the league. The impact of these control measures on the youth league was similar to those on the unions. Whereas the unions were referred to derogatively by workers as departments for managing workers, the CYL is known as the bureaucracy of youth (*qingnian guan*). In 1957 during the Hundred Flowers Blooming campaign, a youth league official stated that "the main contradiction of the League at present is the contradiction between the League and the party" and that "the party's grip on the League is too tight." The main shortcoming of the league, this same official maintained, was "excessive restriction" upon youth, which turned them into yes-men. [76] During the Cultural Revolution, Mao Zedong had stated: "The Youth Association, Women's Federation and the Central organ of the Youth League are all empty frames. . . ." [77] It is telling that when Mao wanted to appeal to students in the beginning of the Cultural Revolution, he made the youth league an *object* of his revolution. After the death of Mao, in the Emancipation of Thought campaign of Deng Xiaoping, a youth league leader commented on the role of the league in the identical terms used by the late Lai Ruoyu on unions: "If the Communist Youth League loses its liaison with the youth, and does not represent the demand of youth, then it will not win the trust of youth and cannot then be a political force with a mass base. It then becomes a 'bureaucracy of youth.'" [78] Hence, just as happened to the unions, the CYL was pushed to the side by students in 1957, in the Cultural Revolution of 1966-76, and in the youth-protest movement of 1978-79.

Like the unions, the youth league of China has been weakened organizationally and ideologically by the Cultural Revolution and social unrest in China. The *China Youth Paper,* organ of the CYL, reported in 1980 that of 2.2 million primary organizations of the league, 30 percent fell into the category of "loose and paralyzed." [79] A CYL leader named Wang Jiangong reported in 1981 that the league had suffered declining membership for the past three years. Since 1978, said Wang, the league had lost 2.9 million members, and in 1980 alone 1.8 million members were lost. Wang attributed this mainly to disorganization of the league. The condition of the youth league in the countryside is especially serious. According to Wang Jiangong, in 1980, 6,548 villages (production brigades) did not have league branches (10 percent of all villages), 1,685 fewer than in 1979.[80] As mentioned earlier in connection with rural organizations, the disorganization of the youth league in the countryside was caused partly by the dismantling of people's communes and peasants' returning to household farming. Wang Jiangong mentions that owing to reversion to household farming, rural leagues found it difficult to gather people or for people to find the time to gather.

A more fundamental difficulty in league work today is youth disaffection. After the death of Mao, the Chinese press candidly reported a serious youth problem in the PRC, similar to the one in East European nations after the death of Stalin. The *China Youth Paper* described the discussion in China on youth as "a social current." [81] According to the *People's Daily,* "The youth problem is frequently talked about by the public and is of concern throughout the party." [82] But one overall diagnosis appears repeatedly: Chinese youth's skepticism of any political ideologizing. Even Wang Zhaoguo, presently head of the CYL, said "This generation of youth was brought up during the ten years of civil unrest. They do not readily believe or blindly follow. They are not satisfied with ready-made explanation or conclusion. They will accept truth only after their own empirical study, personal experience, and analysis." [83] Chinese youth are chiefly responsible for the "three-fold crisis of faith, confidence, and trust" reported in the Chinese press.[84] That is, lack of faith in socialism, lack of confidence in China's four modernizations, and lack of trust in the Communist party. Li Honglin, a major spokesman for reform, wrote in the authoritative *People's Daily* concerning the lack of faith in socialism:

"Do you believe in Marxism?"
"No, I do not."
This is the reply of a young man to a question in a survey. Though the number of people who reply this way is not large, it is still quite shocking. One recalled the time at the beginning of our state when we anxiously studied Marxism. Now thirty years later, some people do not bother to hide their disinterest in Marxism. Is this not shocking? How has this come to be?[85]

Several opinion polls have been taken recently in China to find out the views of Chinese students and youth. A poll of students at Fudan University of Shanghai found that "only one-third of students in the sample replied that they believed in communism" and "a significant 25 percent offered a chilling answer: [they believe] Nothing at all."[86] Another government-sponsored opinion poll of nearly a thousand youths in interior provinces found that 30 percent do not believe in the party line that the socialist system is the most superior one in the world.[87] A survey of 829 junior and senior high school students in the province of Guangxi in 1980 found that of all reading materials and formal subjects of study, students viewed politics the least interesting. On students' desire to join the youth league, 20.3 percent expressed no interest to join. Moreover, the more urbanized the schools are, the fewer the number of students wanting to join the youth league.[88]

Alarmed by youth disaffection, Chinese Communist leaders resort to both hard and soft measures. The hard measures consist of reinstallation of political control by the youth league over students. A system of political work cadres, political assistants, and class heads has been reinstated in Chinese universities to monitor student political activity.[89] In the meantime, ideological instruction, in spite of much evidence of its unpopularity among Chinese students, has been increased in schools. In a national conference on political instruction in school, the Chinese education minister required schools to carry out education in party leadership, basic theories of Marxism-Leninism, and Communist ethics and reimpose manual labor on students.[90] The soft measures consist of youth league's sponsorship of recreational activities such as weekend dances and sports activities. To overcome the widespread notion among Chinese youths that communism is a mere abstraction or illusion, the CYL commenced a campaign of "discovering communism close by" or "looking for the flash of communism." That is, certain meritorious deeds in society by ordinary citizens are treated as "manifestations of communism." But the most dramatic example of this new soft sell of communism was the recent awarding of the honor of "a superior youth leaguer" to a twenty-one-year-old girl named Zhang Haidi, who has been disabled since the age of six by spinal disease. Her heroic struggle with the disease and her will to live earned her the award. In the *People's Daily* report of Zhang, not a single reference, at least not initially, was made to politics or ideology.[91] This is a sharp contrast to the old campaigns of emulating soldier-martyr Lei Feng, who for a decade or so, was the official youth model. Lei Feng was a model because of his total partisanship, in the form of devoting his whole life to Mao Zedong. In Lei Feng, Chinese youth had to reach up for communism. In Zhang Haidi, communism reaches for Chinese youth. As we have discussed with respect to Chinese unions, the Communist party and the youth league of China are now on the defensive. In a 1981 conference of youth league officials, the latter were exhorted by national party leaders to "resolutely oppose and criticize worship of capitalism, bourgeois liberalism, decadent bourgeois idea of 'all for money,' anarchism and extreme form of individualism."[92]

All-China Women's Federation (ACWF)

Among the more prominent parapolitical organizations, such as the ones we have discussed so far, the All-China Women's Federation (ACWF) takes a back seat. The ACWF is not in the same class as the Chinese People's Political Consultative Conference, which is part of the superstructure of the PRC. The ACWF is not formally defined as an advanced group like the Communist Youth League. Neither does the ACWF have a clear class identity like the ACFTU. The inferior status of the women's federation may also be seen in a historical context. Whereas both the trade union and the youth league were established as separate organizations when the CPC was formed, no independent women's organization was established by the CPC until 1945. In that year a "preparatory committee for a women's federation in liberated areas" was organized by the CPC. The head of this preparatory committee, Cai Chang, subsequently assumed the leadership of both the first formal women's group—the All-China Democratic Women's League in 1949—and its successor, the present ACWF. The background of the top leaders of the ACWF, including that of Cai, confirms the inferior status of the women's federation. Cai and two other prominent ACWF leaders, Deng Yinchao and Kang Keqing, are wives of top CPC leaders. Cai is the wife of Li Fuchun; Deng, the wife of Zhou Enlai; and Kang, the wife of Marshal Zhu De. None of the three women leaders of the ACWF had played any active role either in women's affairs or in general politics. Finally, the functions of the ACWF have partly been appropriated by other mass organizations that also have substantial female membership, such as the unions and the youth league. The foregoing makes it clear that the ACWF is more "dignified" than "efficient."

The functions of the ACWF are more diffuse than other mass organizations. In terms of the class composition of its members, the ACWF is supposed to be a united front organization as it is "a mass organization of women of all social strata, nationalities and religious beliefs." However, in terms of activity, the ACWF is a transmission-belt organization. But most significant of all is the strange mix of specific missions that the CPC has assigned the ACWF to carry out. The ACWF is supposed to be, naturally, a school for communism—"to unite and educate women to take the socialist road" and "to thoroughly carry out the policies and directives of the state." Then, rather unnaturally for socialists, the ACWF is also required to teach Chinese women the spirit of "building up the country through thrift and hard work and managing households through thrift and industriousness." The second ethic—"managing households through thrift and industriousness" (*qinjian chijia*)—has a Confucian ring to it. The ACWF's function of "protecting the interest of women and children against feudal influence" comes after ideological and political tasks.[93]

In the first three years of the PRC the women's movement was pushed vigorously by the CPC in conjunction with the campaign to promulgate the New Marriage Law and the Land Reform. According to C. K. Yang:

> A large number of local reports show that peasant women everywhere in the country are coming under an organizational network dominated by the peasants' association and the Democratic Women's League. There are no figures for a nation-wide urban picture, but reports on individual cities show the same trend, women taking to organizations outside the home on an increasing scale.[94]

In retrospect, the mobilization of Chinese women that C. K. Yang described was transitory. In 1949-52 the CPC carried out several class-struggle campaigns such as the Land Reform and the Five Anti (Five Evils) campaigns. Women were organized to create an overall atmosphere of revolution of social relations. But as soon as these campaigns ended, women's organizations were no longer paid much attention by the CPC.

During the 1957 Hundred Flowers campaign, a number of prominent women leaders had accused the ACWF of being a formalistic and impotent organization. On outstanding cases of abuse of women by rape, desertion (especially by cadres who, after 1949, preferred city to peasant women), or "death and injury . . . at the high tide of agricultural cooperation," the ACWF dared not take a stand.[95] Other women leaders, including top-ranking officials of the ACWF, described mutual estrangement among ACWF leaders ("the chairman and vice-chairman . . . had few contacts with each other except during meetings"), formalism (the ACWF "relied too much on administrative orders for its work"), and a tendency to dwell on the trivial while avoiding issues "of strategic importance" to women.[96]

The ACWF before 1978 seemed to be incapacitated by an identity crisis. In the mid-1950s this identity crisis was manifested in the conflict between the ACWF's united front character and the CPC's pressure on the ACWF to exclude female leaders who were not members of the CPC. Then in the mid-1960s the ACWF faced another round of identity crisis. This time the crisis centered on whether the ACWF should concern itself with women's affairs or with class struggle. This conflict on the role of the ACWF was provoked by the Left. The class versus women's affairs conflict was precipitated by an authoritative article in the journal *Red Flag* in October 1964, "How Should We Approach the Problem of Women?" The author, Wan Muchun, wrote:

> It should be clear that if we deviate from class stand and class analysis, we will not be able to see the essence of problems involving women, and we will fail to separate ourselves from the bourgeois stand on feminist issues. To lead some of our comrades, especially female comrades, to focus their attention on things such as happiness in the family, the income of one's husband, or the goal of women in life and thus neglect current political tasks and class struggle is detrimental to our revolutionary task.[97]

Wan's article was specifically aimed at ACWF's journal, *Women of China (Zhongguo Fu Nu)*, which had published a special column under the topic "What Do Women Live For?" in 1963.[98] During this period of 1962-63, when China was still reeling from the famine caused by the Great Leap Forward, the CPC's regimentation of society was relaxed considerably under the leadership of Liu Shaoqi and Deng Xiaoping. Consequently, a degree of literary and professional independence existed. The editors of *Women of China* apparently attempted to turn it into more of a feminist journal by publishing "What Do Women Live For?" Undoubtedly underneath was an effort by some members of the ACWF to make the organization serve the interests of Chinese women in a practical way. To Mao Zedong and his leftist disciples the forum in the *Women of China* was one of the many signs of China's "turning revisionist" or "becoming bourgeois." Earlier we mentioned that on the question of minority nationalities Mao insisted that the race question was, in the final analysis, a class question. Now the same class line was extended to women's affairs.

The Cultural Revolution did not spare the ACWF. In spite of ACWF leader Cai Chang's obsequiousness (in asking Mao to inscribe the title for the journal *Women of China*) and purge of the journal editor, Tung Pien, who had published the column "What Do Women Live For?" the ACWF was suspended just like other mass organizations.[99] As mentioned earlier, Mao Zedong had called both the youth league and the ACWF "empty frames." After the death of Mao in 1978, ACWF leader Kang Keqing reported that the Cultural Revolution had forcibly dismantled women's organizations and cruelly persecuted women cadres, thus forcing the ACWF to stop functioning for about eleven years.[100] However, there were attempts to revive women's organizations in 1971-73. Since the ACWF had been criticized by Mao as an empty frame, the revival stressed grassroots organizations. In 1972 and 1973 numerous women's committees were organized in the countryside. The emphasis was on rural women of "correct class background," i.e., poor and lower-middle peasantry. The aim of the leftists was to promote a substantial number of female activists to cadre positions in the primary organization of the CPC, i.e., county, commune, and production brigade CPC committees. The extensiveness of this campaign was reminiscent of 1949-52 when the CPC had launched a vigorous drive to organize women in connection with the campaigns of class struggle.[101] Now in 1972-73 the leftists around Mao Zedong were literally in a life-or-death power contest with the entrenched CPC bureaucracy. Mobilizing women was part of the leftists' scheme to overturn the established authority pattern in the PRC. But the organization of women in 1972-73, impressive as it was, had inherent limitations. First, because of the emphasis on grassroots women's organizations, women cadres were under the control of local party authorities, which were predominantly male and "feudalistically" inclined. Second, the localized campaign also meant that there was no effective national leadership. We have seen that one important reason for the ineffectiveness of the ACWF before 1978 was lack of active and aggressive national leadership. Though Jiang Qing's power was at a peak in 1972-73, she was never known as a leader of the women's rights movement. All her close colleagues were men, and Jiang even dressed like a man when she appeared in public. Roxane Witke, her biographer, has this to say about Jiang and the women's movement:

> Although in her male-dominated society she had every reason to be a feminist, she was not one in the usual sense. Occasionally she remarked on difficulties faced by Chinese women and on changes in their status (she made no comment on women's condition in the West). But she almost never complained, though it had often been true that men in particular and in general had thwarted her right to an opinion and rise to power.[102]

After her arrest in October 1976, the Chinese press did report that Jiang had accused the CPC Politburo of male chauvinism. But that was an exception. During the Cultural Revolution Jiang had legitimized her rise to power on the ground that she was "a good student of Chairman Mao," and since Chairman Mao recognized class identity as the only legitimate identity for any individual, group, organization, or institution, Jiang could not champion the cause of women without disqualifying herself from national position. In the final analysis, the mobilization of women in 1972-73 was unrealistic. The history of the women's rights movement, be it in China or in the West, shows that it is the well-educated middle-class women who have been most aggressive in pursuing the goal of equality for women. The 1972-73 movement, however, concentrated in the countryside, among the least enlightened and most tradition-bound women of China. The educated middle-class feminists of China were discriminated against and eventually excluded from power by the ACWF even before the Cultural Revolution.

Like the unions and the youth league, the ACWF gained a new lease on life in 1979-80. It was the desire of the reformist group of the CPC, headed by Deng Xiaoping, to grant a certain degree of independence to major mass organizations in order to "mobilize all positive forces in society." The new party line for the ACWF was that the federation should emphasize, as editor Tung Pien did in 1962-63, "the special characteristics of women." In 1979 the ACWF graduated the first group of female cadres from the federation's own school for cadres. Two top ACWF leaders, Deng Yingchao (widow of Zhou Enlai) and Kang Keqing (widow of Marshal Zhu De) transmitted the new party line to the ACWF: "The cadres of ACWF must carry out their work on the principle of laying stress on the *peculiarities of women*" (emphasis added).[103] Following that, in 1980 the Executive Committee of the ACWF, the highest decision-making body of the federation, conducted a limited self-criticism, admitting:

> In the past the ACWF organizations put more emphasis on being responsible to the higherup and less on serving the lower levels; the ACWF had demanded more on women to contribute to China's four modernizations but less in showing considerations for problems that women come across in production, work and

life such as unequal pay for women in the communes, unemployment of young women in cities, the family life of female workers, discrimination and mistreatment of women in general.[104]

In 1983 the powerful Central Secretariat of the CPC transmitted the latest party line: "Turning the ACWF into the authoritative body for the protection and education of women and children."[105] Subsequently, the ACWF has been more active in taking a stand on the resurgence of female infanticide in the countryside as a result of the PRC's stringent one-child-family birth-control policy.[106] The local branches of the ACWF have also been more vigorous than before in protecting battered wives and speaking on behalf of women who have been discriminated against in employment.[107]

From our examination of the four parapolitical organizations—the CPPCC, the unions, the youth league, and the women's federation—a uniform pattern of history emerges. Each had at one time or another attempted to assert a degree of independence by representing the particular interests of their members. But each time, CPC leaders quickly and forcefully suppressed any expression of independence in the name of unified leadership by the party. The Cultural Revolution pushed the emphasis on uniformity to an extreme by making class struggle the guiding principle for all organizations. Underlying this suppression of independence is the revolutionary or military heritage of the CPC. In the minds of many CPC leaders, Mao Zedong in particular, the various mass organizations or groups in society are so many divisions or echelons of a combat-ready army. Naturally in such a military organization, independence of groups is to be minimized. But a normal modern society is a complex federation of numerous groups, each with its distinct interest and "calling." The unity and dynamism of a modern society depends greatly on the degree of mutual accommodation of interests among its numerous informal groups and formal organizations. Riding roughshod over the interests of parties, unions, and organizations of women and youth, as the CPC did before 1978, can result in each group's pushing aside the official organization and forming a different organization and in the accumulation of social problems (as evidenced in China's youth problem) to a dangerous proportion. (The late ACFTU leader Lai Ruoyu warned of the first result.) The attempt of present CPC leaders to "reconnect" mass organizations with their members is hampered not only by a credibility gap but also by the large volume of unfulfilled interests of various groups. It is the latter that has discouraged many party and state officials in Chinese enterprises from organizing Congresses of Workers and Staff. In any case there is no easy solution to the conflict between the Communist party's insistence on unified leadership and the desire of each organized social group to protect or realize its particular interest.

Before we take leave of the parapolitical organizations of the PRC, three points should be made with regard to their political role.

The first point concerns the unequal political power of the parapolitical organizations. Of the four parapolitical organizations that have been discussed here, the CPPCC and the democratic parties clearly have more access to the top-ranking leaders of the CPC than the mass organizations do. Though much distrusted by the CPC, in normal times members of the CPPCC and of the democratic parties meet with national CPC leaders on a regular basis. The speeches by members of the CPPCC and the democratic parties' members are reported by the Chinese national press (again, in normal times). In times of political relaxation such as the present, views of the CPPCC and the democratic parties are genuinely sought by the CPC, and those groups are willing to offer even critical views. In contrast, neither the union nor the youth league nor the women's federation has ever been publicly or regularly solicited by the

CPC for their views with regard to national policy. These transmission-belt organizations, instead, receive endless demands from the CPC. Thus in spite of all the populistic protestation, the CPC is very much elitist inclined.

Second, with regard to the function of the parapolitical organizations, the CPC has sought to ride both horses. On the one hand, the CPC wishes to use these organizations to augment its power by granting them the right to a separate organization. On the other hand, the CPC is extremely wary of each parapolitical group's assuming a strong independent identity and has spared no effort to impose a uniform political perspective on these organizations. Judging by the history of all these groups, the CPC seems to be consumed more and more by the latter effort. The potential for these organizations to make a significant contribution to the Chinese political process and nation building cannot but be diminished by the CPC's preoccupation with stamping out each group's independence.

Finally, the most populous group in Chinese society, the peasantry, is without nationwide representation. The peasant associations in 1949-52 did not outlive the Land Reform campaign. In 1962-64 Mao Zedong wanted to use peasants again to deal with "revisionists," so Associations of Poor and Lower-Middle Peasants were formed in the countryside. But the functions and power of these associations were never made clear.[108] After Mao aborted the Socialist Education campaign in favor of the urban-based Cultural Revolution in 1965, the Associations of Poor and Lower-Middle Peasants again languished.[109] The Gang of Four preferred urban workers' militia to poor peasants. This is an important point to make since in this chapter we have focused entirely on the CPC's dealings with a selected group of parapolitical organizations. But the statecraft of the CPC may be analyzed just as well by examining which group in society is granted the right to a "dignified" representation. The rosters of mass organizations, societies, or associations of the PRC show an unmistakable bias toward urban population on the part of the CPC. Our analysis of the mass organizations in the PRC once more confirms Bianco's observation—"Marxism may be seen as an ideological expression of the age of urbanization and industrialization."

NOTES

1. Tseng Shao-shen, "Memoir of the State-Founding Conference of Chinese People's Political Consultative Conference," *Ming Pao Monthly* 10, no. 9 (October 1974), 17-26.
2. Yuan-tsung Chen, *The Dragon's Village* (New York: Penguin Books, 1981), p. 17.
3. *Survey of China Mainland Press (SCMP)*, no. 1494, pp. 3-6.
4. Roderick MacFarquhar, *The Hundred Flowers Campaign and the Chinese Intellectuals* (New York: Frederick A. Praeger, 1960), pp. 47-48.
5. *Wan-sui*, no. 2, pp. 145-46.
6. Ibid., p. 52.
7. Ibid., p. 83.
8. *Ming Pao Daily News*, May 11, 1983, p. 1.
9. *SCMP*, no. 2001, pp. 2-3.
10. Shi Rugang, "My Understanding of 'Long-term Coexistence and Mutual Supervision,'" *Xuexi*, no. 3 (1957), pp. 9-10.
11. MacFarquhar, *Hundred Flowers Campaign*, pp. 42-143.
12. Yu Gang and Hsu Yung, "The United Front Strategy in a New Era," *Hongqi*, no. 3 (1980).
13. "Open Up a New Situation for the United Front Strategy," *Hongqi*, no. 9 (1982), p. 3.
14. *RMRB*, September 19, 1984, p. 1.
15. *RMRB*, May 8, 1983, p. 4.
16. *RMRB*, April 26, 1983, p. 1.
17. *RMRB*, June 7, 1983, p. 3.
18. *RMRB*, June 15, 1983, p. 2.
19. *RMRB*, February 24, 1983, p. 1; May 6, 1983, p. 3.

20. *RMRB,* May 4, 1982, p. 3.

21. *RMRB,* October 14, 1979, p. 3.

22. Membership figures of all democratic parties are from the Taiwan publication *I-chiu-liu-ch'ih-nien Fei-ch'ing Nian-pao (1967 Yearbook on Chinese Communism)* (Taipei: Institute for the Study of Chinese Communist Problems, 1967), pp. 590-607.

23. Su Doe, "An Analysis of the Historical Tragedy of 'Democratic Alliance,'" *Chung Pao,* July 15-18, 1982. *Chung Pao* is a newspaper published in New York City for overseas Chinese.

24. *RMRB,* January 19, 1981, p. 3.

25. *Wan-sui,* no. 2, p. 70.

26. Ch'ien Tuan-sheng, *The Government and Politics of China, 1912-1949* (Stanford, Calif.: Stanford University Press, 1970), pp. 355-56. Ch'ien also has a brief introduction to several of the democratic parties in China today.

27. *Wan-sui,* no. 2, p. 105.

28. Ibid., pp. 69-70.

29. Ibid., pp. 104-5.

30. MacFarquhar, *Hundred Flowers Campaign,* p. 43.

31. *SCMP,* no. 1737, pp. 3-4. See also *RMRB,* March 17, 1958, p. 1.

32. *RMRB,* October 12, 1979, p. 1.

33. *Beijing Review* 26, no. 45 (November 7, 1983), 27.

34. "Party Central Chung Fa No. 66 File (1980): Teng Hsiao-ping's Speech to the Party Central Political Bureau Enlarged Conference," *Chungkung Yenchiu* 15, no. 7 (July 15, 1981), 104-39.

35. *RMRB,* April 29, 1981, p. 2.

36. *RMRB,* February 6, 1983, p. 4.

37. J. V. Stalin, *The Foundations of Leninism* (Peking: Foreign Languages Press, 1965), pp. 109-10.

38. *Zhongguo Baike Nianjian 1980 (Almanac of the PRC, 1980)* (Peking: Zhongguo Da Baike Quanshu Chuhanshe, 1980), pp. 51-53.

39. *RMRB,* October 11, 1978, p. 4.

40. *RMRB,* October 27, 1983, p. 2.

41. "Constitution of the Trade Unions of China," *Current Background,* no. 484, p. 1.

42. Ibid., p. 1.

43. *China News Analysis,* no. 359 (February 10, 1961), pp. 3-4.

44. Ibid., p. 2.

45. Lai Jo-yu, "Correctly Implement Party Policy of Labor Protection," *Gongren Ribao,* February 20, 1955; *SCMP,* no. 1024, pp. 29-34.

46. Lai Jo-Yu, "Unite the People of the Whole Country. Work Hard and Practice Thrift, and Build the New Socialist China," *Current Background,* no. 492, p. 12.

47. Lai Jo-yu, "How to Treat the Masses," *Gongren Ribao,* December 18, 1954; *SCMP,* no. 1024, p. 34.

48. Alan P. L. Liu, *Political Culture and Group Conflict in Communist China* (Santa Barbara, Calif.: CLIO Books, 1976), pp. 140-51.

49. *RMRB,* November 9, 1979, p. 1.

50. *RMRB,* October 26, 1978, p. 1.

51. *RMRB,* October 22, 1978, p. 2.

52. *RMRB,* September 19, 1980, p. 3.

53. *Gongren Ribao,* February 18, 1981, p. 1.

54. *Beijing Review* 25, no. 26 (June 28, 1982), 5-6.

55. *RMRB,* September 7, 1980, p. 2.

56. *RMRB,* April 1, 1981, p. 1.

57. Yu Yennan, "Promote Advanced Workers' Movement on a Large Scale," *Hongqi,* no. 22 (1982), p. 31.

58. Li Renzi, "On the Congresses of Workers and Staff in State Enterprises," *Hongqi,* no. 2 (1962), pp. 33-37.

59. "March on the Road of Democratizing Our Country," *Hongqi,* no. 18 (1980), p. 4.

60. Yu Yennan, "Correctly Assess the New Generation of Our Working Class," *Hongqi,* no. 17 (1982), pp. 27-32.

61. Shih Baohua and Huang Wei, "A Touching Democratic Discussion," *RMRB,* January 9, 1983, p. 6.

62. *RMRB,* March 1, 1982, p. 2. Also Yu, "Correctly Assess the New Generation," p. 29.

63. *RMRB,* March 1, 1982, p. 2.

64. *RMRB,* August 18, 1980, p. 1.

65. Yu Yennan, "Re-imbue the Working Class with Communist Ideas," *Hongqi,* no. 19 (1982), pp. 35-40.

66. *RMRB,* January 15, 1981, p. 4.

67. *RMRB,* December 25, 1982, p. 2.

68. Carl J. Friedrich and Zhigniew K. Brezezinski, *Totalitarian Dictatorship and Autocracy* (New York: Frederick A. Praeger, 1965), p. 39.

69. Harold D. Lasswell, "Psychopathology and Politics," in *The Political Writings of Harold*

D. Lasswell (Glencoe, Ill.: Free Press, 1951), pp. 177–88; and Erik H. Erikson, *Young Man Luther: A Study in Psychoanalysis and History* (New York: W. W. Norton & Company, 1962), pp. 14–15.

70. "Constitution of the Communist Party of China," *Beijing Review* 25, no. 38 (September 20, 1982), 21.

71. See the biographical sketches in "New Members of CPC Central Leading Organs," *Beijing Review* 25, no. 38 (September 20, 1982), 22–24.

72. Gordon A. Bennett and Ronald N. Montaperto, *Red Guard* (New York: Doubleday & Company, 1972), p. 17.

73. *RMRB*, December 28, 1982, p. 2.

74. *RMRB*, December 25, 1982, p. 4.

75. Tang Hsin-wen, "Chinese Communist Youth League Affairs in the Past Ten Years," *Chungkun Shihnien* (Hong Kong: Union Research Institute, 1960), p. 503.

76. MacFarquhar, *Hundred Flowers Campaign*, pp. 172–73.

77. *I-chiu ch'i-lin Chungkun Nien-pao (1970 Yearbook on Chinese Communism)*, vol. 2 (Taipei: Institute for the Study of Chinese Communist Problems, 1971), sec. VII: pp. 46–49.

78. *RMRB*, November 29, 1980, p. 3.

79. *Zhongguo Qingnianbao*, October 18, 1980, as quoted in Shui Hui, " 'Movement of Educating Qualified Members' Advocated by the Communist Youth League for the Purpose of Strengthening the Organizational Reformation," *Chungkun Yenchiu* 16, no. 9 (September 15, 1982), 101.

80. The text of Wang's speech is printed in full in *Chungkun Yenchiu* 16, no. 8 (August 15, 1982), 101–17.

81. *RMRB*, June 10, 1980, p. 4.

82. *RMRB*, July 29, 1980, p. 1.

83. *RMRB*, December 25, 1982, p. 3.

84. Alan P. L. Liu, "Political Decay on Mainland China: On Crises of Faith, Confidence and Trust," *Issues and Studies*, XVIII, no. 8 (August 1982), 24–38.

85. Li Honglin, "What Does 'Crisis of Faith' Signify?" *RMRB*, November 11, 1980, p. 5.

86. "What Students Believe In," *Time*, November 10, 1980, p. 57.

87. Huang Zijian, "Just How Should One View the Youth of this Generation?" *RMRB*, February 24, 1981, p. 5.

88. Tung Nian, Zhao Ruiqiang, and Yen Xinyi, "An Investigation on the Minds of High School Pupils Today," *Jiaoyu Yenjiu*, no. 4 (1981), pp. 36–40.

89. *RMRB*, August 4, 1981, p. 1; Lin Ke, "Strengthen the Political Education of Young Students," *Hongqi*, no. 17 (1981), pp. 10–14.

90. *RMRB*, August 4, 1981, p. 1.

91. Liu Binyen, "Challenge Fate," *RMRB*, March 8, 1983, p. 3.

92. *RMRB*, January 20, 1981, p. 1.

93. *I-chiu-ch'ih-nien Fei-ch'ing Nien-pao (1967 Yearbook on Chinese Communism)* (Taipei: Institute for the Study of Chinese Communist Problems, 1967), p. 662.

94. C. K. Yang, "The Chinese Family in the Communist Revolution," in C. K. Yang, *Chinese Communist Society: The Family and the Village* (Cambridge, Mass.: MIT Press, 1965), pp. 129–30.

95. *Survey of China Mainland Press (SCMP)*, no. 1556, pp. 2–3; and *RMRB*, June 1, 1957, p. 2. For available translation of some of the women's speeches, see MacFarquhar, *Hundred Flowers Campaign*, pp. 229–30.

96. *SCMP*, no. 1556, pp. 2–3.

97. Wan Munchun, "How Should We Approach the Problem of Women?" *Hongqi*, no. 20 (1964), pp. 23–27.

98. For translations of some of these articles see *Survey of Chinese Mainland Magazine (SCMP)*, no. 374, pp. 27–34; and no. 386, pp. 12–17.

99. *SCMP*, no. 543, pp. 4–12; no. 547, pp. 14–18; and no. 552, pp. 1–7.

100. *RMRB*, September 14, 1978, p. 2.

101. *Hongqi*, no. 2 (1971), pp. 63–71; *Hongqi*, no. 10 (1971), pp. 60–64; also, *China News Analysis*, no. 919 (May 11, 1973), pp. 1–7.

102. Roxane Witke, *Comrade Chiang Ch'ing* (Boston: Little, Brown & Company, 1977), p. 9.

103. *RMRB*, October 1, 1979, p. 3.

104. *RMRB*, October 27, 1980, p. 1.

105. *RMRB*, April 29, 1983, p. 1.

106. *RMRB*, February 23, 1983, p. 3; March 3, 1983, p. 3.

107. *RMRB*, April 12, 1983, p. 4.

108. Richard Baum, *Prelude to Revolution: Mao, the Party and the Peasant Question 1962–66* (New York: Columbia University Press, 1975).

109. For more information on the defunct nature of peasant organization in China's countryside today see William L. Parish and Martin K. Whyte, *Village and Family in Contemporary China* (Chicago: The University of Chicago Press, 1978), p. 39. Also see Anita Chan, Richard Madsen, and Jonathan Unger, *Chen Village: The Recent History of a Peasant Community in Mao's China* (Berkeley: University of California Press, 1984), p. 257 and footnote.

CHAPTER 9

The Communist
Cadre System

So far our analysis of the Chinese Communist political system has focused on the institutional framework of governing. In this chapter we shall concentrate on the "governors." Though we have described national CPC and state leaders, we have not yet dealt with the people who, to the Chinese populace in mainland China, are the real governors of the PRC—the Communist cadres. Effective functioning of the institutional structure and successful promulgation of any national policy depend heavily on the cadres of the PRC.

Generally speaking, "cadres are those who hold responsible positions and wield authority over others."[1] At the lowest level, the leader of a production team in a rural village is a cadre. However, high-ranking leaders such as the late Mao Zedong or the present Deng Xiaoping are, technically speaking, also cadres of the PRC. All hold formal positions in party, state, or mass organizations and make decisions for others. A member of the Communist party may not necessarily be a cadre, but a cadre of any consequence is almost always a party member. At present there are 40 million members of the CPC but the number of cadres is 21 million.

A Chinese Communist cadre is not the same as a civil servant in the Western sense, though cadres are involved in administration. Three things set Chinese cadres apart from Western civil servants. First, since the CPC regards itself as the prototype of a new community, cadres who serve the CPC are the *select*, or *vanguard*, of the proletariat. Western civil servants are functionaries, not regarded as a chosen group. Second, Chinese Communist cadres were at one time professional revolutionaries and are still defined as such after the victory of revolution. Chinese cadres thus have a strong sense of their "ownership" of the PRC. Sociologists Turner and Killian have observed that victors of a long revolution tend to have such a sense of "ownership" of nation.[2] Among Chinese Communist cadres, especially the older ones, the sentiment that "we have *won* the country by fighting" is deeply rooted. The third difference between Chinese Communist cadres and Western civil servants lies in the extent of power that each commands. The power of a Chinese cadre over his or her "clients" is diffuse and unregulated by law. The power of a Western civil servant is limited by his or her technical specialty and the law. Moreover, the vast power of a Chinese Communist cadre over the life of the population under his or her jurisdiction stems also from the central-ized and collectivized Chinese political and economic system. A top rank CPC leader wrote in 1978: "Our country is based on the dictatorship of the proletariat and is highly centralized. The power of cadres is vast. Politics, economy, culture, education and daily necessities such as clothing, food, housing and transportation, all are under the unified management of the state."[3] Until 1983 Chinese Communist cadres as a rule enjoyed life tenure. Hence, in contrast to the civil servants in the West, who are essentially free agents, Chinese Communist cadres are a true ruling class, set apart from the population. To this day the most important and fundamental stratification in Chi-nese Communist society is the distinction between cadres (*ganbu*) and the masses (*qunzhong*). "The term 'masses' is a technical term designating individuals, persons who are not cadres."[4]

COMPOSITION OF CADRES

Chinese Communist cadres have many different ranks and occupations. Cadres are first ranked according to party seniority, which also determines, by and large, a cadre's position in the bureaucracy. A 1981 report describes the ranking according to party seniority:

> There are only about 10,000 cadres who joined the revolution during the First and Second Revolutionary Civil War Periods (1924–27, and 1927–37). They have dedicated themselves to the cause of the revolution all their lives and have rich experiences in leading various fields of work. The 300,000 comrades who joined the revolution during the War of Resistance against Japan (1937–45) are now the mainstay of the ranks of cadres. Seven million cadres took part in the revolution during the War of Liberation (1946–49) and the early 50's, and many of them are the backbone force in the leading posts in various fields of endeav-our. Apart from these, there are about 12 million young cadres who have ma-tured in the last decade.[5]

Next to the ranking in terms of party seniority is ranking of cadres on the basis of power. There are, in the common parlance of the PRC, three classes of cadres—(1) senior cadres (*gaogan* or *gaoji ganbu*), (2) leading cadres (*lingdao ganbu*), and (3) ordinary cadres (*yiban ganbu*). Since these power ranks are not part of official nomen-clature, there is no exact definition of each rank. Generally speaking, senior cadres are national and provincial CPC and government leaders, including PLA commanders of military regions. The leading cadres are generally members of area or institutional party committees, especially party secretaries, since they are the ones who make deci-sions for the rest of the people in an area or institution. The ordinary cadres are ordi-nary in relation to the senior and leading cadres. The ordinary cadres are nevertheless decision makers, though of lesser consequence than senior or leading cadres. Undoubt-edly, the three power ranks of cadres are closely correlated with party seniority, the senior cadres coming mostly from the 10,000 who joined the CPC in 1924-37; the leading cadres are more diversified, including 300,000 of the 1937-45 generation and the 7 million of the 1946-49 and early 1950s generation. The ordinary cadres are composed predominantly of the 12 million who were selected in 1960-80.
Chinese Communist cadres are also distinguished on the basis of their work. The

most important and fundamental occupational distinction among cadres is between political cadres (*zhengzhi ganbu*) and professional cadres (*yewu ganbu*). The political cadres of an institution deal with ideological work, i.e., propaganda and agitation. The professional cadres are in charge of the special task of an organization. The distinction between political cadres and professional cadres corresponds, generally, to sociological concepts of social and emotional versus task-oriented leaders. The main difference between Chinese political cadres and Western social and emotional leaders lies in their genesis. Chinese cadres are always appointed by higher authorities, especially political cadres, given the Communist ideological style of politics. In Western institutions social and emotional leaders emerge naturally from the members of a group.

Another occupational distinction among Chinese Communist cadres is that of professional, which parallels that of political and includes administrative cadres (*xingzheng ganbu*) and specialized cadres (*zhuanye ganbu*). The administrative cadres are like the administrators everywhere: they run an organization. In the PRC, however, administrative cadres have much more power than administrators in a Western nation owing mainly to the CPC's long-standing distrust of professionals or specialists. In 1979 the national leaders of CPC initiated a Reform of the Cadre System campaign, and an outpouring of letters to the national press took place. One letter, for example, describes the relative power of political and administrative cadres on one side and professional and specialized cadres on the other:

> In the current cadre system, leaders give importance to political cadres, not professional cadres. Those political and administrative cadres who are also party members are eligible to be members of the Standing Committee of the Party Committee but party members among professional cadres are not eligible for that. Under the present "party leads all," the power of political and administrative cadres is great. The professional cadres have positions but not power. On economic or other vocational matters, political and administrative cadres often make decisions without consulting professional cadres. (Sometimes these decisions are made in the names of party or Party Branch Committee). It is very difficult for professional cadres to resist any wrong decisions [by political cadres] . . . .[6]

The foregoing is about broad groupings of cadres in terms of their party seniority, power, and work. But since the party and state in the PRC are so totally bureaucratized, cadres are further classified in a complicated system of formal ranks and wages. There are twenty-four grades for the 21 million cadres in the PRC today.

Formal ranks of cadres determine not only wages but also privileges. According to Fox Butterfield:

> Only cadres above grade thirteen are allowed a leather swivel chair, like those used by Western executives. Officials in the grades thirteen to sixteen range get a soft upholstered chair with springs and a velvet-covered seat. Grade seventeen cadres are entitled to a wooden chair with a cushion; those below that, only a plain wooden seat.[7]

The hierarchical ranking of cadres, their perquisites and, until recently, their lifelong tenure have naturally made most cadres bureaucratic careerists. Yet at the same time, CPC requires cadres to have charismatic relationships with the masses. The conflict between these two norms has plagued the cadre system of the PRC ever since 1949.

CADRE RECRUITMENT

When the PRC was established in 1949, the CPC had already developed a viable cadre system, which is resistant to change. In the words of the present director of the Organization Department of the Party Central Committee, Song Renqiong,

> Our party, during the long history of struggle, has formulated a complete system of judging, using, managing and caring for cadres so that, through organizational measures, the fulfillment of our party's political task is insured. However, as the principle contradiction [in our society] changes and the focus of our party activity shifts, the aspects of our cadre system not suited to four modernizations are exposed day by day.[8]

The aspects of the cadre system that Song Renqiong deemed to be unsuited to the requirements of modernization concern, first of all, the criteria for cadre recruitment. Based on its practice in the long civil war in recruiting cadres, CPC stressed: (1) family background (*chushen*), (2) class status (*chengfen*), (3) social connection (*shehui guanxi*), and (4) seniority in the CPC.[9] The first two criteria, family background and class status, are redundant. More specifically, cadres have been recruited predominantly from poor peasants, workers, dependents or relatives of cadres and "revolutionary martyrs." The third criterion, social, is a derivative of the first two criteria. The importance of social connection may be seen in the reason used by most CPC cadres today to exclude intellectuals or members of former "bourgeois" families from cadre recruitment: their social connection is said to be "complicated." A person whose social connection is complicated, i.e., he or she associates with too many different, or "undesirable," people and, hence, is not qualified to be a cadre. Since poor peasants and poor workers associate, as a rule, with their own kind, their social connection is "simple."

In other words, the criteria for recruiting cadres are essentially two: family status and seniority in the CPC. Underlying these criteria of cadre recruitment is, of course, the CPC's overwhelming emphasis on political reliability. The emphasis on the poor peasantry (or the working class after 1949) and seniority in the party was meant to insure, first, receptiveness to CPC political persuasion and, second, having a vested interest in the victory of the CPC.

After victory in the civil war, the CPC persisted in the same cadre recruitment policy as before 1949. Apparently, like the Soviets, Chinese Communist leaders, especially Mao, regarded national reconstruction in peacetime as another form of war. Hence, cadres who are administrators rather than guerrilla fighters are still valued for their political reliability, which continues to be judged in terms of family background, class status, social connection, and seniority in the party. In the early years of the PRC, recruitment of cadres was a simple matter. Each struggle campaign, such as Land Reform, Three-Anti, and Five-Anti, was used by CPC cadres to discover activists from "correct" class background. Those who collaborated with the cadres in charge of a campaign were seen as activists and were recruited as cadres. Obviously the character of new cadres depends very much on the character of the old cadres, who recruit the former. But generally speaking, there is an overall pattern of recruiting those who were most willing to break from the status quo.

Despite the emphasis on poor peasant and worker background in cadre recruitment, the requirements of governing after 1949 did compromise the CPC's standard of cadre recruitment up to the mid-1950s. We may see this trend in the social composition of CPC membership even though, as mentioned before, not every CPC member is necessarily a cadre. In the Eighth Party Congress of 1956, the late Liu Shaoqi (Liu Shao-ch'i) reported that of the party members then, "14 percent come from the ranks of the workers, 69 percent from the peasantry, and 12 percent from the intellectuals."[10] Since then, from other sources, the percentage of workers in CPC has increased to 15, that of peasants decreased to 66, and that of intellectuals rose to 15 in 1961.[11] Obviously the group that suffered the most after 1949 in access to party membership was the peasants, who must have accounted for close to 80 percent of party membership in 1949. There is no reason not to believe that a similar change in the composition of cadres also took place in the same period. But the trend toward increase of intellectuals in cadre recruitment was stopped by Mao Zedong after 1962, in conformity with his renewed emphasis on class struggle. In 1964 at the start of China's third five-year plan, Mao spoke against cadres with formal education:

> Among ordinary cadres many are "three-gate" cadres [leaving family gate, entering school gate, then entering organization gate]. The "three-gate" way is not capable of cultivating good cadres. If our state relies on these cadres, we are in danger. Relying on cadres from the "gate of primary school," "gate of middle school" or "gate of university" will not do either. One must have book learning but too much of that is not good. Ability or skill does not come entirely from book learning; it must also be based on practice. Our country is mainly in the hands of cadres who learn while practicing.[12]

In other words, Mao preferred "cadres not withdrawn from production" (*bu tuochan ganbu*) to those receiving formal education in administration or specialized profession. So after 1964 the emphasis was on promoting cadres directly from workers and peasants. In the Cultural Revolution, recruiting worker-peasant cadres was done through the "shock" method—a whole group of peasants or workers were selected to be cadres at one time. A report from the province of Anhui, for example, states that in 1976 alone 3,403 young cadres were appointed to positions above the deputy commune party secretaries and the deputy directors of the "revolutionary committees" (the state system during the Cultural Revolution") by means of the shock method. Of these, 2,796 were selected directly from peasants and workers.[13] As a result, at least half of the present 40 million members of the CPC were admitted to the party in 1966-76. This shock method has also been extended to the military. As we shall discuss in a later chapter, during the Cultural Revolution Lin Biao also promoted a large number of peasant recruits into the officer corps. All these appointments reflected Mao's conviction that the transformation of China into what he regarded as socialism required the same political qualities that served the CPC so well before 1949.

The emphasis on four modernizations by the present CPC leaders naturally requires a cadre-recruitment policy different from Mao's. In 1980 Song Renqiong announced a major change in cadre recruitment. In a letter to another party member, Song wrote:

> The four modernizations urgently require our cadres to be younger and more specialized. From now on, in recruiting full-time cadres, we shall stress seriously cultural qualification and specialized knowledge. In accordance with the requirement of the new era, cadres will be recruited from graduates of high schools, universities and specialized institutes. As a rule we shall no longer select cadres

directly from peasants and workers whose cultural level is low. Not that we do not want cadres from workers and peasants but that we must select those who are young, educated and with specialized training.[14]

Closely related to cadre recruitment is promotion. Until the 1980s the standards for recruitment and promotion were almost interchangeable. Promotion of cadres is handled in a bureaucratic fashion by the organization departments of the party committees in every institution in the PRC. In each promotion the organization department of a party committee presents to the organization department one step above it two documents: recommendation for promotion and a personal record of the cadre in question. In theory, the higher party committee must discuss each case thoroughly among members of the committee. In practice very little deliberation takes place since the number of cadres and the bureaucratic structure of CPC prevents the higher-up from knowing lower cadres. So promotion is based entirely on recommendation and the highly formalized personnel record. Considerations for promotion are based on the familiar criteria of family background, class status, social connection, and seniority in the party.[15] The performance of a cadre on the job is not stressed. Occasionally, when a cadre's work performance is investigated, it is done behind closed doors. A news story described it:

> In the past evaluation of a cadre's work was done in secrecy. Only the upper-echelon was interviewed, not the lower echelon. Only the views of other cadres were solicited, not that of the masses. So the result of evaluation was often partial. . . . [As a consequence] those who are both "red" and "expert" but have bad family background cannot assume leadership; but those with a mediocre record in ability or performance have become leading cadres for a long time simply because of their good family background.[16]

These exposés are, of course, orchestrated by present CPC leaders bent on reform and modernization. But the important point is that the aspects of cadre recruitment and promotion being exposed do exist and are perceived to be obstacles to China's new direction in national development.

Based on the exposés of the "irrationality" in cadre promotion, the Chinese press carried reports and articles calling for election of cadres.[17] In June 1979 Hua Guofeng, then premier of the State Council, presented to the National People's Congress the proposal to open the lowest cadre positions to election. These positions were confined to people's communes, mines, enterprises, and stores—in other words, the primary organizations of the CPC and the lowest units of China's nationalized production institutions.[18] But even this limited election which was, after all, sanctified by "democratic centralism" quickly provoked a bureaucratic reaction. After February 1979 the discussion in the press on the reform of the cadre system ceased.[19] The Chinese press mentioned various opposition against "mass line" in cadre selection and promotion.[20] A front-page article in the *People's Daily* in August 1980 summed up the objections from the CPC's entrenched bureaucracy. The objections were based on four fears: (1) fear of divulging confidential materials on cadres, (2) fear that masses "muddle things up," (3) fear of promoting "factionalism," and (4) fear that cadres chosen by leaders would be rejected by the masses.[21] Finally, in December 1980 the powerful Organization Department of the Party Central Committee offered a compromise measure, based on its own experiment, combining "mass line" with appointment by existing party bureaucracy. The Central Organization Department had in early 1980 organized a special survey team staffed with representatives from state ministries of heavy industry. The team then went to nineteen factories in Xian, Chengdu, Zhonqing, and Wuhan where they conducted an opinion survey among staff and employees on the most desirable persons to be cadres in each institution. Altogether, 1,758 survey questionnaires were distributed, and 81.5 percent were returned. A total of 570 names were submitted by the employees, 2.7 times the number of present leading cadres of these enterprises. Of these, 100 names were repeatedly nominated by the employees. The educational qualifications of these 100 persons were high; over 65 percent of them had scientific and technical education at or above high school level. Then the team from the Organization Department conducted interviews with each of the 100 persons. After that, the latter were entrusted to the party committees of their institution for a period of "cultivation and observation." Finally, the names of prospective new cadres, together with those designated to be retired, were submitted to the Organization Department one step higher for approval. By October 1980, the 19 enterprises and factories had already promoted, or were in the process of promoting 41 of the 100 persons nominated in the opinion surveys.[22] This is known as a three-in-one (*san wei yi ti*) system. That is, the masses play the role of talent scout, the Organization Department conducts a comprehensive investigation, and final approval is by superiors. In short, the omnipresent bureaucracy of the CPC makes sure that nothing is allowed to pass unless its vested interests are protected.

TRAINING OF CADRES

A vital part of the Chinese Communist cadre system is indoctrination and education. Several things converge to make the CPC stress constantly the importance of indoctrinating cadres. First, the CPC as a normative organization differs from many utilitarian organizations in that it does not entrust the education of its members to society. Just like organized religions, which have its theological seminaries, the CPC has its party schools. The importance of indoctrination was also built into the CPC's past criteria for cadre recruitment. We mentioned one reason that poor peasants and workers are preferred over other groups: they are regarded as more accessible to CPC political persuasion. Easy persuasibility is also one reason for stressing "simple social connection" as a standard for recruiting a cadre. Another reason for the CPC's emphasis on indoctrination is a practical one that can be traced back to the situation that confronted the CPC in the 1930s. The CPC had to recruit from disparate and lower elements of society—"workers, peasants, lumpen-proletarians, men from mercenary armies." Political education was necessary to mold these diverse elements into a unified and disciplined force. After 1949 the requirements of a totalitarian power—expressed in the Stalinist dictum "Once a political line is determined, cadres decide all!"—further stress the need for indoctrination.

When the PRC was established in 1949, the most serious problems that the CPC was faced with in governing were illiteracy and lack of knowledge of Marxism-Leninism among cadres, some 80 percent of them being peasants. Obviously, most CPC cadres were not trained professionally for industrial and other types of management. So the CPC initiated a system of party schools with an ambitious study program. The cadres received indoctrination in Marxist-Leninist classics and also general and professional education. "Cultural extension schools" were opened to give cadres elementary education, and specialized institutes were established for higher education.

The latter included the Central Cadres Institute of Political Science and Law, the Institute of Finance and Trade, and the School for Trade Union Cadres. Chinese colleges and universities were also required to open special classes for cadres. There has been no reliable assessment as to how successful these indoctrination and education programs were. On the whole, it seems that the general education program was the most successful, at least till mid-1959. Success in improving the general literacy of cadres, however, also brought some consequences. For example, in December 1956 the *People's Daily* reported that 3 million cadres had already acquired the equivalent of a junior high school education. But then it criticized some of these cadres for losing interest in their work and wanting to go on to higher education and earn doctoral degrees.[23] Indications are that neither the ideological nor the professional education of cadres accomplished significant results. In 1958 Mao Zedong complained that the leading members of party committees in China were " 'red' but not 'expert.' . . . They are armchair politicians, being alienated from practice."[24] *Red,* should not be construed as mastery of Marxism-Leninism in this saying of Mao's, since he also criticized cadres for lack of self-confidence in ideological study.[25] But the weakest part of the CPC's training and education of cadres was the education of the worker-peasant cadres selected in the Land Reform and collectivization campaigns in the 1950s. Apparently the great majority of worker-peasants were given the most elementary general education and ideological indoctrination in short-term classes in regional party schools and then were quickly returned to their administrative posts. In 1981 a high-ranking CPC leader had this to say about the party's failure to train rural cadres for modernization:

> The cadres that were selected during the Land Reform are now in their 50's. . . . their cultural level is low. . . . We must concede that after liberation one mistake that we have made is not having seriously trained and lifted [the cultural level] of our worker-peasant cadres.[26]

It was Mao Zedong who in a 1964 talk spoke against giving cadres formal schooling. He regarded cadres with formal education as politically dangerous. Mao preferred "cadres learning while practicing."

Mao's opposition to formal education for worker-peasant cadres shows that how cadres should be educated is a very political issue in the PRC. One of the first victims of the Cultural Revolution was the president of the Central Party School in Peking, Yang Xianzhen (Yang Hsien-chen). When Yang came under public attack in August 1964, he had held that important position for ten years. Like other Chinese Communist elites who had issues of conflict with Mao in the Cultural Revolution, Yang was purged. He allegedly emphasized too much "unity of opposites" at the expense of "struggle between opposites." Subsequently, party schools were either suspended or taken over by Mao's disciples as training ground for their followers. Some of these schools were referred to as helicopter fields since cadres from these schools were quickly promoted to leading positions in the Cultural Revolution.

Naturally, after Mao's death a different policy of cadre training and education was necessary. The way post-Mao leaders of the CPC resurrected the cadre-training system also shows their sense of priority. The first institution to be revived was the Central Party School in Peking. The cadets of the Central Party Schools have always been senior party members with positions in national CPC machinery, ministries in national government or party committees in the provinces, municipalities, and autonomous regions. Hence, for any new CPC leader to consolidate his control of the CPC, he must persuade these senior cadres to support the new "line." It is no wonder that among the first formal positions assumed by Hu Yaobang after 1977 was the vice-presidency of the Central Party School so as to make sure that Deng's reform line was acceptable to the members of the party School. That was apparently accomplished. In August 1982 the *People's Daily* reported that 17,883 senior and middle-rank cadres had been graduated from the school since 1977, 2.6 times the number of graduates in the eighteen years before the Cultural Revolution. The graduates went on to be propagandists for the new line. That the Central Party School had at first served Deng's partisan purpose was clearly indicated in the *People's Daily* story:

> A major aim of the teaching at the Central Party School is to require members to grasp Marxism-Leninism-Mao Zedong Thought in a comprehensive and correct way. Taking into consideration the distortion and fabrication of Marxism-Leninism and Mao Zedong Thought by Lin Biao and the "Gang of Four," the school *edited* and *re-translated* a million-word volume of *Selected Readings of Works by Marx, Lenin and Mao Zedong* as its chief teaching text [emphasis added].[27]

Having served its short-term partisan purpose, the Central Party School in 1983 announced a new focus for indoctrination and education of senior cadres. From then on the Central Party School would educate leaders from provincial and prefectural party committees on a long-term basis, each term lasting from two to three years. The curriculum for study includes 55 percent Marxist-Leninist classics, and the remainder consists of science and culture (language and literature, symbolic logic, mathematics, history, and foreign languages) and specialized study (law, international politics, economics, industrial economy, and management). The aim of the national leaders of the CPC is that after five years of systematic education of senior cadres, the cadres will have the literacy and professional knowledge equivalent to high school or vocational school graduates. Gradually CPC leaders hope to see an increase in the percentage of senior cadres with higher education in national CPC and state institutions.[28]

After a degree of support for Deng's reform had been obtained from CPC leaders through the indoctrination at the Central Party School, then regional party schools were reestablished. Song Renqiong reported in October 1982 that 8,100 party schools had been operating and that there were 100,000 instructors in these schools. From 1979 to 1981, some 200,000 "leading cadres" (members of regional party committees) above the county level, half the total number of cadres in those ranks, had been graduated.[29] A hierarchy of party schools and instruction was institutionalized in 1983. The Central Party School in Peking is responsible for the education and indoctrination of provincial and prefectural leaders. The party schools run by provincial, special-municipality, and autonomous-region party committees educate and indoctrinate county party leaders. County party schools educate and indoctrinate party leaders working in townships and primary organizations of the CPC.[30] The curriculum of the regional party schools is naturally modeled after the ones used in the Central Party School, i.e., the core, Marxist-Leninist-Mao classics, supplemented by general and professional education. In the past, members of party schools were recommended by their party superiors. Beginning in 1983, in an attempt to enlarge the pool of prospective party leaders, party cadres have been able to enroll in party schools by passing an admission examination. In 1979 the municipal party school of Peking held its first open admission examination. At first the school feared that few cadres would apply. But 700 cadres took the examination, and 225 were admitted, most of them under thirty-five years of age. They came from factories, offices, and other schools. It is interesting that one of these new cadets' reasons for wanting to be admitted to the party school was "to know genuine Marxism-Leninism-Mao Zedong Thought so we will not be mis-led and manipulated again."[31] They did not give this reason for propagandistic pur-poses. There have been numerous indications over the years that Chinese Communist cadres as a whole are very deficient in their knowledge of Marxist-Leninist works. In a 1982 survey taken in a few provinces and municipalities, it was found that 18 percent of cadres have "a relatively systematic command of basic Marxist works," 56 percent "have a partial understanding of basic Marxist works," and 26 percent "basically do not understand Marxism." As the author of the report put it, "In short, more than 80 percent of cadres do not have a systematic grasp of the basics of Marxism."[32] Given the past criteria for cadre recruitment this result is hardly surprising.

After strengthening ideological education, the next agenda in cadre training has been to improve the general educational qualification of cadres. It is somewhat aston-ishing that more than thirty years after the founding of the PRC, the educational qualification of Communist cadres remains very low. A high ranking CPC leader wrote in the *People's Daily* in 1980 that of the then 18 million cadres, only half had an edu-cation above junior high school level.[33] A 1982 report stated that of the "leading cadres," above county, more than 40 percent had an education of *less* than junior high school level.[34] Moreover, among cadres above county the percentage of those with a college education was lower than the percentage with a college education among all the cadres. "In some places, the higher the rank, the less the number of cadres with college education."[35] In other words, until recently, the CPC systematically discrimi-nated against those with a higher education. All this, of course, is to be expected, given Mao's distrust of cadres with formal education, the criteria for cadre recruitment and promotion, and the emphasis on political cadres over professional cadres. The *People's Daily* described the consequences of the low educational qualification of cadres:

> The effects of cadres' low educational standard have been fully exposed once our focus has been shifted toward four modernizations. Everyday the contradic-tion between their weakness and the requirement of our work is being sharp-ened. Some cadres in charge of industrial production cannot comprehend design drawing, or manage factories well. Some in charge of agriculture know nothing about cultivation of crops or managing farms. Some in charge of commerce are ignorant of circulation of funds and goods. Some in charge of education have neither knowledge nor learning. As a consequence there is no progress in the work under their command, where professionals are suppressed, innovations buried, advanced technique not promoted and confusion in management con-tinued. Wasteful projects have been constructed and continue to be constructed. Astonishing waste of manpower, resources and funds occur frequently.[36]

Lu Dingyi (Lu Ting-i), director of the Department of Propaganda of the party Central Committee until the Cultural Revolution wrote in the Shanghai journal *Democracy and the Legal System*:

> In the early days of liberation we should have sent the worker-peasant cadres to receive formal education, not resorting to short-term training. We should have

subjected them to the full range of education until college graduation. If we had persisted in this way for ten or twenty years, our construction at present would have been much better.[37]

So thirty-one years later, after the death of Mao, the Department of Propaganda in 1980 issued a directive "to strengthen the education of cadres." It called for the establishment of a network of party schools and cadres' schools for specialized education, that is, a repeat of what the CPC did in 1949-50. The aim now is to send all cadres in charge of production to these schools for three or five years.[38]

The last item on the agenda of present CPC leaders for improving the quality of cadres is, of course, scientific, technical, or other types of professional education. Part of the professional training is handled by party schools, the specialized cadre-training schools (such as the old one training cadres in law), and special cadres' classes in universities and colleges. But these have not been enough, since CPC aims at giving all leading cadres in industry and agriculture some basic professional education in four years.[39] So in 1982 a new and quite novel (from the standpoint of CPC tradition) idea was suggested—to use the numerous professional associations in science and technology to educate cadres. These associations were organized to be the CPC's transmission belt, i.e., to politicize professionals whom Mao and some other CPC leaders had always distrusted. It is interesting that this innovative idea originated in the border province of Yunnan, far away from Peking.[40] The most serious problem in the professional training of cadres is a shortage of teachers, which is only to be expected in view of the disruption of Chinese education in 1966-76.

Underneath the metamorphosis of CPC cadre-training policy lies a persistent dilemma. As a normative organization, the CPC cannot entrust the general socialization of its members and cadres to social institutions outside of the party. So a system of party schools has been established to insure that CPC cadres retain their own unique identity and perspectives. But at the same time, cadres must be involved in the social process; otherwise the lofty goal of transforming China could not be accomplished. To solve this dilemma the present CPC leaders follow the Soviet example of dividing the functions of party schools and regular schools. The former *indoctrinate* and the latter *educate*. But Mao's way was more radical and fundamentally different from the Soviet method. Mao trusted neither party nor regular schools. At first glance he seemed to want to entrust cadres' socialization to society since he stressed practice. But in actuality Mao's method was quite radical in controling cadres' socialization. Essentially, Mao wanted to limit the literacy of worker-peasant cadres to the necessary minimum. In this way worker-peasant cadres would be fundamentally closed off from many aspects of society, especially the sophisticated sectors of society. The minds of the worker-peasant cadres would then be accessible to Mao's direction, which was always tuned to "lower-class authoritarianism." In Mao's view, that was the key to CPC victory in the civil war—a mass following of peasant cadres who were strong in willpower but low in literacy. After 1949 Mao believed that the same combination of low literacy and strong will would also be efficacious in national reconstruction. What Mao valued the most in worker-peasant cadres was their unquestioning compliance with his directives and their "heaven-storming determination." Mao desired constant action and quick results; the Great Leap Forward was the finest example of Mao's leadership. Turning worker-peasant cadres into school graduates was, indeed, as Mao put it, "dangerous" to his scheme. The effects of Mao's cadre policy have all been too clear to warrant further comments. But the Soviet way that the present CPC leaders are following runs the risk of causing the party to lose its unique identity unless, of course, the party has quietly made the decision to "secularize" its ideology.

DANGFEN—*CADRES' STYLE OF WORK*

Since 1978 the loftiness of CPC cadres has been questioned from another quarter. After the death of Mao and the final settlement of political succession, the Chinese Communist press launched a large-scale and rather unprecedented campaign—an exposé of the cadres' style of work or, in Chinese, *dangfen.* An extremely critical picture of the cadres has been presented by the Chinese mass media. Cadres are portrayed as being senile, infirm, and bureaucratic. They have been accused of a variety of sins such as mental "ossification" (*jian hua*), disillusionment with socialism, feudal mentality and practice, corruption, and despotism. We shall describe each briefly.

Age and Tenure

One of the first problems concerning cadres tackled by Deng Xiaoping and his colleagues was the life tenure and aging of cadres. An authorized press article described the condition as follows:

> Neither the Constitution of the Chinese Communist Party nor the Constitution of the People's Republic stipulates that leading cadres can stay at their posts all their lives. But there have been no clearly defined terms of office for leading cadres in government organizations and party committees at various levels, especially for top leaders of the party and state. Though some posts require re-election at regular intervals, persons already in leading positions are almost certain to be re-elected every time. For them, therefore, there is also, in fact, no expiration of term of office. At the same time, there is no system for enabling leading cadres to leave office and retire. They can hold on to their posts indefinitely, even if they may have become so old and weak that they have lost their capacity to do any useful work. There are no age limits for them. Thus, a leading cadre, especially a leader of the party and state, can occupy a leading position all his life, so long as he does not commit serious mistakes or is not considered to have serious problems. With the passing of time, the drawbacks of the system which is now in effect are bound to become more and more conspicuous.[41]

The aging of cadres and the de facto life-tenure system account partly for overstaffing in Chinese bureaucracy and extremely low mobility for young cadres. The Chinese press publishes numerous reports of superfluous personnel in public offices. Take, for example, the city of Xianyang of Shaanxi Province. The employees of the city government increased from 462 in 1965 to 1,076 in 1978. The superfluous staff naturally tend to whittle time away by bureaucratic busy work. So from January to October 1978, Xianyang city government turned out 4,207 official documents and 250 "briefs," an average of 15 papers a day. In a 16-day period in November 1978, the city authorities of Xianyang summoned the cadres of a nearby commune to 32 meetings. The *Shaanxi Daily,* which exposed this phenomenon, stated that "this situation [in Xianyang] exists universally in party and state administrations above the counties in the province."[42]

In the meantime, the superfluous administrators have clogged the channel of social mobility. A *People's Daily* "commentator," i.e., a high-ranking CPC leader, stated that although young and middle-age cadres constituted more than 60 percent of the 21 million cadres, "an average of only one young or middle-age cadre has been admitted, in recent years, to the leading core of each of the enterprises under some State Council ministries. The number of young and middle-age cadres being admitted to the leading groups of national or provincial organizations is even smaller."[43] So in 1980 the Organization Department of the CPC Central Committee "suggested" that by 1982, the average age of the members of CPC Standing Committees in the provinces, municipalities, and autonomous regions, the ministers and deputy ministers of national government should be reduced to between fifty and sixty years old. The average age of prefectural leaders should be fifty and that of county CPC committees should be below forty-five years old.[44] By and large, the reorganizations of provincial, municipal, and county CPCs in the spring of 1983 complied with the "suggestion" of the Organization Department (see chapter 6).

The fundamental solution to aging and superfluous personnel in Chinese bureaucracy is, of course, a formal retirement program. But the concept of retirement is alien to many CPC cadres because the Chinese Communist party is more a social movement than a modern political party (in the original sense of the term). The CPC's heritage of revolutionary war has cultivated, in the minds of the old cadres, a strong sense of ownership of both the party and the state. These cadres expect to obtain lifelong sustenance from the party. Moreover, an active position with the party or the state means not only remuneration but, more important, an infinite number of privileges. Without a formal position the privileges could no longer be obtained. That is why, as an interim measure, advisory committees have been established from national to regional CPCs and in state organizations so as to enable old cadres to keep their privileges by being given honorary positions. At lower levels, retiring old cadres is even more difficult than retiring senior cadres. Chinese press reports show that there is no provision made to care for the lives of retired basic-level party cadres.[45]

Jian Hua (Ossification of the Mind)

In 1978-79 when Deng Xiaoping mobilized Chinese public opinion for fundamental reforms of PRC politics, economics, and culture, Chinese press published numerous articles discussing the phenomenon of *jian hua,* ossification, or *ban jian hua,* semiossification, of the minds of cadres. More specifically *jian hua* refers to the deeply ingrained notions of Chinese cadres, which stem partly from their "petty producer" (peasant) background and partly from leftism, i.e., Mao's teaching. Chinese writer Hu Ping has described the various forms of "petty producer" mind: "Ignorance and superstition" (*yumei mixin*), "isolationism" (*biguan zi sou*), "complacency and conservatism" (*gu bu zi fen*), "following the beaten path" (*yinxun soujiu*), "equalitarianism" (*pingjun zhuyi*), "bureaucratism" (*guanliaozhuyi*), and "feudal-bureaucratic style of work" (*yamen zuofen*). People with this mentality, writes Hu Ping, are attracted to the ancient Chinese utopia of *datong,* i.e., great harmony or universal fraternity—the concept that Mao used in "On People's Democratic Dictatorship."[46] Accustomed to the beaten path, the worker-peasant cadres of the CPC fear reform of any kind. "To them, the existing system, no matter how deficient, is acceptable," wrote a *People's Daily* commentator, "but as to any new and improved measure to be undertaken that is bound to have some shortcomings, they would have none of it."[47] Specifically, the beaten path that most worker-peasant cadres are accustomed to is the practice and rationale taken under Mao. The Shanghai newspaper *Liberation Daily* described the legacy of leftism in the minds of many cadres:

You attempt to turn the focus of work to four modernizations and they say: "We should not abandon the key link of class struggle." You want to readjust national economy and they demand to know: "Do you mean to throw out 'Take Steel as the Key Link'?" You want to increase the rights of enterprises and they accuse you of "doing harm to unified leadership." You want to increase profit, enlarge savings and abide by the principle of remuneration according to work and they say: "You are repeating the stuff of 'Profit in Command' and 'Material Incentives.'" You want to thoroughly carry out the policy of respect for intellectuals so that those with professional education and skill shall be employed and they label you "class traitor." You want to import advanced technology from foreign nations and they hit you with the club "Turning Capitalist!" They sound very revolutionary. In actuality they are obstructors.[48]

Though the foregoing description of leftism referred specifically to high-ranking CPC leaders, i.e., like Hua Guofeng, for example, there is no doubt that the same views are shared by most cadres promoted in Mao's times. Moreover, these objections are not simply views or standpoints; various vested interests have been built on and around these leftist views. "Underneath doubts and hesitations," wrote a *People's Daily* commentator "is possible consideration of power and self-interest."[49]

Ideological Disillusionment

A logical accompaniment of most cadres' interest in power and privileges is the absence of idealism or disillusionment with socialism. In our discussion of the youth problem in the PRC, we refer to the phenomenon of "crises of faith, confidence, and trust," i.e., loss of faith in socialism, confidence in China's future, and trust in the Communist party. These crises are by no means confined to the young generation. Communist cadres are as affected as Chinese youth by widespread disillusionment with the socialist system. "There are certain party members," a Shanghai CPC journal commented, "who are passive and prone to complain in view of the colossal damages done in 'the ten years' [1966-76]. They are not very confident about the prospect of four modernizations, having all sorts of worries. Their faith in socialism and Marxism has been shaken. In their view, 'Marxism-Leninism is too abstract; socialism lacks a real example; capitalism has not declined; and Communism is illusory.' So they stress concrete benefit, not ideals."[50] A writer for the official *Hongqi* stated, in 1980, that among party members there were sayings such as: "Building socialism is too difficult and realizing Communism is too remote" or "Remote ideals are empty; concrete benefits are real."[51] Perhaps the most authoritative spokesman on the mental outlook of Communist cadres is Wang Renzhong, director of the Department of Propaganda of the CPC Central Committee. It is telling that on July 1, 1982—the sixty-first anniversary of the CPC—Wang wrote a long article not on the bright prospects of the CPC but on the "ten manifestations of individualism" in the party. These are (1) weak concept of the party, (2) setting self against the party, (3) arrogance and conceit, (4) demanding power and position from the party, (5) graft, (6) clannishness, (7) putting group interest above public interest, (8) absence of moral courage or standard, (9) corruption and materialism, and (10) worship of bourgeois life style.[52]

Present CPC leaders are prone to blame the Cultural Revolution for the lack of idealism on the part of party members or cadres. This blame is certainly true in part. However, incessant elite disputes since 1953, which were always explained publicly on the ground of ideology could not but result in popular disillusionment with socialism.

But an equally important reason, which the CPC does not wish to stress, is lack of real and steady economic improvement of the livelihood of the people in the PRC before 1978. Mao Zedong, his left-wing disciples and even some of the present CPC leaders saw only the "corrosion" of material incentives without being aware of the fact that a long period of material deprivation can also demoralize a person.

Feudalism

Given the composition of Chinese Communist cadres for the past thirty years, it is not surprising that the Chinese press has given a considerable attention to "feudalism" among cadres. "Inside our party," wrote a commentator for the *People's Daily*, "there is a large number of members with peasant background. They have not been educated culturally and remolded by Marxism-Leninism. Their minds cannot but be affected by feudal and patriarchal ideas." [53] More specifically, feudalism in the minds of cadres refers to:

> . . . cult of personality; patriarchalism and dictatorship; privileges in politics and life; remnants of ideas of clans and gangs; life-tenure for cadres; bureaucratic style of work; isolationism and official monopoly in economic work. All these, fundamentally speaking, are reflections of autocracy, monarchism and ideas of imperial authority, perquisites, hierarchy, clanism and obscurantism. [54]

The most conspicuous and glaring display of feudalism takes place in rural areas and among the cadres, from county administration down. As we mentioned before, these rural cadres were given only a very short "training course" and were not supposed to be advanced in literacy. At the same time much of the countryside of the PRC is still in a preindustrial age. Hence, the political socialization of rural cadres remains traditional. In other words, rural cadres model their conduct after traditional Chinese gentry or magistrates, adopting their predilection for pomp, ceremony, nepotism, aloofness, and most interesting of all, the large family ideal. The large-family ideal of county cadres prevents the present CPC leaders' family-planning program from being accepted by some peasants who feel no obligation to limit the size of their family, since cadres have large families. [55] Among leading cadres of the CPC, a very serious problem is that of establishing a special class for their children, in order that the children can enjoy all kinds of privileges, especially access to higher education and desirable occupations. [56]

The Chinese Communist party's exposé of cadres' feudalism adds one more example of the metamorphosis that Western-originated ideas or institutions undergo when they are transplanted to non-Western cultures. Class struggle was regarded by Marx as the motivating force for historical progress. In the PRC, class struggle has led to the domination of China by worker-peasant cadres, who have perpetrated feudalism. The crucial factor in the transplanting of ideas is, of course, the "mediator" between two cultures. In the case of the PRC, the most important mediator was Mao Zedong. The discussion of the Chinese cadres' feudalism also shows a fundamental division in the perspectives of Chinese Communists. The sources that we have used consistently are elite publications. The charge against cadres' feudalism or other forms of misconduct is made by the elite of the CPC, or perhaps only a faction of it that has a relatively cosmopolitan perspective, whereas the majority of middle and lower level cadres have a very different and predominantly parochial or provincial perspective. The division inside the CPC is naturally a result of the CPC's tortuous history from 1921 onward. Most of the cosmopolitans are the remnants of the founding generation of CPC, whereas the majority of provincials joined the CPC after 1930. In the present situation the provincials are powerful owing to their numbers, but the cosmopolitans have access to decision making at the highest echelon.

Corruption

Our discussion of Chinese Communist cadres so far has mentioned several conditions that are necessary and sufficient for widespread corruption in the Chinese Communist bureaucracy. For example, centralization and monopoly of power, low accountability of cadres, life-tenure, absence of civic ethic, clique, feudalism, a strong sense of "ownership" of the party and state, and disillusionment with ideals. Hence, it is no wonder that since 1977 various sources, both domestic and foreign, have reported a pervasive corruption among Chinese Communist cadres.[57]

Pervasive corruption in China is, first of all, reported by law enforcement authorities. According to the director of China's Supreme People's Procuratorate, from January to September 1980 Chinese courts dealt with 10,000 cases of malfeasance, of which some 4,000 were graft, bribe, theft, or other corrupt deeds.[58] During that same period, the courts in the three largest metropolitan cities (Shanghai, Peking, and Tianjin) and ten provinces dealt with 2,600 cases of political corruption, and those cases were particularly endemic in commercial offices, banks, and supply and marketing offices in the countryside.[59] Given the recency of Chinese courts and the gross inadequacy and inexperience of judiciary personnel in China, the cases handled by the courts are at best the tip of the iceberg.

Moreover, the seriousness of corruption among party cadres has obtained bipartisan recognition. Both the leftists, e.g., the Gang of Four, and their enemies, the present party pragmatists, took cognizance and condemned the pervasiveness of venal behavior by the cadres. Yao Wenyuan, one of the Gang of Four, for example, had once accused most old cadres of having the attitude: "They [the capitalists] have grabbed, let me have a go too."[60]

Corresponding to the condemnation of corruption by the highest Communist authorities are complaints to the press by the Chinese public. "The style of work of our party and our social ethic have deteriorated to the point that something must be done about them," three readers wrote to the *People's Daily*. "From leading organs to basic units, anyone with any type of authority resorts to using their office for private ends."[61] Another reader wrote: "Suppose that you want to build a house and need electricity or water, or to obtain a hospital room, to transport or sell goods or purchase equipment, you must send gifts or give feasts [to cadres in charge]. Otherwise nothing could be obtained."[62]

Reflecting public sentiments on corruption are short stories, plays, and novels written after the death of Mao. A recent survey of post-Mao Chinese literature found that a dominant theme is the venality of cadres.[63]

Finally, since the partial lifting of the propaganda wall that used to separate China from the critical eyes of Western journalists, many reports have appeared in the West on the corruptions in the People's Republic of China, which used to enjoy an uncontested reputation as a country that had (allegedly) eliminated political corruption after 1949.[64]

The higher authorities in China concentrated their anticorruption drive at the local level. The largest group of corrupt cadres, according to the press reports, is made up of county cadres, the county being traditionally the breaking point of Chinese bureaucracy. In contrast to the great attention to local cadres' corruption is the relative inattention to that of national leaders. Information about corrupt acts of national leaders, more often than not, circulates only in the rumor network.[65] Publicizing the corruption of regional officials but ignoring the misdeeds of national leaders is also the rule in the Soviet Union.[66] Apparently Communist leaders of China and the Soviet Union are very sensitive to the danger that lower bureaucrats can become the feet of clay of totalitarian states in the double sense that the lower bureaucrats might deprive national leaders of their monopoly of all resources and that the misdeeds of lower functionaries might bring disrepute to the whole establishment.

Another noteworthy aspect of Chinese corruption is the high percentage of corrupt cadres in state firms and state factories—accounting for one-fourth of the reported corruption. These socialized units of production are referred to in China as social entities (*shehui jituan*), and their purchasing power has grown with the state.[67] Cadres in these units are the ones who engage most in embezzlement, extortion, bribery, and appropriation of public goods.

In the thirty-year history of the People's Republic of China, the current anticorruption campaign is the third of its kind. The first nationwide anticorruption drive was the Three-Anti (now known as Three-Evils) campaign in 1951—anticorruption, antiwaste, and antibureaucratism.[68] That was the first indication of the propensity for corruption among Chinese Communist party cadres. The corruption then was caused mainly by political disorganization. The Communist party had not yet consolidated itself after the victory over the Nationalists, and many businessmen were trying to gain access to the new regime.

The second nationwide drive against corruption was the prolonged Four-Cleanups campaign—cleanup of irregularities in accounts, granaries, public properties, and workpoints (units for determining a farmer's wage). Whereas the 1951 Three-Anti campaign was mainly confined to urban areas, the 1963 campaign of Four-Cleanups was aimed at party cadres in rural communes.[69] The corruption in 1963, unlike that in 1951, could not be blamed on Chinese businessmen seeking access to the new regime, for the business class had been liquidated in the Socialist Transition campaign of 1952-55. The causes of corruption in the countryside in 1963-66 lay in the progressive disorganization in rural administration after 1957, particularly after the disastrous Great Leap Forward. Disorganization after 1958 was also accompanied by the CCP's suppression of all dissent from both within and without the party. From then on, surveillance and checks over the conduct of the party cadres deteriorated. It was during the 1958 Great Leap Forward, according to a recent official Chinese commentary, that there was a proliferation of undesirable behavior such as boasting, falsification of gains, and outright lying.[70]

The Four-Cleanup campaign had a catastrophic consequence for the Chinese Communist party when the top party leaders, Mao Zedong, Liu Shaoqi, and Deng Xiaoping, could not agree on how to deal with the widespread corruption among rural party cadres. The result was the great purge of the Cultural Revolution. That in turn produced more of the necessary and sufficient conditions for widespread corruption among cadres, e.g., breakdown of all semblance of law and order, rise of cliques and gangs, dislocation of the economy, and disillusionment with the party and its ideology. Two developments after the death of Mao further contributed to the spread of corruption among CPC cadres. One was the economic reform of Deng Xiaoping. Specifically, expanded foreign trade of the PRC and the rights of enterprises to conduct their own business tended to give more opportunity to venal cadres for smuggling, graft, and bribery. Second, the overall reform of administration under the present CPC leadership temporarily increased confusion, uncertainty, and resentment among cadres. In February 1983, for example, the Organization Department of the CPC issued a five-point directive to cadres who were affected by organizational change.[71] All these elements could not but facilitate more corruption among cadres. The consequence, as put by the deputy director of the PLA General Political Department, was that "the extensiveness and damaging effects of unhealthy trends and evil practices at present are unprecedented in the history of the party."[72]

Corruption among cadres not only impedes administrative reform but also demoralizes the general public. The Chinese press has frequently referred to the fact that among the discontents of the public the main one is corruption.[73] A Liaoning writer reported: "In some enterprises bonuses have been given but workers remain passive. Production does not rise. In addition to inadequate political education, a major reason is the special privileges of cadres who distort policy. As a result, unhealthy trends and evil influences spread unchecked."[74] In a poll taken at Fudan University, Shanghai, 1980, students were asked: "What is China's biggest social problem?" Fifty-five percent replied that it was the special privileges of Communist cadres.[75]

To cope with corruption, the CPC reestablished the judiciary arm of the party—the Central Commission for Discipline Inspection—and the judiciary of the state to handle disciplinary problems and the malfeasance of cadres. Second, in 1980 the national leaders of the CPC issued a code of conduct for CPC members. Last, Chinese Communist *national* leaders appealed to the public. The *People's Daily*, as the organ of the Party Central Committee, has been vigorous and aggressive (relatively speaking) in exposing cadre corruption. In appealing to the public, national CPC leaders and the press have attempted to establish their own credibility by disassociating themselves from the venal behavior of lower cadres.

Each of the measures taken by CPC leaders has met with opposition from other CPC members. The commission for discipline inspection is handicapped in its work because it is subordinated to the CPC committee of an area. Since party secretaries of area CPC committees are often themselves the object of investigation, naturally they are not enthusiastic about the commission for discipline inspection. A commentator on the *People's Daily* reported in 1981, three years after the creation of the commission for discipline inspection, that some CPC committees had called the commission "trouble making" and "mess making." So those party secretaries have deliberately coldshouldered the commission, e.g., have been unwilling to include the work of the commission in the regular agenda of the party committee, have left the commission unstaffed, or have refused to assign the staff of the commission any work.[76] Moreover, the commission for discipline inspection has been impeded by the national leaders' strategy of exposing mainly the misdeeds of subnational leaders. But as the authoritative *Hongqi* pointed out: "The present problem is leading cadres' not executing law strictly. Quite a number of criminal cases involving leading cadres have not been handled in time. This is not proper. . . . The key lies with the upper echelon."[77] The legislation of a code of conduct and media exposure of corruption apparently have had only a limited effect, if at all. The journal *Hongqi* conceded in 1982 that *dangfen* (party style of work) had not significantly turned for the better despite the fact that "we discuss *dangfen* every day in the press."[78] The main reason for that is simply the loss of prestige and credibility of the national leaders of the CPC themselves, a natural result of elite disputes in the CPC for the past thirty years. Appeal to the public might endear the national leaders of the CPC to the people, but ordinary citizens of the PRC cannot play an effective part in the anticorruption drive. One reads frequently of the extraordinary efforts and hazards a Chinese citizen has to make and the hazards he or she must risk to bring a cadre's misdeed to the *attention* of national authorities. Often a PRC citizen has to spend all his savings, even selling property, scattering his family, and making more than ten or twenty trips to the provincial or national party office to have his case heard, let alone acted on.[79]

Despotism

Among the various misdeeds of cadres exposed by the Chinese national press, one that is most contrary to the ideals of Communist cadres is the use of the "third degree" by rural cadres on peasants. For a long time Chinese propaganda portrayed rural cadres as the natural leaders of the masses, sharing "weal or woe" with peasants, although the standard of cadre recruitment and promotion casts doubt on that. Then in August 1978 the *People's Daily* reported on a directive from the then chairman of the CPC—Hua Guofeng—on the despotic practice of the cadres at Xunyi county of Shaanxi Province. The report sent out from the CPC national office read in part:

> The problems in Xunyi county are very serious indeed. The main one is the crude behavior of cadres, including illegality, indiscipline and beating and attacking masses. The practices of indiscriminate withholding [food or money from the masses] and punishment of the masses are widespread.
> County, commune and brigade cadres often resort to beating the masses. County Party secretary Liu Shuren, members of County Party Standing Committee Zhou Jingyu and Liu Quanchi had assaulted people. Of the ten party secretaries, deputy secretaries and directors of Zhetien commune, six have beaten people. . . . Li Yinbin, Party branch secretary of Zhuangli Production Brigade, assaulted some thirty people and for fifty-six times from 1974 to 1977. Once he gathered all those late in reporting for work and whipped them by leather belt. Some twenty people were hit by him. Some commune members have a saying: As soon as one hears the call of Secretary Li, put on your cotton jacket regardless of season so to be ready for the whipping.
> They have designed various ways to punish the masses, including all types of torture. Many communes had organized the so-called "militia squads," humiliating and victimizing the masses at will. Due to the crude practice of cadres, in the past three years, cases of masses committing suicide, being disabled, or driven to madness have occurred.[80]

One must add that Shaanxi is an "old liberated" province and was the base area for the CPC from 1935 to 1949. If the case of Xunyi had been an isolated one, there would not have been the need to publicize it, to transmit a directive from the party Central Committee, or to editorialize in the *People's Daily*. Xunyi was made a cause célèbre to illustrate a trend in the countryside. Subsequent to that, letters from readers and other cases of cadres' assaults on the peasants have been published in the press and journals.[81]

The causes of rural cadres' despotism are basically the same as those of other "nonviolent" misdeeds by cadres. What is noteworthy is that, ever since 1950, in the numerous struggle campaigns, arbitrary detention and abuse of persons designated as "the objects of revolution" have been an established practice. The terror and violence of the Cultural Revolution further aggravated and prolonged the violent tradition of cadres. In the final analysis, the despotism of rural cadres is a built-in aspect of the CPC cadre system in which cadres' accountability to the public is minimal.

CONCLUSION

Perhaps the most ironic, or even tragic, aspect of Chinese Communist cadre policy is that it once had the potential of contributing to Chinese national development. The CPC's emphasis on worker-peasant cadres provided a popular base for the administration. For the first time in Chinese political history, the national government was able to extend its mobilization to the countryside by cultivating grassroots leaders. What prevented the great potential of the CPC's cadre policy from being realized was the adoption of old revolutionary practices in peacetime national reconstruction and unchecked partisanship in politics. The old practice by the CPC of stressing cadres' "willpower" over literacy and accenting class struggle had definite drawbacks in post-1949 national reconstruction. There have been, of course, CPC leaders who advocated a different cadre policy, more in line with Soviet development, but they were thwarted in their effort by Mao's partisanship. Mao's preference of poorly educated cadres who could be relied upon to implement his programs without questioning was an integral part of Mao's lifelong battle against real or imaginary "enemies," intellectuals in particular. Lu Dingyi, former director of the Department of Propaganda, who had earlier acquiesced to Mao's cadre policy, summed up the deficiencies of CPC cadre policy in 1983:

> Lacking in culture and education, of course, means ignorance of democracy and legality. Then [the cadres] are prone to practice feudalism. Making steel was perverted into indiscriminate felling of timber. Taking grain production as the key link in economy was perverted into eliminating all other crops. From above this may be called blind leadership. From below this may be described as blind following. The common point between the two is ignorance. The ignorant, however, look down upon the knowledgeable and so intellectuals were suppressed for a long time.[82]

In 1978 a *People's Daily* commentator wrote: "We want a large number of cadres who dare to think, bring out and solve problems!"[83] A year later the same paper declared: "Without a spirit of vigor and vitality, a sense of honor, responsibility, revolutionary activism and a sense of urgency, it would be impossible to realize four modernizations."[84] These are stirring words; however, they sound more like calling in the wilderness than a description of empirical facts. To have the kind of cadres desired by the writers of these stirring words, something fundamental must be done by the CPC. What the CPC needs is men and women whose personalities differ fundamentally from the personality of Mao's worker-peasant cadres. The latter is akin to what is known in America as authoritarian, that is, conditioned by the custom-bound, hierarchical, and ascriptive traditional society. What the present CPC leaders seem to desire are "innovative personalities" who are alert to new things and are fearless of new problems.[85] However, to obtain what it wants, the CPC will have to change, not just "adjust," many basic aspects of its power, including ideology, organization, and constituency. On the whole efforts have been made in this direction, e.g., shifting national task to modernization, administrative streamlining, legitimizing the role of intellectuals in society and new cadre recruitment standards with emphasis on education and professional skill. It is not easy to predict the success of these reforms. We are much more certain of the strength of opposition to reform among the existing 21 million cadres.

NOTES

1. *China News Analysis,* no. 917 (April 27, 1973), p. 6.
2. Ralph H. Turner and Lewis M. Killian, *Collective Behavior* (Englewood Cliffs, N.J.: Prentice-Hall, 1972), p. 304.
3. *RMRB,* August 19, 1978, p. 2.
4. *China News Analysis,* no. 917 (April 27, 1973), p. 2.
5. *Beijing Review,* no. 31 (August 3, 1981), p. 3. Also, Song Renchiong, "Unity among Old, Middle-age and Young Cadres Is the Guarantee of the Continuation of Our Party Tasks," *RMRB,* June 30, 1981, p. 2.
6. *RMRB,* March 14, 1979, p. 4.
7. Fox Butterfield, *China: A live in the Bitter Sea* (New York: Bantam Books, 1983), p. 67.
8. *RMRB,* October 19, 1979, p. 4.
9. Ren Zhongyi, "Concerning Reform of the Cadre System," *RMRB,* June 10, 1983, p. 5.
10. Liu Shao-ch'i, "The Political Report of the Central Committee of the Communist Party of China to the Eighth National Congress of the Party," in *Eighth National Congress of the Communist Party of China* (Peking: Foreign Languages Press, 1956), p. 95.
11. John M. H. Lindbeck, "Transformation in the Chinese Communist Party," in Donald W. Treadgold, ed., *Soviet and Chinese Communism: Similarities and Differences* (Seattle: University of Washington Press, 1967).
12. *Wan-sui,* no. 2, p. 499.
13. *RMRB,* December 14, 1978, p. 4.
14. *RMRB,* July 19, 1980, p. 2.
15. *RMRB,* January 27, 1979, p. 6; *Hongqi,* no. 15 (1980), pp. 38–40.
16. *RMRB,* January 27, 1979, p. 6.
17. *RMRB,* November 7, 1978, p. 2; November 27, 1978, p. 3; February 26, 1979, p. 3; and September 7, 1979, p. 3.
18. *RMRB,* June 21, 1979, p. 1.
19. *RMRB,* August 30, 1979, p. 3.
20. *RMRB,* September 7, 1979, p. 3.
21. *RMRB,* August 21, 1980, p. 1.
22. *RMRB,* December 3, 1980, p. 3.
23. *RMRB,* December 3, 1956.
24. *Wan-sui,* no. 2, p. 146.
25. Ibid., p. 187.
26. *Hongqi,* no. 2 (1981), pp. 8–9.
27. *RMRB,* August 25, 1982, p. 1.
28. *RMRB,* October 14, 1982, p. 1; March 4, 1983, p. 1; April 29, 1983, p. 3; also, *Ming Pao Daily News,* April 14, 1983, p. 1.
29. Song Renqiong, "Transforming Cadres into Revolutionary, Younger, and Knowledgeable Professionals," *RMRB,* October 2, 1982, p. 2.
30. *RMRB,* March 4, 1983, p. 1.
31. *RMRB,* May 28, 1980, p. 3.
32. *Hongqi,* no. 12 (1982), p. 36.
33. *RMRB,* December 16, 1980, p. 4.
34. *RMRB,* December 22, 1982, p. 1.
35. *RMRB,* March 15, 1983, p. 4.
36. *RMRB,* December 16, 1980, p. 4.
37. *RMRB,* April 29, 1983, p. 5.
38. *RMRB,* March 10, 1980, p. 3.
39. *Ming Pao Daily News,* February 13, 1982, p. 1.
40. *RMRB,* May 10, 1982, p. 5.
41. "The System of Lifelong Leadership Must Be Abolished," *Beijing Review* 23, no. 46 (November 17, 1980), 20.
42. *RMRB,* January 9, 1979, p. 2.
43. *RMRB,* June 26, 1981, p. 1.
44. *RMRB,* December 6, 1980, p. 3.
45. *RMRB,* April 7, 1982, p. 2.
46. *RMRB,* February 6, 1979, p. 3.
47. *RMRB,* July 20, 1979, p. 4.

48. *RMRB*, October 26, 1979, p. 1.
49. *RMRB*, July 20, 1979, p. 4.
50. *RMRB*, January 5, 1981, p. 3.
51. Zhong Can, "The Ideals and Practice of a Communist Party Member," *Hongqi*, no. 13 (1980), p. 8.
52. Wang Renzhong, "Communists Must Persist in Holding Up Communism and Overcome Individualism," *RMRB*, July 2, 1982, p. 1.
53. *RMRB*, October 4, 1980, p. 3.
54. *RMRB*, July 18, 1980, p. 5.
55. See the case of Wenzhou city in *RMRB*, April 11, 1980, p. 4; also, *Ming Pao Daily News*, June 7, 1980, p. 3.
56. *RMRB*, April 22, 1979, p. 3; May 6, 1979, p. 3; August 15, 1979, p. 1; April 14, 1982, p. 2.
57. For a more focused study of cadres' corruption, see Alan P. L. Liu, "The Politics of Corruption in the People's Republic of China," *American Political Science Review* 77, no. 3 (September 1983).
58. *RMRB*, September 17, 1980, p. 2.
59. *RMRB*, October 31, 1980, p. 4.
60. Yao Wen-yuan, "On the Social Basis of the Lin Piao Anti-Party Clique," *Peking Review*, no. 10 (1975), p. 8.
61. *RMRB*, November 1, 1980, p. 3.
62. *RMRB*, November 19, 1980, p. 3.
63. Li Yi, "Chinese Reality as Reflected in New Literary Works," *Ch'ih Shih Nien Tai*, no. 6 (1980), pp. 28-33.
64. Georges Biannic, "AFP Correspondent Reports on 'Corruption' in Peking," *Daily Report—People's Republic of China*, June 28, 1977, p. E1; Fox Butterfield, "Peking Prepares a Drive against Corrupt Officials," *New York Times*, August 1, 1979, p. A5; and John Fraser, "Even Some Top Communists Pull Rank in China," *Christian Science Monitor*, September 26, 1979, p. 7.
65. Butterfield, "Peking Prepares Drive."
66. Steven J. Staats, "Corruption in the Soviet Union," *Problems of Communism*, no. 1 (1972), pp. 40-47.
67. *RMRB*, January 4, 1979, p. 2.
68. Chau Neu, *Corruption in Red China* (in Chinese) (Hong Kong: New Era Press, 1953).
69. Richard Baum, *Prelude to Revolution* (New York: Columbia University Press, 1975).
70. *RMRB*, December 31, 1980, p. 1.
71. *RMRB*, February 12, 1983, p. 1.
72. *RMRB*, January 4, 1982, p. 3.
73. *RMRB*, March 16, 1981, p. 5.
74. Liu Hanqing, "To Persist in and Improve Party Leadership Depends on Improvement of *Dangfen*," *RMRB*, May 22, 1981, p. 5.
75. "What Students Believe In," *Time*, November 10, 1980, p. 57.
76. *RMRB*, April 27, 1981, p. 3.
77. *Hongqi*, no. 4 (1982), pp. 6-8.
78. Ibid., p. 4.
79. *RMRB*, August 10, 1981, p. 3; March 8, 1983, p. 2; March 12, 1983, p. 5.
80. *RMRB*, August 3, 1978, p. 1.
81. *RMRB*, October 18, 1978, p. 2; October 30, 1978, p. 4; *Ming Pao Daily News*, February 27-March 13, 1982, p. 3.
82. *RMRB*, April 29, 1983, p. 5.
83. *RMRB*, December 7, 1978, p. 1.
84. *RMRB*, May 27, 1979, p. 1.
85. I have discussed more of this in "Problems in Communications in China's Modernization," *Asian Survey* XXII, no. 5 (May 1982), 481-99.

PART THREE

Coercive Organizations

CHAPTER 10

The Judiciary
and the Public Security System

The civil administration of the People's Republic of China, which we have analyzed, is complemented by a bureaucracy of coercive organizations. Traditional Chinese political systems always instituted a balance between a civil and a military governor. In modern times both the background of the rise of Chinese Communism and the ideology of the CPC predetermined the fact that the political system of the PRC is high in coercion and low in consensus building. Mao Zedong set the tone in 1949 even before his total conquest of mainland China when he summed up the formula for the CPC success: the tripod of party, army, and united front. On the eve of final victory, Mao stated in "On the People's Democratic Dictatorship":

> Our present task is to strengthen the people's state apparatus—mainly the people's army, the people's police and the people's courts—in order to consolidate national defense and protect the people's interests. . . . The state apparatus, including the army, the police and the courts, is the instrument by which one class oppresses another. It is an instrument for the oppression of antagonistic classes; it is violence and not "benevolence."[*]

As we discussed previously, the need for—in Mao's words—"strengthening the people's state apparatus" did not cease after thirty years of the People's Republic. In this section we shall discuss and analyze the three most important coercive arms of the CPC: the courts and the public security (police), the army, and the militia.

In this chapter we shall deal with the metamorphosis of the judiciary in the PRC and the function of the public security (police) system. Following our previous classification of "dignified" and "efficient" parts of Chinese political institutions, the judiciary (courts and procuracy) is mostly "dignified," whereas the public security apparatus is an "efficient" institution.

*See note 40 in chapter 10, which follows.

Like other "dignified" institutions in the PRC, such as the state constitution, the Chinese judiciary was subject to continuous manipulation by the national leaders of the CPC. The efficient public security apparatus has not been subject to the same degree of fluidity as the courts have been.

Before we describe the various phases that the judiciary in the PRC went through from 1949 to 1980, we must note two fundamental elements of PRC politics that determine the nature and limitation of the judiciary in China. One is the tradition of armed revolution, or as Mao put it, "political power grows out of the barrel of a gun." When the latest constitution of the PRC was published on December 5, 1982, an editorial in the *People's Daily* stated: "The struggle of the Communist party of China was not waged through legal means. It was through armed struggle that we led the people to overthrow the rule of Guomindang. Hence a misleading notion has been cultivated among the people, including part of Communist party membership that . . . rule of law can be dispensed with or it is deemed to be unnecessary." The second element in Chinese Communist politics that crucially affects the judiciary in China is its "ideological style" of politics. Central to the ideological style of politics is that the legitimacy of any activity or program is based less on a set of procedural rules and more on derivation from a "first principle."[1] Carl Friedrich and Zbigniew Brzezinski, for example, wrote: "The totalitarian ideology tends to dissolve the normative in the existential realm and to consider all ordinary laws merely as expressions of laws of nature and history."[2] In addition, the Marxist tradition is that law "is . . . not a guarantee of rights or the protection of a realm of freedom for all, but simply the 'will of the dominant class elevated into a statute' and its tool for the suppression of the laboring classes."[3] This Marxist notion of law was well put by Mao Zedong in 1966: "Legality is reactionary. Illegality is revolutionary. At present the reactionaries are those who would not allow others' having activism and try to restrain revolution. . . ."[4] In other words, to Mao, the work of legal codes and institutions are to be subject to the changing party line.

These two elements, i.e., tradition of armed revolution and law as an instrument of class domination, largely account for the fate of the Chinese judiciary in the first thirty years of the PRC. The post-Mao reform of the Chinese judiciary is also being impeded by these two political traditions of the CPC.

THE JUDICIARY BEFORE 1977

Mainland Chinese legal scholars have recently divided the development of legal institutions in the PRC into five stages: (1) the period of the establishment of the legal system (1949-53), (2) the period of the development of the legal system (1954-56), (3) the period when the legal construction was subject to interference and ceased to develop (1957-65), (4) the period when the legal system was severely undermined (1966-76), and (5) the period of the restoration of the legal system and its further development (1977-present).[5]

Though 1949-53 is referred to as the period of "establishment of the legal system," it is more accurate to characterize this period as one of destruction of the old legal system. The CPC abolished both the legal codes and the judicial institutions of the Nationalist government that were modeled after Western democratic nations. In the meantime, Communist leaders organized large-scale mass campaigns (or movements) to destroy old classes and institutions, and install new ones. Dong Biwu, the highest ranking CPC leader in charge of legal affairs, reported in 1957:

In the past, for the sake of emancipating productive forces, we organized mass campaigns. What is the nature of mass campaigns? A mass campaign is a storm-like revolutionary movement. Its chief means is the direct action of the masses, not law. Land Reform, Suppression of Counter-revolutionaries, Three-Anti [i.e., anti-corruption, waste and bureaucratism] and Five-Anti [anti-bribery, tax evasion, stealing state property, cheating in workmanship and materials and stealing state economic intelligence], all of them were based on mass campaigns. We did not accomplish these things by law and legislation. Our laws have been generated from mass campaigns such as Land Reform Law, Act for the Punishment of Counter-revolutionaries, and Act for the Punishment of Corruption. These were enacted after we summed up our experience in mass campaigns. The thinking of our Party was that that was the only way to liberate the productive forces of the entire nation. . . .[6]

Plainly speaking, the campaigns of 1949–53 consisted of nothing other than kangaroo courts and "revolutionary justice." Consequently, in another speech Dong Biwu stated: "Mass campaigns do not completely abide by laws. So it is possible that a side-effect is created, i.e., making people play down all laws and increasing the difficulty of our party and nation to overcome that frame of mind."[7]

Beginning in 1954, however, the PRC entered into a brief period of normalcy. On September 20, 1954, the first constitution of the PRC was formally promulgated. The constitution contained provisions for civil liberties such as freedom of speech, of the press, of association, and of religion. Subsequently, the PRC organized a Soviet-type judiciary, which consisted of two separate but interlocking hierarchies. The first one was the people's courts, headed by the Supreme People's Court, which had the sole authority to administer justice. The second structure was the people's procuratorates, culminating in the Supreme People's Procuratorate, which had the function of supervising the execution of law. Moreover, the constitution even provided a degree of independence for the judiciary. Article 78 states: "In administering justice, the people's courts are independent, subject only to law."[8] A system of defense lawyers was also established in 1954 albeit of small scale and only in a few metropolitan cities. By 1957, there were 17 lawyers' associations, 800 offices for legal aid, 2,500 professional lawyers, and 300 part-time lawyers.[9]

The judiciary and legal system of 1954–56, nevertheless, was constrained by: (1) supremacy of the CPC over legal matters, hence no real "independence for the judiciary"; (2) class discrimination against "reactionaries" (e.g., landlords, rich peasants, "bureaucratic capitalists"); and (3) continued use of mass campaigns. In 1955 alone, two campaigns of Suppression of Counterrevolutionaries were carried out, resulting in a reign of terror, especially in intellectual circles.[10]

Then came the short-lived free-speech period of May 1957, i.e., the Hundred Flowers Blooming campaign. During this time quite a number of Chinese legal specialists severely criticized and exposed Communist rule, especially party interference in legal proceedings. The PRC, declared these critics, is a land "with neither justice nor law" (*wu fa wu tien*). The CPC, under the leadership of Mao Zedong, took reprisals against both critics and their institutional base in the Anti-Rightist campaign in late 1957. The impact of the Anti-Rightist campaign on the PRC judiciary was well put by Jerome Cohen:

The "antirightist" movement of 1957–58, however, profoundly altered China's legal course, doing away with the evolving Soviet type of judicial system and developing in its stead an administrative apparatus for settling disputes and imposing sanctions. This new system was closely controlled by the Communist party and the Ministry of Public Security (the police). It did not merely give greater emphasis to the P.R.C.'s already impressive institutions for handling most civil disputes and minor offenses in communes, factories, and urban neighborhoods rather than the courts. It also authorized the police and other units—without securing judicial approval—to impose even major, supposedly "noncriminal," deprivations of freedom upon political dissidents and others, and it reduced the role of the courts to virtually rubber-stamping the sentences recommended by the police and party for those formally stigmatized as criminals.

Nothing more was heard about the promised promulgation of codes. Lawyers were phased out. The procuracy, which had frequently questioned the legality of arrests and prosecutions insisted on by the police, was curbed. The experiments with public trials ceased, and legal education and scholarship became more highly politicized than ever.[11]

It was during this period of 1957-65 that the practice began whereby the party secretary decided cases and meted out punishment without having to cite any criminal code.[12] But the worst was yet to come.

In 1966 the PRC was again plunged into mass campaigns: It was the Great Proletarian Cultural Revolution. Since Mao had said that "legality is reactionary; illegality is revolutionary," the judicial organs were "smashed" in 1966-76. The leaders of the Cultural Revolution, said a recent article in a Chinese Communist law journal, "let loose hoodlums and thugs to smash, grab and loot, to break into and ransack homes, illegally detain people, set up kangaroo courts and torture innocent people to extort confessions."[13] After Mao's death and the arrest of the Gang of Four, present CPC leaders reopened those cases of 1966-76 in which the defendants had been accused of committing counterrevolutionary crimes. On an average, two Chinese writers reported, 40 percent of such cases in various localities of China were found to be either questionable or based on false accusations. In some places the percentage of wrongly decided cases reached 60 to 70 percent.[14]

To sum up the Chinese judiciary before 1977, the chief characteristic is paucity of legislation. For thirty years China had neither a criminal nor a civil law. In 1962, reviewing the legal system of the PRC, Franz Michael wrote: "Over twelve years after the establishment of this regime, the Chinese Communists have practically no law of substance" and "a law of substance that provides well-defined norms for human relations does not exist."[15] Eighteen years later, two Chinese writers reported: "Our state has existed for thirty years but our legal legislation, especially concerning rights and duties governing relations among the people, has stagnated for a long time."[16] To most CPC members and cadres, party policy is law. Consequently, in law schools, students were not taught criminal or civil law before 1979, since there was none. Instead, law students learned "party policy on crime" and "party policy on civil matters." The so-called theory of law classes taught "party leadership," "mass line," and "to serve the need of current program of the Party."[17]

The second most important characteristic of the Chinese judiciary before 1977 was interference by numerous extralegal factors. The CPC, especially Mao, continued to rely on mass campaigns to order society. A Chinese writer stated in 1979 that in the past "sentencing by a court always stressed the need [to conform to] current class struggle and mass movement, not on the basis of crime committed."[18] After 1957 sentencing by courts had to be approved by the party secretary in the area. Moreover, during the Cultural Revolution the standard practice was to set up an ad hoc "cadre investigation team" of higher CPC authorities to handle any case involving a party leader accused of certain crimes. In these cases, the court was not permitted to examine evidence or question the defendant. Sentencing in these cases was decided by the ad hoc team. The court merely rubber-stamped it.[19] Finally, court judgment before 1977 was also affected by the "class status" of a person or position in the CPC. If a defendant was a worker, poor peasant, old cadre, or leading cadre, his or her criminal offense was usually dismissed with a light sentence or even none at all. But if a defendant belonged to one of the five "black elements" (i.e., landlord, rich peasant, counterrevolutionary, "bad element," rightist), then severe punishment was always imposed.[20]

THE JUDICIARY FROM 1977

It was against the foregoing history that a comprehensive reform of the Chinese judiciary was carried out after 1977. The third plenary session of the Eleventh Central Committee of the CPC in December 1978 set forth four principles for reform of the Chinese legal system. They are

1. There must be laws for people to follow
2. These laws must be observed
3. Their enforcement must be strict
4. Law breakers must be dealt with

The first principle of reform calls for legislation. In 1979–80 several major laws were enacted: Arrest and Detention Act, Criminal Law, Criminal Procedure Law, Organic Law for Courts, Organic Law for Procuratorate, and Provisional Act on Lawyers. In 1982 a provisional Civil Procedure Law was enacted also. Simultaneously, the court system and procuracy as first established in 1954 were restored in 1978–79. The system of defense lawyers was revived, though mainly in major cities such as Shanghai and Peking. In August 1980 the practice of the party secretary's reviewing court decisions was abolished. But there is no open commitment on the part of the CPC to the principle of an independent judiciary. Article 126 of the current constitution of the PRC states, "The people's courts shall, in accordance with the law, exercise judicial power independently and are not subject to interference by administrative organs, social organizations or individuals." As Hungdah Chiu pointed out, "Since the party is neither an administrative organ nor a social organization, this provision appears not to prohibit party interference in the judiciary."[21]

How much protection can a Chinese citizen expect from the formal law in the PRC today?

The new criminal law attempts to provide a degree of protection for Chinese citizens, especially against the much-dreaded charge of counterrevolutionary crime. The law stresses that before anyone can be accused of committing a counterrevolutionary crime, there must first be established a counterrevolutionary intention or aim. Second, an accused person must have committed some action, not just harbored damaging thoughts against the state.[22] But the trial and imprisonment of young dissident Wei Jingshen in October 1979 show the limitation of the new law. Wei was arrested on March 29, 1979, on a formal charge of supplying military secrets regarding the Sino-Vietnamese War to a foreigner (a British reporter in Peking). Until his arrest, Wei was a prominent young dissident and publisher of a widely read unofficial journal,

Exploration, in Peking. Shortly before his arrest, Wei had demanded democracy in his journal and expressed his skepticism of Deng Xiaoping's commitment to democracy. Every aspect of Wei's trial contradicted the spirit, if not the letter, of the new criminal code (technically, the new criminal code took effect in January 1980). Wei was put on trial six months after his arrest. His trial was not open; only a selected group of citizens were allowed to attend, not including Wei's friends and relatives. No corroborating witness was called by the prosecutor. The prosecution and the defense took just one day. Since the new criminal code was not yet in effect, the court made use of article 16 of the 1951 Counterrevolutionary Act, which is based on the principle of crime by analogy. Wei was sentenced to fifteen years' imprisonment.[23] The case of Wei Jingshen shows, at the least, that so far as political dissenters are concerned, Deng's reform in China's legal system is more apparent than real. Wei's case is not an isolated one, because in the fall of 1978, extending through the spring of 1979, a wave of protest and demand for democracy and human rights arose in major Chinese cities, especially in Peking. The majority of dissenters consisted of young students, or like Wei, workers. Apparently the national authorities of the CPC used Wei's case to warn the rest of the dissenters. Shortly after Wei's "trial," a high-ranking CPC leader wrote an article for the *Guanming Ribao,* a paper designed for highly educated readers, declaring that the human rights question "has become a tool for international political struggle" and that "on the question of human rights it is difficult to find a common language between the proletariat and the bourgeoisie."[24]

As for the majority of ordinary Chinese citizens, the terror of 1966–76 may be a thing of the past, but "protection" under the new legal codes is still handicapped by several things. The first concerns the quality of legal workers in the PRC. In 1980 a deputy to the National People's Congress revealed that on an average there are 1.5 law school graduates in each people's court in China.[25] From 1953 to 1979 a total of 20,000 students graduated from the law institutes of China, a mere 0.6 percent of all college graduates.[26] The second handicap in the protection of Chinese citizens is the paucity of defense lawyers. In 1980, with the Chinese population near a billion, China had 3,000 lawyers.[27] Moreover, defense by lawyers is an alien idea in the minds of the majority of CPC leaders of all ranks. A Shanghai professor reported that a county party secretary forbade any lawyer to practice in his county on the notion that "lawyers always defend bad people."[28] A defendant in the PRC today is tried not only before a judge but also before "people's assessors," who are "representatives of the masses." In principle, people's assessors are elected, but the PRC has not yet established a formal system of such election. At present the people's courts invite the masses to serve as people's assessors. In Peking, for example, in the first seven months of 1979, 32,000 residents were invited to serve as people's assessors.[29] In principle, a people's assessor has the same rights as the judge, e.g., in examining evidence, questioning the defendant or witness, and after a trial, participating in deliberation over sentences.[30] In the few show trials witnessed by American visitors to China, the people's assessors performed their role correctly, but whether the assessors have real substantive functions is still a moot point.[31] It is also a practice of Chinese courts to consult the attending "masses" in the courtroom for opinions, especially those who are associated with the defendant as colleagues in the work place or as neighbors. At best, however, they offer information of mitigating nature in civil and nonpolitical criminal cases. In cases of counterrevolution, consulting the masses means receiving mass assent for court sentences.

Another major handicap in China's attempt to establish a formal judiciary is the attitude of the great majority of Communist party cadres. The Chinese press has commented repeatedly on the following mistaken notions of law among cadres: (1) "Equality before law means absence of class stand";[32] (2) "Defense by lawyers means class surrender";[33] and (3) "Executing party policy is all that is necessary; law abiding is not important."[34] But in the last analysis, the laws of the PRC are, as stated in the new criminal code, "for the defense of the dictatorship of the proletariat." In other words, the authority of the Communist party is still above the judiciary. Huang Huoqing, director of the Supreme People's Procuratorate, laments that interference with the work of the procuratorate still exists.[35] The staff of the procuratorate is often confronted with the demand from those under investigation, "Do you follow the party or does the party follow you?"[36]

So far, our discussion has focused on the formal legal system of China. However, the PRC also operates a vast informal "people's mediation" system to handle numerous civil disputes. In 1981 there were 810,000 such mediation groups with 5,750,000 members.[37] The mediators are mostly neighbors or fellow employees. They often mediate on marital disputes. In the city of Peking, with 9 million residents, there were 10,000 mediation groups and 70,000 members in 1982. In that year alone they handled 77,000 cases, 95 percent of the total civil cases.[38] These mediation groups have multiple functions in Chinese society. On the one hand, they reduce the case load of the people's courts. On the other hand, the mediation groups serve a policing function in keeping "offenders" under close scrutiny. Though a person may not be handed over to the court, thus ostensibly giving him a chance to be rehabilitated while still free from imprisonment, he is likely to become "the object of suspicion and hostility, ostracized by all and pounced upon for the slightest, even imagined, transgression."[39] However, former residents of China have recalled that the mediation by neighborhood groups on marital disputes can serve a positive function and is often effective. The present leaders of the CPC have stressed the function of the informal mediation groups. The change from the political terror of 1966-76 to the current emphasis on "socialist legality" has resulted in an upsurge of both criminal and civil cases in China. Moreover, the various social and economic problems, such as the severe housing shortage, have now come to the fore and contributed to disputes and conflicts among the population. Given the shortage of trained legal workers, it is natural for present leaders to stress the work of mediation groups.

THE PUBLIC SECURITY ESTABLISHMENT

In contrast to the fluctuation and uncertain fate of the formal judiciary in the PRC, the public security (police) establishment has had a stable and active history since the founding of the PRC. It has been a major characteristic of modern radical revolutionary regimes since the French Revolution that a powerful coercive organization accompanied their victory. This is perhaps partly due to the bitter struggle for power that these revolutionary groups have undergone before their political success. And it is also partly due to the ideological outlook of modern revolutionists who wish to impose "a reign of virtue" on society. Shortly before the victory of the CPC in the Chinese civil war in 1949, Mao Zedong spoke about the close connection between coercive power and the long-term transformation of Chinese society. In "On People's Democratic Dictatorship" Mao wrote:

Our present task is to strengthen the people's state apparatus—mainly the people's army, the people's police and the people's courts—in order to consolidate national defense and protect the people's interests. Given this condition, China can develop steadily, under the leadership of the working class and the Communist party, from an agricultural into an industrial country and from a new-democratic into a socialist and community society, can abolish classes and realize the Great Harmony. The state apparatus, including the army, the police and the courts, is the instrument by which one class oppressed another. It is an instrument for the oppression of antagonistic classes; it is violence and not "benevolence."[40]

In the PRC the most powerful organization serving as an "instrument for the oppression of antagonistic classes" is the public security establishment, which is technically subordinated to the State Council, i.e., the Chinese national government. At the top is the Ministry of Public Security, and at each subnational administrative division (province, autonomous region, municipality, and county) a public security bureau is established as part of the "people's government." The lowest public security organizations are the police substations (*paichusuo*) in city districts and the security and defense departments in communes or townships.

The public security system of the PRC performs not only the usual police duties but also other functions that are not within the jurisdiction of police in many other countries. The Ministry of Public Security in Peking, for example, has special departments dealing with:

1. Political defense: investigation and prevention of anti-Communist activity and guard duty for political leaders.
2. Economic defense: prevention of labor unrest such as strikes or peasant riots; protection of public property such as factories, mines, warehouses, and granaries; control of markets to prevent black-marketeering and contrabands.
3. Security administration: control of urban and rural residences through census keeping; investigation of crime and traffic control.
4. Armed defense: training of police, anti-insurgency, control of arms and weapons in society, and surveillance of the armed forces.
5. Border and coastal defense.
6. Internal investigation: collecting intelligence for internal security, and censoring mail, telecommunications, news, and publications.
7. Reform through labor: taking charge of two types of penal labor in China— "labor reform" (*laogai*), i.e., reform of criminals through labor; and "reeducation through labor" (*laojiao*), i.e., forced labor on "undesirable characters" of society.[41]

In 1983, as part of the judicial reform, the control of labor reform was transferred to the Ministry of Justice. In practice it is still the police (i.e., public security establishment) that handles the actual operation of labor reform and reeducation through labor.

In addition, the Ministry of Public Security also commands a people's armed police force, which is equivalent to an independent army. It consists of armed police, a border-patrol force, and a fire-fighting force. The armed police are responsible for guard duty of state property and establishment and prevention or suppression of major internal disturbances. There is no up-to-date information on the size of the people's armed police, which was temporarily suspended during the Cultural Revolution but reinstated in 1983.[42] The late Edgar Snow wrote in 1960 that the total force of the Ministry of Public Security was 1.7 million.[43]

In June 1983 the Chinese premier, Zhao Ziyang, announced the establishment of a new Ministry of State Security to deal with espionage and crime. This new ministry became an umbrella organization encompassing the existing Ministry of Public Security and other security organizations of China.[44] As we mentioned earlier, the change from the terror of Mao's era to the present reform has resulted in an upsurge of protest and crime. The widening contact of China with Western nations after 1978 also tended to make CPC leaders sensitive to problems of infiltration, espionage, and bourgeois corrosion of public morale. The reestablishment of the people's armed police force and the new Ministry for State Security were a response to these developments.

Though formally belonging to the State Council, the Ministry of Public Security has always been closely controlled by the national leaders of the CPC. A report from the ministry stated in 1977:

> Ever since the founding of a new China, Chairman Mao personally supervised all major public security conferences. Chairman Mao commented on a large number of materials dealing with public security.[45]

Moreover, the same report says:

> In accordance with instructions from Chairman Mao, for a long time, the public security agencies have adhered to the policy of obtaining approval from the party center on questions of general line, principle and policy of public security. The party committees at every echelon not only regularly discuss and examine public security work, but also conduct special sessions and systematic inspection of public security work on a yearly basis.[46]

Of the numerous functions of the public security system in China, we shall deal with only three because of their vital importance to the CPC's governing of China.

The first vital political function of the public security establishment in China is to create the right climate in society for the execution of any party policy. On the one hand, the agitation and propaganda machinery of the CPC drums up support of a policy through mass persuasion. On the other hand, the public security complements propaganda work by suppressing opposition. Lo Ruiqing, minister of public security from 1950 to 1959, reported that from June 1955 to October 1957 the public security departments in China carried out a campaign of ferreting out "hidden counterrevolutionaries" among 18 million state employees. The result was that 100,000 "counterrevolutionaries," 65,000 "ordinary counterrevolutionaries" (most likely petty criminals), and 9,000 "counterrevolutionary suspects" were uncovered. In addition, 30,000 "reactionary groups" were dealt with. As a consequence of that, Lo stated, "In many organizations, right spirit rises while evil influence declines. Political spirit is enhanced. Labor discipline has been strengthened. Grievances, strange talks and accidents have been lessened. The productivity of work has been visibly increased."[47] In 1958-59, as the Great Leap Forward was being carried out, Lo Ruiqing called on the public security establishment to "safeguard the big leap forward of socialist construction and insure the . . . progress of the people's commune movement." That meant the public security departments in China must deal not only with political enemies, but also with industrial mishaps, fires, traffic accidents, and control of insecticides and explosives.[48]

Whereas the policy-support function of the Chinese Communist public security system has varied from period to period, the most routine but vital function of public security is control of urban residents. As we stated earlier, the lowest unit of public security in a Chinese city is the police substation (*paichusuo*), which in turn is the linchpin of three basic organizations of self-government by urban residents—a Residents Committee, a Security and Defense Committee, and a People's Mediation Committee.

Of the three basic organizations of urban dwellers, the Residents' Committee is the most important and is closely connected with the police substation. A Residents' Committee consists of from one hundred to six hundred households. Each committee is in turn composed of residents' groups, which consist of from fifteen to forty households. The formal functions of a Residents' Committee include social welfare, security and defense, sanitation, mediation, and women's work. But the most important task of a Residents' Committee is to assist police in keeping track of each household. In every police substation there is a household policeman (*hukou jingcha*), who should be in regular contact with the chairman of a Residents' Committee. Former residents of the PRC report that, in theory, the chairman of a Residents' Committee is to be elected by the residents. But in practice, each local police substation designates the chairman, often a person of poor-worker background who has proven to be loyal to the Communist party. Through the chairman of the Residents' Committee, the household policeman obtains detailed knowledge of each person in the area. According to a 1958 public security publication, a household policeman is required to be familiar with the class status, family history, political outlook, and economic condition of every family in his jurisdiction.[49] Each family must keep a household register (*hukoubu*). In it is information "about addresses of the household, old and new, the names of all family members, with information on sex, age, education, profession, and . . . their current place of work and study."[50] On the basis of this booklet, *the police substation issues food ration cards and purchasing cards to each family.* The close connection between the Residents' Committee and the police substation and the system of the household register enables the public security apparatus to monitor closely the movements of Chinese people. For example, when Chinese people need to travel to another town for more than two days, they are required to obtain from their local police substation permission to depart, documents for travel ("internal passport"), and rice ration coupons to be used on the trip. As they arrive at their destination, visitors must report to the local police substation within three days so that the police can enter the visitor's name in the household register of the host. If he or she fails to report to the local police in three days, the police will visit the local family, demand all the necessary documents, and question the visitor as to reasons for travel. Members of the Residents' Committee usually tip off the police on the arrival of any strangers in the area.[51]

The power of Chinese police in controlling the movement of Chinese citizens received a big boost in 1984 when the central government announced the institution of an individual identification-card system. Since May 1984 each and every Chinese citizen has been required to carry such a card and must produce it upon demand by police at any time and any place. Any public office also has the right to demand such a card from a visitor. This is obviously the government's response to the increased mobility of many Chinese as a result of the economic reforms after 1980 that allow petty private entrepreneurs and peasants to travel about on business.

The police substation in China is also in control of two other residents' groups, the Security and Defense Committee and the People's Mediation Committee. The former is composed of three to eleven members and is set up in offices, factories, enterprises, schools, and residential areas. The functions of the Security and Defense Committee are almost entirely of a political nature, including prevention of counter-revolutionary activity, espionage, treason, and arson.[52] In certain areas, such as hilly villages and towns bordering certain provinces, the Security and Defense Committee also organizes residents against vagrants and criminal activity such as burglary. The People's Mediation Committee is commonly composed of from three to eleven residents. As we mentioned earlier, the Chinese government has stressed the use of this informal mediation group to settle numerous disputes, especially marital problems, among the population.

From the foregoing, it is evident that the public security establishment of the PRC is not an ordinary police institution. It is an intrinsic component of the CPC's comprehensive control and ordering of Chinese society.

The third vital function of the public security apparatus in the PRC is economic, i.e., use of prison labor for various constructions, especially colonizing the border lands in northwestern China. As mentioned earlier, the public security office is in charge of two types of forced labor, reform through labor (*lao gai*) and reeducation through labor (*lao jiao*). The former is applied to prisoners and the latter to people who have not committed any crime but are, for one reason or another, deemed "socially undesirable." The use of prison labor for economic purposes was sanctioned by Mao Zedong, who actually demanded it. On May 15, 1951, Mao told the Third National Conference on Public Security Work: "The large number of criminals who will be sentenced is a big labor force. To reform them, solve difficulties in prisons and forbid criminals from being idle and wasting food, we must immediately take steps to organize them for reform through labor."[53] During the Hundred Flowers Blooming campaign in 1957 critics of the CPC had charged that the public security apparatus was more interested in labor than in reform of prisoners. To this a spokesman of the Ministry of Public Security replied, "Labor . . . is the basic means for the reform of criminals, the material foundation of . . . reform of the political and ideological condition of . . . criminals, and it [labor] plays a decisive role in the transformation of criminals into new people."[54]

The condition and economic role of prison labor forces managed by the Chinese Communist public security apparatus may be gleaned from the accounts of two former inmates of prison labor camps. The better-known account is by Bao Ruo-wang (Jean Pasqualini), who wrote about the economic aspect of labor camps run by the public security system:

> Labor camps in China are a lifetime contract. They are far too important to the national economy to be run with transient personnel. It was convicts who reclaimed and made flourish the vast Manchurian wastelands which had defeated all past efforts and which today still offer the only convincing proof that a Sovkhoze-style state farm can operate profitably; convicts who began China's plastics industry and run some of her biggest factories and agricultural stations; convicts who grow the very rice Mao eats. . . .[55]

The second account of Chinese labor camps run by the public security office is from a former air force veteran of the PRC named Chin Chien-li. After being discharged from an anti-air-artillery unit, Chin was branded a rightist in 1957, since he had said critical things about the CPC during the Hundred Flowers Blooming campaign. But he was imprisoned in 1959 after being caught trying to flee China for Hong Kong. Subsequently, Chin was sentenced on a counterrevolutionary charge in 1961. From then until his escape in 1967, Chin stayed in five different labor camps in northwestern China. According to Chin, "In the Northwest, the number of factories, mines and farms composed of prison labor is countless. They are spaced closely and one comes across them frequently."[56] Chin corroborated Bao's statement that labor reform is a "lifetime contract." In 1965 Chin had served his sentence in Lanzhou but was not allowed to return to his home in Guangdong. Instead, together with some two thousand people who had also completed their sentences, Chin was sent to another farm in Gansu Province; later he was transferred to a camp in Xinjiang. Chin estimates that 80 percent of the workers on the state farms in the Northwest are prison labor.[57] Both Bao's and Chin's accounts have been corroborated by American correspondent Frank Ching, who visited one of the state farms in Xinjiang in 1982. Ching wrote that at first the commander of the state farm spoke only of soldiers and young volunteers on the farm. But when pressed for the number of prison laborers, the commander:

> acknowledged that there were almost 1,000 counterrevolutionaries there from the beginning, and their numbers rose to 3,000 at one time. Statistics on the numbers of counterrevolutionaries who labored in all of Xinjiang aren't available. At least at State Farm 148, all have served their sentence and been released, and *many have been integrated into the state farm* [emphasis added].[58]

Frank Ching's report shed some light on a report in the official *People's Daily* that the state farms in North China had opened up 10 million acres of land for cultivation and were worked by 5 million veterans, poor peasants, and educated youth.[59] If Chin Chien-li is correct that 80 percent of state farm workers are prison laborers, then there could be 4 million counterrevolutionaries on the farms.

The foregoing description is about prisoners' "reform through labor" (*lao gai*). In 1957 the PRC instituted a new form of penal labor known as "reeducation through labor" (*lao jiao*). Ostensibly, this new system of forced labor was for dealing with social parasites and juvenile gangs. In practice, many rightists, i.e., college students and other intellectuals who had, at the urging of the CPC, criticized Communist leadership in the 1957 Hundred Flowers Blooming campaign, were subject to *lao jiao*. This new measure enabled the public security authority to send anyone to forced labor without going through the formal judicial procedure since, in theory, those undergoing *lao jiao* had not committed any crime.[60] The public security authority often lumped political dissenters together with vagrants and delinquents and sent them to farms for "reeducation."[61]

The transition from the Mao era to present reform, however, has not brought any significant change in the function of the public security organization in China. A high-ranking CPC leader wrote in the *People's Daily*, "Our nation has entered the new age of constructing socialist modernization. For that we need a political condition of stability and unity and social order. So, the current mission of public security work is to insure the smooth progress of socialist modernization by strengthening social security and cracking down on criminals."[62] The recent stress on "activeness and comprehensiveness" in security work means a closer connection between police and the basic organizations such as Residents' Committees and the Security and Defense Committee.[63]

The transition from terror under Mao Zedong to present CPC leaders' policy of fundamental reform and socialist democracy has increased anxiety on the part of the Communist party concerning the basic security of the Communist regime. Meanwhile, the deleterious effect of a whole range of early policies and programs undertaken by Communist authorities during 1949-76, such as overpopulation, a sharp disparity in living conditions between urban and rural areas, a gross imbalance between capital industry and consumer industry, and the destruction of higher education, has surfaced, contributing to alarming incidents of crime by juveniles (at one time reaching 60 to 70 percent of all crimes), and graft in the bureaucracy. It is against this background that the Communist party recently strengthened the public security apparatus, e.g., the creation of the Ministry for State Security and the people's armed police force.

NOTES

1. Sidney Verba, "Comparative Political Culture," in Lucian W. Pye and Sidney Verba, eds., *Political Culture and Political Development* (Princeton, N.J.: Princeton University Press, 1965), pp. 545-50.

2. Carl J. Friedrich and Zbigniew K. Brzezinski, *Totalitarian Dictatorship and Autocracy* (New York: Frederick A. Praeger, 1968), p. 118.

3. Franz Michael, "The Role of Law in Traditional, Nationalist and Communist China," *China Quarterly*, January-March 1962, p. 135.

4. *Wan-sui*, no. 2, p. 638.

5. Chen Shouyi, Liu Shengping, and Zhao Zhenjiang, "Thirty Years of Building-up of Our Legal System," *Faxue Yenjiu*, no. 4 (1979), p. 1, as cited in Hungdah Chiu, *Chinese Law and Justice: Trends over Three Decades*, no. 7 (Occasional Papers/Reprint Series in Contemporary Asian Studies, Baltimore, 1982). Much of the discussion on the pre-1977 legal system in the PRC is based on Professor Chiu's study.

6. *RMRB*, October 19, 1978, p. 1.

7. *RMRB*, May 15, 1978, p. 2.

8. Hungdah Chiu, *Chinese Law and Justice*, p. 8.

9. *RMRB*, August 29, 1980, p. 4.

10. Hungdah Chiu, *Chinese Law and Justice*, pp. 10-11.

11. Jerome Alan Cohen, "Will China Have a Formal Legal System?" *American Bar Association Journal* 64 (October 1978), 1511.

12. Hungdah Chiu, *Chinese Law and Justice*, pp. 13-14.

13. "China's Socialist Legal System," *Beijing Review*, no. 29 (January 12, 1979), pp. 26-27.

14. Li Chun and Cui Qingshen, " 'Counter-revolution Crime' Must Be Genuine," *RMRB*, July 24, 1979, p. 4.

15. Michael, *The Role of Law*, p. 137.

16. Fu Zhaozhung and Chu Wenxian, "Is Law Merely a Supplementary Means to Handle Contradictions among the People?" *RMRB*, December 11, 1980, p. 5.

17. Gu Chunde, "There Must Be Law in Addition to Policy," *RMRB*, November 7, 1978, p. 3.

18. Ho Lanjie, "Seriously Study Criminal Code. Strictly Execute Criminal Code," *RMRB*, September 5, 1979, p. 3.

19. *RMRB*, December 28, 1978, p. 1.

20. See the account of the case of a worker accused of embezzlement, in *RMRB*, November 3, 1978, p. 1. For general discussion on equality before law, see Li Buyun, "Insist on Equality Before Law for All Citizens," *RMRB*, December 6, 1978, p. 3.

21. Hungdah Chiu, *Chinese Law and Justice*, p. 20.

22. *RMRB*, May 2, 1983, p. 5.

23. Hungdah Chiu, "Socialist Legalism: Reform and Continuity in Post-Mao Communist China," *Issues and Studies* XVII, no. 11 (November 1981), 66-69.

24. *RMRB*, October 28, 1979, p. 2.

25. *RMRB*, September 15, 1980, p. 4.

26. Zhao Yusi, "Education of Law Must Be Expanded Greatly," *RMRB*, October 10, 1980, p. 5.

27. Li Yuncheng, "The Role of Chinese Lawyers," *Beijing Review*, no. 46 (November 17, 1980), p. 24.

28. *RMRB*, March 30, 1983, p. 3.

29. *Ming Pao Daily News*, July 26, 1979, p. 1.

30. *RMRB*, December 30, 1978, p. 2.

194   *The Judiciary and the Public Security System*

31. Ruth Bader Ginsburg, "American Bar Association Delegation Visits the People's Republic of China," *American Bar Association Journal* 64 (October 1978), 1516-25. Also, "Crime and Punishment in China," *New York Times Magazine*, October 7, 1979, pp. 48-69.

32. Li Buyun, "Insist on Equality."

33. Xiao Weiyun and Wei Dingren, "Protect the Right of Defendants to Legal Defense," *RMRB*, February 17, 1979, p. 3.

34. Zhang Youyu, "Members of Communist Party Must Be Models of Law Abiding," *RMRB*, November 1, 1982, p. 3.

35. Huang Huoqing, "Struggle for the Defense of Socialist Legalism," *RMRB*, August 17, 1979, p. 3.

36. *Ming Pao Daily News*, July 12, 1979, p. 3.

37. *RMRB*, August 27, 1981, p. 1.

38. *RMRB*, April 21, 1982, p. 4; April 22, 1983, p. 4.

39. Ross H. Munro, "China, for Want of a Formal Legal Code, Looks to Community to Re-educate Offenders," *New York Times*, October 12, 1977, p. A3.

40. *Selected Works of Mao Tse-tung*, vol. IV (Peking: Foreign Languages Press, 1967), p. 418.

41. *I-Chiu-Liu-Ch'i-Nien Fei-Ch'ing Nien-pao (1967 Yearbook on Chinese Communism)* (Taipei: Institute for the Study of Chinese Communist Problems, 1967), pp. 456-59.

42. *Ming Pao Daily News*, January 31, 1983, p. 1. Also, *RMRB*, February 2, 1983, p. 1; April 6, 1983, p. 1; and April 29, 1983, p. 4.

43. Edgar Snow, *The Other Side of the River: Red China Today* (New York: Random House, 1962), p. 350.

44. Christopher S. Wren, "China Creates New Security Ministry," *New York Times*, June 7, 1983, p. 4.

45. *RMRB*, November 28, 1977, p. 1.

46. Ibid.

47. Lo Ruiqing, "The Accomplishment of Ferreting out Hidden Counter-revolutionaries and Our Task for the Future," *Xuexi*, no. 1 (1958), p. 2.

48. "Excerpts of Vice Premier Lo Jui-ch'ing's Address at National Conference of Advanced Public Security, Procuratorial, and Judicial Workers," *Cheng-fa Yen- chiu*, no. 3 (June 6, 1959), as translated in *Extracts from China Mainland Magazine (ECMM)* (Hong Kong), no. 177, p. 3.

49. *Gongan Gongzuo Yaojinji* (Peking: Falu Chupanshe, 1958), p. 210.

50. Robert Tung, "People's Policemen," *Far Eastern Economic Review*, August 18, 1966, p. 319.

51. Ibid.

52. *RMRB*, January 19, 1980, p. 4.

53. *Wan-sui*, no. 2, p. 5.

54. Li Shao-sheng, "Refutation of the Slander of the Rightists against the Policy of Reform through Labor for Criminals," *Cheng Fa Yen Chiu*, no. 3 (June 20, 1958), as translated in *Extracts from China Mainland Magazines* (Hong Kong), no. 140, p. 10.

55. Bao Ruo-wang (Jean Pasqualini) and Rudolph Chelminski, *Prisoner of Mao* (New York: Penguin Books, 1976), pp. 11-12.

56. Chin Chien-li, *Pei-kuo Chien-wen-lu (Odyssey in North China)* (Hong Kong: Union Research Institute, 1973), pp. 4 and 524.

57. Ibid., p. 591.

58. Frank Ching, " 'Counterrevolutionary' Wang's Tale," *Wall Street Journal*, June 1, 1982, p. 27.

59. *RMRB*, January 26, 1978, p. 2.

60. Christopher S. Wren, "Ruffians 'Re-educated' in China without Trial," *New York Times*, August 12, 1982, p. 4.

61. Michael Weisskopf, "A Glimpse of Life in China's Prisons," *Washington Post*, September 15, 1981, p. 1. For more on *lao gai*, see Fox Butterfield, *China: Alive in the Bitter Sea* (New York: Bantam Books, 1983), pp. 342-69.

62. *RMRB*, January 14, 1980, p. 3.

63. *RMRB*, August 17, 1981, p. 3.

For students interested in a review of Chinese judicial development from 1950 to 1970, in addition to Franz Michael (see note 3), see Victor H. Li, "The Evolution and Development of the Chinese Legal System," in John M. H. Lindbeck, ed., *China: Management of a Revolutionary Society* (Seattle: University of Washington Press, 1971), pp. 221-55.

CHAPTER 11

The Role of the Military in Chinese Politics

Though the courts and the police of the PRC stood in the frontline to carry out Mao's "oppression of antagonistic classes," the ultimate enforcer of Mao's class line was the People's Liberation Army (PLA). The Chinese Communist army, said a long-time scholar of Chinese Communist affairs,

> is not merely a military organization; it is also an economic colossus, and it is a political weapon. Army units are sent to politically sensitive spots; in many places they lead political indoctrination. The control of the national minorities is in their hands. The army is not something apart from the life of the nation, but something deeply imbedded in it.[1]

The Communist party, Mao Zedong repeatedly stated before 1949, owed its survival and final victory to the Red Army. In 1928, during the most precarious moment of the Communist party's existence, Mao wrote that "the existence of a regular Red Army of adequate strength is a necessary condition for the existence of Red political power" and "even when the masses of workers and peasants are active, it is definitely impossible to create an independent regime . . . unless we have regular forces of adequate strength."[2] A decade later, in 1938, Mao Zedong's emphasis on the political importance of an army was even more pronounced as he spoke at the conclusion of a party conference:

> Every Communist must understand this truth: Political power grows out of the barrel of a gun. Our principle is that the party commands the gun; the gun shall never be allowed to command the party. But it is also true that with the gun at our disposal we can really build up the party organizations. . . . We can also rear cadres and create schools, culture and mass movements. Everything in Yenan has been built up by means of the gun. Anything can grow out of the barrel of the gun. Viewed from the Marxist theory of the state, the army is the chief component of the political power of a state. . . .[3]

Another decade later, in 1949 on the eve of the founding of the People's Republic,

Mao wrote in "On People's Democratic Dictatorship" that the army, police, and courts were the condition to transform China from an agricultural to an industrial society and, ultimately, to reach communism. Hence, any study of Chinese politics would be incomplete without an analysis of the multiple functions of the Chinese Communist military. In this chapter we shall discuss the formal political status of the Chinese military, civil-military relations from 1949 to the present, and the role of the military in Chinese economic development.

FORMAL POLITICAL STATUS OF THE MILITARY

The military in China bears the collective title People's Liberation Army and is granted in both the CPC and the Chinese state constitution an independent status. In other words, just like other recognized groups, such as workers, peasants, intellectuals, and cadres, the PLA is constitutionally given the right to elect its own representatives to both the CPC National Congress and the National People's Congress. Hence, the Chinese Communist political system, unlike others, legally recognizes the military as an independent interest group in society, and in theory the PLA is legally allowed to participate in the political process.

In the national machinery of the CPC, PLA commanders always constitute a significant portion of Central Committee and Politburo membership. As a rule all commanders of the Great Military Region (see subsequent discussion) and the armed services are represented in the Central Committee. The percentage of PLA commanders in the Central Committee of CPC over the years is shown in table 11.1. The represen-

TABLE 11-1   Percentage of military commanders in the Central Committee of the Chinese Communist party (full members only)

CENTRAL COMMITTEE	YEAR	PLA REPRESENTATION
Seventh	1945	38.6[a]
Eighth	1956	27.8[b]
Ninth	1969	43[c]
Tenth	1973	32.3[d]
Eleventh	1977	31.8[e]
Twelfth	1982	23.8[f]

Sources:
[a] Robert C. North and Ithiel de Sola Pool, "Kuomintang and Chinese Communist Elites," in Harold D. Lasswell and Daniel Lerner, eds., *World Revolutionary Elites* (Cambridge, Mass: MIT Press, 1966), p. 384.

[b] Ching Shih-kai, "A Decade of Chinese Communist Party," *Chungkung Shih-nien* (Hong Kong: Union Research Institute, 1960), pp. 13–15.

[c] *I-Chiu-Ch'i-lin Chungkung Nienpao (1970 Yearbook on Chinese Communism)* vol. II (Taipei: Institute for the Study of Chinese Communist Problems, 1970), p. 2.

[d,e] Feng Chun-kuei, "An Analysis of Members of the 11th Party Congress and Personnel in the Central Leading Organs," *Chungkung Yenchiu* II, no. 9 (September 15, 1977), 25.

[f] Kang Feng, "An Analysis of the Members of the 12th Central Leadership," *Chungkung Yenchiu* 16, no. 10 (October 15, 1982), 40.

tation of PLA high command in the Politburo is also substantial. For example, in the eleventh Central Committee of 1977, out of twenty-six members of the Politburo, twelve were PLA commanders.[4] Currently there are eight PLA commanders in the Politburo, 32 percent of the total.[5] The presence of formal representatives of the PLA high command in the innermost chamber of the CPC not only grants high status to the PLA but also enables the military to protect its interests and participate in political decision-making.

While the PLA high command takes part in national policy making, regional PLA commanders also play an important role in the governing of the provinces, municipalities, and counties of China. To understand the governing functions of the PLA we shall briefly describe the structure of the PLA command. The PLA as a whole consists of three parts: the main force units (formerly the field army), the regional armies, and the militia. The main force units are the professional core of the PLA and are equipped with the latest weapons that China possesses. The main force units are mobile and under the direct command of national leaders. Because of their elite status and vital defense function, the main force units are seldom mentioned in the Chinese mass media. The regional armies and the militia have been regarded as part of the regional political structure and are frequently reported on in the Chinese media.

The regional armies of the PLA are organized into Great Military Regions, provincial military districts, and subdistricts. With the exception of that of Xinjiang, each Great Military Region is named after a city and, with the exception of the Jinan Military Region, each has military jurisdiction over more than one province. There are eleven Great Military Regions, covering all the provinces (see table 11-2).

In each of the regional military commands, be it a Great Military Region, a provincial district, or a subdistrict, the two top positions are troop commander and political commissar (or political director). In most cases the position of political commissar of a military region is filled by the first party secretary of the party committee of the area. Thus civil and military leadership are interlocked (see figure 11-1). One may regard the regional PLA commands as the reserve coercive force of CPC authorities at subnational levels. In other words, ordinarily the coercive component of a regional party authority is the public security force, but in case of major disturbance, a party secretary always has the PLA force at his command. Of course, with the civilian party

TABLE 11-2 The Great Military Regions of the PRC

GREAT MILITARY REGIONS	PROVINCES
Guangzhou	Hunan, Guangxi, Guangdong
Chengdu	Sichuan, Tibet
Fuzhou	Fujian, Jiangxi
Kunming	Guizhou, Yunnan
Lanzhou	Gansu, Ningxia, Qinghai, Shaanxi
Nanjing	Anhui, Zhejiang, Jiangsu
Peking	Hebei, Inner Mongolia, Shanxi
Shenyang	Heilongjiang, Jilin, Liaoning
Xinjiang	Xinjiang
Jinan	Shandong
Wuhan	Henan, Hubei

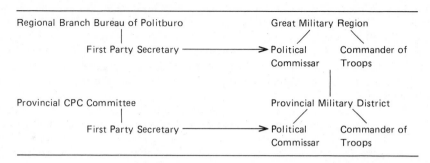

FIGURE 11-1   The regional interpenetration of party and military leadership in the PRC

secretary assuming the position of the political commissar, the CPC enforces its principle that the party commands the gun.

Until 1973 the command of the Great Military Regions was noted for its stability. As a result, regional and provincial party leaders had developed a close working relationship with troop commanders in the area. At the same time, because of the stability of command, scholars outside of China speculated about the possibility of "feudal ownership" of troops by their regional commanders. Even Mao Zedong seemed to respect the power of the commanders of Great Military Regions. During the Cultural Revolution, while Mao did not hesitate to dismiss or denounce any provincial party leader, he did not allow attacks on commanders of Great Military Regions. However, regional commanders reacted, some rather strongly, against the violence and attacks by Red Guards on civil party authorities in the provinces. As a consequence, Mao ordered a transfer of command of the Great Military Regions in 1973, i.e., *after* the most dangerous period of the Cultural Revolution had already passed. But this shakeup was a mere change of command, no commander being dismissed. After the death of Mao, however, there have been two more shakeups of the command, in 1980 and 1982. Present party leader Deng Xiaoping had complained in an inner party conference of the political unreliability of some regional troop commanders. Hence, the changes in 1980 and 1982 included dismissals and a change of command.[6] In 1983 a major change in the command of provincial military districts also took place. All this has been a part of the present leaders' fundamental reform of PRC civil-military apparatus in the direction of promoting younger and better-educated people in order to facilitate the four modernizations of China. Undoubtedly, partisan purposes are always part of this, as is any political action of the PRC.

CIVIL-MILITARY RELATIONS, 1949-79

The foregoing shows how the military is given a formal role to play in civilian politics in China. Formal status in politics, however, does not necessarily mean that PLA commanders will play an active political role or that the political role of the PLA over the years has been invariable. One must remember that while Mao Zedong stressed the political importance of the PLA, he also made it clear that "the party commands the gun; the gun shall never be allowed to command the party." Hence, the formal status of the PLA in party and state may be granted simply to "dignify" the PLA, not necessarily to make the PLA an independent and "efficient" party in the

Chinese Communist political process. In retrospect, we find that the political "efficiency" of the PLA in China, as with military intervention in politics elsewhere, depends largely on the strength of civilian institutions. In other words, the political role of the PLA is in reverse proportion to the strength of the CPC. Our subsequent discussion will bear this out.

The political role of the PLA must be analyzed against the evolution of overall civil-military relations in the PRC, which consists of five distinct periods: (1) the period of civil and military separation (1952-62); (2) the period of Mao's mobilization of the PLA for political leadership (1963-66); (3) the period of army intervention in regional politics (1967-76); (4) the period of the PLA high command's guardianship of national politics (1976-78); and (5) the period of return to civil and military separation (1979 to the present). We have deliberately excluded the period of 1949-51 during which much of China was in the very early stages of Communist takeover. Every locality was then under the rule of a Military Control Commission headed by the commander of the PLA troops that occupied the area. That was a temporary and transitional arrangement. By 1952 the Military Control Commission had been abolished. So it is more meaningful to discuss the civil-military relations in China from 1952 on.

In the first period, 1952-62, the civil-military relations of the PRC, despite Mao's dictum of "political power grows out of the barrel of a gun," was not very different from that of most Western nations. There was a strict separation between civil politics and the military profession. Eric Nordlinger calls this the "liberal model" of civilians' control over the military. According to Nordlinger:

> The liberal model of civilian control is explicitly premised upon the differentiation of elites according to their expertise and responsibilties. Civilians holding the highest governmental office—be they elected, appointed, or anointed—are responsible for and skilled in determining domestic and foreign goals, overseeing the administration of the laws, and resolving conflicts among social, economic, and political groups. Military officers are trained and experienced in the management and application of force, responsible for protecting the nation against external attack and the government against internal violence.[7]

Though the PLA high command was, as always, part of the Central Committee and Politburo of the CPC, there is no evidence that it took any active part in civilian politics. The reason was in part because the PLA was being modernized and turned into a professional force under Soviet advisory during this period. Marshall Peng Dehuai, then minister of defense, was known to be keen on "regularizing" and "professionalizing" the PLA. Moreover, there was also no need for the PLA high command to be active politically since the corporate interest of the PLA was satisfied by civilian leaders. The interest of any military, as pointed out by Nordlinger, is the same as any public institution. "They all share an interest in adequate budgetary support, autonomy in managing their internal affairs, the presentation of their responsibilities in the face of encroachments from rival institutions, and the continuity of the institution itself."[8] According to Mao Zedong, during the first five-year plan (1953-57), expenses for the military amounted to 32 percent of total state budgeted expenses.[9] Furthermore, the industrial construction of the first five-year plan was mostly defense related, with heavy industry as the key. For example, General Tan Cheng, deputy defense minister, claimed in 1955: "In order to strengthen the equipment of our armed forces, the five-year plan put its stress on expanding heavy industry. This is very important and is in conformity with our defense needs."[10] It was also during this period that formal military ranks were established, modeled after the Soviet system. Ten top PLA generals were appointed marshals of the People's Liberation Army. Military uniforms with Soviet-type epaulets and special medals were created. In short, both the material and status needs of the PLA were satisfied by civilian leaders of the CPC in 1952-62.

The separation between civil and military affairs was so complete in 1952-62 that a party propagandist affiliated with the PLA openly criticized the mass media in China in 1958 for its neglect of propaganda for the military. Except for Army Day on August 1 and other standard national occasions, "there is very little propaganda . . . and sometimes for as long as one or two months there are no reports at all on the activities of the army." [11] Marshal Zhu De (Chu Teh) wrote disapprovingly of this period in which "military affairs were emphasized and politics were neglected." [12]

The political quiescence of the PLA in 1952-62, however, was not just due to the fact that the interests of the PLA were being met. Mao and other civilian leaders were strict in enforcing the norm of "the party commands the gun." This may be further illustrated by an exception that proves the rule of civilian control. That was Defense Minister Marshall Peng Dehuai's (Peng Teh-huai) critique of the Great Leap Forward program in a high party conference in July 1959. At that time Marshal Peng was also a member of the Politburo, which was referred to by Mao as China's "political designing institute." Thus in theory Marshal Peng was entitled to voice his critical opinions on the Great Leap Forward. But he was immediately rebuked by Mao, and subsequently Marshal Peng, together with a group of military and civil leaders, was dismissed from all military positions and denounced publicly. It is possible that Marshal Peng was dismissed not because he stepped over the boundary of the civil-military division of function but because of Mao's intolerance of any criticism over the Great Leap Forward program, his brainchild. But the critical point was Mao's accusation that Marshal Peng had formed a "military club" against the party and had threatened the CPC with possible military disaffection. [13] The case of Marshal Peng illustrates what the dire consequences could be for a PLA commander who took his formal political status seriously. The PLA is expected to support the party line, not to contradict it. At the time of Marshal Peng's dismissal, he had served the Communist party loyally for thirty years, from the most precarious days of the late 1920s through the war of resistance against Japan, civil war with Chinese Nationalists and, finally, Chinese intervention in the Korean war. Yet no other military leader came to his defense, and there was no "military reaction" as such. Mao Zedong, of course, cleverly manipulated the rivalry between Marshal Peng and another top PLA commander—Marshal Lin Biao (Lin Piao), who succeeded Marshal Peng to be China's minister of defense in 1959.

As mentioned earlier, in 1958 a political propagandist affiliated with the PLA had openly criticized the Chinese press for neglecting the army. This criticism may well have been the first sign of Mao Zedong's attempt to mobilize the PLA to support his radical socioeconomic program. Mao adroitly capitalized on the emotions of many PLA commanders who felt ambivalent toward professionalization of the military, which, so it was argued, led to an abandonment of the "democracy and equality" of the early days of the Red Army. [14] Under that pretext, an intense political indoctrination campaign was carried out in the PLA after 1959. Marshal Lin Biao, who owed his position to Mao, was the defense minister. At a Central Military Commission (part of the Central Committee) conference in late 1959 Marshal Lin attacked his predecessor Marshal Peng's alleged emphasis on professionalism at the expense of political indoctrination. In the fall of 1960 Marshal Lin convened an enlarged meeting of the Central Military Commission to discuss political work in the army. A decision was made to intensify political indoctrination among troops. A mass political-education campaign was soon initiated in the PLA, consisting of three interrelated and essentially repetitious programs. One was the famous four-firsts movement, which stressed the primacy of man over weapons and of political work over all other kinds. The second movement was the revival of the guerrilla tradition, i.e., ideological commitment, frugality, and discipline. The third movement encouraged learning the works of Mao. It is clear that all three movements were geared to create a cult of personality of Mao among soldiers. Marshal Lin backed up his political education with organizational "cleansing." According to a confidential internal army document, from July 1960 to February 1961 the political departments of the PLA had "cleansed and adjusted" about 83 percent of the party branches in the PLA. Over two thousand cadres (officers and administrators) were either expelled from the party or put on probation. New party members were admitted, and over half of the army squads now had party members. Over 80 percent of the platoons were said to have party groups, and all companies now had party branches.[15] By doing all this, Marshal Lin was preparing the PLA to assume political functions, as Mao wanted. The period of strict separation between civilian and military functions was coming to an end.

The next period of civil-military relations, that of 1963-66, is marked by Mao and Lin's mobilization of the PLA for political leadership. The motive for the PLA's intervention in politics stemmed from Mao's suspicion of his own party and disagreement between Mao and other top party leaders over China's socioeconomic development. So Mao turned for support to Marshal Lin, who had prepared the army for one mass compaign after another used the army as a model and dominated the mass media in mainland China. In February 1964, for example, the nationwide campaign Learn from the People's Liberation Army was started. The methods that Lin Biao had used in indoctrinating and "cleansing" the army during 1960 and 1961 were now applied to the entire nation. Organizations in industry, agriculture, and commerce were told to compare their political education with the army. Under this pretext, army officers and political commissars loyal to Lin's leadership were despatched to various civilian institutions to undertake political indoctrination and "cleansing" of the ranks. In the meantime, Mao attempted to broaden his military support. So he contacted individual commanders of Great Military Regions. General Xu Siyou, former commander of Nanjing Military Region, recalled in a 1978 article:

> In 1965, Chairman Mao was in Hangzhou and he sent for me from Nanjing. He said to me: You must watch out for revisionism, especially revisionism at party center. He asked me: If revisionism were found at party center, what would you do? I replied: If revisionism were found at party center, I would lead my troop marching north to defend Chairman Mao and defend party center. Chairman Mao smiled and answered: That would be too late![16]

In short, Mao was openly inviting PLA commanders to intervene in civilian party politics—of course, on the side of Mao.

Though Mao did not call on General Xu of Nanjing to defend him against revisionism when Mao launched the Cultural Revolution in May, 1966, Mao did call in other army reinforcements to Peking. Mao told a high-ranking Albanian Communist leader: "When we announced the reorganization of Peking Party Committee, we increased xx number of garrison divisions."[17] Then as the Red Guards and worker "rebels" attacked and prevented regional party authorities from assuming their normal functions, the PLA was called in to take control. China reverted to the days of military control commissions. During 1966-76, army control of civilian politics was called a "three-aid two-military" movement: aid leftists, aid industry, aid agriculture, military administration, and military training. Surveying Chinese local politics in 1971, a long-time scholar of Chinese Communist affairs wrote:

> For four and a half years the political vacuum was filled by the army. The army leaders, who had become the backbone of regional administration, became well entrenched in their positions. The result is that 20 of the 29 new first party secretaries (26 provinces and 3 cities) are active soldiers and 93 of the 158 party secretaries are soldiers. Unlike the soldiers in similar positions in the early fifties, these soldiers on entering the civilian administration did not renounce their allegiance to the army.
>
> Soldiers are now the leading officials both in the party and in the government (the revolutionary committees). It has been stated many times that this function of the army will last long, as long as Socialism lasts in China. In such circumstances, solemn statements that the army is subject to the party sound hypocritical. At most it can be said that the soldiers are subject to the party organizations, those within the army. The civilian party as it now stands is no more than an appendix to the army. China is the first military-ruled Communist country in the world.[18]

But army control in 1971 was not confined to regional government. At the national level Marshal Lin had been made a vice-chairman of the CPC and was formally designated in the CPC constitution as the successor to Mao Zedong, chairman of the CPC. Moreover, Marshal Lin had staffed the command of all the services with his own men. Naturally, they were all made members of the Politburo. Thinking that a de facto military takeover of the CPC had materialized, Marshal Lin felt safe enough to cross the civil-military boundary and thus made a fatal error. In a high party conference in August 1970 Marshal Lin, without consulting Mao, presented his own program of restructuring the Chinese national government, especially the restoration of the chairmanship of the PRC. Unlike Marshal Peng, who was falsely accused by Mao of organizing a "military club," Marshal Lin did have such a club. As Mao recounted later, Lin had with him in the August 1970 conference the following people: the chief of staff, the commander of the air force, the political director of the navy, the commander of rear services, and the commander of the Peking Military Region. Marshal Lin's apparent strength in 1970 did not alter the fundamental fact that Mao had invited Lin and other PLA commanders into civilian politics not to turn over political power to the PLA but to use the latter to rid the CPC of Mao's opponents. Hence, Lin's independent move at the conference, like Marshal Peng's critique of the Great Leap Forward in 1959, was immediately rebuked by Mao. But the most astonishing fact is that, even with Lin's deliberation and support from his subordinates, Mao's rebuke was enough to create panic in Lin's "military club." Lin's "big generals" quickly made self-criticism, asking for Mao's pardon, and Lin withdrew his program of reorganizing the state. But too late.

Shocked by Marshal Lin's bold move, Mao made an about face. Until then, Mao had been courting PLA commanders, such as General Xu of Nanjing, to help him fight "revisionism at party center." In 1971 Mao traveled the provinces to court civilian party leaders to help him fight Marshal Lin's "big generals." Whereas in 1965 Mao wanted General Xu Siyou to broaden his concern from military matters to political ideology, in 1971 Mao told provincial party leaders: "You people must be concerned with military affairs. You should not just be civilian leaders; you must be military officers too." [19] In 1964 Mao had called on the whole nation to "learn from the PLA."

In 1971 Mao said: "The People's Liberation Army must learn from the people!"[20] After thus rallying major regional CPC leaders, Mao was ready to convene a high-level party conference to deal with Marshal Lin and his "big generals." Whereupon, according to General Xu of Nanjing, "Seeing that his conspiracy of armed rebellion had been exposed, Lin Biao fled the country in panic and died in 'self-explosion'."[21] Lin's "big generals" were all caught and imprisoned after the Lin Biao incident of September 1971.

After the downfall of Marshal Lin, Mao started to reduce PLA control of regional administration. In 1973 the commanders of the Great Military Regions were transferred, the first transfer since the establishment of the regions in 1954. These powerful PLA commanders "had to abandon their power bases and go to new commands, leaving their own loyal men behind."[22] Soon after that, the PLA command a step below the Great Military Region, i.e., the provincial military district, was also reshuffled. In some places new PLA commanders no longer assumed the civilian position of party secretary. But in society at large the heavy presence of PLA officers remained, as the Cultural Revolution had so disrupted the normal order of things and created so much violence and animosity among various groups in society. A 1975 report by the editor of the *China News Analysis* described the ubiquitous PLA men in China:

> Not only does it [PLA officers] provide material aid, manpower and medical aid; it is also very much in control of the political scene. Assisted by the militia, the soldiers pervade the factories and the villages. They impart the political doctrine; they pursue the class enemy. All this is done—and they proclaim this loudly— "under the guidance of local party committees," i.e., the civilian party committees. The civilian party committees could not do much without the assistance of the military and the militia. The military therefore, even in their humble role, are an indispensable element in the national make-up.[23]

Many PLA commanders, however, had never supported Marshal Lin when he turned the PLA over to Mao for use in the power struggle. These professionally oriented PLA commanders naturally could not voice their opinions while Mao was alive. But the death of Marshal Lin and the subsequent political retreat by Mao did enable the commanders to reduce the political activism of the PLA high command. After Marshal Lin, Mao promoted Marshal Ye Jianying to the most important command post—director of the PLA General Staff Department. Marshal Ye was known to be a professional general and had been politically inactive. Mao had once criticized Marshal Ye's thinking as being "not sharp enough."[24] But before Mao's death, extrication of the PLA from civilian politics was not possible. Whereas Mao had grown wary of "big generals" in the aftermath of the Marshal Lin incident, the Gang of Four attempted to replicate Mao's strategy of using the PLA to consolidate its control over the CPC.

From 1973 till their arrest in October 1976, the Gang of Four mounted a relentless campaign to penetrate the PLA.[25] Mao Zedong had facilitated the work of the Gang of Four by appointing one of the four, Zhang Chunqiao, as director of the PLA General Political Department, which controls the political commissars in the armed forces. Another member of the Gang of Four, Wang Hongwen, was made a member of the Central Military Commission. Although Mao's appointment of two leftist leaders to high military posts may have been due to his reaction to Marshal Lin's attempted military control of the CPC, the four leftists nevertheless , in a power struggle with other CPC leaders, used their position in the PLA high command to build up their own influence. Subsequently, Zhang Chunqiao and Wang Hongwen used their formal military positions to interfere with virtually every issue handled by the PLA high command, from the defense budget to the style of navy uniforms. The second method that the Gang of Four used to influence the PLA was control of the Chinese mass media. The four leftists publicized and praised selected PLA units. Further, they manipulated military historiography, military museum displays, and military film making in order to glorify those PLA commanders who had sided with the leftists politically. They deliberately suppressed the historical roles or merits of other PLA units whose commanders refused to be drawn into party politics. The third method the Gang of Four used was more damaging than the others: their agents carried out a campaign of agitation among the men. From 1974 to 1976 the four leftists conducted a series of political-study campaigns in the armed forces, such as Criticize Lin Biao, Study the Theory of the Dictatorship of the Proletariat, and Criticize Deng Xiaoping. To organize these campaigns they used what is referred to in China as single-line liaison. That is, they sent their agents to various military units with or without the approval of military authorities. By these methods the Gang of Four sought to recruit officers and men to join the radical clique. They also hoped that their agitation among soldiers would put pressure on commanders to pledge their allegiance to the radical leaders. But the four leftists met strong resistance from most PLA commanders except in Peking, Shenyang, and Canton, i.e., places where troops had been under the late Marshal Lin's command.

As the four leftists met strong opposition from PLA commanders, they resorted to a plan for creating a second armed force—an urban workers' militia. In 1973, capitalizing on Mao's shock at Marshal Lin's betrayal, one of the four leftists, Wang Hongwen, who had been a Shanghai factory security guard before being promoted by Jiang Qing to a national position, initiated a nationwide campaign of organizing an urban workers' militia to be modeled after the "Shanghai experience." The Shanghai model consists of three elements: (1) militiamen and women, all factory workers; (2) an independent militia command, under the control of leftist party leaders and in charge of police and fire-fighting forces; and (3) a political mission—to take part in the class struggle. This workers' militia was meant to be a challenge to the PLA since until then Chinese militia had been under the command of the PLA, and moreover, in the past the task of the militia had been to assist the PLA in patrol, intelligence collecting, and logistics. In 1975 Wang Hongwen proposed to organize an independent national militia command with himself as the commander-in-chief. In the end, the urban workers' militia was established in Peking and Shanghai only and was under the close surveillance of the PLA commander and troops in these cities. When the Gang of Four was arrested in October 1976, the urban workers' militia was dissolved.

After the death of Mao and the arrest of the Gang of Four, the PLA high command stepped forward to play the role of "guardian" of the Communist regime. From October 1976 to the end of 1978 the editorials of the *People's Liberation Army Daily* were frequently published on the front pages of national and regional newspapers. Furthermore, these army-press editorials were not confined to military affairs. They dealt with a whole range of civilian matters with respect to three things especially: (1) suppot of Hua Guofang as the chairman of the CPC and of his arrest of the Gang of Four; (2) restoration of the authority of "veteran party cadres," i.e., those in authority positions before the start of the Cultural Revolution; and (3) return to the social and economic order that prevailed before the Cultural Revolution, e.g., industrial discipline. The army paper also spoke strongly in support of the civilian leaders' goal of four modernizations. The Chinese press during this period reprinted a large number of articles from the army press on the highly technical nature of modern war. (The high command of the PLA has an intrinsic interest in China's industrial development.) Finally, the high command of the PLA openly announced its role of political guardianship during this transition period. Take, for example, the statement by the Theoretical Group of the Training Division of General Staff Department:

> Whether the control of the military is in the hands of the proletariat or the bourgeoisie impinges on the survival of the party, the armed forces and the nation. On this we cannot sit idly by and watch it on the sideline. We shall unequivocally and strictly carry out the directives from Chairman Mao and the party center headed by Chairman Hua. As to those ambitious individuals following the line of anti-party, anti-people and anti-Chairman Mao, we will not comply with their will no matter what tricks they employ or excuses they use. To those people we will struggle with them over every inch of the land.[26]

The guardianship by the PLA high command in 1976–78 was different from PLA intervention in politics in 1966–76. In the latter case, the PLA was induced by Mao to be involved in politics. That was largely through the efforts of Marshal Lin Biao. But in 1976–78 it was the more professionally oriented and better-educated senior PLA commanders, such as Marshal Ye Jianying, who took the initiative to arrest the Gang of Four and proclaimed the PLA role of guardian. These professionally inclined PLA commanders put a premium on a hierarchical order, compliance with authority, organizational routine, and ideological orthodoxy. Coming after the anarchy and terror of Mao's Cultural Revolution, the political guardianship of the PLA high command in 1976–78 gave the PRC the necessary stability for the civilian authority of the CPC to transit from Maoist leadership to the present reformist administration.

The pragmatist leaders of the CPC consciously sought to recapture the spirit of the Eighth Party Congress in 1956, with its emphasis on inner party democracy, socialist legalism, and modernization. In the same vein, CPC reformists wished to return to the civil-military relations then, i.e., strict separation between civilian politics and military affairs. The PLA is supposed to concentrate on professionalization, and its sole political role is to support whatever party line was decided by civilian leaders. After 1979 the high command of the PLA had indeed receded from the political front burner, but not completely. The PLA high command apparently has no intention to abandon its guardianship role totally. But the essence of military guardianship, according to Nordlinger, consists of "the preservation of the basic status quo, which is partly defined in terms of a very recent past before the onset of civilian performance failure."[27] The reform of Deng Xiaoping, however, does not really bring the PRC back to pre-Cultural Revolution days. On the contrary, Deng and his reform-inclined colleagues wish to make major changes in the social and economic realm of the PRC. Herein lies the root of a number of conflicts between present CPC civilian leaders and the PLA. In subsequent discussion we shall analyze first the conflicts between civilian leaders and the PLA as a corporate body. After that we shall discuss different reactions to civilian leadership by different groups within the PLA.

CIVIL-MILITARY RELATIONS IN THE 1980s

First of all, PLA commanders as a whole are opposed to any erosion of the status of the PLA elite as a result of Deng's "liberalization." For example, in 1981, when a spate of literature appeared in China that attacked the privileges and abuses of power on the part of high military and party officials, the *PLA Daily* denounced the writers of these works even before the CPC reacted. The army press accused these writers of being affected with "bourgeois liberalism."[28]

A second potential conflict that sets present civilian leaders against the PLA as a corporate body is reduction of state budgetary support to the PLA. China's defense budget was reduced by 30 percent between 1979 and 1980.[29] After the arrest of the Gang of Four and during the 1976-78 period of PLA guardianship, the Chinese military sent abroad numerous "purchasing" missions, seemingly intent on buying advanced weapons from Western nations. But few purchases were actually made. Two American scholars explained the situation: "the military shopping list will be limited by overall economic constraints and by the low priority accorded to defense by the current Peking leadership."[30] In his report to the Chinese National People's Congress in 1983, Premier Zhao Ziyang gave overwhelming emphasis to state expenses in agriculture, light industry, education, and culture. Defense needs were mentioned in a short ritualistic reference to strengthening national defense.[31] General Yang Dezi, chief of staff of the PLA and PLA delegate to the National People's Congress, voiced his support of the national government's policy by saying:

> Economic construction is the foundation of defense construction. Our armed forces began as a single force and [are] now a combined force. Supply and maintenance of these forces in normal times already consume a large amount of money and materials. They are even more costly in war. The equipment of our armed forces is comparatively backward. We need to bridge the gap in weaponry between our forces and that of some foreign countries. But these can be solved only on the basis of continuously developing national economy, culture, science and technology.[32]

One detects a degree of ambivalence in General Yang's speech of "support." The reduced state expenses in military combined with present party leaders' stress on science, technology, and higher education also tends to affect negatively the status of the PLA. For the first time in the history of the PRC, young people do not wish to enlist in the PLA. In a speech to the Communist Youth League in December 1982, Yu Qiuli, director of the PLA General Political Department, mentioned some "incorrect" current sayings among Chinese youth such as, "To be a PLA man is to suffer a loss" or "Nothing is to be learned [if one is enlisted in the PLA] and it is a waste of one's life [to serve in the PLA]."[33]

Another potential point of conflict between civilian leaders and the PLA is a general demobilization drive in China in connection with the overall effort of modernization. In 1981 the civilian leaders of the CPC announced its goal of reducing the four million PLA forces by one-fourth in three or four years.[34] To many peasants-turned-PLA-officers statements by high-ranking party leaders justifying the streamlining measures in the military must sound insulting or "ideologically heretical." For example, Yang Shangkun, secretary-general of the Central Military Commission, wrote in the authoritative *Hongqi* that the human element in a modern army consists not just of the traditional (or Maoist) emphases on bravery, ideological consciousness, or spirit of sacrifice, "but also of intelligence and talent, including a person's grasp and control of science, technology, and culture."[35] Yu Qiuli, director of the PLA General Political Department, stated that henceforth new officers and staff should be recruited from technical units. "The past practice of selecting officers from the rank of infantry no longer meets the requirement of our time," Yu claimed.[36]

The foregoing deals with potential conflicts between civilian leaders and the PLA as a corporate body. But the PLA, as General Yang Dezi has pointed out, is no longer a single force. The PLA, like any modern nation's armed forces, encompasses different services and is subject to interservice rivalry. The various PLA services naturally respond to the civilian leaders' modernization program differently. Moreover, as in the Communist party, the PLA, owing to the numerous elite conflicts in the first three decades of the PRC, is factionalized. During the time of popular political dissent in the fall of 1978 and spring of 1979, a veterans' group put up a wall poster on the Democracy Wall of Peking. It claimed that from 1969 to 1975, some four hundred thousand PLA officers had been persecuted or forced to retire by the late Marshal Lin Biao. These former officers of the PLA now demanded a "reversal of their verdict." [37] Given the nature of political struggle in the Cultural Revolution, there is nothing implausible in this wall poster. Though the official Chinese press is tightlipped about the internal factional struggle in the PLA, occasionally a press report slips out and corroborates the Peking wall poster. [38] These developments in the PLA have a substantial effect on civil-military relations today.

The Chinese air force, probably due to its technically advanced nature, seems to respond most positively to the modernization effort of CPC leaders. The air force of the PLA was for a time under a cloud because of its involvement in Marshal Lin's "conspiracy" since one of Marshal Lin's sons was an air force officer. But apparently the air force has recovered from that. In 1982 the air force, under a new commander-in-chief, proudly declared that it had won the praise of Deng Xiaoping for excellent work in promoting younger and better-educated officers. [39] The *People's Daily* singled out the air force for successfully ridding itself of the influence of the Gang of Four. [40] The air force also vigorously responds to the present civilian leaders' drive to upgrade the educational standard of the PLA. In 1983 the PLA air force established a university to educate its officers and also sent one hundred thousand officers to universities and colleges to receive advanced education. [41]

In contrast to the PLA air force, the Chinese navy is politically less supportive of present CPC leadership. The PLA navy was formed after 1949 and was staffed with former infantry officers. Consequently, the navy is extremely factionalized. The influence of Marshal Lin Biao in the navy was strong. [42] The *People's Daily* spoke obliquely of the navy's being "damaged for a long time by Lin Biao and the Gang of Four and thus suffering from 'internal wounds.' " [43] In contrast to its praise of the air force, the *People's Daily* repeatedly referred to the PLA navy's deficiency in responding to the policy and program of civilian leaders. According to the newspaper, the navy failed to do a serious job in promoting the party line that said that facts were the sole criterion of truth. [44] The navy was said to have "gone astray" in its training because of too much emphasis being put on "political movement." [45] The *People's Daily* also reported that each time a party pronouncement was issued, thousands of naval officers had to be sent from the high command to "basic units" of the navy to insure that the navy was informed of and persuaded by the new party line. [46] In 1983 while the air force was responding actively to the call of modernization, the PLA navy was still pledging to rid itself of leftist influence. [47]

But the most serious opposition to the policy and program of civilian CPC leaders today comes, not surprisingly, from the infantry units in the Great Military Regions. It was in these regional armies that Mao Zedong and Lin Biao established their political stronghold. Specifically, regional army officers were opposed to the campaign of "emancipation of thinking," which was initiated by Deng in 1978 as the ideological underpinning of his reform. They blamed the rise in political dissent in China in the fall of 1978 on that campaign. Second, regional army officers objected to the critical evaluation of Mao's leadership that was part of Deng's campaign of "facts being the sole criterion of truth." The army opponents of Deng maintained that they had "simple and honest" (*chunpu*) feeling for Mao Zedong and rejected statements from Deng and other party leaders that Mao had made mistakes.[48] Basically, as a group of high PLA commanders put it, regional army opponents are accustomed to "surface peace and order" and "uniformity of views," being unwilling and incapable of accepting a diverse and lively political condition.[49] The opposition of regional army officers also encompasses Deng's economic program. General Xiao Hua, one-time director of PLA General Political Department, described the economic critique of leftists among regional army officers:

A few comrades are still accustomed to solve problems in education and economy by the political means of mass movement. They see leftist adventurism as the "revolutionary norm." They are of the opinion that the higher the target of production, the better is the overall economic condition. They do not understand that productive relations must fit productive forces. They cannot accept the various types of production management and free rural market in the countryside today. . . . They are interested in "cutting the tail of capitalism," or "eliminating inequality." They are puzzled by independent accounting, material incentives and reform in economic system.[50]

Deng's new social policy of lifting the label of class enemy from former landlords and rich peasants in the countryside and allowing these formerly outcast groups to improve their living conditions also met opposition from leftists among army officers.[51] Deng's emphasis on the value of intellectuals to Chinese modernization was also criticized by left-wing army officers. For example, General Nie Jungzhen, an ardent supporter of science, technology, and higher learning, wrote in 1982 that his advocacy of paying respect to and nourishing the intellectuals in Chinese society had met with opposition in the PLA and that he had been accused by the opponents of "siding with bourgeoisie."[52]

Taken together, the sentiments and attitudes of regional army opponents to Deng's reforms are a close fit with the phenomenon of *working-class authoritarianism* in Western societies. That concept comes from political sociologist Seymour Martin Lipset. According to Lipset, the manifestations of working-class authoritarianism are a rigid and intolerant approach to politics; viewing politics as black and white, good and evil; preference for extremist movements that suggest easy and quick solutions to social problems; liberalism in economic issues but conservatism in noneconomic issues; anti-intellectualism; and lack of a rich and complex frame of reference. Members of the working class in Western societies tend to display these authoritarian attitudes owing to their low incomes, low-status occupations, and low education. The "intransigent and intolerant aspects of Communist ideology" attract members of the working class.[53] That many PLA officers have the same working-class authoritarianism is not surprising, for they come from a background of low income and poor education. As a Chinese army press article pointed out: "Members of our army are mostly from villages, especially officers in responsible positions. A majority of them come from peasant families." The title of this army press article is telling: "On the Need to Cleanse the Army of Feudalism."[54] The extremism of Mao's ideology naturally attracts many of these peasants-turned-officers. During the Cultural Revolution, Marshal Lin promoted a large number of soldiers with peasant background to officer rank.[55] They must have been the main force of opposition to Deng's reform.

The low educational level and lack of political sophistication of the PLA may be gathered from a 1983 directive from the Central Military Commission on the need to improve the cultural level of the PLA. The directive stated that the PLA must strive to accomplish the goal, before 1985, of the equivalent of a junior high school education for all PLA officers below age forty.[56] A 1980 investigation of 161 PLA divisional and army corps commanders in Peking military regions found that 40 percent had not studied Marxist political economy, 26 percent had studied it briefly in short-term classes, and 34 percent had studied political economy on their own.[57] Similarly a survey of 200 officers of Sichuan troops found that only 12.7 percent had ever studied political economy.[58] For a long time, according to a PLA general, under the influence of the left PLA officers loved to boast of being uncouth and uneducated (*dalaocu*).[59] These PLA officers were the ideal clients for Mao's radical and unsophisticated "thoughts." That these officers would be opposed to Deng's four modernizations was only to be expected.

There are, of course, among PLA commanders those who supported Deng's reforms. But on the whole, these are aged members of the PLA high command, such as General Nie Jungzhen. Thus the opposition to present reform among regional PLA officers also serves to show the internal division of the PLA, especially between the high command and the regional military elite. It is only several years after the death of Mao that younger and better educated officers are being promoted. It was against the complex reaction and opposition in the PLA that CPC civilian leaders undertook an unprecedented action in March 1981—requiring all PLA members to swear an oath of loyalty to the party, the government, and the program of modernization.[60] A Western press report noted the significance of this event:

> This is believed to be the first time since the Communists took power in 1949 that any such oath has been required. The loyalty of members of the army has always been presumed, and the announcement led some non-military Chinese sources and diplomats . . . to speculate that grumbling and questioning in the army, as well as outright resistance to the present Peking leadership's policies and direction, were far more widespread and serious than they had thought.[61]

Finally, for a long time there had been a legend both in and out of China of the PLA's unique relationship with the masses. This legend was based on Mao's famous saying: "The popular masses are like water, and the army is like a fish."[62] But thirty years of building the PLA up into a privileged class plus its intervention in politics in 1966–76 have destroyed the legendary "fish-water" relationship between the PLA and Chinese people. Both official reports and literature in China offer abundant proof of estrangement, even hostility, between the PLA and the public. The editor of *Hongqi* stated: "Our People's Republic was won through revolutionary warfare. So the prestige of our troops was high among the people. But it has suffered during the 'Cultural Revolution.' There is estrangement between the military and the people; it is not as good as it was in the 1950s."[63]

In short, the PLA has lost much of its early populistic character. Nowadays, like praetorian soldiers elsewhere in other developing nations, the PLA is a privileged and basically conservative institution, jealously guarding its interest and opposed to radical reform in the direction of a pluralistic and pragmatic society.

THE PLA AND CHINESE ECONOMIC
DEVELOPMENT

So far, our attention has been on the PLA's role in Chinese politics, which is the preoccupation of commanders and officers mainly. The ordinary soldiers of the PLA participate more in Chinese economic construction than in high-level politics.

Veterans of the PLA, together with soldiers of former Nationalist armies and unemployed students, were organized into production and construction troops for the purpose of colonizing the border areas of China, such as Xianjiang and northeast China. These construction corps were said to have increased the cultivated land of China by 3.6 million acres.[64]

The PLA railway troops constructed major Chinese railways after 1949. In the thirty years from 1949-79, the railway troops constructed 47 railways, amounting to 12,000 kilometers and constituting 37 percent of all railway construction. In 1979 troops began building a line linking Qinghai with Tibet.[65]

The PLA engineering troops participated in China's construction of capital industry. Since 1966, the engineering troops have undertaken construction projects in metallurgy, coal mining, petroleum, chemical engineering, hydropower, transportation, urban subway transport, communications, and defense. Eighty-one projects were completed by the engineering troops in 1966-79.[66] What is significant is that the burden of the PLA engineering troops was increased after 1966 because of the breakdown of industrial discipline in civilian industry due to the Cultural Revolution.

The soldiers of the PLA also perform vast amounts of corvée duty. In the first three years of the PRC (1949-52), PLA soldiers repaired 32,000 kilometers of old highways and constructed 11,000 kilometers of new highways. In 1957 the corvée duty of PLA soldiers was equivalent to the work of 20 million laborers.[67] During the frenzied days of the Great Leap Forward in 1958, PLA soldiers, together with peasants, plunged into the construction of irrigation works and local steel mills in the countryside. To help fulfill the goal of producing 10 million tons of steel in 1958, the PLA made available to the Ministry of Metallurgy 4,120 trucks for transporting iron ore.[68] As one scholar wrote: "The [Chinese Communist] economy could not do without this army work."[69]

While we have dwelled on the close connection between the PLA and Chinese society and politics, we should stress also that the PLA bears the characteristic of, as one scholar put it, "a state within a state" in China. The PLA

> is the best equipped organization in the country. It has better hospitals, more trucks and more responsible men than the corresponding civilian party organizations. The army has its own farms and factories, and of course it has its arms. It is, or could easily become, a state within a state. It is in the army that young men are trained to become good Communists. Demobilized soldiers get leading positions in the localities.[70]

The PLA thus enjoys both autonomy and close connection with Chinese state and society. From the vantage point of civilian leaders, the PLA's multiple roles in society means that no policy could be successfully implemented without the support or acquiescence of the PLA. From the vantage point of PLA leaders, the diverse functions of the PLA have enhanced their self-confidence and sense of righteousness in intervening in civilian politics.

NOTES

1. *China News Analysis,* no. 1011 (August 22, 1975), p. 3.
2. *Selected Works of Mao Tse-tung,* vol. I, abridged by Bruno Shaw (New York: Harper & Row, Publishers, 1970), p. 26.
3. Stuart R. Schram, *The Political Thought of Mao Tse-tung* (New York: Frederick A. Praeger, 1970), p. 290.
4. *Ming Pao Daily News,* August 25, 1971, p. 1.
5. Kang Feng, "An Analysis of the Members of the 12th Central Leadership," *Chungkung Yenchiu* 16, no. 10 (October 15, 1982), 42.
6. *Ming Pao Daily News,* February 9, 1980, p. 1; February 10, 1980, p. 1; Christopher S. Wren, "Military Shake-Up Is Reported in China," *New York Times,* November 9, 1982, p. 3.
7. Eric A. Nordlinger, *Soldiers in Politics: Military Coups and Government* (Englewood Cliffs, N.J.: Prentice-Hall, 1977), p. 12.
8. Ibid., p. 65.
9. *Wan-sui,* no. 2, p. 46.
10. *Guangming Ribao,* October 1, 1955, as quoted in Chiang I-san, "Chinese Communist Military in the Last Decade," *Chungkung Shih-nien* (Hong Kong: Union Research Institute, 1960), p. 380.
11. Hu Ch'ih, "Views on Military Propaganda in the Newspapers," *Hsin-wen Chan-hsien (News Front),* no. 6 (June 15, 1958), as translated in *Extracts from China Mainland Magazines,* no. 151, p. 23.
12. *China News Analysis,* no. 1080 (May 20, 1977), p. 2.
13. *The Case of Peng Teh-huai, 1959-1968* (Hong Kong: Union Research Institute, 1968), pp. 39-44, 315.
14. *China News Analysis,* no. 1080 (May 20, 1977), p. 1.
15. J. Chester Cheng, ed., *The Politics of the Chinese Red Army* (Stanford, Calif.: Hoover Institution Press, 1966), pp. 593-97.
16. Xu Siyou, "Chairman Mao Lives in Our Hearts Forever," *Hongqi,* no. 9 (1978), p. 19.
17. *Wan-sui,* no. 2, p. 664.
18. *China News Analysis,* no. 859, (October 22, 1971), p. 1.
19. "The CCPCC 'Chung-fa (1972) Document #12' plus Supplement: Notes from Chairman Mao's Talks with Leading Comrades on Inspection Trips (mid-August to September 12, 1971)," *Chungkung Yenchiu,* 6, no. 9 (September 10, 1972), 93.
20. Ibid., p. 94.
21. Xu Siyou, "Chairman Mao Lives," p. 20.
22. *China News Analysis,* no. 1011 (August 22, 1975), p. 2.
23. Ibid., pp. 4-5.
24. *Wan-sui,* no. 2, p. 436.
25. For details of the Gang of Four's attempt to use the PLA for political purposes, see my article, "The 'Gang of Four' and the Chinese People's Liberation Army," *Asian Survey* XIX, no. 9 (September 1979), 817-37.
26. *RMRB,* December 4, 1976, p. 1.
27. Nordlinger, *Soldiers in Politics,* p. 25.
28. *Ming Pao Daily News,* November 10, 1981. Ting Wan, "Professional Officers' Dissatisfaction with Pessimistic Literature Exposing the Privilege of High Rank Military Official," *Ming Pao Daily News,* November 17, 1981.
29. *RMRB,* September 3, 1980, p. 4; *Ming Pao Daily News,* August 2, 1981, p. 1; also Charles Mohr, "China Said to Put Military Second to the Economy," *New York Times,* August 10, 1980, p. 10.
30. Drew Middleton, "Caution Shown by China in Buying Western Arms," *New York Times,* February 16, 1981, p. 6.
31. *RMRB,* June 24, 1983, p. 3.
32. *RMRB,* June 10, 1983, p. 3.
33. *RMRB,* December 30, 1982, p. 3.
34. James P. Sterba, "China's Army Follows New Marching Order, Not Happily," *New York Times,* March 1, 1981, p. E5; *Ming Pao Daily News,* July 29, 1981, p. 1; and *RMRB,* August 15, 1981, p. 1.
35. Yang Shangkun, "Build a Great Revolutionary and Modern Armed Forces," *Hongqi,* no. 15 (1982), p. 8.
36. *RMRB,* March 4, 1983, p. 1.
37. *Ming Pao Daily News,* October 28, 1979, p. 1; September 29, 1979, p. 11.
38. See, for example, the article by Li Jiancu in *RMRB,* October 11, 1979, p. 3.
39. *RMRB,* December 26, 1982, p. 1.
40. *RMRB,* November 16, 1981, p. 3.
41. *Ming Pao Daily News,* January 29, 1983, p. 1; May 15, 1983, p. 1.

42. Sheng Tse-ho, "Complicated Factions in Chinese Communist Navy," *Ming Pao Daily News*, May 30, 1980, p. 3; and Sheng Tse-ho, "Complicated Factions in the East Sea Fleet," *Ming Pao Daily News*, May 31, 1980, p. 3.
43. *RMRB*, September 6, 1978, p. 1.
44. *RMRB*, October 5, 1979, p. 1.
45. *RMRB*, July 22, 1981, p. 1.
46. *RMRB*, November 20, 1978, p. 4; September 2, 1981, p. 1.
47. *RMRB*, February 1, 1983, p. 4.
48. *RMRB*, May 3, 1979, pp. 1 and 2; October 11, 1979, p. 4.
49. *RMRB*, March 22, 1981, p. 1.
50. Xiao Hua, "Cleanse 'Leftist' Thought. Implement Party Policy Self-Consciously," *RMRB*, March 27, 1981, p. 3.
51. *RMRB*, July 9, 1979, p. 4; August 24, 1979, p. 1.
52. Nie Jungzhen, "Strive to Open New Era for Scientific and Technical Work," *Hongqi*, no. 24 (1981), p. 9.
53. Seymour Martin Lipset, *Political Man: The Social Basis of Politics* (New York: Doubleday & Company, 1963), pp. 87–116.
54. *RMRB*, November 21, 1980, p. 5.
55. Wei Guoqing, "Bring into Play the Exemplary Role of a Communist," *RMRB*, April 8, 1980, p. 2.
56. *RMRB*, May 5, 1983, p. 1.
57. *RMRB*, July 1, 1980, p. 1.
58. *RMRB*, December 23, 1980, p. 1.
59. *RMRB*, November 2, 1982, p. 1.
60. *RMRB*, March 3, 1981, p. 1.
61. *New York Times*, March 4, 1981.
62. Stuart R. Schram, *Political Thought of Mao Tse-tung*, p. 287.
63. *Hongqi*, no. 24 (1981), p. 4.
64. *RMRB*, October 2, 1979, p. 1.
65. Ibid.
66. Ibid.
67. *RMRB*, February 19, 1958, as reprinted in Chiang I-san, *Chungkung Chunshih Wenchien Huipien (Source Book on Military Affairs in Communist China)* (Hong Kong: Union Research Institute, 1965), p. 538.
68. *RMRB*, September 21, 1958, in Chiang I-san, *Source Book*, p. 540.
69. *China News Analysis*, no. 1011 (August 22, 1975), p. 6.
70. *China News Analysis*, no. 1010 (August 15, 1975), p. 2.

Throughout this chapter I have concentrated on civil-military relations, not on the PLA as a professional institution. Secondary works on the PLA focus predominantly on the PLA as a military institution. Students interested in the latter aspect of the PLA should consult Gerard M. Corr, *The Chinese Red Army: Campaigns and Politics Since 1949* (New York: Schocken Books, 1974); Alexander L. George, *The Chinese Communist Army in Action: The Korean War and Its Aftermath* (New York: Columbia University Press, 1967); John Gittings, *The Role of the Chinese Army* (London: Oxford University Press, 1967); Alice Langley Hsieh, *Communist China's Strategy in the Nuclear Era* (Englewood Cliffs, N.J.: Prentice-Hall, 1962); Robert B. Rigg, *Red China's Fighting Hordes* (Harrisburg, PA.: Military Service Publishing Company, 1951); William W. Whitson with Chen-hsia Huang, *The Chinese High Command: A History of Communist Military Politics, 1927–71* (New York: Frederick A. Praeger, 1973).

CHAPTER 12

The People's Militia

The People's Liberation Army, like the Communist party, has its own parapolitical organization—the People's Militia, whose activity is largely confined to the countryside, especially in border and coastal regions.

Militia as a form of mass mobilization by the CPC has a long history. In the very early stage of the CPC's guerrilla warfare against the Chinese Nationalists, various paramilitary groups were organized by the Communists to assist the small regular force of the Red Army. Names such as Red Guards (*Chiweidui*), Worker-Peasant Insurrectionary Company (*Gongnong Baodongdui*), and Young Pioneer Corps (*Shaoxiandui*) are familiar ones in the annals of the CPC. The development of the militia after 1949 was naturally affected by the shifts and turns of political events in the PRC. However, owing to the unique characteristics and functions of militia, its fortune from 1949 to the present has been different from other parapolitical groups. We can divide the organization of the Chinese Communist militia after 1949 into five periods: (1) peasant militia mainly for public security functions, 1950-57; (2) radical expansion of the militia to all sectors of society in the people's commune movement, 1958-69; (3) militia for defense against Soviet attack, 1970-72; (4) urban workers' militia organized by the Gang of Four in their struggle for power, 1973-76; and (5) retrenchment of the militia, 1977-83.

1950-57

In 1950 when the militia was first organized, its function was clearly for public security or the consolidation of CPC control over China, especially control of the countryside. The specific tasks of the militia then were:

1. Maintenance of social order: assisting the PLA and the public security force in pursuing bandits, informing on enemy agents, maintaining order in social reform, and suppressing the resistance and sabotage of reactionaries.
2. Protection of construction and production: maintaining rural social order for the sake of production; assisting the PLA and the public security force in pro-

tecting railways, bridges, telecommunication lines, warehouses, factories, mines, forests, and irrigation works and in prevention of infiltration, robbery, and arson.

3. Training: undergoing military training and patriotic education and engaging in physical education so as to be ready to shoulder the task of national mobilization.[1]

In this formation stage the Chinese militia was limited to males between eighteen and thirty years old. Membership in the militia was, in theory, voluntary. There was an explicit class requirement: militia members must be "rural laboring people" and recruitment should "start with the activists from campaigns of struggle and gradually expand to include most of the landless peasants, middle and poor peasant youth in the countryside." Members of landlord and rich peasant families were barred from joining the militia.[2] Moreover, the militia was further divided into core members (*jigan*) and ordinary members. The former were allowed to bear arms and had to be the "activists promoted from campaigns of struggle."[3]

The formal status of the militia is somewhat ambiguous. As one official document on militia building puts it: "The militia are an organization of military nature and, hence, it is different from ordinary people's organization. The militia, however, are an organization of the masses so it should be distinguished from the armed forces."[4] Leadership over the militia is equally complex. The militia below the county had its own organization, composed of a representative branch—militia representatives' assembly—and an executive branch—People's Armed Forces Committee. But this militia organization seems to be pointless as it was stressed in all CPC directives that the militia below the county was under the "direct leadership" of the CPC committee of the area. The militia above the county, e.g., militia in some cities, was subordinated to the regional command of the PLA. In general the militia building in 1950-52 was of limited scale and was closely connected with the "campaigns of struggle" that the CPC was carrying out in that period, especially the violent Land Reform in rural areas and the Five-Anti campaign in the cities. Moreover, there was genuine fear on the part of CPC leaders that the PLA and the security forces might not be adequate to cope with social disorder that might accompany the CPC's radical campaigns. At the same time, CPC leaders were very cautious in the organization of the militia. All directives on militia building cautioned against quick expansion and stressed moderate and carefully controlled recruitment from the most reliable activists. A directive from the Central-South sub-bureau of the Politburo in 1950 warned lower party leaders: "The militia are armed and they are scattered. Unified regulation of militia is not easy. Hence militia are prone to be exclusive and alienated from the masses. It might become the tyrant of society and be opposed by the masses."[5] As the PRC passed the period of revolutionary destruction of 1949-52 and embarked on industrialization of the economy, professionalization of the armed forces, and institutionalization of the formal structure of governing in 1953-57, militia organization, such as the peasant associations, were no longer paid attention by the CPC.

1958-69

However, Mao Zedong's radical Great Leap Forward and the people's commune campaign in 1958-60 brought the militia back to the front pages of the Chinese press. Mao Zedong's ideal of communes called for total regimentation of life in the countryside. Each commune was supposed to manage its own industry, agriculture, trade, education, and armed forces. In such a commune, "industry, agriculture and trade constitute the material aspect of life; education, the spiritual aspect of life; and an armed people is for the defense of this material and spiritual life."[6] The people's commune requires, so Mao's thesis goes, a gigantic labor force that combines the functions of workers, peasants, and soldiers. This versatile labor force, an editorial in the army paper commented, "is also the best organization in preparation for people's war."[7] Now the justification for preparation for "people's war" was provided by the PLA's massive artillery attack on two Nationalist-held offshore islands—Quemoy and Matsu—in August 1958 precisely at the beginning of the people's commune movement. Basing its decision on all the foregoing, the CPC issued the call for an "armed people," i.e., turn every able-bodied man and woman in rural areas and even in some cities into militia men. In a talk to regional CPC leaders in November 1958, Mao Zedong attempted to rationalize his ill-fated attack on Quemoy and Matsu by saying: "The shelling in Taiwan Strait is beneficial; otherwise the organization of militia would not have been accomplished so quickly."[8]

Given Mao's emphasis on the people's commune scheme—the countryside must accelerate economic development by its own bootstraps—the militia was most probably intended by Mao as another way of regimenting peasant labor. An editorial in the army paper, *PLA Daily,* stated, for example, "Since the Great Leap Forward, every production front needs a large number of labor. Organizing a labor army of part-worker, part-peasant and part-soldier is one effective way of solving shortage of labor."[9] Another plausible but secondary reason for Mao's expanding the militia may have been to counter the increasing professionalization of the PLA, then under the command of Marshal Peng Dehuai. Both Marshal Peng and General Lo Ruiqing, chief of staff of the PLA in 1959-65, were reported to be opposed to Mao's militia expansion.[10] Thus the functions and status of the militia of 1958 were not entirely clear since partisan motives and the institutional interests of the PLA might well be involved.

The fortune of the 1958 militia, however, was connected with that of the people's communes. Since the latter were soon to be steadily cut back, the militia establishment met the same fate. This may be gathered from a report on militia work by a PLA general named Fu Qiutao, who went on an inspection tour of the militia in November 1960 on behalf of the CPC Central Military Commission. Afterwards, General Fu submitted a startling report to the High Command and Mao on the disarray of the militia organization. According to General Fu, the organization of the militia in 1958 was "impractical" because, first of all, owing to the economic disaster following the Great Leap all able-bodied young men in the countryside had been employed in emergency operations. As a result, many so-called militia units were paper units only. General Fu described the situation:

> It was reported in Chengchow [Henan Province] that there was a militia battalion which was said to be composed of three companies, with 620 members altogether. But after careful check, we found that there are only 16 vegetable watchmen who claimed themselves as militia guards and even these did not know who their squadron and platoon leaders were. They did not know to which platoon or company they belonged either.[11]

It is significant that General Fu selected the province of Henan (Honan) for investigation. Henan was where the first commune was organized in July 1958, and Chengchow was also where urban communes were started. Hence, whatever happened in the commune or militia organization in Henan should reveal some basic problems common to all provinces.

Before 1958 organization of the militia was of limited scale, and careful selection of militia leaders was stressed. The fear then was that the militia might be "the tyrant of society and be opposed by the masses." The expansion of the militia in 1958, in the Maoist style of "doing things in a big way," threw the early cautions to the wind. General Fu found in his 1960 investigation of the militia that "bad elements" had penetrated the militia, who had "robbed, beat up and pushed around the people and raped women." In some places the peasants referred to militia men as mad dogs, gangsters, tiger bands, bandit kings, and little bosses.[12]

The problems of the militia, as revealed in General Fu's report, have sketched for us, in a very clear way, the tremendous gap in the perspective of Mao and other top CPC leaders and that of Communist cadres in basic units of the Chinese state. The communes and militia were legitimized in 1958 by Chen Boda, secretary to Mao, on the basis of: (1) Karl Marx's writing on the Paris Commune—"The first decree of the Commune . . . was the suppression of the standing army, and the substitution for it of the armed people," (2) Lenin's reference in "The State and Revolution" to "the state power of the armed workers," and (3) Marx and Engels' *Communist Manifesto*—"Combination of agriculture with manufacturing industries; gradual abolition of the distinction between town and country. . . ."

It is doubtful that lower CPC cadres, who were almost entirely recruited from poor peasantry on the basis of their activism in the campaigns of struggle, would have been inspired by the Marxist-Leninist ideas that had inspired Mao Zedong and Chen Boda. General Fu's analysis of the low quality of militia cadres points to the gap in perspectives between upper and lower leaders of the PRC.

Subsequent to General Fu's inspection of militia work, the PLA High Command commenced a campaign in 1961 of tightening its control over the militia. By then the people's communes had already been radically "adjusted," and Mao Zedong was no longer in charge of national policy making. This then enabled the PLA high command to restore the nature and status of the militia to the original 1950 pattern. According to a conference of the Central Military Commission in January 1961, PLA commands in military regions and provincial military districts had dispatched thirty-six thousand cadres to various localities to rectify the shortcomings of the militia. But given the size of China and the PLA's concern over its own troops (unrest among troops in 1961 was widespread due to famine in the countryside), the rectification effort of the PLA over the militia was selective. The cadres that the PLA high command sent out had concentrated their cleansing of the militia on city suburbs, places along the railways and thoroughfares, defense areas along the coast and national borders, islands along the coast, and major bridges and warehouses as well as along the provincial and county boundaries. A particularly noteworthy task of the cadres sent by the PLA high command to rectify militia work was tightening control of militia weapons. These PLA representatives found the condition and upkeep of militia arms dismal. "Loss, damage and theft of militia arms was very serious."[13] As a result of the PLA's tightening control over the militia in 1961, the activity of the militia reverted to security and defense. The militia was not allowed to be used in handling ordinary criminal cases or civil disputes. Use of the militia for police action must be approved by higher party and PLA authorities. Party committees were installed in city and county people's armed forces committees that oversaw militia organization.[14] So for the moment, the militia was reined in by the PLA.

The control of the PLA over the militia, however, did not last long. As soon as the worst phase of famine was over, Mao staged a political comeback in 1962. In September of that year at the tenth plenum of the Eighth CPC Central Committee Mao Zedong sounded again his clarion call for class warfare in China. ("We must recognize that classes will exist for a long time and we must recognize class struggle. The reactionaries might be restored to power so we must enhance our vigilance.") Mao was particularly taken aback by the reduction of communal production and the increase in household farming. Class struggle must first be instituted in the countryside, so Mao initiated the Socialist Education campaign soon after the party conference in 1962. The militia would naturally be useful in conducting class struggle. So simultaneously with the Socialist Education campaign, Mao launched his movement to rectify the militia organization. "Militia work must be carried through organizationally, politically and militarily" was the line set by Mao. However, of the three aspects of militia work, Mao clearly wanted to put politics, i.e., class struggle, over organizational and military work. An editorial in the army paper, *PLA Daily,* implicitly repudiated the PLA high command's rectification of the militia in 1961 by saying that militia work must be done in the context of the Socialist Education movement. "If militia work deviates from that [Socialist Education movement] and follows a different line, then it will separate itself from the most important political question of the day. Militia work would then accomplish nothing." To be more specific and explicit, the same editorial stated:

> The organizational, political and military work of the militia are all important. But in actual practice we must put political fulfillment in the first place. This is so because if political work was not done thoroughly then the militia could not be under the absolute leadership of the party and we could not then be sure of the guns' being in the hands of reliable workers, poor peasants and lower-middle peasants. If political work was not thorough then fulfillment in organizational and military work would be formalistic and unreliable. To be thorough in political work means to strengthen the class education of the militia and *to steel the militia in actual class struggle* [emphasis added].[15]

Thus in the militia as in other mass organizations, Mao's class line preempted whatever independent identification any organized group might have. In the case of the militia the most interesting thing is that though the PLA high command was keen in keeping the militia under its wing, Mao's will overrode it. This is hardly surprising since in our discussion of the PLA in politics we have mentioned several instances of the PLA's impotence when faced with opposition from Mao. Another noteworthy aspect of the militia work in 1962-64 is that, as in the collectivization of agriculture, Mao showed little or no interest in problems of operation. We mentioned that in spite of the numerous technical and leadership problems accompanying the higher APCs, Mao launched the people's commune before any solution was found for those problems. Similarly Mao's emphasis on class in militia work in 1962-64 ignored the various problems of the militia organization, especially the quality of both the leaders and the enlisted men, which General Fu Qiutao had described in his report of 1961. Mao's approach would have grave consequences for the rural population in the forthcoming Cultural Revolution. In the meantime, Mao's campaign of political transformation of rural militia in 1962-64 was aborted since the Socialist Education brought out serious divisions between Mao and other top-ranking CPC leaders, such as Liu Shaoqi. It was these divisions that led Mao to launch the Cultural Revolution. His aim was to rid the CPC of "revisionists."

During the long period of the Cultural Revolution of 1966-69 and the leftist reign of 1970-76, the activity of the militia became quite diversified. The rural militia, from the very beginning of the Cultural Revolution and lasting through 1977, became an instrument of terror in the hands of local party and PLA authorities. On November 8, 1980, the *People's Daily*, for example, published a full-page report on the terror of the militia command in a county in Hubei Province. The county party secretary had fabricated a case of corruption and used the militia to torture the accused in order to obtain a false confession. The report stated that the threat of sending an accused to the militia command often was enough to frighten him into agreeing to confess according to the wishes of the party secretary. "The accused knows that that place [the militia command] is where the cruelest beating of people takes place. Passersby often hear terrible screams coming from inside of it. . . . What is startling is that those who beat the people in the most ferocious way are the militia, including veterans of the PLA, who are supposed to be the protector of the people."[16] This case of militia atrocity resulted in six deaths and seventeen disabled. One hundred persons were subjected to "various cruel tortures." During the period of armed conflict among the various Red Guard, or rebel, groups in 1967-68, the arms of the militia, partly because of lack of responsible care, were the first to be made available to the warring factions, thus contributing to group violence in the Cultural Revolution.[17]

1970-72

The militia organization, after being left to itself from 1966 to 1969, received serious attention from Mao and other national CPC leaders in the aftermath of armed conflict between Chinese and Soviet border guards along the Ussuri River in March 1969. Subsequently a war scare was orchestrated by CPC leaders in mainland China. In late 1970 conferences on militia work were convened everywhere in China in which, in addition to the usual emphasis on ideology, stress was put on training for combat readiness. Since Mao and his colleagues had publicly professed faith in the old tactics of luring the enemy deep into Chinese territory and then overcoming it by "people's war," the training of militia in 1970 was entrusted to the provincial PLA command. In sensitive areas, such as the three northeastern provinces (Heilongjiang, Jilin, and Liaoning), Inner Mongolia, and Xinjiang, fully armed militia divisions were organized, and these even took over the duty of border defense from the regular PLA forces. Moreover, according to the CPC leaders' "worst-case scenario," a Soviet attack from the north might also be accompanied by an attack by Indian "reactionaries" along the Tibetan border, an American attack along the Vietnamese border at Yunnan and Guangxi, and a Chinese Nationalist invasion along the coast of Fujian and Guangdong. So the militia in all these areas were greatly strengthened in late 1970. Armed militia forces (full-time, salaried militia men) were established to assume full-time defense duty. In case of actual invasion, the militia would bear the brunt of enemy attack and sufficiently maul the invasion force. The regular PLA would then meet the enemy, whose strength had already been reduced by the militia.[18] So far as the politics of the militia was concerned, the 1970 mobilization of the militia enabled the PLA to reassert its control over the militia and return the function of the militia to its historical mission as the PLA's reserve and assistant.

1973-76

As the threat of Soviet attack receded after 1970, however, the militia was once more, as in 1962-64, entangled in the CPC factional struggle for power. In 1973 a campaign of militia building with a new twist was promoted by the Gang of Four, notably by Zhang Chunqiao and Wang Hongwen. The stress was on the urban workers' militia. The reason behind this emphasis, as we touched upon in our analysis of the role of the PLA in Chinese politics, was the ascendancy of professionally inclined PLA generals in the aftermath of the death of Marshal Lin Biao. The professionals, headed by Marshal Ye Jianying, were now in charge of the PLA high command. Moreover, they were supported by senior CPC leader Deng Xiaoping, who had been rehabilitated by Mao in 1973 to take charge of day-to-day affairs of the CPC and the Chinese national government. Both Ye and Deng wanted to end the political strife in China. But to the Gang of Four returning to normalcy meant their political, if not physical, demise. The formation of the urban workers' militia was a desperate move by the four leftists to provide themselves (so they thought) with a separate armed force. Naturally, the PLA high command was strongly opposed to the urban workers' militia. The issues of contention between the PLA high command and the Gang of Four were long-standing ones. First, on the legitimate function of the militia, the PLA's position since 1950 was clear—the militia being the PLA's reserve and assistant and also, to a limited degree, a back-up force to public security. The militia, the PLA high command maintained, "must not be used to solve contradictions among the people," i.e., the militia should play no role in civilian politics. The stand of the Gang of Four was also clear; theirs was Mao's stand on the militia from the days of 1962-64—the militia being an instrument of class struggle. Second, on the control of the militia, the PLA high command insisted on the traditional system that integrated the main force units, the regional forces, and the militia under the PLA command structure. The Gang of Four naturally sought to establish a separate militia command of the PRC controlled by Wang Hongwen.[19] The conflict between the Gang of Four and the PLA high command over the militia, in its own unique way, parallels the conflicts between the CPC and other mass organizations, i.e., independence of an organized group versus supremacy of the CPC interest. The unique aspect of the dispute over the militia is that the advocates of independence for the urban workers' militia were the ones who ordinarily always insisted on, in Zhang Chunqiao's phrase, "all-round dictatorship of the proletariat." The failure of the Gang of Four in their efforts to create a second armed force by means of the urban workers' militia is symptomatic of the failure of Mao in the Cultural Revolution. In February 1967 Mao explained to an Albanian visitor that all his past efforts to rid the CPC of revisionists had failed until he finally found a way, "a method which openly, comprehensively and coming from below, exposes the dark side of us"—the Cultural Revolution.[20] In other words, Mao and the Gang of Four sought to create a populistic mass organization within the confines of the Communist totalistic framework and, moreover, the mass movement would ultimately steer the Communist party into an even more totalistic power structure. But they failed in the first round—creating a genuinely populistic mass movement within the totalitarian system of the CPC.

1977–83

When the PLA high command assumed the status of "guardian" of the PRC after the death of Mao, the fate of the militia could be easily predicted. The first step of the post-Mao leadership was to abolish Wang Hongwen's militia command and revive the people's armed forces committees as part of the structure of every subnational party committee. The militia were to be formally subordinated to these people's armed forces committees. But regional party committees provide only general leadership over the militia; the actual training and other operational activity of the militia are in the hands of regional PLA commands.[21] In other words, the PLA has reestablished its control over the militia. A more significant step taken by the present leaders of the CPC in militia matters was announced in March 1983. The militia has been consolidated, i.e., reduced in number and streamlined in organization. More important, the militia today have been formally transformed into the PLA's reserve. Membership in the militia is now classified as active reserve duty for the PLA. The 1983 report maintains that the reduction of the numerical strength of the militia and reform of its military training have curtailed the claims of the militia on the time and service of civilians, thus lessening the burden of the public.[22]

CONCLUSION

We have stated that in its use of the parapolitical organizations, the CPC shows an unmistakable urban bias and that there is no nationwide and prominent organization representing Chinese peasants, as the ACFTU represents workers. The People's Militia, however, may be regarded as a peasants' association since it is composed mostly of peasants. But note the difference in the roles of the People's Militia and other parapolitical organizations. The militia lacks the dignified status that is granted the democratic parties, unions, youth leagues, and even women's associations. When we relate the status of the militia to our early discussion of the CPC's rural policy (administration and development) we can see clearly that Chinese peasants are perceived by the CPC to be of two major uses only: (1) as beasts of burden for China's industrialization and (2) as professional subduers at the beck and call of the CPC.

NOTES

1. *Zhangjiang Ribao,* August 17, 1950, in Chiang I-san, *Chungkung Chunshih Wenchien Huipien (Source Book on Military Affairs in Communist China)* (Hong Kong: Union Research Institute, 1965), p. 632.
2. Ibid., p. 635.
3. Ibid., pp. 635–36.
4. Ibid., p. 636.
5. Ibid., p. 637.
6. *Jiefangchunbao (People's Liberation Army Daily),* August 16, 1958, in Chiang I-san, *Source Book,* p. 646.
7. Ibid.
8. *Wan-sui,* no. 2, p. 255.
9. *Jiefangchunbao,* August 16, 1958, in Chiang I-san, *Source Book,* p. 645.
10. Hsiang Chuan-she, "Militia Work of the Chinese Communists," *Chungkung Yenchiu* 6, no. 6 (June 10, 1972), 57.
11. The original text is in Chiang I-san, *Source Book,* pp. 658–66. The present translation is from J. Chester Cheng, ed., *The Politics of the Chinese Red Army* (Stanford, Calif.: Hoover Institution Press, 1966), pp. 117–18.

12. Ibid., p. 119.

13. Chiang I-san, *Source Book,* p. 671.

14. Ibid., pp. 675–76.

15. Ibid., p. 677.

16. Zuo Hui, "Oh, My Brothers and Kinsmen!" *RMRB,* November 8, 1980, p. 5.

17. Hai Feng, *Kuangchou Tich'u Wenke Lichen Sulueh (An Account of the Cultural Revolution in the Canton Area)* (Hong Kong: Union Research Institute, 1971), pp. 175–76.

18. Hsiang Chuan-shu, "Militia Work," pp. 56–66. See also William Beecher, "Shift in Strategy by Peking Is Seen," *New York Times,* July 25, 1972, p. 1.

19. *RMRB,* December 30, 1976, p. 2; and *RMRB,* March 15, 1977, p. 2. Though these are partisan accounts by the PLA high command, I do not see anything implausible in them. After all, Wang Hongwen and Zhang Chunqiao were rather explicit in what they hoped to do with the militia. For more on the subject, see *RMRB,* January 27, 1976, p. 2; April 21, 1976, p. 4; June 19, 1976, p. 1; June 20, 1976, p. 1; September 29, 1976, p. 2.

20. *Wan-sui,* no. 2, p. 664.

21. Yu Yang, "Restoration of People's Armed Force Committee," *Chungkung Yenchiu* 14, no. 3 (March 15, 1980), 107–110.

22. *RMRB,* March 18, 1983, p. 4.

PART FOUR

The Political Process

CHAPTER 13

Ideology and Ideological Style

So far we have discussed the "hard tools" of governing in the People's Republic of China, i.e., the formal governing organizations. These, however, are used and enlivened by Chinese leaders at all levels, whose actions are guided by their peculiar predispositions that are, in turn, based on their life experience. We mentioned the major predispositions of the CPC at the conclusion of our discussion of the origin of Chinese Communism (see chapter 2), namely, faith in the ideology of Marxism-Leninism, personalistic leadership, campaigns as a working style, communalization of life, and a political ethos of struggle. We might call these predispositions the political culture of Chinese Communists.

How the political culture of the CPC shapes the operation of the Chinese Communist political system is discussed in subsequent chapters. We shall first deal with the impact of the Communist political culture on the total system, to which it imparts an overall characteristic—the ideological style of Chinese politics. Next we shall analyze the manifestations of the CPC political culture at the elite level, namely the cliquish process and the overall decision-making pattern. Finally, we shall describe the linkage between the elite and the masses in the PRC by studying Chinese Communist political communication and public opinion.

The Communist party of China, as we have noted, is a "normative organization" whose goal is to create a new culture. Moreover, the CPC regards itself as the prototype of the new society and seeks thus to transform China after its own image. As a consequence, the operation of the Chinese Communist political system is pervaded with an "ideological style." According to Sidney Verba, ideological-style politics "involves a deeply affective commitment to a comprehensive and explicit set of political values which is hierarchical in form and often deduced from a more general set of 'first principles.'" The contrast to the ideological style is the pragmatic style politics, which "consists of an evaluation of problems in terms of their individual merits rather than in terms of some preexisting comprehensive view of reality."[1]

The politics of ideological style resembles closely a theocracy in which the government and officials are "divinely guided." In ideological politics, the government and officials are doctrinally guided. Similar to organized religion, ideological-style politics puts a premium on sacred texts, authoritative spokespersons (prophets), hierarchically positioned cadres, and institutionalized enemies (devils). Simon Leys, a longtime sinologist and resident of mainland China, wrote: "Ecclesiastical metaphors are virtually irresistible when describing the People's Republic. . . . Those who harbor a certain nostalgia for totalitarianism and unconsciously regret the passing away of the Inquisition and the Pope's Zouaves will find in Maoist China the incarnation of a medieval dream, where institutionalized Truth has again a strong secular arm to impose dogma, stifle heresy, and uproot immorality."[2]

In ideological-style politics, any or every aspect of public or often even private activity is legitimized by referring to precepts from the formal ideology. The vital political question, Who gets what, when and how? for example, is answered in China (or any other Communist nation) by referring to the works of Marx, Lenin, and in the PRC, "Mao Zedong thought." Ideology in the PRC thus takes the place of an electorate, which in Western democracies is the final legitimizer of political actions.

The overwhelming importance of a formal ideology such as Marxism, Leninism, and "Mao Zedong thought" in the PRC has several specific implications for the Chinese political system. First of all, political power is in the hands of a *select*, whose power and position are justified on the ground that they are ideologically proficient. In this respect the Chinese Communist political system may be defined, following Lasswell and Kaplan, as an *ideocracy*, in which the predominant forms of power are those resting on the manipulation of symbols.[3] Specifically, this means that the elite of the PRC are duty bound to make authoritative pronouncements on the state of the nation in terms of its progress toward the "new culture." These authoritative pronouncements (religious edicts) are a highly formalized and ritualized affair. Each of the pronouncements has three components. There is first a historical review, which is meant to reassure that the nation, under the guidance of the elite, is progressing along the "historical path" to the final goal of a "good society." Often in the historical review certain "deviations" are noted, and the perpetrators are thus denounced, but above all, the tenor of the review is that the "main current" of development is correct. After the historical review comes a "diagnosis," often presented in a spectacular fashion, of the current situation, which is said to mark a "turning point" or a "new page" in history. Lessons of the past have been learned, and corrective actions have been undertaken. Ideological reinterpretation is made in order to adapt to the demands of the situation. Then comes a call on the nation to fulfill certain important tasks—political, social, or economic. Finally, the authoritative statement from the party concludes with a bright "prognosis," urging the nation to march into another phase of "history" toward the ultimate "new society." (For a sample of such an authoritative statement, see the appendix.)

Second, ideological-style politics is premised on an authoritarian and hierarchical power structure. At the top of the hierarchy is "the Word" and "God"—Marxism-Leninism and Marx, Engels, and Lenin. Below that are "gospels" and "apostles"—"Mao Zedong thought" and Mao. Further down the line are the lesser apostles, i.e., the cadres. As noted previously, the cadres are, in theory, *selected* on the basis of their ideological proficiency, which is assured by making the cadres study in party schools (religious seminaries).

Third, ideological-style politics requires a myth of unanimity. "This myth can rest either on the divine inspiration of the ruler or, as it did with Calvin and Marx, upon the assumption that no rational person can come to any other conclusion—i.e., that the ideology or theology is 'scientific' or 'rational,' and that no other one is or can be."[4] The requirement of unanimity further leads to two tendencies in ideological-style politics. One is continuous need for "symbol manipulation," i.e., interpretation and reinterpretation of ideology, which is necessary to cope with the complexity of society and economy. Reinterpretation of ideology is designed to maintain an image of infallibility. The drive to maintain unanimity in ideological politics also leads to a continuous battle against heretics. "In such societies, the pursuit of heretics is considered necessary and is both widespread and fierce, for heretics represent a threat to power as well as to ideological interests."[5] Actual power conflicts among leaders are also presented in ideological terms, which ultimately brings disrepute to ideology itself. The "crisis of faith, trust, and confidence" in the PRC today, which we discussed earlier, is an example of how ideology was discredited owing to Mao's continuous manipulation of it to mask power conflicts. Yet at the same time, the stress on unanimity and the hierarchical power structure of ideological politics tend to generate internal conflict. Moreover, the distinction of conflict over means and over ends in ideological-style politics is blurred, breeding more conflicts. The history of the first thirty years of the PRC fully bears this out.

THE FORMAL IDEOLOGY OF THE CPC

So far we have focused our discussion on the way that the PRC elites regard their formal ideology. We shall now briefly describe the substance of the CPC's formal ideology.

There are three components, arranged in a hierarchical manner, to the formal ideology of the CPC. The first principle is, naturally, the works by Marx and Engels. Next are the works of Lenin and Stalin. Finally, there is the "thought of Mao Zedong," which is often referred to as "creative adaptation of Marxism-Leninism to the Chinese situation."

From the works of Marx and Engels, Chinese Communists learn the basic concepts of society, economy, and politics, the most prominent ones being a dialectical view of the universe, class struggle in social relations, interaction of productive forces and productive relations (superstructure) in social and economic development, and two-stage historical development (or revolution), i.e., from bourgeois-democratic to socialist revolution. The dialectical view of the universe predisposes Chinese Communists to view everything in a polarized, mutually antagonistic, and fluid state. Struggle between the bourgeoisie and the proletariat, which inevitably ends in the destruction of the former, is regarded by the CPC as the essential force to move society forward. In the development of social and economic institutions, Chinese Communists follow Marx's prescription that productive relations must align themselves with productive forces. Productive relations means the organization of human society, such as government, factory, or agricultural collectives. Productive forces refer to actual production. According to the materialist view of Marx, productive forces develop first, and then the corresponding productive relations follow. Finally, according to Marx, a society must first undergo a bourgeois-democratic revolution to destroy feudalism and allow capitalism to liberate the productive forces. If productive forces have gone further ahead, then the capitalist productive relations would no longer suffice. Socialist revolution is the natural result, and the form of ownership will be transformed from private into public. During the early transition to socialist construction, workers will organize the dictatorship of the proletariat to replace bourgeois democracy. These basic Marxist concepts constitute the world outlook of the leaders of the CPC. As Mao Zedong once observed, after 1949 the national development of China followed two principles: the law of social development—establishing "a unitary system of the ownership of the means of production by the whole people [community]"—and class struggle.[6]

From Lenin and Stalin, Chinese Communists learned practical steps and programs of revolution and national development. The essential ingredients of Leninism that the Chinese Communist party accepted wholeheartedly are organization of the Communist party around a core of revolutionary intellectuals, indoctrination of workers and peasants with Marxist concepts, seizure of political power without waiting for the "inevitable turn" of history to socialism, and use of political power to create foundations of socialism, for instance, dispossessing capitalists' means of production and collectivizing agriculture. In other words, Lenin put a tremendous emphasis on the omnipotence of political power, or in Marxist terms, the productive relations. Contrary to Marx's theory, Lenin put productive relations before productive forces.

While it is relatively simple to sketch the essentials of Marxism and Leninism, it is much more difficult to do so with "the thought of Mao Zedong." That Mao made no theoretical breakthrough in Marxism-Leninism is the consensus among Western students of Chinese Communism.[7] Mao's distinct role both in China and in the international Communist movement was his practical leadership of the CPC in winning political power. In ideological matters "the thought of Mao Zedong" is distinguished by the way Mao held the few basic Marxist and Leninist concepts. In other words, it was Mao's attitudes toward Marxism and Leninism, not his theoretical contribution, that made him unique. Basically there are two aspects of Mao's approach to Marxism. One is his literalism, especially with regard to, in his words, "the law of social development, i.e., unitary ownership of the means of production by the whole people." Chinese Communist historian Hu Sheng alluded to Mao's literal attitude toward Marxism when he wrote:

> The public ownership of the means of production and the principle of distribution "to each according to his work" as well as the planned and proportionate development of the national economy represent only the general laws of the socialist system. If we rely solely on these general laws but fail to integrate them with our concrete conditions, we will accomplish nothing. If we design a "pure" and "perfect" socialism according to these laws and become obsessed with such abstract concepts as "pureness" and "perfectness" we can get nothing but guiding principles that are estranged from reality and *spoil things that could have been done well* [emphasis added].[8]

Mao adhered to the Leninist stress on productive relations (i.e., the omnipotence of political power) with the same degree of literalism as he did with Marxist law of social development. He declared:

> The history of all revolutions has shown that it is not the case that there must first be new productive forces before the obsolete productive relations can be transformed. Our revolution started with a propagation of Marxism-Leninism so to create a new public opinion and thereby facilitating revolution. While in revolution we overthrow the outdated superstructure and destroy the old productive relations . . . paving the road for great expansion of productive force.[9]

The second noteworthy attitude of Mao toward ideology is his radicalness, which we defined previously as an attempt to align all undertaking to a single principle (see chapter 3). In other words, Mao was a *reductionist,* e.g., he believed in reducing all social relations and human activity to the principle of class struggle, thus denying the complexity of contexts in everyday life. The principle of class struggle as the key link of society best exemplifies Mao's radicalism.

Mao's literalness and radicalism apply not only to the few master Marxist and Leninist concepts that he accepted without reservation but also to the revolutionary legacy of the CPC that we discussed in chapter 3. In other words, "the thought of Mao Zedong" means applying the whole range of practice acquired during the Communist revolution to post-1949 national reconstruction, e.g., use of mass campaigns, communal life, egalitarianism, and political motivation. As Mao stated in 1962 in opposition to giving material incentives to workers: "We once fought for some twenty years and had relied on the system of supply of provisions. . . . Up till the early days of liberation [of China] we generally lived an egalitarian life and all of us worked very hard and fought very bravely. These were not based on material incentives, but on revolutionary spirit."[10]

Toward the end of his life Mao, frustrated by the fact that there was no prospect of turning China into what he regarded as a Communist society and by the increasing alienation of other Communist leaders from him, withdrew further and further into ideological abstractions. This can be seen in his 1967 talk to an Albanian military delegation, explaining the Cultural Revolution:

> I once said at a rally of seven thousand people in 1962: "In the struggle between Marxism-Leninism and revisionism, it is yet uncertain as to which will win and which will be defeated, it being highly possible that revisionism will triumph and we will be defeated. We used the possibility of defeat to alert the public, and we found this to be highly conducive to heightening our vigilance against revisionism, as well as to preventing and opposing revisionism. . . ." Actually, the struggle between the two classes and the two lines within the Communist party has always existed. . . . Since that rally, the struggle between the two classes within our party has manifested itself in the forms of "left" in appearance but "right" in essence and the opposition to same, a denial of the existence of class struggle and emphasis on the existence of class struggle, and in compromises and accentuation of proletarian politics.[11]

Hu Sheng wrote in 1983 that in later years, when Mao "believed that he was blazing a new trail for socialism, he was actually bound hand and foot by a number of abstract concepts and formulas which were divorced from reality."[12]

POST-MAO IDEOLOGICAL TRENDS

The death of Mao in September 1976 gave the party pragmatists the long-awaited chance for a fresh start. However, the numerous policy blunders of Mao, especially the Cultural Revolution, brought an unprecedented legitimacy crisis to the CPC. The "threefold crises of faith, trust, and confidence" (the Chinese public's lack of faith in socialism, of trust in the CPC, and of confidence in China's future), which we discussed previously (see chapters 8 and 9), best exemplifies this legitimacy crisis. Moreover, the ideological-style politics that the CPC adheres to demands that the party maintain an image of infallibility. The task that post-Mao leaders of the CPC are faced with is to find a way to maintain the validity of socialism and even of "the thought of Mao Zedong" and at the same time acknowledge the blunders made by Mao and the party in the past thirty years. Fortunately for the post-Mao Chinese Communist leaders, the history of both the CPC and Communist parties elsewhere provides precedents for the necessary ideological interpretation that the CPC must do. The method is to "sum up" history, acknowledging the past mistakes but relegating them to aberrations, and then declaring a new turning point. Subsequently the history of the past is rewritten and ideology reinterpreted to legitimize the "new line" and new leadership. In 1945 during the Seventh CPC Congress, Mao did exactly these things to firm up his leadership of the CPC when he repudiated the past deeds of his opponents, the Stalin-trained "returned students' clique." So Deng Xiaoping followed suit after the death of Mao. In June 1981 the CPC issued a long authoritative statement to accomplish what we have just described: "On Questions of Party History—Resolution on Certain Questions in the History of Our Party Since the Founding of the People's Republic of China." [13] It was complemented by numerous other ideological statements by the CPC intended to cope with the legitimacy crisis. Specifically, these statements attempt to reinterpret the meanings of: the thought of Mao Zedong, class struggle, dictatorship of the proletariat, unitary ownership of the means of production by the whole people, use of mass campaigns, and China's policy of self-reliance with regard to the world.

Undoubtedly the most difficult ideological question for the post-Mao leaders to tackle is the role of Mao and his "thought." From 1945 until his death in 1976, Mao Zedong was not only the symbol of Communist revolution (i.e., his life and personality were regarded as the expression of the national struggle) but also the ultimate decision maker of public policy. Being such, Mao appropriated all the credits of accomplishments but also all the blame. Unfortunately for Mao and the CPC, after 1949 there were major blunders to account for. As Mao was so closely identified with the CPC, complete repudiation of Mao, as Khrushchev repudiated Stalin, was not possible for the CPC. That Khrushchev could so unconditionally repudiate Stalin was because there was still the foundation of Lenin to fall back on. But for the CPC Mao was both Lenin and Stalin. Thus in drafting "On Question of Party History," Deng Xiaoping was preoccupied with the question of legitimizing the thought of Mao Zedong without, however, condoning Mao's blunders. Hence, Deng instructed his party historians that " 'On Question of Party History' must contain a section that expounds Mao Zedong Thought because what is involved here is not merely a theoretical question but, in particular, a political question of great domestic and international significance." [14] Deng then laid down the ground rules for his historians: "On no account can we discard the banner of Mao Zedong Thought. Otherwise, we would be negating the glorious history of our Party." [15] In the end the post-Mao leaders hit upon a formula to solve their dilemma with regard to Mao. What the present Communist leaders uphold is "scientific Mao Zedong Thought," which contains all the "correct" ideas of Mao and excludes all Mao's "later mistakes." In the words of a chief Communist Chinese theoretician, Mao's mistakes "are opposed to scientific Mao Zedong thought and therefore Comrade Mao Zedong's thinking in his late years must not be confused with Mao Zedong Thought. Mao Zedong Thought is a scientific theory which does not embrace Comrade Mao Zedong's mistakes." [16]

Next on the ideological agenda of post-Mao Chinese leaders is the question of class struggle. Under Mao class struggle was the "key link" of society and national development. It was in the name of class struggle that Mao carried out one mass campaign after another, which culminated in the Cultural Revolution. Tens of millions of

Chinese were made the objects of Mao's class struggle. The irony is that after 1956, the so-called exploiting classes in China, e.g., landlords, rich peasants, and capitalists, had all been eliminated, their property having been taken over by the state (the "whole people"). In the Cultural Revolution, class struggle was aimed at the top leaders of the CPC. As we mentioned previously (see chapter 3), in 1956 the party pragmatists had tried to alter the platform of the Eighth Party Congress so that it stated that class struggle was no longer the primary concern of the CPC, economic development (developing the productive forces) being the main task. But the pragmatists were quickly thwarted by Mao. Finally, after Mao's death, Deng and his fellow pragmatists were able to reinterpret the role of class struggle in Chinese society. Party pragmatists have dealt with it the way they dealt with Mao Zedong Thought. They want, so to speak, to have the class-struggle cake and eat it too. So the official line presently is that class struggle still exists in China owing to "the remnants of exploiting classes and other hostile elements," the survival of "the system of exploitation" in Taiwan, the "imperialists and hegemonists (i.e., the Soviets)," and the influence of "decadent Western bourgeois ideology and bourgeois life styles." But class struggle is no longer the major concern ("principal contradiction") of the PRC. Moreover, "The chief targets of the current [class] struggle are serious economic criminals . . . [those] who embezzle, steal, speculate and profiteer." And the method to deal with them is not through the past "tempestuous mass movements" (e.g., the Cultural Revolution) but through the judicial system.[17]

Following the reinterpretation of the meaning of class struggle and of its role in China, the CPC likewise revised its formula for the dictatorship of the proletariat. In 1979 the CPC declared that the intellectuals of China had long since become a part of the working class and that the landlords, rich peasants, and bourgeoisie, as exploiting classes, no longer existed. Logically then, the dictatorship of the proletariat had lost many of its targets. So the CPC revised the formula for the People's Democratic Dictatorship with the accent on *democratic*. A senior Communist leader wrote in 1981: "Today, the task of our people's democratic dictatorship is to unite all the people and build China into a socialist country with material modernization, highly developed political democracy and a highly advanced spiritual civilization."[18]

One might, with a degree of justice, dismiss all the foregoing as mere manipulation of symbols. At best, these actions were designed simply to earn the new CPC leadership a period of grace. But we cannot dismiss so lightly the reforms that post-Mao leaders have carried out in the economic structure. It is there the most substantive "deradicalization" or "de-Maofication" has taken place. As we mentioned in chapter 3, the pragmatists of the CPC have declared that "there are laws of revolution and there are laws of production; one cannot be substituted for the other!" Today the people's commune is practically a thing of the past; Chinese peasants have returned to household farming under the new "responsibility system" (see chapter 7). As for industry, while state enterprises still constitute the overwhelming majority, in 1981 a Chinese writer listed eight other forms of industrial ownership, ranging from joint ventures between state and collective enterprises to enterprises backed by foreign investments. This writer justified these new economic structures on three grounds: the fact that state enterprises still constituted 95 percent of the economy, the precedent of Lenin's New Economic Policy, and the simple fact of the backwardness of Chinese farming. "That is to say, at the present," he concluded, "the productive forces in China are many-tiered, and we must, therefore, build a many-tiered socialist economic structure, i,e., an economy which includes various economic sectors, ranging from the state to the individual economy, with socialist public ownership occupying the dominant position."[19]

With their emphasis on economic development and disavowal of "mechanical" application of revolutionary practice to national reconstruction, the CPC pragmatists declared in 1978 that its method of operation would no longer be "large-scale political movement." The new watchword is "scientific planning."

Finally, the party pragmatists, whose outlook has always been more cosmopolitan than that of Mao and his radicals, established a "golden mean" in relations with the rest of the world. "On Question of Party History" states:

> China's revolution and national construction are not and cannot be carried on in isolation from the rest of the world. It is always necessary for us to try to win foreign aid and, in particular, to learn all that is advanced and beneficial from other countries. The closed-door policy, blind opposition to everything foreign and any theory or practice of great-nation chauvinism are all entirely wrong. At the same time . . . we must maintain our own national dignity and confidence and there must be no slavishness or submissiveness in any form in dealing with big, powerful or rich countries.[20]

This kind of reformulation of a long-held (or imposed) faith always brings some serious consequences in ideology and power relations. Though designed to reaffirm the validity of the original ideology, reformulation might actually further dilute and discredit the original doctrine. But world history shows that if a reformulated faith is successful in winning mass converts, then the original faith might acquire a new lease on life, albeit in a much "revised" form. Meanwhile, reformers must face opposition from above and below. The vested interests of the old regime would fight tooth and nail against the reformulation. So Deng Xiaoping had to cope with the so-called *whatever* clique in the CPC, who declared in 1978-79: "We must resolutely support whatever policy decisions Chairman Mao made and consistently follow whatever directives Chairman Mao issued."[21] (See also chapter 3.) Whereas the "whateverists" pulled Deng to the left, *aroused* Chinese public opinion sought to push Deng further to the right. As mentioned earlier, in the autumn of 1978 and through the spring of 1979 wall posters mushroomed on Peking's Democracy Wall, calling for democracy, freedom of speech, free elections, and human rights.[22] Poor peasants, workers, veterans, unemployed students, youths returned from the countryside, and victims of the Cultural Revolution streamed into Peking to demonstrate and petition for redress of the wrongs that they had suffered in the past.

Hemmed in between the whateverists from above and the democrats from below, Deng Xiaoping and his colleagues did what Mao did in the 1957 Hundred Flowers Blooming campaign—they issued a post facto standard of freedom of speech and, moreover, declared the outer limits of reform. The former was designed for the democrats, or dissidents, whereas the latter was meant to placate the whateverists. On April 7, 1979, an editorial in the authoritative *People's Daily* announced that the CPC was the fundamental guarantee of the success of the four modernizations, so "any speech deviating from and weakening the leadership of the party is most harmful and must be resolutely corrected." Those were almost the exact words that Mao had used in June 1957 to turn the Hundred Flowers Blooming around into an Anti-Rightist campaign. On April 18, 1979, a senior Communist leader (presumably one of Deng's colleagues) wrote in the *People's Daily* that all reforms must adhere to four principles—socialism, dictatorship of the proletariat, leadership of the Communist party, and the thought of Mao Zedong.

From then on the party pragmatists have been almost permanently caught in the classic dilemma of reformers. Reaffirming the old faith, such as announcing the four principles, encourages the vested interests to ignore the reform programs. Not long after declaring the four principles, the army paper denounced the comments among PLA officers and men that if only the four principles had been made known earlier, then there would not be so many problems in society.[23] For a short while the pragmatists were on the verge of repudiating the four principles so as to clip the wings of the vested interests. The *People's Daily* editorialized in May 1979 that though the "socialist road" must be followed, the "concrete forms" of socialism were "open" for study.[24] But then, not even the pragmatists are sure just how much openness they themselves are willing to put up with. We must not forget that the pragmatists, such as Deng Xiaoping, Hu Yaobang, and Zhao Ziyang, share with Mao Zedong the long years of revolutionary experience. There is a significant degree of "common socialization" between the pragmatists and the radicals. The reforms that Deng and his colleagues have advocated and carried out are, in their eyes, absolutely necessary to stave off a violent revolution against the CPC. They are not about to carry reforms to the extent that the party changes its colors. Since 1983, Deng and Hu have commenced campaigns that are more left than right, e.g., campaigns against "spiritual pollution" from "decadent capitalist ideology"[25] and rededication to the thought of Mao.[26]

The divided hearts of the pragmatists of the CPC mean that the success of their reformulation of faith is in doubt and that they are actually undermining their own efforts to rid the CPC of the leftists.

NOTES

1. Sidney Verba, "Conclusion: Comparative Political Culture," in Lucian W. Pye and Sidney Verba, eds., *Political Culture and Political Development* (Princeton, N.J.: Princeton University Press, 1969), p. 545.
2. Simon Leys, *Chinese Shadows* (New York: Penguin Books, 1978), pp. 34-35.
3. Harold D. Lasswell and Abraham Kaplan, *Power and Society: A Framework for Political Inquiry* (New Haven: Yale University Press, 1950), p. 212.
4. William E. Griffith, "Communist Esoteric Communications: Explication de Texte," in Ithiel de Sola Pool and Wilbur Schramm, eds., *Handbook of Communication* (Chicago: Rand McNally College Publishing Company, 1973), p. 513.
5. Ibid.
6. *Wan-sui,* no. 2, p. 132.
7. Stuart R. Schram, *The Political Thought of Mao Tse-tung* (New York: Frederick A. Praeger, 1969).
8. Hu Sheng, "Marxism and the Reality of China," *Beijing Review* 26, no. 15 (April 11, 1983), 17.
9. *Wan-sui,* no. 2, p. 334.
10. *Wan-sui,* no. 2, pp. 362-63.
11. "Speech to the Albanian Military Delegation" (May 1, 1967), in *Miscellany of Mao Tse-tung Thought (1949-1968), Part II* (Arlington, Va.: Joint Publications Research Service, 1974), p. 456. Students interested in English translations of *Wan-sui* should read this reference and also part I.
12. Hu Sheng, *Marxism,* p. 17.
13. "On Question of Party History," *Beijing Review* 24, no. 27 (July 6, 1981), 10-39.
14. Deng Xiaoping, "Suggestions on the Drafting of the 'Resolution on Certain Questions in the History of Our Party Since the Founding of the People's Republic of China'" (March 1980-June 1981), *Beijing Review* 26, no. 30 (July 25, 1983), 19.
15. Ibid., p. 18.
16. Lu Zhichao, "China Upholds Principles of Mao Zedong Thought," *Beijing Review* 24, no. 24 (June 15, 1981), 16.
17. Zhou Yan, "On China's Current Class Struggle," *Beijing Review* 25, no. 33 (August 16, 1982), 17-19.

18. *Guangming Ribao* Special Commentator, "The People's Democratic Dictatorship Is in Essence the Dictatorship of the Proletariat," *Beijing Review* 24, no. 19 (May 11, 1981), 20.

19. He Jianzhang, "New Emerging Economic Forms," *Beijing Review* 24, no. 21 (May 25, 1981), 18.

20. "On Question of Party History," p. 34.

21. Deng, "Suggestions on the Drafting," p. 23.

22. For translation of these wall posters and dissidents' publications, see James D. Seymour, *The Fifth Modernization: China's Human Rights Movement, 1978-1979* (Stanfordville, N.Y.: Human Rights Publishing Group, 1980).

23. *RMRB*, May 22, 1979, p. 1.

24. *RMRB*, May 5, 1979, p. 1.

25. "The Initial Stage of Communism," *Beijing Review* 26, no. 22 (January 31, 1983), 22.

26. Zhang Gong, "Mao Zedong's Thought on Socialist Economic Construction," *Beijing Review* 26, no. 51 (December 19, 1983), 14-23; and Wang Qi, "Inheriting and Developing Mao Zedong Thought," *Beijing Review* 26, no. 52 (December 26, 1983), 20-26.

CHAPTER 14

Factions, Cliques, and Clientelism

The two major characteristics of the Chinese Communist political system—centralization and ideological style—that we have discussed so far perhaps have already led the reader to infer that competition for power in the CPC takes the form of factional, or cliquish, struggles. Given the fact that political power, like money in economics, is a scarce good, a totalitarian and doctrinal political system such as that of the PRC, by proscribing open political competition, merely shifts the location and nature of the power struggle from the public into the internal and personal sphere of the system.

For the purpose of subsequent discussion, we shall define *faction, clique,* and *clientelism.* Following Lasswell and Kaplan, we define a faction as a subgroup of a decision-making group, "organized in relation to interests distinct from those of the rest of the group."[1] But one should not infer from this definition that the rest of the group is united in interests. Lasswell and Kaplan amplify further: "The characteristic interests of different factions within a group are likely to be in conflict *with one another. . . .*"[2] Whereas a faction is organized around interests, a clique is defined by Lasswell and Kaplan as primarily organized around a person and for expedient purposes. "A clique is an informal, impermeable, and highly personalized demigroup."[3] "A clique is not as well-organized as a party or faction, nor does it like them formally participate in decision-making. . . . The clique ordinarily exercises its power conspiratively (behind the scenes), but it may organize a faction of which it then serves as the leadership."[4] In the Cultural Revolution, for example (see chapter 3), Mao Zedong at first organized a "clique"—the Gang of Four—and promoted it to a "faction" in 1966; the Gang of Four then became the leading core of the formal Central Cultural Revolution group. The extension of the power or influence of a central faction or clique to local organizations or groups is through clientelism, which refers to "a patron-client relationship . . . an alliance between two persons of unequal status, power or resources each of whom finds it useful to have as an ally someone superior or inferior to himself."[5] Patron-client relationship, however, may be established between organizations. Carl Lande calls it *corporate clientelism.*[6] As subsequent discussion will bear out, Chinese Communist bureaucracy below the national echelon is pervaded with corporate clientelism.

The history of the CPC has been littered with factional or cliquish struggles. From the late 1950s to his death in 1976, whenever Mao Zedong was about to punish some opponents or dissenters in the party, he would justify it by reminding his colleagues of the factional history of the CPC. In 1958 when Mao was cleansing the party of rightists, he remarked:

> We must prevent possible big disasters, such as world war, or party splits. Our party underwent four splits, involving Chen Tu-hsiu [Chen Duxiu], Lo Chang-lung [Luo Zhanglong], Chang Kuo-t'ao [Zhang Guotao], and Kao Kang [Gao Gang]. They set up their own Central Committees and collapsed. Wang Ming appeared in a legal way with his "leftist" line three times. . . . New splits may occur. As long as there is a party, splits are possible. They are possible even 100 years from now.[7]

At the start of the Cultural Revolution in 1966 Mao declared: "So far as our party is concerned, we have parties outside and factions inside. This has always been so and is quite normal."[8] Since 1927 almost at every crucial juncture of the growth of the CPC, when a major decision was to be made, a factional conflict broke out (see table 14-1).

TABLE 14-1　Factions in the Communist party of China, 1927–80

TITLE	YEAR	ISSUE
"Right capitulationist" Chen Duxiu	1927	Breakup of the united front between the CPC and KMT
"Liquidationism" Luo Zhanglong	1931	Failure of urban uprisings led by Li Lisan
"Splittism" of Zhang Guotao	1938	Split of armed forces between Zhang and Mao during the Long March; Zhang's defection to the KMT in 1938
"Leftist" line of Wang Ming (Returned Student Clique)	1930 1931 1938	Urban uprising versus peasant war Guerrilla war versus positional war Cooperation with the KMT
"Anti-party Clique" of Gao Gang and Rao Shushih	1953	Start of first five-year plan
"Right opportunism" of Marshal Peng Dehuai	1959	Result of the Great Leap Forward
"Revisionism" of Liu Shaoqi	1966	Overall social and economic policy after the Great Leap Forward and the three years of famine; the Cultural Revolution
"Ultra-leftism" of Chen Boda	1970	Rebuilding of the CPC after the Cultural Revolution
"Counterrevolutionary Clique" of Marshal Lin Biao	1971	As in 1970; alleged coup against Mao
"Rightist and restorationist" Deng Xiaoping	1976	Post-Cultural Revolution social and economic policy
"Counterrevolutionary Clique of Jiang Qing" (Gang of Four)	1976	Death of Mao and succession struggle
"Whateverist" group of Hua Guofeng and others	1979 through 1981	Policy and program after death of Mao Zedong

To analyze the dynamics of factionalism in Chinese Communist politics, we shall discuss: (1) structural conduciveness of factionalism, (2) precipitants to factions after 1949, (3) type of faction, (4) clientelism, and (5) post-Mao leaders' attempt to cope with factionalism.

STRUCTURAL CONDUCIVENESS

Though factions exist in all political systems, the degree of factionalism varies from one system to another. The prevalence, intensity, and destructiveness (of group interest) of factions are closely related to the basic structure of a political system. As pointed out by anthropologists and political scientists, centralized and hierarchical systems tend to facilitate factionalism.[9] "But authority is most forcibly challenged when it is concentrated," wrote Lasswell and Kaplan.[10] According to Griffith, "An authoritarian, theologically or ideologically oriented elite is prone to internal conflict, either to gain the leadership or to curry favor of an already existing leader."[11] A possible reason for the faction-proneness of centralized and hierarchical political systems is that it is simply not possible for a single authority to represent all the interests of society. Since in a totalitarian system like the PRC, no organization other than the party-state bureaucracy is allowed to make decisions, the entire range of social interests is incorporated into a single structure. Factions are likely to be formed within such a unitary system.

Second, an authoritarian system tends to exaggerate the power of the leader. This is especially true in a totalitarian system with a charismatic leader whose position is built on a revolutionary movement. In this kind of system the distribution of power among other officials is most often based on the changing personality preferences of the leader.[12] The insecurity of power among these officials encourages them to form factions to win the favor of the leader and protect their own interests against other factions.

Third, an authoritarian and ideologically oriented political system tends to promote doctrinal conflicts, which further enhance insecurity among its members, thereby encouraging them to form factions or cliques for self-protection. That internal conflicts tend to proliferate in an authoritarian and doctrinal party is due to the blurring of differences of conflicts over means and ends. The impulse to maintain a facade of infallibility suppresses all conflicts or elevates all differences to fundamental "line" struggles. The document "On Question of Party History," for example, states that in the Socialist Education campaign of 1963–65, "problems differing in nature were all treated as forms of class struggle or its reflections inside the party," or as a general rule, owing to its revolutionary legacy, "normal differences among comrades inside the party came to be regarded as manifestations of the revisionist line or of the struggle between the two lines."[13]

Fourth, in connection with the structural reasons for factionalism in the PRC that have been mentioned, an additional and somewhat paradoxical reason is that once a system of highly concentrated authority shows signs of division or actually does divide its authority, factionalism is further aggravated. The key to this is again insecurity of status and power and uncertainty of their legitimacy among lesser officials. Mao Zedong, for example, stated that it was after his decision in 1953 to divide the functions of CPC leadership into front and rear lines, with himself in the rear, that "independent kingdoms" in the CPC began to rise.[14]

So far our discussion has mainly concerned the factionalism at the upper echelon of the CPC. To account for the prevalence of cliques at the middle and lower echelons of the CPC two additional reasons must be mentioned here. One is that owing to the totalitarian and collectivistic nature of the PRC political system, formal political position is *the* key to all other forms of power and privileges. As a result, interests of social or private groups such as family and friends must be realized through the political system. Complementing that is the long tradition of personal rulership in the CPC, which was cultivated during the civil war in China. Mao stated in 1959:

> Our party was in reality a united council, with many mountain-tops. The First Army Corps had four mountain-tops. The Fourth Corps had four mountain-tops. The Second Corps had two mountain-tops. North Shaanxi had two mountain-tops. There are small mountain-tops in other base areas. While in Yannan we said that we must recognize these mountain-tops, take care of them and then we may be able to destroy them.[15]

Each "mountain-top" was naturally led by a "chief," based on personal rulership.

The collective way of life before 1949 practiced by the CPC further enhanced personal rulership. For example, Chinese Communist leaders employ their wives in formal governmental functions: as Mao and Jiang Qing, Liu Shaoqi and wife Wang Guangmei, and Lin Biao and wife Ye Chun. An interesting report was published in the authoritative *People's Daily* in 1978 describing how the late Lin Biao had used his wife and children to handle important matters in the Ministry of National Defense even before the Cultural Revolution.[16] That this practice is a carryover from the days of civil war is perhaps only half the explanation. The other possible reason for the high degree of personalization of the CPC political system is a pervasive sense of insecurity and distrust among leaders.

PRECIPITANTS

The structurally conducive reasons for factions that we have discussed are galvanized by several "precipitants" that account for the proliferation of factions, cliques, and clientelism in the PRC today.

Perhaps the most frequent precipitant to factionalism is serious failure of a group to achieve its collective goal. Responsibility for the failure must be placed, and a group thus splinters into factions. Moreover, failure to achieve an important group task undermines the legitimacy of the leader, and a power struggle starts among aspirants for power. Looking over the factions in the history of the CPC as presented in table 14-1, we can see that a majority of factional struggles were caused by serious failures of the CPC.

Another major precipitant to factionalism is a major transition in the authority pattern of a group, especially involving what Max Weber calls the "routinization of charisma." That is the transition from subjective- to objective-type authority. As Weber points out, this transition is always desired by the disciples of a charismatic leader. In the words of Weber, they need "to legitimize their social and economic conditions, that is, to transform them from mere resultants of power relationships into acquired rights, and hence to sanctify them."[17] The best examples of factionalism due to routinization of charisma in the history of the CPC are the cases of Gao Gang and Rao Shushih in 1953 and Chen Boda and Lin Biao in 1970–71. Both conflicts followed a period of revolution and occurred in the process of the system's return to normalcy. As Deng Xiaoping recalled in 1980, Gao had expressed his dissatisfaction over Mao's appointing Liu Shaoqi vice-chairman of the CPC. Gao had wanted several vice-chairmen, himself as one of them.[18] In 1970–71 Chen Boda and Lin Biao clashed with Mao over very similar issues, i.e., Chen and Lin wanted the position of the presidency of the PRC restored, and Lin sought that position for himself (see chapter 3).

Third, factions are precipitated by factions. In social conflict, for example, once a hostile action breaks down the barrier of social control, then a barrage of conflicts follows. Smelser refers to this process as conflict in the initial (or real) phase and in the derived phase.

> In the initial or real phase the hostility and its expression result from the build-up of specific conditions of strain, precipitating factors, etc. Once hostile outbursts begin, however, they become a *sign* that a fissure has opened in the social order, and that the situation is now structurally conducive for the expression of hostility. As a result, a rash of hostile actions appears, many of them motivated by hostility unrelated to the conditions giving rise to the initial outburst.[19]

The same dynamics occur in factionalism. The surge of factions in the Cultural Revolution and afterwards was apparently caused by factionalism at the top level of the CPC. To this day the CPC is not able to stop factionalism throughout the rank and file of the CPC.[20]

TYPES OF FACTIONS

The factions that have plagued the CPC since 1949 may be initially divided into two types according to their organizational status, i.e., those at the highest echelon of the CPC and those at the subnational level. The former consists of members of the most "efficient" parts of the national offices of the CPC—the staff departments of the Central Committee, the Politburo, and the Standing Committee of the Politburo. Together these powerful national organizations of the CPC are referred to in China as *the Center* or *zhongyang*. The basis for the factions at the Center is different from that of cliques at provincial, municipal, and county levels.

Factions at Party Center

We can discern three types of factions at the Center before the Cultural Revolution. One type was comprised of the radicals and the pragmatists between whom there was a gross division in terms of their perspectives or attitudes on the formal ideology of Marxism-Leninism and the legacy of the Communist revolution. Though neither the radicals nor the pragmatists were "organized," as Lasswell and Kaplan's definition of faction seems to require, the differences between these two groups were real and grew sharper over the years. By and large, the perspectives or interests of the two groups persisted throughout the first three decades of the PRC. For example, it was the same pragmatists who wrote the party platform at the Eighth CPC Congress in 1956 and took charge of the Chinese economy and national development after the disaster of the Great Leap Forward, i.e., Liu Shaoqi, Chen Yun, and Deng Xiaoping. In the post-Mao period, it is again this same group, with Chen Yun and Deng Xiaoping in the lead, that had initiated major reforms consistent with their earlier policies and programs.

In general, this division between the radicals and the pragmatists at the uppermost echelons of the CPC corresponds to the observation by Turner and Killian that in social movement there is a continuous conflict "between leaders who are more value oriented and those more concerned with the power and organization of the movement itself."[21]

The second type of faction at the Center of the CPC was based on the changing personality preferences of Mao Zedong. In almost every totalitarian regime, one finds an inner circle consisting of top officials who are personally favored by the charismatic leader—Stalin or Mao or Hitler, to mention some notable examples.

> There was no defined route nor any set of prescribed qualifications for gaining or losing membership in the inner circle. Members were not assigned to specific offices with defined responsibilities and authority. Instead each member received a vague commission from the [leader] and sought to extend his power at the expense of others among the inner circle. "Purges" resulted when individuals or factions within the inner circle fell from favor.[22]

The highly subjective way this inner faction was formed precipitated factionalism around the leader. The best example of this in the CPC is the Gao Gang and Rao Shushih case. As mentioned earlier, Gao was dissatisfied with Mao's choice of Liu Shaoqi as the vice-chairman of the CPC.

But the most dramatic illustration of the crucial importance of the inner circle, or faction, around Mao is the dynamics of the Cultural Revolution. The revolution began with Mao's changing the composition of his inner faction—ousting Liu Shaoqi and admitting Lin Biao. Moreover, Mao organized a radical clique, which was at first led nominally by his secretary, Chen Boda, but in reality was controlled by Mao's wife, Jiang Qing, and her two confidantes—Zhang Chunqiao and Yao Wenyuan. The line between the radicals and the pragmatists was then sharply drawn by Mao, who escalated the differences between the two groups to a "struggle between two lines" (socialism versus capitalism). In 1967 the violence that was provoked by the radical faction of Mao, formally known as the Central Cultural Revolution Group, had affected the entire CPC and even the army. This temporarily compelled all those senior CPC leaders who were against the Cultural Revolution to form into a large and temporary faction, confronting the radicals face to face at a meeting in February 1967. The radicals referred to this confrontation as the February Countercurrent.[23] But the temporary faction of senior CPC members interested in the survival of the CPC could not overcome the radicals who were supported by Mao. So the large faction disintegrated once Mao gave his support to the radical faction. In 1970, however, the original inner faction of Mao underwent change because of Mao's shifting preference. Perhaps alarmed by the chaos in society and possible military resistance to further violence and anarchy, Mao decided to call a halt to revolution and rehabilitated much of the old party establishment. Now conflict broke out inside Mao's inner faction, resulting in the purge of secretary Chen Boda in 1970 and the death of Lin Biao in 1971. The composition of Mao's inner faction after that was no longer purely radical since Mao, after the Lin Biao affair, relied more and more on Zhou Enlai, who seemed to play forever the role of middle man between the two large factions at the Center. In 1973, through Zhou Enlai, Mao Zedong readmitted Deng Xiaoping to his inner faction. Owing to the chaos and paralysis in government and industry throughout the period of 1967-73, when Deng was rehabilitated he was able to organize a loose alliance between his pragmatist group and the veteran cadres, i.e., those who were in charge of various party offices and state ministries before the outbreak of the Cultural Revolution. The interests of the pragmatists and the institutionally-based factions coincided in 1973–76. The Gang of Four naturally fought tooth and nail with this large alliance between Deng and the veteran cadres. Their factional conflicts spilled over to lower levels of the party and state bureaucracy and to society. The riot in Tiananmen Square on April 5, 1976, was related to the factional struggle between the Gang of Four and Deng's veteran cadres.

As a result of the riot, Deng was once more ousted from Mao's inner circle. By that time Zhou Enlai had died. Mao's inner faction underwent another change when Hua Guofeng, Wang Dongxin (commander of the guard division in Peking), and several other civil and military leaders were brought into Mao's inner circle. After Mao's death, it was this new group led by Hua and Wang who sought to placate Deng and the veteran cadres by arresting the Gang of Four. But as we recounted previously, Deng, with his power based on party and state bureaucracy, was able to oust the Hua-Wang group—the whateverists—from the Center.

The third type of faction is relatively permanent and is based on institutional interests. Powerful departments in the national offices of the CPC and the ministries of the State Council develop into such factions—what Mao called independent kingdoms. For example, Mao made no secret of the fact in the 1950s that he was at odds with two staff departments of the Central Committee: the rural work department (with Deng Zihui in the lead) and the finance and economic department. The latter was often referred to by Mao as an independent kingdom for its habit of presenting him with a completed program that left no room for change.[24] As we mentioned previously, the rural work department under Deng Zihui was opposed to Mao's acceleration of agricultural collectivization (see chapter 7). Another example of faction based on institutional interest is the united front department of the Central Committee. Assigned to do "work among intellectuals," the united front department tended to be much less inclined than Mao to conduct struggle campaigns against prominent intellectuals. Mao accused the united front department of surrendering to "the bourgeoisie" in 1962 and attempting to turn "bourgeois parties" (the "democratic parties") into "socialist parties."[25]

However, it was the post-Mao reforms under Deng Xiaoping and Chen Yun that really brought out the "face" of the institutionally based factions. Deng's priority in light industry and agriculture in order to upgrade the living standard of the people immediately threatened the interests of the ministries in charge of heavy and defense-related industries. Throughout Mao's era, those heavy and defense industries were protected and given top priority in national planning. The turnaround that Deng achieved in the Chinese economy after 1978 brought about the conflict between the so-called New Economic Group, which had Deng's support for reform, and the entrenched Oil Faction, which centered around the Petroleum Ministry and its allied steel industry. The New Economic Group used the sinking of a $25 million drilling platform in the winter of 1980 in the Gulf of Bohai to discredit the Oil Faction and the interest group of heavy industry and push ahead the reforms of pragmatist leaders.[26] Figure 14-1 illustrates the foregoing description of the factions at the Center in schematic fashion.

Cliques at Subnational Level

The factionalism at the top echelons of power inside the CPC provoked a proliferation of cliques that are often indiscriminately referred to both in and out of China as factions. We shall, however, adhere to the definitions of faction and clique

PERIOD	BASIS OF FACTION		
	MAO'S PERSONALITY (INNER CIRCLE)	INSTITUTIONAL INTERESTS	PERSPECTIVES ON IDEOLOGY
Before GPCR*	Mao Zedong–Liu Shaoqi vs. Gao Gang–Rao Shushih	Rural work dept. United front dept.	Deng Xiaoping, Chen Yun—the pragmatists
During GPCR	Central Cultural Revolution group (Lin Biao, Gang of Four, and Chen Boda)	Zhou Enlai and Veteran cadres in February Countercurrent	
After GPCR	Gang of Four plus Zhou Enlai and Deng Xiaoping, 1973–76 Gang of Four plus Hua Guofeng and Wang Dongxin, 1976 until death of Mao	Zhou Enlai and Deng Xiaoping (veteran cadres and pragmatists in loose alliance)	
After Mao	(Inner circle around the personality of Deng Xiaoping, e.g., Chen Yun, Hu Yaobang, and Zoao Ziyang)	Factions and cliques within the PLA Oil Faction vs. New Economic Group	Party pragmatists vs. Maoists (whateverists)

*Great Proletarian Cultural Revolution (1966–69)

FIGURE 14-1 Political factions in the national offices of the Communist party, 1950–81

provided by Lasswell and Kaplan. As mentioned previously, cliques do not participate in decision making and are relatively impermeable.

The complicated nature of cliques and clientelism in the Chinese party and the state bureaucracy is best illustrated in the case of a certain Wang Zhong, formerly county party secretary in Haifeng County of Guangdong Province. Wang was executed in January 1983 for large-scale graft and smuggling.[27] An analysis of Wang's operation by the authoritative *People's Daily* throws into sharp relief the interconnection of three loyalty ties that crisscross Chinese bureaucracy today. The most fundamental tie is kinship (*qinbang*); members of Wang's extended family were all involved in the graft and smuggling. Next to kinship is clique (*pengdang*). In Wang's case it consisted of his colleagues at work. Family and colleagues are further connected with a patron (*houtai*), a superior party authority with whom they have a clientelist relationship.[28] The interconnection of these three loyalty ties is illustrated in figure 14-2. We shall discuss briefly each of the three loyalty ties among Chinese Communist cadres, around which the cliques and patron-client relations are organized.

First, almost every kind of information from the PRC, official or unofficial, testifies to the persistence and strength of Chinese kinship ties, particularly among cadres who have access to political power. Kinship, however, is not the only diffuse tie on which Chinese cliques or clientelism is based.

Another loyalty tie, which is closest to kinship in terms of its diffuse nature, is old acquaintanceship. In the Chinese language, relationships of acquaintanceship

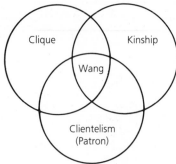

FIGURE 14-2

always carry the prefix of *old*—old colleagues, old superiors, old subordinates, old comrades-in-arms, or old acquaintance. These ties developed from one-time formal associations now being "magnetized" by the strong particularism in Chinese society. The old acquaintanceship, unlike kinship, is, strictly speaking, entirely voluntary and more reciprocal than the kinship tie. Nevertheless, the former has claims over every Chinese as strong and diffuse as the obligatory kinship tie. When one city textile bureau hired 1,520 new workers, the bureau director's telephone began to ring incessantly. The calls, 297 in total, came from old superiors, old comrades, old friends, old acquaintances, old followers, and relatives who requested the director to assign the children of the callers' old acquaintances to choice locations.[29] The force of old acquaintanceship is a major obstacle to the reimposition of discipline within the Communist party of China today.

Beyond kinship and old acquaintanceship, the cliques in Chinese bureaucracy are based on a complex network of what Lande calls *dyadic alliances,* which are linked together to exchange favors and to come to each other's aid in time of need.[30] There are two main reasons that these alliances emerge in the Chinese Communist bureaucracy. One is the centralized structure of the Chinese Communist system, which inhibits lateral communication and exchange. Hence, to facilitate their work, cadres organize informal alliances to exchange goods and services. The second reason for the prevalence of alliances in the Chinese Communist bureaucracy is insecurity, which was enhanced to an infinite degree by the violence in the Cultural Revolution.

The personal alliances inside the Chinese Communist or state apparatus are primarily of two kinds: horizontal or vertical. Horizontal alliances are between persons of more or less equal status and are usually confined in a delimited geographic area. The vertical alliances are between persons of different status and positions. Both types, however, are variants of political clientelism—the dyadic alliances mentioned above.

The horizontal alliances in the Chinese bureaucracy can be further distinguished on the basis of the alliances: individual cadres or entire party/state organizations. The dyadic alliances based on individual cadres usually overlap with formal organizational linkage. In other words, cadres in a county, city, or public firm develop informal and personal relationships out of their formal interactions. They build what the Chinese call a hornet's nest (*mafeng-wo*). For instance, when the provincial party authorities of Jiangsu sent an investigation team to the city of Taizhou on a case of housing irregularity and reprisal against an informer, the team met collective resistance. A reporter accompanying the investigation wrote: "The population of Taizhou is small and the cadres know each other well. When the disciplinary office handles a case, they often encounter people who intercede on behalf of the persons under investigation."[31]

Some horizontal alliances in the Chinese bureaucracy were based on the rebel groups formed during the Cultural Revolution of 1966-70. To combat party opposition then, Mao had called upon lower party cadres to revolt against their superiors who were suspected of not supporting Mao. Many daring lower cadres responded to Mao's appeal by forming rebel associations, or rebel groups. As rewards, leaders and members of these groups were promoted to formal positions, though mostly at regional and basic party echelons. They became "natural" cliques inside the Communist party and the state apparatus after 1970. Members of these cliques refer to each other as gang brothers (*bang xiongdi*). A case in point is a cadre named Yu Xinfa in the city of Wenzhou. Yu was accused of taking reprisal against a young female accountant in a factory by having her imprisoned illegally. In 1978 when his actions were exposed he was the chief of a material supply division in one of the city's several bureaus on light industry. But Yu had two political resources: (1) He had been the leader of a large rebel group during the Cultural Revolution whose members were at Yu's beck and call, and (2) he had control of raw materials and was thus a lifeline to numerous factories in the city. Building upon these two resources, Yu opened a score of illegal—underground—factories and shared the profits from those factories with other party leaders in the city. With that he was able to control the hiring in many factories, and he used the hiring power to establish ties with numerous party and state officials in the city. For six years, from 1973 to 1978, Yu was able to resist provincial party authorities' investigation of his persecution, including torture, of the woman because she refused to agree to his placing his own kin and those of his allies in her factory. Even after Yu's case was exposed, he received merely a serious warning from party authorities.[32]

The alliances that we have described so far have been relatively extensive in size and coincide with either a formal organizational unit or an entire administrative district, but the Chinese Communist party is also plagued with smaller alliances existing within a formal unit and giving rise to what is known as pervasive factionalism.[33] Cliques of this genre stem mainly from the power-seizure movement in 1967-68. The main incentive for joining such cliques seems to be hostility toward some members of the opposing cliques. These groups surface, as one report has it, "as soon as promotion or job assignment is discussed. . . ."[34] They are known in China as alliances for offense and defense or little brotherhoods and are numerous among both young and middle-aged party functionaries. Members of these cliques extend every favor in job assignment, admission into the Communist party, election of leaders, hiring, merit evaluation, promotion, wage raise, and housing allocation to their comrades and deliberately obstruct members of opposing groups from having access to those benefits.

CLIENTELISM IN COMMUNIST BUREAUCRACY

In addition to horizontal alliances, the Chinese bureaucracy is also rife with vertical alliances. The vertical alliance is commonly known as a patron-client relationship, i.e., "alliance between two persons of unequal status, power or resources each of whom finds it useful to have as an ally someone superior or inferior to himself."[35] Furthermore, patron-client relationships tend to pyramid on each other like a multilayered cake. As Lande puts it: "Several patrons, each with their own sets of clients, are in turn the clients of a higher patron who in turn is the client of a patron even higher than himself."[36] We can classify the patron-client relationships in China, according to the position of the "ultimate" patron, as national, regional, and local.

The most powerful patron-client relationship is naturally the national type, i.e., the patron is a national party leader. And the most powerful national patron was, of course, Mao Zedong himself before his death in 1976. A well-known case with Mao as the patron involved the commune of Dazhai (Tachai) and its leader, Chen Yonggui (Ch'en Yung-Kuei). The Mao-Chen relationship was an authentic patron-client relationship. First, the status between Mao and Chen could not have been more different—Mao was like a monarch while Chen was the leader of a basic rural production unit. Second, the monetary assets of Mao and Chen were quite different. Mao used his power to promote Chen to national leadership and transform Chen's commune into a prosperous, prestigious model. What Chen offered to Mao was basically "vanity." That is, Chen's commune was touted as a shining example of Mao's way of socializing the Chinese countryside. Furthermore, the Mao-Chen relationship was based on face-to-face contact. The alliance between the two was established in a crucial meeting at the request of Chen in 1964, which was publicized in the authoritative *People's Daily* with a front-page picture of "Chen's smiling face . . . alongside that of the Chairman."[37] Thus the Mao-Chen relationship had all three essential elements of a patron-client relationship as defined by John Powell: (1) inequality in status, wealth, and influence; (2) reciprocity in the exchange of goods and services; and (3) proximity—resting heavily on face-to-face contact between the two parties.[38] Moreover, according to Powell, an important aspect of patron-client relationships is that the needs of the client tend to be critical while the needs of the patron tend to be marginal. Thus it is important to note that when Chen requested the audience with Mao in 1964 Chen's career was at a dangerous point, as his claim of a production increase was being severely questioned by his immediate superior. Mao's patronage saved Chen's career. It was not until July 1980 that the public learned that Chen was a fraud. As a result of the relationship between Mao and Chen, the Dazhai commune received massive state aid to build up its fields, irrigation network, roads, and public housing though Dazhai was held up to the nation as an example of building up the countryside through "self-reliance."[39] Chen's kin and fellow village cadres were rapidly promoted and transferred to upper levels. Some of them engaged in corruption or other misdeeds with impunity.[40]

Another case of national patronage concerned the Communist Party Committee at Luda city in Liaoning Province. The chief figure was the first secretary of the Luda Municipal Party Committee, Liu Decai, who was also chairman of the Municipal Revolutionary Committee (i.e., mayor), commander of Luda Garrison District, and deputy commander of Shenyang Garrison Company—all at the same time. Thus Liu exemplified the principle of concentration of power and functions in the Chinese Communist political system. Liu had organized a horizontal alliance with a colleague, Xuan Shimin, secretary of the Party Committee. Xuan in turn was a member of a horizontal alliance, based on a rebel group in the Cultural Revolution, which included two leaders of the Municipal Public Security Bureau (police) and the staff of several factories. But Liu had a powerful provincial and national patron—Mao Yuanxin, nephew of Chairman Mao and de facto head of Liaoning Province to which the city of Luda belongs. The patron-client relationship of Liu is diagrammed in figure 14-3. The result of this linkage between vertical and horizontal alliances was "aggravated corruption." Liu and his company embezzled public funds, extorted contributions from other organizations, and employed free prison labor to build sixty-four unauthorized constructions including twenty-eight clubhouses and a score of office buildings, theaters, and department stores.[41]

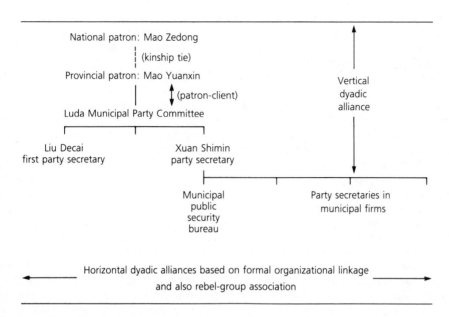

FIGURE 14-3 The patron-client relationship between the Luda Municipal Party Committee and the national leadership

Next to the patron-client relationships that have their ultimate patrons in Peking are those whose patrons are at provincial or county level. The most well-known case involved a woman named Wang Souxin, manager of a county fuel company in the province of Heilungjiang. Wang was a cashier in the company when the Cultural Revolution began. During that time of disorganization, the de facto power of Wang's county was in the hands of a military representative known as Commissar Yang, who became Wang's patron. Wang then formed a rebel group and seized the managership of the fuel company. Using the supply of coal to various organizations, factories, and households as a political resource, Wang soon established connections with all party officials in the county. After her initial patron, Commissar Yang, was promoted to a provincial post, Wang extended her connections to the provincial party establishment. In exchange for valuable goods from provincial party leaders, such as cement, chemical fertilizers, and tractors, Wang offered to place the sons and daughters of high provincial party leaders in her fuel company so that they would not be exiled to the countryside. In other words, Wang became the link between the county and the province. To her employees, Wang was their patron. She supplied them with coal, food, and clothing. When she was arrested for embezzlement in 1979, she declared: "You go to the county and inquire about me. You will learn that I, Mrs. Wang, always have the welfare of the masses as my chief concern."[42]

Finally, one also finds the type of patron-client relationship that is often found in southern Europe, Italy in particular, where an entire village has a patron who represents the interests of the village in the national political process. For example, many villagers in Fengren County in Hebei (Hopei) Province were given jobs outside the county because the county was an old revolutionary-base area. Whenever the county was in need of something, such as materials for agricultural mechanization, the county sought out those villagers who were lucky enough to work outside and in the upper echelons of the government.[43] The main difference between Chinese and Italian rural clientelism lies in the fact that Chinese rural clients have very few concrete benefits to exchange with their patrons since elections are not part of the Chinese political process. Italian or other Western rural clients can often repay their patrons by electing them to public office. Chinese rural clients appeal to their patrons on the basis of their vague tie as fellow townsmen, which like the old acquaintanceship has a strong influence over the Chinese.

By now the reader is entitled to see a close resemblance between the Chinese Communist bureaucracy and the traditional bureaucracy, which as we mentioned earlier was pervaded with personal alliances and cliques. Students of comparative communism undoubtedly see parallels in factionalism between the Chinese Communist system and that of other Communist nations. Robert Dahl summed up the pattern of conflicts in East European Communist regimes: First, there are "struggles by men who seek to win the dictator's favor and avoid his wrath." Second, there are "efforts by members of the highest party and governmental decision-making bodies to change the personnel or policies of the party-state." Third, there is "the seemingly unavoidable maneuvering among leaders who wish to protect or improve the position of specific segments and institutions of the society: the military, heavy industry, consumer goods, education, sciences, the arts."[44] The two underlying dynamics of factionalism, cliques, and clientelism that we have just mentioned, one cultural (or traditional) and the other system-bound, are closely related. Ithiel de Sola Pool has shown, for example, that the Communist approach to communication—the lifeline in any bureaucracy—is very similar to the approach in a traditional society. Both see "communication as embedded in a process of elaborately organized particularistic relations among persons rather than as a uniform output from the media to a faceless mass."[45] The Chinese Communist press itself points out the connection between cliques and Chinese feudalism. The cliques and factionalism in the Chinese Communist bureaucracy add another twist to the transplanting of Marxism, a European ideology, to Chinese society. In the original Marx-Engels conception, society would be so urbanized and secularized by capitalism that after the socialist revolution public functions would "lose their political character and be transformed into simple administrative functions of watching over social interests."[46] Instead, we witness Communist revolution succeeding in traditional societies such as Russia and China. There, the Communist party imposes a highly centralized system, which masks an advanced social, cultural, and political heterogeneity. The result is that totalitarianism "merely leads to a highly centralized variant of personal governance under which the ruler has maximum discretion."[47]

COPING WITH FACTIONALISM

Given the cultural and "systematic" causes of factionalism and cliques in the Chinese party–state bureaucracy, there is very little that the present leadership of the CPC can do to change it significantly short of another revolution. Nevertheless, some attempts have been made to reduce the incentives of party leaders and cadres to form factions or cliques.

At the upper echelon, Deng Xiaoping sought to dampen the ideological style of the party in order to reduce the chance of elevating differences of opinions into "line struggles." Thus Deng instructed his colleagues to review the past "struggles of lines" and to reinterpret them in less ideological terms. As Deng stated it, "In the past, we often talked about the ten struggles between two opposing lines. How should we look at them now? The struggle against Comrade Peng Dehuai cannot be viewed as a struggle between two lines. Nor can the struggle against Comrade Liu Shaoqi. Thus, the number is cut by two."[48]

But the institutional measures to reduce factionalism and cliques by ridding the party-state system of concentration of power and establishing "inner party democracy" have gained little substance. The Communist party and the state remain hierarchical and monopolistic.

The present Communist leadership has attempted to lessen the insecurity that cadres have on their status by declaring the abandonment of the "large-scale and turbulent political struggle." That, however, is cancelled out by the reform measures that have momentarily enhanced the feeling of insecurity among so many party members and cadres who were recruited during the Cultural Revolution.

The two major factors that at one time imposed a degree of discipline on the party—a unified central leadership and an unambiguous goal—remain largely absent today. Four modernizations as the goal of the CPC are too amorphous for most party members and cadres. In the meantime, a considerable number of party, state, and military leaders and the rank and file do not regard the present reform as legitimate. Factionalism in this circumstance is unlikely to be curtailed.

In the meantime, as long as the sharp rural-urban gap exists in Chinese society and economy, feudalism as a source of cliques and clientelism cannot be uprooted.

NOTES

1. Harold D. Lasswell and Abraham Kaplan, *Power and Society: A Framework for Political Inquiry* (New Haven: Yale University Press, 1963), pp. 171–72.
2. Ibid., p. 172.
3. Ibid., p. 173.
4. Ibid.
5. Carl H. Lande, "Introduction: The Dyadic Basis of Clientelism," in Steffen W. Schmidt, Laura Guasti, Carl H. Lande, and James C. Scott, eds., *Friends, Followers, and Factions* (Berkeley: University of California Press, 1977), p. xx.
6. Ibid., p. xxxi.
7. *Miscellany of Mao Tse-tung Thought (1949–68),* part I (Arlington, Va.: Joint Publications Research Service, February 20, 1974), p. 113.
8. *Wan-sui,* no. 2, p. 652.
9. Bernard J. Siegel and Alan R. Beals, "Pervasive Factionalism," *American Anthropologist,* no. 62 (1960), pp. 399–407.
10. Lasswell and Kaplan, *Power and Society,* p. 166.
11. William E. Griffith, "Communist Esoteric Communications: Explication de Texte," in Ithiel de Sola Pool and Wilbur Schramm, eds., *Handbook of Communication* (Chicago: Rand McNally College Publishing Company, 1973), p. 513.
12. Ralph H. Turner and Lewis M. Killian, *Collective Behavior,* 2nd ed. (Englewood Cliffs, N.J.: Prentice-Hall, 1972), p. 391.
13. "On Question of Party History," *Beijing Review* 24, no. 27 (July 6, 1981), 20, 25.
14. *Wan-sui,* no. 2, p. 657.
15. *Wan-sui,* no. 1, p. 30.
16. Hao Zhiping, "In Memory of Beloved Comrade Ruiqing," *RMRB,* September 1, 1978, p. 3.
17. Max Weber, *Economy and Society: An Outline of Interpretive Sociology,* vol. 3, edited by Guenther Roth and Claus Wittich (New York: Bedminister Press, 1968), pp. 1146–47.
18. Deng Xiaoping, "Suggestions on the Drafting of the 'Resolution on Certain Questions in the History of Our Party Since the Founding of the People's Republic of China,'" *Beijing Review* 26, no. 30 (July 25, 1983), 15–16.
19. Neil J. Smelser, *Theory of Collective Behavior* (New York: Free Press, 1962), p. 259.

20. For a survey of factionalism in China after the Cultural Revolution, see *China News Analysis*, no. 1012 (September 5, 1975) and no. 1013 (September 12, 1975). For an overall and questionable analysis of Chinese Communist factions, see Lucian Pye, *The Dynamics of Chinese Politics* (Cambridge, Mass.: Oelgeschlager, Gunn & Hain, 1981).

21. Turner and Killian, *Collective Behavior*, p. 395.

22. Ibid., p. 391.

23. Ji Xizhen, "A Round of Great Struggle in Defense of the Party," *RMRB*, February 26, 1979, p. 2.

24. *Wan-sui*, no. 2, pp. 150, 429.

25. *Wan-sui*, no. 2, p. 479.

26. Michael Parks, "Rig Accident at Sea Sinks China's 'Oil Faction,'" *Los Angeles Times*, February 13, 1981, part I-A.

27. *RMRB*, January 18, 1983, p. 1.

28. *RMRB*, February 22, 1983, p. 8.

29. *RMRB*, February 15, 1981, p. 3.

30. Lande, *Dyadic Basis of Clientelism*, and John Duncan Powell, "Peasant Society and Clientelist Politics," *American Political Science Review* LXIV, no. 2 (June 1970), 411-25.

31. *RMRB*, April 20, 1979, p. 1.

32. *RMRB*, September 15, 1978, p. 2.

33. Siegel and Beals, "Pervasive Factionalism."

34. Zhang Tingfa, "Leading Cadres Must Be the First to Be Qualified Party Members," *Hongqi*, no. 13 (1980), pp. 2-7.

35. Lande, *Dyadic Basis of Clientelism*, p. xx.

36. Ibid., p. xxi.

37. Richard Baum, *Prelude to Revolution* (New York: Columbia University Press, 1975), p. 121.

38. Powell, "Peasant Society."

39. Zhou Jinhua, "Appraising the Dazhai Brigade," *Beijing Review* 21, no. 16 (1981), 24-28.

40. *RMRB*, November 8, 1980, p. 3.

41. *RMRB*, April 6, 1978, p. 1.

42. Liu Binyen, "Between Human and Monster," *Ch'ih Shih Nien Tai*, no. 12 (1979), pp. 22-38.

43. *RMRB*, October 25, 1977, p. 3.

44. Robert A. Dahl, ed., *Regimes and Oppositions* (New Haven: Yale University Press, 1973), p. 12.

45. Ithiel de Sola Pool, "The Mass Media and Politics in the Modernization Process," in Lucian W. Pye, ed., *Communications and Political Development* (Princeton, N.J.: Princeton University Press, 1963), pp. 241-42.

46. Quoted in V. I. Lenin, *State and Revolution* (New York: International Publishers, 1943), p. 53.

47. Guenther Roth, "Personal Rulership, Patrimonialism, and Empire-Building in the New States," *World Politics* XX, no. 2 (January 1968), 203.

48. Deng Xiaoping, "Suggestions on the Drafting," p. 15.

CHAPTER 15

The Policy-Making Process

The major characteristics of the Chinese Communist political system that we have discussed so far, such as monopoly of power by the CPC, centralization, ideological style, and factionalism, are in the final analysis, meaningful only as each bears upon the policy-making process. Like the blood circulation in a human body the policy process not only gives life to a political system but also provides us with a strategic vantage point to observe how various parts of a political system work (or fail to work) together. This chapter will deal with the two major groups involved in the Chinese Communist policy-making process: the elite and the masses.[1] Though it is the elite who make policy, the masses are involved in the application of policy. Lasswell and Kaplan write, "Since the decision-making process includes application as well as formulation and promulgation of policy, those whose acts are affected also participate in decision-making: by conformity to or disregard of the policy they help determine whether it is or is not in fact a decision."[2]

IDEOLOGY: SUM AND PARTS OF POLICY

Before discussing the actual process of Chinese Communist policy making, we must first note that policy decisions of whatever type of political systems are determined by basic values. According to Lasswell and Kaplan, "policy is a projected program of goal values and practices."[3] Values of an elite are often formalized and made explicit in ideology. Thus Mao Zedong wrote in 1961:

Planning is ideology which is a reflection of reality but in turn affects reality. In the past we did not plan to build new industry in coastal areas until 1957. We thus wrongly delayed that for seven years. After 1958 we started large-scale construction (in coastal areas) and achieved great expansion in two years. This shows the great impact of ideology on economic development, determining whether economy will develop or how high the speed of development.[4]

Ideology determines both the substance and the practice of the policy-making process. Major domestic policies of the PRC before 1976 were almost all made in the 1950s. These policies, such as the first five-year plan of economic development and agricultural collectivization, stemmed from the Marxist-Leninist law of social development as Mao perceived it.[5] Specifically, by the law of social development is meant the transformation of a nation into "a unitary system of the ownership of the means of production by the whole people."[6] That is, Mao sought to turn China into a nation consisting of several giant state-owned collectives each handling a specific aspect of production. All major policies before 1976 originated from this ideological perspective of Mao Zedong and his associates in the CPC.

But there is another aspect of Chinese Communist ideology that determines the practices of policy. The Marxist-Leninist law of social development sets the "goal-values" but does not decide the specific programs and ways of coping with intermediate events. For those two elements of policy making, Chinese Communists were guided by two references before 1976. The first reference for specific or contingency planning was Soviet experience. In a 1958 talk, Mao, for example, admitted that in economy, education, and, in part, military work the CPC mechanically copied Soviet experience.[7] The Soviet experience, however, was not simply copied by the CPC; Mao sometimes also regarded Soviet experience as "minimal goals," to be surpassed by China. For example, when Mao accelerated steel production in 1958, he was partly motivated by a wish to outperform Soviet steel production. In 1961 Mao recalled the 1949 "election speech" of Stalin, in which the latter stated that between 1921 and 1940 steel production in the Soviet Union had risen to 18 million tons, 14 million tons more than the steel production under the tsar. That was regarded by Mao to be a low rate of increase.[8] Subsequently, Mao planned a one-fold increase in steel production in China in one year, from 5.3 to 10 million tons—the Great Leap Forward of 1958.[9]

The second specific reference in Chinese Communist policy making before 1976 was Mao's own experience in revolutionary war. The two most important points of this indigenous reference are an overwhelming emphasis on the impact of institutional change and the practice of learning by doing as opposed to careful planning before action. Mao's stress on the effect of institutional change, in Marxist terms, means that he regarded the productive relations (ideology and organization) more important than productive forces (technology and capacity for production) in effecting change. Commenting on a Soviet text on political economy, Mao stated, "The history of all revolutions has shown that it is not the case that there must first be new productive forces before the obsolete production relations can be transformed. Our revolution started with a propagation of Marxism-Leninism so to create a new public opinion and thereby facilitate revolution. While in revolution we overthrow the outdated superstructure and destroy the old productive relations . . . paving the road for great expansion of productive force."[10] Mao disputed another statement from the same Soviet text— "spontaneity and absence of leadership are incompatible with the survival of the collective ownership of the means of production." Mao maintained that in a socialist society spontaneity and actions without leadership are still possible because planning is never perfect. Planning is not perfect because human cognition is not perfect. "Take, for example, our own experience. At first we did not understand socialism. Our understanding of socialism is obtained through practice."[11] In Chinese Communist policy making before 1976 there was a strong preference of applying a rudimentarily worked out policy to careful planning. The belief was that practice and planning should be carried out simultaneously.

THE ELITE: POLICY MAKING

The Chinese Communist policy-making process can be divided into an initial and a derived phase. The initial phase of a policy consists of: (1) genesis of policy, (2) preliminary validation of policy, (3) persuasion, (4) formalization (legitimation), and (5) feedback (application). The derived phase is a response to the initial feedback or application and has its own sequence consisting of: (1) spot investigation, (2) rule making, (3) persuasion, and (4) formalization.

Initial Phase

Genesis. Since the formal ideology of Marxism-Leninism determines both the sum and the parts of Chinese Communist policy making, the genesis of any policy in Chinese Communist political system is always in the hands and heads of the top Communist leaders. In other words, the policy-making process takes the form of "trickling down" rather than "bubbling up." Take, for example, the first major decision of the CPC after 1949—the General Line for Socialist Transition in 1952, i.e., to take preliminary steps such as nationalization of industry and collectivization of agriculture toward turning China into "a unitary system of the ownership of the means of production by the whole people." Mao, in a talk in July 1957 used the metaphor of the digestion process of a cow to describe the genesis and promulgation of the General Line: "Every sector of society has studied the General Line but there has been no debate on it, neither within the party nor in society. It is like a cow eating grass—first you take it down and then you come back to chew it slowly." [12] Later he amplified it. The general line was at first suggested by Mao in a party conference on finance in 1952. [13] The decision then was to not even inform the whole CPC about it (though the leading cadres up to county level were informed). It was in 1953 that Mao first publicized the General Line to the non-CPC elites of the CPPCC. The process was clear: first, the genesis of the General Line came from Mao, in an innerparty conference, motivated obviously by ideological reasons. Then the rest of the Communist party and the Chinese population, like a cow eating grass, took "the General Line down" and then gradually gained understanding and, ideally, accepted it.

The General Line for Socialist Transition, however, was just as its title had it, a general line. For it to have impact on society, a general line had to be turned into policy, program, and institution. [14] Determining a general line and its specific programs were the prerogatives of the most efficient organizations of the CPC: the Standing Committee of Politburo, the Politburo, and the Central Secretariat.

Preliminary validation. In conformity with Mao's preference for quick application of a generally conceived policy, the second step of CPC policy making was testing a policy or program at certain testing points (*shidian*). Formally speaking, the functions of testing points, like pilot projects, were to determine the feasibility of a project or policy. In practice, Mao used the testing points mainly to obtain information supportive of his policy and rally support from regional CPC leaders. In the meantime, the measure of the testing point lent a scientific or objective flavor to Mao's policy-making process. Take, for instance, the program Forty Articles of Agricultural Development publicized in 1956. This was Mao's radical plan to collectivize and accelerate agricultural production. [15] According to Mao, the genesis of the Forty Articles was the Politburo—the "institute for political designing." After that, the forty articles were put to "practice" for two years. The result of practice through testing points was a sweeping plan to increase grain production in China in twelve years by assigning an output quota for each region of China—"2,700 pounds per acre north of the Yellow River, 3,300 pounds north of Huai River and 5,300 pounds south of Huai River." [16] Similarly, the goals and means of the Great Leap Forward came from the testing points in Henan Province, where Mao had visited a number of times. [17] In Mao's talks one frequently comes across statements to the effect that if a program worked in one area, it must work in the rest of China. In 1955 Mao said that since agricultural collectivization had been accomplished in Zhejiang and Anhui Provinces, the other provinces could do the same. [18]

Persuasion. After the testing point, with specific information obtained on implementation and political support from regional leaders, a policy was usually regarded as "mature" enough to be propagandized to the whole nation. Hence, the next step was persuasion. For example, Mao made known the General Line of Socialist Transition to the CPPCC in late 1953, and then the Department of Propaganda of the Central Committee prepared an outline of propaganda for the general line for mass persuasion. [19] In the case of the Forty Articles of Agricultural Development, after two years of practice, Mao directed the forty articles to be discussed by the joint session of the Standing Committee of National People's Congress and the CPPCC. Afterward, they were discussed in the press, in villages, factories, and mass organizations and among the democratic parties. [20]

In reality, the *persuasion* was merely a euphemism for *transmission.* The discussion consisted simply of party propagandists' refuting "incorrect" views and the masses' acclaiming a new policy.

Formalization. The conclusion of persuasion was "formalization" of a policy by "dignified" institutions. In the case of the forty articles, after discussion by the parapolitical organizations and the masses in villages and factories, the forty articles were first formalized into a CPC policy through a National Party Congress. After that, formality dictated that the CPC handed the articles to the State Council, which in turn sent them to the National People's Congress to be acclaimed as national policy. [21] By the time a policy had gone this course, usually it had already been applied for some time.

The foregoing describes the standard procedure. Mao, of course, felt no obligation to always follow the standard. As mentioned before, the convening of the National People's Congress was up to the wishes of the Communist party.

Application and feedback. Since the genesis of a policy in the Chinese Communist political system was a "trickling down" process, the only major correcting mechanism was "feedback of decision"—"knowledge of the consequences of actions taken." This type of feedback through the consequence of a policy has been common in Communist policy making. [22] The way a policy *should be* monitored and fed back to top leaders was set forth by Mao in 1955 in connection with organizing cooperatives in the countryside:

1. Convene several meetings a year; big ones and small ones.
2. Solve a problem without delay; do not let problems accumulate. All one needs is to know a few cooperatives well; then a general conclusion can be made.

3. Use telegrams and telephones.

4. Conduct inspection tours; ride in jeep or on horseback or walk.

5. Improve journals. . . . Every province and autonomous region must compile a book every year to be available to the public. . . . *How to Establish An Agricultural Producers' Cooperative* should be published by the People's Publishing House and copies distributed to all the people.

6. Publish brief bulletins. Every ten days the county party committee must submit a brief report to the prefectural party committee and the prefectural committee must submit one to the provincial committee. If the situation is urgent, then submit a report every five days. The substance of these reports should be, What problems have taken place and what is the state of its development? The provincial party committee must submit a brief report to the party center fortnightly. If the situation is urgent, then submit a report every ten days. The content must be brief; a few hundred words would do.[23]

The foregoing prescribes merely the form of feedback, not its substance. The efficiency of feedback in Chinese Communist policy making has been severely lowered by the ideological and partisan nature of policy. For example, the feedback formality presented here was made by Mao in September 1955. Two months earlier, in July, Mao had for all practical purposes foreclosed critical feedback in another speech, a very crucial one at that, entitled "The Question of Agricultural Cooperation." In it Mao spoke with scorn of those who had reservations about the cooperatives: "But some of our comrades are tottering along like a woman with bound feet, always complaining that others are going too fast. They imagine that by picking on trifles, grumbling unnecessarily, worrying continuously, and putting up countless taboos and commandments, they are guiding the socialist mass movements in the rural areas on sound lines. NO. This is not the right way at all; it is wrong."[24] Throughout this July talk Mao made numerous disparaging and even threatening references to those who were opposed to the acceleration of collectivization, such as accusing the latter of taking "the viewpoint of the bourgeoisie, rich peasants or well-to-do middle peasants," trying "to cover up their dilatoriness by quoting the experience of the Soviet Union," or "paint[ing] a pessimistic picture of the present situation in the Party's work in guiding agricultural cooperation."[25] Mao then reminded party cadres of the party's reprimand to those who dissolved cooperatives in 1953: "Do not commit the 1953 mistake of mass dissolution of cooperatives again, otherwise self-critical examination will again be called for."[26] Mao all but blocked any critical feedback by saying that "in such a movement some deviations are inevitable" and that "criticism should be made in good time; *do not get into the habit of criticizing only after something has happened.*" (emphasis added).[27]

The result of the blockage of critical feedback in institutionalized channels is predictable—only when the consequence of a policy takes the form of massive resistance or national catastrophe will a policy be corrected. This is best exemplified in the people's commune movement of 1958-59. Mao, for example, conceded in March 1959 that he was "a prophet after fact" concerning the passive resistance of Chinese peasants to the people's commune.[28] Mao stated that he was "thankful" to several hundred million peasants who had resorted to "falsification of amount of production and private distribution of produce," for that had taught him to let the production teams own land and have control over farming.[29] But the most telling of all regarding feedback of decision in 1958-59 was Mao's admission in September 1959 that only after the catastrophe of the Great Leap Forward did he begin "learning economic work."[30]

In the same year Mao, apparently for the first time, read a Soviet book on political economy.[31] Some of Mao's unnamed critics observed about Mao policy making: (1) "Only when a mistake has gone to the extreme will it be turned back" and (2) "Turning back means a 180 degree turn!"[32]

Derived Phase

The catastrophic consequences of the Great Leap Forward triggered the second round of the policy-making process. This derived phase of policy making starts with top-ranking leaders personally conducting inspection at certain spots.

Spot investigation. The feedback of decision in 1958–59 not only impressed, finally, top leaders on the urgency of the situation in the countryside, but at the same time also made it clear that the regular institutional channels of the CPC were not able to inform them on the actual conditions in rural areas. To obtain accurate information in order to rectify the original decision of the Great Leap, central leaders, including members of the Standing Committee of the Politburo such as Mao, Liu Shaoqi, and Zhou Enlai, had to conduct spot investigations themselves. Liu, for example, made several tours to Henan and Hunan to see the people's communes in these two provinces.[33] Liu found that getting lower cadres to make critical reports was not easy because of punitive campaigns against dissenters earlier. Before Liu's talk with commune cadres, the leading cadres of production brigades had already "unified" the speeches of production-team cadres. But then, according to one account, because of Liu Shaoqi's "superior technique of Marxist-Leninist leadership," he was able to obtain a *"relatively* complete picture" of a commune" (emphasis added).[34] Other leaders conducted similar spot investigations in factories. The late Li Fuchun, then a member of the Central Secretariat in charge of economic planning, industry, and transportation, spent six months in a Peking lathe factory in 1961 looking for problems in industry.[35]

It must be pointed out that even this high-level feedback was not without political risk. The late Marshal Peng Dehuai had also conducted spot investigations in 1958, but his critique of the people's commune led to his dismissal and the initiation of a purge of "right-wing opportunism" by Mao. It seems that Marshal Peng had made known the results of his investigation too early before the feedback of decisions made its full impact on Mao, who thus had to respect the report by other leaders.

Rule making. The result of spot investigation by central leaders was the drafting of specific rules to rectify the original policy. The spot investigation by Liu Shaoqi and other CPC leaders resulted in the promulgation of Rules on Work in Rural People's Communes or Sixty Articles on Commune Management in March 1961, thus eliminating many radical measures of the original commune organizations and legitimizing pre-commune activities in the countryside, such as private plots and free markets. Spot investigation of factories such as the one conducted by Li Fuchun led to the drafting of Seventy Articles on Industry, also in 1961, which reestablished the authority of managers in factories and tightened central control over industrial construction.[36]

To the extent that Chinese Communist policy making also had a "bubbling-up" component, albeit extremely weak, it took place in this rule-making stage. Before the articles on commune management and industry were drafted during the spot investigations, lower cadres did get a chance to express their views to top decision makers. Even Mao Zedong allowed this policy and personally practiced it. For example, the Twenty-Three Points of 1965 (full title: "Some Problems Currently Arising in the Course of the Rural Socialist Education Movement"), according to Mao, was drafted by him after consulting with "several cadres from regions." In this case, however, Mao was prone to solicit views only from leftist regional leaders.[37]

After specific articles are drafted, they go through the routine of persuasion and formalization. Implementation of these rules, however, in practice preceded the formality of persuasion and formalization.

Chinese Communist policy making produced articles for every line of work. Mao, in a talk in 1962, mentioned Sixty Articles on Agricultural Work (i.e., commune management), Seventy Articles on Industry, Sixty Articles on Higher Education, and Forty Articles on Scientific Research.[38] These articles, according to Mao, represented the specific principles, policies, and programs of the General Line of Socialist Transition. These articles were meant "to persuade the masses and cadres [and] be the educational materials so that they [the masses and cadres might] have a unified understanding and action."[39] In other words, both the input and the output of a policy in the PRC were ideology, i.e., to realize the law of social development as perceived by Mao before 1976.

Our discussion of the policy-making process under Mao has emphasized almost exclusively factors intrinsic to the Chinese Communist political system (see table 15-1). That, of course, is not sufficient. There were external factors, domestic or foreign, that affected CPC policy making. For example, Mao Zedong had stated that his decision to start the radical people's commune movement in 1958 was in response to the "frenzied attack" on the Communist party by "bourgeois rightists" in the 1957 Hundred Flowers Blooming campaign. Since according to Mao, the "bourgeois rightists" denied the "achievement of socialist construction," Mao decided to speed up agricultural communization, hoping to "change the face of China in three years."[40] In a talk in

TABLE 15-1 Policy-making process of the Chinese Communist political system

PROCESS	INSTITUTION
I. Initial phase	
1. Genesis	Standing Committee of Politburo
	Politburo, Central Secretariat
2. Preliminary validation (Testing point)	(as genesis) plus Provincial CPC
3. Persuasion	National Congress of CPC
	Standing Committee of National People's Congress
	Standing Committee of CPPCC
	Mass organizations
4. Formalization	State Council, National People's Congress
5. Application and feedback	Provincial, municipal, county, and township CPCs
II. Derived phase	
1. Spot investigation (*dundien*)	(as genesis) plus grassroot cadres
2. Rule making	(as genesis)
3. Persuasion	(as initial phase)
4. Formalization	(as initial phase)
5. Application and feedback	(as initial phase)

1964 Mao mentioned other factors that had influenced decision making but were beyond the control of the Communist party:

> Come natural disaster and it makes sure that you do not have that much grain. . . . War cannot be figured into our planning either. We are not the chief of staff of the United States. We do not know when they will start a war. And then there are revolutions in other nations. That is difficult to put into our planning. In some countries the people's revolutions succeed. They then want economic assistance from us. How can this be predicted?[41]

But even without such contingency factors as natural disaster and revolution in other nations, it is clear that the policy-making system under Mao was strong in commitment to action but weak in gathering and analysis of information. As a result, Mao's policies seemed to be a continuing series of miscalculations. In July 1957 Mao estimated that in three years more than 90 percent of the peasants would have an increase in income due to the superiority of cooperatives.[42] This was never realized since a year later people's communes superseded the cooperatives. The Great Leap Forward of 1958, Mao predicted, would greatly expand productive forces, so that in 1960 production would increase "in a big way."[43] In 1959 Mao expected that in three, five, or at most, seven years, the whole Chinese countryside would be managed by large people's communes, and farming would be mechanized, all other forms of ownership of means of production having been abolished by then.[44] Then in 1960, Mao envisaged that by 1969 the PRC would have realized the four modernizations, i.e., modernization of agriculture, industry, science, and defense.[45] Underlying these faulty expectations of Mao's was his faith in the power of productive relations, i.e., ideology, leadership, and organization. Strange as it may seem, there was a great similarity between the policy-making process and the cadre policy under Mao. Both lay stress on ideology and will power and played down the role of knowledge, information, and education.

The Maoist mode of policy making should be familiar to students of Soviet studies because of the similarities between the Maoist and Stalinist pattern of decision making. Both preferred to base their plans on feedback of decision rather than on the views and opinions of various groups and leaders. The result, both in the PRC and the Soviet Union, was that commitment to an unviable policy was made before its possible effect was known. By the time the effect was known, commitment to it had advanced to such an extent that a leader such as Mao could not retreat without bringing discreditation to himself and the commune system. So both Mao and Stalin resorted to terror to sustain policy, in Mao's case, the Cultural Revolution.[46]

POLICY MAKING AFTER MAO

Some interesting changes have occurred since the death of Mao and the conclusion of the struggle for succession. The first and foremost characteristic of the post-Mao period is that the entire decision-making process belongs to the derived phase. In other words, present Chinese Communist policy making is in response to the feedback of thirty years of Mao's decisions. Consequently, as in earlier decisions made in the derived phase, present CPC policy making is closely connected with Chinese social and economic conditions. The second characteristic of post-Mao policy making is that though the general institutional framework of present policy making remains much the same as in Mao's era, significant changes have taken place in the operation of the institutional framework.

The genesis of policy is still in the hands of the CPC but no longer in that of one man. As we said earlier, major policy-making is now done by the Secretariat of the Central Committee of the CPC. More significant than that is change in ideology. Being part of the derived phase of policy making, post-Mao (after 1978) decisions of the CPC have been determined much less by the "first principle" of Marxism-Leninism and more by the consequences of Mao's decisions. This not only introduces a new set of values (see, for example, the debate on "the real objectives of socialist production"[47] in the Chinese press), but the very fact of responding to the consequences of Mao's decisions means taking into account Chinese public opinion. Further, not only the *value* but also the *practice* aspect of ideology is being changed by CPC leaders today. The Maoist emphasis on productive relations, spontaneous action, and campaigns has been repudiated.[48] Hu Qiaomu, the top-ranking CPC ideologue today, for example, publicly advocated the "objective character of economic principles" and criticized CPC's past reliance on administrative means to manage economic development.[49] CPC leaders at present play up the role of information over "spontaneous action" in policy making. In September 1979 the State Council announced the establishment of four research groups under the Finance and Economy Commission—to look into reform of the economic system and of the economic structure and into the importation of technology and of economic theory and methodology—to facilitate China's overall economic reform.[50] In 1983, it was reported that there were over seven hundred agencies in China specializing in "information and intelligence on science and technology" organized by state enterprises.[51]

The old practice of testing point remains an integral part of the policy making of post-Mao leaders. For example, the reform measure of granting more autonomy to enterprises was at first tested in the province of Sichuan (home province of Deng Xiaoping) and then extended to Anhui and Zhejiang Province.[52] However, the testing-point phase nowadays is not associated immediately with a disruptive mass campaign. Present CPC leaders are much more willing than Mao to allow regional differences in adopting testing-point experience. As a matter of fact, it is the lower cadres who are still accustomed to the old ways and are prone to apply testing-point programs indiscriminately.

Probably the most visible and significant change in the post-Mao policy-making process is the enlargement of participation in policy deliberation. The critical discussion in the Chinese mass media of various problems in Chinese economy, politics, education, and society since 1978 has been unprecedented. This is a sharp contrast to the days of Mao's rule when the press and the media as a whole rarely discussed but mostly acclaimed Mao's policies. Furthermore, as we mentioned before, members of the National People's Congress, especially the Standing Committee and that of the CPPCC, also play some part in policy deliberation, mainly in the rule-making stage. The norm of policy making at present is to conduct various opinion forums before a party or state organization plans a program. Take, for example, the regulation on sanitary standards of food. Before the regulation was formalized by the State Council in 1982, the Ministry of Public Health conducted some twenty forums or conferences to solicit opinions from experts. After that, a draft of proposed food regulations was circulated to various provincial and municipal state agencies for more opinions. Reportedly, some fourteen hundred suggestions were gathered and were eventually incorporated into the final regulations.[53]

Compared with the decision making under Mao, the present one puts more emphasis on building consensus than on mobilization. Accordingly, present CPC leaders attempt to elicit opinions from a variety of extra-CPC groups and regional authorities. In the application of policies, present CPC leaders are more tolerant of regional differences than Mao was. The technical specialists employed by state ministries are also given more authority than they were under Mao. All these practices naturally increase the feedback to the CPC. The logical consequence of the measure of post-Mao policy making is reduction of central control, which in turn gives rise to problems of integration. Hence, we see a trial-and-error process since 1978; Chinese Communist leaders after Mao have been groping for a formula combining "trickling down" with "bubbling up."

So far, our analysis has been on the policy-making cycle. But we mentioned at the outset that the policy-making process, in China as elsewhere, is the focus of other major forces of politics such as ideological style, centralism, and factionalism. The foregoing discussion has made abundantly clear the central role of ideology in Chinese Communist policy-making, largely because of the causative role played by Mao in Chinese Communist politics. Mao initiated all the major policies of the PRC: the Socialist transition of 1952, the agricultural collectivization of 1955, the Great Leap Forward of 1958, and finally the Cultural Revolution of 1965–69. As mentioned throughout this study, these policies were believed by Mao to be necessary to carry out the law of social development. However, as pointed out throughout this study, there were high-ranking Chinese Communist leaders whose views on social development did not entirely concur with Mao's, e.g., the party pragmatists. Hence, each policy initiation by Mao brought forth factional dispute at the highest echelon of the Communist party. For example, the Gao Gang and Rao Shushih case occurred in 1953 at the start of the first five-year plan. Mao's initiation of the agricultural collectivization plan in 1955 provoked dissent from the members of the Rural Work Department of the Central Committee. The result of the Great Leap Forward prompted Marshal Peng Dehuai to remonstrate with Mao and the latter's purge of Marshal Peng and his associates. Each such flareup of dissent or factionalism caused both disorientation and opportunity for lower party leaders. Disorientation enhanced a sense of insecurity and so brought about the formation of cliques among lower leaders for self-protection. High-level factionalism also created opportunities for lower-level leaders to ingratiate themselves to Mao, for instance, by establishing clientelist alliances. Finally, the centralist political process under Chinese Communism is extremely conducive to both factionalism and clientelism. Some scholars might argue that Mao attempted to break the centralist process and factionalist confines by initiating mass campaigns such as the Three-Anti, the Hundred Flowers Blooming, and the Cultural Revolution. However, Mao always returned to the centralist structure at crucial points. The present leaders of the CPC do not fundamentally deviate from the Maoist course, though Deng, at least on the surface, tries to create the image of an enlarged participation circle in policy making.

MASS CAMPAIGNS

Though the Chinese Communist policy-making process involves predominantly the elites, the party stresses mass participation in policy application. The form of mass involvement in policy execution is mass campaign.

There seem to be two reasons for Chinese Communist leaders' attempt to supplement elite decision making with mass involvement. First, the Communist party grows out of a social movement and, hence, fully recognizes the force of mass participation. Second, the Leninist component of the CPC ideology stresses the educational function of the mass participation in political process. Though the masses play no part in the genesis of policy, participation in policy execution, so goes the Leninist thesis, would transform the masses into Communists. A CPC propagandist explains this Leninist concept in connection with the function of propaganda:

> A prevailing skepticism has it that since one cannot eat propaganda why should we devote so much effort and energy to it? It's correct that if we rely on propaganda alone, without simultaneously undertaking other organizational works, then nothing can be accomplished. But correct propaganda can enhance people's patriotic passion and political consciousness, making them comprehend the correctness and necessity of the policies. Hence, they will actively implement the policies and transform the demand of the party and the state into practice.[54]

In other words, mass propaganda and campaigns play the crucial transformation role in the Chinese Communist political process, i.e., transforming policies decided by the leaders of the Communist party into policies "of the people and by the people."

Based on this Leninist notion of political leadership, numerous campaigns were carried out by the Chinese Communists after 1949. Almost every policy of the Communist party was accompanied by a campaign to involve all the population in its application. Each campaign sought to induce genuine involvement. At the same time, each campaign was also a highly orchestrated affair. Specially trained campaign cadres were dispatched to all localities to supervise the campaign work of an area. Local activists were recruited to assist campaign cadres. The mass media concentrated reports and commentaries on the campaign while it was being carried out. During a campaign everyone had to take part and play a role. There were daily group meetings at work places and in neighborhoods. In these meetings campaign documents—directives from the CPC or important speeches by CPC leaders—were studied. There were large rallies and parades that everyone had to attend. A Chinese citizen's conduct in a campaign was closely watched by cadres, for that determined one's political stand. Anyone who stood aloof from campaigns or displayed indifference was, in the eyes of cadres and activists, a suspect. For those who sought to advance themselves politically, campaigns offered a good opportunity for them to show their support for the party. In short, when a campaign was launched, the entire Chinese population was mobilized like an army ready for combat. In the scheme of Mao, the mass campaigns arranged Chinese people in serried ranks marching forward at the direction of Mao and the CPC—the general staff of the proletariat.

Before 1952 campaigns were used to eliminate groups that were suspected to be "natural" enemies of the CPC, e.g., landlords, rich peasants, businessmen, religious leaders, and former members of the Nationalist party. As mentioned in our previous discussion of the Chinese judiciary, campaigns before 1952 were also used to enact laws such as the Act for the Punishment of Counterrevolutionaries following the campaign Suppression of Counterrevolutionaries of 1950-51. In the mid-1950s each new economic measure was accompanied by a mass campaign. The most well-known economic campaign was the 1958 campaign to make steel in "backyard furnaces"— so that China might realize Mao's goal of increasing steel production by 100 percent in one year. But starting in 1957, campaigns became predominantly vehicles for "political study" as Mao was preoccupied by the fear of China's turning "revisionist."

One campaign after another for studying the precepts of Marx, Lenin, or Mao was launched. This kind of campaign reached a peak in the ten years from 1966 to 1976. Campaigns also became increasingly coercive and violent, as exemplified by the "Cultural Revolution."

The campaigns, originally designed to be the "schools" of communism for the masses, ended up being objects of fear and resentment. Campaigns are seen by the Chinese people as the most serious disruption of their life. Naturally the impact of campaigns is directly associated with the unviable programs such as making steel in backyard furnaces of 1958 and the incessant elite conflict from 1957 to the present. Instead of making the masses enthusiastic supporters of communism, the mass campaigns in the PRC generated mass disillusionment and cynicism. In 1976 shortly before Mao's death, the Chinese press, then controlled by the Gang of Four, decried the popular saying: "The struggle between two lines, two classes and two roads [is] a front for sectarian struggle for power."[55]

In response to the Chinese public's resentment and fear of mass campaigns, one of the very first new policies of present CPC leaders was to decree the end of campaigns as the standard practice of the party. "Experience from history," Deng Xiaoping reported in an internal party meeting in 1980, "testifies to the ineffectiveness of using mass campaigns, instead of reasoning and discussion, to deal with problems of ideology or using mass campaigns, instead of taking practical measures in a careful way, to deal with reform of old system and establishing new ones."[56] Nevertheless, Deng Xiaoping's administration has not abandoned the use of campaigns entirely. But he has been very selective in their campaigns in contrast to Mao's view of campaigns as the panacea of social, economic, and political problems. In 1982, for example, the present leaders of the PRC initiated the campaign of Five Stresses and Four Points of Beauty—"stress on decorum, manners, hygiene, discipline and morals; beauty of the mind, language, behavior and the environment." This campaign is designed to counter the public mood and manner in mainland China that was marked by a mean and rough streak after the terror and violence of the Cultural Revolution. Naturally this new campaign is neither coercive nor disruptive of people's lives. Unlike previous campaigns under Mao, which counterposed the CPC against the public, the campaign of Five Stresses and Four Points of Beauty coopts the old morality of society so that the party stands on the side of Chinese society. In a larger sense, the change in the policy toward mass campaigns represents present CPC leaders' overall acceptance of the diversity and complexity of a society in peacetime reconstruction. Campaigns have their own realm—for moral renewal—just as economics has its own laws.

NOTES

1. The description of Chinese Communist policy making at the elite level is based primarily on *Mao Tse-tung Shih-hsiang Wan-sui (Long Live the Thought of Mao Tse-tung)*, which was issued in two volumes in 1969, apparently, by the leftists. The two volumes contain hitherto unpublished talks of Mao in various conferences and meetings from 1949 to 1968. These were originally intended as "internal documents" for the leftists to indoctrinate their new recruits in the Cultural Revolution. After the death of Mao, the fifth volume of *Selected Works of Mao Tse-tung* was published (Peking: Foreign Languages Press, 1977) incorporating some of the same materials as *Mao Tse-tung Shih-hsiang Wan-sui* (hereafter *Wan-sui*), thus establishing the authenticity of the materials in *Wan-sui*. The two volumes of *Wan-sui* are invaluable in obtaining information and insights into the decision-making process of the Chinese Communist elite.

Michel Oksenberg has written two quite identical articles on Chinese Communist policy making ("Policy Making under Mao, 1949–68: An Overview," in John M. H. Lindbeck, ed., *China:*

Management of a Revolutionary Society (Seattle: University of Washington Press, 1971); "Policy Making under Mao Tse-tung, 1949-68," *Comparative Politics* 3, no. 3 (April 1971). However, Oksenberg's discussion is not really focused on policy making as such; his articles deal with Mao's leadership in general. Nowhere in his articles is there any analysis on just how a policy is made. Rather Oksenberg speculates on the many dimensions of Chinese Communist political process such as Mao's self-perceived roles, his state of health, relationship with colleagues, and use of various forms of meetings. Curiously, Mao's causative role in all the major policies of the PRC is never pointed out. Oksenberg's image of Mao the decision maker seems to be heavily influenced by American political experience in which the top executive is often the object of various demands from various groups and institutions. Thus Oksenberg misses the most important contrast in policy making between a totalitarian system such as the PRC and a pluralistic system such as the United States. The totalitarian system is structured to shield the top executive from demands from below in order for him to exercise his causative influence.

2. Harold D. Lasswell and Abraham Kaplan, *Power and Society: A Framework for Political Inquiry* (New Haven: Yale University Press, 1950), pp. 74-75.

3. Ibid., p. 71.

4. *Wan-sui,* no. 2, p. 355.

5. In a Supreme State Conference in October 1957 Mao stated that for the rightists to approve the policies of the CPC, they must "understand the law of social development." See *Wan-sui,* no. 2, p. 132.

6. *Wan-sui,* p. 348.

7. Ibid., pp. 161-62.

8. Ibid., p. 395.

9. *RMRB,* July 14, 1981, p. 5.

10. *Wan-sui,* no. 2, p. 334.

11. Ibid., pp. 354-55.

12. Ibid., p. 115.

13. *Wan-sui* (p. 122) seems to have made an error in date since it has Mao stating that he first made the suggestion in 1953 and then publicized it in a CPPCC meeting also in 1953. But the *People's Daily* on July 10, 1981, in recounting the first thirty-year history of the PRC, stated that Mao suggested the General Line in 1952.

14. *Wan-sui,* no. 2, p. 118.

15. For more discussion on Chinese policy making, see Parris H. Chang, *Power and Policy in China* (University Park: Pennsylvania State University Press, 1975).

16. *Wan-sui,* no. 2, p. 141.

17. Ibid., pp. 201-2.

18. Ibid., p. 26.

19. Ibid., p. 122.

20. Ibid., p. 141.

21. Ibid., pp. 141-42.

22. Walter D. Connor, "Public Opinion in the Soviet Union," in Walter D. Connor and Zui Y. Gitelman with Adaline Huszczo and Robert Blumstock, *Public Opinion in European Socialist Systems* (New York: Frederick A. Praeger, 1977), p. 107.

23. *Wan-sui,* no. 2, pp. 19-20.

24. Mao Tse-tung, *The Question of Agricultural Cooperation* (Peking: Foreign Languages Press, 1959), p. 1.

25. Ibid., p. 30, 26, and 20.

26. Ibid., pp. 11-12.

27. Ibid., pp. 1 and 30.

28. *Wan-sui,* no. 1, pp. 40-41.

29. Ibid., p. 47.

30. Ibid., p. 99.

31. Ibid., pp. 116-20 and 167-247.

32. Ibid., p. 88.

33. *RMRB,* March 29, 1980, p. 5; May 19, 1980, p. 2; May 21, 1980, p. 2.

34. *RMRB,* May 19, 1980, p. 2.

35. *RMRB,* January 9, 1980, p. 4.

36. *RMRB,* July 14, 1981, p. 5.

37. *Wan-sui,* no. 2, p. 599.

38. Ibid., p. 415.

39. Ibid.

40. Ibid., pp. 260 and 395.

41. Ibid., p. 497.

42. Ibid., p. 78.

43. Ibid., p. 321.

44. Ibid., pp. 15 and 30.

45. Ibid., p. 346.

46. Walter D. Connor, "Public Opinion in the Soviet Union," p. 107.

47. *RMRB*, October 20, 1979, p. 1.

48. Chen Hanping, "On 'Concentrate Forces to Wage a War of Annihilation'—A Debatable Slogan in Economic Construction." *RMRB*, August 11, 1980, p. 5.

49. Hu Qiaomu, "Act According to Economic Principles to Accelerate the Realization of Four Modernizations," *RMRB*, October 6, 1978, pp. 1-3.

50. *RMRB*, September 4, 1979, p. 1.

51. *Ming Pao Daily News*, January 24, 1983, p. 1.

52. Lin Zili, "The Beginning of the Reform of Our Nation's Economic System," *RMRB*, April 4, 1980, p. 5.

53. *RMRB*, November 13, 1982, p. 4.

54. Fu Chengshen, *Dong Bei Qu Jian Li Shuan Zhuan Wang Di Jing Nien* (Beijing: Renmin Chupanshe, 1951), pp. 20-21.

55. *RMRB*, May 5, 1976, p. 1.

56. "Teng Hsiao-ping's Speech to the Party Central Political Bureau Enlarged Conference," *Chungkung Yen-chiu (Studies on Chinese Communism)* 15, no. 7 (July 15, 1981), 130.

CHAPTER 16

Public Opinion
and Political Communication

So far our discussion of the Chinese Communist political process has stressed the overwhelming role of the elites of the Communist party. This is as it should be since the Chinese Communist system, as with all Communist systems, is designed to give maximum discretion to the national elite. However, both the previous chapter on Chinese Communist policy-making process and other works of modern totalitarianism have pointed out that the public in a Communist nation does play a role in the political process.[1] The present chapter will focus specifically on public opinion in the Chinese Communist political system.

Generally speaking, public opinion in any nation is greatly affected by the overall political system, the communication system, and leadership.

THE OVERALL POLITICAL SYSTEM

To begin with, the conceptualization and organization of a political system affects public opinion significantly. It is the general system of politics that determines what opinion is allowed, how it is expressed, and with what effect. For example, in a democratic and representative system public opinion is ordinarily expressed through the parliament, parties, interest groups, and mass media. The underlying assumption of the democratic system is that people are expected to have opinions on public affairs and their opinions do matter. In many political systems, however, the forums of opinion such as parliament and the mass media have been turned around by the regime to air the views of the government. As a result, public opinion in the sense of spontaneous opinions of the people on any aspect of the community must be expressed in other channels, which are usually suppressed by the government.

Thus the role of public opinion in China is necessarily constrained by the essential elements of the Chinese Communist political system, to-wit:

1. The Communist party acquired political power by force of arms, not through ballot box.

2. The normative nature of the Communist party makes public opinion the object of Communist transformation.

3. The principle of unified leadership of the Communist party denies the autonomy of any other social group.

4. The ideological style of rule demands that all opinions conform to Marxism-Leninism-Mao Zedong thought as defined by the ruling faction of the Communist party.

The foregoing puts the relationship between the Communist party and the public opinion of China in a master-subject or teacher-pupil pattern. The Communist party regards itself as superior to the views of ordinary people. Thus members of the Communist party have often been instructed not to "sink to the level of the consciousness of general mass." Mao Zedong required Communist cadres to be good at dividing the mass into "the relatively active," "the intermediate," and "the relatively backward."[2] The task of every Communist cadre, according to Mao, is to unite with the active, win over the intermediate, and isolate the backward. In other words, the Communist party's attitude toward public opinion closely resembles fighting a battle.

The formal ideology of Marxism-Leninism further constrains the Chinese Communist party's treatment of public opinion. Central to the Marxist-Leninist view of public opinion is that the latter is class determined. Moreover, an equally important ideological tenet of Leninism is that the class consciousness of the proletariat is deficient and needs the Communist party to enhance it. So the Communist party is in a position to deny the legitimacy of any opinion in terms of class category or refuse to respond to opinions from the proletariat on account of the latter's "deficiency in class consciousness."

The attitudes of Chinese leaders toward the ideology further restrict the range of opinions that could be expressed openly in China. As we discussed earlier, Chinese Communist politics are of the "ideological style"—the leaders being emotionally committed to a comprehensive, explicit, and highly formalized ideology. Political action, be it speech or policy making, must *explicitly* conform to the formal ideology of Marxism-Leninism. This is in contrast to a system that is of pragmatic style, with implicit and informal sets of beliefs. Whether a political system is founded on an explicit or implicit ideological system has immediate bearing on public opinion. Sidney Verba, for example, wrote: "Once one's ultimate goals are made explicit it becomes more difficult to compromise them in a specific case. An implicit goal system allows more flexibility since the goals of the culture are not present as overt criteria for judging any policy, and so it is possible to justify a policy in terms of the expediencies of the situation without explicitly violating the cultural goals."[3] Under the rule of Mao, all issues or opinions were conceived of as representing a single scale, i.e., either socialist or capitalist. Naturally this unidimensionality restricted the range of legitimate opinions severely. Even when Communist leaders change their policy in order to meet situational crises, they have to justify it in terms of Marxist-Leninist precepts. When reinterpretation of Marxism-Leninism was required each time a Communist party such as the CPC repeatedly changed its party line, either the party or the ideology gradually lost its credence in the minds of the public.

THE POLITICAL-COMMUNICATION SYSTEM

Given the characteristics of the overall system, the forums of public opinion and political communication in China are closely regulated and controlled by the Communist party. The party regards itself as the "gatekeeper" of Chinese society and relegates to itself the prerogative of deciding what information and how much of it is to be made available to the public. Political communication is structured to enable the party to perform such a gatekeeping function.

We can divide the opinion forums or communication system of the PRC into two types, the formal-institutionalized and the informal-noninstitutionalized. The formal-institutionalized system is in turn divided into intra- and extraparty communication. The main difference between the formal and informal system of opinion expression and communication is that the formal system is legitimized (hence controlled) by the Communist party whereas the informal system is not legitimized by the party and is the object of Communist suppression. These divisions of communication and opinion forums are shown schematically in figure 16-1.

The Representative Organization: The Elite Forum

As dealt with in chapters 5, 6, and 8, the National People's Congress and the Chinese People's Political Consultative Conference are severely restricted as opinion forums. To be the deputies of these elite organizations is a form of political patronage by the Communist party. The social composition of the deputies is a reflection of the current party line. Only when the Communist party allowed it, as in 1956 and 1980, could or would the deputies of the NPC and CPPCC speak up, and their views were in conformity to the current line. There has been no institutionalized procedure for the deputies to maintain contact with their constituents. As a high-ranking Communist leader put it in 1981: "Specific provisions are lacking to ensure that people's deputies meet their constituents at regular intervals, solicit and reflect their opinions, and report their work to them."[4] Owing to lack of regular and frequent contact with their constituents, the deputies of the NPC and CPPCC cannot do as the parliamentarians in Western democracies do—aggregate the "raw" interests of the public into broad alternatives so that both the voters and policy makers can take action readily. Instead, we find that the deputies of the NPC and CPPCC, when opportunity avails, articulate raw interests simply as individual citizens of China. The "representation" function of the deputies is thus largely lost.

FIGURE 16-1   Divisions of communication and opinion forums in the PRC

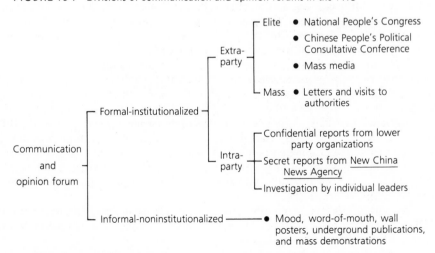

The Mass Media

The NPC and the CPPCC constitute neither an effective opinion forum representing the public nor a regular channel of communication linking the public with the Communist elite, since the functioning of these two organizations has been highly episodic. In contrast, the mass media in the PRC, like mass media everywhere, face the public of the PRC on a daily, and in broadcasting media an hourly, basis. Because of the power of the mass media in affecting public opinion, they have been made an appendage of the Communist party. The underlying assumption of the Communist party is that the social effect of news or information is much more important than truthfulness of content. To change society, according to the Communist viewpoint, one must first change the perspectives of the people. To control and manipulate information is to influence people's perspectives. Once the perspectives of the people have been changed (to conform to socialism), so goes this Communist philosophy, then they will create a new society and culture. Based on these conceptions, the Chinese Communists use mass media to affect public opinion instead of allowing the media to be an outlet of public opinion.

Accordingly, the system of mass media in the PRC is integrated with the formal bureaucracy of the Communist party and the government. The media are organized in a hierarchical pattern just as the Communist party is. At the apex of the media hierarchy stand the national media, which present the authoritative party line of the Central Committee of the CPC: (1) the newspaper *Renmin Ribao (People's Daily)*, (2) the journal *Hongqi (Red Flag)*, and (3) the news agency, Xinhuashe (New China News Agency). These comprise the commanding voice of the People's Republic, all other media being subordinated to these three. Top Communist leaders, including Mao before his death, often write commentaries and editorials under pseudonyms for the *People's Daily* and *Red Flag*. The New China News Agency (NCNA), the PRC's counterpart of the Soviet TASS, is *the* news gatekeeper of the PRC. The agency transmits all news from China to foreign nations and all foreign news to Chinese leaders and the public. Moreover, the agency also transmits all national news to provincial and local media. The NCNA thus controls the news or information "gate" for the Communist party. In addition, the NCNA assembles confidential foreign news reports to higher party leaders.[5] Sharing that authoritative status with the national press, though with somewhat less political emphasis, are the two broadcasting stations, the Central People's Radio Broadcasting Station (Radio Peking to the international audience) and the Central Television Broadcasting Station. Both are formally subordinated to the Central People's Government. But all of these are under the strict control of the Propaganda Department of the Central Committee of the CPC.

The national media structure is replicated at provincial and municipal levels. The Communist party of every province and municipality publishes a newspaper and a journal, representing the authoritative stand of the party. "It was regarded as a pretty sure guess that no important article could appear in provincial newspapers without the approval of the first Party secretary. Editorials in newspapers always present the official line and give the necessary guidance."[6] Every city in China, in turn, operates its own radio station, and some cities have television stations. All these media are naturally under the strict control of the Propaganda Department of the area's Communist party, which is in turn subordinated to the Propaganda Department of the National Central Committee of the CPC.

As part of its overall political structure, major parapolitical organizations all publish their newspapers. The ACFTU, for example, publishes *Gongren Ribao (Work-*

ers' Daily) and the Communist Youth League, *Zhongguo Qingnian Bao (China Youth Paper)*. The members of the CPPCC and the democratic parties are, in theory, represented by three newspapers: the *Guangming Ribao (Brightness Daily)*, *Wenhui Bao (Literary Paper)*, and *Dagong Bao (Impartial Paper)*. The first two are for intellectual and literary circles whereas *Dagong Bao* is for commercial and business readers. These papers do as their organizations do: serve as transmission belts from the Communist party to the members of these organizations. The editorial policy of these newspapers is in the hands of the party organization, sometimes known as the party fraction, inside each parapolitical organization. The party fraction is in turn subordinated to the propaganda department of the party committee in the area.

Thus in contrast to the mass media in Western democracies where the media are autonomous and often in an adversarial relationship with the government, the mass media in China are an integral part of the government. Underlying this contrast is the different history of the media in the West and in most developing nations. The mass media in the West developed from social process, reflecting the changing social intercourse of Western societies. Thus, according to Robert Park, the natural history of the press in the West began as a device for organizing gossip.[7] In contrast, the mass media in most developing nations, including China, began as a device, in the hands of a small group of radical intellectuals, for organizing nationalist revolution against colonial control. In other words, "politicization" and partisanship are the birthmarks of modern mass communication in China (or for that matter, in most developing nations).

Accordingly, the substance of the mass media in China is determined by the Communist party to serve its grand design of mobilizing and transforming society. Generally speaking the substance of Chinese mass media may be characterized as ideological, didactic, hortatory, and partisan. It is ideological, as all news content in the Chinese media is phrased in Marxist-Leninist terminology. Whatever is printed or spoken in the media must be *explicitly* put in the context of the Communist doctrine. It is didactic in that Chinese Communist media are also used as instructional tools for political or other purposes. Thus Chinese media publicize "model" persons, deeds, and organizations with the aim that the public at large will learn from these reports. It is hortatory in the sense that the communication in Chinese Communist media is designed specifically to persuade readers or audiences to accept the perspectives of the Communist party. The truthfulness of information is less important than the need to achieve "desirable" social effect. For example, Chinese Communist leader Hu Yaobang cautioned Chinese journalists in a 1982 speech on reporting about capitalist nations:

> We must take a solemn and cautious attitude toward reporting the capitalist world. We should be analytical and critical. Prettying [the capitalist nations] is absolutely not allowed, neither will the so-called objective reporting do. News reporting belongs to the realm of ideology so it has a class content. . . . We may report or even learn from, based on our own needs and situation, the advanced technology, management technique and results of scientific research of the capitalist nations. As to the social system and the decadent ideas [of the capitalist nations] we should absolutely not praise it.[8]

Finally, the content of Chinese media is partisan in that although all information is to be put in Marxist-Leninist context, specific interpretation of Marxism-Leninism is in the hands of whichever ruling faction of the party is currently in control. In chapter 13 we discussed how the present leaders of the Communist party redefined the meanings of the thought of Mao Zedong, class struggle, dictatorship of the proletariat, and forms of economic management. For Chinese citizens who wish to keep in step with the government, careful reading of the Communist press is important so to learn the new line each time a different group of leaders reaches the apex of power.

Since the Chinese media are a political tool in the hands of the Communist party, they do not report what is known in the West as social, or human-interest, news. Absent largely from Chinese media are reports on crime, accident, tourism, personalities, food, and other "gossipy" items that are part of the usual content in Western media. Instead, we find in Chinese media verbatim reports of party policy, program, speeches by party leaders, successful completion of production assignments in factories or farms, and superior deeds of Communists and world news slanted to favor the foreign policy of the current party leadership. It is clear that the Communist party wishes to structure the people's range of interest. But when something is absent from the Chinese media, that does not necessarily mean that the public is not interested in it. Rather, the information that is left out of the party-controlled media finds its way into the informal communication channels: rumor and covert publications.

The grand design of the Communist party to control and alter the perspectives of the Chinese people is thwarted, however, by the underdevelopment of the Chinese media. Take, for instance, newspaper circulation. There are 70 copies of newspapers per 1,000 people in China, the comparable figures for Taiwan and the United States being 120 and 300 (1970 figure) respectively.[9] In radio ownership, there are 50 radios for every 1,000 people in China, compared with 200 on Taiwan and 400 in the Soviet Union (1970 figure). With regard to television sets, there are 10 television sets for every 1,000 people in China, compared with 203 in Taiwan. A unique component of the Chinese media system is the loudspeaker system in the countryside, which is composed of regular radio stations at county seats, amplifying stations at townships (formerly communes), and loudspeakers in villages. By 1980 every county of China (2,300 altogether) had a radio station, every township (or commune) an amplifying station (the total number of townships or communes being 49,000 to 50,000), and 107 million loudspeakers in villages, amounting to 88 percent of all the villages.[10] This is an unprecedented penetration of the central authority to the countryside of China. However, the Chinese press and reports from former residents of China testify to the fact that a considerable number of speakers in the villages do not operate regularly owing to lack of repair and lack of interest on the part of local peasants. This is substantiated by the fact that whenever the national authority in Peking has wanted to transmit a policy widely in the countryside, it almost always had to begin with a campaign to reinstall the speakers in the villages.[11]

Undoubtedly the most serious flaw in the circulation of mass media in China is the relative isolation of the countryside. First of all, most of China's 200 million illiterates are in the countryside, where only a third of the counties have achieved universal education. Most of the rural illiterates are women since 70 percent of the total number of illiterates are women.[12] In 1981, of the 2,300 counties in China only 51 had published their own newspapers. Of the total circulation of newspapers and journals only 10 percent are in the countryside. Thus most of the rural population, which amounts to 80 percent of the total Chinese population, are *not even reached* by Communist propaganda, let alone persuaded. As we discussed in a previous chapter, most of the programs of the Communist party were implemented in the countryside through administrative measures by cadres, not through the "raised consciousness" of the peasants.

So far, the opinion forums that we have described—the representative organizations and the mass media—belong to the elites of China. Their linkage with the masses of China is at best intermittent. For ordinary Chinese citizens the most direct means to air views that are regarded by the Communist party as legitimate are letters and visits to the press and higher authorities, most preferably the authorities in Peking.

Mass Forums: Letters and Visits

Writing letters to the newspapers or leaders is one means of communication for the masses that the Chinese Communist regime explicitly approves. As early as 1950 when the People's Republic had just been established, the Communist party initiated a letter-writing drive among the public, ostensibly to enable the party to correct its mistakes in the spirit of criticism and self-criticism. It is clear that the real purpose of the letter-writing campaign of 1950 was public relations, i.e., the Communist party's desire to create a favorable image for itself among the public. Since then the CPC has launched letter-writing drives in times of repression and in times of serious social and economic breakdown. Letter-writing drives during a period of repression are designed to make people spy on each other. For example, letters from the public were encouraged during the Suppression of Hidden Counterrevolutionaries campaign of 1955 and the Anti-Rightists campaign of 1957-58. During years of serious social and economic breakdown, such as 1962 and 1977-80, the Communist party promotes letter writing in order to stem mass disaffection. For Chinese Communist leaders, letters perform four important functions: information, feedback, surveillance, and building popular support for the regime. To Chinese citizens the chief asset of letters is the autonomy they afford the writer. People can choose whichever issues that concern them and express themselves in relative privacy.

From 1978 to 1980 a great outpouring of letters to the Communist party (mostly provincial and national leaders) took place in China. In the first eight months of 1978, as the Chinese public followed closely the victorious struggle of party pragmatists over the leftists, letters to the authorities increased thirty-fold.[13] In 1979 alone the Central Committee of the Communist party and the Chinese national government received 1.082 million letters, "one third of them asking for aid with problems of incorrect policies."[14] By the end of 1982 the Central Commission for Discipline Inspections of the national Communist party had received (since 1979) 7.65 million letters and interviewed 2.63 million visitors.[15] The *People's Daily* receives, on an average, 2,000 letters a day.[16]

The chief reason for the massive volume of letters to the higher authorities in 1978-80 was the political persecution during the ten years of the Cultural Revolution, which according to the Communist party's own admission victimized 100 million people, one-tenth of the population.[17] The letters to the authorities dealt largely with personal matters. For example, in 1979 the letters to the party first secretary of Henan Province, one of the leftist strongholds during the Cultural Revolution, fell into six categories (in descending order): persecution of the letter writers during the Cultural Revolution, factionalism among local party leaders, criticism of provincial party leaders, request for job adjustment, unlawful and violent deeds of local party cadres, and undesirable developments in production and management.[18] The letters to the press, however, are screened before they are published. The *People's Daily,* for example, forwards most of the letters it receives to appropriate authorities. So the published ones, like the speeches made in the NPC and CPPCC, are designed to support current party line. They deal with matters such as poor quality of products, bad manners of public functionaries, environmental destruction and pollution, and negligence of local officials.

Overall the role of letters in the Chinese Communist political system is very similar to the role of letters in the Soviet Union. As Fainsod put it: "The letters provided one of the few direct links which the leadership had with grass-roots experience; the outpourings of the letter-writers and the responses they elicited represented the nearest approximation to a spontaneous dialogue between the leaders and their subjects."[19]

Another outlet for expression of opinion is a visit to higher authorities. However, visits to authorities, especially to the national leaders in Peking, are usually a last resort. There are several reasons. Unlike letter writing, a visit is a highly conspicuous and identifiable action and thus invites prompt reprisal by local authorities. Second, travel in China for most Chinese citizens, especially those in rural areas, is not easy for both political and economic reasons.[20] One frequently reads about Chinese citizens having to sell all their belongings and even, in some cases, deserting wives and children in order to go to Peking to make a petition. Moreover, there is no guarantee that the visitor will be received by national authorities. The *People's Daily* reported a case on August 8, 1979, in which a member of a rural commune had made repeated visits to the provincial authorities for fifteen years in order to right the wrongs done to him by commune party officials. Whereas the Communist party unequivocally approves the letter writing, its attitude toward visits is ambivalent. A high Communist official wrote: "We are for solving problems locally and do not advocate people's leaving their homes, carrying their children, and traveling over long distances to Peking to visit higher authorities. However, when local solution is not possible and the masses have descended on Peking, then we cannot just shut doors in their faces."[21] From the vantage point of authorities, visits have the potentiality of creating a "social contagion." They bring, in a dramatic way, disrepute to the Communist party and can overload the system. From late 1978 and through the spring of 1979 a large number of people gathered in Peking petitioning national leaders for justice in their personal misfortunes. "During August–September 1979, an average of seven hundred persons arrived in Beijing [Peking] every day appealing to the government for help."[22] Not all visitors came for individual problems; sometimes delegates were sent to Peking by special groups such as the case involving a farm in Yunnan Province where most members were urban youths sent forcibly by the Communist party in 1966–76 to the countryside.[23] Apparently a great number among the visitors to Peking in 1979 consisted of displaced groups. The Communist party of China had, over the years, forcibly repatriated millions of urban residents to the countryside or frontier areas because of the inability of the urban economy to employ them. In 1960–61 in the wake of the disaster of the Great Leap Forward, for example, some 20 million members of the urban labor force were returned to the countryside. In 1966–76 a total of 17 million youths were sent to the countryside and frontier areas. Beginning in 1977, 10 million of these youths abandoned their rural and frontier settlements and returned to the cities of their origin, thus creating unprecedented urban unemployment.[24] Since some of these problems were rooted in the Chinese economic system, many visitors to Peking did not receive satisfactory responses from the government; the danger of hostile outbursts was real in Peking in 1979. To defuse the situation quickly, the Chinese government dispatched more than one thousand officials from Peking to various localities to take prompt remedial actions in each locality, so to stem the tide of visitors to Peking. Here is a good example of a totalitarian system that has been "overloaded" as a result of its overall social and economic policy. Moreover, the danger of overloading the system and the possible "social-contagion" effect of the stream of visitors to Peking, combined with the ascendancy of a less radical ruling group, finally produced a goal-changing result. After 1979, the Communist party terminated the policy of forcing urban youths to settle in the countryside. That, in turn, compelled the party to make more changes in the economic structure. To solve the employment of millions of urban youths, shops and stores owned by private entrepreneurs have been allowed to return. Since 1980 the rate of growth of employment in the newly revived private sector has outstripped that in the public sector. Thus in this case the mass response produced a "goal-changing feedback" that the elites of the NPC or CPPCC have not been able to achieve.

The foregoing deals with the opinion forums in China that have been approved by the Communist party to operate openly. The opinions expressed intermittently by the representative organizations, the letters, and the visits all deal with the operative aspects of the Communist system, not with goals. "Goal-seeking feedback" is the term coined by Karl Deutsch to describe these opinions. It is feedback that is aimed to accomplish the existing goals.[25] Opinions that might bring a change in the goals of the Communist party cannot be expressed in the forums that we have discussed so far. The Communist party is undoubtedly aware of the fact that whatever is expressed in the approved forums is but a small part of the genuine opinions of Chinese people. Denied legitimate expression, much of the genuine opinion of the Chinese public finds its way in numerous noninstitutionalized channels. The Communist party is concerned with these opinions because of their possible social effects. So a separate intraparty communication system, which reports to the top leaders on the critical opinions of society, exists. Thus in the PRC as in the USSR, a paradoxical situation results. The Soviet dissident Andrei Amalrik put it well: "It is . . . paradoxical that the regime should devote enormous effort to keep everyone from talking and then waste further effort to learn what people are talking about and what they want."[26]

Intraparty Communication

To learn what people are talking about and what they want, the Chinese Communist party depends on several covert channels of opinion gathering. The first is of course the regular bureaucratic channel of the party itself and other organizations, especially the Public Security Ministry. For example, during the food-crisis period of 1961–62, rural party organizations were required to submit reports to higher party leaders on the "ideological condition" of peasants, the rumors and complaints of peasants, the conduct of cadres, and the activity of "class enemies" (former landlords, rich peasants, rightists, counterrevolutionaries).[27] However, this routine bureaucratic feedback is often distrusted by higher authorities for, as is with every lower bureaucracy, there is a built-in constraint in the truthfulness of its feedback. Too critical a feedback from lower leaders is virtually political suicide. So there is the natural tendency of local leaders to anticipate what upper leaders wish to hear and then manipulate their reports accordingly. That is why in modern totalitarian systems we find that often national leaders rely more on police reports which, however, tend to exaggerate the negative sides of the social condition so as to justify more police work.[28] In our discussion on public security, we mentioned that Mao Zedong paid special attention to materials submitted by the Public Security Ministry.

A second major covert channel of communication is the numerous reports stamped with the phrase "For internal reference," especially reports from the correspondents of the New China News Agency and the *People's Daily*. These correspondents enjoy high status and act as the eyes and ears of the top-ranking party leaders. Their visits to every corner of the nation result in two types of reports, one for mass consumption, which is always positive and hortatory, and the other for internal circulation, which deals with the critical aspects of society.

A third channel of opinion gathering is, as we already mentioned in the previous chapter on policy making, visits and investigations by top-level leaders in time of crisis when quick remedial action is required. National leaders, including the late Liu Shaoqi, conducted a number of such special surveys in 1962–65 in order to find out the true conditions of society. In 1961, for example, the current leader Deng Xiaoping took charge of a large investigation team, descended upon the northeastern city of Shengyang, and conducted an in-depth and comprehensive survey of every aspect of the city. Reportedly, Deng concluded that Shengyang had three outstanding characteristics: shortages, disrepair, and dirtiness.[29] What is noteworthy is that these elite surveys are all retrospective and are fraught with political consequences. There were always suspicions on the part of Mao that other leaders used these surveys to prevent him from realizing his "socialism."

A fourth channel of opinion gathering, which the Communist party used only sparingly before the death of Mao, was commissioning scholars to conduct surveys. As early as 1941 Mao had expressed his contempt for the inability of the "immature Chinese bourgeoisie" to provide reliable social data for the Communist party.[30] After 1949 sociology and political science as academic learning were abolished and were not reinstated until recently. In 1956 and 1959, however, some Chinese sociologists and economists (who had received their education before 1949) were permitted to survey some areas of the countryside, mainly about the results of collectivization. In 1959, for example, the Economic Research Institute, headed by the late economist Sung Yefang, was allowed by the party to study peasants' opinions on communal mess halls, which were regarded as an essential part of Mao's people's communes. Sung's report was not received well by the leftists within the party for he found that the peasants disliked the mess halls as a permanent institution, though they accepted them on a temporary basis. Sung's survey was subsequently denounced as antisocialist, though Sung maintained that Mao had not endorsed that judgment.[31] The case of Sung points up again the political risk of passing on critical feedback to higher leaders in the totalitarian context.

Finally, after the death of Mao and the start of reform under current party leadership, opinion polls have been used to learn about the attitudes of youths, students, and workers. Most of these polls, however, have not been made public. Their results are reported in confidential internal publications. For example, the confidential *Qingnian Yanjiu (Research on Youth)* publishes surveys of youth attitudes toward various topics such as the problems of sex and juvenile crime and outlook on life. These studies are done by universities, individual scholars, and the Communist Youth League branches.[32]

Thus the Communist party has a significant number of covert channels for opinion gathering. But the irony is that these channels are frequently ignored. In February 1959, for example, amid the growing evidence of the disastrous consequences of the Great Leap Forward, which must have been reflected in the confidential NCNA publication, *For Internal Reference*, Mao stated: "The *For Internal Reference* from the NCNA should be read *but not too frequently*. For instance, in 1957 it reported about the frenzied attacks [on the party] by the rightists at Peking University; the situation [there] seems to be rather serious. Well, Chen Po-ta [Chen Boda] went there to take a personal look and reported that it was not too bad. . . . the *For Internal Reference* reports history. It should be read but not too frequently" (emphasis added).[33] The special surveys conducted by Liu Shaoqi and Deng Xiaoping in 1961-65 were later used as incriminating evidence against them during the Cultural Revolution. Thus we see yet another paradox in the communication system of totalitarian societies. At first the party suppresses genuine public opinion and then it makes great effort, in a covert way, to find out what people's thoughts are. However, when these thoughts are collected in covert communication channels, they are often ignored. The Chinese Communist case is certainly not unique; these paradoxes are quite common in authoritarian political systems. Bushkoff wrote: "Aggressive leaders, confident of success and eager for victory, hardly provide the neutral atmosphere in which intelligence can be gathered honestly. Resenting bad news, they denounce those who bear it, and find solace instead in a world of illusions and scapegoats."[34]

NONINSTITUTIONALIZED COMMUNICATION

As we have stated on several occasions, the Communist suppression or ignoring of genuine public opinion simply means that the latter is expressed in nonofficial and informal, but by no means insubstantial, channels of communication. A most important indication of the importance of these informal communications and expressions of opinion is the anxiety of the Communist regime toward them.

Mood

Perhaps the informal opinion that is most pervasive and most resistant to suppression is public mood. When necessary conditions are obtained, mood can be quickly activated into action. Thus public mood has always been the concern of any authoritarian regime. In China the mood of the public is variously referred to in the mass media as people's "spiritual countenance" (*jingshen mienmao*), "social trend" (*sichao*), or "wind" (*feng*). Moreover, these references are always used in a negative way. In other words, whenever the Communist media refer to a certain social trend it is always for the purpose of countering it.

In September 1955, after the establishment of the higher Agricultural Producers' Cooperatives in the countryside, Mao noted in a conference that there was "tension in the countryside."[35] In January 1957 Mao spoke about "a current of rightism moving below heaven and above earth" and said that "the wind of deviation in society must be hit and suppressed."[36] After the people's commune movement, Mao reported in March 1959 that "quite a bit of tension exists between us and peasants over some matters."[37] In December 1964 Mao stated in a conference that he had learned from others that "the situation was bad, and that there was such a general atmosphere."[38]

During the food crisis of 1961 a low mood was prevalent among the general public and soldiers. Lo Ruiqing, who was then chief of staff of the PLA, declared: "There is a distinct absence of the cheerful, vigorous spirit that makes group life bearable. The men . . . are truly 'not active as a dragon nor lively as a tiger' but dull and inanimate. An army with its men going around with puckered brows and unhappy faces, weighed down by an air of heavy moodiness, cannot have strong fighting power."[39]

The incessant conflicts among top party leaders and their consequent reversals in policies since 1966 had naturally affected the mood of the public, particularly that of cadres. The outbreak of the riot in Tiananmen Square in April 1976, the subsequent dismissal of Deng Xiaoping, and the imminent death of Mao resulted in a wave of pessimism and gloom in China. To counter this, the *People's Daily* editorialized:

> The bourgeois revolutions in England, France and the United States had taken, respectively, forty-eight, eighty-six, and about a hundred years. . . . The proletariat aims at the total destruction of the bourgeoisie, all exploiting classes and systems. Naturally it will take longer time and experience more twists and reversals. . . . Class struggle, Line struggle, one after another; this is entirely in accordance with law. There is no need to be alarmed, let alone troubled.[40]

The mood of the public in China underwent a dramatic change after the purge of the Gang of Four and the institution of a new economic policy by the Deng regime. American journalist Fox Butterfield reported from Peking in August 1977 that a sense of humor had returned to the Chinese:

> For a foreigner traveling in China, it is always difficult to penetrate beyond the surface of life, to do more, as the Chinese saying goes, than "view flowers from horseback." But almost everywhere in China these days it is possible to see signs of the changes that have begun to transform the lives of the country's 900 million people since the death last year of Mao Tse-tung and the arrest of his widow Chiang Ching.
>
> The new sense of humor is one such change. Now people are also more candid, relaxed and openly interested in the kinds of things familiar to Americans, from better education and higher wages to buying television sets and taking vacations.[41]

However, the initial euphoria after the arrest of the Gang of Four did not last long. The promised changes came very slowly and were met with opposition by the left. The public mood in the PRC changed to a fundamental questioning of the ideological and organizational bases of the Communist system. This mood is expressed in the "crises of faith, confidence and trust."[42] The most active and militant groups in Chinese society turned their mood into political protest in 1978–79. Naturally public mood, like other forms of public opinion, is subject to variation according to social characteristics such as age, occupation, and locality. Lacking survey data, we cannot be more precise about the mood of various subgroups in Chinese society.

Word of Mouth: Side-Lane News

An informal mass medium as pervasive and resistant to official suppression as mood is word of mouth, which is often misleadingly referred to as *rumor*. The Chinese term for this mass medium is probably most apt—*side-lane news (xiaodao xiaoxi)*. The word *rumor* suggests falsity. But scholars who have done research have pointed out that in the real world rumors are, more often than not, far from false. According to Ithiel de Sola Pool: "Experiments have . . . shown that in free, real-life situations people do not pass on rumors unless they make sense to them. The result is that the rumors, as they are relayed, are generally corrected for plausibility and are delivered to target persons who can use and understand them."[43] Similarly, Shibutani points out that the notion of rumor being used for emotional satisfaction regardless of objective truth is not valid. Rumor is simply another form of collective decision making in which personal "wish-fulfillment is definitely secondary."[44] Rumor, to use Shibutani's words, is "improvised news" and arises whenever and wherever institutionalized channels of communication are no longer available or credible.

Totalitarian regimes such as the PRC provide a fertile soil for the rise of rumors in society. First, all public media of communication have been monopolized by the authorities. Second, politics is conducted in secrecy with no meaningful role for the public to play. Third, though without any meaningful participation in the process, the public is affected directly by the outcome of elitist politics of secrecy. Whereas in democracies rumors arise only in extraordinary situations when institutionalized media are not available, in totalitarian regimes rumor, or word-of-mouth transmission of news, is a daily affair. Numerous eyewitness accounts show that rumor, or word-of-mouth communication, is a very prominent mass medium in China. Even the official media have acknowledged the wide circulation of side-lane news in China. The following is a dramatic account, published in the *People's Daily,* of the way the president of Peking University, Dr. Zhou Beiyuan, learned about the arrest of the Gang of Four. The time was early October 1976 and the place, the campus residence of Dr. Zhou:

> . . . Enter a middle-age teacher.
> He is an intimate comrade of Zhou Beiyuan. In these days they would not talk even when they met; all they did was nod to each other. He has not come to Zhou's house for a long time.
> "What is up?"
> There is excitement in the face of this teacher.
> He looks around and then tightly grabs the hands of Zhou Beiyuan, whispering: "They have been arrested!"
> "What?" Mrs. Zhou joins them.
> "I just heard that the Center had learned that they were about to move [alleged coup by the Gang of Four]. So, the night before yesterday Premier Hua and Marshal Ye arrested them: Jiang Qing, Yao Wenyuan, Zhang Chungqiao and Wang Hungwen, all four of them!"
> Daughter of Zhou exclaims: "That's great! That's just great!"
> Zhou Beiyuan: "Is that true?"
> "News from underground," says Mrs. Zhou, "not credible."
> Daughter of Zhou objects: "On the contrary, the news from the official media is often not credible nowadays. More often than not it is the underground news that is true, though its details might not be entirely correct."[45]

Like mood, the rise of side-lane news in China is closely related to the social, political, and economic situations that mainland Chinese have experienced over the years. In 1962, for example, a Fujian County party document revealed that rumor in the countryside made "hostile" elements "think that the world had changed."[46] The domestic situation in 1960–62 was the right one for the rise of side-lane news as famine stalked the countryside and severe food shortages debilitated the urban population.

The Cultural Revolution was another extraordinary situation that gave rise to rumors. The seemingly endless purges and policy reversals after 1969 made China a land of side-lane news. In 1971, for example, the disappearance of Lin Biao was the substance of most rumors. It was reported in November of that year:

> All over southern China, peasants and workers are openly discussing the fate of Marshal Lin Biao. . . . The astonishing feature of these reports from a great variety of districts is the lack of any confusion about who was involved in Lin's downfall and the date on which it took place. Rarely is common gossip so unani-

mous, and even less frequently does the Chinese man-in-the-street identify with precision the rank of those he names as Lin's fellow conspirators in a plot against Mao.[47]

When the power struggle between the leftists and party pragmatists gathered momentum in 1974-76, rumors again became rampant in China. Rumors were then fed by wall posters, the content of which was copied by readers who then relayed it by word of mouth. The earlier rumors about Lin Biao's death and his alleged plot to assassinate Mao seem to have colored later rumors. In 1974 rumors about political assassination were common. Joseph Llelyveld reported from Hong Kong in February 1974:

> Rumors of at least four political shootings have made their way out of China in the last five years. All of them may be baseless but their persistence testifies to a fear that political struggle in the Chinese leadership may not always be confined to the realm of ideological debate.[48]

The death of Zhou Enlai in January 1976 provoked another spate of rumors on mainland China about Zhou's alleged "last will." At times four versions of Zhou's "will" circulated in various parts of China. But journalist David Bonavia perceptively observed: "The important thing now is not whether Zhou actually left such a testament, but the fact that large numbers of people in China believe he did. The different versions circulating seem to reflect both what people thought of Zhou and his policies, as well as their own thoughts about the way China needs to be run."[49] Rumors, wrote Shibutani, "are usually a better index of the preoccupations of a public than most other forms of verbalization."[50]

That the CPC had paid close attention to rumors is borne out in the open polemics on "counterrevolutionary public opinion" in April 1976 both before and immediately after the riot at Tiananmen Square. Chinese newspapers then referred regularly to the "rise of rumors in society." The most harmful effect of these rumors, stated the *People's Daily,* was to mislead people to regard the ideological question as "mere sectarian struggle for power." It is clear from this that the "rumors" in 1976 were not "false beliefs" but "beliefs that are inconvenient for the regime in power."

The prominence of word-of-mouth communication was so widespread in 1974-76 that a semiprofessional corps of "inside dopesters" appeared in China. One report stated:

> Some diffused the different opinions inside the Party Committee to the masses outside without any sense of shame. On the contrary they are proud of doing this. Some enjoyed talking the so-called "inside information" as soon as they learned it. They damage the prestige of the Party Committee and hurt unified leadership by the party.[51]

The significant role of the side-lane ("byroad") news in China was pointed out by a former resident of the PRC to Miriam London and Ivan London:

> American scholars should really try to understand that America is a democracy and news in the United States appears in newspapers. . . . [In China] every news release has gone through numerous stages of censorship. What comes out is in stereotyped format, is always and only in the interest of the powerholders, and

has with time lost all credibility. . . . However, byroad news, which always comes from the top, is informative about the political situation and is backed by facts, which are confirmed by subsequent events.[52]

At the beginning of 1983, however, the *People's Daily* declared victory over side-lane news, which is said to be no longer in vogue in China.[53] If so, this is largely due to a degree of stability in the leadership after 1980 and the fact that the mass media itself began to acknowledge many critical aspects of Chinese society and politics, such as the mistakes of Mao, corruption and privileges among cadres, and the inferior production system in China. Thus it is the side-lane news that is the victor, for by its very existence it has forced the media controlled by the party to publicize facts that have been circulating through side-lane news for sometime.

Wall Poster: Dazibao

The informal channels of opinion such as public mood and side-lane news that we have described so far not only prove that there is much genuine public opinion in China that is not reflected in the official mass media but also indicate that the informal opinion has a distinct structure of its own, in terms of explicitness and concreteness. Compared with mood, for example, the side-lane news is more explicit and concrete in opinion substance and expression. Ascending the ladder of explicity and concreteness is another mass medium, the "wall poster," which is sometimes translated as "big-character poster" (*dazibao*). Actually it is more accurate and faithful to its original meaning to translate *dazibao* into "big-letter newspaper." In terms of its format, the wall poster in China is a crossbreed of written notes and graffiti. That is, Chinese citizens write their opinions on a piece of paper—often old newspapers—in broad letters with the traditional Chinese brush and stick it up on a wall so that passersby can see it. This is truly a "mass paper" in that individuals have complete freedom to choose the topic, write in private, and then publicize it. The wall poster thus substitutes for the official printed media.

For more than two decades, from 1957 to 1979, the wall poster was used by Chinese citizens whenever conditions permitted. It was first used by university students, especially those in Peking, during the Hundred Flowers Blooming campaign of 1957. The wall posters were used by the youth then to protest to the one-party dictatorship of the CPC.[54] The effectiveness of the posters in mobilizing opinion both impressed and shocked the Communist party. Thus after 1957, the Communist party sought to use the poster to serve the interest of the government. Mao, for example, stated:

> *Dazibao* is a good thing. Let us take it over. It is better to use *dazibao* to carry out rectification in factories. The more of them, the better. *Dazibao*, like language, is classless. . . . *Dazibao* . . . is a light weapon, like rifles, pistols or machine guns. Newspapers . . . are like airplanes and artillery. . . .[55]

From 1957 until the suppression of the posters in late 1979, almost every political campaign in China was accompanied by an upsurge of posters, which appeared on university campuses, factory grounds, and street corners. But as Mao suggested, the Communist party took the poster over to use it for partisan purposes. So after 1957 two types of posters appeared in China, one clearly a weapon of the party and the other still in the hands of Chinese citizens. The latter, however, must ride on the coattails of the former. Whenever the party sponsored a campaign of posters for its own purpose, we witness an upsurge of posters reflecting the spontaneous opinions of the public. This became more and more evident, as the leftists of the CPC used posters to attack the party establishment from the beginning of the Cultural Revolution to the end of the left in 1979.

Posters, in terms of their substance, are generally of three types. The first type is clearly an extension of the factional struggle inside the CPC, so this category of posters attacked hitherto sacred figures such as Liu Shaoqi during the Cultural Revolution (posters with the title: "Liu Shaoqi Is the Number One Revisionist in Our Country!"). That these are officially instigated posters can be readily proved in that only this category of posters is reported in the Chinese news media. During the struggle for succession period in 1976-77, the officially inspired posters would name party leaders, such as Deng Xiaoping, whom many party rank and file would like to see restored to power.

The mass-inspired posters are primarily of two categories, those dealing with individual matters (personal misfortunes or misconduct of individual officials) or in-depth commentaries of the Chinese Communist political system. The latter was one of the chief media of the dissidents in China. The long poster that appeared in the city of Canton in November 1974 signed with the pseudonym Li Yizhe is a case in point. Entitled "Concerning Socialist Democracy and Legal System," this poster was unique in two ways. First, its length. The poster was said to have "extended for a hundred yards in length" and "contained no less than sixty-seven sheets of news-print paper." Second, it was unique in its content, for it was a comprehensive critique of the political system under Chinese Communism.[56] Much had been done to prepare this poster, as stated by the author. Li claimed that the document had been written on September 13, 1973, and a revised version was completed on December 12 of the same year. It was then circulated underground before it was posted in the public on November 10, 1974. In terms of its content, the poster by Li is a rambling critique of various aspects of the Communist regime such as the growth of a new class, cult of personality, official's nepotism, and Lin Biao's dictatorship. This poster is no longer what Mao called a light weapon but, like newspapers in their clout, "artillery and airplanes." According to an eyewitness, Li's poster created a traffic jam in the city as tens of thousands of people congregated to read it. Some wrote on the poster: "You have said it well! You have expressed what my heart wanted to say!" Others wrote on the margin of the poster: "Right! My own experience is just like yours." Even more people copied the poster so it could be transmitted to others. The local party authorities did not effectively silence Li until March 1975.[57]

That Li was able to publicize his poster in late 1974 was due to the renewed factional struggle between the leftists (Gang of Four) and the party pragmatists headed by Deng Xiaoping, who had been rehabilitated by Mao in 1973. Before Li's poster appeared, Peking had already witnessed a wave of officially (i.e., by the leftists) instigated posters attacking Deng's followers. Thus Li was able to capitalize on the political instability in China in 1974 to air his views. What is more significant about Li's poster is that actually Li was a collective name of three young men whose education had been disrupted by the Cultural Revolution. They were disillusioned by the factional conflicts and other aspects of Chinese Communist society. While workers in a factory they organized an informal group, and the poster represented their group opinion. Thus Li's poster not only revealed that group dynamics, *independent* of Communist regimentation, continued in China but also that a new generation of Chinese had come of age under Communist rule. This new and young generation is fearless and most disillusioned with the Communist regime.

The golden opportunity for posters came in November 1978 when the current party leader Deng Xiaoping mobilized public opinion to overcome the remnant leftists in the party Center, which was then in the crucial meeting—the third plenum of the Eleventh Central Committee. The trickle of posters that had appeared after Mao's death in Peking, Shanghai, and some other cities now suddenly mushroomed, especially in Peking.[58] A brick wall, originally known as the *xidan* wall near a bus station in Peking, became known as Democracy Wall since all the major posters were found there. Students, petitioners, workers, soldiers and, above all, Western correspondents congregated in front of this wall to read the posters, the topics of which now became, more and more, fundamental critiques of the Communist system. Criticism of Mao, demand for democracy, denunciation of the "Fascist dictatorship" practiced by the leftists, and other similar topics attracted large crowds. As usual, people read, copied, and passed along the substance of the posters. Democracy Wall soon became the center of youth dissent as underground journals printed by dissidents were sold there. The famed dissident Wei Jingshen circulated his journal, *Exploration,* in which he called for a "fifth modernization—democracy." In the meantime, a social contagion took place as thousands of petitioners and demonstrators streamed into Peking. Elsewhere in China in provincial capitals, posters appeared and protests took place. Deng's use of public opinion for partisan purposes threatened the entire Communist regime.

So in April 1979 the Communist party commenced a campaign of suppression of posters and repression of "human rightists" in Peking and elsewhere. The CPC announced the limits of speech; all speeches and actions against the four principles— "socialism, proletarian dictatorship, leadership of the Communist party, and Marxism-Leninism-Mao Zedong thought"—were outlawed and punishable by "physical labor, education, and discipline." Mass arrests of youth dissidents lasted through the year of 1979. In September 1980 the National People's Congress, at the "request" of the CPC, abolished the four rights hitherto guaranteed by the Chinese constitution: "speaking out freely, airing views fully, holding great debates, and writing big-character posters." To compensate for the suppression of youth dissent the Communist party unprecedentedly published verbatim the questioning and criticism by deputies of the National People's Congress and the Chinese People's Political Consultative Conference. The speeches in these elite forums were safer than the posters and underground journals.

Though suppressed by the Communist party, the wall poster, like the side-lane news, scored a victory. The wall poster made the Communist party use it, too, a forcible "channel sharing"—itself a measure of failure of Communist-controlled mass media. Second, the wall poster exposed effectively the other side of the Chinese Communist society for all in the world to see. Third, the wall poster, in conjunction with side-lane news compelled the official media to acknowledge many social and economic problems in China and, unwittingly, granted the elite forums a rare opportunity to air their views.

Underground Publications

The upsurge of the posters in Peking and elsewhere in China in 1978-79 was accompanied by the appearance of underground publications, the Chinese equivalent to the *samizdat* in the Soviet Union. These were journals published by dissenting youth groups in China. At their height, there were around fifty such publications in Peking alone.[59] At first, these journals were appropriately called "publications among the people" (*minjian chubanwu*) or "spontaneous publications" (*zifa chubanwu*) because unlike the mass media, they were not controlled by the CPC and did not reflect the orchestrated opinions of the elite. That these publications emerged in China after the death of Mao is hardly surprising, given the existence of a large number of educated and disillusioned youths in China. Moreover, the post-Mao underground publications were precipitated by the Red Guard publications during the Cultural Revolution. Thus just like the medium of posters, the underground publications were the unwitting by-product of officially sponsored Red Guard papers that Mao had used in 1967–69 to intimidate his real or imaginary enemies inside the Communist party.

The circulation of these publications is necessarily limited, partly because of the official monopoly of all printing facilities and partly because of police repression. Fox Butterfield wrote an eyewitness account of the production of one such publication in Peking, the *April Fifth Forum (April Fifth* referred to the mass riot against Mao and his leftist disciples in Peking in 1976):

> Few of them had more than a high school education. But in their spare time they had been laboriously using a primitive mimeograph machine to print *The April Fifth Forum* and then sell the copies at Democracy Wall. The old wooden-frame machine sat on a bench. Each page had to be copied by hand on a cloth matrix. Then a sheet of paper was placed beneath and an inked cylinder roller over the matrix, printing the magazine one page at a time. Still they had managed to churn out 1,000 copies a month of the fifty-to-sixty page journal.[60]

Consequently, many of the journals were barely legible. Nevertheless it was a tribute to the young editors of these journals that, according to eye-witness accounts, they were quickly sold out when they appeared in front of Democracy Wall.[61]

It is important to note that though the underground journals in Peking were the most well-known both inside and outside of China, they existed in many cities of China. Indeed, the very first post-Mao underground journal was published in Guiyang city, capital of the southwestern province of Guizhou, a backward area where many educated youths were forcibly sent by the Communist party during the 1960s and 1970s. Moreover, on September 14, 1980, editors of several underground journals gathered in the city of Canton and declared the formation of the Chinese Association of People's Publications. The eventual fate of these publications was the same as the poster. An official campaign of suppression and arrest was commenced in late 1979. By June 1981 most of the underground publications had disappeared, and most of the prominent dissenters had been imprisoned.[62]

Since the underground publications were in the class of countermedia, their content was designed to crack the official monopoly of information. Thus in the underground publications we find political commentaries that subjected the Communist system to a fundamental and comprehensive critique, exposé of conditions that the official media glossed over, such as inhuman treatment of political prisoners, news about dissenters and their activities elsewhere in China, international news that the official media either ignored or distorted—for instance, the workers' movement in Poland—and finally literary works devoid of political propaganda. These topics corresponded closely to those in the Soviet *samizdat*.[63] Both testified to the existence of an intelligent, critically minded, and concerned public in totalitarian societies. Moreover, this group is a postrevolution generation, not the so-called remnants of the bourgeoisie. The dissenters in China were predominantly young men and women who grew up under Communist rule. Some of the editors of the underground journals were sons of high-ranking party officials, Wei Jingshen being the best example. A number of them had at one time been enthusiastic supporters of Mao. Their participation in the Cultural Revolution and personal experience in the countryside made them question and ultimately oppose the Communist system.[64]

Though both the posters and the underground publications lasted only for a while, they served their purpose. First of all, the posters and the underground journals broke the pluralistic ignorance in Chinese society. By that we mean that the political repression of the Communist party often results in a situation in which people are not aware of other people's true feelings since everyone puts on a mask in dealing with others for fear of official informers. The social atomization that follows political repression is what a totalitarian regime desires. Now the posters and the dissenters' journals informed Chinese citizens that their concerns and opinions were shared by others. Second, the posters and underground journals informed the world of the other side of Chinese politics and society, which hitherto had been hidden behind the facade of official orchestration. Finally, though the Communist party might have been successful in suppressing the channels of dissent such as posters and underground publications, it will not succeed in stamping out dissent since the social base for the rise of side-lane news, posters, and underground publications still exists. As long as that is true, channels other than posters and covert journals will carry the views of dissenters. The campaign "against spiritual pollution" that the CPC initiated in 1983 is a case in point. The CPC will be fighting a continuous war with the "guerrillas" of Chinese public opinion.

Demonstrations

Of all the informal channels of public opinion in China, certainly the most explicit and concrete form is public protest and demonstration. Unbeknown to most Westerners, demonstrations by various social groups in China have been continuous in the PRC since the mid-1950s.

We can view the demonstrations in the PRC first in a developmental context. Seen in the developmental perspective, the demonstrations in China were provoked by programs of the CPC aimed at realizing Mao's goal of a "unitary system of the ownership of the means of production by the whole people." The result of that is a cumulative increase of social displacement or deprivation. To this category belong the demonstrations of peasants in 1956–57 against the establishment of the higher form of Agricultural Producers' Cooperatives and especially the Unified System of Purchase and Marketing. A wave of demonstrations by peasants demanding food from party leaders occurred in the countryside in 1956 and 1957. Mao mentioned in January 1957 that in one instance thirty thousand peasants staged a demonstration in one county.[65] Another example of a demonstration caused by the Communist party's imposition of socialism was the massive revolt by the Tibetans against Communist rule in 1959. After 1960 more and more displaced or deprived groups demonstrated against the government. Among them were the youths forcibly sent to settle in the countryside and a group known as contract or temporary workers, most of whom were rural migrants in cities, dispossessed intellectuals, and educated youth. These two groups demonstrated first during the chaotic days of the Cultural Revolution in 1967 and 1968. The displaced youths were the most persistent, and they carried out some of the largest and most disruptive demonstrations after the death of Mao (in Shanghai in particular). A displaced group that has demonstrated continuously against the government, not necessarily for reasons of "socialist transformation," is made up of the veterans, who were one of the most violent groups during the Cultural Revolution. The veterans were among the first to be disillusioned with the Communist party and joined with the critics in the Hundred Flowers Blooming campaign in 1956.[66]

We can also analyze the demonstrations in the PRC in terms of the aims of demonstrators. The demonstrations by peasants from 1956 through 1979 were specifically aimed at improvement of their economic situation, e.g., they were demonstrating for food and land. Similarly the various reports about strikes by workers in 1957 and in the decade of 1966–76 made it clear that the workers' aim was largely economic. However, the riot at the Tiananmen Square on April 5, 1976, which at its peak involved some one hundred thousand people was not aimed at any specific economic issue. It was an expression of generalized hostility toward the entire regime. First, the social composition of this riot was broadly representative. Second, while the riot was triggered by a seemingly trivial action—premature removal of wreaths in memory of Zhou Enlai—the outburst was an expression of general resentment against Mao's regime. The pattern of this riot corresponded closely to the universal pattern of hostile outburst. The long duration of elite dispute since 1966, Peking as the seat of the central government, and the Tiananmen Square itself with its symbols of authority, such as the Great Hall of the People, the Monument to the Martyrs of the Revolution, the Museum of Chinese Revolution, and the Ministry of Public Security, provided what sociologists call the conduciveness of mass action. The lack of any significant amelioration of the numerous discontents in society that were first disclosed to the full extent in the Cultural Revolution, such as the low wages of workers, the lack of employment for students, the persecution of intellectuals, the abuse of power by party cadres, the special privileges enjoyed by high-ranking civil and military officials constitute "social strains." Rumors and other word-of-mouth news, together with posters, a form of protest used since 1975, provided the "ideological basis" for protest. In the meantime, "social control," which in the past had depended on the effectiveness of party bureaucracy at every level, was greatly eroded after the years of public criticism that had been launched by the radicals. The death of Zhou Enlai in January 1976 added a note of urgency to the already volatile situation. The outpouring of public sentimentalism toward Zhou in the traditional *qinmin* festival (memorial to ancestors) in April 1976 finally rallied the public in Peking. The removal of the wreaths in memory of Zhou that had been deposited by various groups since March 29 became the precipitating event (the straw that broke the camel's back) that triggered the riot at Tiananmen Square on April 5, 1976.

The demonstration on April 5, 1976, was not confined to Peking. Similar demonstrations took place in over half a dozen other major Chinese cities.[67] As in Peking, the demonstrations hailed Zhou Enlai and denounced the radicals led by Mao. As in 1957, the demonstrators were severely dealt with. An uncertain number of participants were shot on the spot. Subsequently the radicals instituted a reign of terror with massive arrests and two public executions. Zhang Chunqiao, one of the radicals, reportedly told a study class in June, 1976, that forty to fifty thousand persons were arrested in Peking alone.[68] In Shanghai, some three thousand in schools and colleges were arrested.[69] Not even the military were exempted from this ferocious reprisal against the public.[70]

One can discern from the demonstrations that the focus of public protest steadily shifted from the "output" aspect of the Communist system to the whole system. This became clearer with the posters and the underground journals in Peking in 1978–79. The various demonstrations that occurred in Peking during this time included both those who protested for specific reasons, such as peasants, and those who demanded a new system of government. In October 1980, for example, college students in the city of Changsha, provincial capital of Hunan, protested against party officials' manipulation of local elections.[71] Similar student activities occurred in some campuses in Peking.[72]

The hypothesis is inescapable that all the informal opinions described so far, coupled with the changing focus of opinion, i.e., from the output of the system to the system as a whole, ultimately forced the CPC to make some important changes in its policy—abandonment of the people's commune, termination of the youth-to-the-countryside program, permission for private shops and stores, and reinterpretation of the objectives of socialism.

An ancient Chinese saying has it that preventing people from expressing their opinions is more difficult than damming a river. Our study of the communication system of the PRC fully bears out this ancient Chinese wisdom. The public, after all, is composed of living human beings, who have mind, will, and most important of all the capacity to learn and innovate. As the Communist party has turned all public media of communication into tools of authority, the public of the PRC has developed its own system of communication in which genuine opinions of the people circulate.

LEADERSHIP

Public opinion, in China or elsewhere, is to a significant degree a reaction to leadership. This does not mean that public opinion is manipulated at will by leaders. Rather it means that the speeches and actions of leaders provide the public with a focus. Moreover, in a highly coercive political system such as the Chinese Communist, the public learns to adapt to the particular practices of its leaders in order to survive. Hence, the various characteristics of Chinese public opinion today are to a large degree a reaction to the thirty-some years of Chinese Communist rule.

The Chinese Communist rule, as we have mentioned several times in this study, is characterized by ideological style, accent on conflict, and primacy of political power. The Chinese Communists believe, as Mao Zedong did, that the most effective way to mobilize the public is to give "symbolic definition" to every public issue. That is, no matter how mundane an issue is, e.g., draining a fish pond in order to have more land for crops, it must be translated into the struggle between socialism and capitalism.[73] Mao Zedong strongly agreed with those American scholars of public opinion who said, "It is not what things are, but what they can be made to seem to be, that counts."[74] Hence, central to Chinese Communist leadership practice is to politicize every action, nothing being free of ideological or symbolic significance. Second, the Chinese Communists extol the virtue of conflict. Mao held the belief that society is rent with latent conflict between the proletariat and the bourgeoisie. Because the masses are deficient in culture and education often they are not aware of such hidden conflict. So, in Mao's scheme, the Communist party had to activate the latent conflict in society by politicizing every action and speech. Once the latent conflict was brought to the surface, Mao believed, then a massive force would be unleashed in favor of socialism. Hence, from 1949 to the death of Mao in 1976, campaign upon campaign of class struggle was initiated by the CPC in order to realize Mao's scheme. The best example of this was the Great Proletarian Cultural Revolution, with its opinion unidimensionality (struggle between *two* lines, *two* roads, or *two* thoughts) and violence.

Third, as the derivative of the above two, Chinese Communist leadership implicitly and explicitly puts an overwhelming emphasis on political power. With power everything is possible.

The impact of these leadership characteristics on Chinese public opinion, however, did not conform to Mao's design. First of all, instead of activating the supposed latent conflict between the proletariat and the bourgeoisie, Chinese Communist promotion of conflict resulted in polycentrism. The Cultural Revolution created pluralistic conflicts. Numerous student, youth, and workers' groups emerged and carried on a continuous process of conflict among themselves. Taken aback by the pluralistic conflicts in society, Mao expressed his bewilderment—"there is no reason why workers should be divided."[75] Instead of promoting a sharpened sense of class consciousness, the Cultural Revolution led to a quick rise of local and personal interests. In the countryside Chinese peasants promptly reverted to parochialism, and the government had difficulty requisitioning grain. The Cultural Revolution precipitated the rise of factionalism in the Communist party and the state bureaucracy.[76] Denunciations of "factionalism," "mountain-top-ism," and "polycentrism" have appeared regularly and prominently in Chinese newspapers since 1967.

At present, we can discern at least four distinct "publics" in Chinese society: (1) subjective-participant, (2) alienated-passive, (3) alienated-active, and (4) parochial.

The subjective-participant public consists of those who have chosen to live within the system and who air their views through the legitimate and institutionalized channels. Their opinions are almost exclusively on the "output" side of the political system, and the feedback from these views is naturally of the goal-seeking type. In other words, the opinions and feedback of the subjective-participant do not require any change in the internal arrangement of the present political system, especially power relations; the views of the subjective-participants are, in principle, to facilitate the regime's goals. Because of these qualities the opinions of the subjective-participants are almost the only ones acknowledged explicitly and approvingly by the Chinese Communist mass media. The subjective-participants use the institutionalized means of opinion expression, such as the NPC, CPPCC, mass media, letters, and visits. Thus a degree of rapport exists between the Communist system and the subjective-participants. In contrast, the alienated-passives are the ones who have ideologically separated themselves from the system ("internal exile"); they have become spectators in politics. They have no real opinion to air except for the fact that having no opinion is a form of opinion. They engage in what is known in China as idle talk or empty talk (*qing tan*), and they are active in passing side-lane news. As several Communist writers have described them, the alienated-passives have no respect for the formal communication of the party; they follow rumors instead. They often assume the posture of "people in the know" and shift their public stand as "the direction of wind changes."[77] Most of them are lower officials who have been alienated by the constant changes in party lines. They have concluded that "the so-called struggle between two lines is merely a mask for sectarian power struggle."[78] Whereas the alienated-passives are at least organizationally in, though ideologically out, of the Communist system, the alienated-actives are outsiders in both an organizational and an ideological sense. They are political dissidents, and most of them are young or late adolescents. They are active in that they openly or secretly oppose the Communist system in a fundamental way, so the channels of communication that they employ are all noninstitutionalized, such as side-lane news, wall posters, underground publications, and demonstrations. Finally, there is the parochial public, consisting of predominantly

Chinese peasants who, as we mentioned before, are isolated from modern mass media and often illiterate. It is clear from all sources that the mentality of Chinese peasants remains in the traditional mode; their views are still encased in magical beliefs and clan relations. We shall have more to say on this in a later chapter.

The Maoist leadership was not a total failure, however. Among the subjective-participant public there is a subgroup, the leftists among the cadres. The opinions of these cadres have already been discussed in chapter 9. They are opposed to the present reforms on the grounds that they go against the Maoist principles, such as "class struggles as the key link," "steel as the key link," "unified leadership of the party," and "two-line struggle." These are the cadres who have been promoted from the ranks of poor peasants, whose literacy level is low. Their views, however, must also be understood in the context that the present reforms, which emphasize modernization, threaten the career of these cadres.

The foregoing analysis of Chinese public opinion tends to substantiate the view among American scholars of public opinion that, in the final analysis, people judge an issue according to their own frame of reference, which "hinges on the person's knowledge of what goes with what is in his or her immediately relevant social environment."[79] A person's past experience with the government is another component in his or her frame of reference. Much of Chinese youth's disillusionment with the Communist system is due to their own experience in the countryside. The lack of saliency of class struggle in the minds of Chinese peasants is another example of the importance of people's independent frame of reference. It is also due to people's autonomous political analysis that they viewed the two-line struggle in the Cultural Revolution as being "between this and that group of people, between this and that person."[80] As the implausibility of Chinese Communist "symbolic definition" persists, it reinforces the private frame of reference of Chinese citizens. The editor of the *China News Analysis* wrote:

> . . . it is highly doubtful that Chinese public opinion is easily changed by organized "culture." There are countries, even some countries that are far advanced technically, in which public opinion changes rapidly under the influence of the mass media. One day everyone is pro-Russia, the next day anti-Russia. One day communist China is condemned, the next day it is embraced. Chinese public opinion is much less volatile; internal convictions do not change at the bidding of the mass media. An obvious pointer to this is that throughout the years great numbers of young people, leaving China legally or illegally, have promptly expressed a desire to continue their studies in the U.S., the country that the Chinese mass media have always depicted in the darkest colors.[81]

THE POST-MAO APPROACH TO PUBLIC OPINION

The death of Mao in 1976 and the ascendance of the party pragmatists to power after 1978 provided the CPC with the opportunity to review its past critically and to initiate reforms. Consequently, a relatively new approach toward public opinion has been adopted by the leaders. We have mentioned that one of the first measures implemented by the present leaders is the public disavowal of large and turbulent mass campaigns. In our discussion of ideology we have also noted the new interpretation of class struggle made by present leaders. Moreover the "primacy in politics" is also being criticized. As a Chinese writer put it: "The contradictions among the people that stem from differences in material interests must ultimately be resolved through economic means."[82] Chinese propagandists have been instructed to connect propaganda with the "immediate interests of the masses."

Finally, a major change from Maoism is in the inventory of the key symbols that the Communist party employs to mobilize Chinese public opinion. Mao had followed the parsimony principle—the fewer symbols used, the better. So ultimately, Mao translated every difference into a two-line struggle. The present leaders chose the pluralistic principle. Since 1981 the Communist party has tried to rally people under patriotism as well as socialism.

The pluralizing of key symbols in the post-Mao period is fraught with problems. That is evidenced by the recent Chinese campaign of countering "spiritual pollution," which is a reaction to the growing contact of the Chinese public with Western culture. The campaign itself testifies to the fear and ambivalence of party leaders regarding the social and political ramifications of diversifying symbol inventory. The short-livedness of the campaign points to the serious conflict within the Communist party, for the leftist cadres quickly turned the campaign of "antispiritual pollution" into another mass repression of the Cultural Revolution genre, compelling the national leaders to call a halt to the campaign.

In the final analysis, in the public opinion and communication in China we see once more the powerful influence of the CPC's revolutionary legacy in the post-1949 situation. The Maoist concept of leadership was based primarily on the Communist party's experience of war mobilization before its victory in 1949. In war, differences in society are indeed condensed into a simple polarity. The mass and the elite are drawn closer in war so that symbolic definition is an effective way of organizing the masses. These conditions are not readily replicated or obtained in time of peace when people operate in pluralistic contexts.

NOTES

1. Ithiel de Sola Pool, "Communication in Totalitarian Societies," in Ithiel de Sola Pool and Wilbur Schramm, eds., *Handbook of Communication* (Chicago: Rand McNally College Publishing Company, 1973), pp. 462–511.

2. *Selected Works of Mao Tse-tung*, vol. III (Peking: Foreign Languages Press, 1965), p. 118.

3. Sidney Verba, "Conclusion: Comparative Political Culture," in Lucian W. Pye and Sidney Verba, eds., *Political Culture and Political Development* (Princeton, N.J.: Princeton University Press, 1965), p. 546.

4. Feng Wenbin, "Reforming the Political Structure," *Beijing Review* 24, no. 4 (January 26, 1981), 17.

5. Henry G. Schwartz, "The *T'san-k'ao Hsiao-hsi*: How Well Informed Are Chinese Officials about the Outside World?" *China Quarterly*, no. 27 (July–September 1966); Alan P. L. Liu, "Control of Public Information and Its Effects on China's Foreign Affairs," *Asian Survey* XIV, no. 10 (October 1974); and Alan P. L. Liu, "Ideology and Information: Correspondents of the New China News Agency and Chinese Foreign Policy Making," *Journal of International Affairs* 26, no. 2 (1972).

6. *China News Analysis*, no. 1070 (February 18, 1977), p. 2.

7. Robert E. Park, "The Natural History of the Newspaper," in Wilbur Schramm, ed., *Mass Communications* (Urbana: University of Illinois Press, 1960), p. 10.

8. Hu Yaobang, "On Problems in Political Thought Affairs," *Hongqi*, no. 1 (1983), p. 10.

9. The newspaper-circulation figure for China is from Zhou Zheng, "Newspapers in China," *Beijing Review* 24, no. 20 (May 18, 1981), 23. The circulation figures for the press and other media on Taiwan are from *Chung-yang Jih-pao* (overseas edition), October 12, 1981, p. 1. The circulation figures for the media in the U.S. and USSR are from Frederick W. Frey, "Communication and Development," in de Sola Pool and Schramm, *Handbook of Communication*, pp. 442–59.

10. *Zhongguo Baike Nianjian, 1980 (1980 China Yearbook)* (Peking and Shanghai: Zhongguo Da Bakike Quanshu Chubanshe, 1980), p. 604.

11. Alan P. L. Liu, *Communications and National Integration in Communist China* (Berkeley: University of California Press, 1976), p. xxxvi.

12. *RMRB*, December 16, 1982, p. 3; February 18, 1983, p. 3; "The Fifth National Women's Congress," *Beijing Review* 26, no. 38 (September 19, 1983), 6.

13. *RMRB*, June 12, 1978, p. 1.

14. Zhou Zheng, "Visits and Letters from the People," *Beijing Review* 25, no. 25 (June 21, 1982), 23–28.

15. *RMRB*, October 3, 1983, p. 1.

16. Zhou Zheng, "Newspapers in China," *Beijing Review* 24, no. 20 (May 18, 1981), 25.

17. Fox Butterfield, "Peking Indictment Accuses Radicals of Killing 34,000," *New York Times*, November 17, 1980, p. A3.

18. *RMRB*, August 29, 1979, p. 3.

19. Merle Fainsod, *Smolensk under Soviet Rule* (New York: Random House, 1963), pp. 407–8.

20. Frank Ching, "Thousands in Peking Resort to Vagrancy in Pursuit of Justice," *Wall Street Journal*, June 26, 1979, p. 1.

21. *RMRB*, January 27, 1979, p. 2.

22. Zhou Zheng, "Visits and Letters," p. 24.

23. *RMRB*, February 10, 1979, p. 1.

24. Feng Lanrui and Zhao Lukuan, "Urban Unemployment in China," *Social Sciences in China*, no. 2 (1982), pp. 123–39.

25. Karl W. Deutsch, *The Nerves of Government* (New York: Free Press, 1966), p. 92.

26. Zvi Y. Gitelman, "Public Opinion in Communist Political Systems," in Walter D. Connor and Zvi Y. Gitelman with Adaline Huszczo and Robert Blumstock, *Public Opinion in European Socialist Systems* (New York: Frederick A. Praeger, 1977), p. 2.

27. Samples of these party reports are found in *Rural People's Communes in Lien-Chiang.* Edited, with an introductory analysis, by C. S. Chen and translated by Charles Price Ridley (Stanford, Calif.: Hoover Institution Press, 1969).

28. See, for example, Aryeh L. Unger, "The Public Opinion Reports of the Nazi Party," *Public Opinion Quarterly*, winter 1965–66, pp. 565–82.

29. This information is from the Red Guard paper, *Weidong*, no. 24 (May 15, 1967), as reprinted in *Hung-wei-ping-pao Ling-chien Huipien* by the Center for Chinese Research Material (Washington, D.C.: Association of Research Libraries, n.d.). I have obtained this material from the East Asian collection of the library at the Hoover Institution at Stanford University.

30. Mao Tse-tung, "Second Preface to 'Village Investigations,'" in *Mao's China: Party Reform Documents, 1942–44*, translated, with introduction, by Boyd Compton (Seattle: University of Washington Press, 1966), p. 57.

31. *RMRB*, March 16, 1978.

32. A former student of mine obtained a copy of this publication while touring China, and he was very generous in letting me read it.

33. *Wan-sui*, no. 2, p. 272.

34. Leonard Bushkoff, "German Intelligence," *New York Times Book Review*, June 18, 1978, p. 18.

35. *Wan-sui*, no. 2, p. 17.

36. Ibid., p. 73.

37. Ibid., p. 281.

38. *Miscellany of Mao Tse-tung Thought (1949–1968)*, part II (Arlington, Va.: Joint Publications Research Service, February 20, 1974), p. 430.

39. J. Chester Cheng, ed., *The Politics of the Chinese Red Army* (Stanford, Calif.: Hoover Institution Press, 1966), p. 203.

40. *RMRB*, August 6, 1976, p. 1.

41. *New York Times*, August 30, 1977.

42. Alan P. L. Liu, "Political Decay on Mainland China: On Crises of Faith, Confidence and Trust," *Issues and Studies* XVIII, no. 8 (August 1982).

43. de Sola Pool, "Communication in Totalitarian Societies," p. 473.

44. Tamotsu Shibutani, *Improvised News: A Sociological Study of Rumor* (Indianapolis: Bobbs-Merrill Company, 1966), p. 93.

45. *RMRB*, March 20, 1978, p. 2.

46. Ridley, *Rural People's Communes*, p. 96.

47. *Far Eastern Economic Review*, November 20, 1971, p. 5.

48. *New York Times*, February 9, 1974.

49. *Far Eastern Economic Review*, June 18, 1976, p. 25.

50. Shibutani, *Improvised News*, p. 65.

51. *RMRB*, June 6, 1977.

52. Miriam London and Ivan D. London, "China's 'Byroad' News Leaks: A New People's Channel," *Freedom at Issue*, no. 47 (September–October 1978), p. 9.

53. Zhen Weiwei, "The Rise and Fall of Side-land News," *RMRB*, January 12, 1983, p. 3.

54. Roderick MacFauquhar, *The Hundred Flowers Campaign and the Chinese Intellectuals* (New York: Frederick A. Praeger, 1960); Dennis J. Dollin, *Communist China: The Politics of Student Opposition* (Stanford, Calif.: Hoover Institution Press, 1964).

55. *Wan-sui*, no. 2, p. 115.

56. The text of Li's poster is in *Issues and Studies* (January 1976), pp. 110-48.

57. Lo Chuan, "The Li I-che That I Knew," *Ming Pao Daily News*, January 24, 1979, p. 3, and January 25, 1979, p. 3.

58. Roger Garside, *Coming Alive: China after Mao* (New York: Mentor, 1981). For other studies of the posters and underground journals in China, see Gregor Benton, ed., *Wild Lilies: Poisonous Weeds* (London: Pluto Press, 1982); Fox Butterfield, *China: Alive in the Bitter Sea* (New York: Bantam Books, 1983); David S. G. Goodman, *Beijing Street Voices* (London: Marion Boyars, 1982); and James D. Seymour, ed., *The Fifth Modernization* (Stanfordville, N.Y.: Human Rights Publishing Group, 1980).

59. My sources for the underground publications consist mainly of original Chinese publications, which are available at the Universities Service Center in Hong Kong. For students interested in English sources see note 58 above and Kjeld Erik Brodsgaard, "The Democracy Movement in China, 1978-1979: Opposition in Movements, Wall Poster Campaigns, and Underground Journals," *Asian Survey* XXI, no. 7 (July 1981), pp. 747-74.

60. Butterfield (1983), p. 407.

61. Chen Jo-hsi, "Democracy Wall and People's Publications," *Hai-wai Hsueh-jen*, no. 106 (May 1981), pp. 25-33. This is a Chinese journal for overseas Chinese scholars and students, mainly in America. Chen Jo-hsi is the author of *The Execution of Major Yin* (Bloomington: Indiana University Press, 1978).

62. Ta-ling Lee and Miriam London, "Wei Ching-sheng Defends Himself," *Freedom at Issue*, no. 56 (May-June 1980), pp. 10-13; "Let a Hundred Flowers Wilt," *Time*, September 21, 1981, p. 34; "A Voice from Peking's Gulag," *Time*, September 21, 1981, p. 35; Michael Weisskopf, "A Glimpse of Life in China's Prisons," *Washington Post*, September 15, 1981, p. 1.

63. Compare, for example, the description of political dissent in the Soviet Union in Gayle Durham Hollander (Gayle Durham Hannah), "Political Communication and Dissent in the Soviet Union," in Rudolf L. Tokes, ed., *Dissent in the USSR: Politics, Ideology, and People* (Baltimore: Johns Hopkins University Press, 1975), pp. 263-68.

64. "A Dissenter's Odyssey through Mao's China," *New York Times Magazine*, November 16, 1980.

65. *Wan-sui*, no. 2, pp. 87 and 104.

66. For more on the demonstrations of various groups in the Cultural Revolution, see Alan P. L. Liu, *Political Culture and Group Conflict in Communist China* (Santa Barbara, Calif.: Clio Books, 1976).

67. Fox Butterfield, "Demonstrations for Chou Not Confined to Peking," *New York Times*, April 14, 1976.

68. *New York Times*, May 19, 1976; Fox Butterfield, "Some Chinese Uneasy over Peking Demonstrations," *New York Times*, January 11, 1977.

69. *Ming Pao Daily News*, April 11, 1978.

70. *RMRB*, December 1, 1977.

71. Fox Butterfield, "A Student Protest Reported in China," *New York Times*, October 15, 1980.

72. Kuan Pin-shu, "On the Student Movement at National Qinghua University," *Cheng Ming*, no. 42 (April 1981), pp. 43-44.

73. For examples of this line of reasoning, see *Philosophy Is No Mystery* (Peking: Foreign Languages Press, 1972).

74. W. Lance Bennett, *The Political Mind and the Political Movement* (Lexington, Mass.: D. C. Heath and Company, 1975), p. 51.

75. *China News Analysis*, no. 1012 (1975), p. 2.

76. Lucian W. Pye, *The Dynamics of Chinese Politics* (Cambridge, Mass.: Oelgeschlager, Gunn & Hain, 1981). Pye's analysis is questionable, however.

77. Zhang Mingshu, "An Ugly Performance of Splitting the Party," *RMRB*, June 6, 1977; Chu Yan, "Treat Party Documents Seriously," *RMRB*, December 19, 1980; and Xue Ming, "The Current of 'Idle Talk' Should Not Be Allowed to Expand," *Hongqi*, no. 17 (1980).

78. *RMRB*, May 5, 1976, p. 1.

79. Bennett, *Political Mind*, p. 13.

80. *China News Analysis*, no. 946 (1974), p. 4.

81. *China News Analysis*, no. 870 (1972), p. 4.

82. Yang Chunggui, "The Contradictions among the People Must Be Analyzed in a Concrete Manner," *RMRB*, May 23, 1980, p. 5.

PART FIVE

Economic and Social Transformation

CHAPTER 17

The Chinese Political Economy

The various characteristics of the Chinese Communist political system that we have discussed so far might give the impression that Chinese Communist leaders are interested in power for the sake of power. Undoubtedly political power is a very major consideration of Chinese leaders. However, Chinese Communist leaders are equally concerned with building up China's economy and transforming Chinese society. Indeed, those two objectives might even be regarded as *the* goal for which the Communists waged a life-or-death struggle with their enemies for more than two decades. After 1949, as we have seen, economic questions often provoked serious elite dispute. Therefore a study of the Chinese Communist economy and social change is essential to the understanding of Chinese Communist politics.

The two chapters that follow deal with the economic and social transformation of China under Communist rule. The analysis of Chinese Communist economic development provides the necessary background for the discussion of social change. As there are numerous studies on the Chinese Communist economy, our emphasis is on the strategy and the major results of economic development from 1949 to the present. Similarly, our analysis of social change is more macroscopic than microscopic, examining fundamental constituents of society such as population, occupation, family, stratification, social mobility, education, public health, and social integration. Throughout our discussion we point out the intimate relation between manmade decisions and the social consequences that compound the further development of Chinese economy and society.

In 1949 when the PRC was established, the Chinese economy and society were, indeed, as Mao said, "poor and blank." It is customary to speak of the Chinese economy at that time as having been composed of three segments. There was first the vast interior, largely self-sufficient traditional agriculture. Second, there was a modern coastal sector where Western business since the Opium War of 1842 had made its impact; this sector was mainly noted for its light industry, especially textiles. These two sectors were poorly linked, and the effect of the poor linkage is not entirely clear.

There is the suggestion that the modern textile industry ruined the handicraft industry of the agricultural communities in the interior, thus further impoverishing Chinese peasants. At the same time, modern cities on the coast provided Chinese agriculture with the outlet for export and cash income for commercial crops. But the underdevelopment of modern transport prevented these two sectors from having a regular and substantial interconnection. Then there was the third segment of Chinese economy: the heavy industry in the Northeast (Manchuria) that was built by the Japanese in the 1930s and controlled by them until the end of the Second World War. That sector was not linked with the rest of China until after 1949. Moreover, during the brief Russian occupation of the Northeast after Japan's surrender, many key industrial installations in the region were dismantled by the Soviet army and moved to the Soviet Union.[1] In actuality, there was a fourth segment in Chinese economy, the pastoral economy of the ethnic minorities in Inner Mongolia, Xinjiang, Qinghai, and Tibet. This segment was, like the Northeast, almost entirely detached from the rest of China. As we mentioned at the outset, economic regionalism has been the rule rather than the exception throughout the history of China.

The "poor and blank" picture of China in 1949 may be further illustrated by a few figures. "Agriculture, accounting for 75 percent of the population, contributed 40 percent to national product, while the urban sector, with only 15 percent of the population, made roughly the same contribution. At least an additional 10 percent of China's people lived in rural areas, engaged mostly in non-farm tasks and producing about 20 percent of total national output. Thus it took three out of four Chinese workers to feed the country . . . as opposed to one out of seven in the United States, and one out of two in Japan and the Soviet Union."[2] The number of workers in modern industry was about three million and, with their families, comprised less than 3 percent of the total population then.[3] At the upper strata, in 1949 "there were in China some 5 million college and middle-school graduates plus about 40 million with an elementary education. The literate formed about 10 percent of the population."[4] As to the number of "intelligentsia," i.e., those with a modern education and working in modern professions, they numbered about 1 percent of the total population.[5]

The facts of Chinese economy that we have just mentioned, such as economic regionalism and the overwhelming rural framework, were assets to the CPC in waging guerrilla warfare against the Kuomintang. These same facts in 1949 became "difficulties" and challenges to the CPC. Mao articulated the dilemma of the Communists on the eve of the conquest of mainland China: "We shall soon put aside some of the things we know well and be compelled to do things we don't know well. This means difficulties. The imperialists reckon that we will not be able to manage our economy; they are standing by and looking on, awaiting our failure."[6] Mao professed modesty and humility in overcoming the difficulties in the economic task. As he said, "We must learn to do economic work from all who know how, *no matter who they are*" (emphasis added).[7] However, as in numerous instances, Mao's deeds belied his words. For it mattered a great deal to Mao from whom he would learn to manage the Chinese economy. We turn now to the strategy of Chinese economic development.

THE STRATEGY OF ECONOMIC DEVELOPMENT

The strategy of economic development of any nation revolves around two interrelated decisions: saving and investment. The question of the former is primarily on the optimal rate of saving. Too high a rate of saving affects the productivity of the people adversely and is thus counterproductive, whereas too little saving hinders the growth of a nation's economy. The question of investment concerns what type of goods to invest in. "Generally speaking, a large investment in producer goods—transportation, the production of raw materials, factories, and heavy machinery—will result in more rapid economic development but will impose a heavier burden on the population. A large investment in consumer goods, on the other hand, will benefit the population but will reduce the productive capacity of the economy."[8] In the final analysis, all these questions for China in 1949 hinged on *from whom* the CPC, especially Mao, would learn. Though he professed open-mindedness in learning economic work, Mao's mind was already made up. He declared in "On People's Democratic Dictatorship," "the Communist party of the Soviet Union . . . under the leadership of Lenin and Stalin . . . learned not only how to make the revolution but also how to carry on construction. It has built a great and splendid socialist state. The Communist party of the Soviet Union is our best teacher and we must learn from it."[9]

In actuality, the development strategy of the CPC was a hybrid, a combination of Soviet economics and Maoist politics. Learning from the Soviets, Chinese Communist leaders, especially Mao, put the development of heavy industry (or producer goods) as their first priority, followed by light industry and agriculture. Similarly, the Chinese Communists emulated the Soviets in stressing a high rate of saving as expressed in the Chinese saying, "Production first, livelihood second." Moreover, Chinese Communist leaders adopted the Soviet pattern of "extensive form of development," which means continuous massive state investment in new projects (of heavy industry) with little provision for renovation or depreciation of the existing enterprises. Finally, the CPC structured the economy after the Stalinist bureaucratic centralized model. The economy was organized by a hierarchical system of planning and management, the State Planning Commission constituting the peak of the pyramid. Enterprises were not allowed independence of decision making, being bound by centrally decided targets and other indicators. Probably the only significant Chinese input into the economic strategy was the emphasis in the 1950s on developing industries in the interior in order to redress the overconcentration of modern industry on the coast.

The Soviet developmental strategy was combined, in China, with Maoist politics which emphasized "productive relations" (organizational changes), "uninterrupted revolutions," "high speed," and "mass line." The rural developmental plan of the CPC best expressed this Maoist strategy with its emphasis on continuous changes in production management, e.g., from the mutual aid teams to people's communes and mass movement in making steel and managing local industry. In 1981, reviewing the past strategy of economic development, a high-ranking Chinese Communist leader summed up the Maoist model of development as follows:

> The main mistake that we made in the past in guiding socialist construction is "belief in accelerated growth." . . . This belief was exemplified in two respects that were evident after 1958. One was that so many changes in the "productive relations" were made not in accordance with the level of productive forces. We persisted in "uninterrupted revolutions," wishing to transit quickly to socialism. The second was that the scale of construction, more often than not, exceeded the practical capability of our nation. We insist on high targets, high speed and high saving. The result is that our advancement was often blind and rash.[10]

After 1958 more and more Maoist politics were added to the basic Soviet pattern of Chinese economy, such as the principle of local autarky, which called for each province to develop an independent and complete economy so that the national government could concentrate maximum resources to develop major heavy industries.

Another Maoist program was to substitute class struggle and egalitarianism for material incentives for workers; offering material incentives was regarded as the bourgeois way of motivating workers and so was rejected. As Mao put it in 1964: "If we grasp only production struggle and scientific experiment without stressing class struggle, then the spirit of the people could not be enhanced." [11]

THE PERFORMANCE OF THE ECONOMY

Following the Soviet way, beginning in 1953 Chinese Communist planners subjected the Chinese economy to a series of five-year plans. These did achieve some notable results, mainly in heavy industry; at the same time, the five-year plans were interrupted by serious breakdowns and, in 1958–62, nationwide catastrophe.

The first five-year plan of 1953–57 best exemplified the Soviet strategy of investment. Of the total state investment in new constructions (capital construction), 46.5 percent went to heavy industry, 5.9 to light industry, and 7.8 to agriculture. Further, the heavy industry was steel centered, for 10.14 percent of the capital construction in heavy industry was in metallurgical industry.[12] Heavy industry, in principle, may serve light industry, agriculture, or itself. The heavy industry in the first five-year plan served mainly itself. Of the 156 new projects constructed in the first five year plan, only one tractor plant and three chemical fertilizer plants were included.[13] The strains of this lopsided investment in the first five-year plan on the Chinese economy and society were already apparent at the start. Two Chinese economists wrote in 1980: "As a matter of fact, while the first five-year plan was being carried out, food and light industrial goods were already in short supply. Thus a state monopoly over grain and other products was established, requisition purchases of farm produce were conducted among the peasants, and food grain, cotton cloth and edible oil were rationed among office and industrial workers." [14] The shortages of agricultural and consumer goods were even more acute by the end of the first five-year plan in 1957, which we mentioned in relation to the rural administration and development (see chapter 7). The crux of the matter was that in neglecting agriculture, Chinese Communist planners undermined the most important source of Chinese industrial development. According to a Chinese economist writing in 1957, one half of the total value of heavy industrial output then was dependent on the supply of agricultural materials, and the proportion of the value of agricultural materials in light industrial output was as high as 80 percent. Of the total value of Chinese export goods then, 75 percent came from agricultural products.[15] It is no wonder that the lopsided investment in the first five-year plan, which was actually worked out by Soviet advisers to China, in the end threatened to undermine heavy industry itself. It was against this background that Mao invented his Great Leap Forward in 1958.

The strategy of the Great Leap Forward, which, formally speaking, constituted the second five-year plan (1958–62), is clear from the Maoist slogan—"Taking Steel as the Key Link!" According to Yang and Li, "Steel output was untenably set to be doubled to 10.70 million tons in 1958 and hit 18 million tons in 1959. The result was a serious imbalance in the economy." [16] New iron and steel works proliferated in 1958–59. Since these plants needed a large amount of steel, timber, cement, equipment, and energy (coal supply and power generation), overall investment in heavy industry rose precipitously. Other consequences followed. The number of heavy industrial workers was increased to 35.5 million in 1958 from 5.57 million in 1957, a rise of 29.93 million in one year. "At the same time, the nonagricultural population grew from 106.18 million in 1957 to 122.10 million in 1958, a rise of 15.92 million. The urban population increased from 99.49 million in 1957 to 107.21 million in 1958, a rise of 7.72 million." [17] The new urban labor force was mainly recruited from the countryside. Since there was no significant rise in agricultural productivity per acre, the great reduction in the agricultural labor force spelled disaster, let alone the fact that the rural program of the Great Leap Forward demanded a significant increase in agricultural production. By 1959 the strains in the Chinese economy were very clear. "The total output value of agriculture dropped by 13.6 percent from the 1958 figure, while the growth rate of national income decreased to 8.2 percent from 23.1 percent in 1957." [18] At the same time, the saving rate reached "the disastrous level of 43.8 percent" (the optimal rate being 22 to 25 percent). [19] The Chinese economy was on the brink of catastrophe. The average grain ration for each person, which was 203 kilograms in 1957, dropped to 198 kilograms in 1958, 186.5 kilograms in 1959, and 163.5 kilograms in 1960. The edible oil and meat rations decreased sharply, and less cotton cloth was distributed. [20] Millions of Chinese peasants perished in the famine years of 1960-62 (for details, see chapter 7, on rural development). The overall decline of Chinese economic development is shown in table 17-1.

So for the moment, another five-year plan was not possible. The years 1963 to 1965 were known in China as the adjustment period, when the Chinese economy was handled by party pragmatists. The state investment in capital construction was reduced by 85 percent between 1960 and 1962. Some 44,500 enterprises were closed down, and the saving rate was reduced from 40 percent in 1960 to 10 percent in 1962. About 28 million members of the urban labor force were returned to the countryside. [21]

By 1965 the Chinese economy had bounced back from the catastrophe of the Great Leap Forward, and Mao Zedong again pushed for a resumption of the same strategy that had brought Chinese economy to disaster in 1958-62. The third and fourth five-year plans (1966-75) were carried out amidst the violent Cultural Revolution (1966-76), which was started partly to forestall opposition to Mao's industrial development. In the third five-year plan, for 1966-70, two options were made available to Mao, a higher and a lower target. Mao chose the former, naturally. Investment in heavy industry amounted to 61 percent of all the capital construction, and steel was again the chief target. The strains brought on by this third round of lopsided investment are shown in table 17-2. But the overall slump in 1966-72 did not bring about the starvation and other sufferings of 1960-62 "because the stocks of grain, cotton cloth and other commodities put aside as reserves in the 1963-65 period of economic readjustment were used to tide over the difficulties." [22] Chinese economic planning under Mao resembled the psychology and behavior of a gambler.

TABLE 17-1 Increases or decreases over the previous year in the total output value of agriculture, light industry, and heavy industry

	AGRICULTURE	LIGHT INDUSTRY	HEAVY INDUSTRY
1958:1957	+2.4%	+33.7%	+78.8%
1961:1960	−2.4%	−21.6%	−46.6%

Source: Yang Jianbai and Li Xuezeng, "The Relations between Agriculture, Light Industry and Heavy Industry in China," *Social Sciences in China* I, no. 2 (June 1980), 185.

TABLE 17-2   Increases or decreases over the previous year in the total output value of agriculture, light industry, and heavy industry

	AGRICULTURE	LIGHT INDUSTRY	HEAVY INDUSTRY
1965:1964	+8.3%	+47.7%	+10.2%
1968:1967	−2.5%	− 5.0%	− 5.1%

Source: Yang and Li, "The Relations between Agriculture, Light Industry and Heavy Industry in China," *Social Sciences in China* I, no. 2 (June 1980), 186.

In 1970 the Chinese economy, probably because of the conclusion of the most violent phase of the Cultural Revolution (e.g., the convening of the Ninth Party Congress in 1969), was momentarily on good footing. The agricultural production increased by 11.5 percent and industrial production by 30.7 percent. This was taken (or mistaken) as the sign of "the advent of a new period of leaps forward." The 1975 steel target was set at 35 to 40 million tons as against only 13 million in 1969.[23] Investment in heavy industry once more amounted to 59 percent of all investment in new construction. "During 1970–72, the number of office and industrial workers increased by 12,750,000, reaching 56,100,000 in 1972. The total sum of wages increased by 7,700 million *yuan*, and the consumption of commodity grain went up by 4,750 million kg. Such a sharp increase in investment and in the number of workers repeated the mistakes of 1958–60."[24] Soon the targets of the fourth five-year plan proved to be unrealistic, and in 1973 readjustments began. At this juncture factional struggle broke out at the top level between the Gang of Four and the pragmatists led by Deng Xiaoping, who had just been rehabilitated. Though the strains of the fourth five-year plan did not lead to the same disaster as in 1958–60, according to two mainland Chinese economists writing in 1980, "Its deep, chronic effects [of imbalance] last even to this day."[25]

From 1976 through 1978, the Maoist economic strategy was carried out without Mao. In February 1978 the CPC chairman, Hua Guofeng, announced the ambitious program of constructing 120 large-scale projects "including ten iron and steel complexes, nine nonferrous metal complexes, eight coal mines, ten oil and gas fields, thirty power stations, six new trunk railways and five key harbors." The state's outlay for new capital construction was increased by 32 percent from 1977 to 1978. The rate of saving was raised from 32 percent in 1977 to 36.6 in 1978. Moreover, since by 1978 China had already broken away from Mao's self-reliance policy, a new method of rapid development of new heavy industry was available—importation from the West of complete plants. In 1978 alone twenty-two projects were planned to be purchased from Japan and Western Europe. This was, as a Chinese writer put it, an "old mistake in new form."[26] The importation of advanced Western or Japanese steel plants was not carefully planned in terms of supply of needed fuel and transport facilities. Gross waste and cost overruns were the consequence, as in the notorious example of the multi-billion-dollar Baoshan Steel Mill in Shanghai.[27] In 1979 Hua was forced by Deng Xiaoping and other pragmatist leaders to cancel his ambitious plan, and the Chinese economy went into another period of adjustment and retrenchment.

The one-sided developments of all the five-year plans are shown dramatically in the overall growth figure of the Chinese economy. According to a Chinese economist writing for the authoritative *Hongqi* in 1981, from 1949 to 1978, the heavy industry of China increased 90.5 times, light industry 19.7 times, and agriculture 2.4 times.[28] In 1949 the value of industrial output was 30 percent of the total output value of industry and agriculture. By 1978 the proportion of industrial contribution to the total output value of industry and agriculture had risen to 74 percent.[29] The strategy of extensive development of industry had made its mark. In 1947 there were 14,078 enterprises in major Chinese cities, with 680,000 workers and employees. By 1978, the number of enterprises had increased to 400,000 and that of workers and employees to 40 million.[30] As the *People's Daily* proudly claimed in 1979, those figures meant that since 1949, an average of 21 new enterprises had been added to the Chinese economy every day.[31] Chinese economy is no longer "blank," but China remains poor. Underneath these impressive statistics are some very serious imbalances and qualitative weaknesses (see table 17-3).

Two prominent Chinese economists, Yang Jianbai and Li Xuezeng, wrote in the journal *Social Sciences in China* in 1980 that Chinese economy manifests three serious imbalances.[32] First, agriculture "is still *extremely backward*" (emphasis added). The "per capita grain output shows that in 1978, while each producer in China reaped 1,036 kilograms, his counterpart in the United States brought in more than 50,000. . . . Agricultural labor productivity remains at roughly the same level as during the first five-year plan period (1953-57). Over the last 20 years and more, China's agricultural production, which is predominantly grain production, has hardly improved its ability to take the burden of industry and the economy as a whole."

The second serious imbalance in the Chinese economy is obviously the light industry. Chronic shortages of consumer goods were evident in China until very recently.

In 1977, the per capita output of cotton cloth was just over 10 meters, or less than half of that in the Soviet Union, Japan, France and some other countries. The per capita output of sugar was under 2 kilograms, against 36 kilograms in the Soviet Union, 29 in the United States, and 25 in France and West Germany. The number of bicycles averaged 78 among every 10,000 people in China, which was one-third of the figure in the United States and one-sixth of that in Japan. As to the number of television sets, there were 3 for every 10,000 people in China, over 300 in the United States and over 1,300 in Japan.[33]

TABLE 17-3   Output of major industrial and agricultural products

PRODUCTS	1980 ANNUAL OUTPUT	INCREASE OVER 1949 (TIMES)
Coal	620 million tons	19.4
Crude oil	109.95 million tons	883.0
Electricity	300,600 million kwh	70.0
Steel	37.12 million tons	232.0
Timber	53.59 million cubic meters	9.4
Cement	79.86 million tons	121.0
Chemical fertilizer	12.32 million tons	2161.0
Machine tools	134,000	83
Cotton yarn	2.93 million tons	8.9
Sugar	2.57 million tons	12.8
Bicycles	13.02 million	930.0
Grain	318.22 million	2.8

Source: Liang Xiufeng, "China's Economic Achievements," *Beijing Review* 24, no. 40 (October 1981), 19, 21.

Third, imbalances occurred in the heavy industry too. Heretofore much emphasis was put on production of crude steel at the expense of other necessary developments, most notably fuel and industrial materials. Many Chinese industries operate below full capacity for lack of electricity. "At the same time, there is a serious waste of fuel and other energy resources. Estimates by energy departments in 1978 showed that mismanagement caused a waste of 30 billion kwh of electricity and 50 million tons of coal during the year. The rate of fuel utilization is as low as 28 percent, against 50 percent in Japan and more than 40 percent in Western Europe." [34] Furthermore, much steel produced in China is of little or no use. "Thus some of the steels for the equipment for the farm machinery, fertilizer, pesticide, fiber, and petro-chemical industries have to be imported . . . but the trouble is that, while millions of tons of steel are imported every year, over ten million tons of home-made steel are uselessly stockpiled." [35] In 1981 over 20 million tons of steel made in China were stockpiled. [36]

Yang and Li concluded their discussion on the imbalances between agriculture, light industry, and heavy industry on a depressing note:

> For thirty years the Chinese people have worked hard to build up the country, trying their best to attain a high rate of accumulation while keeping the rise in their level of consumption to a minimum. The purpose was to achieve a faster growth of industrial and agricultural production and, on that basis, a better living standard for the nation. But things have gone contrary to their wishes. Although China is one of the few countries maintaining a high rate of accumulation, she lags far behind many countries in the modernization of productive forces and in raising the standard of living. The crux of the matter lies in the fact that the enormous funds accumulated have not been distributed properly. Little has been done to achieve an overall balance, and too much stress has been laid on heavy industry to the neglect of light industry and agriculture. Besides, the funds were used ineffectively as they were spread over too many projects which took too long to complete. And there has been an astonishing waste of funds and other material resources. [37]

So far, our discussion of the Chinese Communist economy has not yet touched the regional imbalance of the economy, which was very pronounced in 1949. During the first five-year plan, Chinese Communist planners did put an emphasis on developing the inland provinces.

> Of the 694 major projects to be started during 1953–57, more than two-thirds were to be located in the inland area. During the first three years of this period (1953–55), investment in the inland area accounted for 55 percent of the total, compared to about 50 percent during 1950–52. The new industrial centers to be developed included Lanchow [Lanzhou], Tai-yuan [Taiyuan], Sian [Xian], Loyang in northwest, north and central China. Provinces in the southwest and south China were assigned lower priorities. [38]

Developing industry in these hitherto traditionally agricultural regions, however, is time consuming, and the result of it is not immediate. Consequently, in the second five-year plan, i.e., the Great Leap Forward, Mao and his radical planners shifted their emphasis once more to the coastal areas because of Mao's wish for quick results. In the 1970s, owing to Peking's fear of war with the Soviet Union, inland areas were again emphasized in industrial investment. The total result of all this is that while there was significant development of industry in the inland provinces, the sharp contrast between the inland provinces and the coastal areas remains today. American scholars Charles Roll, Jr., and Kung-cha Yeh, after a careful study of Chinese Communist industrial development in coastal areas and the inland provinces, reported, "The distribution of population between the coastal and inland areas hardly changed in the last two decades despite the emphasis on the interior. The share of total population in the coastal area remained at 40 percent throughout the period (1953-73)."[39] Moreover, they found that the distribution of industrial production between the coastal and inland regions is somewhat similar to total population. There had been a slight shift away from the coastal area during the first five-year-plan period. But this was followed by a balanced growth since 1957.[40] Chinese reports show that while there had been growth in the industry of inland regions, its quality is questionable. According to one report, from 1952 to 1978 the annual average rate of industrial growth in the coastal areas was 9.9 percent, whereas in inland regions it was 11.6 percent. Of the total value of industrial output, the proportion from inland industry rose from 29.2 percent in 1952 to 36.7 percent in 1978.[41] Nevertheless, the inland industry is referred to in China as a "burden" of Chinese economy. As to the nine provinces or autonomous regions (Xinjiang, Tibet, Inner Mongolia, Guangxi, Ningxia, Yunnan, Guizhou, Qinghai, and Gansu) in border areas, their total industrial output in 1981 amount to 60 percent of the industrial output of the city of Shanghai.[42] It is no wonder that in 1982 a Chinese governmental report called for an east-west dialogue inside China.[43]

Hence, in both the overall investment pattern and the regional developmental record the Maoist economic strategy stresses short-term gain at the expense of long-term development. The Chinese economy is truly a "political" economy.

STRUCTURAL STRAINS

The chronic effects of imbalances in the investment pattern of the Chinese Communist economy are aggravated by numerous strains caused by the Stalinist bureaucratic centralized model. Chinese enterprises had little or no independent decision-making power. Their production targets were assigned centrally by the planning commission of the national or provincial government. Distribution of products was handled by another state ministry. Labor force was allocated by the state. Equipment was also distributed by a state ministry. All profits of an enterprise were submitted to the state, and the state also bore all the losses. In the words of the PRC's top economic planner Xue Muqiao: "With one kick, we got rid of the market economy which capitalist nations developed for two to three hundred years and is most conducive for large-scale modern production. We established another economic model which, to a certain extent, has put a limit to the expansion of productive forces."[44]

The over-centralized economic system that the PRC took over from the Soviets has had several consequences for the Chinese economy. First of all, without the market mechanism, production was divorced from social demand. Thence followed the anomalous situation that, on the one hand, there was a stockpile of unwanted goods, and on the other hand, there was a shortage of much needed goods. Second, as two Chinese economists wrote in the *People's Daily,* the bureaucratic centralized model deprived the enterprises of their internal dynamism and relieved them of external pressure.[45] There was no incentive to innovate or to institute quality control. Today, only 10 percent of the products from Chinese machine-tool industries are of the genre of the 1970s or the 1980s.[46] Most homemade machinery is of the 1950 or 1960 type and has been in that state for the past twenty years. Take, for example, the famous Shoudu Iron and Steel Company. The annual output value of this company was over half a billion U.S. dollars. But until recently, the company was allowed only $400 for its own independent use—and sometimes not even that amount. As the general manager put it:

> In the past, each enterprise put aside an annual depreciation fund equivalent to 3.3 percent of the total value of its fixed assets. In addition, it had to hand over 50 percent of the fund to the state, so in actuality it ended up with a depreciation fund of 1.65 percent of its fixed assets. Our company uses much very old equipment, such as the US Ford Company's boilers made in 1918 and outdated steam engines left over by the Qing Dynasty (1644–1911). It will take the company 60 years to replace or transform all its old equipment with such a limited depreciation rate.[47]

It is no wonder that Chinese newspapers nowadays run stories such as "Loyang Steel Company Alters the Condition of 14 Years of Deficit"[48] or about the notorious Guangzhou Tractor Plant that produced a total of seven thousand *unusable* tractors in twelve years.[49] As late as November 1983 the Chinese press reported a deficit of over a billion dollars sustained by state-run enterprises.[50] Third, the bureaucratic centralized model facilitates the imposition of a "political line" over economics. For example, the scandal of the Guangzhou Tractor Plant was brought about by its former party secretary whose only interest was a statistical record of tractors produced, not the quality of them. Those in the factory objecting to the secretary were accused of committing the sin of "rightist tendency." Last, the bureaucratic centralist system created in China a vertically segregated economy. Each enterprise belonged to a vertical chain of command, the longer one being the national and the shorter one the regional bureaucracy. Lateral communication and coordination were extremely difficult if not impossible. This further contributed to the imbalances and bottlenecks in Chinese economy. It also directly promoted the informal alliances and cliques that we discussed previously.

The strains caused by the use of the Soviet bureaucratic centralized model in China have been compounded by the Maoist ethos of anti-intellectualism. A significant reason for the low productivity and quality of Chinese industry in general is discrimination against well-educated specialists. This discrimination is known in China as "amateurs leading specialists." Most Chinese enterprises are led by poorly educated political cadres. Their leadership in Chinese industry has been justified by Mao's line of primacy of politics. Under this pretext numerous "reasons" were used by party cadres in Chinese enterprises not to respect trained technical experts, such as bad family status, bad political qualifications (again based on family or class status), or lack of leadership experience. Most party leaders, learning from the repeated campaigns from 1949 to 1976, regarded "political task" much more important than "professional task."[51] The impact of the Maoist anti-intellectualism is shown not only in the dwindling number of technically trained persons in Chinese industry as a whole but also in the low educational qualifications of Chinese workers. According to the authoritative *People's Daily*, based on a survey of some 20 million Chinese workers and staff in 1979, it was found that 80 percent had education below junior high school, and of these 7.8 percent were illiterate or semiliterate. The majority of workers had low skills (below third grade in the Chinese system of skill classification), and most staff members had no knowledge of modern management. In industrial departments the technically trained personnel were a mere 2.8 percent of the total, and among these a considerable number had no higher education.[52] Given the lopsided pattern of investment, the share of technically competent personnel is extremely uneven in Chinese industry and agriculture. In 1978, for example, the technically trained personnel in Chinese light industry constituted 0.78 percent of total staff and workers.[53] In Chinese agriculture the technicians amounted to 4 percent of the rural population.[54] But China, as we mentioned earlier, had made notable progress in heavy industry, especially in defense industries such as aviation, rocketry, and space. Undoubtedly technically trained persons have been mainly channeled to these few elite industries.

Owing to all the foregoing, Chinese industrial development was grinding to a halt by the time that Mao died. This was dramatically demonstrated by the fact that it took longer and longer to complete new construction. A plant that took six years to construct in 1953-57 now takes more than ten years.[55] In 1978, for example, the *People's Daily* reported that the new harbor project at Guangzhou (Canton) city could not be completed in time due to nondelivery of promised cement and steel.[56] The late Sun Yefang, a top-ranking Chinese Communist economist and himself a victim of Mao's repression, wrote in 1983 shortly before his death: "Every year, more than one thousand large and medium-sized new projects (mainly industrial and transport and communication projects) go into construction, but only around one hundred of these are completed and functioning within the year."[57]

It is somewhat astonishing that the industrialization drive in the PRC ran its course in less than thirty years. Sometimes it is suggested that England today needs a second industrial revolution, but in contrast to the experience of China, the first industrial revolution took more than a century to run its course.

REFORM

Given the foregoing discussion, it is not surprising that high-ranking Chinese Communists described Chinese economy at the time of Mao's death as being "on the brink of collapse,"[58] which directly refuted those in the West who groundlessly stated that the Maoist model of development seemed "to be developing stronger capabilities for dealing with its domestic and international problems."[59] The state of the Chinese economy in 1978 was described by Li Xiannian, who was then a vice-chairman of the CPC. Li told the delegates of the National People's Congress that about 10 percent of China's 950 million people did not have enough to eat. Thousands were on relief, and factory workers received grain rations of only thirty-one pounds a month, not enough to sustain hard work. A rise in population and a lack of increase in productivity combined to prevent any real change in the Chinese people's living standard. In 1978 alone there were 20 million unemployed workers in urban areas. Complicating the problem were the 8 million people who lost their jobs in the Cultural Revolution.[60]

Li's dismal picture of the Chinese economy left behind by Mao paved the ground for drastic readjustment and reform in the hands of CPC pragmatists. The ambitious plan of Hua Guofeng to construct 120 large-scale projects from 1978 to 1985 was scrapped. The pragmatist leaders, such as Chen Yun and Deng Xiaoping, announced a three-year period of rehabilitation of Chinese economy, from 1979 to 1981. During this period Chinese leaders would "readjust, reconstruct, consolidate, and improve" the national economy in order to bring it step by step into the orbit of sustained, proportionate, and high-speed growth. The national budget of investment was revised as presented in table 17-4. Even the revised budget shows a high degree of lopsidedness in the low proportions assigned to light industry and agriculture. Nevertheless the adjustment policy made its mark. From 1979 to 1982 the value of agricultural output rose an average of 7.5 percent a year, that of light industry, 11.8 percent, and that of heavy industry, 3.4 percent. The relative proportions of agricultural, light industrial, and heavy industrial output value in the total output value of the three sectors also changed by 1982. The agricultural proportion increased from 27.8 to 33.6 percent, the light industry proportion increased from 31.1 to 33.4, and the heavy industry proportion decreased from 41.1 to 33 percent.[61] At the same time, the government raised the price of mandatory purchases of agricultural goods from peasants and reduced some agricultural taxes for the first time in twenty years so that the incomes of Chinese peasants began to rise. In urban areas workers' wages were also raised. One result of all this was several consecutive years of budget deficit, from 1978 to 1980. Another consequence of readjustment was an overall decline in the rate of economic growth which in the past had been kept up by the strategy of "extensive development" and massive investment in heavy industry. The rate of economic growth, owing to decline in heavy industry, slowed from 8.7 percent in 1980 to 1 percent in the first months of 1981.[62] As a reaction to this slump, in late 1981 the government had to re-emphasize heavy industry in order to arrest the demoralization of industrial workers.

The reform so far mentioned deals with investment function. The pragmatist leaders of the CPC also implemented reform in the organization and structure of Chinese enterprises. To reduce centralized control of enterprises, the government at first increased the portion of profit they retained for their own use. Then in June 1983 the law was changed so that now state-owned enterprises—the "mainstay of the national economy"—are required to pay taxes to the state instead of sharing their profits with the state. The state will no longer bear the responsibility for the gains and losses of the enterprises. Funding of development is now done mostly through bank loans. This, according to the government, is a "major step toward scrapping the 'big public pot' system which has long crippled the initiative of enterprises and workers."[63] Another measure allows more diverse forms of ownership of enterprises instead of the past uniform state or collective (regional units) ownership. There are today about eight different types of industrial and business ownerships, ranging from joint ventures between state and local enterprises to joint ventures between Chinese and foreign investors to individual enterprises.[64]

Within enterprises a *production-responsibility* system, similar to the responsibility system in farming, has been instituted. "The new system clearly defines the rights and responsibilities of each position in the enterprise, from the leadership down to the least skilled jobs. It also assigns specific wages (remuneration) to each job and defines

TABLE 17-4 National investment budget, 1979–81

	1978	1979
Investment in heavy industry	54.7%	46.8
Light industry	5.4	5.8
Agriculture	10.7	14.0

Adapted from Fox Butterfield, "China Releases Figures Indicating Budget Deficit," *New York Times,* June 22, 1979, p. D1.

how bonuses are awarded. It includes practical provisions for enforcing the principle of 'more work, more pay.' "[65] A Chinese writer compared the old system of Chinese enterprises to a building in which each individual enterprise is like a brick, entirely immobilized and lifeless. The new policy after 1978 was designed to make the Chinese enterprise system more like a living organism in which each enterprise is like a living cell, with a life of its own.

By far the most radical economic reform by the post-Mao leaders of the PRC is their attempt to connect the economy of eastern coastal China with the market economies of the West (thus reverting to the policy of the Nationalist government before 1949). Implicitly emulating Taiwan, Hong Kong, and Singapore, the PRC established four special economic zones, three in the province of Guangdong and one (Xiamen) in Fujian in 1980. Of these, Shenzhen, adjacent to Hong Kong, is the most successful so far. These special economic zones are primarily areas for foreign (Western and overseas Chinese) investment. As the mayor of Shenzhen described it, "These investors build factories, which in turn import advanced technology, create jobs, bring in foreign exchange and promote general economic development." [66] These areas are special in the sense that their economy is operated according to market economy, not the command economy prevalent in the rest of China. Enterprises in the special zones manage their business independently and produce goods for profit. These foreign factories produce primarily for export, and the Chinese government provides for low rates of taxation and custom duties, cheap labor, and social overhead (e.g., cheap land). By the end of 1983 Shenzhen had already concluded 2,506 agreements with foreign and overseas Chinese businesses and had imported 20,000 pieces of machines and equipment from abroad.[67] The other three special economic zones, lacking Shenzhen's unique advantages—proximity to Hong Kong (hence, availability of modern transport and cheap land) and availability of cheap labor—have accomplished much less than Shenzhen. In 1984 the Chinese government announced the opening of fourteen eastern and coastal cities (Qinhuangdao, Tianjin, Dalian, Yantai, Qingdao, Lianyungang, Nantong, Shanghai, Ningbo, Wenzhou, Fuzhou, Guangzhou, Zhanjiang, and Beihai) to trade with the West. These cities are allowed to have flexible economic policies. As the government communiqué explained: "Some of the cities may take measures to set up economic development zones in designated sections away from the existing urban areas. Essential services should be brought to those designated areas to provide sites for Chinese-foreign joint ventures, cooperative enterprises and enterprises with exclusive foreign investment." [68] In other words, these cities will have enclaves of special economic zones. All this, of course, is reminiscent of the old treaty ports in late nineteenth-century China.

How, then, does one evaluate the short-term and long-term consequences of these reforms under Deng Xiaoping? Robert Dernberger's overall assessment is worthy of mention. According to Dernberger, in the short run,

The new Chinese economic development model of the 1980s—one that rejects giving operational priority to the Maoist economic principles, adopts a rate and allocation of investment that is a compromise between the Stalinist "big push" and the "balanced growth" strategies, and to a lesser or greater extent allows for decentralized decisions based on market forces to supplement central control and planning in the allocation of resources and products—will be a considerable improvement over the Chinese model of the past in the post-Mao leadership's search for the path of sustained growth and ultimate modernization of the Chinese economy.[69]

However, Dernberger also writes:

> It is important to note that the adoption of an improved Chinese economic development model by the post-Mao leadership is only a necessary condition, not a sufficient condition, for solving both the current short-run economic problems they face—budget deficits, inflation, unemployment, import surpluses, etc.—and the fundamental long-run obstacles to the modernization of China's economy—the problems of agriculture, population, technology, etc.[70]

Of the long-run problems agriculture still ranks as the first and foremost obstacle. Reviewing Chinese agricultural development under Communist rule, Nicholas Lardy wrote in 1981:

> While state policy toward agriculture has moved in the right direction over the last few years, the steps actually taken seem quite modest and a significant undervaluation of agriculture persists. The state has not raised farm level investment significantly and failed to follow through on promised reductions in the prices of machinery and other agricultural means of production. While agricultural output has grown rapidly in the short run due to increased price incentives and greater freedom to pursue comparative advantage cropping, Chinese agriculture remains less commercialized and more of a subsistence character than it was in the 1950s. It is difficult to foresee how the Chinese economy can be modernized without more concerted efforts to provide improved price incentives to increase production, specialized cropping and marketing.[71]

Last but not least, there is always the fundamental problem of ideological legitimacy and political integration of the new programs under Deng. On the special economic zones, for instance, a Chinese Communist economist wrote:

> In the special economic zones, it is not only the law of value but also the law of surplus value that is operating. There is exploitation of surplus value in the form of profits earned by guest investors, whether joint ventures or foreign-owned enterprises. The exploitation of surplus value exists objectively in China's special economic zones, which is in contradiction with China's socialist system.[72]

On the ultimate question of political integration of the economic reforms, the remarks by the Nobel Prize winning economist Milton Friedman, after visiting mainland China in 1980, are quite germane:

> On an absolute level, China is a very poor, backward economy. The great bulk of its enormous population is engaged in agriculture . . . and the level of productivity in industry is terribly low. . . . With respect to change, as opposed to level, the situation is more complex. There clearly has been a decided improvement in the economy over the past three years or so. The Chinese attribute this to the new "pragmatic" policies adopted under Vice Premier Deng, who is clearly the person in charge. My own impression is somewhat different. It is a common observation that the restoration of order in a society that has been in a state of turmoil is capable of producing a rapid improvement in the economy. . . . The mere restoration of order on the death of Mao and the gaining of power by Deng was bound to permit a rapid recovery and a jump in economic level. I believe that is a far more fundamental explanation than the Deng reforms, most of which are so far only on paper. The reforms—the attempt to introduce market elements,

the opening up of contacts with the West, the encouragement of foreign invest-ment, and so on—are in a desirable direction. But the test of whether they will be carried out and what their effects will be is still for the future. . . . My own conjecture is that there will be a considerable progress in the next few years as some of the newly announced policies work themselves through the system. At the same time, I am pessimistic that the progress will be long continued. Opening up the system involves dispersing power and responsibility and that will produce threats to the security of the centralized political apparatus. It is likely to re-spond by closing down again.[73]

NOTES

1. W. W. Rostow in collaboration with Richard W. Hatch, Frank A. Kierman, Jr., and Alex-ander Eckstein, *The Prospects for Communist China* (New York: John Wiley & Sons; and Cam-bridge, Mass.: Technology Press of MIT, 1954), pp. 223–29.

2. Ibid., p. 224.

3. Ibid., p. 156.

4. Ibid., p. 134.

5. Ibid.

6. *Selected Works of Mao Tse-tung,* vol. IV (Peking: Foreign Languages Press, 1967), p. 422.

7. Ibid., p. 423.

8. C. E. Black, *The Dynamics of Modernization: A Study in Comparative History* (New York: Harper & Row, Publishers, 1966), p. 19.

9. *Selected Works of Mao Tse-tung,* vol. IV, p. 423.

10. Special commentator, "Rectify the Mistakes in the Guiding Thought of Economic Work," *RMRB,* April 9, 1981, p. 5.

11. *Wan-sui,* no. 2, p. 476.

12. Yang Jianbai and Li Xuezeng, "The Relations between Agriculture, Light Industry and Heavy Industry in China," *Social Sciences in China* I, no. 2 (June 1980), 190.

13. Ibid., p. 199.

14. Ibid., p. 189.

15. Jiang Dong, "We Want Both Heavy Industry and the People," *Xuexi,* no. 11 (1957), p. 20.

16. Yang and Li, "Agriculture, Light Industry and Heavy Industry," p. 189.

17. Ibid., p. 195.

18. Ibid., p. 190.

19. Ibid.

20. Ibid., p. 193.

21. *RMRB,* July 14, 1981, p. 5.

22. Yang and Li, "Agriculture, Light Industry and Heavy Industry," p. 191.

23. Ibid., p. 192.

24. Ibid.

25. Ibid., p. 191.

26. Special commentator, "Rectify the Mistakes," p. 5.

27. Frank Ching, "Ambitions Gone Awry: Problems Building Big Steel Mill Reflect Failure of China's Modernization Drive," *Wall Street Journal,* September 2, 1981, p. 42.

28. Song Jiwen, "On Greatly Increasing the Production of Consumer Goods," *Hongqi,* no. 6 (1981), p. 9.

29. *RMRB,* October 2, 1979, p. 1.

30. Lu Liping, "A Preliminary Inquiry into Economic Alliance," *RMRB,* April 23, 1981, p. 5.

31. *RMRB,* October 2, 1979, p. 1.

32. Yang and Li, "Agriculture, Light Industry and Heavy Industry," pp. 186–88.

33. Ibid., p. 187.

34. Ibid., p. 188.

35. Ibid.

36. Liu Fengchang, "An Urgent Task in the Adjustment of Economic Structure," *RMRB,* May 6, 1981, p. 5.

37. Yang and Li, "Agriculture, Light Industry and Heavy Industry," pp. 193–94.

38. Charles Robert Poll, Jr., and Kung-chia Yeh, *Balance in Coastal and Inland Industrial Development in the People's Republic of China* (Santa Monica, Calif.: RAND Corporation, April 1975), pp. 7–8.

39. Ibid., pp. 14-16.
40. Ibid.
41. Li Yueh, "Correctly Handle the Relations between Coastal and Inland Area Industry," *RMRB*, December 15, 1981, p. 5.
42. *Kuang Ming Ribao*, January 31, 1981, p. 4.
43. "'East-West Dialogue' in China," *Beijing Review* 25, no. 33 (August 16, 1982), 23-25.
44. Xue Muqiao, "The Reform of Economic Structure and System," *Hongqi*, no. 14 (1980), p. 7.
45. Wu Jinglien and Zhou Sulien, "Correctly Handle the Relation between Reform and Adjustment," *RMRB*, December 5, 1980, p. 5.
46. *RMRB*, December 7, 1983, p. 1.
47. Sun Yefang, "Expand Industry through Technical Transformation," *Beijing Review* 26, no. 9 (February 28, 1983), 24.
48. *RMRB*, May 23, 1981, p. 1.
49. *RMRB*, January 7, 1979, p. 3.
50. *Ming Pao Daily News*, November 18, 1983, p. 1.
51. *RMRB*, February 11, 1979, p. 2; March 21, 1979, p. 2; also, Fox Butterfield, "A Little Knowledge Is Dangerous to Many of China's Leadership," *New York Times*, June 1, 1980, p. 3.
52. *RMRB*, April 1, 1981, p. 1.
53. You Xinchao, "We Must Emphasize the Projection of Manpower Requirement," *RMRB*, December 10, 1981, p. 3.
54. Ho Chukang, "Firmly Grasp the Key Facets of Education and Science," *RMRB*, November 15, 1982, p. 5.
55. *RMRB*, March 24, 1979, p. 1.
56. *RMRB*, November 1, 1978, p. 1.
57. Sun Yefang, "Expand Industry," p. 22.
58. Special commentator, "Rectify the Mistakes," p. 5; also, Li Zhengrui and Zhang Choyuan, "High Speed Based on Proportionate Development," *RMRB*, March 16, 1979, p. 3.
59. James R. Townsend, *Politics in China* (Boston: Little, Brown & Company, 1980), p. 341.
60. Fox Butterfield, "China's Modernization Said to Cause 1978 Deficit," *New York Times*, June 15, 1979, p. D1.
61. *RMRB*, September 30, 1983, p. 1.
62. Fank Ching, "China's Planners Reemphasize Heavy Industry after Recent Years' Stress on Consumer Products," *Wall Street Journal*, September 30, 1981, p. 48.
63. "An Important Economic Reform," *Beijing Review* 26, no. 21 (May 23, 1983), 15-18.
64. He Jianzhang, "Newly Emerging Economic Forms," *Beijing Review* 24, no. 21 (May 25, 1981), p. 15.
65. "New System Improves Industry," *Beijing Review* 26, no. 15 (April 11, 1983), 24.
66. Liang Xiang, "China's Special Economic Zones," *Beijing Review* 27, no. 4 (January 23, 1984), 24.
67. Ibid., p. 28.
68. "14 More Coastal Cities to Be Opened," *Beijing Review* 27, no. 16 (April 16, 1984), 6.
69. Robert F. Dernberger, "The Chinese Search for the Path of Self-sustained Growth in the 1980's: An Assessment," *China under the Four Modernizations*, part 1, Joint Economic Committee, Congress of the United States, August 13, 1982, p. 76.
70. Ibid.
71. Nicholas Lardy, "Chinese Agricultural Development Policy," *Mainland China's Modernizations: Its Prospects and Problems* (Berkeley: University of California, Institute of International Studies and Institute of East Asian Studies, 1981), p. 183. For Lardy's general study of Chinese economic development, see his *Economic Growth and Distribution in China* (Cambridge: Cambridge University Press, 1978).
72. Xu Dixin, "Salient Feature: State Capitalism," *Beijing Review* 27, no. 4 (January 23, 1984), p. 31.
73. Milton Friedman, "Report to the Committee on Scholarly Communication with the People's Republic of China on Trip to China," quoted in Dernberger, "Chinese Search," p. 76.

For other major works on the Chinese economy, see Chu-yuan Cheng, *China's Economic Development: Growth and Structural Change* (Boulder, Col.: Westview Press, 1982); Jan S. Prybyla, *The Chinese Economy: Problems and Policies* (Columbia: University of South Carolina Press, 1981).

CHAPTER 18

Social Change
and Modernization

The various characteristics of Chinese Communist politics and economics that have been discussed so far have necessarily changed Chinese society in a profound way. In analyzing the changes in Chinese society since 1949 we shall note that actually two processes are involved. One is the universal "secular" change that all societies undergo as they are transformed from traditional and agrarian to modern and industrial states. It consists of urbanization, growth in literacy, rising per capita income, enhanced social mobility and equality, improvement in health, and social integration. The second change that one notes in Chinese society since 1949 is particular to China; it is the change brought about by Chinese Communist politics and economics, most notably the emphasis on class struggle, the use of turbulent and violent campaigns, dictatorship by the Communist party, and the various imbalances in Chinese Communist economic development. We shall analyze the impact of these two forms of change on Chinese society by focusing on population and occupation, family, education, social stratification and mobility, status of women, public health, and social consensus and integration.

POPULATION AND OCCUPATION

Undoubtedly the most significant and even catastrophic social change in mainland China after three decades of Communist rule is the population explosion. In 1949 when the People's Republic of China was established, the Chinese population in mainland China stood at 540 million. By 1964, the Chinese population had risen to 700 million, having increased annually by an average of 10.6 million for fifteen consecutive years. "In the fourteen years from 1964 to 1978, there was a net population increase of 250 million; from 1978 to 1979, 20 million more babies were born, pushing the population up to 970 million by the beginning of 1979. The annual growth rate averaged over twenty per thousand, much higher than the seven per thousand figure for the world's advanced countries."[1] In July 1982 the PRC conducted its third and most rigorous census. By that time the Chinese population had already broken the 1 billion mark. In October of the same year, the State Statistical Bureau announced that the Chinese population stood at 1,008,175,288—double the 1949 figure.[2] The length of time needed for each increment of 100 million Chinese has been steadily shortened from eight to seven to six years in the past thirty-three years.[3] Qian Xinzhong, chairman of the State Family Planning Commission, wrote in 1983:

> In 1981, the natural growth rate of China's population was 14.55 per thousand. At this rate of growth, the total population would top the mark of 1,300 million by the end of this century.
>
> The added expenditures to support 100 million extra people are staggering. If 2,200 yuan are needed to support a child until he reaches sixteen, the total to support 100 million will be 220,000 million yuan, nearly half of the total value of China's present fixed assets.
>
> From 1964 to 1982, China's population increased by 310 million. It can only increase by just over 190 million in the next eighteen years, with an average annual growth rate of less than 9.5 per thousand. This is extremely important, but difficult to achieve.[4]

As two Chinese economists put it, "Such rapid increase of population and the work force would have retarded the economic development of an economically advanced country, let alone a country like China."[5]

No effective birth control or family planning was possible before the death of Mao, whose opinion on population was set forth in the 1949 essay, "The Bankruptcy of the Idealist Conception of History":

> It is a very good thing that China has a big population. Even if China's population multiplies many times, she is fully capable of finding a solution; the solution is production. The absurd argument of Western bourgeois economists like Malthus that increases in food cannot keep pace with increases in population was not only thoroughly refuted in theory by Marxists long ago, but has also been completely exploded by the realities in the Soviet Union and the Liberated Areas of China after their revolutions.[6]

In 1957 when the chancellor of Peking University, Ma Yinchu, proposed in the National People's Congress that the government take up the population question seriously, he was quickly denounced by the Communist party as a Malthusian and anti-Marxist, subjected to a campaign of vilification, and forced to resign his chancellorship of the university. It was only in 1974 that even Mao had to acquiesce to a birth-control program, which, however, could not be effectively implemented owing to the factional struggle between the Maoist radicals and the party pragmatists. The former suspected any economic measure as an attempt by the latter to divert people's attention from the class struggle.

In the meantime, with the tremendous rise in population as a whole in mainland China, one would expect a large-scale migration from rural to urban areas, as the universal pattern of industrialization would suggest. However, the rate of urbanization in China is comparatively low, even among Third World nations. Only 20 percent of the Chinese population resides in cities. In contrast to the overall low urbanization rate, China has more cities with a population over one million than any other country. In 1950 there were only five cities in mainland China with populations over a million. By 1981 the number of cities with populations over a million had risen to fifteen. At the present time, 42 percent of Chinese urban population and 50 percent of the value of Chinese industrial output are concentrated in 43 cities (out of a total of 225 cities in mainland China), each with a population over 500,000.[7] The overall urban population, as the general population, has nearly tripled since 1949.[8] The imbalance in Chinese urbanization is a direct result of the economic strategy of the CPC, especially the stress on capital-intensive heavy industry.

In terms of occupational structure, China remains today an agrarian society, with 80 percent of the population engaged in farming. However, owing to the lopsided investment policy of the CPC, the number of industrial workers increased significantly in the past three and a half decades. From around 3 million in 1949, China's urban workers (including staff) rose to 110 million in 1982. Of these, 36 percent were women, almost a three-fold increase since 1955.[9] The internal composition of urban workers and staff today reveals both the overall pattern of Chinese economic development for the first thirty years of the PRC and the changes in Chinese economic policy since 1978. For example, of the 110 million workers and staff today, 76 percent are employed in state-run enterprises, while 24 percent are employed in "collective enterprises," i.e., private groups that have been allowed to operate since 1978. From 1978 to 1982, the collective enterprises grew by 29 percent, in contrast to 15.8 percent growth in state-run enterprises.[10] Many of the collective enterprises that have come into being since 1978 are in the service sector, which was a mere 6.4 percent of all the workers in 1978.[11] (In industrialized societies, the service sector typically amounts to 30 percent of all employed.) The tremendous increase in collective enterprises in the last five years has resulted in the service sector's rising to 20 percent of all the urban workers today.[12] This is by far the most dramatic change in China's urban occupational structure since the death of Mao. That the Chinese economy is organized along the Soviet bureaucratic centralized model is reflected in the number of "staff" members among urban workers. In 1982 the number of "nonmanual" workers (staff) amounted to 22,670,000, or 20 percent of the total workers in cities. It is highly likely that the technical and scientific professions are included in the nonmanual workers. In 1983 there were 5.7 million technical workers, a mere 0.57 percent of the population.[13] Of the manual workers, 50.5 percent are employed in heavy industry as compared (or contrasted) with 9.5 percent in light industry.[14] In terms of regional variation, the growth of workers in the coastal areas is higher than that in inland provinces, being more than 20 and 17 percent respectively from 1978 to 1982.[15]

In sum, the Chinese Communist occupational structure faithfully reflects the economic strategy of the CPC. That is, the development of the modern industrial sector is at the expense of the countryside. Moreover, in the modern sector, development concentrated in heavy industry at the expense of light industry and the service and intellectual professions.

Owing to the overcommitment to heavy industry and the rapid growth in population in the last three decades, unemployment in cities has become an increasingly serious social problem. When the Communist party first took power in 1949, it was faced with 4 million unemployed in urban areas. By 1956, most of the unemployed had been absorbed into the expanding industry. The total nonagricultural employment increased from 8 million in 1949 to 24.51 million by the third quarter of 1956.[16] Then came the artificial "boom" of the Great Leap Forward in 1958, and Chinese cities had serious labor shortages. So in addition to the annual 1.2 million new members of the labor force, some 20 million people were recruited from the countryside. The urban labor force swelled to 45 million in 1958. After the "bust" of the Great Leap, the 20 million labor force recruited from the countryside had to be "persuaded" to return to the countryside, where there was serious famine. The drastic adjustment made by the pragmatist leaders of the CPC after the disaster of the Great Leap reduced the proportion of workers in heavy industry from 80 percent in 1958 to 52.6 percent in 1965, and the proportion of workers in light industry rose to 47.4 percent from 19.6 percent in 1958. Ever since, Chinese leaders have been faced with urban unemployment, especially among the young. That is why in 1960 the Chinese Communist government launched the youth-to-the-countryside movement—to mask urban unemployment. From 1966 to 1976, an estimated 17 million Chinese youths from cities were disposed of by the government in this way. What is anomalous is that while millions of youths were being sent to the countryside, the government recruited 14 million workers from the countryside to carry out the lopsided third and fourth five-year plans (1966–75) (see chapter 17). It was only in 1974 that the government took measures to reduce this anomaly by allowing the only child of a family and sick or disabled youths to remain in cities and be employed. The youth-to-the-countryside movement was extremely unpopular among Chinese youths, who fully understood the real reason for their fate in spite of the high-sounding principle used by the government to justify the program. The poverty and misery in the Chinese countryside further disillusioned Chinese youth. Hence, given a chance, most of the youths in the countryside streamed back to cities, for instance, during the Cultural Revolution. After the death of Mao and the downfall of the Maoists, the present Chinese Communist leaders abandoned the youth-to-the-countryside program. About 10 million youths returned to the cities from 1977 to 1980. This movement, in addition to the 15 to 16 million new members of the labor force in the cities (annual number of youngsters entering the labor market being 5 million), created over 20 million unemployed in 1979–80. As the youths returning from the countryside were mostly already in their thirties and their desperate mood was highly disruptive socially, they were given priority in job placement over the youths just entering the labor market.

Since most state-run enterprises are capital-intensive heavy industry that do not employ many people, the government now allows private enterprises to operate under the euphemistic name "collective enterprises." The role of such enterprises in absorbing unemployed people can be seen in the statistics of employment made public by the government. In 1982 the percentage of those assigned to state-owned enterprises dropped to 20.9 percent from 29 percent in 1981. The proportion of those absorbed by collective enterprises increased to 50.4 percent in 1982 from 49 percent in 1981.[17] In September 1983 the Chinese government announced that 46.5 million people had been given employment from 1977 and the rate of unemployment had fallen from 5.5 to 2.6 percent.[18] Nevertheless, because of the growth of population and the irrationalities in the Chinese economic structure, it is estimated that each year there will be 4 to 5 million people seeking employment from the state.[19]

The employment pattern, like other sectors of the Chinese economy, reflects the imbalances in the Chinese politicalized economy. For example, light industry takes less investment, employs more people, and improves people's living standard faster than heavy industry. As two Chinese economists have pointed out, "With one million yuan of fixed assets, a state-owned light industrial enterprise can absorb 257 workers, but a heavy industrial enterprise can only take in 194 workers."[20] Similarly, the "third sector"—commerce, service, trades, public utilities, and scientific, cultural, educational, and health facilities—can create a great many jobs without much investment. "With one million yuan of fixed assets, for instance, 800 to 1,000 jobs can be created in these sectors."[21] However, the service trades and commerce were almost entirely eliminated after 1958 in order to satisfy Mao's preference for "a unitary system of the ownership of the means of production by the whole people." In 1953 there were 9 million self-employed Chinese in the third sector. After the "transition to socialism," only 150,000 of them were left by 1966.[22] Just as in rural collectivization, the thirty-year experience of "unitary system of the ownership of the means of production by the whole people" in the third sector of employment led to the demise of that system after the death of Mao. By now, however, a deep-rooted attitude has been formed among the workers of China, the young ones in particular. The most coveted jobs among urban Chinese youths today are in state-run enterprises in which one enjoys lifelong security, higher pay, and superior fringe benefits. In 1981 two Chinese sociologists surveyed 150 Shanghai senior high school students as to their choices of employment after graduation. Of thirty-eight suggested jobs, the students ranked "self-employed" thirty-eighth, the very last (the first choice being engineer, followed by doctor); peasant, or farming, was ranked thirty-fifth.[23] The students are only being realistic since Chinese publications are rife with reports of Communist cadres' discrimination against self-employed persons or collective enterprises. A study in 1980 of the collective enterprises in Shanghai by the students of Fudan University found that party cadres regarded the profits of collective enterprises as legitimate loot. In the name of "borrowing," the profits of collective enterprises were taken away, never to be returned.[24]

Perhaps the chief lesson of the Chinese experience with population growth and occupational change is that the universal process of urbanization in a predominantly agrarian society such as China is already stressful enough without being compounded further by the "particularistic" process of Maoism. Mao was poorly informed on the Soviet experience. As mentioned previously, he believed that the Soviet example showed that a big population was not an impediment to economic growth. But the Soviet Union did not have a big populati in 1928 when Stalin's drive to industrialization began. Moreover, both Soviet industrial technology and productivity and skilled manpower in 1928 were far superior to China's in 1952 when the first five-year plan began.[25] It is, however, difficult to argue with a true ideologue like Mao who, in 1962 when China was still reeling from mass starvation, boasted that Chinese industrialization had achieved the highest rate in world history because the socialist revolution had gone furthest in China.[26] He also claimed at the same time that collectivization in China was the most successful in the world.[27]

THE CHINESE FAMILY

The industrialization and urbanization process in China, as elsewhere, has brought fundamental changes to the Chinese family. In the universal process of modernization, larger kinship units normally associated with agrarian life give way to much smaller nuclear families consisting only of parents and younger children. In China this universal pattern is more true in cities than in the countryside. Rural Chinese families are affected more by the particularistic programs of Maoism than by industrialization.

In Chinese cities the process has been going on for a long time, starting long before the Communist takeover.[28] The rapid rise in urban population and the industrial labor force after 1949 further contributed to the growing number of nuclear families. What is significant in recent findings about urban Chinese families is not that nuclear families are in the majority but that there are still a considerable number of extended families, i.e., three or more generations living under one roof. For example, in a 1981 study of the families in a Peking residential area, sociologist Xiaotong Fei (Fei Hsiao-tung) reported that nuclear families constituted 56 percent of the families, but extended families still accounted for 18 percent of the rest. According to Fei, one very important reason for the persistence of extended families in significant numbers in his study is the housing shortage, yet another manifestation of the Communist policy of "production first, livelihood second."[29] In 1978 the average living space of an urban Chinese resident was 3.6 square meters, a 20 percent decline since 1949. Based on a survey of 182 cities in 1978, i.e., 95 percent of the cities, it was found that 36 percent of urban residents lacked adequate housing and that half of urban houses were in disrepair.[30] Another reason for the persistence of extended families, according to Fei's study, also has to do with the lopsided economic development in the PRC. That is the lack of child-care facilities, which has made the help of grandparents in taking care of young children a necessity for many Chinese families.

Another study, by two Chinese sociologists, of urban families in the city of Tianjin found that the percentage of nuclear families is correlated positively with the age of the parents. Of those families in which the husbands and wives were born before 1926, 31.32 percent were nuclear families. Among those families in which the husbands and wives were born after 1951, however, 67.21 percent were nuclear families. In contrast to Fei's study of Peking, in the Tianjin sample of 452 families, nuclear families constituted 82.9 percent and extended families, 0.7 percent.[31] This tends to confirm Fei's reasoning, which attributed the large number of extended families in his sample to "particularistic" causes. The universal pattern of the nuclear family accompanying urbanization and industrialization is irresistible in China as elsewhere in the world.

The pattern of the Chinese family in the countryside is subject mostly to Chinese Communist policies on rural development. Xiaotong Fei's longitudinal study of the Jiang Village in Jiangsu Province may be used as an example. Based on his investigation of the families in this village in 1936, 1964, and 1981, Fei presented a breakdown of families as shown in table 18-1. Now the most interesting aspect of the composition of families in Jiang Village is that from 1964 to 1981, the percentage of nuclear families went down while that of enlarged nuclear and extended families went up substantially.

Another noteworthy phenomenon among the families of Jiang Village was the significant rise in broken families from 1936 to 1964. Fei's explanation reveals the fate of Chinese peasants after "liberation." According to Fei, from 1954 to 1961, the population of Jiang Village declined steadily; in some years the death rate exceeded the birth rate. This is quite startling given the overall rising birth rate in the whole nation. It is relevant to mention here that Fei had also visited Jiang Village in 1957, and the very first complaint that the villagers made known to Fei was the lack of food since the collectivization.[32] In our discussion of the Chinese economy, we cited a study by two Chinese Communist economists, who testified that the food supply was already inadequate in 1953 when the first five-year plan began and that the government used collectivization and compulsory purchase to take grain from the countryside to feed the rising number of industrial workers in the cities. That was the background to Fei's report that 1962 was the year that the population in Jiang Village reached the lowest point (obviously due to the famine that followed the Great Leap Forward). The large percentage of broken families in 1964 was said to be partly due to young peasants' going out of the village to find a living. In other words, large numbers

TABLE 18-1   Breakdown of families in Jiang Village

	1936	1964	1981
I. Broken family			
(incomplete husband-wife team)	27.6%	32.7%	19.6%
II. Nuclear family	23.7	45.9	38.7
III. Enlarged nuclear family			
(husband-wife plus one			
grandparent)	38.4	15.9	21.1
IV. Extended family			
(two or more husband-wife teams)	10.3	6.1	20.6

Based on the paper, "The Problem of Support to the Old in a Time of Change in Family Structure—More on Change in Chinese Family Structure" by Fei Xiaotong, presented at the Conference on Modernization and Chinese Culture at the Chinese University of Hong Kong, March 7–11, 1983.

of peasants either died in the aftermath of the Great Leap Forward or fled the village to find work in cities. Starting in 1963, however, the population in Jiang Village began to increase, thanks to the policies of party pragmatists. The birth rate in the village reached an all-time high of 3.28 percent in 1963. The total population of the village increased from 1,412 in 1964 to 1,761 in 1981. But owing to the leftist policies during the Cultural Revolution (1966-76), no significant rise in living standard took place. There were few resources for peasants to build new houses, so the number of enlarged nuclear families and extended families increased quickly. According to Fei, only when the annual income of a peasant reached 300 yuan ($150) could he afford to build a house. But before 1978, the per capita income in a well-off village like Jiang remained around 100 yuan ($50). Even to this day, the average per capita annual income in the countryside is below 300 yuan. The crowded conditions in rural housing are exemplified by one case where three families used to live in a three-house courtyard in 1936; Fei found that eighteen families now live in the same courtyard.

In this connection we must point out that the growing number of nuclear families in the Chinese countryside should not be viewed in the same context as nuclear families in Chinese cities. Long ago, in traditional times, China abandoned the practice of primogeniture in favor of equal division of land among sons after the death of the father. So the development of the nuclear family in the countryside is not necessarily associated with modern influences. Rather, the number of nuclear families in a Chinese village is related to the income of peasant families. According to Fei, for example, nuclear families increased soon after the Land Reform, but rural collectivization, especially the disaster of the Great Leap Forward, reversed that trend. Today, after the dismantling of the people's commune and the subsequent prosperity in most Chinese rural areas, one may expect a rising trend toward nuclear families in the countryside. That the number of nuclear families in Chinese villages is associated with peasant income, not necessarily with modernity, is given further credence by the persistence of clan relations in the Chinese countryside. The resurgence of clans was first made evident during the Cultural Revolution when the Communist party was disintegrating amidst violence among numerous rebel and Red Guard groups. A long-time student of Chinese affairs reported in 1971: "The village clans have probably persisted throughout the twenty-two years of the People's Republic, but for most of the time they were kept in subjection and were rarely, if ever, mentioned. Politically they were insignificant. They are highly significant today; in the villages they constitute a social and political force that the military, though ruling all the counties, have been unable to handle."[33] The reversion to family farming after the death of Mao has certainly given the clans a new lease on life. Chinese visitors to the villages nowadays report almost full restoration of traditional social relations, such as ancestral worship, nativistic religion, and of course arranged marriages. Given the lopsided economic development in mainland China for the past thirty-some years, it is not surprising that the Chinese countryside remains tradition bound. In 1977 an anonymous Chinese citizen wrote a wall poster in Peking bemoaning the strange paradox in Chinese economy and society: "We have a satellite flying in space, but on earth our farmers must still pull plows with their shoulders."[34]

EDUCATION

In addition to the switch in occupation from agriculture to industry and the rise in the number of nuclear families, growth in education and literacy is a significant measure of the degree of modernization of a society. "Formal education," says James Coleman, "has a cardinal role in producing the bureaucratic, managerial, technical, and professional cadres required for modernization [and] education is unquestionably the master determinant in the realization of equality in a modernizing society dominated by achievement and universalist norms."[35] But educational development in the PRC did not escape the two forces that have affected all Chinese economic and social development—the lopsided investment pattern and the ideology of Mao Zedong, especially his strong anti-intellectualism. We shall review the accomplishments and problems in Chinese education in the context of Chinese economic development and Maoist politics.

In sheer quantity, the PRC has made great strides in the education of Chinese people as shown in the number of schools and students in tables 18-2 and 18-3. The rate of illiteracy has declined dramatically, from an estimated literacy of 10 to 20 percent in 1949 to 75 percent today. Nevertheless, the illiterates in 1982 still accounted for one-fourth of the people above twelve years old. Universal education remains a goal to be achieved, especially in rural areas. In 1982 only about one-third of China's two thousand counties reported universal education.[36] The quality of middle-school

TABLE 18-2   The growth of schools in the PRC, 1949–82

	1949	1957	1965	1978	1982
Institutions of higher education	205	229	434	598	715
Secondary schools	5,216	12,474	80,993	165,105	107,829*
Primary schools	346,800	547,300	1,681,900	949,300	880,516
Schools for the deaf and mute	—	66	266	292	312
Kindergartens	—	16,400	19,200	164,000	122,107

Source: Beijing Review 26, no. 40 (October 3, 1983), 26.

*Correction of the number of secondary-school students to 107,829 was published in *Beijing Review* 27, no. 4 (January 23, 1984), 5.

TABLE 18-3   The growth of number of students in the PRC, 1949–82 (in thousands)

	1949	1957	1965	1978	1982
Institutions of higher education	117	441	674	856	1,154
Secondary schools	1,268	7,081	14,∶8	66,372	47,028
Primary schools	24,391	64,283	116,209	146,240	139,720
Schools for the deaf and mute	–	7.5	22.9	30.9	33.7
Kindergartens	–	1,088	1,713	7,877	11,131

Source: *Beijing Review* 26, no. 40 (October 3, 1983), 26.

education is very low. The authoritative *People's Daily* reported in 1981 that even in such a reputedly cultured city as Peking, only one-third of the ninth-grade graduates that year met graduation qualifications.[37] The number of students in higher learning is embarrassingly small. "The proportion of students at schools of higher learning per 10,000 people is 11.4 in China, 58.4 in India, 106 in the USSR, 210 in Japan, and 507 in the United States."[38] Opportunity for higher education is severely limited. "Although about 4 million students have graduated from general senior middle schools each year since the examinations were restored in 1977, less than 300,000 were admitted to institutes of higher learning annually," said a report in 1982.[39] "As a result, more than 90 percent of senior high school graduates entered the labor market directly without the necessary professional knowledge or job skills. Many required two or three years additional training following graduation. This led to low labor productivity in numerous enterprises that are the key to economic construction," so wrote a senior Chinese education official in 1982.[40] Chinese educational development could have achieved much more than it did if it had not been affected seriously by the Maoist economics and politics.

After the death of Mao in 1976 and the arrest of the Gang of Four, more and more mainland Chinese scholars have been forthright in pointing out the debilitating impact on education of the state's lopsided investment in the national economy. Whereas after 1959 the state increased its investment in new industry by several fold, expenditure in education steadily declined.[41] In 1975 only 6.3 percent of total state expenditure was on education, and in terms of state expense on education per person, mainland China ranked 141st in the world.[42] Even in 1979 the state budget allocated only $8.14 per person for education, health, science, and culture.[43] In the sixth five-year plan (1981–85), the state investment in education, science, culture, health, and physical culture has been increased only marginally to $9.60 per person. As a Chinese educator pointed out in the *People's Daily*, most nations in the world allocate on an average 15 percent of the budget to education, but in China it was 10 percent in 1982, in spite of the Chinese government's avowed commitment to education.[44] He Tong-chang, minister of education, stated in 1982 that the state allocation in education has been used mostly to subsidize the wages of teachers and staff. As a result, school buildings, libraries, and equipment have been neglected and are in an appalling state.[45] The condition of rural schools is even worse than that of urban schools. According to a study in 1981, 70 percent of rural school teachers are academically unqualified to teach.[46] According to the Chinese press, owing to the severe shortage of construction materials, such as glass for windows in rural areas, peasants frequently loot schools for wood and glass. In an Anhui school students shivered in winter because of "glassless" windows. In 1981 Chinese industry could provide only 40 percent of the glass needed by the whole country.[47] A Chinese educator wrote in the authoritative *Red Flag (Hongqi)* that for decades the state was interested mainly in "the reproduction of materials" at the expense of improving the intellectual and physical quality of people."[48]

The extreme unevenness in the economic development of the PRC is also institutionalized in the structure of education. From 1949 to 1978 the state assigned most high school and college graduates—and all the brightest ones—first to defense industry, then to heavy industry, and third, to light industry.[49] The agricultural schools were slighted throughout the first thirty years of the People's Republic. Before 1966 only 7 percent of the students in higher learning were in special agricultural institutes. In 1979 that percentage had declined to 4.4.[50] Another imbalance in China's educational system is the ratio of general middle schools to vocational schools. In 1980 that ratio was 32:1.[51] According to a high-ranking Chinese educational minister, before the Cultural Revolution there was a general balance between academic middle schools and vocational schools. More than half the secondary school students (52.1 percent, or 4 million students) were enrolled in technical schools and vocational schools before 1965. But during the Cultural Revolution Mao and his left-wing disciples charged the educational leaders with class discrimination against students in vocational schools. Marshal Lin Biao called the two-track system (general middle schools and vocational schools) a "bourgeois tracking system." Consequently, "many secondary technical schools and workers' training schools were summarily closed; agricultural middle schools and vocational schools were *completely* dismantled" (emphasis added).[52] The result was that, on the one hand, the majority of Chinese received substandard general education, while on the other hand, Chinese factories lacked highly skilled workers. In the meantime, China showed off to Western visitors her impressive accomplishments in space, rocketry, and aviation. After a visit to Chinese space facilities in 1979, members of the American Institute of Astronautics and Aeronautics reported:

> In many cases our preconceived notions based on briefings and reports given by earlier U.S. delegations proved misleading. We were quite surprised at the advanced state of development in several technological areas as shown by work conducted in the last two or three years.
> Certain solid-state devices and techniques appeared to be advancing space with those in the U.S. Certainly we would discount any sweeping observation that "Chinese technology is x years behind the U.S."[53]

Thus the educational system of the PRC mirrors closely the lopsided economic development of China. Instead of integration, Communist policy in economy and education results in segregation.

The Chinese educational system before 1976 was affected significantly not only by the lopsided economic development but also by the Maoist politics. The latter probably has done more damage to Chinese education than the former. That educational policy is a political issue is recognized in and out of China. As James Coleman put it: "Since Plato and Aristotle, political philosophers have affirmed principles embodied in the phrases, 'As is the state, so is the school,' or 'What you want in the state, you must put into the school.' "[54] So it was with the PRC. What should be taught and how and who would be allowed to learn became issues of intensive elite conflict in the Communist party, especially between Mao and the party pragmatists.

Since 1949, Chinese educational policy has gone through five changes. At the beginning, from 1952 to 1957, China adopted the Soviet system of education with stresses on science and technology; large numbers of technical and vocational schools were opened to train technicians to support the policy of "extensive development" of industry. Changes in middle and primary schools from the pre-1949 days were more quantitative than qualitative. There was no rigid imposition of social-class qualifications of students, and learning was based on universal academic criteria. More drastic changes took place in a score of quality universities that had at one time been sponsored by American missionaries. The Communist party disbanded the social-science departments in these institutions and turned them into technical institutes. By and large, academic standards were maintained during this period.[55] Today 1950s graduates of the universities and colleges are valued more than those who graduated later.

But the Hundred Flowers Blooming campaign of 1957 radically changed Mao's attitude toward education. He was appalled by the criticisms of the Communist regime by intellectuals, professors, and college students, especially those in Peking.[56] From then on Mao worked steadily to destroy the higher-education institutions of China. The first measure imposed by Mao after 1957 and through 1960, coinciding with the Great Leap Forward, was to increase ideological indoctrination in school curricula. This was accompanied by two other measures: imposing social-class qualifications of students (students from proletarian background were given priority in college and university admission) and combining academic learning with common labor. During the 1958 "mass making of steel" campaign, almost all colleges were closed so that students and faculty could build backyard furnaces to make steel. At the same time, students and faculty were required to carry out a "reforming-the-teaching-methods" campaign. One student described this campaign: "The idea was to change the teaching system in the colleges and to emphasize the policy that education must serve the interests of the proletariat, that it must be integrated with productive labor, and that politics must always take command."[57] The key slogan used by the leftists then was, "Every student must be both red and expert" (politically sound and technically competent). Academic standards in Chinese higher education began their long decline until their eventual disintegration in the Cultural Revolution.

The failure of the Great Leap Forward after 1960 temporarily put a stop to Mao's educational policy. Under the leadership of party pragmatists, school life was returned to pre-1957 days. Academic learning and scientific and technical specialization were again emphasized in colleges and universities. A major reason for this reversal was the abrupt withdrawal of Soviet advisers from China in the summer of 1960 because of conflict between Mao and the Soviet leader Khrushchev. So China had to rely on her own scientists and technicians to industrialize. This period of "normality" in education lasted from 1961 through 1965.

Then came the Cultural Revolution of 1966–76 when all colleges and universities were closed so students could "make revolution." Professors and scholars suffered greatly during this period. Most of them were exiled to the countryside to do manual work, and a significant number of them died at the violent hands of their Red Guard students. All these actions were carried out in the name of "reform of education." The Maoist program for new schools consisted of shortening university education to two or three years and simplifying the curriculum to consist mainly of ideological learning (works of Mao, Marx, Lenin, and Stalin) and manual labor, with some professional training. Mao Zedong particularly favored factory-run schools so that students could learn while working. No one was allowed to go to a university until he or she first worked as a peasant for a number of years, and after that the student had to be recommended by party authorities in the countryside. In other words, admission criterion was political soundness, not academic merit. The students who were enrolled in the universities were known as worker-peasant-soldier students. In the 1970s, when the power struggle between the Gang and Four and the rehabilitated party pragmatists such as Deng Xiaoping gathered momentum, the former turned the universities in Peking into centers of radical agitation; students and faculty were made to write wall posters and articles for the press denouncing revisionism. For all practical purposes, higher learning in China ceased to exist from 1966 to 1976.[58] What Mao actually tried to do was to replicate his own experience. Mao and most of the Chinese Communist leaders had not spent their adolescent years in formal university learning; instead they had become student-agitators and revolutionaries in the 1920s. Thus Mao regarded university learning as luxurious at best and politically dangerous at worst. The middle schools and even the primary schools were also severely disrupted during the Cultural Revolution as the leftists encouraged students to pay no respect to teachers, in the name of "daring to innovate" and "daring to make revolution."

After 1977, with the party pragmatists in control, the Chinese educational system was returned to normality. However, the present leaders are now faced with a generation of uneducated or poorly educated youth and a badly wounded teaching profession.

These then are the reasons for the numerous horror stories told in the Chinese press about the low cultural standards of Chinese youth today. A professor of Chinese language and literature, for example, wrote to the *People's Daily* that a test of ninety-four juniors at a teachers' college found that 84 to 97 percent of the students did not know the most elementary method of locating source materials, such as making use of the *Guide to Periodical Literature*.[59] Semiliterate "college graduates" abound in post-Mao China.[60]

According to Talcott Parsons, as societies advance from primitive to modern, "they tend to become decreasingly subject to major change from narrow, particularized, conditional causes operating through specific physical circumstances or individual organic or personality differences."[61] The ill fate of the mainland Chinese educational system, especially higher education, before 1976 was largely the responsibility of Mao, who, as we have pointed out, had a deep antipathy toward university learning (with the exception of defense-related subjects). As mainland Chinese scholars eloquently testified after the death of Mao, "feudalism" is still predominant in Communist Chinese politics, economics, and society.

SOCIAL STRATIFICATION AND MOBILITY

The disruption of Chinese education before 1976 had serious implications for social stratification and mobility, which were further affected by the monolithic Communist political structure and the lopsided economic development in the PRC. The situation was reflected in the social stratification of the PRC.

Revolutionaries since ancient times have invariably promised "equality" to their constituents, though the evidence from world history shows that they have usually replaced old stratification with a new one. The Chinese Communist party is no exception. Despite claims to the contrary by Chinese Communist propagandists and some of their sympathizers in the West, mainland China is still a highly stratified society. Interviews with former residents of mainland China and other evidence show that the social stratification in mainland China closely resembles the stratification in the Soviet Union. Generally speaking there are eleven major social-class groups in mainland China:

1. The ruling elite, a small group consisting of high party, government, economic, and military officials, prominent scientists (the majority being in defense industries), and selected artists and writers.
2. Senior cadres, composed of the intermediary ranks of the categories mentioned above, plus certain important technical specialists such as senior engineers or architects.
3. Middle cadres, incorporating most of the middle ranks of the bureaucracy, junior military officers, technicians, most professionals, and some skilled workers.
4. The working class "aristocracy," consisting of those working in sophisticated industries such as instrumentation, computer, and semiconductor and defense industries such as space, missiles, and aviation.
5. General white-collar group, encompassing most employees and lower party cadres.
6. Average workers, e.g., in the steel industry and textiles.
7. Lower workers, those working in sanitation, sales, and restaurants.
8. Peasants in well-to-do villages, most in the areas surrounding modern cities like Shanghai.
9. Disadvantaged workers, i.e., "contract workers," who are not unionized and whose employment is seasonal; perhaps the youth sent to settle in the countryside should also be included in this class.
10. Average peasants.
11. Five groups of outcasts: former landlords, rich peasants, counterrevolutionaries, "bad elements," and rightists.

There are some important features of Chinese Communist social stratification that are not shown in the above hierarchy. The first is that to most Chinese youths on the mainland, the higher party-government-military elite is regarded as a caste, closed to all outsiders. The successors to this triumvirate elite are the members' children. Second, compared with 1949, the one social group that gained significantly in status over the decades was the military. A young Chinese, if of the "correct" family background, would choose the military as the second career preference, the first always being a college education in science or engineering. A military background gives a mainland Chinese a marked advantage over others in gaining access, later, to university education, party membership, and preferred position in industry. Third, the gain of the military in mainland China is contrasted with the loss of status of teachers. In traditional China teachers were esteemed. Now after thirty years of Mao's campaigns against intellectual elitism, teachers have become an unenviable group in China. There have been frequent reports in the mainland Chinese press of beatings of teachers by cadres and their relatives.

Another group whose status is quite revealing about the social stratification is the peasants. Despite all the official proclamations about the peasants' being "the purest" or "cleanest" people on earth, every mainland Chinese except the mentally retarded can see that peasants are shabbily treated and are only one step higher in status than the outcast classes. The Chinese press frequently refers to the *qing nong* ("looking down on peasants") attitude among the public. The lack of recognition of peasants in Chinese Communist society was demonstrated in the speeches and representations of the Fifth National People's Congress in September 1980. The official *People's Daily* had unprecedentedly devoted page after page to the views expressed by the delegates at the Congress. Of all the delegates, only two from Hubei aired the views of peasants. Subsequently, several readers wrote to the paper with the query: "Why are there so few who speak on behalf of peasants?"[62]

As anomalous as the status of Chinese peasants is that of Chinese intellectuals. The term *intellectual* in Chinese lacks a precise definition. Generally it refers to all those who have received a modern education that qualifies them as professionals, literary or technical. According to a senior Chinese scientist, in 1982 there were 20 million intellectuals in the PRC of whom 5.7 to 6 million were technical and scientific intellectuals.[63] Given their small number and their crucial role in China's modernization, intellectuals should receive national esteem and support. But this has not been true. Instead, before the death of Mao the Communist party carried out an inconsistent and self-contradictory policy toward Chinese intellectuals. On the one hand, the CPC followed the Soviet practice of rewarding senior intellectuals with high pay and material comfort, but on the other hand, the party repeatedly subjected intellectuals to vilification and even, during the Cultural Revolution, violent treatment. The root cause of this self-contradictory policy toward intellectuals was, of course, Mao's deep antipathy toward Chinese intellectuals. Like other modern-day totalitarian leaders, such as Lenin and Hitler, Mao professed to have great respect for the common man (or the masses) but contempt for intellectuals. In Mao's view, intellectuals were social parasites. He declared in 1957: "The intellectuals used to find sustenance in feudal, bourgeois and self-employed system of production. . . . Now they have climbed unto our body. The workers and peasants, through the Communist party, allow them work and let them eat."[64] Because of Mao's hostility, Chinese intellectuals have led an extremely precarious life under Communist rule. This is a historical irony since most Chinese intellectuals were ardent supporters of the Communist party during the civil war of 1947–49. Mao's persecution of Chinese intellectuals reached a peak during the Cultural Revolution. The intellectuals then were branded as the "stinking ninth category," coming after the eight kinds of class enemies: landlords, rich peasants, counterrevolutionaries, "bad elements," rightists, renegades, enemy agents, and capitalist-roaders.[65] The agents of the Gang of Four used extreme measures to deal with intellectuals. For example, it was reported in 1978 that while the radicals were in control of Qinghua University in Peking, three thousand professors and staff were deliberately sent to an area infested with contagious disease; as a result, more than a thousand members of the faculty and staff fell victim to disease.[66]

Whereas the Communist party has granted senior intellectuals high pay, the overwhelming majority of Chinese intellectuals have been paid extremely low wages. A senior scientist or artist (actors and actresses) may get as much as 1,000 yuan a month, but most Chinese intellectuals receive wages lower than those of workers, who earn an average of 50 yuan a month. Most intellectuals have to endure three hardships: low pay, poor living conditions, and contempt from the rest of society.[67] After the death of Mao, the pragmatist party leaders adopted a new policy toward intellectuals, who are now regarded as part of the working class. Substantial improvement in the income and living conditions of intellectuals (but not all of them) has been made since 1980. More and more intellectuals have been admitted into the Communist party. In 1980 intellectuals constituted 19 percent of the new members of the CPC; in 1982 the percentage had been raised to 23.6.[68] Nevertheless, the present leaders admitted that there are obstacles to the new policy toward intellectuals. The Maoist anti-intellectualism is deeply entrenched among party cadres, who are mostly from worker-peasant backgrounds. Present CPC leaders have to contend with sentiments among cadres such as, "While we fought for the empire, the intellectuals sat on the sideline" or "The social background of intellectuals is too complicated" or general references to intellectuals as "they."[69]

Finally, the most significant change in Chinese social stratification after 1949 was the establishment of formal "outcast" groups or, in Mao's term, *nonpeople*. The outcasts are landlords, rich peasants, counterrevolutionaries, "bad elements," and rightists. These appellations are hereditary, designating not the individual but the family. Persecution and discrimination have been imposed by the Communist party. "This type of pariah," said a long-time scholar of Chinese affairs, "is new to Chinese society . . . the most striking development under Communist rule."[70] An official report revealed that in 1977 there were 6 million former landlords, rich peasants, counterrevolutionaries, and "bad elements" in China. After Deng Xiaoping's "declassification" campaign of 1979, the number of those "four elements" had been reduced to 100,000. In 1948 the Communist party had designated 36 million people as landlords and rich peasants, to be made "the object of revolution."[71]

Another aspect of modernization is change within the system of stratification. For example, according to Alex Inkeles, modernization brings forth social homogenization and equilibration with the stratification system. By the former, Inkeles means "reducing the gap or range separating the top and the bottom of the scale in the several stratification subsystems based on income, status, power, experience (self-expression, knowledge, and skill). . . ."[72] By equilibration, Inkeles refers to the phenomenon in which "an individual's rank in any one of the several stratification hierarchies tends to be the same or similar to his rank in any other hierarchy of the set."[73] Let us look into these two aspects of social change.

On the degree of social homogenization within each social stratum, we know that there is a complicated system of ranks and wages and that the system is different in different professions. With the party and government, for example, there are about twenty-four ranks. The differential between the highest and lowest levels, before 1956, was 28:1 and after 1956, 25.2:1.[74] The late Alexander Eckstein found, while in mainland China, that the range of wage differential in Chinese industry was between 3:1 and 5:1 and, in his words, "quite typical for industries in many other countries, both developed and underdeveloped."[75] But these formal differences are only part of the story. Conversations with former residents of mainland China reveal that the inequality extends beyond wages, to special privileges for the higher-ups. The description of the privileges of high party officials written by the editor of *China News Analysis* is worth quoting:

> The salary of a top man may be ten times that of the lowest grades, but in itself, particularly when compared with salaries in the Western world, it is not high. Nevertheless the higher cadres enjoy privileges, which are admired and envied by the lower cadres.
>
> Fairly reliable sources say that in Canton the highest army and government officials of the present regime live now in the modern villas once occupied by the Nationalist high officials. The men in the highest brackets have cars at their disposal. Their entertainment expenses are met by the State, as are also their own and their families' medical expenses. Their wives do not go to the market, and if they go shopping, they do so in private cars with the car-curtains drawn.

Lines of distinction between the ranks are sharply drawn. A section has several cars and its leaders may use one when on an official errand; on trains they travel hard-berth; for lodging each has a flat with two bedrooms and a sitting room.

The head of a Department lives in a house with three bedrooms and a sitting room. He has a car at his personal disposal, but only for official purposes. On trains he travels soft-berth. If necessary, he can travel by plane. When he or a member of his family is sick, the hospital gives the case preferential treatment.

The head of a Bureau has his own private car; all he has to pay for is the petrol. If he travels with some of his subordinates he can reserve a special coach on the train; and he may always travel by plane. He lives in a house with a garden, or if no such house is available, in a flat with four bedrooms and a sitting room. He has a special body-guard and a chauffeur and his family has a woman servant. The head of a province may have several body-guards and servants, and he may travel on a special plane.[76]

More than the above-mentioned privileges tied to a party cadre's formal position is the hereditary nature of these privileges. After the death of Mao, there was an exposé in the media on the conduct and privileges of the children of high cadres. Those children have become a special class on the mainland.[77] They have taken special routes to position and privilege, especially if their fathers were of high rank. In the late 1960s children of high party cadres avoided the youth-to-the-countryside movement by entering the armed forces. Once inside the military, these privileged youngsters were given the least onerous and most civilian oriented work such as in logistic departments and military hospitals. When colleges and universities were revived in the early 1970s, the children of high party cadres quickly left the armed forces and entered universities. In the late 1970s they were given the first opportunity to go abroad to study in America and Europe.[78]

By all accounts, the most glaring inequality is between life in the countryside and in the cities. According to Martin Whyte, "In spite of the official policy of reducing the urban-rural income gap, a large differential remains, and it is not clear that it has been reduced to any extent since 1949."[79] Whyte has suggested that the urban-rural differential in income is on the order of 2:1. According to the State Statistical Bureau, however, in 1980 the average income of an urban resident was $319, whereas that of a rural resident was $88, a differential of 3.6:1.[80] Nick Eberstadt further elaborated on the urban-rural differential in China:

> The most surprising fact about the inequality between city and countryside in China is that there are no clear signs it is diminishing. It was about 2:1 not only in the 1950s but also in the 1930s, the era of impoverished peasants and grasping urban capitalists. Income inequality *within* cities or rural regions may have declined, but there is no evidence that nearly three decades of socialism have brought . . . "equality" between rural "peasants" and urban "workers."
>
> Even greater than the difference between city and country, however, is the difference between rich and poor provinces. Partly by historical accident and partly by design, China's wealth lies along a coastal rim which extends up into Manchuria. . . . In 1957, the last year for which there are reliable and comprehensive figures, the ratio of per capita agricultural and industrial income between Honan, the poorest province, and Shanghai, the richest, was well over 7:1.[81]

Eberstadt's analysis was confirmed by a 1981 official report, which stated that 10 percent of the two thousand-odd counties had experienced no improvement in life since the 1950s. These counties are located in the northwest and southwest frontier regions. Economically, counties leading the nation are in the Songhua-Liao Valley in the Northeast, on the Changjiang (Yangtze) Delta and the Hangzhou-Jianxing-Huzhou Plain in the East, and on the Zhujiang (Pearl) River Delta in the South. In 1979, 1,622 outstanding production brigades (about 2.3 percent of the total in the country) whose per capita income was $210,400 were on the periphery of Shanghai.[82] So the image of mainland China as a dual society, one urban and one rural, is once more being reinforced.

In sum, we cannot say categorically that Inkeles's social homogenization took place from 1949 to 1980. We see little change in urban-rural differential from the 1930s to the present. Though the formal wage system does not show extreme disparity, there is a vast difference in privileges between the high and the low.

The political stratification also shows little tendency toward homogenization in the access to power. The activities of the Cultural Revolution bear that out. Mao Zedong had originally induced a large number of youngsters to support his Cultural Revolution with a vague promise of more access to power. In the end, the Cultural Revolution merely replaced one group of veteran party cadres with another. That is why to this day the phenomenon of "aging" among party leadership at every level of the bureaucracy remains a national issue.

On Inkeles's concept of social equilibration, which refers to the consistency in an individual's rank in several stratification subsystems, we do not have much information pertaining to mainland China. According to Inkeles, "The educational measure is particularly useful in highlighting the tendency of modern society to bring the different stratification measures 'into line.'"[83] Before 1976, however, Mao took several measures to cancel the equilibrating effect of education, such as sending educated youths to settle permanently in the countryside, stressing "politics taking command" or "amateurs leading experts," and so on. Impressionistic evidence suggests that individuals must possess two crucial aspects to enable them to use their rank to get ahead in other stratification subsystems (e.g., power, income, status, style of life). These assets are seniority in the Communist party and urban residence. A former resident of mainland China explained to Lynn White the reasons for people's wanting to move to Shanghai:

> They come mainly for material benefit. A worker is usually paid higher wages in Shanghai than in other cities, not to mention the rural areas. And in Shanghai he can enjoy the facilities of China's most modern city. There he will have more rationed food, cooking oil, and sugar. He can buy a greater variety of commodities than is available even in Peking. And because Shanghai is more developed in all respects, the people enjoy more freedom of ideology, so to speak. Even the meetings in hours after work are fewer than elsewhere.[84]

As to the numerous benefits that come with party seniority, we have already made them clear in our discussion of privileges. Our point is that, at least before 1976, education or general knowledge did not play an important role in gaining access to urban residence or party membership. However, in certain selected areas not even Mao could stop the equilibrating effects of modern education and occupation. These are the defense-related subjects such as nuclear physics, computer science, and space science. To these lucky few (many of the young ones in these fields are children of high party cadres) social equilibration is real. But for the vast majority of the people, their rank in each stratification system has very little "carryover" effect on other systems. Mainland Chinese society is in fact highly segregated and traditional. In traditional society, says Inkeles, "there is relatively sharp separation between many of the different stratification realms, because of religious and quasi-religious restrictions on certain types of activity."[85] Former residents of mainland China bear witness to the existence of political restrictions on people's choice of career and profession.

It should surprise no one that social mobility is subject to the influence of those broad events that we have already mentioned: the gap between city and countryside, destruction of the educational system during 1966–76, the norm of "politics taking command," and the priority in heavy industry. In retrospect, social mobility for the young and the lower classes in mainland China was relatively high in 1950–57. For example, in the period of 1949–59 the number of students in institutions of higher education increased from 117,000 to 812,000, and the students in specialized vocational schools increased from 229,000 to 1,490,000.[86] In the same period Chinese industrial production grew at an annual rate of 18 percent. Moreover, as mentioned before, during the first five-year plan the government invested significantly in interior China in order to even the spread of industry. But by 1959 Chinese Communist state investment had shifted back to the coastal areas.

After 1959 several factors emerged to lower social mobility in mainland China: a rise in population, destruction of the educational system, imposition of stringent political criteria on career choices, and forced migration of millions of people from cities to the countryside. Nationalization of commerce, service trades, and handicrafts after 1958 also tended to restrict social mobility. By 1965, according to Michel Oksenberg, social mobility was characterized by: (1) an extremely limited range of career choices, (2) intense competition and accompanying risks and dangers, (3) generally limited career options within an organization, and (4) permanent exclusion from the political system if, for one reason or another, one does not accept the first career offer by the system.[87] The Cultural Revolution, by destroying the higher-education system and paralyzing industry, depressed social mobility as a whole.

Today career opportunities for Chinese youths are as limited as ever. Even for those lucky enough to be in colleges or universities, changing one's initial choice of study is very difficult, if not impossible. To the majority of peasant youths, social mobility means, as it has meant since ancient times, joining the army. Unemployment in large cities has reached such an extent that when a district sanitation office in Shanghai wanted to hire twenty-six female sanitation workers (considered very low in employment status) in 1981, eight hundred high school graduates *within the district* applied.[88] It is estimated that from 1981 to 1985, jobs have been needed for 30 million youths.[89] There is no doubt that lack of career opportunity ranks as the number one social problem and is one of the most important causes of the "crisis of faith in socialism" in China.

In sum, the development of social stratification and mobility in the PRC for the past thirty-some years has paralleled China's economic development—initial spurt followed by decline and breakdown. Though the effects of modernization are real, as in the rising number of people in the modern labor force, they have been more than offset by the underdevelopment of peasants and intellectuals. In the meantime, social mobility has been restricted to a tiny minority, i.e., college graduates and children of the party elite. Undoubtedly, the post-Mao policies of the party pragmatists, especially with respect to intellectuals and self-employed professionals, will bring about a degree of mobility and pluralism in stratification. But the large population, particularly the young generation, and the limited capacity of China's industry to absorb new manpower and womanpower will keep a lid on Chinese social development.

STATUS OF WOMEN

Modern revolutions always raise the hopes of the underdogs in society, including the underdog in the sex hierarchy. In one of his most memorable essays, "Report of an Investigation of the Peasant Movement in Hunan," written in 1927, Mao Zedong wrote that whereas Chinese people as a whole were subject to three forms of authority—state, clan, and religion—Chinese women had to endure the additional authority of males. "These four authorities—political, clan, religious, and masculine," Mao wrote, "are the embodiment of the whole feudal-patriarchal system and ideology, and are the four thick ropes binding the Chinese people. . . ."[90] The CPC thus, in principle, was committed to the liberation of women.

Aside from the Communist revolutionary ideology, modernization as an empirical process also tends to erode male domination over women. The advanced technology that modernization brings strikes at the root of male domination by making physical labor increasingly unnecessary. Education is the principal vehicle for the emancipation of women, making professional, managerial, and clerical occupations available to them.[91]

How then have the women fared since 1949? We shall look briefly at Chinese women's access to education, employment, and political power in the PRC.

According to a mainland Chinese writer, before 1949 girls constituted at most one-fourth of primary school enrollment and one-fifth of middle school enrollment, and 17.8 percent of college students were women. In 1981 female enrollment in primary schools was slightly less than half the total enrollment. In middle schools female enrollment was 40 percent and in colleges and universities, 25 percent. Before 1949 the percentage of females in the work force was 7.5.[92] The total number of female workers increased from 31.28 million in 1978 to 40.93 million in 1982, accounting for 36.2 percent of the total number of workers and staff members as against 32.9 percent in 1978.[93] Compared with the rest of the world, the gains of Chinese women in acquiring higher education are more or less on a par with those in developing nations; the percentages of women in higher education in Latin America, Africa, the Middle East, and Asia in 1970 were respectively 33, 26, 23, and 30. In the USSR the proportion of women studying at institutions of higher education was 42 percent in 1968, and in North America the percentage was 40. However, China's record of female employment in 1983 had caught up with the developed nations of the world. In 1970, according to the Department of Economic and Social Affairs of the United Nations, "Women comprise[d] 40 percent or more of the labor force in a number of countries, especially in Eastern Europe, and between 30 and 40 percent in most of the Western European and North American countries."[94]

However, in spite of the impressive statistical record of the achievement of Chinese women after 1949, we see a persistent pattern of discrimination against women. For example, according to Kang Keqing, the chairwoman of the Fourth Executive Committee of the All-China Federation of Women, in 1983 "about 70 percent of the 200 million illiterates in the country are women."[95] Undoubtedly, most of the female illiterates are in the countryside. In primary and middle schools, female teachers constituted half of all the teachers in 1981. But at the university level, female instructors and professors were 26 percent of the total university faculty.[96] The destruction of higher learning in the Cultural Revolution was definitely detrimental to the status of women. As Phyllis Andors found, the highly trained female specialists in industry, education, medicine, and the arts before 1965 were a product of the educational system of the 1950s and early 1960s.[97]

In terms of access to political power, according to the head of the Organization Department of the Central Committee of the CPC, there were 4.7 million female cadres in 1981, constituting 26 percent of total cadres, representing a thirteen-fold increase over 1951. But among leading cadres, the percentage of female cadres went from 3 to 6 percent.[98]

The above discussion, however, does not reveal the tremendous difference in the fate of women in cities and in the countryside. Phyllis Andors, for example, pointed out that the institutional order in the countryside of the PRC did not provide conditions for women's liberation. She was referring to the overwhelming importance of physical strength in work, the workpoint-allocation system before 1980, the lack of child care or other services to relieve women of domestic duties, the absence of technological development to enable women to use their talent, and, above all, the equivocation of Communist authorities over the role of women in society.[99] Perhaps the most telling and gruesome indication of the lack of improvement of women's status in the countryside is the sudden rise of female infanticide since 1981 as a result of the government's stringent birth-control policy ("one family, one child"). The *People's Daily* reported in March 1983: "At present, the phenomena of butchering, drowning and leaving to die female infants and maltreating women who have given birth to female infants have been very serious. It has become a grave social problem."[100] In some poor Chinese counties the murder of female infants resulted in a radical change in the sex ratio of living infants. In two counties in Anhui Province, the proportion of male to female infants was 103.1 to 100 in 1979 but 116.4 to 100 in 1981. In two communes the ratios of male and female infants were respectively 175 to 100 and 180 to 100.[101] The Communist government characteristically, while playing down the seriousness of the problem, blamed it on "old feudal ideas" of male superiority, though it did not explain why, after more than thirty years of Communist "liberation," the fate of females in the countryside and even in cities to a certain extent was still in the days of feudalism. Two mainland Chinese scholars studying in the United States wrote anonymously to the *New York Times:*

> We are filled with boundless indignation that during this last quarter of the twentieth century such atrocities take place in our country. They reflect, on the one hand, the persistence of feudal thought and traditional indifference to the welfare of women and female children, and, on the other, the backward, benighted conditions of poverty and ignorance under which most parts of China still live.
>
> But traditional prejudice and economic backwardness notwithstanding, we strongly feel that all elements of our Government concerned with implementation of the new population policy should be held directly accountable for the prevalence of such tragic incidents. Infanticide need not be an inevitable outcome of the policy. Apparently, the affected units and organizations have not adopted a policy of "gentle persuasion and education" to achieve the desired goal of birth control and population control but have callously exerted political pressures and adopted extreme political measures for implementation of the policy.[102]

Embarrassed by the publicity about female infanticide, the Communist government announced in May 1983 that the sex ratio of China's newborns was "normal."[103]

Meanwhile, the Chinese press has reported other instances of violence against women. For example, in the countryside, peasants use their daughters to make prospective husbands pay a large sum of money or give a generous dowry and then have them quickly sue for divorce so that their daughters can be used again. The *China*

Youth News published a special column, "Marriage by Sale," in November 1978 and within three months, it received more than four thousand letters in response from readers.[104] The 1981 year-end issue of the journal *Women of China* reported that kidnapping of countryside girls to be sold elsewhere was on the rise.[105] The official *Beijing Review* reported in 1981: "Many young people below thirty did not even know that there was a marriage law in China." [106] The new "responsibility system" in farming has caused farmers to withdraw their daughters from schools since now a family's income depends on its own efforts. Thus illiteracy among Chinese women will remain high for some time to come. So on the status of Chinese women in the PRC, we are once more faced with the stark contrast between urban and rural areas. But 80 percent of the Chinese reside in rural areas where female laborers amount to 150 million—half the labor force. The lopsided economic strategy of the PRC under Mao, who once wished to free Chinese women from masculine authority, instead confined rural women to the old authorities of the "feudal-patriarchal system and ideology."

PUBLIC HEALTH

Commensurate with the rise in literacy, urbanization, social mobility, and the status of women is the great improvement in health, owing to the availability of modern health care. That is the universal pattern. But each nation adapts to this universal process in its own way. Two important questions are whether the improvement in health is relatively even among the population and whether health care is based on an overall improvement of living conditions such as the supply of potable water, adequate nutrition, housing space, and sanitary environment. As subsequent discussion will show, the imbalances in overall Chinese economic development are an important factor in public health in the PRC.

Many claims have been made about improvement in public health since 1949. In reality, growth of public health in China, like the overall economic development, has been more quantitative than qualitative. Let us look at the most commonly used indicators of the health status of a population: the mortality rate, the hospital bed/population ratio, and the doctor/population ratio. Table 18-4 presents the latest Chinese health statistics.

The most dramatic improvement in the health of the Chinese population since 1949 was the decline in the mortality rate. By world standards, a mortality rate below

TABLE 18-4   Mortality, hospital bed/population ratio and doctor/population ratio in the People's Republic of China (unit: per thousand)

	1949	1957	1965	1975	1980	1982
Mortality	20.0	10.8	9.5	(6.3 in 1978)		6.6
Hospital beds	0.15	0.46	1.06	1.74	2.02	2.03
City	0.63	2.08	3.78	4.61	4.70	4.76
Countryside	0.05	0.14	0.51	1.23	1.48	1.46
Doctors*	0.67	0.84	1.05	0.95	1.17	1.29
City	0.70	1.30	2.22	2.66	3.22	3.59
Countryside	0.66	0.76	0.82	0.65	0.76	0.81

*Includes traditional Chinese medicine

Source: "Health Service," *Beijing Review* 26, no. 46 (November 14, 1983), 23.

15 per 1,000 entitles a country to be ranked among the developed nations. In some developing nations the mortality rate ranges from 100 to 200 per 1,000.[107] Because of the greatly lowered mortality rate, the average lifespan of Chinese in 1982 was sixty-eight years as compared with thirty-five years in 1949.[108] Undoubtedly, the end of the war in 1949 and the extension of basic medical care account for that result. Historically, as we mentioned at the outset, the Chinese population always increased rapidly after the founding of a new dynasty.

While improvement has also been made in hospital bed/population and doctor/population ratios in the PRC since 1949, it is moderate compared with the world standard, and moreover, there are sharp contrasts between urban and rural areas. In terms of hospital bed/population ratio, the world average in 1970 was one bed for every 229 persons. In China overall it was one bed for every 500 persons in 1982. But Chinese cities have attained the world average of hospital bed/population ratio, whereas the countryside is far below the world average. In the availability of doctors, China is ahead of most developing nations but behind the USSR (2.4 doctors per 1,000 in 1970).[109] But again it is the Chinese cities that are impressive by world standards while the availability of doctors in the countryside is very much in the norm of developing nations. Moreover, one can see the deleterious effects of the Cultural Revolution in the availability of doctors; note the decline of the doctor/population ratio from 1965 to 1975, especially in the countryside, where the ratio reverted to the 1949 level. Yet one of the rallying cries of the radicals in the Cultural Revolution was to make more physicians available to the peasants.

The development of Chinese medical services is essentially of the "extensive" type at the expense of quality. According to the Ministry of Public Health, one-third of the hospital beds are of makeshift type. The shortage of "specialized beds" is acute. In many cities, two or three women giving birth have to share one bed.[110] In 1983 a high Chinese finance official complained to the minister of public health that even the medical facilities in the *clinics for high cadres* were in poor condition, not to mention those in the *hospitals for ordinary people*.[111] The cause of that was the same as in other sectors of "nonmaterial production": lack of funds, which were diverted to heavy industry. The nationally circulated *Jiankang Bao (Health Newspaper)* cited the province of Guangdong as an example "where public health expenditures in 1979 were 3.94 percent of the total expenditures of the province, 6.12 percent less than the 1952 figure. . . . From 1950 to 1981 annual investment in public health capital construction was gradually reduced to only 0.68 percent of the province's total investment in capital construction."[112]

Though much publicity has been given to Chinese Communist extension of modern medicine to Chinese peasants, particularly the "barefoot doctors," the real situation is less rosy than the official accounts, which are usually accepted uncritically by the outside world. It is reported that all of China's two thousand-odd counties have a modern hospital and that each commune (fifty thousand of them) has a clinic. But the problem is that thse rural medical facilities are financed locally. As a consequence, the availability of medical care in the countryside depends on the prosperity of an area and the fluctuating condition of the harvest. In times of poor crops, commune medical service has to be suspended.[113] Because of the poverty in the countryside, Chinese peasants regard medical service as they regard schools—as a luxury that they cannot afford. So as soon as the new "responsibility system" in farming was established in 1980, peasants refused to contribute to either local schools or clinics. Consequently, the livelihood of the barefoot doctors (paramedics) was immediately threatened. The number of barefoot doctors has been declining steadily since 1977: 1.76 million in 1977, 1.67 million in 1979, 1.46 million in 1981, and 1.39 million in 1982.[114] One reason for the decline was the return of urban youths to the cities after 1978. Many of the barefoot doctors were urban youths sent by the government to the countryside to relieve the burden of unemployment in urban areas.

Then there are other qualifications that one must make on the public health in China, based on more recent reports in the Chinese press. First, in the past much of the public-health work was carried out in the form of mass campaigns, for instance, to kill rats, flies, fleas, and schistosomiasis. Since campaigns were staged by the party in a top-to-bottom manner, once the party slackened its effort, there was little or no incentive for the people to follow up. Thus in 1977-79, the press reported that there had been relapses in public sanitation. Most significantly, there was an urgent appeal by the government to combat schistosomiasis, which was reported to have been wiped out a decade or so ago through a Maoist-style mass campaign.[115] Second, there are reports that medical workers in preventive medicine have been demoralized and have changed their profession in large numbers.[116] Third, there are an increasing number of reports in the Chinese Communist press on the need to pay attention to the "quality of population." Two demographers reported in 1980 that some two thousand congenital diseases have been discovered. A health survey of 300,000 children under the age of seven in ten provinces found that "a relatively large proportion" of the children had birth defects such as heart disease, deformation, and mental retardation. In some areas the instances of these diseases are on the rise.[117] Another health survey conducted in 1978-80 found that 33 percent of a sample of 110,031 children below the age of three suffered from rickets. This sample was drawn from twenty-one provinces and cities on the mainland.[118] In 1983 a Shanghai newspaper reported that because of deficiency of calcium in the diet, in some areas of China 80 percent of young children suffered from rickets.[119]

As stated before, the health of a people cannot be isolated from the general living condition, such as nutrition, housing, and environmental sanitation. The nutrition level of Chinese people has registered some marked improvement since 1978. The consumption of oil, sugar, and meat in 1978, as compared with the world average, is shown in table 18-5. In 1982 the State Statistical Bureau published new figures to show the improvement in the diet of Chinese after the institution of the new economic policy of party pragmatists. The average caloric instake was 2,666 a day in 1981, compared to 2,311 in 1978 and an estimated 2,099 in 1975 (diets in industrialized countries range from 3,000 to 3,500 calories per person a day). In the countryside, the peasants' average diet amounted to 2,598 calories, a 17 percent increase in three years. "The Chinese diet, however, is still largely based on rice and wheat. The average Chinese consumed 482 pounds of grain (in 1981), up 52 pounds from 1978.

TABLE 18-5   Consumption of oil, sugar, and meat in 1978

	MAINLAND CHINA	WORLD
Oil	3.85 lb./capita	33 lb.
Sugar	5.17	44
Meat	18.15	51.7

Source: *Renmin Ribao*, July 8, 1980, p. 5.

In contrast, the average consumption of 24½ pounds of pork, the principal meat, is up 7½ pounds over three years ago [1978] but still less than half a pound a week."[120] Still low in the Chinese diet are beef, fish, mutton, milk, vegetables, and fruit.

It is sometimes forgotten that living space is correlated with the health of a people. A study found that in England during the period of industrialization and urbanization the number of rooms in a dwelling was related with remarkable consistency to child mortality. "Those with only one room had child mortality rates roughly two times that of those with four to six rooms."[121] As we had occasion to mention previously, crowding is a serious social problem in the PRC. The average living space of a citizen of the PRC is 3.6 square meters. This is a direct result of the Communist party's strategy of "production first, livelihood second."

Finally, contrary to some early reports, there has been very serious environmental pollution and destruction. It is reported that of all the countries in the world mainland China ranks near the bottom in pollution by sulphur dioxide.[122] Pollution of rivers, destruction of forests and pastures, and other forms of destruction of the environment are extensive.[123] In 1982-83 the Communist government carried out a campaign of environmental sanitation in the countryside and reported that about 40 percent of peasants in China now had "*relatively* potable water to drink."[124] In urban areas 85 percent of the people had potable water.[125]

In 1981 the Environmental Fund, an American organization, published a world survey on the quality of life, based on the Physical Quality of Life Index, developed by the Overseas Development Council. The survey rated countries on a scale of 1 to 100. Three factors were used to determine the rating—infant mortality, life expectancy at age one, and literacy. On the scale Sweden got top marks with a 97 rating. The United States rated a 94. China was rated 69, behind Hong Kong and Taiwan (86), Singapore (83), South Korea (82), and the Philippines (71). But China was ahead of Burma (51), Indonesia (48), India (43), and Cambodia (40).[126] That China was rated higher than India must have gladdened the hearts of a number of Western scholars who hold the view that if China is doing better than India, then China is not doing too badly. Be that as it may. However, given our discussion so far and the rating by the Environmental Fund, it would be difficult for anyone to trumpet the thesis that gained popularity for quite a while that the PRC is a "model" of development in the third world.

SOCIAL CONSENSUS AND INTEGRATION

Modernization as the secular process in which a predominantly agrarian society is transformed into a predominantly industrial society must eventually culminate in a reintegrated society. In this last phase of modernization "the great movement of peoples from the countryside to the city transforms the structure of society from one of relatively autonomous regional, organizational, and occupational groupings to one that is highly fragmented and in which the individual is relatively isolated." That means that "the individual's ties with local, regional, and other intermediate structures are reduced at the same time that his ties with the larger and more diffuse urban and industrial network are strengthened."[127]

Economically, the most satisfactory index of integration is the proportion of the population engaged in manufacturing and services as distinct from agriculture and other forms of primary production. Politically, integration is based on institutionalization of power, and the exercise of power is divided into many specialties and shared by many people. The ruling groups come to depend more on merit than on privilege. Socially, wealth tends to be more evenly distributed and the standard of living of rural and urban workers tends to approximate that of salaried employees. The result is a great enlargement of the middle ranks of society. "When societies reach this phase there is also a much greater consensus than ever before among interest groups regarding the policies of modernization that should be followed. . . . If there is not an end to ideological controversies within integrated societies, at least the range of controversy is greatly narrowed."[128]

Measured in the foregoing terms, the society in mainland China is far from being integrated. Fully 80 percent of the population is still engaged in agriculture. Owing to the lopsided strategy of economic development of the CPC, over the decades the gap between agricultural and industrial product per worker has been widening.[129] Moreover, following the failure of the Great Leap Forward, the Communist authorities deliberately segregated urban from rural development. This tactic may be seen in the transformation of the urban working class. Today a large proportion of the new and younger workers in Chinese factories are from urban working-class families, no longer first-generation rural migrants, as they were in the 1950s. Of the workers employed after 1966, 80 percent have come from families of the city working class.[130] Deprived of contact with urban areas, Chinese rural residents naturally remain tradition-bound; as we mentioned previously, clan activity has been on the rise in the countryside ever since the Cultural Revolution. Since the death of Mao and the implementation of the new economic policy, there have been more exchanges between urban and rural areas. But two obstacles have put a severe restraint on these exchanges: the opposition of rural cadres, who were used to living off Chinese peasants, and overpopulation in the cities. The policy of the present administration in the PRC is to stress the need for the countryside to modernize "on the spot" without following the universal route of migration to the cities. That was also the strategy of Mao. But for the Chinese countryside to develop, it needs input from the cities. Our discussion on Chinese economic strategy shows that even the present government is not willing or able to transfer a significant amount of urban resources to the countryside. Seen in this light, Deng Xiaoping's strategy is, fundamentally speaking, not very different from Mao's in that both sought to rely on the manipulation of the "productive relations" of farming to develop the countryside. The main difference between Mao and Deng is that Mao used collectivization and Deng, decollectivization. The latter is naturally more popular with Chinese peasants than Mao's way, but the long-term development and integration of the urban and rural sector of Chinese society cannot be based on a strategy that does not channel a significant amount of urban resources to the countryside.

Also, when judged in political terms, Chinese society today lacks significant integration. In our discussion of the evolution of the Communist party since 1949, we observe the trend of ever narrowing access to power. At the top echelon, the Communist party gradually evolved into Mao's "family circle." For the rest of the Communist party the policy of Mao was to narrow recruitment increasingly to worker-peasant cadres at the expense of the knowledgeable members of society. The Cultural Revolution threw this process of restriction into sharp relief. The present leaders of the CPC have been making an effort to widen the basis of party members, especially admitting intellectuals in recent years. But just as in agricultural policy, the party reformers have run into serious opposition from the entrenched party bureaucracy, whose view toward the new recruitment policy of the party is exemplified by the sentiment, "While we fought for the empire, the intellectuals sat on the sideline." The process of turning the Communist party from a party of privileges to a party of merits has barely begun. When we measure the degree of integration in Chinese society in terms of equalization of wealth, we immediately run into the familiar contrast between urban and rural areas. Based even on the latest and most optimistic statistics released by the Communist government, the gap between the income of the peasant and urban employee remains substantial. Premier Zhao Ziyang reported to the Sixth National People's Congress in June 1983 that the average annual income of Chinese peasants was 270 yuan and that of an urban employee, 500 yuan.[131] The government recently claimed that the gap between rich and poor peasants has narrowed considerably. In 1978 high-income rural households (annual income between 400 and 500 yuan) had 3.6 times the income of low-income families (annual income at or below 150 to 200 yuan); this figure decreased to 3.1 in 1982.[132] It is quite possible that the recent improvement in the living standard of Chinese peasants is due to the immediate benefits of the dismantling of the communes. It is uncertain as to how long the present trend of rural development will continue without a major change in the strategy of the Communist party. Sooner or later the lack of urban input to the countryside *in substantial amounts* will arrest the development in the countryside and the urban-rural gap in living standard will widen radically.

Throughout our discussion on social integration, we see the clash between the universal process of modernization and the particular process of Chinese Communist politics. But it is in social consensus that the contradiction between the integrating force of modernization and the disintegrating force of Chinese Communist (or Maoist) politics is most sharply presented. First, we are not certain whether the Chinese Communist party wishes to see a consensual society, or whether Mao did, their public pronouncements notwithstanding. As we mention throughout this study, Mao believed in the key link role of class struggle. Under this conception, the social policy of the Communist party became a self-fulfilling prophecy; since the Communist party treated society as if divided by mutually antagonistic classes, the people adapted to Communist policy and reacted as the party wished. The escalating politics of class struggle culminated in the Cultural Revolution in which the party itself was on the brink of disintegration. As the violence and political insecurity of the 1960s and 1970s continued without end in sight, Chinese people increasingly reverted to private and traditional solidarities to protect themselves. According to the editor of *China News Analysis* (writing in 1971):

> Things that had been buried deep and scarcely seemed to exist any more are now emerging from the yellow earth—things that have nothing to do with the official ideals of moral behavior, with the total subjection to the impersonal Moloch, be it called the Thoughts of Mao, the Party, or sacrifice for the liberation of mankind.
>
> These ghostly revenants are elementary human values, mutual aid and solidarity among closely linked people, among people of common interests—factionalism in the official parlance—and among those united by the most ancient of all ties, the ties of the family clan.
>
> Both factionalism and the family spirit made their appearance on the political scene during the cultural revolution. At a time when party and government machinery were crumbling and human existence was becoming hazardous, people with common interests were gathered together by an instinctive urge for self-preservation.[133]

Another reason for our uncertainty about whether the Communist party wishes to see an integrated and consensual society in China stems from our observation of the Communist strategy of the development of the communications network. In a nutshell, the Communist party, for the past thirty-some years, stressed much more the development of major railways and roads to facilitate political control than communication facilities such as telephone and postal service, which promote social integration. From 1949 to 1982 the railway mileage of mainland China doubled, from 21,000 to 50,000 kilometers. In 1949 there were only 80,700 kilometers of road in China's 9.6 million square kilometers territory; by 1980 there were 900,000 kilometers of highway, an eleven-fold increase.[134] These railways and highways primarily link the major regions of China, especially between the coastal regions and the inland provinces. The new lines that have been built in the Southwest and the Northwest are especially impressive. These modern transport lines are one of the most outstanding accomplishments of the Communist party after 1949. But they serve primarily political rather than social purposes. In contrast, the underdevelopment of telecommunication shows the low priority that the Communist party puts on social communication and integration. A Chinese press report of 1979 revealed that from 1949 to 1977, whereas the total value of industrial output increased by thirty times, the postal routes and long-distance telephone lines increased by only seven times and intracity telephone lines by five times.[135] In 1983 there was an average of one telephone for every 200 Chinese people. With a population of over a billion, China has 1.3 million dial phones, compared with 3.3 million telephones in Taiwan with a population of 18 million and 1.8 million telephones in Hong Kong with a population of 4.5 million.[136] In the countryside, with more than 800 million residents, the number of telephones in 1983 was 2.5 million.[137] Undoubtedly the rural phones in China are the exclusive property of the bureaucracy, and rural roads, according to former residents of the PRC, are used primarily to transport grains to cities under the government's system of "unified purchase." Even in urban areas, phones are found mainly in the homes of the chairpersons of the Residents' Committees. The segregation of rural from urban areas also shows up in the postal service. Daily delivery of mail is extended to 62 percent of the brigades (i.e., rural districts that are one step removed from natural villages). Chinese newspapers are rife with reports of the hit-and-miss character of rural postal delivery. From 1973 to 1978, whereas subscriptions to newspapers and journals in the countryside increased by 30 percent, the number of postmen in rural areas decreased by 10,000.[138] Most likely, as in the case of barefoot doctors, many of the former rural postmen were urban youths sent forcibly to the countryside before 1976 who have since returned to cities. One might argue that the reason for the imbalances in the development of communications is purely economic, i.e., the heavy-industry-first strategy. Undoubtedly that may be part of the reason. But one must consider the policy of the Communist party that allowed most new telephones to be installed, after 1949, in the homes of cadres in city Residents' Committees. Moreover, we must also mention a study by Frederick Frey on world communications development. Frey discovered that in East European countries, mass communications are stressed over telecommunications. As he puts it, "One obvious hypothesis to explain this difference . . . is to assume that these nations wish to emphasize social control in their communications policy."[139] Apparently the social integration that the Communist party in China or elsewhere desires resembles a strange wheel in which all spokes are connected to the hub at the center but without a rim to connect the spokes.

Now it does not make sociological sense to expect a consensual society to develop from the combination of the Maoist ideology of class struggle and his lopsided economic development. The Chinese mass media, as well as former residents of the PRC, testify to a high degree of social tension and conflict. They repeatedly refer to the sharp differences between the radicals, or leftists, and the party pragmatists; a large-scale "party consolidation" (i.e., purge) is being conducted. Factionalism and cliques pervade the body politic. The extent of group or interpersonal conflicts in the PRC can be gathered from the mass campaigns that the current leaders have launched. One campaign is establishing "civilized villages" throughout the countryside. Peasants are urged to set up "village rules and people's compact" (*xianggui minyue*) in order to deal with such things as superstition, clan revival, gambling, theft, fights, land grabbing, looting of public property, and trafficking in women.[140] Another campaign promotes "hygiene, decorum, and courtesy." Even before the violent Cultural Revolution, Mao and his radical disciples spared no effort to cultivate an ethos of incivility and violence among the youth of China. During the Cultural Revolution, incivility degenerated into what a Chinese writer called barbarism.[141] When this new ethos of incivility was combined with material deprivation in China, social ethic disintegrated. American correspondent Michael Parks observed in 1982:

> Snarling, angry voices do seem to predominate in stores and other public places. Ordinary conversations are filled with vulgarities and obscenities, and "please," "thank you" and "excuse me" have all but disappeared from everyday usage.
> Social order and self-discipline as a whole also seem to have degenerated in China, pushing and shoving are routine, and street corner scuffles are nearly as common. . . . Rowdiness is an increasing problem at sports events. . . .[142]

Chinese Premier Zhao Ziyang made an appeal in a nationwide radio and television address: "When people in both urban and rural areas pay attention to hygiene, decorum and courtesy, they will be able to improve their health, shape themselves up, consolidate public disorder, strengthen their unity and mutual help, reduce disorder, raise working efficiency and improve the general mood of society."[143] The view (in a widely used textbook on China) that "social life in the PRC has been relatively orderly and free of crime and corruption" is demonstrably false.[144]

Of all the social stresses in the PRC today, the youth problem concerns the Communist party and Chinese people in general the most. The disaffection of Chinese youth not only brings disrepute to the entire Communist system but also depresses the general social mood. Let us deal briefly with the youth problem as it is discussed by Chinese writers and commentators in the PRC.

To the youth today Chinese commentators have applied a rich array of epithets, such as "a contemplative generation," "a wounded generation," "a wasted generation," "a lost generation," and "a fallen generation."[145] Moreover, Chinese youth today are often contrasted with the youth in the 1950s and early 1960s. The most detailed contrast is provided by a teacher from a Shandong teachers' college:

> 1. Generally speaking, the youth in the 50s and 60s lacked social experience and tended to be simple-minded. Their ability in physical and social activity was deficient. But the youth today, being through ten years of struggle with Lin Biao and the "Gang of Four," has seen more. Their experience in society is relatively rich. Their minds are complex. The questions that they ponder are numerous. Their physical and labor capability is high.
> 2. The youth of the 50s and 60s were good at imagination and full of hope for

the future, though tainted, sometimes, with romanticism and unrealism. Today's youth are relatively "practical." They do not like to think about the future of the motherland or the fate of mankind, regarding these as pompous talks. In the 50s and 60s, youth in general, let alone party or youth league members, never thought of not complying with job assignment, taking it rather for granted. Anyone who refused to comply with a job assignment then would be ostracized. But this is different today. Nowadays a student, after being assigned to the countryside, thinks first and foremost of getting back to the city to find a better job.

3. The youth of the 50s and 60s had lofty thoughts regarding our party. But today the attitude of youth toward the party is rather distant. Their opinion of party membership is not high and they treat socialism as a mere slogan, even doubting the superiority of socialism.

4. The conduct of the youth of the 50s and 60s was relatively proper. Their knowledge was adequate and they were courteous and civil. Nowadays, generally speaking, youths are not very civil and courteous. Some have learned to be boastful, dishonest and arrogant. They are prone to commit physical assault upon a slight provocation.[146]

To complete their picture of Chinese youth today, mainland Chinese writers also use various typologies. For example, an editor of the official *Chinese Youth* divides the youths on the mainland into five categories. First, there is the "Europeanized youth." "These are young people who have become . . . skeptical about the basic theory of Marxism-Leninism and Mao Tse-tung thought. . . . They have had greater exposure to European democratic and other contemporary ideas. They have broader vision; they are more dynamic in their thinking and consequently are the most dissatisfied with the current situation in China and most urgently desire reform." Then there are the " 'dedicated' optimists," who "have a better understanding of the basic theory of Marxism-Leninism and do not place blind faith in anyone." Third, there are " 'nice' young dupes who . . . must still painfully be weaned from the false theories of the 'Gang of Four.' " The fourth type of youth consists of "philosophical 'nihilists' who have 'seen through' " and, finally, the saddest of all categories, "the young who have become criminals."[147]

In addition to impressionistic surveys of the psychology of Chinese youth, discussion on youth also focuses on four specific areas: disillusionment of youth with the socialist system as exemplified in present Chinese reality, their failure to find meaning in life, their disinterest in political education, and young criminals.

As a measure of the pervasiveness of the first two concerns—disillusionment with socialism and finding life meaningless—Chinese authorities have deliberately provoked public discussion of them, obviously attempting to bring them into the open and overcome them through reasoning. Furthermore, Chinese propagandists have aimed at specific groups. The discussion on disillusionment with socialism was aimed at high school pupils who are rapidly becoming avid watchers of television. It was through television that most mainland Chinese pupils became aware, for the first time in thirty years, of the consumer society in the West. The discussion on the meaning of life was also meant for late adolescents, whose education was disrupted by the Cultural Revolution and are now already working; this is the "wasted" or "wounded" generation.

Discussion on each of those two topics—disillusionment with socialism and searching for meaning in life—began with publication of a student essay or letter. For example, in May 1979 a Shanghai newspaper publicized an essay by a high school pupil who was depressed by the sight of a peasant woman with a baby in her arms begging in the street. His essay provoked other students to make their views known. One wrote:

> So far as our generation is concerned, we have been taught, ever since primary school, how good is our socialist motherland and how bitter and hard are the lives of the people in capitalist nations. . . . Now we see from television the skyscrapers, modern facilities, parks and cultural centers in foreign countries. Compared with that, our country is backward. How can you expect us to turn our thinking around to continue believing the superiority of socialism?[148]

Soon students from other schools joined in the discussion and questions were raised such as, Why are the lives of the workers in capitalist countries better than ours? and Why, after thirty years of building socialism, are we not as good as the capitalist countries?[149] Underlying the disillusionment, says a perceptive Chinese writer, is the process of "proceeding from blind faith to skepticism and from skepticism to awakening."[150]

The discussion on the meaning of life began with the publication of a young woman's letter in the journal *Chinese Youth,* organ of the Communist Youth League, with the title: "Ah, the Path of Life; How Is It That It Gets Narrower and Narrower!" The writer was a twenty-three-year-old woman named Pan Xiao, whose once warm family was broken up by the Cultural Revolution and she was abandoned by her mother. Working in a factory now, Pan was appalled by the selfish and materialistic behavior of her coworkers. Pan's despair was also precipitated by her one-time close friend's betraying their private conversation to the authorities and also by the desertion of her boyfriend, who belonged to a higher class of party cadres. Pan Xiao concludes: "Everyone is selfish. . . . When it comes to a crucial moment, everyone acts according to his selfish instinct. . . . Everyone, on the surface, acts altruistically but, deep down, seeks to benefit himself."[151] The letter of Pan Xiao touched a sensitive chord in the minds and hearts of mainland Chinese youth. In twenty-five days, *Chinese Youth* received 18,603 letters in response.[152] With that, a press campaign was organized "to establish a correct view toward life." As the object of this discussion was young workers, the *Workers' Daily* took the lead in the campaign. From June 5 to August 1, 1980, the paper received 6,600 readers' letters on this topic.[153]

Given the foregoing, it is not surprising that another major concern of the Chinese Communist authorities is a prevalent disinterest by students in political instruction. "Nowadays," admits Wang Renchong, Director of the Department of Propaganda of the Party Central Committee, "many students do not like to attend political instruction; this is a fact."[154] It is revealing that in 1982 the Department of Propaganda of the Communist party, together with the Chinese Ministry of Education, warned universities and colleges against canceling political-instruction classes or replacing them with nonpolitical subject matter.[155] At the same time, Chinese authorities acknowledge that the old sermon-type political instruction must be abandoned. Political instructors are being told to use flexible methods and indirection and to combine "the spiritual with the material interest" of youth in order to arouse their interest in politics.[156]

So far, Chinese discussion of youth problems has been of a generalized nature. One youth subgroup, however, has received special attention: the young criminals. It was reported in 1978-80 that crimes committed by juveniles accounted for 70 to 80 percent of all the crimes in China.[157] One reason given for the high incidence of youth crimes is that the Cultural Revolution not only sanctioned violence and open flouting of the law but also broke up homes, leaving many youngsters to subsist by themselves. Second, many cases of youth crimes are a direct result of the Communist party's action in sending millions of high school and even college graduates to settle in the countryside. As one account puts it: "The productive forces of Chinese rural areas were very backward. People in some places earn only ten to twenty cents a day. Educated youths were hardly able to support themselves on such incomes. . . . Under the pressure of poverty, many educated youths were forced to commit crimes."[158] Third, Chinese schools and industry in the 1970s could no longer accommodate the large number of youths who came of age every year. Not being able to continue their education or to find jobs turned many youths to crimes. Finally, youth crimes are also attributed to young people's resentment of the existence of a privileged class of party elite. To cope with the problem of juvenile crimes, the Institute for the Research on Youths and Juveniles and the Chinese Society for Research on Juvenile Delinquency were established in 1981 and 1982.

The youth problem is not restricted to the student population of China. As we mentioned previously, today 60 percent of Chinese urban workers are below the age of thirty-five and are poorly educated. The morale and discipline of this young working force are of acute concern to the authorities, since the prospects of China's modernization are significantly dependent on them.

Historically, in China and elsewhere, significant youth disaffection often portends social disintegration. Revolutionary leaders come from the ranks of young dissidents, Chinese Communist leaders themselves being the best examples. However, a dynamic and well-integrated society obtains from its youth an ever renewed source of strength for further growth and progress. Judged in these terms, the Chinese Communist system has indeed failed.

Overall, after thirty-some years of Communist rule, Chinese society remains as divided as ever (if not more). The root causes of the divisions in Chinese society are the Chinese Communist political and economic strategies. For a while, the social divisions in China were masked by Communist monopoly of the means of mass communication and liberal use of coercion. But over the long run, the imbalances in the Communist strategy of development manifest themselves in numerous ways that gradually gather force and intensity. Eventually, the authorities are forced to accommodate to the reaction from society before another revolution occurs. But when the Communist party finally comes around to redress the old imbalances it finds that whereas social reaction has gathered strength over the decades, so have the vested interests. The party reformers thus have to walk a tightrope between the upsurge of social discontent and the resistance of the existing power groups. In short, Chinese society will remain stressful and mal-integrated (if not disintegrated) for some time to come.

NOTES

1. Feng Lanrui and Zhao Lukuan, "Urban Unemployment in China," *Social Sciences in China*, no. 2 (1982), p. 128.
2. *RMRB*, October 28, 1982, p. 1.
3. Tian Xueyuan and Zhen Yukuan, "Population and Economic Adjustment," *RMRB*, May 11, 1981, p. 2.
4. Qian Xinzhong, "Controlling Population Growth," *Beijing Review* 26, no. 7 (February 14, 1983), 21.
5. Feng and Zhao, "Urban Unemployment in China," p. 128.

6. *Selected Works of Mao Tse-tung*, vol. IV (Peking: Foreign Languages Press, 1967), p. 453.

7. Ai Feng, "Our Cities Are Beckoning for Reform," *RMRB*, April 15, 1983, p. 3; Yi Zi, "The Strategic Significance of Developing Small Towns," *RMRB*, June 18, 1981, p. 5.

8. Zhang Qingwu, "Control the Growth of Urban Population," *RMRB*, August 21, 1979, p. 3; also, *RMRB*, October 28, 1982, p. 4. For more on Chinese urban development, see Laurence J. C. Ma and Edward W. Hanten, eds., *Urban Development in Modern China* (Boulder, Co.: Westview Press, 1981).

9. For 1982 figures, see *RMRB*, May 1, 1983, p. 2. For 1955 figures, see "China's Workers in 1955: Their Number, Composition and Distribution," in *Tung Chi Kung Tso Tung Hsin* (Statistical Work Bulletin), no. 23 (December 14, 1956), as translated in ECMM, no. 68, pp. 27-34.

10. *RMRB*, May 1, 1983, p. 2.

11. The percentage of the service sector in 1978 is given in Wang Jiye, "Adjust Structure of Enterprises and Enhance the Efficiency of Macroeconomics," *RMRB*, April 27, 1981, p. 5.

12. Calculated on the basis of the figures in *RMRB*, May 1, 1983, p. 2.

13. Hu Ji, "Updating Science and Technology," *Beijing Review* 26, no. 7 (February 14, 1983), 14.

14. I have calculated the number of workers employed in light and heavy industry of China according to the figures given for total workers in *RMRB*, May 1, 1983, p. 2, and the number of technical personnel in light industry (81,500 or 0.78 percent of total workers and staff in light industry) given in Yu Kinchao, "We Must Emphasize the Projection of Manpower Requirement," *RMRB*, December 10, 1981, p. 3.

15. *RMRB*, May 1, 1983, p. 2.

16. All the figures on employment in this paragraph are from Feng and Zhao, "Urban Unemployment in China."

17. "Millions Put to Work in 1982," *Beijing Review* 26, no. 23 (June 6, 1983), 5.

18. "46.5 Million People Employed Since 1977," *Beijing Review* 26, no. 38 (September 19, 1983), 7.

19. Zhuang Qidong and Sun Keliang, "The Employment Problem in the Period of Adjustment," *Hongqi*, no. 11 (1981), p. 28.

20. Feng and Zhao, "Urban Unemployment in China," p. 129.

21. Ibid.

22. *RMRB*, August 19, 1980, p. 5.

23. Lang Zhengdong and Zhang Chongru, "The Choice of High School Graduating Class," *She Hui (Sociology)*, no. 2 (1981), pp. 22-25.

24. The Street Enterprises Survey Team of the Department of Political Economy, "Report of Survey of the Street Enterprises of Shanghai," *Fudan Xuebao*, no. 4 (1980), pp. 5-10.

25. Alexander Eckstein, *Communist China's Economic Growth and Foreign Trade* (New York: McGraw-Hill Book Company, 1966), pp. 18-19.

26. *Wan-sui*, no. 2, p. 398.

27. Ibid., p. 424.

28. See, for example, Olga Lang, *Chinese Family and Society* (New Haven: Yale University Press, 1946); and Marion J. Levy, Jr., *The Family Revolution in Modern China* (Cambridge, Mass.: Harvard University Press, 1949).

29. Based on the paper, "On the Change of Chinese Family Structure" by Fei Xiaotong, presented at the Conference on Modernization and Chinese Culture at the Chinese University of Hong Kong, March 7-11, 1983. I was a participant at this conference.

30. Zhou Sulien and Lin Shengmu, "On Housing," *RMRB*, November 10, 1980, p. 5.

31. Pan Yunkang and Pan Naigu, "Urban Family Structures and Their Changes," *Beijing Review* 26, no. 9 (February 28, 1983), 25-29.

32. Xiaotong Fei, "Revisit to Jiang Village," *Xinkuancha*, no. 11 (June 1, 1957), p. 3.

33. *China News Analysis*, no. 864 (December 10, 1971), p. 4. For more on rural Chinese family structure, see William L. Parish and Martin K. Whyte, *Village and Family in Contemporary China* (Chicago: University of Chicago Press, 1978).

34. Fox Butterfield, "Chinese Poster Deplores Backwardness of Economy," *New York Times*, February 2, 1977.

35. James S. Coleman, "Introduction to Part I," in James S. Coleman, ed., *Education and Political Development* (Princeton, N.J.: Princeton University Press, 1965), p. 17.

36. "Facts and Figures: Education," *Beijing Review* 26, no. 40 (October 3, 1983), 26.

37. Commentator, "A Phenomenon in Middle School Education That Is Worthy of Our Attention," *RMRB*, November 12, 1981, p. 3.

38. *Beijing Review* 26, no. 40 (October 3, 1983), 26.

39. Wen Xiajie, "Tailoring Education to Fit China," *Beijing Review* 25, no. 42 (October 18, 1982), 23.

40. Ibid. For more on the Chinese educational system see Suzanne Pepper, "Education and Revolution: The 'Chinese Model' Revisited," *Asian Survey* XVIII, no. 9 (September 1978); Jonathan Unger, *Education under Mao: Class and Competition in Canton Schools, 1960-1980* (New York: Columbia University Press, 1982).

41. Li Hai and Xu Yapin, "Educational Growth Must Be Kept up with Growth in Economic Construction," *RMRB,* April 19, 1980, p. 3.

42. Ting Wang, "From Peking: The Total Number of Illiterates Is 150 Million," *Ming Pao Daily News,* August 12, 1981, p. 3.

43. *New York Times,* July 5, 1979.

44. Zhong Peizhang, "The New Awakening of China," *RMRB,* June 29, 1983, p. 3.

45. *RMRB,* October 3, 1982, p. 5.

46. *RMRB,* October 13, 1981, p. 3.

47. *RMRB,* December 19, 1981, p. 1. For reports on peasants looting schools for construction materials, see *RMRB,* June 18, 1982, p. 1; October 19, 1982, p. 3; and November 4, 1983, p. 5.

48. Yuan Baohua, "To Improve the Education of Workers and Staff Is a Major Strategic Task of Four Modernizations," *Hongqi,* no. 5 (1982), p. 17.

49. *RMRB,* May 24, 1981, p. 3.

50. *RMRB,* December 20, 1980, p. 4.

51. Duan Wuyon, "We Must Break Shackles in Order to Change the Composition of Middle School Education," *RMRB,* July 8, 1980, p. 3.

52. Wen Xiajie, "Tailoring Education," p. 24.

53. Burton Edelson, Sheldon Haas, James Harford, Leonard Jaffe, Ralph Nansen, Abraham Schnapf, and Michael Yarmovyth, "Eye-Witness Report on Chinese Satellite Work," *Astronautics & Aeronautics,* February 1980, pp. 38–44.

54. James S. Coleman, *Education and Political Development,* p. 6.

55. For more on Chinese education during this period, see Stewart Fraser, ed., *Chinese Communist Education, Records of the First Decade* (New York: John Wiley & Sons, 1965).

56. For a sample of student criticism of the Communist party, see Dennis J. Doolin, *Communist China: The Politics of Student Opposition* (Stanford, Calif.: Stanford University, Hoover Institution Press, 1964).

57. "Interview: 'Politics Must Always Take Command,'" *Current Scene* I, no. 26 (March 5, 1962), 6.

58. Jan S. Prybyla, "Notes on Chinese Higher Education: 1974," *China Quarterly,* no. 62 (June 1975), pp. 271–96.

59. Pan Xuguan, "It Is Necessary for Colleges to Offer Courses on Locating Source Materials," *RMRB,* August 25, 1981, p. 3.

60. Xia Yan, "Letter to a Young Reader," *RMRB,* November 5, 1979, p. 3.

61. Talcott Parsons, *Societies: Evolutionary and Comparative Perspectives* (Englewood Cliffs, N.J.: Prentice-Hall, 1966), p. 10.

62. *RMRB,* October 19, 1980, p. 3.

63. *RMRB,* December 4, 1982, p. 2.

64. *Wan-sui,* no. 2, p. 102.

65. "Combating Bias against Intellectuals," *Beijing Review* 26, no. 9 (February 28, 1983), 4.

66. *RMRB,* February 5, 1978, p. 1. For more on Chinese intellectuals see Merle Goldman, *Literary Dissent in Communist China* (Cambridge, Mass.: Harvard University Press, 1967); and *China's Intellectuals: Advice and Dissent* (Cambridge, Mass.: Harvard University Press, 1981).

67. Li Chun, "We Must Be Concerned with the Living Conditions of Intellectuals," *RMRB,* August 7, 1980, p. 4.

68. *RMRB,* December 9, 1983, p. 3.

69. *RMRB,* August 2, 1980, p. 8; January 27, 1981, p. 4; and February 6, 1983, p. 1.

70. *China News Analysis,* no. 774 (September 19, 1969), p. 4.

71. Wu Min, "The Number of Landlords and Peasants Is as Numerous as 36 Million," *Ming Pao Daily News,* May 22, 1981, p. 3. This report is based on a Chinese Communist publication, *An Anthology of Class and Class Struggle for the Past Thirty Years (Sanshih Nianlai Jieji He Jieji Douzheng Lunwenji),* published by the Institute of Philosophy of the Chinese Academy of Social Sciences in 1981. For secondary works on class and class conflict in the PRC see Richard C. Kraus, *Class Conflict in Chinese Socialism* (New York: Columbia University Press, 1981).

72. Alex Inkeles, *Social Change in Soviet Russia* (Cambridge, Mass.: Harvard University Press, 1968), p. 138.

73. Ibid., p. 139.

74. Martin King Whyte, "Inequality and Stratification in China," *China Quarterly,* no. 64 (1975), pp. 684–711.

75. Alexander Eckstein, *China's Economic Revolution* (Cambridge: Cambridge University Press, 1977), p. 299.

76. *China News Analysis,* no. 966 (1974).

77. *RMRB,* April 22, 1979, p. 3.

78. Mu Min, "Going into Army, Engineering College, Going Abroad," *Ch'ih Shih Nien-Tai,* no. 12 (1979), pp. 8–9; also, Jan Wong, "China's Leap to American Campuses," *New York Times Magazine,* November 15, 1981, pp. 82–100.

79. Whyte, "Inequality and Stratification," p. 686.

80. *Ming Pao Daily News,* October 4, 1981, p. 1.

81. Nick Eberstadt, "China: How Much Success?" *New York Review of Books* XXVI, no. 7 (1979), 40.

82. Commentator, "Let Some Localities and Peasants Prosper First," *Beijing Review,* no. 3 (1981), pp. 19-22.

83. Inkeles, *Social Change,* p. 147.

84. Quoted in Lynn T. White III, *Careers in Shanghai* (Berkeley: University of California Press, 1978), p. 210.

85. Inkeles, *Social Change,* p. 145.

86. Li Hai and Xu Yapin, "Educational Growth Must Be Kept up with Growth in Economic Construction," *RMRB,* April 19, 1982, p. 3.

87. Michel Oksenberg, "The Institutionalization of the Chinese Communist Revolution: The Ladder of Success on the Eve of the Cultural Revolution," *China Quarterly,* no. 36 (1968), pp. 61-92.

88. *RMRB,* August 27, 1981, p. 1.

89. Zhuang Qitong and Sung Keliang, "Urban Employment During the Period of Adjustment," *Hongqi,* no. 11 (1981), pp. 28-32.

90. *Selected Works of Mao Tse-tung,* vol. I (Peking: Foreign Languages Press, 1965), p. 44.

91. C. E. Black, *The Dynamics of Modernization: A Study in Comparative History* (New York: Harper & Row, Publishers, 1967), p. 22.

92. Wu Cangping, "Control the Growth of Population and a Further Emancipation of Women," *RMRB,* January 20, 1981, p. 5.

93. *Beijing Review* 26, no. 38 (September 19, 1983), 6.

94. Department of Economic and Social Affairs, *1974 Report on the World Social Situation* (New York: United Nations, 1975), pp. 244-45.

95. *Beijing Review* 26, no. 38 (September 19, 1983), 6.

96. Wu Cangping, "Control the Growth of Population," p. 5.

97. Phyllis Andors, "Politics of Chinese Development: The Case of Women, 1960-1966," *Signs: Journal of Women in Culture and Society* II, no. 1 (1976), 89-119.

98. *RMRB,* March 4, 1981, p. 2.

99. Andors, "Politics of Chinese Development," pp. 89-119.

100. Quoted in Li Jianguo and Zhang Xiaoying, "Infanticide in China," *New York Times,* April 11, 1983.

101. *RMRB,* April 7, 1983, p. 4.

102. Li and Zhang, "Infanticide in China."

103. *Beijing Review* 26, no. 18 (May 2, 1983), 9.

104. *RMRB,* February 13, 1979.

105. *Ming Pao Daily News,* December 19, 1981, p. 3; also, Michael Parks, "Trafficking in Women on the Rise in Rural China," *Los Angeles Times,* April 23, 1982, part IA, p. 5; and Christopher S. Wren, "China Fights Old Abuse: Sale of Young Women," *New York Times,* January 6, 1983, p. 4.

106. *Beijing Review* 24, no. 3 (January 19, 1981), 7.

107. Department of Economic and Social Affairs, *1974 Report,* p. 216.

108. *Ming Pao Daily News,* December 20, 1982, p. 1. This report is based on a *New China News Agency* dispatch from the National Conference on Medical Supply held in Chengdu city.

109. Department of Economic and Social Affairs, *1974 Report,* p. 216.

110. *RMRB,* October 7, 1982, p. 3.

111. *RMRB,* March 18, 1983, p. 3.

112. "Funds for Public Health Inadequate," *Beijing Review* 26, no. 46 (November 14, 1983), 26.

113. David Lampton, "Performance and the Chinese Political System: A Preliminary Assessment of Education and Health Policies," *China Quarterly,* no. 75 (1978), pp. 509-39.

114. Pi-chao Chen and Chi-hsien Tuan, "Primary Health Care in Rural China: Post-1978 Development," *Social Sciences and Medicine* 17, no. 19 (1983), 1414; also, Tao Zhenni, "China's Primary Health Care," *Beijing Review* 25, no. 29 (July 19, 1982), 18.

115. *RMRB,* April 5, 1977, p. 1; and *RMRB,* December 26, 1979, p. 4.

116. *RMRB,* February 23, 1982, p. 2.

117. Tian Xueyuan and Liu Zhaoxian, "Population, Four Modernizations and Investment in People," *RMRB,* July 22, 1980, p. 5.

118. *Ming Pao Daily News,* January 19, 1981, p. 3.

119. *Ming Pao Daily News,* January 16, 1983, p. 3, based on a report from the Shanghai paper *Wenhui Bao.*

120. "Nutrition Improved in China," *Beijing Review* 25, no. 23 (June 7, 1982), 7; also, Michael Parks, "Chinese Eating Better, Peking Says," *Los Angeles Times,* April 2, 1982, p. 8.

121. Cited in Paul K. C. Liu and Ching-lung Tsay, *Health, Population and Socioeconomic Development in Taiwan* (Taipei: Conference on Experiences and Lessons of Economic Development in Taiwan, the Institute of Economics, Academia Sinica, 1981), p. 20.

122. Yi Zhi, "Protecting the Environment and Benefiting the People," *RMRB*, November 10, 1980, p. 5.

123. Vaclav Smil, "Environmental Degradation in China," *Asian Survey* XX, no. 8 (1980), 777-88.

124. *RMRB*, September 26, 1982, p. 3.

125. *RMRB*, October 23, 1983, p. 3.

126. "Sweden Top-ranked Country in Quality of Life Survey," *Santa Barbara News-Press*, November 12, 1981, p. C9.

127. C. E. Black, *Dynamics of Modernization*, p. 81.

128. Ibid., pp. 82-84.

129. Eckstein, *China's Economic Revolution*, p. 231.

130. Yu Yannan, "Correctly Assess the New Generation of the Working Class of Our Country," *Hongqi*, no. 17 (1982), pp. 27-32.

131. *RMRB*, June 8, 1983, p. 2.

132. "Gap between Rich and Poor Narrows," *Beijing Review* 26, no. 39 (September 26, 1983), 27.

133. *China News Analysis*, no. 864 (December 10, 1971), p. 2.

134. *RMRB*, October 1, 1983, p. 2; and Wang Zhanyi, "Highway Construction in China," *Beijing Review* 24, no. 45 (November 9, 1981), 21.

135. *RMRB*, May 25, 1979, p. 2.

136. *RMRB*, May 15, 1983, p. 5; and *Ming Pao Daily News*, July 31, 1982, p. 3.

137. "Development of China's Post and Telecommunications," *Beijing Review* 26, no. 44 (October 31, 1983), 19.

138. *RMRB*, May 4, 1980, p. 3.

139. Frederick W. Frey, "Communication and Development," in Ithiel de Sola Pool and Wilbur Schramm, eds., *Handbook of Communication* (Chicago: Rand McNally College Publishing Company, 1973), p. 358.

140. *RMRB*, November 13, 1983, p. 4.

141. Niu Ping, "Barbarism and Civility," *RMRB*, June 5, 1979, p. 3.

142. Michael Parks, "Leaders Press Chinese to Keep a Civil Tongue in Their Head," *Los Angeles Times*, April 1, 1982, part IC.

143. Ibid.

144. James Townsend, *Politics in China* (Boston: Little, Brown & Company, 1980), p. 323.

145. Zhong Peizhang, "Opening up Careers for the New Generation," *RMRB*, July 12, 1980, p. 4; Huang Zijian, "Just How Should One View the Youth of This Generation?" *RMRB*, February 24, 1981, p. 5.

146. *Jiaoyu Yanjiu*, no. 1 (1981), pp. 46-47.

147. M. London, T. L. Lee, and I. D. London, "China: The Generation in the Wings," *American Spectator* 13, no. 2 (1980), 21-25.

148. *RMRB*, May 18, 1979, p. 3.

149. Pan Yida, "Reflection on an Essay," *RMRB*, August 13, 1979, p. 4.

150. Ibid.

151. "What Is the Meaning of Life?" *Ch'ih-shih Nien-tai*, no. 1 (1981), pp. 82-85.

152. *RMRB*, June 10, 1980, p. 1.

153. *RMRB*, August 2, 1980, p. 3.

154. Wang Renchong, "Unify Thought: Seriously Rectify Party Style of Work," *Hongqi*, no. 5 (1983), pp. 2-13.

155. *RMRB*, December 25, 1982, p. 2.

156. *RMRB*, June 10, 1980, p. 1, and March 1, 1982, p. 2.

157. *RMRB*, August 19, 1980, p. 4; and Wei Min, "Reforming Criminals," *Beijing Review* 24, no. 8 (February 23, 1981), 22-29; Ying Tzu, "Roundup of the Situation of PRC Youth and Juvenile Delinquency," *Foreign Broadcast Information Service-PRC*, December 21, 1978, pp. 14-15.

158. Ying Tzu, ibid. For recent English works on Chinese youth, see David M. Raddock, *Political Behavior of Adolescents in China: The Cultural Revolution in Kwangchow* (Tucson: University of Arizona Press, 1977); Susan Shirk, *Competitive Comrades: Career Incentives and Student Strategies in China* (Berkeley: University of California Press, 1982).

PART SIX

Conclusion

Politics, as we stated at the outset, essentially involves conceptualization and organization for joint action. It is thus appropriate that we conclude this study by critically reviewing the conceptual and organizational development of the PRC.

Conceptually, the thirty-some years of the PRC throw into relief the genesis, solidification, and ossification of the two key concepts that have steered the Chinese Communist political system: socialism and the CPC's revolutionary legacy. Neither of the two was a result of rational deliberation that took into account the social and economic conditions of China. Socialism as the only way for China had been accepted by Chinese Communist leaders as a matter of faith ever since their late adolescence, when the Communist party was organized. The hard road to power that the CPC traversed further strengthened the emotional nature of the Chinese Communists' commitment to socialism. Not only was Mao's ego invested in building China according to socialism but also the collective ego of the Communist party. Under this circumstance no rational discussion of the suitability of socialism for China was possible. Facts must be made to conform to ideology, not the other way around.

Both socialism and the CPC's revolution legacy were reactions to a particular situation. Socialism was embraced by the leaders of the CPC against the emotionally charged era of post-Republican China, when Chinese intellectuals were radicalized by warlordism, imperialist aggression, and socioeconomic disintegration. Socialism was regarded as the cure-all solution to China's problems. The CPC's revolutionary legacy was based on the imperatives of survival in the barren and backward areas of China's northern interior. By 1949 adolescent commitment to socialism and two decades of revolutionary wars had hardened in the minds of Chinese Communists into a world outlook. But even more important, these key concepts had become the iron will of Mao Zedong, who by 1949 had been built by the CPC into a godlike figure. Conceptual ossification was the logical result of all these developments.

Our study has shown that a major reformulation of the party line was possible only after the death of Mao in 1976, and the effectiveness of this reformulation is not yet entirely clear. Today, more than five years after the memorable third plenum of the Eleventh Central Committee (December 1978) in which the party pragmatists finally took the helm of national development, the CPC is still faced with serious dissension among cadres and party members, many of whom regard the reforms after Mao's death as a betrayal of socialism. Though no political system ever achieves complete consensus on basic values, the Chinese Communist political system, because of its totalitarian nature, cannot function well without an overall agreement among the party rank and file on basic values and norms.

All the foregoing tends to corroborate Lasswell's observation: "Politics is the transition between one unchallenged consensus and the next. It begins in conflict and eventuates in a solution. But the solution is not the 'rationally best' solution, but the emotionally satisfactory one. The rational and dialectical phases of politics are subsidiary to the process of redefining an emotional consensus."[1] It would be inaccurate to say that no "rational and dialectical" consideration took place in the CPC after the death of Mao, for the reforms by party pragmatists after 1978 were partly a result of rational and dialectical analysis. However, that process of analysis was always shadowed by the CPC's emotional commitment to socialism and the revolutionary legacy. Most recent developments in the PRC fully bears this out. In late 1983 a revival of the Mao cult, albeit focusing on the "good Mao," took place in the PRC and was followed by a full-scale attack on the so-called spiritual pollution of Chinese socialism, which was blamed on the influence of "decadent bourgeois culture."

Thus it is not at all certain just how "pragmatic" the Party pragmatists are. To the extent that China's numerous social and economic problems such as population explosion, youth mobility, agricultural underdevelopment, inefficiency in industrial organizations, and venality in administration require a truly genuine reformulation of the conceptual basis of Chinese Communist politics, the latest "ideological throwback" is a reminder of the limitation and uncertainty of significant changes in the Chinese Communist political system.

As with conceptualization, a reformulation of the organizational development of the PRC is required. The essential characteristics of the CPC's organizational framework, as we pointed out in this study, are those of a combat unit with accents on centralization, hierarchy, and monopoly of decision making. These the CPC initially copied from the Soviet Union. In both countries the present organizational measures were installed during a revolutionary struggle for power. The Chinese Communists were even more in need of a combat party than the Soviets given the prolonged civil war in China. Thus the organizational principles that the CPC followed were adapted to combat, not to postwar reconstruction.

Modernization, as a number of Western scholars have hypothesized, requires large, complex, but flexible, organizations.[2] The prevalence of particularism in Chinese society further demands flexible institutions. However, the organizations that the CPC established after 1949 are large and complex but not flexible. We have referred to some Chinese commentators' comparisons of Chinese enterprises to buildings in which every component is nailed into place, unlike living organisms in which every cell is a living being. Moreover, centralization necessarily leaves a considerable distance between the decision-making center and the operating field. When centralization is marked by extensive local particularism, as in China, it often leads to gross miscalculation and blunders such as the Great Leap Forward.

Overall, Chinese Communist institutions have been fraught with conflict of norms. On the one hand, the Chinese Communist system demands strict compliance with centrally decided goals. On the other hand, the inflexible system of the PRC is rife with bottlenecks that have made it extremely difficult if not impossible for lower functionaries to comply with and fulfill the goals set by national authorities. To deliver the desired results, an informal system of corruption develops underneath or outside the formal system, such as private trades among agencies, establishing "connections," and offering bribes. These informal measures, however, have a multiplying effect; soon the connection necessary to attain state-assigned goals is extended to use for self-enrichment. Not only is the formal organizational routine thus corroded but also social morale.

This structural reason for the prevalence of corruption in Chinese bureaucracy is of course greatly aggravated by factional strife at the top echelon of the CPC. The total consequence of all this is what the social psychologist calls *anomie*, i.e., normlessness.

Anomie, as Talcott Parsons points out, is the antithesis of institutionalization. It means either a decline in, or even absence of, stable role expectation and commitment to institutionalized values.[3] Anomie, says Merton, engenders deviant behavior such as graft, fraud, superstition, and gambling.[4] The numerous problems in the Chinese state and society that we have mentioned throughout our study were diverse manifestations of anomie. They included factionalism, venality, corruption, "crises of faith, confidence and trust," and social disorder in the countryside, in which superstition and gambling were prominent.

Anomie in the PRC was caused by Mao's style of leadership (privatization of the party, accent on struggle, continuous conflict with other leaders, reversals of policy and programs), structural anomaly, and the lopsided strategy of economic development. The lack of a stable system of values and norms to follow and the years of material scarcity compelled Chinese people to revert to a purely private ethos—maximization of self-interest and the assumption that everyone else was doing the same.

It is sometimes suggested that with all its flaws, the Communist political system, in contrast to developing nations as a whole, is at least good at governing.[5] The performance of the Chinese Communist political system casts severe doubt on that suggestion. The degree of corruption and inefficiency in administration that Chinese news media nowadays report on a daily basis does not compare favorably with the situation in any developing nation. Neither is the Chinese Communist system any more stable than other developing nations, unless one ignores all the substances of Chinese politics and sees only the shell of Communist one-party dictatorship. The Chinese Communist political system impresses outsiders as being more capable of purposive actions than other developing nations are. However, the results of the Great Leap Forward, the Great Proletarian Cultural Revolution, and after the death of Mao, abandonment of collectivized farming and the return of private entrepreneurship (to a limited degree) make one pause. As some Chinese writers pointed out in the great outpouring of self-criticism in 1978–79, the Maoist "doing things in a big way" is indistinguishable from "doing things in a foolhardy way."

The performance of the Chinese Communist political system in national integration is, impressionistically, not superior to other developing nations. With overwhelming numbers and arms, the Chinese Communist armed forces have been able to insure Chinese rule of the ethnic minority areas. But our study shows that Chinese Communist rule is far from being genuinely accepted by the various minority nationalities. Communist forcible "socialization" drove the Tibetans to armed rebellion in 1959, and the present government in Peking has seen fit to invite the Dalai Lama to return from his exile in India, which, however, is not an indication of genuine acceptance of

Chinese rule by the Tibetans. The situation in Xinjiang and Inner Mongolia is not too different as far as integration between Chinese and the native population is concerned. In Inner Mongolia the massacre of Mongolians (little known to the outside) during the Cultural Revolution left behind a virulent anti-Chinese attitude among the outnumbered Mongolians and a strengthening of ethnic identity.[6]

The record of economic development in the PRC does not constitute a positive model for developing nations either. The economic fragmentation that existed in 1949 has changed but little. The lopsided development strategy of the CPC has made the contrasts between industry and agriculture and between city and countryside as sharp today as in the past. The social and economic symptoms of most developing nations, such as population explosion, congested cities with poor living conditions, primitive farming, subsistence living in the countryside, lack of opportunity for the young, extreme social inequality and social demoralization, are just as real in China.

Some Western scholars, nevertheless, maintain that Mao's rule achieved "positive" results such as building an industrial system, maintaining price stability, autonomy in dealing with the international economy, preventing large rural migration to urban areas, a better or stronger "welfare 'safety net'" than before 1949, and self-sufficiency in food (though on a minimal basis).[7] We will now address the specific points which are current among certain circles.

As mentioned earlier, the Maoist industrial system is seriously imbalanced and is in need of drastic overhaul. Whether an industrial system such as China's that has run its course in a little over two decades is a sound one is glossed over by these defenders of Mao's rule. As to price stability and autonomy in dealing with international economy, the crucial question is, On what condition are these obtained? In China these supposedly Maoist "feats" have been achieved by keeping the overwhelming majority of Chinese living at subsistence level and isolating Chinese economy from the world market. The real strength of a national economy, however, is derived from its ability to improve the living standard of its people continuously and also hold its ground *even while* interacting and competing with the economies of other nations. Moreover, if the Maoist model of economy was as successful as these American scholars have alleged, then why would the present leaders of the PRC want to change it in such an urgent manner? The so-called stronger welfare safety net under Mao's rule apparently did not save the 20 to 25 million Chinese people who died of hunger in 1960-62 (see chapters 7 and 17). According to some Western estimates, "Forty million Chinese died in the turmoil and famine of the first three decades of Communist rule."[8] The minimal self-sufficiency in food, however, should not obscure the fact that as late as 1977 China needed to import 6 million tons of grain to feed its people (mostly urban population).[9] According to the most recent Western analyses: "While the national average picture is one of small overall gains, problems of regional and local food shortages remain. Grain production in some provinces is well below the national average. . . . The poorer regions of the country face tight food supplies even in good years and find themselves very hard pressed in years of poor harvests. Central government resources are inadequate to eliminate local disparities."[10] China, as we acknowledged in the previous chapter, has a low rate of rural-urban migration (compared with other Third World nations). However, this low urbanization in China must be put in its proper perspective. According to China's most well-known sociologist, Fei Xiaotong, the structure of Chinese cities is extremely imbalanced. Fei reports that next to cities with over a million population are cities with twenty thousand population.[11] A huge gap thus exists not only in the size of cities but also in the overall condition of social and economic development. Basically, this overall imbalance in Chinese rural-urban migration is similar to the colonial situation in much of the Third World, where a few modern cities, built by Western colonial capital, exist amidst a vast surrounding premodern countryside. The Communist party of China, Mao in particular, had vowed, upon their coming to formal power in 1950, to end the colonial or semicolonial structure of Chinese society.

Those Western scholars who defend Mao's economics also support his politics. They maintain that the post-Mao changes are anticipated by Mao (even prepared by him). As perceived by these scholars, Mao's strategy was that the central control could be loosened only after the state's priorities were implemented. Mao, these Western scholars admit, may have been in command too long. However, so we are told, Mao had fulfilled his "historical role." This thesis is neither scientifically nor empirically accurate. Scientifically, this interpretation is meaningless since it is nonfalsifiable and tautological (e.g., Mao did not loosen state control because the time had not arrived to do it; Deng loosened control because the right time had arrived). Empirically, this defense of Mao is flawed in numerous ways. First, unlike Sun Yat-sen, who had an explicit theory of first tightening state control ("political tutelage") and then loosening it ("political democracy" in which "the government returns 'politics' to the people"), Mao had advanced no theory similar to Sun's. On the other hand, Mao stressed the ultimate goal of establishing "a unitary system of the ownership of the means of production by the whole people," which, if the people's commune can serve as a guide, means dissolving society into polity—the very opposite of the hypothesis suggested by these Western scholars bent on the defense of Mao's rule. Second, Mao's action directly refutes the above-mentioned hypothesis. In 1963–65 when the Party pragmatists loosened state control and Chinese economy and society responded with dynamism and growth, Mao put a stop to all that by launching the Cultural Revolution. (Of course, those who defend Mao would say: That is because Mao judged that the time had not arrived to loosen control.) Third, the defenders of Mao seem to neglect the tendency for state control to be self-perpetuating. In other words, state control creates the condition for more state control. There is a saying in China to the effect that loosening of central control leads to confusion, which necessitates reimposition of central control, which in turn causes the revival of the original condition of stagnancy. These defenders of Mao perhaps unwittingly confirm that by saying that perhaps Mao occupied the stage too long. The history of the PRC up until Mao's death makes it abundantly clear that Mao always ensured that his role would never be "historical" but rather would be "contemporary." Fourth, the present reforms of Deng are not the results of having waited for Mao to complete his "historical role." Deng and his pragmatic associates had wanted to carry out their "less politics but more economics" program as early as 1956 and continued to want that thereafter. Each time they were thwarted by Mao. Finally, almost anything, including holocaust, may be judged *after the fact* to have some "positive" effects in history. Following the logic of our defenders of Mao's rule, one might even regard the Nazis as having fulfilled their historical role, e.g., creation of a free Jewish state. So much for Mao's rule and his defense.

Today the Communist rule of mainland China, in some respects, has a twice-born appearance. Reform and change have affected every aspect of state and society. It was at the third plenum of the Eleventh Central Committee of the CPC in December 1978 that Deng Xiaoping unfurled his reform agenda. The general shape of Deng's reform is now relatively clear—more substantial change in economics than politics. It seems unmistakable that the present ruling trio—Deng Xiaoping, Hu Yaobang, and

Zhao Ziyang—have adopted the strategy of the fast-growing East Asian states of Taiwan, South Korea, and Singapore. Specifically, these three states have shown that a high rate of economic growth and social prosperity can be obtained under authoritarian rule. Whether the PRC will reap the same result as these three East Asian states with the same strategy, however, is a moot question. The other states are not (as China is) burdened with 800 million peasants still remaining in subsistance farming, a Stalinist heavy industry that serves itself, and a bureaucracy that is not based on modern standards of meritocracy. Moreover, though lacking a North American type of democracy, none of the fast growing East Asian nations ever developed the state stranglehold over economy and society that the PRC did, and still enforces to a large degree. It is difficult to envisage that the CPC would allow a market sector as dynamic and open as in the three other East Asian states. (We see all types of entrepreneurs in Taiwan, Singapore, and South Korea.) Last but not least, although the economies of Taiwan, Singapore, and South Korea grew initially under authoritarian rule, all three states have been subject to increasing demand for more political participation. Now at least in these three states, demand for political participation comes *after* economic growth, which dampens the degree of intensity of pressure on the government. In the PRC today, demands for economic growth and political participation are made simultaneously. So in political science terms, the PRC faces the problem of "loading" more urgently than the three other East Asian states do.

In the short run, the political and economic development of post-Mao China has brought a substantial degree of fragmentation. Politically, the party and state bureaucracy are affected by such phenomena as "obstruction at the middle" and sabotage and paralysis at the basic level. Factions and cliques pervade the political system. In minority-nationality regions, ethnic identity has had a new lease in life. Economically, the eastern seaboard has achieved more beneficial results from Deng's reforms more quickly than other regions of China. It appears very likely that the coastal areas will be a self-sufficient sector that is tied more with the world market than with the rest of China, much like China before 1949. Socially, with the reduction of terror and the resumption of a degree of market forces, the Chinese family and clan have reasserted their influence in the lives of the people.

The party pragmatists led by Deng have proved their capability to end the worst abuses of Mao's rule, alter national priority, and revive a degree of dynamism in society. They have yet to prove their capability in establishing new and flexible institutions (political or economic) to integrate and further induce dynamic forces in Chinese society.

NOTES

1. Harold D. Lasswell, *Psychopathology and Politics* (New York: Viking Press, 1960), p. 185.

2. Lucian W. Pye, *Politics, Personality, and Nation Building: Burma's Search for Identity* (New Haven: Yale University Press, 1963), pp. 38–42; also, Samuel P. Huntington, *Political Order in Changing Societies* (New Haven: Yale University Press, 1969), chap. 1.

3. Talcott Parsons, *The Social System* (New York: Free Press of Glencoe, 1964), p. 39.

4. Robert K. Merton, *Social Theory and Social Structure* (New York: Free Press of Glencoe, 1957), chap. 4.

5. Huntington, *Political Order*.

6. Information supplied by a young scholar who spent two years doing research in Inner Mongolia in 1981 and 1982. For occasional official reference to the killing and jailing of Mongolians during the Cultural Revolution, see *RMRB*, February 9, 1979, p. 3; and *Ming Pao Daily News*, June 28, 1981, p. 1.

7. These views are often heard in scholarly conferences and are especially current among those who had at one time professed unconditional admiration for Mao.

8. Christopher S. Wren, "China Reagan Will Visit Unlike That Nixon Saw," *New York Times,* April 24, 1984.

9. Frederic M. Surls, "China's Grain Trade," in *Chinese Economy Post-Mao.* A compendium of papers submitted to the Joint Economic Committee, Congress of the United States, vol. 1, "Policy and Performance," November 9, 1978 (Washington, D.C.: Government Printing Office), p. 655.

10. Frederic M. Surls and Francis C. Tuan, "China's Agriculture in the Eighties," in *China under the Four Modernizations,* part 1. Selected papers submitted to the Joint Economic Committee, Congress of the United States, August 13, 1982 (Washington, D.C.: Government Printing Office), p. 423.

11. Talk by Fei Xiaotong at the Conference on Chinese Culture and Modernization at the Chinese University of Hong Kong, March 8, 1983.

Hu Yaobang's Speech

This is the speech delivered on July 1, 1981 by the present top-ranking leader of the CPC, Hu Yaobang, on the sixtieth anniversary of the founding of the Communist party of China. It is presented here as an illustration of Chinese Communist ideological style.

As noted in chapter 13, the leaders of the PRC feel duty bound to instruct the Chinese population with authoritative and ideological speeches in order to realize the normative goals of the Communist party. Hu's speech consists of the three major components—historical review, diagnosis, and prognosis—that we find in all CPC ideological statements.

The historical review presented by Hu depicts the CPC and China as being on the correct path and marching toward a predestined stage of communism. To impress the reader with this historical process, Hu refers to "stages," e.g., from new democracy to socialism. Moreover, the historical march is led by the Communist party as the "leading force" and guided by the ideology of Marxism-Leninism and Mao thought.

The diagnostic part of Hu's speech begins with the subtitle "A Decisive Turning Point." Here Hu wishes to impress the Chinese people that the mistakes of the past have been corrected, i.e., the "left orientation." But there are important tasks to be carried out, mainly the restrengthening of the Communist party. The various passages beginning with "We must" should be interpreted as indirect admissions of deficiencies in Communist party affairs.

As with every ideological statement from the CPC, the prognosis is bright: Hu's concluding passage is entitled "Unite and Look Forward."

Comrades and Friends:

We are gathered here today to celebrate the 60th anniversary of the founding of the Communist party of China. At this moment, we are all deeply aware that our party and state are in an important historical period, a period in which we are bringing order out of chaos, carrying on our cause and forging ahead.

Adapted from *Beijing Review*, no. 28, July 13, 1981.

To bring order out of chaos, carry on our cause and forge ahead, we must undo all the negative consequences of the "cultural revolution," advance the great cause pioneered by the party under the leadership of Comrade Mao Zedong and other proletarian revolutionaries of the older generation, and pave the way further to socialism and communism for the Chinese people.

HISTORICAL REVIEW

The Sixth Plenary Session of the 11th Central Committee of the Communist party of China, which has just ended, adopted the Resolution on Certain Questions in the History of Our Party Since the Founding of the People's Republic of China. The resolution reviews the party's 60 years of struggle, sums up the basic experience it has gained in the 32 years since the founding of the People's Republic, makes a concrete and realistic evaluation of a whole train of crucial historical events, analyses what was right and what was wrong in the ideology behind these events and the subjective factors and social roots giving rise to them, evaluates Comrade Mao Zedong's role in history and expounds Mao Zedong Thought scientifically, and indicates our way forward more clearly. The plenary session also took decisions on other important matters. History will prove that it too was a meeting of paramount importance for our party – a new milestone for our party and state in the course of bringing order out of chaos, carrying on our cause and forging ahead.

Looking back over the path our party has traversed, we are keenly conscious of the fact that the Chinese revolution has not been smooth sailing. We can say that the 60 years since the founding of the Communist party of China have been years of unflinching, heroic struggle for the liberation of the Chinese nation and the happiness of the Chinese people, years of ever closer integration, through repeated application, of the universal truth of Marxism-Leninism with the concrete practice of the Chinese revolution, and years when right prevailed over wrong and positive aspects prevailed over negative aspects in the party. They have been years during which we marched on to a number of victories despite untold hardships and setbacks.

Why do we say that the history of the Chinese Communist party is one of unflinching, heroic struggle for the liberation of the Chinese nation and the happiness of the Chinese people?

In modern Chinese history, between the Opium War of 1840–42 and the outbreak of the May 4th Movement of 1919, the Chinese people waged protracted, heroic struggles against imperialism and feudalism. The 1911 Revolution led by the great revolutionary Dr. Sun Yat-sen overthrew the Qing Dynasty monarchy, thus bringing to an end more than 2,000 years of feudal autocracy. However, the way to China's salvation was not discovered through any of these struggles. It was not until the Communist party of China was born after the October Socialist Revolution in Russia and the May 4th Movement in China that new vistas were opened up for the Chinese revolution, as a result of the integration of Marxism-Leninism with the rising workers' movement in China, and with the help of the international proletariat.

The enemy of the Chinese revolution was formidable and ferocious. But none of the hardships overwhelmed the Chinese people and the Communist party of China. In a dauntless revolutionary spirit, our party led the people in rising up to fight the enemy. We Communists and the people depended on each other for survival: we relied closely on the people, and the people had deep faith in us. Our party steeled itself in the grim struggle and became the most advanced and most powerful leading force in the history of the Chinese revolution and built a new and well-trained people's army. After 28 years of arduous struggle in four great people's revolutionary wars (the Northern Expedition, 1924–27, the Agrarian Revolutionary War, 1927–37, the War of Resistance Against Japan, 1937–45, and the War of Liberation, 1946–49), our party led the people of all our nationalities in finally overthrowing in 1949 the reactionary rule of imperialism, feudalism and bureaucrat-capitalism and winning the great victory of the new-democratic revolution, a victory which led to the founding of the People's Republic of China, a state of the people's democratic dictatorship.

After the founding of the People's Republic, our party led the entire people in sustained advance. We thwarted the threats, attempts at subversion, sabotage and armed provocations of the imperialists and hegemonists, and safeguarded the independence and security of our great motherland. Except for Taiwan Province and a few other islands, we have achieved and consolidated the unification of our country. We have achieved and strengthened the great unity of the Chinese people of whatever nationality and of the workers, peasants and intellectuals throughout the country. We have formed and consolidated the broadest possible united front of all socialist workers, patriots who support socialism and other patriots who uphold the reunification of the motherland—a united front led by the Chinese Communist party in full co-operation with all the democratic parties. And we smoothly effected the decisive transition of our society from new democracy to socialism. Thanks to the arduous struggle of the whole party and people, we in the main completed the socialist transformation of the private ownership of the means of production and embarked on large-scale, planned socialist economic construction. Thus, our economy and culture registered an advance unparalleled in Chinese history. However numerous the shortcomings and mistakes in our work and however imperfect some aspects of our social system, we have eliminated the system of exploitation and the exploiting classes and have established the socialist system. Hence, with nearly a quarter of the world's population, China has entered upon a socialist society, a brand new society in the history of mankind. Beyond the shadow of a doubt, this is the most radical social change in Chinese history. It is a leap of the most far-reaching significance in the progress of mankind and a tremendous victory for and a further development of Marxism.

The change is indeed striking. In the 80 years between the Opium War and the birth of the Chinese Communist party, the ceaseless struggles of the people had all failed despite their heroism, and their hopes and lofty aspirations were sadly frustrated. The picture has been altogether different in the 60 years since the birth of the Chinese Communist party. A new epoch in Chinese history was ushered in. The Chinese people have taken their destiny into their own hands: they have stood up in the East. Never again will the Chinese nation be bullied and oppressed.

In celebrating the 60th anniversary of the founding of the Chinese Communist party, we feel with deep emotion that the splendid fruits of the Chinese people's revolution have been truly hard-won. They have been won by the Chinese people in 60 long years of hard struggle under the leadership of the Chinese Communist party. They have been nurtured with the blood of millions of Communists and non-party revolutionaries who died before the firing squad, on the battlefield or at their posts.

Let us rise and pay our sincere tribute to the memory of all the revolutionary martyrs: all the revolutionary leaders and cadres, Communists and Communist Youth League members, veteran revolutionaries and young fighters, non-party comrades-in-arms and foreign friends who laid down their lives for the Chinese people at different stages of the Chinese revolution over the past six decades.

Why do we say that the history of the Chinese Communist party is one of ever closer integration, through repeated application, of the universal truth of Marxism-Leninism with the concrete practice of the Chinese revolution?

From the moment of its inception, our party adopted Marxism-Leninism as its guiding ideology. However, the general principles of Marxism provide no ready-made recipe for revolution in a particular country, especially a big, oriental, semi-feudal and semi-colonial country like China. During its formative years, the 1920s and 1930s, our party suffered again and again from the "infantile malady" of turning Marxism into a dogma and deifying foreign experience—a malady which could not but leave the Chinese revolution groping in the dark and even lead it into a blind alley. Comrade Mao Zedong's great contribution lies in the fact that, in the course of combating this erroneous tendency and in the struggles waged collectively by the party and the people, he succeeded in integrating the universal truth of Marxism with the concrete practice of the Chinese revolution and in summing up freshly gained experiences. In this way Mao Zedong Thought took shape as the guiding scientific ideology conforming to Chinese conditions. It is this scientific ideology that has guided the sweeping advance of the Chinese revolution from one triumph to another.

Mao Zedong Thought, coming into being and developing in the course of the Chinese revolution, is the crystallization of the collective wisdom of our party and a summing-up of the victories in the gigantic struggles of the Chinese people. Its theories on the new-democratic revolution, on the socialist revolution and socialist construction, on the strategy and tactics of revolutionary struggle, on the building of a revolutionary army, on military strategy, on ideological and political work, on cultural work, and on the building of the party, as well as its theories concerning scientific modes of thought, work and leadership which will be even more important in guiding all our work in the future, have all added new and original ideas to the treasure house of Marxism. As a theory and as the summing-up of experiences verified in practice, as the application and development of Marxism in China, Mao Zedong Thought has been and will remain the guiding ideology of our party.

However, Comrade Mao Zedong had his shortcomings and mistakes just like many other outstanding figures in the forefront of the march of history. Chiefly in his later years, having been admired and loved for so long by the whole party and people, he became overconfident and more and more divorced from reality and the masses and, in particular, from the party's collective leadership, and often rejected and even suppressed correct opinions that differed from his. Thus, he inevitably made mistakes, including the comprehensive, long-drawn-out and gross blunder of initiating the "cultural revolution"; this was a tremendous misfortune for the party and the people. Of course, it must be admitted that both before the "cultural revolution" and at the time of its inception, the party failed to prevent Comrade Mao Zedong's erroneous tendency from growing more serious but, instead, accepted and approved of some of his wrong theses. We veterans who had been working together with him for a long time as his comrades-in-arms, or who had long been following him in revolutionary struggle as his disciples, are keenly aware of our own responsibility in this matter, and we are determined never to forget this lesson.

Although Comrade Mao Zedong made grave mistakes in his later years, it is clear that if we consider his life work as a whole, his contributions to the Chinese revolution far outweigh his errors. He had dedicated himself to the Chinese revolution since his youth and had fought for it all his life. He was one of the founders of our party and the chief architect of the glorious Chinese People's Liberation Army. At the most trying times in the Chinese revolution, he was the first to discover the correct road for the revolution, work out a correct overall strategy and gradually formulate a whole set of correct theories and tactics, thus guiding the revolution from defeat to victory. After the founding of the People's Republic, under the leadership of the Party Central Committee and Comrade Mao Zedong, New China quickly consolidated its position and embarked on the great cause of socialism. Even in the last few years of his life, when his errors had become very serious, Comrade Mao Zedong still remained alert to the nation's independence and security and had a correct grasp of the new developments in the world situation. He led the party and people in standing up to all pressures from hegemonism and instituted a new pattern for our foreign relations. In the long years of struggle, all comrades in our party drew wisdom and strength from Comrade Mao Zedong and Mao Zedong Thought which nurtured successive generations of our party's leaders and large numbers of its cadres and educated the whole Chinese people. Comrade Mao Zedong was a great Marxist, a great proletarian revolutionary, theorist and strategist, and the greatest national hero in Chinese history. He made major contributions to the cause of the liberation of the world's oppressed nations and to the cause of human progress. His immense contributions are immortal.

While celebrating the 60th anniversary of the founding of the Communist party of China, we deeply cherish the memory of Comrade Mao Zedong. We deeply cherish the memory of the great Marxists, Comrades Zhou Enlai, Liu Shaoqi and Zhu De, and the memory of Comrades Ren Bishi, Dong Biwu, Peng Dehuai, He Long, Chen Yi, Luo Ronghuan, Lin Boqu, Li Fuchun, Wang Jiaxiang, Zhang Wentian, Tao Zhu and others, all of whom were outstanding leaders of our party and, together with Comrade Mao Zedong, made important contributions to the victorious Chinese revolution and to the formation and development of Mao Zedong Thought. We deeply cherish the memory of Comrades Li Dazhao, Qu Qiubai, Cai Hesen, Xiang Jingyu, Deng Zhongxia, Su Zhaozheng, Peng Pai, Chen Yannian, Yun Daiying, Zhao Shiyan, Zhang Tailei, Li Lisan and other prominent leaders of our party in its formative years. We deeply cherish the memory of Comrades Fang Zhimin, Liu Zhidan, Huang Gonglue, Xu Jishen, Wei Baqun, Zhao Bosheng, Dong Zhentang, Duan Dechang, Yang Jingyu, Zuo Quan, Ye Ting and other outstanding commanders of the people's army who early laid down their lives for the party and the country. We deeply cherish the memory of Comrade Soong Ching Ling, a great contemporary woman fighter who fought together with us over a long period of time and became a member of the glorious Chinese Communist party before her death, of Cai Yuanpei, the prominent Chinese intellectual forerunner, and of Lu Xun, the great standard-bearer of our proletarian revolutionary culture. We deeply cherish the memory of Liao Zhongkai, He Xiangning, Deng Yanda, Yang Xingfo, Shen Junru and other close non-party comrades-in-arms of ours who consistently supported our party. We deeply cherish the memory of Comrades Zou Taofen, Guo Moruo, Mao Dun and Li Siguang, Mr. Wen Yiduo and other distinguished fighters in the fields of science and culture. We deeply cherish the memory of Yang Hucheng, Tan Kah Kee, Zhang Zhizhong, Fu Zuoyi and other renowned patriots who made important contributions to the victorious Chinese people's revolution. We deeply cherish the memory of Norman Bethune, Agnes Smedley, Anna Louise Strong, Dwarkanath S. Kotnis, Edgar Snow, Inejiro Asanuma, Kenzo Nakajima and other close friends of the Chinese people and eminent internationalist fighters.

Why do we say that the history of the Chinese Communist party is also the history of the triumph of right over wrong and of the triumph of the party's positive aspects over its negative ones?

The revolutionary cause our party has embarked upon is a sacred cause involving the radical transformation of Chinese society, a completely new cause never undertaken by our forefathers. The enemy of the revolution was formidable and the social conditions under which the revolution took place were extremely complex. Therefore, it was only natural that we should make mistakes of one kind or another, and even grievous ones, in the course of our revolutionary struggles. The important thing is to be good at learning through practice once a mistake has been made, to wake up in good time and endeavour to correct it, to strive to avoid a blunder which is long-drawn-out and comprehensive in character, and to avoid repetition of the same grievous blunder.

Our party was born and grew to maturity in the old society. At the hightide of the revolution, large numbers of revolutionaries joined our ranks. This boosted our strength, but a few careerists and opportunists, too, wormed their way into the party. This could hardly be avoided. The point is that while transforming society, our party must pay attention to remoulding itself, and be good at educating and remoulding those who have diverse non-proletarian ideas when they join our party and good at recognizing careerists and conspirators for what they are, so as to be able to foil their schemes and conspiracies.

The greatness of the party does not lie in any readiness to guarantee complete freedom from any negative phenomena but in its ability to overcome shortcomings and rectify errors and to defeat sabotage by all alien forces. Let us look back: Isn't this precisely how our party has fought in the past? Its history contains the grave errors of Chen Duxiu's Right capitulationism and Wang Ming's "Left" dogmatism. There were also conspiracies to split the party hatched by Zhang Guotao and by Gao Gang and Rao Shushi. There were even the Lin Biao and Jiang Qing counter-revolutionary cliques. However, none succeeded in destroying our party. The extremely treacherous careerists and conspirators Lin Biao and Jiang Qing exploited the "cultural revolution" to seize supreme power; they committed every conceivable sin against our nation and people, with the gravest consequences. Yet they were finally unmasked and swept into the garbage bin of history by the party and the people. Isn't this an incontrovertible historical fact? Instead of being destroyed by sabotage or crippled by reverses of one kind or another, our party has emerged each time refreshed and reinvigorated from the struggle to overcome mistakes and prevail over what is negative. It is our party that is invincible.

The past 60 years prove that our party is indeed a proletarian party armed with Marxism-Leninism and Mao Zedong Thought and a party wholeheartedly serving the people, entirely dedicated to their interests and with no particular interest of its own. It is truly a long-tested party which has acquired rich experience, learnt many lessons and is capable of leading the people in braving difficulties to win victory after victory in the revolution. The role of this great party as the force at the core of the Chinese people's revolutionary cause and its leadership in this cause are the dictates of history and of the will and interests of the people of all our nationalities, dictates which no force on earth can change or shake.

A DECISIVE TURNING POINT

Comrades and friends!

With widespread popular support, our party smashed at one stroke the Jiang Qing counter-revolutionary clique in October 1976. This saved the revolution and our socialist state and ushered in a new period of historical development. The Third Plenary Session of the 11th Central Committee held in December 1978 marked a decisive turning point in the post-1949 history of our party.

The tremendous significance of this plenary session lies in the fact that it really started to correct matters in an all round, determined and well-considered way by relying on the masses. Since then, right through the Fourth, Fifth and Sixth Plenary Sessions, our party has been working hard with concentrated energy and attention and under difficult and complex conditions, and has adopted and implemented step by step a series of major policy decisions in ideological, political and organizational matters and all aspects of socialist construction, thus correcting the erroneous "Left" orientation. Moreover, in the light of the new historical conditions, our party has gradually charted a correct course for socialist modernization that is suited to China's conditions.

The most striking change of all is the shift of the focus of work of the whole party and nation after the liquidation and repudiation of the Lin Biao and Jiang Qing counter-revolutionary cliques. The leading organs from the central down to local levels are now concentrating their energy and attention on socialist modernization. Now that liquidation of the long prevalent "Left" deviationist guiding ideology is under way, our socialist economic and cultural construction has been shifted to a course of development that takes into account the basic conditions of the country and the limits of our ability, proceeds step by step, and seeks practical results and steady advance. With the implementation of the party's policies, the introduction of the system of production responsibilities and the development of a diversified economy, an excellent situation has developed in the vast rural areas in particular, a dynamic and progressive situation seldom seen since the founding of the People's Republic.

In socio-political relations, our party has resolutely and appropriately solved many important issues which had been wrongly handled over a long period of time, eliminated a number of major factors detrimental to stability and unity and put an end to the social unrest and upheaval fomented in the "cultural revolution." We are now striving to foster socialist democracy, improve the socialist legal system and reform and perfect the socialist political system. This gives a powerful impetus to the consolidation and development of a political situation of stability, unity and liveliness.

Through organizational consolidation and rectification of the style of work, tangible progress has been made in the normalization of party life, the development of inner-party democracy and the strengthening of the party's ties with the masses. The party's prestige, grievously damaged during the "cultural revolution," is gradually being restored.

To ensure the proper implementation of the principle of emancipating the mind, our party has reiterated that it is necessary to uphold the four fundamental principles of the socialist road, the people's democratic dictatorship (i.e., the dictatorship of the proletariat), the Communist party's leadership, and Marxism-Leninism and Mao Zedong Thought. These principles constitute the common political basis for the unity of the whole party and the unity of the entire people and provide the fundamental guarantee for the success of socialist modernization.

The great change which began with the Third Plenary Session of the party's 11th Central Committee and our correct line and policies fulfil the common aspirations of the people and the party. Speaking of the general orientation and major policy decisions taken since the session, many comrades have said, "They suit us fine." These words reflect the thoughts and feelings of the masses and of the majority of cadres. They explain why the change is so dynamic and irresistible.

Needless to say, many difficulties confront us. We have yet to finish the process of correction, and in various fields many problems remain to be resolved. Our material resources, expertise and experience are far from adequate for the achievement of the four modernizations. The people's living standards are still very low and many pressing problems demand solution. We have yet to introduce further improvements in the party's leadership and style of work. It is wrong to take these difficulties lightly. Only by taking them into full account will we be invincible. The road before us is still long and tortuous. It is like climbing Mount Taishan; when we have reached the Half-Way Gate to Heaven, we find that the three Eighteen Bends lie ahead of us, demanding Herculean efforts. Until we have negotiated these bends, however, we won't be able to reach the South Gate to Heaven. Still climbing, we will find it relatively easy to mount the Peak of the Jade Emperor, our destination, and only then can we claim to have accomplished the splendid cause of socialist modernization. Once at the South Gate to Heaven, we shall be in a position to appreciate the great Tang Dynasty poet Du Fu's well-known lines, "Viewed from the topmost summit, all mountains around are dwarfed." The hardships that once towered like "mountains" will then look small and we will be able to negotiate the obstacles on the way to the "topmost summit" more or less easily. In the course of our long journey, we will certainly be able to conquer the Eighteen Bends, reach the South Gate to Heaven and then ascend the Peak of the Jade Emperor. Once there, we shall push towards new summits.

PARTY BUILDING

Comrades and friends!

The historical experience of the past 60 years can be summed up in one sentence: there must be a Marxist, revolutionary line and a proletarian party capable of formulating and upholding this line. Faced with the gigantic task of socialist modernization centering around economic construction in the new historical period, we are deeply aware that the key to the fulfillment of this task lies in our party.

Now, the entire people has placed its hopes on our party, and other peoples of the world are closely watching it. Whether or not we can steer the ship of the Chinese revolution onward through storm and stress in the new historical period, whether or not we can modernize our agriculture, industry, national defence and science and technology fairly smoothly, avoid suffering such serious setbacks and paying such a huge price as in the past, and achieve results that will satisfy the people and win the praise of posterity, all depends on the efforts of all comrades in the party in the next decade or two. We must not let our people down.

With higher political awareness, we must make our party a solid core which is more mature politically, more unified ideologically and more consolidated organizationally, and more able to unite with all our nationalities and lead them in socialist modernization.

1. All members of the party must work with selfless devotion for China's socialist modernization and in the service of the people.

We Chinese Communists must always proceed from our basic standpoint with the objective of wholeheartedly serving the people. Serving the people in essence means that our party must rally the masses round it and, by virtue of its correct guidelines and policies, its close ties with the masses, its members' exemplary role and its propaganda and organizational work, help them to see where their fundamental interests lie and to get united to strive for them.

The people are the makers of history. Both the people's revolution and the construction of socialism led by our party are the people's very own cause. At all times party members comprise only a small minority of the population; so we must rely on the people in all our work, have faith in them, draw wisdom from them, set store by their creativeness and subject ourselves to their supervision. Otherwise, we will accomplish nothing, we will fail. Since victory was won in the revolution, the people have become the masters of the country and society. To organize and support them in fulfilling this role and building a new life under socialism is the very essence of the party's leadership over affairs of state.

For us Communists, serving the people means primarily dedication to the cause of communism and readiness to sacrifice ourselves for the interests of the people. In the years of war, many of our party members were the first to charge at the enemy and the last to pull back; they remained staunch and unyielding in captivity, dying as martyrs; and they were invariably the first to bear hardships and the last to enjoy comforts. What an inspiration and encouragement they were to millions upon millions of our people! Today, in peacetime construction, and particularly after the decade of havoc of the "cultural revolution," we need this revolutionary spirit even more. Although our party's fine style of work was corroded by the counter-revolutionary cliques of Lin Biao and Jiang Qing, there are still large numbers of fine party members who have maintained and carried forward this revolutionary spirit, a spirit characterized by readiness to sacrifice one's individual interests and even one's own life, for the interests of the people. They have won high praise from the people, and they have earned it. It is utterly wrong to think and act as though the revolutionary spirit may be discarded in peacetime construction and party members no longer need to share weal and woe with the masses whose interests they may subordinate to their own. That would be to debase our party spirit.

The style of work of a party in power vitally affects its very existence. As Comrade Mao Zedong pointed out in 1942, "Once our party's style of work is put completely right, the people all over the country will learn from our example. Those outside the party who have the same kind of bad style will, if they are good and honest people, learn from our example and correct their mistakes, and thus the whole nation will be influenced. So long as our Communist ranks are in good order and march in step, so long as our troops are picked troops and our weapons are good weapons, any enemy, however powerful, can be overthrown." Let us firmly resolve to strive to our utmost to restore and carry forward the fine style of work which our party and Comrade Mao Zedong cultivated, and to lead the whole Chinese nation in building a high level of socialist civilization.

2. We must be good at carrying forward Marxism-Leninism and Mao Zedong Thought in the light of the new historical conditions.

We have obtained great successes in revolution and construction in the past under the guidance of Marxism-Leninism and Mao Zedong Thought. We will obtain new and greater successes in our long march into the future by relying on Marxism-Leninism and Mao Zedong Thought for guidance. If we Communists have any family heirlooms to speak of, by far the most important one is Marxism-Leninism and Mao Zedong Thought. It has always been our basic and unshakable principle to uphold Marxism-Leninism and Mao Zedong Thought and persist in taking the tenets of Marxism as our guideline.

Marxism is the crystallization of scientific thinking on proletarian revolution; it is our most powerful weapon for understanding and transforming the objective world. Its tenets are truths that have been repeatedly verified in practice. However, it does not embrace all the truths in the unending course of human history, nor can it possibly do so. For us revolutionaries, the theory of Marxism is the guide to action and by no means a rigid dogma to be followed unthinkingly. All revolutionaries true to Marxism have the responsibility to ensure that it does not become divorced from social life and does not stagnate, wither or ossify; they must enrich it with fresh revolutionary experiences so that it will remain full of vitality. Therefore, our fundamental approach to Marxism is that we should apply and advance Marxism-Leninism and Mao Zedong Thought; such is our unshirkable historical duty as Chinese Communists. This is not easy of course. It requires us to make an arduous, lifelong effort to achieve a better integration of the tenets of Marxism with the concrete practice of China's socialist modernization.

We must continue to apply ourselves to the study and investigation of the history of the Chinese revolution. For the China of today has grown out of the China of yesterday, a China about which we know, not too much, but too little. We should especially study present-day China because our efforts to create a radiant future must first of all be based on a comparatively correct understanding of the present. And the trouble is that we don't know much; in fact we still know very little, about Chinese realities today and the objective laws governing the building of socialism.

Our cause is an integral whole and has a single goal. Yet, ours is a vast country with extremely diverse conditions. Therefore our study and understanding of the overall situation and of the situation in different regions must be closely co-ordinated. If we overlook the whole and disregard uniformity, we shall make the mistake of acting blindly and thoughtlessly and with no consideration for the whole in directing the work in specific regions. If we ignore the regions' specific conditions in directing the work of the whole country, we shall make the mistake of being guided by our own conjectures and fancies which may have no relation to reality. We Chinese Communists should be revolutionaries who are at once far-sighted and realistic in our approach.

We lay stress on self-reliance and strive to solve our problems by our own efforts and treasure our own experience. But we must never be conceited and underrate the experience of others. We should through analysis absorb whatever is useful in others' experience and lessons. We must therefore earnestly study and analyse the experience of other countries, other regions and other people while studying and summing up our own.

The integration of the universal truth of Marxism with Chinese reality is a long process of repeated cycles of practice, knowledge, again practice and again knowledge. In the new historical period, we should emancipate our minds and constantly identify and grapple with the new conditions and problems in our practice and thus equip ourselves with rich, varied and living perceptual knowledge. At the same time, we must set our minds to work and learn more social and natural sciences and their methods in order to raise perceptual knowledge to the plane of rational knowledge, logical knowledge that is more or less systematic, and verify it again and again in practice. We must therefore study diligently, learn from specialists and heed differing views and opinions and, at the same time, delve deep into reality and carry out thorough, systematic investigation and study so as to successfully synthesize our direct and indirect experience.

So long as we proceed in study and work in accordance with this stand, viewpoint and method, we shall be able to put all our party work on a scientific foundation, make discoveries and function creatively for socialist modernization, thus ensuring the triumphant advance of our great cause.

3. We must put democratic life in the party on a sounder basis and strengthen party organization and discipline.

One of the fundamental reasons why the grievous errors of the "cultural revolution" remained unrectified for so long is that the regular political life of our party, inner-party democratic centralism and the collective leadership of the Central Committee in particular, had been disrupted. As a result, the personality cult, anarchism and ultra-individualism all prevailed. This afforded the Lin Biao and Jiang Qing counter-revolutionary cliques and other scoundrels an opportunity they exploited to the full. No comrade in the party must ever forget this bitter lesson and we must all take warning from it.

We are historical materialists. We do not deny the significant role that outstanding individuals play in history or the significant role of outstanding leaders in a proletarian party. But at the same time we maintain that our party must be placed under collective leadership to be exercised by those who combine ability with political integrity and who have emerged in the course of mass struggles, and that we must ban all forms of the personality cult. Party organizations should commend all comrades, irrespective of their rank or position, who have made special contributions and achieved outstanding results in their work, so as to encourage other party members and people to learn from their example. But such public commendation must be truthful and unvarnished.

Appropriate relationships should be established between the leaders and the led in our party organizations at all levels. Comrades at a lower level must respect and obey the leadership of comrades at a higher level. They must not feign compliance while actually violating or resisting instructions from the higher level. On the other hand, comrades at a higher level must heed the opinions of their subordinates, respect their functions and powers and accept their supervision. Leaders should take part in inner-party activities just like ordinary party members, abide by party rules and discipline and the law of the state, and maintain their ties with the rank-and-file and the masses in general; they must not put themselves in a special category just because they are in leading positions.

Decisions concerning important matters must be made after collective discussions by the appropriate party committee, and no one individual is allowed to have the final say. All members of a party committee must abide by its decisions. Party committees at all levels must practise a division of labour and responsibilities to be discharged under the collective leadership of the party committee, with each member doing his share conscientiously and responsibly and in the best and most efficient way possible.

All party members are entitled to criticize, at party meetings, any individuals within the party, including leading members of the Central Committee; retaliation is impermissible. Party organizations at all levels and all party members should give full play to their initiative and dare to work independently and conscientiously in a spirit characterized by boldness in thinking and action. But no party member is allowed to impair the party's interests and the common goal by turning the department or unit entrusted to him by the party into his own independent kingdom.

Our party's fighting strength lies in its vitality and strict discipline. Now that we are committed to the socialist modernization of the country and our task is most challenging and difficult, we have still greater need to promote this fine party tradition.

4. We must be good at keeping ourselves politically pure and healthy and under all circumstances maintain our revolutionary vigour as members of a party in power.

Ours is a large party with a membership of 39 million and it is a party in power. This can easily make some of our comrades feel conceited and succumb to bureaucratic practices. Confronted as we are with so many new things and new problems, we can hardly avoid making mistakes. Besides, class struggle continues to exist to a certain extent in our society, and the ideological influences of the exploiting and other non-proletarian classes still survive. These facts, combined as they are with the complexities of contemporary international relations, put us in daily contact with the undesirable phenomena of capitalism, feudalism and small production. The contradictions between proletarian and non-proletarian ideology and between correct and erroneous thinking within our party demand that we make more effective use of the best weapon Communists have for remoulding themselves, namely, the practice of criticism and self-criticism.

Communists should take a clear-cut stand on questions of principle and should uphold truth. Every party member should uphold the party spirit and be unequivocal in his position on questions of right and wrong which involve the interests of the party and the people and should show clearly what he is for and what he is against. The rotten and vulgar practice of trying to be on good terms with everybody at the expense of principle is incompatible with the proletarian character of our party.

Our party's fine tradition of criticism and self-criticism, gravely undermined in previous years, is now being revived and carried forward, and some new and useful experience has been gained in this respect. In making either criticism or self-criticism, one should base oneself on facts and rectify existing mistakes without trying to hide or magnify them. Criticisms should be offered in a well-reasoned way and should be instructive so that they can help the comrades concerned raise their level of political consciousness; they must not be based on speculation or aimed at intimidating others. We should induce the comrades concerned voluntarily to examine themselves and correct their mistakes. In our criticisms we must not make far-fetched interpretations and unduly involve other comrades at a higher or lower level. So long as the comrades concerned have recognized their mistakes and are willing to correct them, we should encourage them to go on working boldly. Our main mistake in the past was to engage in excessive struggle that yielded results contrary to our expectations; people became reluctant to make self-criticism and were afraid to criticize others. We must change this unhealthy tendency.

We Communists need to practise criticism and self-criticism so that our party will become more, not less, united and militant. Provided we fully revive and carry forward this fine tradition, our party will undoubtedly continue to show inexhaustible vitality and will never show signs of decay.

5. We must select more cadres who combine ability and political integrity and who are in the prime of life and appoint them to leading posts at all levels.

Insofar as experience in struggle is concerned, it may be said that our party's cadres belong to three or four generations, which shows that ours is a long-standing and well-established cause. It is indeed fortunate that our leading cadres at all fronts are largely veterans who have been tempered in prolonged revolutionary struggle. If cadres can be called valuable party assets, then these numerous senior comrades are most valuable.

But the laws of nature cannot be changed and, after all, most of our senior comrades are physically not as strong and active as before. In order to ensure that there is an adequate number of successors to carry on our cause and guarantee continuity in our party's guidelines and policies, we must devote much of our energy from now on to the selection and training of thousands upon thousands of cadres who combine ability and political integrity and are in their prime and give these comrades the opportunity to take part in leadership in various fields so that they may be better and more effectively tempered through practice. It is now a pressing strategic task facing the whole party to build up a large contingent of revolutionary, well-educated, professionally competent and younger cadres.

The older comrades have an especially significant role to play in fulfilling this strategic task. Comrades Ye Jianying, Deng Xiaoping, Chen Yun and Li Xiannian have said more than once that although the old comrades may be pardoned for other mistakes, they would be committing an unforgivable historical error if they did not redouble their efforts to train younger successors. The old comrades should work personally with the organizational departments of the party and the masses in the selection and training of younger cadres and eagerly and enthusiastically guide them to front-line posts of leadership. At the same time, they should free themselves from the onerous pressure of day-to-day work and advance their views and judgments on key and long-range problems. The Central Committee of the party earnestly hopes that all veteran party comrades will have the depth of insight and foresight to discharge this crucial historic responsibility to the best of their ability. Meanwhile, it hopes that party organizations at all levels and all comrades in their prime who have been selected for higher posts will respect and take good care of our veterans and learn as much as possible from them.

At present, we are facing the major task of learning anew. It is the hope of the Central Committee of the party that all party comrades and the younger comrades in particular will brace up, strengthen their party spirit, enhance their political consciousness, set stricter demands on themselves, diligently study Marxist-Leninist works and works by Mao Zedong and the history of the party, our nation and the world, acquire more theoretical and practical knowledge, and learn more about management and technology as required by their own occupations and specific jobs. The results of our study will determine the quality of our leadership and work and will have a direct bearing on the progress of the socialist modernization of our country. Since we have successfully learnt to destroy the old world, we can surely learn even more successfully how to build a new one.

6. We must forever uphold internationalism and cast in our lot with the proletariat and the people of the whole world.

We Chinese Communists have always integrated patriotism with internationalism.

We are patriots. We have invariably fought might and main for our national liberation, for the well-being of our people and the unification and prosperity of our motherland. We have never knuckled under to any pressure from any foreign power. We have never flinched in our determination to be independent and to rely on ourselves, no matter how formidable the difficulties we have faced. Our country is still relatively backward economically and culturally; but we have always maintained our national self-respect in the face of hegemonist threats of force or in our relations with all stronger and richer countries, and will not tolerate any servility in thought or deed. We are resolved to strive together with the people of the whole country, not least including those in Taiwan, for its return and for the sacred cause of the complete reunification of our motherland.

At the same time we are proletarian internationalists. We have always cast in our own lot with the other peoples of the world in their just struggles and with the cause of human progress. Our struggles have throughout enjoyed the support of the other peoples of the world, and we on our part have always supported the struggles of the world's oppressed nations and people for emancipation, the cause of world peace and the cause of human progress, and we have consistently opposed imperialism, hegemonism, colonialism and racism. Our cause of socialist modernization is at once patriotic and internationalist. Its success will be a tremendous contribution to the cause of world peace and human progress. We hereby wish solemnly to proclaim once again that the Communist party of China will always live in friendship and co-operation and on an equal footing with all the political parties and organizations in the world which are dedicated to human progress and to national liberation and will learn from their useful experience, and that we will never interfere in the internal affairs of any foreign political party. Even when it becomes stronger and more prosperous, socialist China will belong to the third world and forever stand by the other peoples of the world, strive for world peace and friendly intercourse among peoples, abide faithfully by the Five Principles of Peaceful Coexistence, and continue to promote more economic, cultural, scientific and technological exchange and co-operation with other nations; it will never seek advantage at the expense of others or bully weaker nations and will never under any circumstances seek hegemony.

UNITE AND LOOK FORWARD

Comrades and friends!

The decisions of the Sixth Plenary Session of the 11th Central Committee of the party were adopted after ample and extensive exchanges of views and discussions both prior to and during the session. Its outcome fully testifies to our party's ability to safeguard and strengthen its unity on the basis of Marxist principles and to the fact that the political life of our party has now become much healthier.

Some well-intentioned friends at home and abroad have been worried about our party's ability to achieve complete unity, while a handful of people harbouring evil designs placed their hopes on successfully sowing dissension so as to undermine the unity of our party. Now, reality has given them a clear answer: No force on earth can break the Chinese Communist party's strong unity based on Marxist principles.

Comrades and friends!

We, the proletariat, are the class which commands the future, and our party has lofty ideals and aspirations. The best way for us to celebrate this grand festival, our party's birthday, is to learn from historical experience and thus unite and look forward, focusing our attention on unresolved problems.

Socialist modernization is a great revolution. We are undertaking this great revolution in a huge oriental nation left economically and culturally backward by ruthless imperialist oppression and plunder. The fact that China entered upon socialism before developed capitalist countries is due to its specific historical conditions, to the correct leadership exercised by our party and the arduous struggles of the entire people. It represents a development of scientific socialism and is a credit to our party and the Chinese people. On the other hand, our socialist cause is bound to meet many difficulties arising from our economic and cultural backwardness. This in turn calls for more strenuous and protracted struggle. We are still living under the threat of aggression and sabotage from outside. Therefore, our whole party, our whole army and our whole people must more actively apply their revolutionary spirit, heighten their revolutionary vigilance and steel their revolutionary will so as to win victory in this great revolution.

We have suffered severe setbacks in our advance to socialism and paid heavily for our errors. However, these errors and setbacks have made us firmer, more experienced, more mindful of our actual conditions, more sober and more powerful. We have learnt much from our reverses and mistakes and shall go on learning more. In this sense, our grievous errors and reverses are but fleeting phenomena. We must not overlook that we have a vast contingent of cadres steeled in struggle, that we have built up a substantial material base, that the whole party, army and people fervently desire a prosperous motherland, and that we enjoy the superiority of our socialist system. All this and the fact that we now have correct ideological, political and organizational lines, constitute the decisive factor that will apply for a long time to come. There is no doubt whatsoever that our socialist cause and the hundreds of millions of Chinese people have a bright future.

The internal unity of the party and the party's unity with the people are the essential condition for the triumph of our cause. While celebrating the 60th anniversary of the founding of the Communist party of China, we wish to pay our sincere respects to the workers, peasants and intellectuals who are fighting valiantly on the different fronts, to the glorious People's Liberation Army, the Great Wall of steel that defends our motherland, to the vast numbers of hard-working cadres, to our party's close aides, the Communist Youth League members who are full of vigour and vitality, and to our fellow-countrymen in Taiwan, Xianggang (Hongkong) and Aomen (Macao) and to Chinese citizens overseas! We wish to extend our heartfelt thanks to all the democratic parties and non-party personages and friends of all circles who have co-operated with our party and rendered invaluable support to the people's revolution and to construction.

The unity of the Chinese people with the other peoples of the world is another essential condition for the triumph of our cause. In celebrating the 60th anniversary of the founding of the Communist party of China, we wish to express our deep gratitude to all friendly countries which have entered into relations of equality and mutual assistance with us, and to all our foreign friends and comrades who have rendered our party and people invaluable help.

Let all comrades in the party and the people of all nationalities in our country unite as one under the great banner of Marxism-Leninism and Mao Zedong Thought and work hard to make China a modern and powerful socialist country, which is prosperous, highly democratic and culturally advanced! Let us all strive for the supreme ideal of communism!

Index

Agriculture. *See* Economy; Government, rural
    administration and development
Amalrik, Andrei, 269
Andors, Phyllis, 321, 322
Anomie, 340-41

Bianco, Lucien, 132, 156
Bittner, Egon, 39
Bolsheviks. *See* USSR
Bonavia, David, 89, 274
Borodin, Michael, 21
Boxer Rebellion, 16-17
Bureaucracy tradition, 9-12. *See also*
    Communist party of China; Government
Bushkoff, Leonard, 271
Butterfield, Fox, 272, 278
Brzezinski, Zbigniew, 182

Cadres, 159-80
    aging and tenure, 170-71
    composition, 160-61
    corruption, 174-77
    in Cultural Revolution, 49
    definition, 159
    despotism, 177-78
    feudalism, 173-74
    ideological disillusionment, 172-73
    number of, 159
    ossification, 171-72
    recruitment of, 162-65
    style of work, 170-79
    training of, 165-70
Cai, Chang, 152, 153
Census. *See* Population

Chang Kia-ngau, 33
Chang Tsun-ming, 11
Chang Xueliang, 28
Chang Kai-shek, 140
    campaigns against Communists, 27
    commander of revolutionary army, 21
    head of Nationalist government, 32
    kidnapped in Sian (1936), 28
    leader of resistance against Japan, 29
    attack of Communists in Shanghai, 22
    talk with Mao Zedong, 31
Chen Boda, 216, 235-37
    head of Central Cultural Revolution Group,
        48
    denounced by Mao Zedong, 50-51
Chen Duxiu, 20, 24
Chen Peixian, 66-67
Chen Xilian (General), 53-54
Chen Yi (Marshal), 51
Chen Yonggui, 129, 242
Chen Yun, 45, 236, 238, 297
Chin Chien-li, 191
Chinese People's Political Consultative
    Conference (CPPCC), 57-58, 136-39,
    263
Ching, Frank, 192
Chiu, Hungdah, 185
Ch'u, T'ung-tsu, 11, 12
Clans, 309-310
Class struggle. *See* Ideology
Clientelism, 241-45
Clique. *See* Faction
Cohen, Jerome Alan, 183
Coleman, James S., 310, 312
Collectivization. *See* Government, rural
    administration and development

Communist International (Comintern). *See*
    USSR
Communication
  highways, 329
  north and south, 3
  railways, 4, 329
Communist party of China
  constitution, 59-60
  democratic centralism, 46
  factions
    pragmatists, 39, 45, 46
    radicals, 39
    "whateverists," 54
  history
    Canton Commune, 24
    Chinese Soviet Republic, 27
    first united front with Kuomintang, 21
    establishment of, 19-20
    incubation in Yenan, 29-30
    Long March, 27-28
    membership decline, 22
    membership in 1945, 30
    peasant wars, 25-28
    second united front with Kuomintang,
      28-30
    Shanghai massacre, 22
    urban uprisings, 22-25
    urban mass movement, 20-22
    war of liberation, 30-34
  local organization, 72-74
  membership, 21, 38, 60
  national organization, 61-69
    background of leaders, 20
    Central Advisory Commission, 68
    Central Commission for Discipline
      Inspection, 68
    Central Committee, 62-65
    Central Cultural Revolution Group, 237
    Central Military Commission, 68
    Congress, 61-62
      eighth (1956), 43
      ninth (1969), 49-50
      seventh (1945), 30
      tenth (1973), 51
    Politburo (Political Bureau), 65-66
    Secretariat, 65-67
    staff department of Central Committee,
      63-64
    Standing Committee of Politburo, 65-66
    third plenum of the Eleventh Central
      Committee, 54
  primary organization, 74-75
  provincial organization, 69-72
  revolutionary legacy, 34-36, 338-39
  stresses, 76-85
    alienation and dissension, 77-80
    bureaucratization, 81-83
    clique proliferation, 80-81
    party rectification (1978), 83-85
    personalization, 76-77

Communist Youth League (CYL). *See* Youth
Congress. *See* Communist party of China;
    Government
Constitution. *See* Communist party of China;
    Government
Corruption, 10-11, 340. *See also* Cadres
Counterrevolutionaries, suppression of. *See*
    Mass campaign
Court. *See* Government, judiciary
Cressey, George B., 2
Cultural Revolution
  crisis phase, 49
  effects on schools, 312-14
  formation of Red Guards, 48
  formation of Revolutionary Committees, 49
  ideological phase, 48
  mass movement phase, 48
  power seizure phase, 49
  victims of, 48

Dahl, Robert A., 244
Deng Liqun, 66-67
Deng Xiaoping, 35, 45, 62, 63, 66, 71, 90, 92,
    142, 145, 149, 153, 159, 171, 175,
    205, 219, 227, 230, 236, 237, 238,
    244, 255, 270, 271, 272, 276, 277,
    292, 297, 314, 317, 327
  on bureaucratism, 81
  on campaigns, 258
  chairs Central Military Commission, 68, 93
  concentration of power, 69
  coping with opposition, 229
  dismissed by Mao Zedong, 52
  drafting three major guidelines, 52
  on Gao Gang and Rao Shushih, 236
  launching reform, 54-55
  on minority nationalities, 113
  praise of the air force, 207
  reform agenda, 342-43
  rehabilitation (1973), 51
  on reinterpretation of Mao thought, 227
  reorganizing Central Committee, 64
  relationship with army commanders, 198
Deng Yanda, 140
Deng Yinchao, 152, 154
Deng Zihui (Teng Tzu-hui), 119, 238
Dernberger, Robert F., 299-300
Deutsch, Karl W., 269
Dictatorship of proletariat. *See* Ideology
Dong Biwu, 40, 182-83
Dowager Ci-Xi (Tsu-hsi), 16-17

Eberstadt, Nick, 318
Eckstein, Alexander, 317
Ecology, 2-7
  land area, 2
  terrain
    Grand Canal, 3
    hills and plains, 2

Yangtze River, 3
Yellow River, 3
Xi River, 3
Economy, 287-302
  agriculture (1949), 288
  first five-year plan, 290
  food supply, 341
  Great Leap Forward, 290-91
  imbalances, 293-94
  investment after 1980, 298
  the Maoist model, 289-90
  performance (tables), 290-95
  reform after Mao, 297-300
  reform of enterprises, 298-99
  regional imbalance, 294-95
  special economic zones, 299
  State Planning Commission, 289
  strategy of development, 288-90
  structural strains, 295-97
  third and fourth five-year plan, 291-92
Education, 310-14. *See also* Students;
    Youth
  five stages of development, 313-14
  growth of number of students (table),
    310
  growth of schools (table), 311
  number of students in 1949, 288
  "red and expert" policy, 313
  state expenses on, 311-12
  structure of schools, 312, 313
Election. *See* Government, Congress
Employment. *See* Occupation
Engels, Frederick, 223
Environmental destruction, 326
Erikson, Erik, 148

Faction, 232-45
  in Communist party history (table),
    233
  definition of, 232
  at local level (clique), 238, 241
  at Party center (chart), 236-38
  precipitants of, 235-36
  structural conduciveness, 234-35
Fainsod, Merle, 85
Fairbank, John King, 12
Family, 307-10
Famine, number of deaths, 45
Fei Xiaotong, 308, 309, 341
Feng Wenbin, 149
Five-Antis. *See* Mass campaign
Five-year plans. *See* Economy
Food. *See* Economy
Four modernizations, 52, 54
Four principles. *See* Ideology
Frey, Frederick W., 329
Friedman, Milton, 300-301
Friedrich, Carl J., 182
Fu Qiutao (General), 215-17

Gang of Four. *See* Jiang Qing; Wang Hongwen;
    Yao Wenyuan; Zhang Chunqiao
Gao Gang, 42, 77-78, 235-37, 256
Geography. *See* Ecology
Government
  constitutions, 88-91
  judiciary, 181-94
    people's assessors, 186
    people's mediation system, 187
  national organization, 88-99
  People's Congress, 88, 89, 91-94, 97, 98,
    136-37
    election, 41, 52, 91
    as opinion forum, 363
  presidency, 94
  provincial (table)
    executive, 105-8
    legislative, 103-4
    minority nationalities (table), 108-13
  Public Security (police), 187-93
    Ministry of State Security, 189
  rural administration and development,
    116-34
    agricultural cooperatives, 42
    Agricultural Producers' Cooperatives
      (APCs), 120-24
    Kuomintang policy, 117
    Mutual Aid Teams, 119-20
    People's Communes (diagram), 124-29
    production responsibility system, 130-31
    townships, 130-31
  State Council, 95-97
Great Leap Forward. *See* People's Commune
Griffith, William E., 234
Gu Mu, 66, 67

Hao Jianxiu, 66, 68
He Tongchang, 311
Health, 323-26
  barefoot doctors, 324-25
  children's condition, 325
  diet of people (table), 325-26
  doctors and hospitals (table), 323-24
  quality of life index, 326
Hitler, Adolf, 316
Hsiao, Kung-chuan, 9, 57
Hu Feng, 42
Hu Qiaomu, 255
Hu Qili, 66-68
Hu Sheng, 225, 226
Hu Yaobang, 62, 63, 90, 113, 148, 230
  as chairman of Communist party, 55
  on Communist party organization, 59-60
  as general secretary of Communist party, 64,
    66
  on news reporting, 265
  speech, 345-58
  as vice-president of Central Party School,
    167

Hua Guofeng, 89, 93, 139, 164, 172, 177, 238, 292, 297
  heir to Mao Zedong, 53–54
  successor to Zhou Enlai, 52
Huang Huoqing, 187
Hundred Flowers Blooming campaign. *See* Mass campaign
Hurley, Patrick J., 31

Ideology. *See also* Engels; Lenin; Mao Zedong; Marx; Stalin
  class struggle, 227–28
  dictatorship of proletariat, 228
  formal components, 224–26
  four principles, 229–30, 277
  ideological style, 222
  Leninism, 225
  Mao Zedong thought, 225–26
  Marxism, 1, 19, 224
  people's democratic dictatorship, 89–90
    definition, 58–59
  post-Mao development in ideology, 226–30
  productive relations, 228
  role in policy-making, 247–48
  role in state structure, 222–31
  on self-reliance, 229
Industry. *See* Economy
Intellectuals. *See also* Education; Occupation
  in modern Chinese revolution, 15, 20
  social status, 316, 317
Inkeles, Alex, 317, 319, 320

Japan
  attack at Marco Polo Bridge, 29
  in Boxer rebellion, 17
  design on China, 19
  occupation of Manchuria, 28
  surrender, 31
Jiang Qing, 46, 51, 52, 79, 154, 204, 237

Kang Keqing, 152–54, 321
Kaplan, Abraham, 223, 232, 234, 236, 239, 247
Khrushchev, N. S., 227, 313
Killian, Lewis M., 55, 237
Kuomintang
  causes of defeat, 31–33
  elites' background, 20
  formation of, 19
  inflation under, 32–33
  loss of energy, 20
  record of accomplishments, 31–33
  reorganization (1923), 21

Labor reform, 191–92. *See also* Trade Union; Workers

Lai Ruoyu, 144, 150
Land reform, 40. *See also* Government, rural administration and development
Lande, Carl H., 232, 240, 241
Lardy, Nicholas, 300
Lasswell, Harold D., 148, 223, 232, 234, 236, 239, 247, 339
Legislature. *See* Government, People's Congress
Lenin, V. I., 63, 148, 216, 223, 227, 257, 313, 316
Leninism. *See* Ideology
Levy, Marion, Jr., 132
Leys, Simon, 223
Li Fuchun, 252
Li Honglin, 81–83
Li Lisan, 24, 25
Li, Shi-heng, 17
Li Xiannian, 53, 71, 297
Liang Ch'i-ch'ao, 7, 8, 12, 15, 18
Lin Biao, 145, 163, 200, 235–37, 273, 276, 312
  alleged plot against Mao, 50–51
  attitude toward Mao, 77
  control of Communist party center, 202–3
  death in 1971, 50–51
  as heir to Mao, 49–55, 77
  influence in army regional command, 207
  influence in the navy, 207
  Mao cult in the army, 46, 200–201
  purge of army officers, 207
Lipset, Seymour Martin, 208
Literacy, 310. *See also* Education
Liu Shaoqi, 35, 146, 153, 163, 175, 217, 235–37, 245, 252, 270–71, 276
  attacked in the Cultural Revolution, 49
  chairman of People's Republic, 45, 94
  establishing Mao cult, 76
  on Land Reform, 117–18
Llelyveld, Joseph, 274
Lo Lungji, 137, 141–42
Lo Ruiqing (General), 189, 215, 271
London, Ivan D., 274
London, Miriam, 274
Lu Dingyi, 168, 178

Ma Yinchu, 304
Mao Yuanxin, 242
Mao Zedong, 1, 2, 13, 94, 159, 173, 175, 183
  on agricultural cooperatives, 42
  on alienation within the Communist party, 78–79
  on association of poor and lower-middle peasants, 156
  attending funeral of Marshal Chen Yi, 51
  attitude toward education, 313–14
  attitude toward intellectuals, 316
  building militia, 214–18
  on cadre recruitment, 163, 166, 178

on cause of the Cultural Revolution, 47-48, 226
chairman of Chinese Soviet Republic, 27
charismatic leadership, 39-40
on CPPCC, 137
on Chinese society, 1
on class struggle, 39, 46, 290
on coercive organizations, 181
on collectivization, 118-19
compared with Sun Yat-sen, 342
conflict with Lin Biao, 202-3
on constitution, 90
cultivating the Red Army, 29-30
death, 53
on "democratic parties," 140, 141, 142
denigrating other Party leaders, 63
denouncing Red Guards, 49
on dictatorship of proletariat, 58-59
dispute on rural collectivization, 64-65
disputes with other leaders, 77
on dissolving the cooperatives, 121
on economic problems in 1949, 288
on education of cadres, 169-70
at eighth Party congress, 43
on expenses for the military, 199
on extrinsic factors in planning, 254
on faction and splits, 233
founding People's Republic, 31
on Gao Gang and Rao Shushih, 78
as Godlike figure, 338
on Great Leap Forward, 124-28
guerrilla leader, 22, 24, 25, 26
impact on rule making, 252-53
on "independent kingdoms," 234-35
on industrialization, 307
influence in army command, 207
on internal reporting, 79
launching Great Leap, 44-45
launching Hundred Flowers Blooming campaign, 43-44
learning from Soviet economy, 289
on local cadres, 74
on local government, 100
Long March, 27-28
making self-criticism (1962), 46
on manipulation of public opinion, 262
on mass organization, 155
meeting with Chiang Kai-shek, 31
miscalculation of policy effect, 254
mobilization army for politics, 200-202
on peasant demonstrations, 279
peasant movement, 21, 47
on peasant resistance to communes, 127-28
personal control of Party, 29-30
personality of, 237
personalizing the Communist party, 76-77
on planning, 247-48
on policy making, 95-97
on Politburo, 65
on the political role of the military, 195-96

on population, 304
promotion of incivility, 330
promoting Tachai brigade, 128-29
on public mood, 271
reinterpretation of Mao thought, 227
relationship with provinces, 107
relationship with regional army command, 198
resigning chairman of People's Republic, 45
on revolution of production, 225
role in Dazhai (Tachai) model, 242
role in five-year plans, 291-92
role in Hu Feng campaign, 42
role in policy feedback, 251-52
role in rural development, 327
role in tenth Party congress, 51
thoughts of (*see* Ideology)
on the use of force, 182, 187-88
on use of prison labor, 191
view on agricultural cooperatives, 251
views on public opinion, 281
on victory of the Communist party, 33-34
on wall poster, 275
on women's federation, 153
on women's status, 321
on youth league, 148-49
Marriage law. *See* Mass campaign
Marshall, George C., 31
Marx, Karl, 88, 216, 223, 313
Marxism. *See* Ideology
Mass campaign, 35, 40-41
Anti-America, Aid-Korea, 40
Anti-Rightists, 43, 44, 140, 141, 142, 183, 267
"civilized villages," 330
"criticize Lin Biao and Confucius," 52
Five-Antis (Five-Evils), 41, 152
Four-Cleanups, 175
Hundred Flowers Blooming, 43, 93, 111, 123, 136-37, 140, 141, 144, 183, 191, 229, 253, 256, 275, 280, 313
"Hygiene, decorum and courtesy," 330
New Marriage Law, 40
public health, 325
role in policy making, 256-58
Socialist education, 46
Suppression of Counterrevolutionaries, 40-41
Suppression of Hidden Counterrevolutionaries, 42, 267
Thought Reform of Intellectuals, 41
Three-Antis (Three-Evils), 40, 175
Mass media. *See* Public opinion
Mencius, 8, 13
Merton, Robert K., 340
Michael, Franz, 184
Military, 195-212
civil-military relations, 198-210
conflict with Gang of Four, 203-4
demobilization (1981), 206
educational level of officers, 209

Military (*cont.*)
  emulation of Lei Feng, 47
  formal representation in the Party, 196
  Great Military Region, 197, 198, 203
  guardianship of nation, 204–5
  intervention in politics, 49
  Military Control Commission, 199
  number of Red Army (1949), 38
  political attitude
    air force, 207
    navy, 207
    regional army, 207–8
  relationship with public, 209
  rise to power in China, 20
  role in economy, 210
  role in regional government, 197–98
  social status, 315
  "three-aid two-military" movement,
    202
Militia, urban workers', 204, 213–21
Minority nationalities, 108–13
Modernization, 303–33

Nationalists. *See* Kuomintang
Nie Jungzhen (General), 208, 209
Nordlinger, Eric A., 199, 205
Northern Expedition, 22, 26

Occupation, composition of, 305–7
Oksenberg, Michel, 258–59, 320
Outcasts, 317

Pao-chia system. *See* Government, rural
    administration and development
Parapolitical organizations, 135–80
  All-China Federation of Trade Unions (*see*
    Trade Union)
  All-China Women's Federation (*see* Women)
  Communist Youth League (*see* Youth)
  Democratic parties, 139–42
    All-China Association of Fellow
      Countrymen from Taiwan, 141
    All-China Federation of Industry and
      Commerce, 141–42
    China Zigong Party, 140–41
    Democratic Construction Society, 140
    Democratic League, 139–40
    Democratic Party of Workers and Peasants,
      140
    "Heart surrendering" movement, 142
    League for Democratic Self-Government of
      Taiwan, 141
    Promotion of Democracy Society, 140
    The Revolutionary Committee of
      Guomindang, 139
    September 3rd Society, 141
Paris Commune, 127, 216

Park, Robert E., 265
Parks, Michael, 330
Parsons, Talcott, 314, 340
Parties. *See* Parapolitical organizations
Peasant. *See also* Government, rural
    administration and development
  border region strategy, 26
  peasant association, 118
  rebellion in nineteenth century, 16–17,
    18–19
  social status of, 315–16
  traditional life, 6–7
Peng Bai, 21
Peng Dehuai (Marshal), 25, 45, 48, 77, 78, 199,
    200, 215, 245, 252, 256
People's Commune, 124–29
People's Democratic Dictatorship. *See*
    Ideology
People's Liberation Army. *See* Military
People's Mediation Committee, 191
People's Militia, 45, 118, 127, 213–21
People's Republic of China, history
  The Great Leap Forward, 44–45
  The Great Proletarian Cultural Revolution,
    47–50
  rehabilitation (1962–65), 45–47
  revolutionary destruction (1949–52),
    40–41
  socialist construction (1953–57), 41–44
  the struggle for power after Mao, 53–55
  struggle for succession (1970–76), 50–52
Po I-po, 76–77
Police. *See* Government, Public Security
Policy-Making, 247–60
  application and feedback, 250–52
  formalization, 250
  genesis of, 249
  impact of revolutionary legacy, 248
  persuasion stage, 250
  post-Mao development, 254–56
  preliminary validation, 249–50
  role of Soviet model, 248
  rule making, 252–54
  spot investigation, 252
Political tradition, 7–13
  alien rule, 12–13
  bureaucratic centralism, 9–12
  regionalism, 8–9
  revolutionary tradition (table), 7–8
Population, 303–4
  census of 1982, 2
  density, 3
  growth after 1949, 303–5
  mortality (table), 323
  rise in Qing dynasty, 16
  rural, 116
Postal service, 329
Powell, John Duncan, 242
Presidency. *See* Government
Productive relations. *See* Ideology

Public opinion, 261–86
  the communication system, 262–81
  elite forum
    mass media, 263, 264–67
    the representative organizations, 263
  four publics, 282–83
  impact of the Cultural Revolution, 282–83
  impact of Marxism-Leninism, 262
  intraparty communication, 269–71
  mass forum, letters and visits, 267–69
  noninstitutionalized communication, 271–81
    democracy wall, 229, 277–78
    demonstrations, 279–81
    public mood, 271–72
    underground publications, 277–79
    wall poster, 275–77
    word of mouth news, 272–75
  overall system impact, 261–62
  post-Mao approach, 283–84
  role of Communist party leadership, 281–83
Pye, Lucian W., 60

Qian Xinzhong, 304
Qiao Shi, 66–67
Qing dynasty, 7–11, 15–19
Qu Qiubai, 24

Rao Shushih, 42, 77, 78, 235–37, 256
Regionalism, 8–9
  dialects, 4
  economic, 287–88
  in Guangdong, 73–74
  political division, 8–9
  in Yunnan, 73–74
Residents' Committee, 190
Revolution, Republican (1911), 16–19
Rightist. *See* Mass campaign
Riot, 55. *See also* Tiananmen Square riot
Roll, Charles, Jr., 295
Roosevelt, Franklin D., 31

Scalapino, Robert A., 77
Schwartz, Benjamin I., 132
Security and Defense Committee,
  190–91
Serruys, Paul L. M., 4
Shibutani, Tamotsu, 272, 274
Skinner, G. William, 6, 128
Smelser, Neil J., 236
Social change, 303–37
  equilibration, 319–20
  homogenization, 317–19
  mobility, 320
  stratification, 314–20
Social consensus, 326–33
  communication, 329–30
  lack of, 328–30

Social integration, 326–33
  effect of the Cultural Revolution, 327–28
  inequality, 328
  rural areas, 327
  sharing of power, 327–28
Socialism, 338–39
Socialist construction. *See* People's Republic
  of China
Socialist education. *See* Mass campaign
Socialist transition, 42
Song Renqiong, 162, 163, 167
Stalin, 24, 31, 148, 227, 248, 313
  denunciation by Khrushchev, 43
  on mass organizations, 142–43
State Council. *See* Government
State Economic Commission. *See* Economy
Stereotyping, 4
Students. *See also* Education; Youth
  in Cultural Revolution, 48–50
  in Great Leap Forward, 44
  in Hundred Flowers Blooming campaign, 43
  in Socialist education, 46
  student association, 149
  used by radicals, 51–52
Sung Yefang, 45, 270, 297
Sun Yat-sen, 140, 342
  collaboration with USSR, 21
  death, 22
  life and career, 16–20
  president of Republic, 18

Tachai (Dazhai) brigade, 128–29
Taiping rebellion, 7, 16–18
Taiwan, 33
Tang Cheng (General), 199
Tawney, R. H., 6, 7, 9, 122
Teachers, 315
Telecommunication, 329
Tian Jiayin, 65
Tiananmen Square, 274
Tiananmen Square riot, 238, 272, 280
Township. *See* Government, rural
  administration and development
Trade Union
  All-China Federation of Trade Unions,
    143–47
  in the Cultural Revolution, 144–45
  Congress of Workers and Staff, 146
  Democratic Reform, 41
  in Hundred Flowers Blooming campaign, 144
  post-Mao development, 145
  social composition of workers, 147
Transmission belt, definition, 142–43
Treaty of Nanking, 16
Turner, Ralph H., 55, 237

Unemployment, 305–6
Union. *See* Trade Union

United front, 135-39
United States, 30-31
Urbanization, 304-5
USSR. *See also* Lenin; Stalin
   aid to China, 28
   Comintern, 19-21, 24, 28
   economic assistance to People's Republic of
      China, 42, 288-90
   occupation of Manchuria, 288
   organizational influence in China, 339
   role in the history of the Communist party,
      19-21, 24
   unequality treaty in China, 19
   withdrawal of advisors, 313

Verba, Sidney, 222, 262

Wallace, Henry A., 31
Wan Li, 66, 67, 106, 113
Wang An-shih, 11
Wang Guangmei, 235
Wang Hongwen, 51, 203, 204, 219, 220
Wang Jiangong, 150
Wang Renchong, 65, 172, 332
Wang Zhaoguo, 150
Warlords, 19-20
Weber, Max, 10, 39, 235
Wei Jingshen, 185-86, 277, 279
White, Lynn, III, 319
Whyte, Martin K., 318
Women
   employment, 321
   enrollment in schools, 321
   federation (ACWF), 151-56
   infanticide of females, 322
   percentage in cadre system, 322
   rate of illiteracy, 321
   social status, 321-23
Wong Dongxin, 53-54, 64, 238
Workers. *See also* Trade Union
   composition of, 305, 327
   educational qualification, 146
   militia, 145
   number in 1949, 288
   unrest in 1974-75, 51-52
Wu Han, 48

Xi Chongxun, 66-67
Xiao Hua (General), 208

Xie Fuzi, 50
Xie Xue-hong, 141
Xu Siyou (General), 201, 203
Xue Muqiao, 295

Yang, C. K., 6, 35, 152
Yang Dezi (General), 206, 207
Yang Jinren, 113
Yang, Martin C., 6
Yang Shangkun, 206
Yang Xianzhen, 166
Yang Yung (General), 66
Yao Wenyuan, 46, 51, 52, 79, 174,
   237
Yao Yilin, 66, 67
Ye Chun, 235
Ye Jianying (Marshal), 53, 203, 205
Yeh, Kung-cha, 295
Young, Arthur N., 32, 33
Young Pioneers, 148-49
Youth, 330-33
   association, 149
   attitude, 150-51
   crimes committed, 332-33
   disillusionment, 330-32
   political indoctrination of, 46, 332
   protest, 55
   sent to countryside, 306
   youth league, 41, 147-51
      in the Cultural Revolution, 150
      in Hundred Flowers Blooming campaign,
         149
      relationship with the Communist party,
         148-49
Yuan Sikai (General), 19
Yu Qiuli, 66, 67, 206

Zhang Bochun, 136, 137, 140
Zhang Chunqiao, 46, 51, 203, 219, 237,
   280
Zhang Haidi, 151
Zhao Ziyang, 55, 62, 71, 189, 206, 230, 330,
   343
Zhou Beiyuan, 273
Zhou Enlai, 24, 28, 67, 79, 152, 237, 238, 252,
   274, 280
   death, 52
   on intellectuals, 43
   leadership of Communist party, 51-52
Zhu De (Marshal), 24, 25, 27, 152, 200